Writing with POWER

Contributing Author
Joyce Senn

Senior Consultants
Constance Weaver
Peter Smagorinsky

Language

Composition

21st Century Skills

Editorial

Editorial Director	Carol Francis
Executive Editor	Jim Strickler
Editorial Team	Gay Russell-Dempsey, Terry Ofner, Kate Winzenburg, Sue Thies, Andrea Stark, Paula Reece, Sheri Cooper

Design

Art Director	Randy Messer
Design Team	Tobi Cunningham, Deborah Bell, Emily Greazel, Mike Aspengren, Jane Wonderlin, Dea Marks, Lori Zircher, Jill Kimpston
Illustration/Diagrams	Mike Aspengren, Sue Cornelison
Image Research	Anjanette Houghtaling

Joyce Senn taught both middle and high school before putting her experience and love of language to work in her distinguished career as educational consultant and author. Specializing in grammar, Senn was a pioneer in textbook publishing in her use of themed activities, helping to provide a context for once-isolated grammar, usage, and mechanics practice. Senn's other publications include the acclaimed children's reference book *Quotations for Kids* (Millbrook Press, 1999) and *Information Literacy: Educating Children for the 21st Century* (with Patricia Breivik, National Education Association, 2nd Ed., 1998).

Special thanks to Joan McElroy, Ph.D., for contributions to the research strand of *Writing with Power,* and to David Kulieke, English instructor and consultant, for his review of the grammar, usage, and mechanics chapters.

Printed in the United States of America

by Perfection Learning® Corporation
1000 North Second Avenue
P.O. Box 500
Logan, Iowa 51546-0500
Tel: 1-800-831-4190 • Fax: 1-800-543-2745
perfectionlearning.com

3 4 5 6 7 RRD 16 15 14

ISBN 13: 978-1-61563-634-1
ISBN 10: 1-61563-634-x

Senior Consultants

Peter Smagorinsky wrote the activities that form the project-centered "structured process approach" to teaching writing at the heart of the composition units of *Writing with Power*. A high school English teacher for fourteen years, Smagorinsky has also taught in the English Education programs at the University of Oklahoma (1990-1998) and University of Georgia (1998-present). In addition to numerous articles, he has published books through Heinemann (*Teaching English by Design*, 2007, and *The Dynamics of Writing Instruction: A Structured Process Approach for the Composition Teacher in the Middle and High School,* with Larry Johannessen, Elizabeth Kahn, and Thomas McCann, 2010); through Teacher's College Press (*Research on Composition: Multiple Perspectives on Two Decades of Change*, ed., 2006); through Cambridge University Press (*Vygotskian Perspectives on Literacy Research: Constructing Meaning through Collaborative Inquiry*, with Carol D. Lee, 2000); and through the National Council of Teachers of English (NCTE) Press (*Standards in Practice, Grades 9–12*, 1996). For NCTE, he also chaired the Research Forum, co-edited *Research in the Teaching of English*, co-chaired the Assembly for Research, chaired the Standing Committee on Research, chaired the Research Foundation, and served as President of the National Conference on Research in Language and Literacy.

Constance Weaver developed the "power" concept and features for *Writing with Power,* identifying strategies for using grammatical options to add power to writing and thinking as well as developing the "Power Rules," beginning with ten "must know" conventions for success in school and the workplace and expanding into features more relevant for advanced writers. Weaver has shaped English education for more than thirty years, illuminating the relationship between grammar and writing and providing practical, effective teaching guidance, from her earliest works on the subject, the best-selling *Grammar for Teachers* (NCTE, 1979) and the widely acclaimed *Teaching Grammar in Context* (Boynton/Cook, 1996), to her most recent *Grammar Plan Book* (Heinemann, 2007) and *Grammar to Enrich and Enhance Writing* (with Jonathan Bush, Heinemann, 2008). She has also long been a leader in literacy and reading. Her book *Reading Process and Practice* (Heinemann, 1988) is authoritative in its field. In 1996, Weaver was honored by the Michigan Council of Teachers of English with the Charles C. Fries award for outstanding leadership in English education. Weaver is the Heckert Professor of Reading and Writing at Miami University, Oxford, Ohio, and Professor Emerita of English at Western Michigan University, Kalamazoo.

National Advisory Panel

Writing with Power was developed under the guidance of outstanding educators—teachers, curriculum specialists, and supervisors—whose experience helped ensure that the program design was implemented in a practical, engaging way for every classroom.

Middle School

DeVeria A. Berry
Curriculum Specialist
Frank T. Simpson-Waverly School
Hartford Public Schools
Hartford, Connecticut

Marylou Curley-Flores
Curriculum Specialist
Reading/Language Arts
Curriculum and Instruction
San Antonio Independent School District
San Antonio, Texas

Karen Guajardo
Curriculum Specialist
Reading/English Language Arts
Curriculum and Instruction
San Antonio Independent School District
San Antonio, Texas

Tina DelGiodice
English Teacher/Staff Developer (retired)
Jersey City Public Schools
Jersey City, New Jersey

Julie Hines-Lyman
Curriculum Coach
Agassiz Elementary School
Chicago Public Schools
Chicago, Illinois

Marcia W. Punsalan
Language Arts Department Chair
Clay High School
Oregon City Schools
Oregon, Ohio

Melanie Pogue Semore
Director of Upper School
Harding Academy
Memphis, Tennessee

High School

Nathan H. Busse
English Language Arts Teacher
Fox Tech High School
San Antonio Independent School DIstrict
San Antonio, Texas

Joyce Griggs
Instructional Specialist
Peoria Unified School District
Peoria, Arizona

Jill Haltom
English Language Arts/Reading Director
Coppell Independent School District
Coppell, Texas

Lynn Hugerich
Retired English Supervisor
Secaucus Public School District
Secaucus, New Jersey

Linda M. Moore, M.Ed.
English Instructor
Coppell High School
Coppell Independent School District
Coppell, Texas

Debora Stonich
Secondary Curriculum Coordinator of
English Language Arts
McKinney Independent School District
McKinney, Texas

Student Contributors

Writing with Power proudly and gratefully presents the work of the following students, whose writing samples—from effective opening sentences to in-depth literary analyses—show so clearly the power of writing.

From Lucyle Collins Middle School
Fort Worth, Texas
Marbella Maldonado
Victor Ramirez

From Evanston Township High School
Evanston, Illinois
Morgan Nicholls

From Sunrise Mountain High School
Peoria, Arizona
Griffin Burns

From Canton South High School
Canton, Ohio
Cody Collins
Marti Doerschuk
Reanna Eckroad
Erica Gallon
Lindsay Kerr
Elise Miller
Katie Smith
Natalie Volpe

Contents in Brief

COMPOSITION

UNIT 1 Style and Structure of Writing 2

Common Core State Standards Focus

W.5 Develop and strengthen writing as needed by planning, revising, editing, rewriting, or trying a new approach, focusing on addressing what is most significant for a specific purpose and audience.

L.5 Demonstrate understanding of figurative language, word relationships, and nuances in word meanings.

Common Core State Standards Focus

W.4 Produce clear and coherent writing in which the development, organization, and style are appropriate to task, purpose, and audience.

Composition

Common Core State Standards Focus

W.3 Write narratives to develop real or imagined experiences or events using effective technique, well-chosen details, and well-structured event sequences.

Common Core State Standards Focus

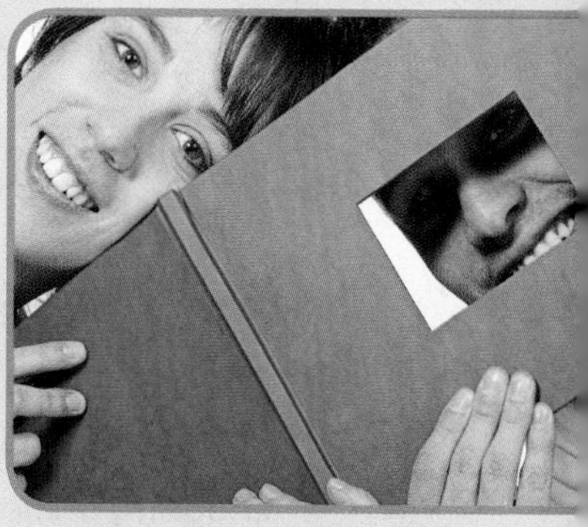

W.3 (d) Use precise words and phrases, telling details, and sensory language to convey a vivid picture of the experiences, events, setting, and/or characters.

Common Core State Standards Focus

W.3 (a) Engage and orient the reader by setting out a problem, situation, or observation and its significance, establishing one or multiple point(s) of view, and introducing a narrator and/or characters; create a smooth progression of experiences or events.

Common Core State Standards Focus

W.2 Write informative/explanatory texts to examine and convey complex ideas, concepts, and information clearly and accurately through the effective selection, organization, and analysis of content.

Common Core State Standards Focus

W.1 Write arguments to support claims in an analysis of substantive topics or texts, using valid reasoning and relevant and sufficient evidence.

Common Core State Standards Focus

W.9 Draw evidence from literary or informational texts to support analysis, reflection, and research.

Common Core State Standards Focus

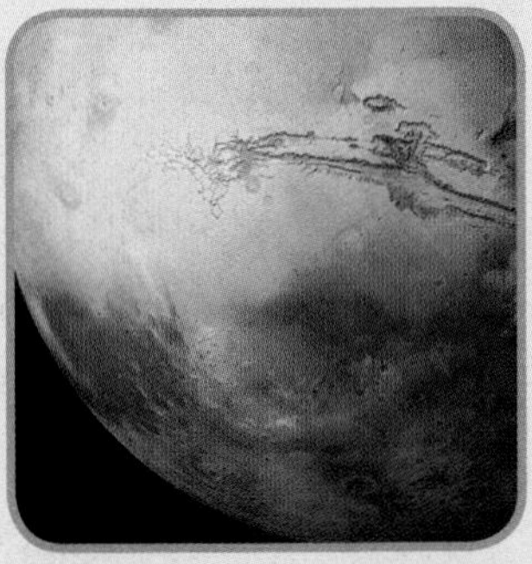

W.8 Gather relevant information from multiple authoritative print and digital sources, using advanced searches effectively; assess the strengths and limitations of each source in terms of the task, purpose, and audience; integrate information into the text selectively to maintain the flow of ideas, avoiding plagiarism and overreliance on any one source and following a standard format for citation.

12 Research: Synthesizing, Organizing, and Presenting 434

Common Core State Standards Focus

W.7 Conduct short as well as more sustained research projects to answer a question (including a self-generated question) or solve a problem; narrow or broaden the inquiry when appropriate; synthesize multiple sources on the subject, demonstrating understanding of the subject under investigation.

W.1 Write arguments to support claims in an analysis of substantive topics or texts, using valid reasoning and relevant and sufficient evidence.

COMPOSITION

Common Core State Standards Focus

L.5 Demonstrate understanding of figurative language, word relationships, and nuances in word meanings.

Part II Communication and Collaboration

Common Core State Standards Focus

L.4 Determine or clarify the meaning of unknown and multiple-meaning words and phrases based on grades 11–12 reading and content, choosing flexibly from a range of strategies.

SL.6 Adapt speech to a variety of contexts and tasks, demonstrating a command of formal English when indicated or appropriate.

Composition

Common Core State Standards Focus

SL.1 Initiate and participate effectively in a range of collaborative discussions (one-on-one, in groups, and teacher-led) with diverse partners on grades 11–12 topics, texts, and issues, building on others' ideas and expressing their own clearly and persuasively.

Common Core State Standards Focus

W.6 Use technology, including the Internet, to produce, publish, and update individual or shared writing products in response to ongoing feedback, including new arguments or information.

GRAMMAR

UNIT 4

Grammar 616

Common Core State Standards Focus

L.1 Demonstrate command of the conventions of standard English grammar and usage when writing or speaking.

Common Core State Standards Focus

L.3 (a) Vary syntax for effect, consulting references (e.g., Tufte's *Artful Sentences*) for guidance as needed; apply an understanding of syntax to the study of complex texts when reading.

GRAMMAR

Common Core State Standards Focus

W.3 (d) Use precise words and phrases, telling details, and sensory language to convey a vivid picture of the experiences, events, setting, and/or characters.

Common Core State Standards Focus

W.1 (c) Use words, phrases, and clauses as well as varied syntax to link the major sections of the text, create cohesion, and clarify the relationships between claim(s) and reasons, between reasons and evidence, and between claim(s) and counterclaims.

Common Core State Standards Focus

L.1 Demonstrate command of the conventions of standard English grammar and usage when writing or speaking.

Common Core State Standards Focus

L.1 (b) Resolve issues of complex or contested usage, consulting references (e.g., *Merriam-Webster's Dictionary of English Usage, Garner's Modern American Usage)* as needed.

Common Core State Standards Focus

L.1 Demonstrate command of the conventions of standard English grammar and usage when writing or speaking.

UNIT 6 Mechanics 888

Common Core State Standards Focus

L.2 Demonstrate command of the conventions of standard English capitalization, punctuation, and spelling when writing.

Common Core State Standards Focus

L.2 Demonstrate command of the conventions of standard English capitalization, punctuation, and spelling when writing.

Common Core State Standards Focus

L.2 (a) Observe hyphenation conventions.

L.2 (b) Spell correctly.

Common Core State Standards Focus

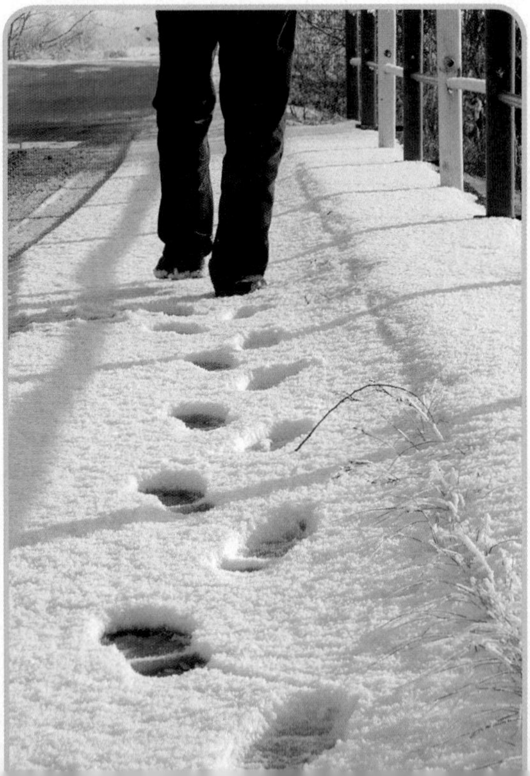

Writing with POWER

Language

Composition

21st Century Skills

Perfection Learning®

Unit 1

Style and Structure of Writing

On a hot summer night when the tiny light of an insect blinks randomly in the darkness, you give it a sideways glance. But when a bolt of lightning electrifies the sky, you jump. So it is with words. The almost-right word is worthy of a glance, but the right word electrifies a sentence. In this unit you will develop your skills of writing with such power. You will learn the value of collaborating with others to brainstorm and develop ideas and to convey them through a meaningful structure. You will continue to develop a unique style and appropriate voice and gain the skill and confidence to replace the lightning bugs in your writing with bolts of real power.

The difference between the right word and the almost right word is the difference between lightning and the lightning bug. — *Mark Twain*

A Community of Writers

This book is called *Writing with Power.* Its goal is to help you develop powerful writing and necessary and useful communication skills for today's world. You may ask, What does it mean to write with power? What makes communication skills in today's world any different from communication skills in earlier times? This chapter will provide the answers and lay the foundation for the writing instruction and activities presented in future chapters.

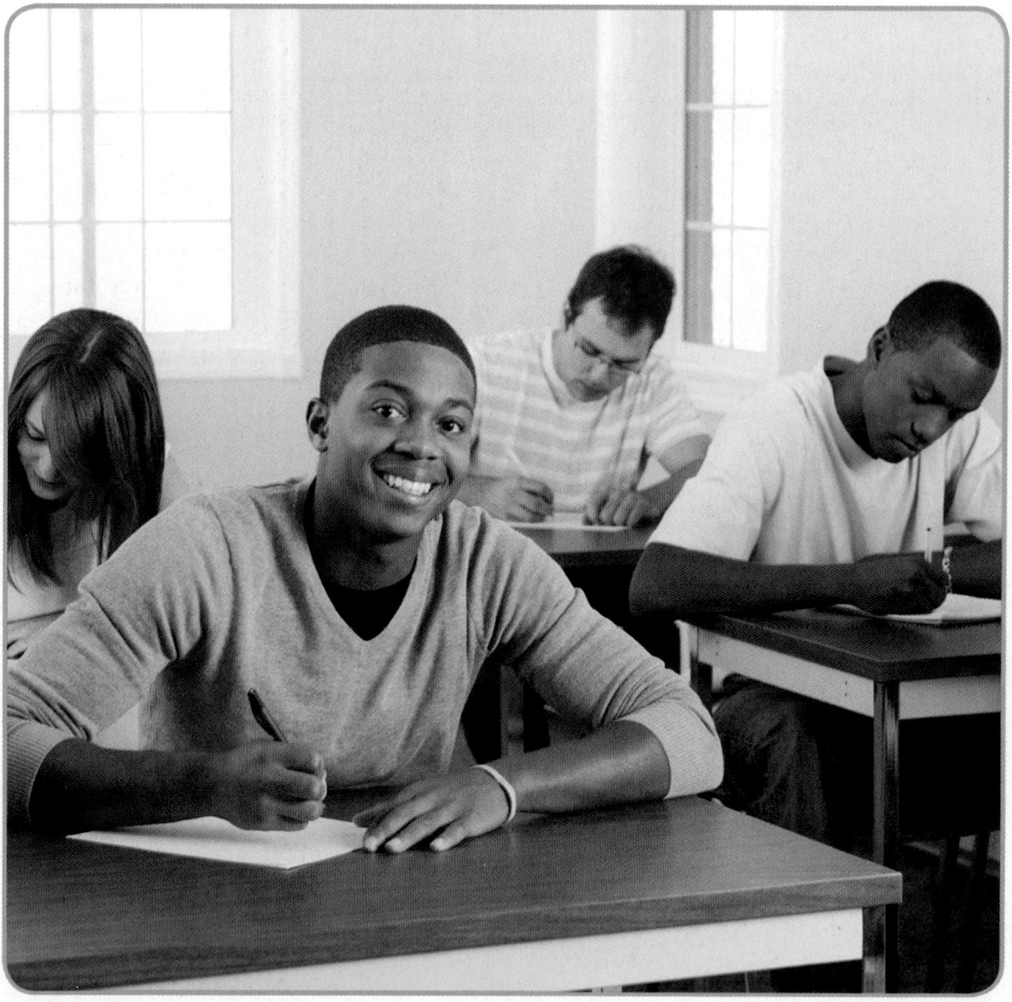

Writing with Power

You read something just about every day. You can usually distinguish a text that has been written with power from one that has not. Texts written with power usually

- demonstrate the **six traits** of good writing
- use **language in varied, interesting ways** to show relationships and provide details
- follow the **conventions** appropriate for the purpose, occasion, audience, and genre

This program will help you to write with power and enable you to accomplish your goals through your writing.

1 The Six Traits

Ideas

Strong writing includes a clear idea, message, or theme. Writers add potent and vivid details that help explain or support their ideas. Powerful writing helps you focus your thinking so that readers can easily follow what you are trying to say.

Organization

Well-organized writing typically has a clear beginning, middle, and ending. It presents details in a logical order, often using the transitional words and phrases listed in the chart below.

WRITING PURPOSE	ORGANIZATIONAL PATTERNS	COMMON TRANSITIONS
Expository (to explain or inform)	Order of importance	*First, next, most important*
	Comparison/contrast	*Similarly, in contrast, on the other hand*
	Cause/effect	*As a result, for that reason, because*
Narrative (to tell a real or imaginary story)	Chronological (time) order	*First, yesterday, the next day, last year, next, until*
Descriptive	Spatial (location) order	*At the top, near the middle, to the right, on the other side, next to, behind*
Persuasive	Order of importance	*The most important, equally important, in addition, also, in fact*

Voice

Voice gives your writing a unique personality. It provides your writing with a personal signature in your expression of ideas. Your writing voice should fit the expectations for the situation, such as the different voices you'd use to write an essay on a college application or to write an entry on a friend's social networking page. The following chart identifies appropriate voices for different writing occasions.

WRITING PURPOSE	WHAT THE WRITER'S VOICE SHOULD CONVEY
Expository and persuasive writing	Genuine interest in the subject, often including personal insights about why the subject is important to the writer and what the reader might expect to gain from it; respect for differing viewpoints; confidence without swagger
Descriptive and narrative writing	A genuine, not phony, personality; often some personal statements that show a willingness to trust readers with sensitive ideas

Word Choice

You can get your readers' attention by using specific and lively language appropriate to the situation. Strategies for producing vivid texts include using active-voice verbs, employing precise nouns and modifiers, and adding colorful and figurative language that meets the expectations of your readers. (You will learn more about word choice in Chapter 2.)

Sentence Fluency

Your sentences can flow together when you employ transitional words or phrases, repeated words, and pronouns that refer back to an earlier word. These devices enable you to connect your sentences fluidly to one another. Most writers return to their texts and revise some parts so that readers can follow their thinking easily and clearly. To help your readers follow your points, you can add transitions, repeat a key word, or replace a word with a pronoun, a synonym, or a substitute. (You will learn more about sentence fluency in Chapter 2.)

Conventions

Writing that readers find clear is generally free of problems with spelling, capitalization, punctuation, and word choice. Sentences follow appropriate rules for grammar and usage, and paragraph breaks occur where you change topics. Writing that follows these rules can make a positive impression on readers. If you use conventions that are inappropriate for the occasion, such as using text messaging abbreviations in a college application essay, you may confuse or turn off your readers. (You will learn more about some of the most important conventions on pages 9–11.)

2 The Power of Language

There are an infinite number of words and sentence structures that you could conceivably combine to produce sentences. Simple pictures can communicate an idea such as "Hank swung at the pitch," but language can add detail, meaning, subtlety, and feeling to that idea in seemingly endless ways: "With his team down 7-3, with a full count, and with two outs in the 9th inning already, Hank steadied his nerves, kept his eye on the ball, and swung at the pitch with more strength than he'd ever felt go through his arms before."

Fluent writers generate power through their careful use of language. To help you develop this ability, each composition chapter in this program includes a warm-up activity called "The Power of Language." These activities help you create interesting and varied sentence patterns and add meaningful detail to your writing. Most language strategies have two names. The first identifies the language concept. The second name, after the colon, reflects its purpose or function. The "Power of Language" strategies in this book are:

- Semicolons: Catch and Release, page 65
- Dashes: Dash It All, page 93
- Fluency: Let It Flow, pages 145 and 440
- Appositives: Who or What? page 175
- Adjectives: Come Early or Lately, page 202
- Parallelism: The Power of 3s, page 250
- Adverbial Clauses: Tip the Scale, page 307
- Participial Phrases: Getting Into the Action, page 351
- Adjectival Clauses: Which One, What Kind? page 376

Using these strategies will help you transform your writing from "Hank swung at the pitch" to an endless variety of detailed, interesting, and original expressions, giving your language real *power*.

Learning Tip

With a partner, take the simple sentence "Hank swung at the pitch" and use your language power to expand it with details and subtlety of meaning. Share your revised sentence with the class.

3 The Power Rules

The ways in which you use language can help you get where you want to go. The kind of language that you use—the words, the arrangement of words in your sentences, the rules you follow—signifies your membership in a social group. With friends and family, you speak casually and comfortably. Your participation in these situations teaches you whether to say "Y'all be cold" or "All of you are cold." The language you use usually sounds like the speech of the people with whom you spend time or hope to spend time. This kind of speech is the language of power in the social situations you choose for yourself. It feels natural to you.

However, the language of power with friends and family is not necessarily the language of power in other situations. In many situations, "Standard English," such as the language used in many workplaces, is expected. Its conventions may differ from the speech you use most naturally. However, if you hope to succeed in school, college, or a profession, you benefit from learning the language used by people who occupy positions of power in those settings. The speech conventions you follow are therefore not absolutely right or wrong. Rather, good communicators learn how to "code switch": They learn to adjust their speech so that the conventions that they follow meet the expectations for each particular situation.

English professors have found that certain usage patterns, such as non-mainstream subject-verb agreement, create more negative impressions than others. Since these patterns can influence how people perceive you, you should learn how to edit your writing so that it meets the standards of workplaces and educational settings. The following list identifies 10 of the most important conventions to master. Check for these Power Rules whenever you edit.

Editing for Mainstream Conventions: The Power Rules

1. Use only one negative form for a single negative idea. (See page 853.)

Before Editing	After Editing
After I dropped it, my mp3 player *wasn't* worth *nothing.*	After I dropped it, my mp3 player *wasn't* worth *anything.*
There *wasn't nowhere* to keep my old comic book collection.	There *wasn't anywhere* to keep my old comic book collection.

2. Use mainstream past tense forms of regular and irregular verbs. (See pages 742–766.) You might try to recite and memorize the parts of the most common irregular verbs.

Before Editing	After Editing
I *swum* at the YMCA last night.	I *swam* at the YMCA last night.
Otto *fix* my car engine.	Otto *fixed* my car engine.
You should not have *did* that.	You should not have *done* that.
You *brung* me the wrong hammer.	You *brought* me the wrong hammer.

3. Use verbs that agree with the subject. (See pages 814–839.)

Before Editing	After Editing
She *don't* have any.	She *doesn't* have any.
The brussels sprouts and the shitake mushroom *tastes* good together.	The brussels sprouts and the shitake mushroom *taste* good together.
Either the shrubs or the tree *are* diseased.	Either the shrubs or the tree *is* diseased.
Neither the cat nor the dogs *is eating* the bird food.	Neither the cat nor the dogs *are eating* the bird food.

4. Use subject forms of pronouns in subject position. Use object forms of pronouns in object position. (See pages 781–789.)

Before Editing	After Editing
Her and Carla are wearing boots.	*She* and Carla are wearing boots.
Him and his hiking partner are going in the wrong direction.	*He* and his hiking partner are going in the wrong direction.
Her and *me* have much in common.	*She* and *I* have much in common.

5. Use standard ways to make nouns possessive. (See pages 944–946.)

Before Editing	After Editing
The *frogs* legs are powerful.	The *frog's* legs are powerful.
Carly was scratched by the *cats* claws.	Carly was scratched by the *cat's* claws.
Sybil marched across the *citys* border.	Sybil marched across the *city's* border.
The *trucks* brakes squealed loudly.	The *truck's* brakes squealed loudly.
All three *bikes* tires deflated over the winter.	All three *bikes'* tires deflated over the winter.

6. Use a consistent verb tense except when a change is clearly necessary. (See pages 753–766.)

Before Editing	After Editing
The power *goes* off during yesterday's storm.	The power *went* off during yesterday's storm.
I *play* video games for two hours yesterday.	I *played* video games for two hours yesterday.

7. Use sentence fragments only the way professional writers do, after the sentence they refer to and usually to emphasize a point. Fix all sentence fragments that occur before the sentence they refer to and ones that occur in the middle of a sentence. (See pages 663–664.)

Before Editing	After Editing
Today. Tanya is wearing sunglasses.	*Today,* Tanya is wearing sunglasses.
Writing a paper. *While the school band is playing next door is hard.* So I'm moving to the library.	Writing a paper *while the school band is playing next door is hard, so* I'm moving to the library.
We contributed half of our money to the charity. *The reason being that we wanted to help their worthy cause.*	We contributed half of our money to the charity *because we wanted to help their worthy cause.*

8. Use the best conjunction and/or punctuation for the meaning when connecting two sentences. Revise run-on sentences. (See pages 728–730.)

Before Editing	After Editing
Celia got an A in English, she celebrated.	*When* Celia got an A in English, she celebrated.
It snowed, I got out my sled.	*After* it snowed, I got out my sled.
I took a guess, my answer was wrong.	I took a guess, *but* my answer was wrong.

9. Use the contraction *'ve* (not *of*) when the correct word is *have,* or use the full word *have.* (See pages 872, 881, and 883.) **Use *supposed* instead of *suppose* and *used* instead of *use* when appropriate.**

Before Editing	After Editing
They should *of* sung the national anthem in the right key.	They should *have* sung the national anthem in the right key.
We might *of* gone a bit overboard with the sugar.	We might *have* gone a bit overboard with the sugar.
The songs would *of* sounded better if they'd been sung instead of played on a kazoo.	The songs would *have* sounded better if they'd been sung instead of played on a kazoo.
I was *suppose* to be home by dinnertime.	I was *supposed* to be home by dinnertime.
I *use* to take piano lessons, but then I switched to cello.	I *used* to take piano lessons, but then I switched to cello.

10. For sound-alikes and certain words that sound almost alike, choose the word with your intended meaning. (See pages 860–887.)

Before Editing	**After Editing**
Atticus wanted *too* clean the kitchen. (*too* means "also" or "in addition")	Atticus wanted *to* clean the kitchen. (*to* is part of the infinitive *to clean*)
I have *to* jobs, but I probably need three. (*to* means "in the direction of")	I have *two* jobs, but I probably need three. (*two* is a number)
You're tendrils could use a trim. (*you're* is a contraction of *you are*)	*Your* tendrils could use a trim. (*your* is the possessive form of *you*)
They're problem is obvious. (*they're* is a contraction of *they are*)	*Their* problem is obvious. (*their* is the possessive form of *they*)
Their you go again. (*their* is the possessive form of *they*)	*There* you go again. (there means "in that place")
Its unfortunate that Marcus lost in the first round of the chess tournament. (*its* is the possessive form of *it*)	*It's* unfortunate that Marcus lost in the first round of the chess tournament. (*it's* is a contraction of *it is*)

CHAPTER 1

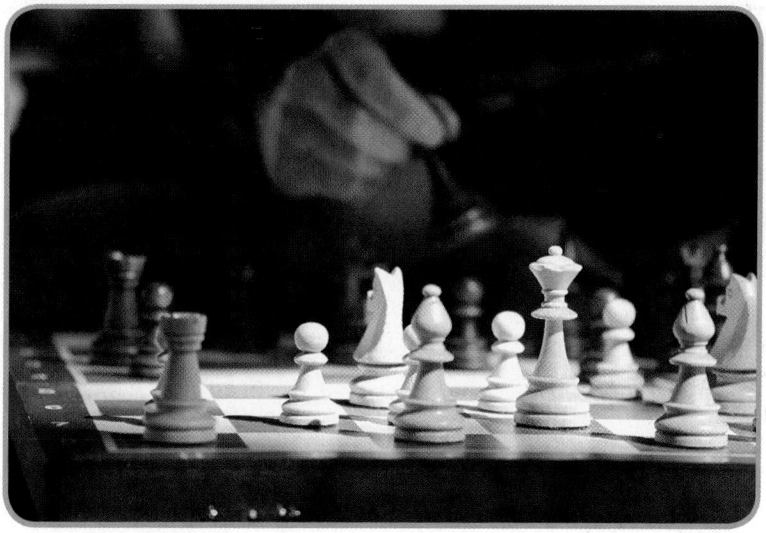

Learning Tip

With a partner, think of one more **Before Editing** and **After Editing** example for each rule. Write your examples down and share them with the rest of the class while someone records them on the board or on a large sheet of paper.

Writers often use the following proofreading symbols to indicate where they need to make changes when they edit. These symbols help writers know where their writing should be revised to follow the Power Rules.

PROOFREADING SYMBOLS

Symbol	Meaning	Example
^	insert	We went on a ^fantastic journey.
^,	insert comma	Meg enjoys hiking, skiing^, and skating.
⊙	insert period	Gary took the bus to Atlanta⊙
ℊ	delete	Refer ~~back~~ to your notes.
¶	new paragraph	¶ Finally Balboa saw the Pacific.
no ¶	no paragraph	no ¶ The dachshund trotted away.
. . .	let it stand	I appreciated her sincere honesty.
#	add space	She will be^#back in a moment.
⁐	close up	The airplane waited on the run way.
tr	transpose	They only have two dollars left.
≡	capital letter	We later moved to the south.
/	lowercase letter	His favorite subject was Science.
(SP)	spell out	I ate 2 oranges.
∨"∨ ∨"∨	insert quotes	I hope you can join us, said my brother.
=^	insert hyphen	I attended a school=related event.
∨'∨	insert apostrophe	The ravenous dog ate the cats food.
◯→	move copy	I usually on Fridays go to the movies.

Learning Tip

Write the following sentence on a piece of paper, just as it's written here:

Have you scene that new movie withthe amazing specail affects, Maria asked, trying to make conversation?

Add proofreading symbols to show corrections and to show how to move the last phrase to the beginning of the sentence. Compare your work with a partner's.

4 Writing in the 21st Century

If you are like most teenagers, you are already an expert in much of 21st century writing. You send at least 100 text messages every day. You spend at least an hour a day on the Internet, often on social networking Web sites. You may blog; write e-mail, text, and instant messages; maintain a social networking site; and write notes to friends on theirs. You upload photos, videos, and music files, and people often respond to them. You "talk" with friends in chat rooms, often carrying on several conversations at the same time. You might complement these interactions with video technology so that you can see the people with whom you converse. For each type of 21st century writing, you probably follow unique and often evolving conventions.

You also write in school. You answer essay questions on tests, write papers for English, take notes in social studies, write research reports for various classes, and write appropriate sorts of texts for other classes.

Outside school, you may submit reports as part of your job, keep a log of various activities, write poems and perform them, and keep a journal as a way to think about your life.

The Right Kind of Writing?

With all these kinds of writing, what is the "right" way to write? There is no single way to write that is "right" for every occasion. The right way to write is the way that's appropriate for the situation, your reasons for writing, and the expectations of your readers. In other words, writing should be "in tune" with what is appropriate for the purpose, audience, occasion, and genre.

Global Interactions

Technology makes it easy for you to get and stay connected with people. Life today spans the globe: The Internet enables you to buy music from distant lands, the Web sites you visit may have versions in several different languages, and the computer you use may be assembled from parts produced in several different countries.

Those who work, play, and thrive in this wired world benefit from **creative thinking** and the ability to **work cooperatively with others.** To make it in the 21st century, you need to be able to **think critically, reason logically,** and **solve all manner of problems** effectively. You will need to know how to **communicate** and **master the technologies** through which you engage in virtual exchanges with others. Writing can help you develop all of those skills and prepare you to live a satisfying and fulfilling life in the 21st century.

Learning Tip

For one day, keep a log of how many times you write, and under what circumstances. Include text messaging. Compare your log to those of your classmates and look for patterns.

Collaborating Through the Writing Process

The writer is often depicted as a solitary scribe, working with a personal muse but otherwise sequestered from the rabble. Some parts of the writing process are indeed accomplished alone, but most people write as a joint activity. People talk over their ideas with others, get feedback as they work, have an editor or supervisor read and critique their writing, and complete other similar activities. For the writing in this program, you and your classmates will create and participate in a **community of writers** and work in **collaboration** throughout the writing process, often in groups of three to four students.

1 Prewriting: Getting Started

Strategies for Finding a Subject

The following prewriting strategies involve pondering your interests, skills, and experiences to discover a store of ideas for writing.

Taking an Inventory of Your Interests Thinking about your life and even dreams about the future is one way to discover good subjects for writing. Ask yourself questions like the following and write your answers.

- What is the most difficult decision I have ever had to make?
- What accomplishment am I especially proud of?
- What advice would I give to someone younger?

Keeping a Journal A **journal** is a daily notebook in which you explore your responses to people and events in your own life and in the larger world. Many writers find their journal an indispensable source of writing ideas. It is a place to ask questions, to dream, to be angry, to list words and ideas for writing, to draw pictures, to be yourself, or to make sense of the world.

Keeping a Learning Log A Learning Log is a section of your journal where you can write down ideas or information about math, science, history, health, or any other subject that interests you. You can use it to capture what you know about a subject and what you still need or want to learn about it. You can also use it to record your progress as a writer.

Reading, Interviewing, Discussing Use the following strategies to develop ideas for subjects. In each case, take notes to remember the ideas that surfaced.

HERE'S HOW

Strategies for Thinking of Subjects

- Do some background reading on general topics that interest you. If you are interested in aviation, for example, find some recent articles to read in the library or on the Internet.
- Interview someone who knows more about a subject than you do.
- Discuss subjects of mutual interest with classmates, friends, and/or family to find interesting and fresh angles on a subject.

Choosing and Limiting a Subject

Review your ideas from prewriting work and select the ones that meet the requirements of your particular assignment. Then apply the following guidelines.

HERE'S HOW

Guidelines for Choosing a Subject

- Choose a subject that will really engage you and your readers.
- Choose a subject you can cover well through your own knowledge or through a reasonable amount of research.
- Consider your purpose for writing, the occasion for writing, and the readers of your work. (See pages 16–17 for more on purpose, occasion, and audience.) Be sure your topic is appropriate for each of those factors.

Once you have chosen a subject, you may need to limit it so that it is more manageable. General topics such as *inventions, education,* or *China* are too broad, and they tend to promote poorly organized, over-generalized essays. Something more limited, on the other hand, is more manageable because it focuses on just one facet. To limit your subject, use one or a combination of the following strategies.

HERE'S HOW

Guidelines for Limiting a Subject

- Limit your subject to just one person or example that represents the subject.
- Limit your subject to a specific time or place.
- Limit your subject to a specific event.
- Limit your subject to a specific condition, purpose, or procedure.

Notice how a student writer, Sarah, limited the subject of her essay on getting a job.

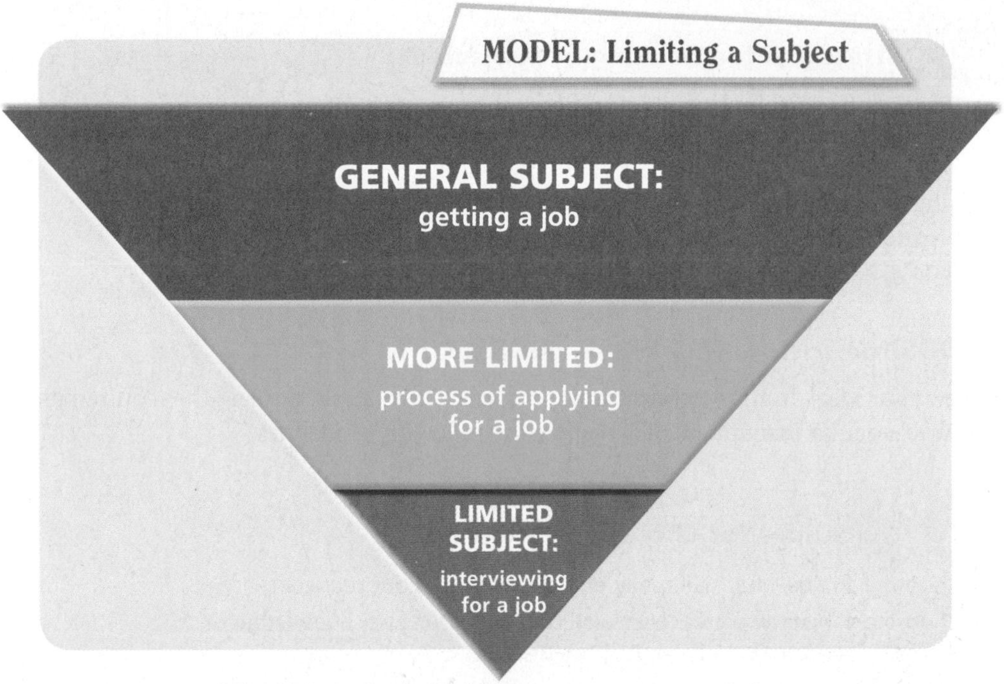

Considering Your Purpose, Occasion, Audience, and Genre

Purpose is your reason for writing or speaking. In successful communication, the purpose of your message is appropriate to both the occasion that prompts it and the audience who will receive it. The following chart lists the most common purposes.

RHETORICAL PURPOSES	POSSIBLE FORMS
Expository to **explain** or **inform;** to focus on your subject matter and audience	**Factual writing** scientific essay, research paper, business letter, summary, descriptive essay, historical narrative, news story
Creative (literary) to **create;** to focus on making imaginative use of language and ideas	**Entertaining writing** short story, novel, play, poem, dialogue
Persuasive to **persuade;** to focus on changing your readers' minds or getting them to act in a certain way	**Convincing writing** letter to the editor, persuasive essay, movie or book review, critical essay (literary analysis), advertisement
Self-expressive to **express** and **reflect** on your thoughts and feelings	**Personal writing** journal entry, personal narrative, reflective essay, personal letter

Occasion is your motivation for composing—the factor that prompts you to communicate. Occasion usually can be stated well using one of the following sentences.

- I feel a need to write for my own satisfaction.
- I have been asked to write this by [name a person].
- I want to write an entry for [name a publication].
- I want to enter a writing contest.

As you plan your writing, you also need to remember the **audience** you will be addressing. Who will be reading your work? What are their interests and concerns? How can you best communicate to this particular audience?

CHAPTER 1

HERE'S HOW

Audience Profile Questions

- Who will be reading my work?
- How old are they? Are they adults? Teenagers? Children?
- What do I want the audience to know about my subject?
- What background do they have in the subject?
- What interests and opinions are they apt to have? Are there any words or terms I should define for them?

The **genre,** or form of writing, you choose will have an impact on your subject. (See the chart on the previous page for a listing of common forms or genres of writing.) Each genre has its own defining characteristics, and readers expect these to be present when they read. If you are reading a science fiction story, for example, you expect a story of imaginary events set in the future. If you begin reading and find that instead of a futuristic story, you are reading a nonfiction essay exploring the role of women in Victorian England, you would not know how to interpret the text. In the same way, if a college asked for a personal essay as part of your admission application, you would be wise to provide one within the bounds of their expectations: a thoughtful, nonfiction, reflective, and interpretive essay about yourself, not, for example, a collection of haiku.

Collaboration in Action

Prewriting

Orell, Sarah, and Joe are in a writing group together. This is their first meeting as a group, though they've known each other for years. Their task is to come up with a topic and choose the purpose and audience for their writing. Here's how their discussion might go:

Orell: Hey Sarah, where were you all summer?

Sarah: I was mainly around, but I was a counselor at the YMCA camp for a month.

Joe: I had to work all summer.

Sarah: Where did you work?

Joe: I worked in the kitchen at Porky's Rib Shack.

Orell: I don't think I'd like that job very much.

Joe: So, where would you work?

Orell: I'd work in an office somewhere.

Joe: Yeah? How would you get a job like that?

Orell: I don't know. Maybe I'll find out.

Sarah: Write your paper on it! I'm going to do mine for high school students on how to interview for a job.

Orell: I think I will. Mine could also be be a how-to paper for high school students. I'll have to research it though, because I really don't know how to get an office job.

Joe: You could probably find out a lot online. Mrs. Tanforth also has those books in her office about getting a job.

Orell: Good ideas, thanks.

Joe: You know, Orell, you say you wouldn't have wanted my job, but it actually wasn't too bad. I'll bet a lot of kids don't know what goes on in a kitchen like that. I could write about that, for people who don't know.

Collaboration Practice

Meet with a small group for 10 minutes. Use what you have learned to try to come up with a good writing topic for each member.

2 Prewriting: From Ideas to a Plan

Developing a Subject

At this point, you have chosen a subject, limited it, and considered your occasion, audience, purpose, and genre. Now you can begin to collect **supporting details** such as facts, examples, incidents, reasons, sensory details, and other specifics that will give life and meaning to your subject. The following strategies will help you gather material.

Brainstorming In **brainstorming,** your goal is to work with a partner or a group of classmates and freely list all ideas related to your subject as they occur to you. Just let them flow from one to another until you have unearthed a large store of ideas.

HERE'S HOW

Collaboration: Guidelines for Brainstorming

- Set a time limit, such as 15 minutes.
- Write the subject on a piece of paper and ask someone to be the recorder. If your group meets frequently, take turns recording ideas.
- Start brainstorming for details—facts, examples, incidents, reasons, connections, and associations. Since you can eliminate irrelevant ideas later, contribute and record any and all ideas.
- Build on the ideas of other group members. Add to those ideas or modify them to make them better.
- Avoid criticizing the ideas of other group members.

You can learn more about cooperative learning on page 588.

When you have finished brainstorming, you should get a copy of all the supporting details from the group recorder. Then, from the group list, select the details that are best for your own essay.

Clustering **Clustering** is a visual form of brainstorming in which you not only jot down details as you think of them but also make connections among those details. As with oral brainstorming, in which you note your ideas in a list, a useful cluster of ideas is uncensored. A cluster may be as simple or as complex as needed to capture all of the ideas that occur to you. The important thing in a cluster is to show the connections between ideas, either as they occur or later, when your ideas are down on paper and you are trying to organize them. Sarah developed the following cluster on the subject of interviewing for a job.

MODEL: Clustering

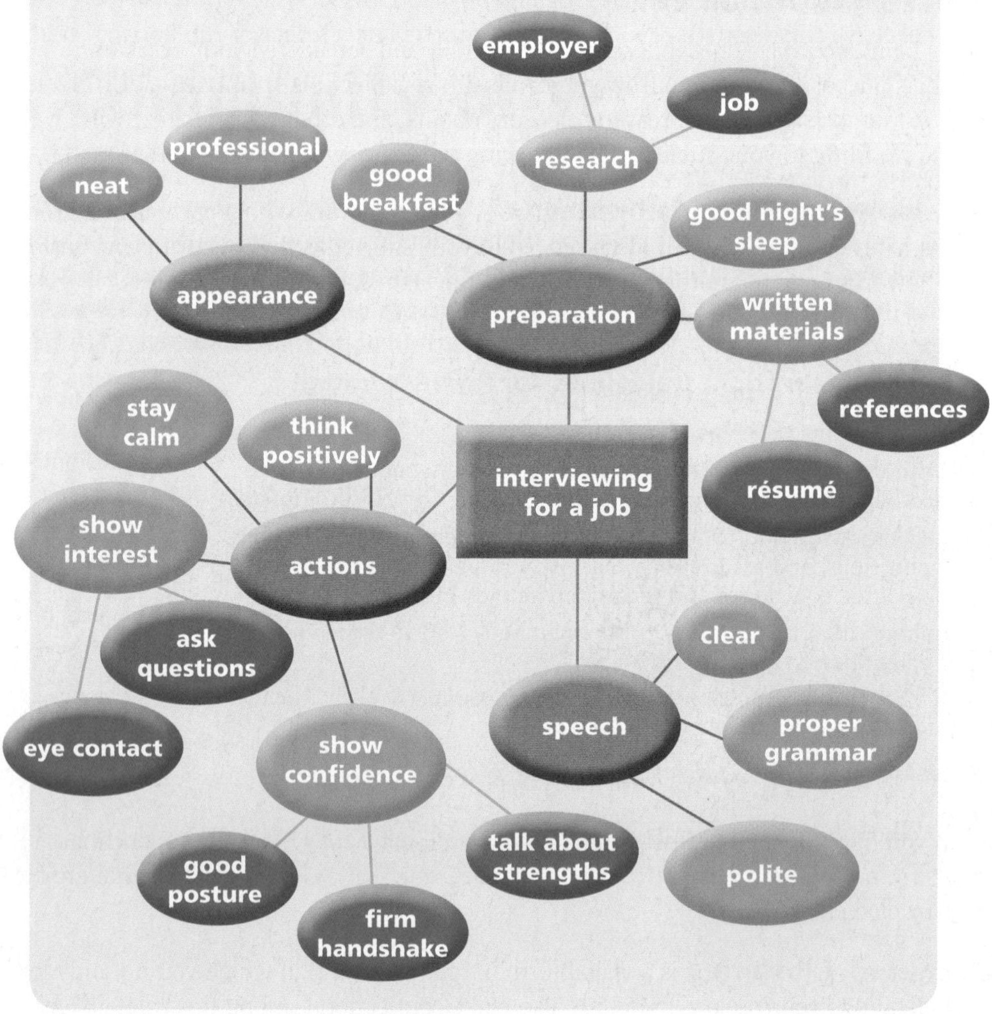

Inquiring Inquiring is a way to explore a subject as journalists do. Asking and answering questions that begin with *who, what, where, when, why,* and *how* can be a good way to develop details for an essay. Notice that a number of questions can emerge from each word. The following model shows how one writer used this technique on the subject of acid rain pollution.

MODEL: Inquiring to Develop Supporting Details

SUBJECT: ACID RAIN POLLUTION

Who	studies acid rain pollution? first discovered the effects of acid rain?
What	is the definition of acid rain pollution? causes acid rain? are the effects of this type of pollution?
Where	does acid rain pollution occur? are the effects most harmful?
When	were the effects of acid rain first noticed?
How	are the effects of acid rain studied? if possible, can the effects be reduced? can citizens become involved in solving this problem?
Why	do the causes vary in different regions? should people study acid rain pollution?

CHAPTER 1

Organizing Details

Focusing Your Subject Before organizing your information, determine the focus, or **main idea,** of your writing. A main idea is also called a **controlling idea** because all the other ideas in the text must relate to it.

Learning Tip

With a partner, use brainstorming, clustering, or inquiring to develop ideas for a topic of your choice. Share your work with the rest of the class.

HERE'S HOW

Guidelines for Deciding on a Focus

- Look over your details. Can you draw meaningful generalizations from some or all of the details? If so, the generalization could be the focus of your writing.
- Choose a main idea that intrigues you.
- Choose a main idea that suits your purpose and audience.

Sarah has decided to focus on how best to succeed in a job interview. This main idea grew out of a generalization she made about some of her details. Since she has had success in interviewing for jobs, she is eager to exploit this main idea for her essay. Her assignment is to write an essay that informs her audience—her classmates—about something. Her idea clearly suits this purpose and the genres associated with it, and her classmates are apt to find the subject both interesting and informative.

CHAPTER 1

Classifying and Ordering Details Organize your material by **classifying** your details—that is, grouping related details that support the main idea. Sarah has decided to group her details into three categories. She will explain strategies to use (1) before, (2) during, and (3) after a job interview. This logical grouping will allow the reader to track the ideas easily.

Next, place your details in the best order to achieve your writing purpose.

WAYS TO ORGANIZE DETAILS

Type of Order	Definition	Examples
Chronological	the order in which events occur	story, explanation, history, biography, drama
Spatial	location or physical arrangement	description (top to bottom, near to far, left to right, etc.)
Order of Importance	degree of importance, size, or interest	persuasive writing, description, evaluations, explanations
Logical	logical progression, one detail growing out of another	classifications, definitions, comparison and contrast

Following is the list of details Sarah developed, arranged here in chronological order.

MODEL: Ordering Details

Before the Interview

- learn about job and employer
- prepare written materials—résumé, references
- get good night's sleep
- establish neat appearance

During the Interview

- arrive on time
- greet interviewer with handshake
- keep good posture
- use clear, proper speech
- emphasize strengths
- listen carefully, make eye contact, ask questions

After the interview

- thank interviewer
- leave with firm handshake
- write thank-you note

3 Drafting

In writing your first draft, you pull together all of your prewriting notes into complete sentences and form a beginning, a middle, and an end—an introduction, a body, and a conclusion. As you draft your essay, you will learn whether you actually have a workable subject with enough pertinent details or if you will need to rethink your subject. Remember, your goal here is not to struggle over individual words but to present your ideas in a coherent, understandable form. Here are some strategies to help you prepare a first draft.

HERE'S HOW

Strategies for Drafting

- Write an introduction that will capture the reader's interest and express your main idea. You may want to return to your introduction at a later stage to evaluate its effectiveness in reaching your audience and addressing your purpose.
- After you write your introduction, use your notes as a guide, but depart from them as needed.
- Write fairly quickly. Don't worry about spelling or phrasing. You will have the opportunity to revise.
- Stop frequently and read what you have written. This practice will help you move logically from one thought to the next.
- Do not be afraid to return to the prewriting stage. You can always stop and freewrite, brainstorm, or cluster to collect ideas.
- Write a conclusion that drives home the point of the essay.

Sarah did some research about interviewing for a job and wrote the following first draft. Notice that a number of mechanical errors in this draft will need to be corrected later on in the editing stage.

MODEL: First Draft

Learning how to interview for a job is one of the most valuable skills you can develop. Wether you are applying for a part-time summer job, an internship, or a full-time professional position, it is important to know how to interview good. There are several things you can do to make sure that the interview is a success. This will improve your chances of getting a job.

It is important to think in advance about how to make the best possible impression on your interviewer. It is always a good idea to start by learning as much as you can about the job and the employer. Start off by carefully reading the job description. Then, research your prospective employer by asking for and reading any company brochures. Do some online research on the company's Web site. You should also take some time to prepare additional written materials about. It is always a good idea to bring along several copies of your résumé, as well as something to take notes on. Try to get a good night's sleep the night before the interview.

On the day of the interview, dress as neatly as possible—never allow yourself to look disheveled! Leave plenty of time to get to the interviewer's office on time. When you arrive, shake hands with the person inter-viewing you and assume a confident posture when you sit. Explain your background and experience. To do this, use clear, proper speech and emphacise your strengths and skills. Be sure to point out how your skills will help you do the job well. In addition, show your interest and enthusiasm by asking questions and maintaining eye contact. Be sure to listen carefully.

Closing the interview and following up on it. This is very important to your success. Thank the interviewer for his or her time and leave with a firm hand shake. Be sure to write a brief thank-you note, or follow-up letter, to the interviewer expressing thanks once again for meeting with you. The sooner you do this, the better the impression you will make, and the fresher you will remain in your interviewer's mind.

Preparation, performing, and follow-up is the critical things for Success when interviewing for a job and my experience has taught me that following and carrying out these steps for interviewing will help ensure that you have you're fare share of job offers!

Drafting a Title

The final step in drafting your essay is to think of an accurately descriptive, captivating title. Often titles can be taken directly from words and phrases in the essay itself. Others can read like a newspaper headline and express the main idea in an eye-catching way. Whatever your approach, remember that your title should capture the reader's interest *and* suggest your main idea.

HERE'S HOW

Guidelines for Choosing a Title

- Choose a title that identifies your subject or relates to your subject focus.
- Choose a title that is appropriate for your purpose and audience.
- Choose a title that will capture the reader's interest.

4 Revising

Following are some strategies you can use to improve your draft.

REVISING STRATEGIES	QUICK FIXES
Check for Clarity and Creativity • Are your ideas interesting, fresh, and original, rather than ones that people have heard over and over? • Does the text satisfy its purpose?	• Insert a personal experience or example. • Think of an unlikely comparison between your subject and something else. • Talk with others to get ideas. • Explore your subject from someone else's point of view.
Elaborate by Adding Details • Does your writing seem fully developed? • Are your ideas fully supported? • Have you used details that would help bring a scene or idea to life for a reader?	• Use one of the prewriting strategies on pages 14–15 and 18–21 to come up with lively elaborations. • Add extra information between dashes (page 93), tell who or what with appositive phrases (page 175), add details with adjectives come lately or early (page 202), get into the action with participial phrases (page 351), tell which one or what kind with adjectival clauses (page 376), add details through a subordinate clause (pages 62, 307, 376, and 712–722). • Show, don't tell. • Take a mental snapshot of a scene and write what you see.
Rearrange Out-of-Order Items • Check the organization of your words, sentences, and ideas. Does one idea lead logically into another? • Can any ideas be combined?	• Use your word processor to rearrange and reorganize your sentences or paragraphs so the reader can easily follow your thoughts. • Use transitions to show the relationships between ideas.
Delete Unnecessary Words or Details • Do all the details in your draft relate to your controlling idea?	• Cut unrelated details. Also delete any extra or unneeded words and repetitive sentences and paragraphs.
Substitute Words and Sentences • Are all parts of your draft as clear as possible? • Are all of your words precise and vivid?	• Ask a "test reader" to tell you where you need to provide more or clearer information. • For a dull, general word, find a richer and more vivid synonym.

Using a Six-Trait Rubric

A rubric like the one below can help you determine what you need to do to improve your draft. You can also use it to evaluate the work of your writing group partners.

Ideas	**4** The main idea is clear. Plenty of details such as facts, examples, and anecdotes provide support.	**3** The main idea is clear. There is enough support for the main idea to back it up adequately.	**2** The main idea could be clearer. There are some supporting details, but more details would be helpful.	**1** The main idea statement is missing or unclear. Few examples and facts are provided in support.
Organization	**4** The organization is clear with abundant transitions.	**3** A few ideas seem out of place or transitions are missing.	**2** Many ideas seem out of place and transitions are missing.	**1** The organization is unclear and hard to follow.
Voice	**4** The voice sounds natural, engaging, and unique.	**3** The voice sounds natural and engaging.	**2** The voice sounds mostly natural but is weak.	**1** The voice sounds mostly unnatural and is weak.
Word Choice	**4** Words are specific, powerful, and appropriate to the task.	**3** Words are specific and language is appropriate.	**2** Some words are too general and/or misleading.	**1** Most words are overly general and imprecise.
Sentence Fluency	**4** Varied sentences flow smoothly.	**3** Most sentences are varied and flow smoothly.	**2** Some sentences are varied but some are choppy.	**1** Sentences are not varied and are choppy.
Conventions	**4** Punctuation, usage, and spelling are correct. The Power Rules are all followed.	**3** Punctuation, usage, and spelling are mainly correct and Power Rules are all followed.	**2** Some punctuation, usage, and spelling are incorrect but all Power Rules are followed.	**1** There are many errors and at least one failure to follow a Power Rule.

Using a Checklist

A checklist like the one on the next page is another tool for improving a draft.

Evaluation Checklist for Revising

✓ Did you clearly state your main idea? (pages 21–24 and 85–86)
✓ Does your text have a strong introduction, body, and conclusion? (pages 112–124)
✓ Did you support your main idea with enough details? (pages 19–22, 25, and 90–91)
✓ Do your details show instead of merely telling what you want to say? (pages 19–22 and 90–91)
✓ Did you present your ideas in a logical order? (pages 5 and 22)
✓ Do all of your sentences relate to the main idea? (pages 22–23 and 90–91)
✓ Are your ideas clearly explained? (page 25)
✓ Are your words specific? (pages 6 and 49)
✓ Have you removed any words or ideas that are repeated unnecessarily? (pages 25 and 68)
✓ Are your sentences varied and smoothly connected? (pages 59–66)
✓ Is the purpose of your text clear? (pages 5–6 and 16)
✓ Is your writing suited to your audience? (pages 16–17)
✓ Is your title effective? (page 24)

CHAPTER 1

CONFERENCING

You have been **conferencing,** meeting with others to share ideas or identify and solve problems, throughout the writing process. Conferencing is especially helpful during revising when weaknesses in the writing can be addressed. However, offering something that might sound like criticism isn't an easy thing to do. At the same time, you don't help your writing group members if you are not honest with them. The trick is to be positive and specific and to offer praise as well as any suggestions for improvement.

HERE'S HOW

Guidelines for Conferencing

Guidelines for the Writer

- List some questions for your peer. What aspects of your work most concern you?
- Try to be grateful for your critic's candor rather than being upset or defensive. Keep in mind that the criticism you are getting is well intended.

Guidelines for the Critic

- Read your partner's work carefully. What does the writer promise to do in this text? Does he or she succeed?
- Point out strengths as well as weaknesses. Start your comments by saying something positive like, "Your opening really captured my interest."
- Be specific. Refer to a specific word, sentence, or section when you comment.
- Be sensitive to your partner's feelings. Phrase your criticisms as questions. You might say, "Do you think your details might be stronger if ... ?"

Collaboration in Action

Revising

Sarah's writing group has already discussed Orell's and Joe's drafts. They made notes on their papers about where they could make improvements based on their peers' feedback. Now it is Sarah's turn to have her paper discussed.

Sarah: All right everybody, what do you think of my paper on job interviews?

Joe: Well, you've got some good information, and the organization is clear.

Orell: I thought it was really good. The only things I noticed were some repetition and some mistakes that need editing.

Sarah: Okay, I can fix that stuff. I just wrote it all out and didn't bother to go back and revise. Where do you see repetition?

Orell: In the first paragraph, for example. your first sentence says that interview skills are very important. Then at the end of your second sentence, you say the same thing.

Sarah: Wow, you're right, I do.

Joe: I really liked the way you summed up the three most important things in your conclusion.

Sarah: Thanks.

Orell: That last sentence seems too long though.

Collaboration Practice

Choose a paper you are working on or have completed previously and make two copies, one for each member of your group. Conference with one another to improve your drafts.

USING FEEDBACK FROM YOUR TEACHER

Your teacher is a member of the community of writers and an excellent collaborator. He or she is probably with you for each stage of the writing process. The chart shows different ways your teacher can provide feedback and how you can use that feedback to improve your writing.

TEACHER FEEDBACK	HOW TO USE FEEDBACK
During prewriting your teacher might • meet briefly with you to discuss and approve your topic • suggest ways you might gather information and other supporting materials • comment on your organization	**You can use this feedback to improve your work by** • rethinking if necessary to come up with a sharply focused topic • following the suggestions with an open mind • experimenting with different organizational patterns
During drafting your teacher might • move from desk to desk to offer suggestions on your process of drafting (for example, continually going back and rereading what you've written) • offer suggestions or concerns about a direction your draft seems to be taking	**You can use this feedback to improve your work by** • trying out the suggestions, even if they are uncomfortable at first • saving your work and then coming back to it with a fresh eye to try to see the concerns your teacher raised • asking questions if don't understand the concerns your teacher has
During revising your teacher might • meet with you to go over some issues face to face • make written comments on your work about ideas, organization, and flow	**You can use this feedback to improve your work by** • making a good effort to change the things you discussed • using the comments as positive guides rather than negative criticisms
During editing your teacher might • identify errors • offer mini-lessons on challenging points	**You can use this feedback to improve your work by** • making corrections and adding items to your personalized checklist
During publishing your teacher might • give you presentation ideas • help you reach your audience	**You can use this feedback to improve your work by** • gaining confidence in sharing your work with readers and being willing to take risks

5 Editing and Publishing

Editing for Wordiness: Editing Star

Any large home appliance certified by the Environmental Protection Agency ensures customers of its "energy star" efficiency. A clothes dryer that is marked with an energy star is guaranteed to get the same results as a clothes dryer that uses more energy. The less power required to do a job, the more energy-efficient the product is.

Word power is similar to energy power in that efficiency is often desirable. The fewer words needed to get the job done, the more efficient the writing is. In the following two examples, note how much stronger the efficient version is.

Word Guzzler	It seems that Beverly was cooking the morning breakfast meal and being that she liked waffles, she made those for breakfast.
Fuel Efficient	Beverly made waffles for breakfast.

EDITING STAR

Throughout the composition chapters in this book, you will see the language arts version of the energy star logo: the editing star. It will accompany a brief activity that can remind you to cut out wordiness.

Using a General Editing Checklist

Writers often use an editing checklist. The best way to use such a list is to go over your paper several times, looking for a different kind of problem each time. For instance, you might look for spelling errors in one reading and comma errors in the next. You might also want to read your essay backward, word by word. You will find that you are able to spot many errors that you might otherwise miss. The following checklist will help you guard against common errors.

Editing Checklist

- ✓ Are your sentences free of errors in grammar and usage?
- ✓ Did you spell each word correctly?
- ✓ Did you use capital letters where needed?
- ✓ Did you punctuate each sentence correctly?
- ✓ Did you indent paragraphs as needed?

Using a Manual of Style

Writers often consult style guides or handbooks to review rules for grammar, usage, and mechanics. As you edit, you may wish to consult one of the following guides.

- *A Manual for Writers of Research Papers, Theses, and Dissertations.* Kate Turabian. 7th ed., Chicago: University of Chicago Press, 2007.
- *The Chicago Manual of Style: The Essential Guide for Writers, Editors, and Publishers.* 15th ed. Chicago: University of Chicago Press, 2003.
- *MLA Handbook for Writers of Research Papers.* 7th ed. New York: Modern Language Association of America, 2009.

Creating a Personalized Editing Checklist

You may want to reserve eight pages at the end of your journal for a Personalized Editing Checklist. Write one of these headings on every other page: Grammar, Usage, Spelling, and Mechanics (capitalization and punctuation). Use these pages to record recurring errors in each category. Consult the index in this book to find the pages on which each problem is addressed. Write those page numbers next to the error, along with some examples of the corrected problem. Add to this checklist throughout the year and refer to it each time you edit an essay.

Proofreading

Proofreading during the editing stage helps you pick up mistakes that you missed earlier. **Proofreading** means carefully rereading your work and marking corrections in grammar, usage, spelling, and mechanics.

HERE'S HOW

Proofreading Techniques

- Focus on one line at a time.
- Exchange essays with a partner and check each other's work.
- Read your essay backward, word by word.
- Read your essay aloud, very slowly.
- Use a dictionary and a handbook to check spelling, grammar, usage, and mechanics.

The following model shows how Sarah edited part of her essay about achieving success in a job interview. Notice how she used proofreading symbols to correct errors in grammar, usage, spelling, and mechanics.

Interviewing for a Job

Learning how to interview for a job is one of the most valuable

skills you can develop. Wether you are applying for a part-time
(h)

summer job, an internship, or a full-time professional position, it is

important to know how to interview good. There are several things
steps

you can do to make sure that the interview is a success. This will
take

improve your chances of getting a job.
ing   *that you really enjoy*

It is important to think in advance about how to make the best

possible impression on your interviewer. It is always a good idea to start
way

by learning as much as you can about the job and the employer. Start off

by carefully reading the job description. Then, research your prospective

employer by asking for and reading any company brochures. If the

company has a Web site, do some online research. You should also take

yourself, such as recommendations and references from previous employers
some time to prepare additional written materials about. It is always a good

idea to bring along several copies of your résumé, as well as something to

Finally
take notes on. Try to get a good night's sleep the night before the interview.

PUBLISHING

Here are just a few ways you could share your writing.

HERE'S HOW

Publishing Options

In School

- Read your work aloud to a small group in your class.
- Display your final draft on a bulletin board in your classroom or school library.
- Read your work aloud to your class or present it in the form of a radio program or video.
- Create a class library and media center to which you submit your work. The library and media center should be a collection of folders or files devoted to different types of student writing and media presentations.
- Create a class anthology to which every student contributes one piece. Use electronic technology to design a small publication. Share your anthology with other classes.
- Submit your work to your school literary magazine, newspaper, or yearbook.

Outside School

- Submit your written work to a newspaper or magazine.
- Share your work with a professional interested in the subject.
- Present your work to an appropriate community group.
- Send a video based on your written work to a local cable television station.
- Enter your work in a local, state, or national writing contest.

CHAPTER 1

Using Standard Manuscript Form The appearance of your essay may be almost as important as its content. A marked-up paper with inconsistent margins is difficult to read. A neat, legible paper, however, makes a positive impression on your reader. When you are using a word-processing program to prepare your final draft, it is important to know how to lay out the page and how to choose a typeface and type size.

Use the following guidelines for standard manuscript form to help you prepare your final draft. The model on pages 34–35 shows how Sarah used these guidelines to prepare her final draft on job interviews.

CHAPTER 1

HERE'S HOW

Standard Manuscript Form

- Use standard-sized 8-1/2 by 11-inch white paper. Use one side of the paper only.
- If handwriting, use black or blue ink. If using a word-processing program or typing, use a black ink cartridge or black typewriter ribbon and double-space the lines.
- Leave a 1.25-inch margin at the left and right. The left margin must be even. The right margin should be as even as possible.
- Put your name, the course title, the name of your teacher, and the date in the upper right-hand corner of the first page. Where it is applicable, follow your teacher's specific guidelines for headings and margins.
- Center the title of your essay two lines below the date. Do not underline or put quotation marks around your title.
- If using a word-processing program or typing, skip four lines between the title and the first paragraph. If handwriting, skip two lines.
- If using a word-processing program or typing, indent the first line of each paragraph five spaces. If handwriting, indent the first line of each paragraph 1 inch.
- Leave a 1-inch margin at the bottom of all pages.
- Starting on page 2, number each page in the upper right-hand corner. Begin the first line 1 inch from the top. Word-processing programs give you the option of inserting page numbers.

MODEL: Final Draft

1 inch

Sarah Crenshaw
English: Ms.
DiLorenzo
September 18, 2015

2 lines

Interviewing for a Job

4 lines

Whether you are applying for a part-time summer job, an internship, or a full-time professional position, learning how to interview for a job is one of the most valuable skills you can develop. There are several steps you can take to make sure that the interview is a success, thus improving your chances of getting a job that you really enjoy.

1.25 inches

1.25 inches

It is important to think in advance about how to make the best possible impression on your interviewer. Learning as much as you can about the job and the employer is always a good way to start. Carefully read the job description. Then research your prospective employer by asking for and reading any company brochures. If the company has a Web site, do some online research. Also take some time to prepare additional written materials about yourself such as recommendations and references from previous employers. It is always a good idea to bring along several copies of your résumé, as well as something to take notes on. Finally, try to get a good night's sleep the night before the interview.

On the day of the interview, dress as neatly as possible—never allow yourself to look disheveled! Leave plenty of time to get to the interviewer's office on time. When you arrive, shake hands with the person interviewing you and assume a confident posture when you sit. As you explain your background and experience, use clear, proper speech and emphasize your strengths and skills. Be sure to point out how your specific skills will help you do the job well. In addition, show your interest and enthusiasm by asking questions and maintaining eye contact as you listen carefully.

1.25 inches

1.25 inches

Closing the interview and following up on it are very important to your success. Thank the interviewer for his or her time and leave with a firm handshake. Be sure to write a brief thank-you note, or follow-up letter, to the interviewer expressing appreciation once again for meeting with you. The sooner you do follow up, the better the impression you will make, and the fresher you will remain in your interviewer's mind.

Preparation, performance, and follow-up are the critical elements for success when interviewing for a job. My experience has taught me that following and carrying out these steps for interviewing will help ensure that you have your fair share of job offers!

1 inch

Keeping a Writer's Portfolio

As you begin your writing, think of yourself as an apprentice learning a craft. Ideally, with each new essay you write, you come a step closer to developing your own composing processes. A good way to track your progress is to keep a **portfolio**—a collection of your work that represents various types of writing and your progress in them. The following guidelines will help you make the most of your portfolio.

CHAPTER 1

HERE'S HOW

Guidelines for Including Work in Your Portfolio

- Date each piece of writing so that you can see where it fits into your progress.
- Write a brief note to yourself about why you included each piece—what you believe it shows about you as a writer.
- Include unfinished works if they demonstrate something meaningful about you as a writer.

Occasionally, you will be asked to take "Time Out to Reflect." Reflecting on your experience as a writer will give you an opportunity to develop your process even further. Your written reflections are suitable additions to your portfolio.

Time Out to Reflect

Take a moment to write down your understanding of the writing process. How closely does this process match your previous experiences as a writer? What might account for any differences between the writing process as described in this chapter and the writing process as you have previously experienced it? How did you collaborate through this process?

Timed Writing: On Your Own

There are times in school, such as during testing, when you will not be able to benefit from collaboration. The more you collaborate when you can, however, the less alone you will feel in those situations. You will no doubt be able to remember things your writing partners have said during your group meetings and then use them in your solo writing as well. For example, you might catch yourself writing a word or phrase that your group members thought was overused and too general. Or you might remember that, time after time, your group members reminded you to use transitions to connect ideas. Use these memories to help you do your very best on timed writing tasks.

CHAPTER 1

The following chart shows the stages of a timed writing experience. In each, imagine what your writing partners would be saying to help you.

HERE'S HOW

Working Through Timed Writing Tasks

- Begin by understanding the task. Read the prompt carefully. Identify the key words in the directions: they will tell you what kind of writing to produce. Ask yourself what your audience—the examiners—will be looking for, and try to provide it.
- Think about the time you have for the test and make a budget. Leave the most time for drafting, but build in time for planning and revising as well.
- Plan your writing by jotting down ideas, making lists, or using any other format that helps you (such as a cluster diagram). When you have good ideas to work with, arrange them in a logical order.
- Think through how to begin your writing. Begin drafting when you know what your main idea will be and you have ideas for introducing it.
- Use your notes to draft the body of your work.
- Remember what you have learned about strong conclusions and write a good ending to your work.
- Read over your work. If something seems confusing or out of place, fix it.
- Check your work for errors in grammar, usage, mechanics, and spelling. Try to remember the mistakes you have made in the past so that you can avoid them.

Like everything else, writing under time pressure gets easier with practice. Each composition chapter in this book ends with a timed writing activity you can use to practice.

You can learn more about preparing for timed writing experiences on pages 500–501.

CHAPTER 2

Developing Style and Voice

Your writing style is the distinctive way you express yourself through the words you choose and the way you shape your sentences. Your **voice** is the quality in your writing that makes it sound as if there is a real and unique person behind the words, your verbal fingerprint.

As you discover and develop your writing style and voice, always keep your purpose and audience in mind. When you take time to develop your own writing style, the end result will be writing that says what you want it to say and fulfills your purpose—in a style that readers will want to read.

Writing Project: Travel Narrative

From Here to There ***Write a narrative with style about the events that happened when you took a memorable journey.***

Think Through Writing "Travel writing" is a genre in which the author describes in detail events that take place during travel. Think about a remarkable trip you have taken. It might be exotic, as when people travel to foreign countries; it might be seemingly simple, as when people take the subway across town. Write about your travel as a narrative. What was your destination? How did you get there? What events took place during your trip? How did you feel about them? What distinctive things happened? What did you see, hear, smell, touch, and taste? In this draft, do not worry about grammar, spelling, and other aspects of form; just write about your trip and what made it seem remarkable to you.

Talk About It In your writing group, discuss the trips you took and the ways you wrote about them. What is common to them? What is unique about each? How might each piece be expanded on and improved?

Read About It In the following selection, author Truman Capote describes a train ride through Spain during which he made many observations. Read Capote's piece as an example of travel writing, similar to the piece you will develop in this chapter.

MODEL: Style

A Ride Through Spain

Truman Capote

Certainly the train was old. The seats sagged like the jowls of a bulldog, windows were out and strips of adhesive held together those that were left; in the corridor a prowling cat appeared to be hunting mice, and it was not unreasonable to assume his search would be rewarded.

". . . like the jowls of a bulldog" is a vivid simile, a figure of speech.

Slowly, as though the engine were harnessed to elderly coolies,[1] we crept out of Granada. The southern sky was as white and burning as a desert; there was one cloud, and it drifted like a traveling oasis.

Capote uses more figurative language here when he compares the sky and cloud to a desert and oasis.

We were going to Algeciras, a Spanish seaport facing the coast of Africa. In our compartment there was a middle-aged Australian wearing a soiled linen suit: he had tobacco-colored teeth and his fingernails were unsanitary. Presently he informed us that he was a ship's doctor. It seemed curious, there on the dry, dour plains of Spain, to meet someone connected with the sea. Seated next to him there were two women, a mother and daughter. The mother was an overstuffed, dusty woman with sluggish, disapproving eyes and a faint mustache. The focus for her disapproval fluctuated; first, she eyed me rather strongly because as the sunlight fanned brighter, waves of heat blew through the broken windows and I had removed my jacket—which she considered, perhaps rightly, discourteous. Later on, she took a dislike to the young soldier who also occupied our compartment.

Well-chosen words and a variety in sentence length and structure make the scene easy to visualize and follow.

The soldier, and the woman's not very discreet daughter, a buxom girl with the scrappy features of a prizefighter, seemed to have agreed to flirt. Whenever the wandering cat appeared at our door, the daughter pretended to be frightened, and the soldier would gallantly shoo the cat into the corridor: this byplay gave them frequent opportunity to touch each other.

The young soldier was one of many on the train. . . . They seemed to be enjoying themselves, which apparently was wrong of them, for whenever an officer appeared the

1 **coolies:** Laborers who are unskilled.

CHAPTER 2

soldiers would stare fixedly out the windows, as though enraptured by the landslides of red rock, the olive fields and stern stone mountains. Their officers were dressed for a parade, many ribbons, much brass: and some wore gleaming, improbable swords strapped to their sides. They did not mix with the soldiers, but sat together in a first-class compartment, looking bored and rather like unemployed actors. It was a blessing, I suppose, that something finally happened to give them a chance at rattling their swords.

This sentence foreshadows an event to come and creates a sense of anticipation in the reader.

The compartment directly ahead was taken over by one family: a delicate, attenuated, exceptionally elegant man with a mourning ribbon sewn around his sleeve, and traveling with him, six thin, summery girls, presumably his daughters. They were beautiful, the father and his children, all of them, and in the same way: hair that had a dark shine, lips the color of pimientos,[2] eyes like sherry. The soldiers would glance into their compartment, then look away. It was as if they had seen straight into the sun.

Visual details, including more figures of speech, paint a clear image.

Whenever the train stopped, the man's two youngest daughters would descend from the carriage and stroll under the shade of parasols. They enjoyed many lengthy promenades, for the train spent the greatest part of our journey standing still.

No one appeared to be exasperated by this except myself. Several passengers seemed to have friends at every station with whom they could sit around a fountain and gossip long and lazily. One old woman was met by different little groups in a dozen-odd towns—between these encounters she wept with such abandon that the Australian doctor became alarmed: why no, she said, there was nothing he could do, it was just that seeing all her relatives made her so happy.

At each stop cyclones of barefooted women and somewhat naked children ran beside the train sloshing earthen jars of water and furrily squalling *Agua! Agua!*[3] For two *pesetas*[4] you could buy a whole basket of dark runny figs, and there were trays of curious white-coated candy doughnuts that looked as though they could

---

2 **pimientos:** Sweet red peppers used for stuffing olives.
3 ***agua:*** Water. (Spanish)
4 ***pesetas:*** Spanish monetary unit.

be eaten by young girls wearing Communion dresses. Toward noon, having collected a bottle of wine, a loaf of bread, a sausage and a cheese, we were prepared for lunch. Our companions in the compartment were hungry, too. Packages were produced, wine uncorked, and for a while there was a pleasant, almost graceful festiveness. . . .

These details appeal to the senses of taste and smell.

Afterward everyone was sleepy; the doctor went so solidly to sleep that a fly meandered undisturbed over his open-mouthed face. Stillness etherized the whole train; in the next compartment the lovely girls leaned loosely, like six exhausted geraniums; even the cat had ceased to prowl, and lay dreaming in the corridor. We had climbed higher, the train moseyed across a plateau of rough yellow wheat, then between the granite walls of deep ravines where wind, moving down from the mountains, quivered in strange, thorny trees. Once, at a parting in the trees, there was something I'd wanted to see, a castle on a hill, and it sat there like a crown.

It was a landscape for bandits. Earlier in the summer, a young Englishman I know (rather, know of) had been motoring through this part of Spain when, on the lonely side of a mountain, his car was surrounded by swarthy scoundrels. They robbed him, then tied him to a tree and tickled his throat with the blade of a knife. I was thinking of this when without preface a spatter of bullet fire strafed the dozy silence.

Because of the device of foreshadowing, readers have been anticipating a development like this.

It was a machine gun. Bullets rained in the trees like the rattle of castanets,[5] and the train, with a wounded creak, slowed to a halt. For a moment there was no sound except the machine gun's cough. Then, "Bandits!" I said in a loud, dreadful voice.

"Bandidos!" screamed the daughter.

"Bandidos!" echoed her mother, and the terrible word swept through the train like something drummed on a tom-tom. The result was slapstick in a grim key. We collapsed on the floor, one cringing heap of arms and legs. Only the mother seemed to keep her head; standing up, she began systematically to stash away her

5 **castanets:** Hollowed out pieces of wood connected by a cord and clicked together with the fingers.

CHAPTER 2

CHAPTER 2

treasures. . . . Like the crying of birds at twilight, airy twitterings of distress came from the charming girls in the next compartment. In the corridor the officers bumped about yapping orders and knocking into each other.

Suddenly, silence. Outside, there was the murmur of wind in leaves, of voices. Just as the weight of the doctor's body was becoming too much for me, the outer door of our compartment swung open, and a young man stood there. He did not look clever enough to be a bandit.

"Hay un médico en el tren?"[6] he said, smiling.

The Australian, removing the pressure of his elbow from my stomach, climbed to his feet. "I'm a doctor," he admitted, dusting himself. "Has someone been wounded?"

"*Sí, Señor*. An old man. He is hurt in the head," said the Spaniard, who was not a bandit: alas, merely another passenger. Settling back in our seats, we listened, expressionless with embarrassment, to what had happened. It seemed that for the last several hours an old man had been stealing a ride by clinging to the rear of the train. Just now he'd lost his hold, and a soldier, seeing him fall, had started firing a machine gun as a signal for the engineer to stop the train.

Now in the midst of telling the story, Capote uses more direct language to keep events moving, though the words are still well chosen to create the scene.

My only hope was that no one remembered who had first mentioned bandits. They did not seem to. After acquiring a clean shirt of mine which he intended to use as a bandage, the doctor went off to his patient, and the mother, turning her back with sour prudery, reclaimed her pearl comb. Her daughter and the soldier followed after us as we got out of the carriage and strolled under the trees, where many passengers had gathered to discuss the incident.

Two soldiers appeared carrying the old man. My shirt was wrapped around his head. They propped him under a tree and all the women clustered about vying with each other to lend him their rosary; someone brought a bottle of wine, which pleased him more. He seemed quite happy, and moaned a great deal. The children who had been on the train circled around him, giggling.

6 ***"Hay...el tren?"***: "Is there a doctor on the train?" (Spanish)

We were in a small wood that smelled of oranges. There was a path, and it led to a shaded promontory; from here, one looked across a valley where sweeping stretches of scorched golden grass shivered as though the earth were trembling. Admiring the valley, and the shadowy changes of light on the hills beyond, the six sisters, escorted by their elegant father, sat with their parasols raised above them like guests at a *fête champêtre.*[7]

Now that the height of the story has passed, Capote stretches out into longer descriptive passages once again.

The soldiers moved around them in a vague, ambitious manner; they did not quite dare to approach, though one brash, sassy fellow went to the edge of the promontory and called, *"Yo te quiero mucho."*[8] The words returned with the hollow sub-music of a perfect echo, and the sisters, blushing, looked more deeply into the valley.

A cloud, somber as the rocky hills, had massed in the sky, and the grass below stirred like the sea before a storm. Someone said he thought it would rain. But no one wanted to go: not the injured man, who was well on his way through a second bottle of wine, nor the children who, having discovered the echo, stood happily caroling into the valley. It was like a party, and we all drifted back to the train as though each of us wished to be the last to leave. The old man, with my shirt like a grand turban on his head, was put into a first-class carriage and several eager ladies were left to attend him.

In our compartment, the dark, dusty mother sat just as we had left her. She had not seen fit to join the party. She gave me a long, glittering look. *"Bandidos,"* she said with a surly, unnecessary vigor.

The train moved away so slowly butterflies blew in and out the windows.

7 ***fête champêtre:*** A festival held outdoors. (French)
8 ***"Yo...mucho.":*** "I like you very much." (Spanish)

CHAPTER 2

Respond in Writing Respond to Capote's travelogue. How does he hold your attention? What parts of the narrative do you like best? What does he do as a writer to make this story interesting to those who have never been to Spain?

CHAPTER 2

Develop Ideas Work with your classmates to develop ideas for writing your own travelogue.

Small Groups: In small groups, construct a list of devices that Capote has used to make his writing vivid and compelling. Use a graphic organizer like the following to identify the devices of an effective travelogue, providing an example of each device and explaining its effect on readers.

Device	Example	Effect

Whole Class: Make a master chart of all of the devices of travel writing that the writing groups have identified, and discuss the relative effectiveness of the examples provided. As a result of this discussion, you should have a list of many literary devices and an understanding of why you find them effective in different examples from Capote's text.

Write About It You will next write a travel narrative about a trip you have taken. Your travelogue might take any of the following directions.

Possible Topics	Possible Audiences	Possible Forms
• a family vacation • a short but eventful local trip • a school field trip • travel to a new or foreign place • a trip with friends	• other teenagers • parents • people in the community explored through travel • people who sponsored your trip • people "back home" who are interested in your travels	• a teen-oriented magazine • a blog • a travel diary • a letter to a friend or loved one • a formal report

Understanding the Varieties of English

English is a very rich language spoken by millions of people, but not all words in the language are spoken alike by all people. Besides the differences in pronunciation by Americans in different regions, English speakers from different countries speak the same words in various ways. The different ways of speaking the same language are called **dialects.** Using dialects in your writing helps to shape its voice and style.

CHAPTER 2

1 American Dialects

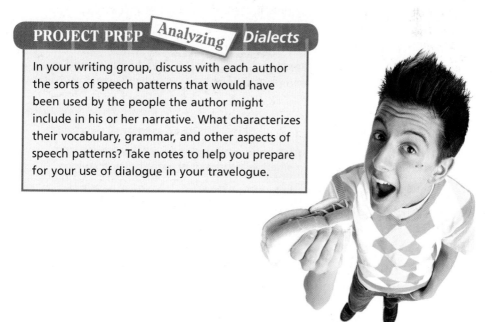

In the past four centuries, slight variations of English have developed from country to country and even within different sections of the same country. Dialects differ from one another in vocabulary, spelling, pronunciation, and even grammar. For example, a Bostonian may call a hot dog a *frankfurter*, and a person from Vermont may pronounce *cow* as "ka-ow." Although dialects differ across the United States, few are so different that one group cannot understand another. In fact, different dialects add color and richness to American English.

Practice Your Skills

Identifying Dialects

With a small group discuss the dialect that you speak. Provide examples of your vocabulary, pronunciation, and grammar that characterize the dialect. What culture has influenced your dialect? Share your examples with another group.

PROJECT PREP Analyzing Dialects

In your writing group, discuss with each author the sorts of speech patterns that would have been used by the people the author might include in his or her narrative. What characterizes their vocabulary, grammar, and other aspects of speech patterns? Take notes to help you prepare for your use of dialogue in your travelogue.

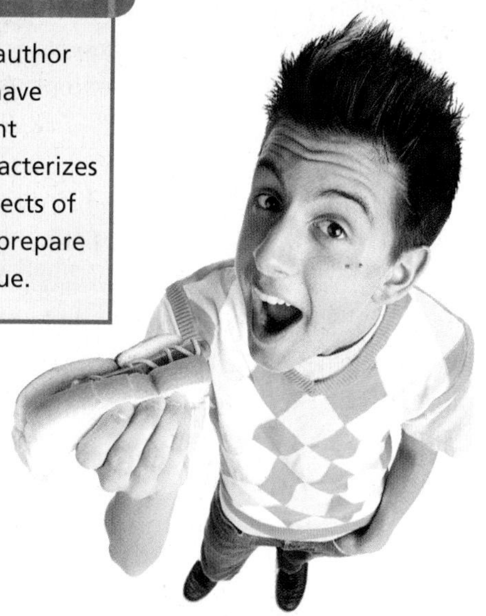

2 Formal and Informal American English

Standard English

Dialects can help you create believable characters when writing fiction and poetry. William Faulkner and Zora Neale Hurston were masters of the southern dialect; Howard Frank Mosher and David Budbill are two contemporary writers who write in a northern Vermont dialect. However, none of these writers would use dialect in a formal speech or in expository writing. They would use Standard English. **Standard English** is the formal English taught in school and used in newspapers, scholarly works, and many books. It is also called "mainstream English."

CHAPTER 2

Practice Your Skills

Comparing Dialects with Standard English

Compare and contrast your examples of dialect with Standard English and with the dialects of other parts of the country (a Southern dialect compared to a Western dialect, for example). Make a chart, index, or dictionary of words to introduce your regional dialect to people from other parts of the country.

Writing Tip

Use **Standard English** when writing for school and for a large general audience.

Colloquialisms, Idioms, Slang, and Jargon

Many words and phrases come into the English language through everyday conversation and usage. Such expressions include colloquialisms, slang, idioms, and jargon. These informal types of language are usually not appropriate for formal written English.

Informal Language	Definition	Example
Colloquialism	informal expressions used in conversation but usually not in writing	When Scott saw Sadie he smiled and said, "What's up?"
Idiom	a phrase or expression that has a meaning different from the literal translation of the words	The doctors are keeping tabs on the patient's recovery.
Slang	colorful or exaggerated expressions and phrases that are used by a particular group	The concert last night really raised the roof.
Jargon	a specialized vocabulary most often used in a technical, scientific, or professional field	The film director told the talent to get set for a trailing dolly shot.

Practice Your Skills

Using Appropriate Standard English

Read the following selection of sentences. Identify colloquialisms, idioms, slang, and jargon.

1. The batter hit a Texas League blooper that fell like a dying quail just behind the keystone sack.
2. Mr. Hargroves okayed our science project, so we've got the green light to build an apiary behind the school.
3. Teal bought herself a pre-owned car, and she's been driving it all over town.
4. There's no doubt about it—Willard sure is way cool.
5. The police lieutenant spoke off the record when the reporter questioned him.

Writing Tip

Idioms, colloquialisms, slang, and **jargon** can make your fiction and poetry convincing and lively. They are not, however, appropriate for formal writing such as that you will do in school and work.

Developing Your Voice

If you choose words carefully and match your level of usage (standard or nonstandard) with your situation and purpose, you can develop a satisfying writer's voice. The rubric below shows the qualities of more and less successful writer's voices.

Voice Rubric

4 The voice is engaging throughout. It sounds natural and unique.	**3 The voice is engaging almost always. It usually sounds natural and unique.**	**2 Sometimes the voice doesn't connect with the reader. Parts may not sound natural or unique.**	**1 The voice does not make a connection with the reader and there's little sense of a unique person.**

PROJECT PREP Prewriting *Voice*

1. In your writing group, discuss with your writing partners the appropriate voice for the narrator of your writing. Will the narrative be presented in Standard English? Will there be a clear contrast between the diction, or word choice and speech patterns, of the characters in the narrative and the diction of the narrator? Why or why not?
2. In your writing group, discuss the colloquialisms, idioms, slang, and jargon you might hear in the setting of your narrative. A train conductor, for instance, might call "All aboard!" while a fellow teenager might say "Get in the car!" What sorts of distinctive language would you hear on this trip? Which speakers would use it? What would they say, and how would others respond? Keep lists of the ideas you develop.

In the Media

In the Media

Dialects

In "A Mother in Mannville" (pages 323–329), Marjorie Kinnan Rawlings creates the character of the young boy, Jerry, in part through how he speaks: "Size don't matter, chopping wood," he says. "Some of the big boys don't chop good. . . ."

Knowing as the reader does that this story takes place in the Carolina mountains, the reader may also mentally hear a Southern accent when Jerry speaks. If this story were dramatized on stage or in film, the speech characteristics would be even more noticeable.

Some writers go to great trouble to capture accurately the speech patterns of their characters, even in print. Sometimes, whole cultures seem to come to life in the colorful rhythms and tones of a local dialect.

Media Activity

Think of a character from a book, movie, or television show that you identify with a noticeable dialect or regional or ethnic accent. Write a sentence from the mouth of your character that reproduces accurately exactly how that character pronounces his or her words.

Then ask yourself if the writer or producer has also given that character other qualities that tend to be associated with a certain culture. What media images come to mind when you think of this culture? Chances are they fall into the general category of **stereotypes,** untrue generalizations. Write a paragraph analyzing the stereotypes with examples from your own experience or knowledge.

Choosing Vivid Words

One key to developing an effective writing style is to *show* rather than to tell. A skillful writer creates an image in the reader's mind by using specific and vivid words that bring writing to life. Notice how Katherine Mansfield's precisely chosen words help you visualize the following scene.

MODEL: Vivid Words

Then, after six years, she saw him again. He was seated at one of those little bamboo tables decorated with a Japanese vase of paper daffodils. There was a tall plate of fruit in front of him, and very carefully, in a way she recognized immediately as his "special" way, he was peeling an orange.

—Katherine Mansfield, "A Dill Pickle"

CHAPTER 2

1 Specific Words

In the following pairs of examples, notice how specific words replace general words to create a more precise meaning.

General Noun	We went to see a science fiction **movie.**
Specific Noun	We went to see a science fiction **thriller.**
General Adverb	Martin played the drums **well.**
Specific Adverb	Martin played the drums **passionately.**

Practice Your Skills

Choosing Specific Words

Write two specific words for each of the following general words.

1. dog
2. hungry
3. slowly
4. sound
5. funny
6. attractive

Writing Tip

Choose **specific words** over general words.

The Language of Power Possessive Nouns

Power Rule: Use standard ways to make nouns possessive. (See pages 944–946.)

See It in Action Vivid, specific words are one key to the effectiveness of Capote's description. Another is error-free writing, which allows experienced readers to focus on the description and not be distracted by mistakes. In the first example below, the mistakes in the treatment of possessive nouns are bumps in the road, drawing the reader's attention away from the content of the sentence.

Errors in the Use of Plural Possessive Nouns	Thinking she heard **bandits** voices, she hushed her **childrens** crying.

When the writing is error free, as Capote's is, the reader can give full attention to the dramatic events.

Correct Use of Plural Possessive Nouns	Thinking she heard **bandits'** voices, she hushed her **children's** crying.

To form the possessive of a plural noun, add only an apostrophe to a plural noun that ends in *s* or add *'s* to a plural noun that does not end in *-s*. To form the possessive of a singular noun, simply add *-'s*.

Singular Possessive	Fearful, she hid her **mother's** ring.
Singular Noun Ending in *-s*	We attended **James's** recital.

Remember It Record this rule and examples in the Power Rule section of your Personalized Editing Checklist.

Use It Read through your project to make sure you have formed possessives correctly. Identify all the possessive nouns in your composition. Determine if each is singular or plural and form the possessive according to the rules above.

PROJECT PREP Prewriting *Vivid Language*

In your writing group, discuss how you could present certain events in vivid language. What events call for expressive language? What choices result in descriptions that are clear and open to visualization? Keep notes of the specific suggestions you receive from your writing group members.

CHAPTER 2

In the Media

Newspapers

As you study ways to improve your writing style, you may want to analyze the way newspapers use style. In standard journalistic style, straight facts are presented to answer the questions *who, what, when, where, why,* and *how*. Rarely do hard news stories contain figurative language or complex sentence structure. A feature story, however, may begin with a brief portrait of someone dealing with the issue covered in the article before getting involved in the facts. The use of photographs is usually restrained.

Tabloid newspapers are another matter. A tabloid is usually half the size of a standard newspaper. It carries a condensed version of the story and features large, eye-catching photographs. The choice of material and its presentation are usually distinct from more traditional newspapers. Even when a tabloid leads with the same story that a hard-news daily does, the focus is likely to be on the more sensational aspects.

Headlines in each type of periodical reveal a similar stylistic distinction. Tabloid headlines tend to be brief, set in large, colorful type, and aimed at the most titillating aspects of the story. Traditional papers reserve large type for events of national or international significance.

Most online newspapers also provide a forum for readers to respond in posted comments to the articles or editorials. The style of the comments about a tabloid article is often very different from the style of the comments from a mainstream newspaper such as the *Washington Post,* with more formal language associated with the latter. However, both styles of comments are distinctive from the style of the newspaper itself, reflecting the informality of many online communications.

Media Activity

Investigate how newspapers with different audiences treat the news. Look in your school library or media center for recent issues of your community's major newspapers. For a more expansive range of examples, search the Internet for the Web sites of major news dailies. Make notes of the differences you find. List the newspapers you find and identify each as a tabloid or traditional paper. Also note the kinds of words each uses in headlines, lead paragraphs, and reader comments. Then, with a partner, choose one story from a traditional newspaper and rewrite the headline and lead paragraph in tabloid style. Create a few comments to your story in the style that readers might actually use.

2 Denotation and Connotation

Words sometimes have two meanings: the **denotative** meaning, which is the dictionary definition of a word, and the **connotative** meaning, which is how the word is emotionally perceived by a reader. For example, *movie* and *film* have a similar denotative meaning. *Film,* however, connotes (or suggests) more sophistication than *movie*. Choosing the word with exactly the connotation you want to convey will help you add subtlety and depth to your writing.

Practice Your Skills

Identifying Denotation and Connotation

The following pairs of words all have similar denotative meanings. Describe their connotative differences.

1. cinema, multiplex
2. football field, gridiron
3. sleep, snooze
4. work, toil
5. midnight, witching hour

Practice Your Skills

Exploring Denotation and Connotation

Create five word pairs of your own, using the dictionary as needed. Your pairs should all have similar denotative meanings but different connotative meanings. When you have completed your five pairs, share them with the class.

PROJECT PREP Prewriting *Subtlety of Meaning*

In your writing group, consider your word choices in your first quick draft (see page 49). Which words have connotations that bring the scene to life? Which sections are drab and would benefit from new word choices? Does your word choice have a consistent set of connotations that create a consistent tone (pages 112–113)? How might you improve your travel writing according to each of these concerns?

3 Figurative Language

Literal language uses words for their exact, direct meaning. Because literal language is often inadequate in creating clear mental images, writers use **figurative language,** or figures of speech, also called **tropes.** Figurative language is an important tool in developing an effective writing style because it allows writers to use words in inventive ways to create strong images.

Literal Language	Her constant sighing annoyed me.
Figurative Language	Listening to her sighing made me feel like I was at a leaky tire convention.

CHAPTER 2

Similes and Metaphors

The two most common figures of speech are similes and metaphors. Both create vivid impressions through the use of comparisons. **Similes** use the word *like* or *as* to express a comparison between two essentially different things. **Metaphors** imply comparison without using the word *like* or *as*. Notice the vivid images created by the following examples.

Writing Tip

Use **figurative language** to make ideas vivid for your readers.

Simile	Think of the storm roaming the sky uneasily like a dog looking for a place to sleep. —Elizabeth Bishop
Metaphor	The kitchen was the great machine that set our lives running; it whirred down a little only on Saturdays and holy days. —Alfred Kazin

Elizabeth Bishop uses *like* to compare an impending storm to a restless dog. Alfred Kazin *implies* a comparison—without using *like* or *as*—between his kitchen and a great whirring machine.

CHAPTER 2

Personification

This figure of speech attributes human qualities to lifeless objects or ideas.

Personification	The sunny skies smiled on the farmer's crops.

Skies cannot actually smile. When you use personification, you invite the reader to see objects and ideas in new ways.

Onomatopoeia

Another way to appeal to the reader's imagination is to use words with sounds that match their meanings. Some examples of onomatopoeia are *sizzle, thump, splash, crackle, shoo, slosh, swoop,* and *whisk.*

Practice Your Skills

Identifying Figurative Language

Identify the figure of speech underlined in each sentence by writing *simile, metaphor, personification,* or *onomatopoeia.*

1. The dawn <u>embraced</u> the rich landscape <u>with arms</u> of warmth.
2. Time <u>is a taskmaster whipping us on</u>.
3. The child <u>slurped</u> her melting ice-cream bar.
4. Worries pounded in her brain <u>like angry waves</u>.
5. The <u>thirsty</u> sand <u>drank up</u> the desert shower in minutes.

Practice Your Skills

Using Vivid Words

Write a paragraph that describes the approach of a storm. Use specific, literal language in one sentence, a simile or metaphor in another, and personification in a third. In all three sentences, use language as creatively as you can.

PROJECT PREP Prewriting *Using Tropes*

In your writing group, think about how the use of tropes can help your narrator present the story in an engaging way. For example, Truman Capote opens his travel writing about his train ride in Spain by saying that on the train, "The seats sagged like the jowls of a bulldog." What comes to mind with this simile? How does it help Capote give an impression of the train to his readers? Where might you employ figurative language to convey the images of *your* trip? Jot down specific ideas.

Think Critically

Comparing

Writing often involves making comparisons. When you **compare,** you find similarities between people, places, things, or even ideas. Creating a simile or metaphor is one effective way to compare by showing how two essentially dissimilar things are similar. For example, if you compare a short-distance runner to a gazelle, you can find some revealing similarities. Both move swiftly and gracefully, and both strive for high speeds in running.

Effective similes and metaphors use creative, thought-provoking comparisons to allow people to see things in a new light.

The storm, like a bird of prey, swooped down on the town.

Creating a chart like the following will help you write original comparisons. Begin by identifying the qualities of your subject that you wish to convey.

COMPARISON CHART

Identify: What are the subject's (storm's) qualities?	**Ask:** What other subjects share those qualities?	**Choose:** Which conveys the connotation or feeling I am after, and why?
–comes on suddenly	–enemy warplane	The bird of prey comes closer because it is tied to unstoppable natural forces rather than human forces.
–does terrible damage	–bird of prey	

Thinking Practice

Make a comparison chart for one of the following phrases. Then write the resulting simile or metaphor.

1. The moon is (like). . .
2. The school hallway is (like). . .
3. Success is (like). . .

Think Critically

CHAPTER 2

4 Language to Avoid

Clichés

Some figures of speech have been so overused that they no longer create a strong mental image. Such words and phrases are called **clichés,** and you should avoid them.

CLICHÉS		
hungry as a bear	crystal clear	pretty as a picture
sweet as honey	cold as ice	smooth as silk

Tired Words, Euphemisms, and Loaded Language

When choosing what words you use to express yourself, it is important to realize that certain common expressions have become so overused that they are no longer precise or vivid. Similarly, there are other expressions that are misleading.

Type of Expression	Definition	Example
Tired Words	language that has been exhausted of strength or precision through overuse	Virtually everything she said made sense. That was an amazing movie. She felt quite pleased that she was chosen for the role. We had an awesome time.
Euphemism	the substitution of a mild, indirect term for one considered blunt or offensive	Miss Coles excused herself to take a trip to the powder room. Samuel works for the city as a sanitation engineer.
Loaded Language	words that are weighted with meaning or emotional importance	If you think your home might have lead paint, you should take steps to protect your family. All his life, Mr. Sudbury worked as a bureaucrat.

Practice Your Skills

Identifying Language

Read the following sentences. Identify clichés, tired words, euphemisms, and loaded words.

1. When Catalina first set foot on the stage, the butterflies in her stomach took flight.
2. After reading the novel, Jamal thought the book was really very interesting.
3. The city council voted to spray the neighborhood for mosquitoes in order to defeat the small but virulent enemy of the people.
4. Suh Jung puts her money in the bank, citing the old adage, "A penny saved is a penny earned."
5. The battalion of peacekeepers suffered several personnel losses during the unfriendly fire.
6. One aspect of the concept "Freedom of Speech" is that we have the right to express ourselves.
7. Steer clear of Georgie, the schoolyard bully; he's as mean as a junkyard dog and as sly as a fox.
8. Henrietta stared at the pretty dress in the department store window.
9. Six-month-old Emily is the apple of her father's eye.
10. The sanitation engineer tossed the smelly bag of garbage into the truck.

Using a Word Choice Rubric

Evaluate your word choice with the following rubric.

4 Words are specific and powerful, rich in sensory images.	3 Words are specific and some words appeal to the senses.	2 Some words are overly general and/or tired.	1 Most words are overly general and tired.
• I used Standard English if required. • I used Nonstandard English, with colloquialisms, if appropriate. • I used words with connotations that match my intended meaning. • I used fresh, not tired, words. • I used words with punch and sparkle that appeal to the senses of sight, sound, touch, smell, and taste. • I used tropes to to add different levels of meanings to my words.	• I was aware of differences between Standard and Nonstandard English and made reasonable choices. • My word choice conveys my meaning but may not have sparkle and punch. • I made a good effort to appeal to the senses, but now see where I might have done more. • I used some figurative language, especially comparisons such as metaphors and similes.	• I was not always aware of differences between Standard and Nonstandard English and made some choices that might confuse a reader. • I still need to work on finding the best, most specific word to give sparkle and punch to my writing. • I used a few tired expressions. • I appealed to only one or two senses and used no figurative language.	• I was not aware of differences between Standard and Nonstandard English and made some confusing choices. • Few of my words are as specific and vivid as they need to be. • I used a number of tired expressions. • I didn't really appeal to the senses and I used no figurative language.

PROJECT PREP Revising *Vivid Words and Style*

Return to the draft you wrote and review all the notes and ideas you now have as a result of meetings with your writing group. Write a second draft of your essay putting the suggestions and improvements into place. Be sure to watch out for tired words and other language that interferes with your reader's experience. When each writer has finished a second draft, share your work with the other members of your writing group and invite feedback. Use the rubric above to evaluate your own and one another's word choice.

Creating Sentence Variety

If a passage has sentences of varying lengths and patterns, the resulting rhythm is natural and pleasing. If all the sentences follow the same pattern, however, the rhythm becomes monotonous. You can achieve sentence variety in your writing style by combining sentences, varying sentence structure, and varying sentence beginnings.

One way to achieve sentence variety is to combine short, choppy sentences into longer ones that read more smoothly. Combining related ideas into one sentence can also clarify the relationship between ideas.

Short Sentences Mica liked to play video games with Seth. Mica and Seth were best friends. They were rivals in the gaming world. Mica enjoyed scoring more points than Seth during a game. He also felt bad about beating Seth.

Combined When Mica beat Seth while playing a video game, he enjoyed the win, but he also felt bad about scoring more points than his best friend and chief rival in the gaming world.

Writing Tip

Vary the length and structure of your sentences.

1 Combining Sentences with Phrases

In the following examples, short sentences are combined into a longer sentence that includes at least one phrase.

A. Polar explorers wear heavy parkas. These parkas have hoods. The hoods have drawstrings.
Polar explorers wear heavy parkas **with drawstring hoods.** (prepositional phrase)

B. The drawstrings help keep the person warm. They prevent warm air around the head from escaping.
The drawstrings help keep the person warm, **preventing warm air around the head from escaping.** (participial phrase)

C. Balaclavas keep the face warm. Balaclavas are tight-fitting woolen head masks.
Balaclavas, **tight-fitting woolen head masks,** keep the face warm. (appositive phrase)

Practice Your Skills

Combining Sentences with Phrases

Combine each set of short sentences, using the type of phrase indicated in parentheses. Remember to use commas where needed.

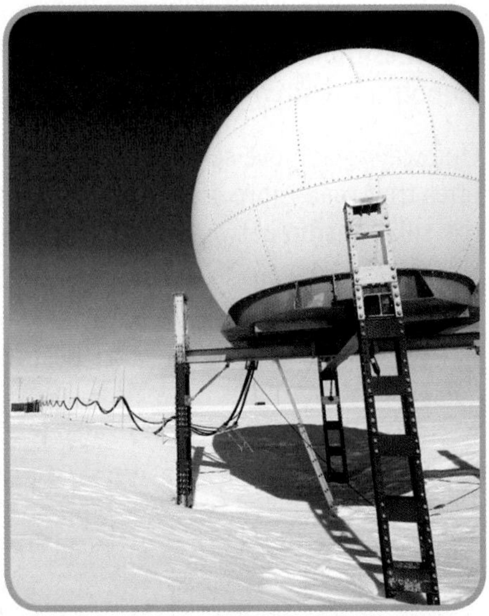

1. Explorers in Antarctica burn up energy quickly. They require 1,000 more calories per day than their usual intake. (participial phrase)

2. Well-balanced diets are carefully selected. They consist of fats, carbohydrates, and proteins. They are selected before an expedition sets off. (prepositional phrase)

3. Glaciologists now go to Antarctica and brave the climate that threatened the early explorers. Glaciologists are experts who study ice formations. (appositive phrase)

4. Other experts go to Antarctica to study. They are experts in biology, geophysics, meteorology, and geology. (prepositional phrase)

5. Scientists are highly dedicated people. They endure great loneliness as they study and learn. (participial phrase)

6. Scientists who go to Antarctica are particularly intrepid. Antarctica is one of the planet's most hostile climates. (appositive phrase)

PROJECT PREP Revising *Sentence Length*

In your writing group, discuss what sort of mood you wish to convey, and how your sentence structures could contribute to that mood. For instance, short, staccato sentences are often used to tell a fast-paced story; longer sentences slow down the reader and are appropriate for a slower pace and reflective mood. What types of sentences should the author use to tell this story? Help each author experiment by drafting a few sentences of different lengths.

2 Combining by Coordinating and Subordinating

Combining Sentences by Coordinating

Ideas of equal importance can be joined to form one sentence by using a **coordinating conjunction,** such as *and, but, or, for, yet,* and *so.* The resulting sentence will contain compound elements.

A. "Mississippi Rag" is an early example of ragtime piano music. "Harlem Rag" is an early example of ragtime piano music.
"Mississippi Rag" and "Harlem Rag" are early examples of ragtime piano music. (compound subject)

B. Scott Joplin performed ragtime. Scott Joplin composed ragtime.
Scott Joplin **performed and composed** ragtime. (compound verb)

C. Joplin's ragtime piano pieces were influenced by show music. They were influenced by a popular dance called the cakewalk.
Joplin's ragtime piano pieces were influenced **by show music and a popular dance called the cakewalk.** (compound object of a preposition)

D. Ragtime melodies were hard to sing. Most rags were written without words.
Ragtime melodies were hard to sing, **so** most rags were written without words. (compound sentence)

E. Ragtime rhythms are syncopated. They are energetic.
Ragtime rhythms are **syncopated and energetic.** (compound predicate adjective)

F. Scott Joplin was a famous ragtime composer. Thomas Turpin was a famous ragtime composer.
Two famous ragtime composers were **Scott Joplin and Thomas Turpin.** (compound predicate nominative)

Practice Your Skills

Combining Sentences by Coordinating

Combine the following sentences, using the preceding model and coordinating conjunction indicated in parentheses. Remember to use commas where needed.

1. A high fever was a symptom of the bubonic plague. Swollen glands were a symptom of the bubonic plague. (A—*and*)

2. The plague reached London in 1592 through wharves. It reached London through river mouths. (C—*and*)

3. Rats from ships carried fleas. The fleas spread microorganisms throughout the city. (D—*and*)

4. Home remedies against the plague were creative. They were ineffective. (E—*but*)
5. The only medicines were herbs. The only medicines were spices. (F—*or*)

Combining Sentences by Subordinating

With the technique of subordinating, ideas of unequal importance can be combined by changing the less important ideas into a **subordinate clause.** The following words often begin subordinate clauses.

CHAPTER 2

WORDS USED TO BEGIN SUBORDINATE CLAUSES			
Relative Pronouns (to introduce adjectival clauses)		**Subordinating Conjunctions (to introduce adverbial clauses)**	
who	that	after	because
whom	which	until	whenever
whose	whoever	unless	although

The following examples show how to combine by subordinating.

A. Sunspots look like dark blotches on the sun. They are 2,000 degrees cooler than the surrounding surface.
Sunspots, **which are 2,000 degrees cooler than the surrounding surface,** look like dark blotches on the sun. (adjectival clause)

B. Sunspots can interfere with radio communications. They hurl electrically charged particles into space.
Because they hurl electrically charged particles into space, sunspots can interfere with radio communications. (adverbial clause)

Practice Your Skills

Combining Sentences by Subordinating

Combine the following sentences, using the preceding model and the joining word indicated in the parentheses.

1. The outermost layer of the sun reaches a temperature of one million degrees. It is called the corona. (A—*which*)
2. The corona can be seen during an eclipse. Usually it is invisible. (B—*although*)
3. The sun is expected to burn for another 5,500 million years. The sun is about halfway through its life cycle. (A—*which*)

4. The medium-sized sun will last longer than more massive stars. Massive stars burn up their fuel at a very fast rate. (B—*because*)
5. A red giant is a star in the first stages of its death. A red giant is typically 100 times larger than the sun. (A—*which*)

CHAPTER 2

PROJECT PREP Revising *Coordinating and Subordinating*

Review your draft, looking for opportunities to combine sentences by coordating and/or subordinating. Make those revisions and bring your revised work to your writing group. For each author, compare the original to the revision and discuss the differences in rhythm and effectiveness.

3 Varying Sentence Structure

The sentence-combining techniques you have just studied will help you achieve a variety of sentence types. As you develop your writing style, strive for a mixture of the four basic sentence types.

Simple	Puppies show their obedience to other dogs by rolling onto their sides or backs. (one independent clause)
Compound	Most puppies will let an older dog intimidate them, but some insist on being the boss. (two or more independent clauses)
Complex	Because they do not know the rules of obedience, very young puppies can get hurt by older dogs. (one independent clause and one or more subordinate clauses)
Compound-Complex	After a puppy reaches the age of four months, it has learned the social rules, and an owner can leave it safely with an older, friendly dog. (two or more independent clauses and one or more subordinate clauses)

Practice Your Skills

Varying Sentence Structure

The following paragraph contains only simple sentences. Using the combining techniques of coordinating and subordinating, revise the paragraph so that it contains a variety of the four different sentence types. Remember to use commas where needed.

Daily Rhythms

Humans experience a lull in energy level in the middle of the day. Lower animals often pursue quiet activities in the early afternoon. Animals spend early morning and early evening hours in active feeding. They reserve the early afternoon hours for grooming and play. People all over the world slow down after lunch. Many make mistakes during this period. Eating lunch is not believed to be the cause of the slowdown. Some scientists believe these patterns stem from a body clock. All creatures carry a body clock within them.

PROJECT PREP Revising *Varying Sentence Structure*

Revise your draft to include at least one of each type of sentence and evaluate the results. Is your writing more interesting to read? Discuss the changes with your writing group.

The Power of Language

Semicolons: Catch and Release

Throughout this section you have been reading about combining separate sentences into one. What if there were a way to both combine and separate? There is—the semicolon serves that purpose. You can think of a semicolon as a hybrid between a comma and a period. The comma part joins two sentences closely related in meaning (catches); the period part separates them grammatically (releases). When you use a semicolon, you usually do not use a conjunction, so you invite the reader to figure out the nature of the relationship between the two sentences. That invitation draws readers in and is one reason the semicolon is such an effective stylistic device. Here are a few examples from Truman Capote's "A Ride Through Spain."

> The seats sagged like the jowls of a bulldog, windows were out and strips of adhesive held together those that were left; in the corridor a prowling cat appeared to be hunting mice, and it was not unreasonable to assume his search would be rewarded.

> The southern sky was as white and burning as a desert; there was one cloud, and it drifted like a traveling oasis.

> Afterward everyone was sleepy; the doctor went so solidly to sleep that a fly meandered undisturbed over his open-mouthed face.

> Stillness etherized the whole train; in the next compartment the lovely girls leaned loosely, like six exhausted geraniums; even the cat had ceased to prowl, and lay dreaming in the corridor.

What effect does the string of semicolons in the last example have on the reader? In what way might it reinforce the content of the sentence and suggest stillness?

Try It Yourself

On your project topic, write three pairs of related sentences. Then join each pair into one sentence using a semicolon. Compare the effectiveness of the revision from separate sentences into one sentence and identify what the semicolon invites the reader to supply.

Punctuation Tip

To simply connect and/or separate two complete sentences, there are usually three punctuation options. Which you choose is a stylistic decision.

- **Separate with a period:** The comma part joins. The period part separates.
- **Join with a comma plus *and*:** The comma part joins, and the period part separates.
- **Join/separate with a semicolon:** The comma part joins; the period part separates.

4 Varying Sentence Beginnings

Beginning every sentence with a subject can become monotonous. Use the following sentence starters to vary syntax for effect. References such as *Artful Sentences: Syntax as Style* by Virginia Tufte offer a variety of models.

Subject	**Grant Wood** was born in 1892 on a farm in Iowa.
Adverb	**Gradually** he began sketching the animals and scenery on his farm home.
Adjective	**Industrious,** he worked odd jobs to buy art supplies.
Infinitive Phrase	**To learn his craft,** he studied at the Handicraft Guild in Minneapolis.
Participial Phrase	**Taking the first job offered him,** Wood worked as a caretaker in a morgue to pay expenses while studying art.
Prepositional Phrase	**In later years** he studied in Chicago and Paris.
Adverbial Clause	**Although he studied in Europe,** Wood developed a distinctly American style.

CHAPTER 2

Practice Your Skills

Varying Sentence Beginnings

Begin each of the following ten sentences with the construction or part of speech suggested in parentheses. Remember to use commas where needed.

1. Most sports have a long history because they were played in one form or another by the ancients. (adverbial clause)
2. You need to look back no further than 1891 to find the beginnings of basketball. (infinitive phrase)
3. Dr. Luther Gulick, a YMCA leader, began looking for a new sport in that year. (prepositional phrase)
4. Dr. Gulick wanted a sport that could be played indoors to fill the gap between the football season and the baseball season. (infinitive phrase)
5. He also wanted a sport without too much body contact, believing that soccer and rugby were too rough. (participial phrase)

PROJECT PREP Revising *Varying Sentence Beginnngs*

Review your draft looking for places where you can vary the beginnings of your sentences. Use at least three of the sentence starters in the list above, and evaluate and compare the effectiveness of the original and the version with a varied beginning.

Writing Concise Sentences

For your vivid, specific words to have their most powerful effect, cast them into concise sentences. By eliminating redundancy, empty expressions, and wordiness from your sentences, you will communicate your ideas clearly and powerfully.

1 Rambling Sentences

Too many phrases or clauses in one sentence can bury the main point. To avoid confusion, separate long, rambling sentences into several shorter ones.

Writing Tip

Keep your sentences **concise** by eliminating needless words and phrases.

CHAPTER 2

Rambling The word *bonanza* is a Spanish word that means "fair weather at sea" and that signifies good luck for sailors, travelers, and fishers, but the word was also used in gold rush days in Nevada, and when miners found a vein of gold, they would shout, "Bonanza!" which gradually came to mean that someone had struck it rich.

Improved The word *bonanza* is a Spanish word that means "fair weather at sea." *Bonanza* signifies good luck for sailors, travelers, and fishers. The word was also used in gold rush days in Nevada. When miners found a vein of gold, they would shout, "Bonanza!" This expression gradually came to mean that someone had struck it rich.

Practice Your Skills

Revising Rambling Sentences

Revise the following rambling sentences into shorter sentences. Capitalize and punctuate the new sentences correctly.

December on State Street in Chicago is a hectic time, for holiday shoppers crowd the streets and stores, and even though the street is turned into a mall that allows buses only, traffic on surrounding streets is still congested, yet the hectic feeling adds to the holiday excitement, and the store windows re-create fanciful wonderlands, and volunteer musicians play festive music on the street corners.

PROJECT PREP Revising *Rambling Sentences*

Look for and eliminate rambling sentences in your draft.

CHAPTER 2

2 Unnecessary Words

Redundancy

One way to keep your sentences concise is to eliminate unnecessary repetition, or **redundancy.** Notice how the following sentences are improved when the redundancy is trimmed away.

Redundant	Lynne **shouted loudly** to warn her brother of the **dangerous risk.**
Concise	Lynne **shouted** to warn her brother of the **danger.**

Empty Expressions

Empty expressions are phrases that add no meaning to a sentence. You should eliminate these expressions entirely or replace them with single words or concise phrases.

Empty	**It seems as if** advertisers often appeal to emotions.
Concise	Advertisers often appeal to emotions.
Empty	**Due to the fact that** it was a legal holiday, schools were closed last Monday.
Concise	Because of the legal holiday, schools were closed last Monday.

EMPTY EXPRESSIONS	
on account of	due to the fact that
what I want is	the reason that, the reason being
in my opinion	what I'm trying to say is that
it seems as if	the thing is that
it is/was	there is/are/was/were
because of the fact that	I believe/think/feel that

editing

Save "fuel" in the following sentences by eliminating redundancy and empty expressions.

There was a movie called *The Great Train Robbery*, made in 1903, that was the first Western. It was in the 1920s that some of the best movies made were Westerns, including *The Spoilers* and *The Virginian*.

Practice Your Skills

Eliminating Redundancy and Empty Expressions

Create two different revisions of the following sentences. Eliminate redundancy and empty expressions and also look for ways to combine the sentences.

> Our senses link us to the external world outside of our bodies. Messages received by our eyes travel instantaneously to our brain at lightning-fast speed.

CHAPTER 2

Wordiness

Another way to make sentences concise is to eliminate wordy phrases and clauses. You should also simplify inflated language for conciseness.

Wordy Phrases and Clauses An idea can often be expressed in a number of ways—in a clause, in a phrase, or in a single word. Constructions that use more words than necessary are referred to as **wordy.** Because wordiness detracts from your writing style, try to reduce each wordy construction to a shorter phrase or a single word.

	Phrase to Word
Wordy	Sailors aboard a submarine perform their tasks **on a routine basis.** (prepositional phrase)
Concise	Sailors aboard a submarine perform their tasks **routinely.** (adverb)
	Clause to Phrase
Wordy	A sailor **who is on watch** may be assigned to the engine room, the radio, the periscope, or the bridge. (adjectival clause)
Concise	A sailor **on watch** may be assigned to the engine room, the radio, the periscope, or the bridge. (prepositional phrase)
	Clause to Word
Wordy	Food **that is plentiful** is a must on submarines. (adjectival clause)
Concise	**Plentiful** food is a must on submarines. (adjective)

Inflated Language

Some writers tend to use **inflated language**—words with many syllables that sound impressive but do not communicate as effectively or concisely as simple, direct words. Avoid using long or pretentious words merely to impress your reader.

Inflated	The governor has availed herself of every opportunity to enlarge her knowledge of recently published economic theories.
Concise	The governor has studied recent economic theories.

Practice Your Skills

Eliminating Wordiness and Inflated Language

Revise each sentence by eliminating wordy phrases and clauses or by translating inflated language into simpler words. Remember to use commas where needed.

1. The report that I am working on which is about Jacques Cousteau is due Friday.
2. The book that was sitting on my desk is about the science of astronomy.
3. Joan and Marie met at a campsite that was near the river.
4. Students who cannot successfully function in a mathematical learning situation must be reprocessed until they acquire this skill.
5. The galley, which is the kitchen of a ship, is busy every hour of the day.
6. The candidate was the victim of incorrect thinking and made a misstatement.
7. Generals Grant and Lee agreed to peace terms that were honorable.
8. Experience has shown that a suitable course of conduct is to adhere to one's own standards of behavior and allow others the opportunity to operate according to theirs.
9. The brothers talked in a brief manner about happier periods in their lives.
10. Julie, a friend of mine, who is a person who loves animals, has two dogs and two cats.

PROJECT PREP **Revising** ***Concise Sentences***

Exchange papers with a member of your writing group. Carefully read each other's draft and make notes about places where sentences could be revised to be more concise. Suggest a possible revision for each place you find. Discuss your findings with your partner and make any changes to your draft that you think will improve it.

Correcting Faulty Sentences

The hallmark of an effective writing style is clarity. To achieve clarity, good writers reread everything they write, asking, "Is this really what I mean? Will my reader understand this?" If they find a problem, they revise their sentences, adding words, eliminating phrases, or correcting mistakes.

1 Faulty Coordination

By using the technique of coordination, you can add variety to your sentences and clarify your ideas. Coordination is used to join ideas of equal importance. **Faulty coordination,** however, leaves the reader puzzled over the relationship between those ideas. Faulty coordination results from (1) using the wrong conjunction, (2) combining unrelated ideas, or (3) combining unequal ideas.

In the following examples, the wrong coordinator fails to express the precise relationship between two ideas. Notice how the correct coordinating conjunction clarifies how the ideas are related.

Faulty Coordination	It was raining, **and** we decided to cancel our afternoon practice.
Precise Coordination	It was raining, **so** we decided to cancel our afternoon practice.
Faulty Coordination	My best friend recommended the movie about space travel, **and** I didn't like it very much.
Precise Coordination	My best friend recommended the movie about space travel, **but** I didn't like it very much.
	or
	My best friend recommended the movie about space travel; **however,** I didn't like it very much.

Coordinating words have different uses. Some show similarity, some show contrast, and others show result. The following chart lists some common coordinators according to their use.

SOME COMMON COORDINATORS		
To Show Similarity	**To Show Contrast**	**To Show Result**
and	but	so
both/and	yet	therefore
not only/but also	however	consequently
just as/so also	instead	thus
besides	on the other hand	hence
indeed	still	accordingly
furthermore	or, nor	as a result
moreover	nevertheless	for this reason

CHAPTER 2

Faulty coordination can also result if you try to combine two unrelated ideas. To correct this problem, express the ideas in separate sentences.

Faulty Coordination Developing your own photographs can be fun, and my friend Gail has her own darkroom.

Correct Developing your own photographs can be fun. My friend Gail has her own darkroom.

Another common problem arises if you coordinate ideas that are not of equal importance. Subordination is the proper technique for such a situation. To subordinate correctly, change the less important idea into a phrase or subordinate clause. Notice how faulty coordination is corrected in the following examples.

Faulty Coordination Toby broke a drinking glass, and she was washing the dishes.

Correct **Washing dishes,** Toby broke a drinking glass. (phrase)

Correct **As she was washing dishes,** Toby broke a drinking glass. (subordinate clause)

PROJECT PREP *Revising* *Faulty Coordination*

Check your draft for faulty coordination and fix any problems you find, clarifying the relationship between the coordinated ideas.

2 Faulty Subordination

Subordination is used to show the relationship between ideas of unequal importance. **Faulty subordination** occurs when (1) the wrong subordinator is used or (2) the wrong idea is subordinated in a sentence. To avoid faulty subordination, use the subordinator that expresses the precise relationship between ideas. In each of the following examples, notice how the correct subordinator clarifies how the ideas are related.

Faulty Subordination	Michael excelled in gymnastics **even though** he practiced for three hours every day.
Precise Subordination	Michael excelled in gymnastics **because** he practiced for three hours every day.
Faulty Subordination	Carla went outside, **since** she could watch the eclipse.
Precise Subordination	Carla went outside **so that** she could watch the eclipse.

The following chart lists some common subordinators according to their use.

SOME COMMON SUBORDINATORS			
To Show Time	**To Show Cause**	**To Show Purpose**	**To Show Condition**
after	because	that	if
before	since	so that	even though
until	as	in order that	unless

To avoid faulty subordination, express the more important idea in an independent clause.

Faulty Subordination	Although we found it difficult, we had prepared for the marathon race.
Correct	Although we had prepared for the marathon race, we found it difficult.
Faulty Subordination	Jake is the smallest on the team, although he is the fastest runner.
Correct	Although Jake is the smallest on the team, he is the fastest runner.

The following guidelines will help you correct faulty coordination and faulty subordination as you revise your writing.

HERE'S HOW

Correcting Faulty Coordination and Faulty Subordination

- Use the connecting word that best shows the relationship between your ideas.
- Express unrelated ideas in separate sentences.
- If the ideas in a sentence are of unequal importance, express the less important idea in a phrase or a subordinate clause.
- Express the most important idea in an independent clause.

CHAPTER 2

Practice Your Skills

Correcting Faulty Coordination and Faulty Subordination

Using the preceding guidelines, revise each of the following faulty sentences. Use commas where needed.

1. Bees use no words, and they communicate with one another.

2. Male bees hatch from eggs laid by worker bees, because female bees hatch only from eggs laid by the queen bee.

3. A female worker bee finds food, and she returns to the hive to let the other bees know.

4. She dances in a circle; nevertheless, this dance is called a round dance.

5. The bee dances in a circle, and the other bees follow her movements, keeping their antennae close to her body.

6. Because one of the other bees leaves and finds the food, she has learned from the dancer where the food is.

7. The newly fed bee returns to the hive, yet she also begins a new dance.

8. The process continues, and many bees have learned of the feeding spot.

9. Because the other bees hold their antennae close to the dancer's body, she carries the scent of food.

10. The bees pick up the scent; nevertheless, they are able to trace down the food when they leave the hive.

11. In the dance movements, a bee can communicate the direction and distance of the food, and scientists have charted these dancers carefully.

PROJECT PREP Revising *Faulty Subordination*

Check your draft for faulty subordination and fix any problems you find, clarifying the relationship between the subordinated ideas.

3 Faulty Parallelism

A sentence with parallelism uses the same grammatical construction to express similar ideas. **Parallelism,** as its name suggests, points out parallels that help a reader group certain ideas together. It is one of several **schemes** a writer can use to vary the word order or grammatical structure to emphasize a point. Faulty parallelism occurs when similar ideas are expressed in different grammatical constructions.

Faulty	Jeffrey's hobbies are **playing the piano** and **to work on cars.** (one gerund phrase; one infinitive phrase)
Parallel	Jeffrey's hobbies are **playing the piano** and **working on cars.** (two gerund phrases)
Faulty	Jessye Norman's voice is **clear, warm,** and **with a heavenly quality.** (two adjectives and a prepositional phrase)
Parallel	Jessye Norman's voice **is** clear and warm and **has** a heavenly quality. (two verbs)

Practice Your Skills

Correcting Faulty Parallelism

Revise each of the following sentences so that the grammatical constructions are parallel.

1. To keep the peace, to uphold human rights, and feeding the hungry—these are the goals for which nations strive.
2. Cross-country skiing and to swim are good exercise for the heart, lungs, and legs.
3. Eating out is more expensive than to eat at home.
4. My best friend is sympathetic, understanding, and of a kind nature.
5. The car was rusty and with a broken-down look.
6. I want to go outdoors and that I exercise every day.
7. To surprise his mother and hoping to make her laugh, Roberto appeared at the back door in a disguise.
8. Ellen likes to fish, to ride her bicycle, and run.
9. Carl wanted driving lessons and that someone inform him about buying a car.

PROJECT PREP Revising *Faulty Parallelism*

Revise your draft once again, this time looking for faulty parallelism and eliminating it. Also look for opportunities to introduce parallelism to strengthen a point, and be sure the parallel structures are really parallel.

CHAPTER 2

4 Active Voice

In grammatical terms, the **active voice** places emphasis on the performer of the action. The **passive voice** places emphasis on the receiver of the action.

Active	I ate the sandwich.
Passive	The sandwich was eaten by me.

In some cases the performer of the action is missing entirely from a passive construction.

Passive	The decision was made to add two extra hours to the school day.

When you wish to place emphasis on the receiver of the action, the passive voice is proper and useful.

Emphasizing the Receiver	Miguelina was named the top student by her peers. Sandy was elected class president.

Overuse of the passive voice, however, drains writing of its vitality. Use the active voice whenever possible.

CHAPTER 2

Practice Your Skills

Eliminating the Passive Voice

Revise each sentence by changing the passive voice to the active voice.

1. A cake was baked by Mr. Gianelli.
2. It was decided by the student council to cancel the spring dance.
3. A lie was told by Tracy about the spilled paint.
4. The bed was made and the room was cleaned by Mark.
5. The musical was rehearsed for weeks by the acting club.

Writing Tip

Revise your sentences to eliminate **faulty coordination, faulty subordination,** or **faulty parallelism.** Avoid **rambling sentences** and overuse of the **passive voice.**

PROJECT PREP Revising *Active Voice*

Look over your draft one more time. Circle all the active-voice verbs you find and underline all the passive-voice verbs. Evaluate each passive-voice use: would it be better in active voice? If so, revise accordingly.

Using a Fluency Rubric

Evaluate your sentence fluency with the following rubric.

4 Sentences are varied in length, structure, and beginnings. Every sentence matters.	3 Sentences are mostly varied in length, structure, and beginnings. A few words and sentences seem unnecessary.	2 Many sentences are the same in length, structure, and beginnings. A number of words and sentences seem unnecessary.	1 Most sentences are the same in length, structure, and beginnings. A number of words and sentences seem unnecessary.
• I combined short, choppy sentences into varied, longer ones. • I used coordinating and subordinating conjunctions to improve the flow and show the relationship of ideas. • I started my sentences in a variety of ways, not always with the subject first. • I avoided rambling and faulty sentences.	• I combined some short, choppy sentences into varied, longer ones, but in a few places there is still some choppiness. • I sometimes used coordinating and subordinating conjunctions to improve the flow and show the relationship of ideas. • I started most of my sentences in a variety of ways, not always with the subject first. • I avoided rambling and faulty sentences.	• A few parts of my work flow, but there is still choppiness. • I used a few conjunctions to improve the flow and show relationships, but I see now that I could have used more. • Many of my sentences start the same way, with the subject. • Some of my sentences ramble or contain unnecessary information or faulty structure.	• I didn't quite achieve a flow. My writing seems to start and stop. • I didn't often combine ideas into one sentence to improve the flow and show relationships. • Most of my sentences start the same way, with the subject. • Many of my sentences ramble or contain unnecessary information or faulty structure.

PROJECT PREP Evaluating *Using a Rubric*

Use the rubric to evaluate your work and make as many changes as you feel necessary. Then publish it through an appropriate medium, such as a class Web site.

TIME OUT TO REFLECT

You have now learned and practiced some important stylistic skills. Which of these skills are most relevant to your own writing style? How can you continue to develop your writing style? Record your thoughts in the Learning Log section of your journal.

Writing Lab

Project Corner

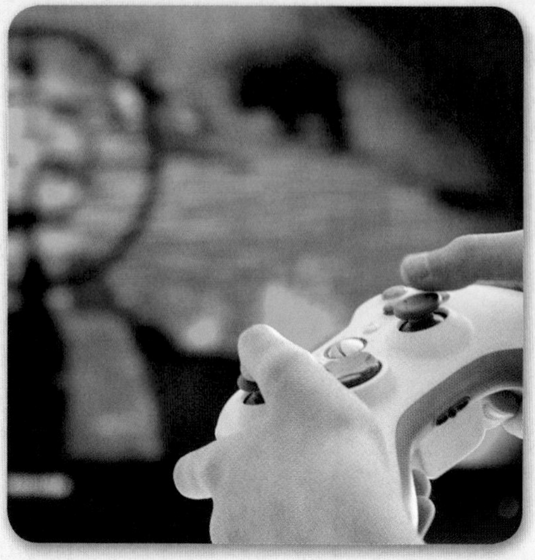

Get Creative
Make a Storyboard

Create a storyboard for a film or video game based on the narrative you wrote. (See page 599 for information on storyboards.) What key scenes do you want to emphasize? What would they look like in these images? Sketch out the main scenes of your travel-based film or video game.

Get Technical Create a Podcast

Create an audio podcast of the story you told about your travel experience. Practice reading it aloud so you can use your voice as dramatically as possible to tell your story. For inspiration, check the listings of your local public radio station for broadcasts of "Selected Shorts," a series of short stories read by well-known actors. You can also find podcasts of these stories online if you search for "PRI (Public Radio International) Selected Shorts."

Investigate Further
Research and Report

Using a variety of sources, from the Internet to printed or spoken news, **investigate the subject of your composition further**. What else might you have included in your narrative? Undertake a larger research project in which you depict—through writing, film, images, sounds, or other media—a more comprehensive range of information and impressions about the site of your travel than you were able to provide in your composition.

CHAPTER 2

In Everyday Life
Postcard to a Celebrity

Apply and Assess

1. A friend of yours is an agent for some of Hollywood's biggest stars. Yesterday she told you that you can write a postcard to your favorite celebrity, and she will send it! ***Compose a vivid and concise postcard*** to the celebrity of your choice, describing what you admire most about him or her. Be sure to eliminate unnecessary words, clichés, and rambling sentences. Correct sentences that use faulty parallelism or passive voice. Remember to keep your writing style cordial and clear so your reader can understand you.

CHAPTER 2

For Oral Communication Advertising Slogan

2. This Thursday you will record a commercial for AussieCakes, a new snack from Australia that will be coming to stores in your area. It is your job to create a short advertising slogan to market the cakes. ***Write a television or radio slogan*** to introduce AussieCakes to your class. Describe the taste and texture of the product. Use specific words and figurative language, including at least one instance each of personification and onomatopoeia.

Timed Writing Memo

3. You hold a part-time job with Amicus Amusements, a company manufacturing toys and games for young children. They are marketing My Talking Stone—a painted rock with a ribbon and bow that, your bosses claim, will "make the perfect pet." Your boss has asked you to write him a short memo offering marketing strategies for My Talking Stone.

   Before You Write Consider the following questions: What is the subject? What is the occasion? Who is the audience? What is the purpose?

   Prewrite to focus on what makes My Talking Stone so special. Use vivid and specific words, figurative language, and sentence variety to present your ideas. Do not use clichés or tired words. Your marketing strategies should target a wide group of potential customers. You have 20 minutes to complete your work. (For help budgeting time, see pages 37 and 500–501.)

   After You Write Evaluate your work using the rubrics on pages 26 and 77.

CHAPTER 3

Structuring Your Writing

The structure of a written text is the arrangement of its parts.

Text structures vary. The following examples show a variety of organizational forms for different kinds of texts.

- **Your favorite song begins with a drum solo** and continues with a verse sung by a solo voice followed by a chorus sung in harmony. A second verse and chorus, followed by another drum solo, round out the song and bring it to an end.
- **The letter you receive from the Red Cross** begins "Dear Donor," continues with sincere appreciation for your recent blood donation, and ends "Gratefully yours."
- **A science fiction story begins with** "Somewhere in a far-away galaxy," moves on to tell a story with a conflict, and ends with a gripping conclusion.
- **A science experiment follows the steps of the scientific method:** ask a question, do background research, construct a hypothesis, test the hypothesis by doing an experiment, analyze data, draw a conclusion, and communicate results.

Writing Project — Analytical

It's Not Easy ***Write an essay that defines what a hero is and illustrates a hero in action.***

Think Through Writing Everyone has heroes—famous athletes, powerful writers, the mom down the street who heals broken wings. Who are your personal heroes? Select someone who has inspired others through the example he or she sets. Write briefly to define what makes this person a hero.

Talk About It In your writing group, discuss the heroes you have identified. What do they have in common? In what ways are they different? How would you define the qualities that make them heroic?

Read About It In the following passage, author Shanlon Wu writes about the heroes he had as a youth, especially martial arts film star Bruce Lee. Think about your own heroes as you read about Wu's.

MODEL: Analytical Article

From

In Search of Bruce Lee's Grave

Shanlon Wu

It's Saturday morning in Seattle, and I am driving to visit Bruce Lee's grave. I have been in the city for only a couple of weeks and so drive two blocks past the cemetery before realizing that I've passed it. I double back and turn through the large wrought-iron gate, past a sign that reads: "Open to 9 P.M. or dusk, whichever comes first."

The first sentence of this paragraph draws the reader in and implies a main idea. The two sentences that follow it provide examples that support the main idea.

It's a sprawling cemetery, with winding roads leading in all directions. I feel silly trying to find his grave with no guidance. I think that my search for his grave is similar to my search for Asian heroes in America.

This is the framing metaphor and main idea: Wu's search for Asian male heroes felt as guideless as his search for Lee's grave.

I was born in 1959, an Asian American in Westchester County, N.Y. During my childhood there were no Asian sports stars. On television, I can recall only the most pathetic of Asian characters, Hop Sing, the Cartwright family houseboy on *Bonanza*. But in my adolescence there was Bruce.

I was 14 years old when I first saw *Enter the Dragon*, the granddaddy of martial-arts movies. Bruce had died suddenly at the age of 32 of cerebral edema, an excess of fluid in the brain, just weeks before the release of the film. Between the ages of 14 and 17, I saw *Enter the Dragon* 22 times before I stopped counting. During those years I collected Bruce Lee posters, putting them up at all angles in my bedroom. I took up Chinese martial arts and spent hours comparing my physique with his.

In the next few paragraphs, Wu writes about Lee's life while also revealing things about his own.

I learned all I could about Bruce: That he had married a Caucasian, Linda; that he had sparred with Kareem Abdul-Jabbar; that he was a buddy of Steve

McQueen and James Coburn, both of whom were his pallbearers.

My parents, who immigrated to America and had become professors at Hunter College, tolerated my behavior, but seemed puzzled at my admiration of an "entertainer." My father jokingly tried to compare my obsession with Bruce to his boyhood worship of Chinese folk-tale heroes.

"I read them just like you read American comic books," he said.

But my father's heroes could not be mine; they came from an ancient literary tradition, not comic books. He and my mother had grown up in a land where they belonged to the majority. I could not adopt their childhood and they were wise enough not to impose it upon me.

Although I never again experienced the kind of blind hero worship I felt for Bruce, my need to find heroes remained strong.

In college, I discovered the men of the 442nd Regimental Combat Team, a United States Army all-Japanese unit in World War II. Allowed to fight only against Europeans, they suffered heavy casualties while their families were put in internment camps. Their motto was "Go for Broke."

I saw them as Asians in a Homeric epic, the protagonists of a Shakespearean tragedy; I knew no Eastern myths to infuse them with. They embodied my own need to prove myself in the Caucasian world. I imagined how their American-born flesh and muscle must have resembled mine: epicanthic folds[1] set in strong faces nourished on milk and beef. I thought how much they had proved where there was so little to prove.

As Wu analyzes the heroes he encountered, he presents his discoveries in chronological order. That typically narrative organization and Wu's use of first person make this article more a personal narrative than an analytical essay, which would use third person and might be organized in a different pattern.

After college, I competed as an amateur boxer in an attempt to find my self-image in the ring. It didn't work. My fighting was only an attempt to copy Bruce's movies. What I needed was instruction on how to live. I quit boxing after a year and went to law school.

1 **epicanthic fold:** A prolongation of a fold of the skin of the upper eyelid over the inner angle or both angles of the eye.

I was an anomaly there: a would-be Asian litigator. I had always liked to argue and found I liked doing it in front of people even more. When I won the first year moot court competition in law school, I asked an Asian classmate if he thought I was the first Asian to win.

He laughed and told me I was probably the only Asian to even compete.

The law-firm interviewers always seemed surprised that I wanted to litigate.

"Aren't you interested in Pacific Rim trade?" they asked.

"My Chinese isn't good enough," I quipped.

My pat response seemed to please them. It certainly pleased me. I thought I'd found a place of my own—a place where the law would insulate me from the pressure of defining my Asian maleness. I sensed the possibility of merely being myself. . . .

I was surprised and frightened . . . by my still-strong hunger for images of powerful Asian men. That hunger was my vulnerability manifested, a reminder of my lack of place.

The hunger is eased this gray morning in Seattle. After asking directions from a policeman—Japanese—I easily locate Bruce's grave. The headstone is red granite with a small picture etched into it. The picture is very Hollywood—Bruce wears dark glasses—and I think the calligraphy looks a bit sloppy. Two tourists stop but leave quickly after glancing at me.

I realize I am crying. Bruce's grave seems very small in comparison to his place in my boyhood. So small in comparison to my need for heroes. Seeing his grave, I understand how large the hole in my life has been, and how desperately I'd sought to fill it.

I had sought an Asian hero to emulate. But none of my choices quite fit me. Their lives were defined through heroic tasks—they had villains to defeat and wars to fight—while my life seemed merely a struggle to define myself.

But now I see how that very struggle has defined me. I must be my own hero even as I learn to treasure those who have gone before.

I have had my powerful Asian male images . . . I may yet discover others. Their lives beckon like fireflies on a moonless night, and I know that they—like me—may have been flawed by foolhardiness and even cruelty. Still, their lives were real. They were not houseboys on *Bonanza.*

The concluding paragraph sums up the author's quest for a hero and his discovery about himself.

CHAPTER 3

Respond in Writing Respond to Shanlon Wu's article about heroes. Do you see Bruce Lee and the other role models Wu mentions as heroes? How do they compare to the hero you have identified and defined?

Develop Your Own Ideas Work with your classmates to develop criteria for heroes.

Small Groups: In your writing group, use a graphic organizer like the following to outline each member's hero. Use the writing you have done, the article by Shanlon Wu, and any other knowledge or sources available to help you develop your ideas.

Name of hero	Qualities that make this person heroic

Whole Class: Make a master chart of all of the ideas generated by the small groups, and use these ideas for further discussion of heroes.

Write About It You will next write a paragraph and then an essay in which you define and illustrate "hero." You may choose from any of the following possibilities.

Possible Topics and Examples	Possible Audiences	Possible Forms
• a person you know personally • a person whose achievements are in an area in which you hope to excel • a person very different from you whom you have read about and admired	• other teenagers • parents • school administrators • the student council • your personal hero	• a teen magazine • a blog • an e-mail • an opinion column for a newspaper

1 Paragraph Structure

No matter what its length, a good composition needs a clear structure. In a **paragraph**—a group of related sentences that present and develop one main idea—the topic sentence, supporting sentences, and concluding sentence are the structural elements. Notice how they function in the paragraph below.

MODEL: Paragraph Structure

A student of yoga can learn to meditate by practicing three activities. One activity is called "watching inwardly." In this exercise the student tries to watch all the words and thoughts that come to mind. A second exercise for meditating is called "seeing simply." This activity calls for looking at objects without attaching a word to them. A chair, for example, should be experienced for its shape and color, rather than classified as something to sit on. A third activity, called "following the breath," moves in stages—from concentrating on breathing, to watching inwardly, and finally to keeping the mind quiet. People who use these techniques feel refreshed afterward, as if they had rested.

Topic Sentence: States the main idea

Supporting Sentences: Develop the main idea

Concluding Sentence: Creates a strong ending

The structure of a paragraph can vary. In the model paragraph above, the main idea stated in the **topic sentence** appears as the first sentence. The **supporting sentences** are in the middle, and the **concluding sentence** is the paragraph's last sentence. You may choose to construct your paragraph differently by placing your topic sentence in the middle of the paragraph or even at the end. You may not need a concluding sentence if you end with a topic sentence. Whatever the structure, your main idea must be clear.

HERE'S HOW

Guidelines for a One-Paragraph Composition

- Make your main idea clear.
- Develop your main idea fully.
- Provide a strong ending.

Topic Sentence

The topic sentence often comes at the beginning of a paragraph, although it can also appear in the middle or at the end. Wherever it is placed, however, its purpose and character are always the same.

A **topic sentence** states the main idea of the paragraph.

The topic sentence is more general than the other sentences in the paragraph. It gives an overall summary of what the paragraph will cover while being specific enough to focus on the one main point of the paragraph.

CHAPTER 3

FEATURES OF A TOPIC SENTENCE

A topic sentence

- states the main idea
- focuses the limited subject to one main point that can be adequately covered in the paragraph
- is more general than the sentences that develop it

The topic sentence in the following paragraph is suitably specific.

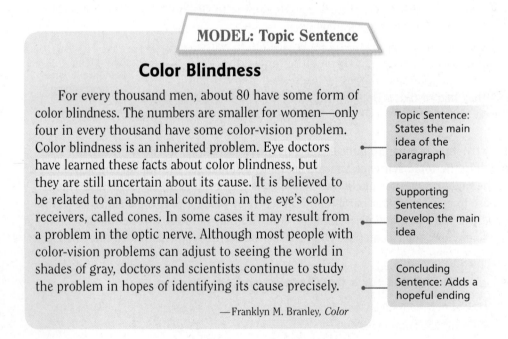

MODEL: Topic Sentence

Color Blindness

For every thousand men, about 80 have some form of color blindness. The numbers are smaller for women—only four in every thousand have some color-vision problem. Color blindness is an inherited problem. Eye doctors have learned these facts about color blindness, but they are still uncertain about its cause. It is believed to be related to an abnormal condition in the eye's color receivers, called cones. In some cases it may result from a problem in the optic nerve. Although most people with color-vision problems can adjust to seeing the world in shades of gray, doctors and scientists continue to study the problem in hopes of identifying its cause precisely.

—Franklyn M. Branley, *Color*

Topic Sentence: States the main idea of the paragraph

Supporting Sentences: Develop the main idea

Concluding Sentence: Adds a hopeful ending

Practice Your Skills

Identifying Topic Sentences

Find and write the topic sentence for the following paragraph.

Jobs and Concrete Thinking

The architect is a good example of a person who must be able to visualize solid objects or structures. Civil engineers, who build bridges, work with solids of three-dimensional objects; so do mechanical engineers who design and build machines. The die-maker, who makes patterns and molds, must be able to visualize the finished product. The sculptor, too, must be able to "see" the finished statue. Surgeons must have a clear picture in mind of the structure of that part of the body on which they are operating. The same is true of the builder, the mechanic, the dressmaker, the fashion designer—anyone whose job deals with shapes and solids. They all need an aptitude for concrete thinking.

—George Francis Barth, *Your Aptitudes*

Supporting Sentences

The supporting sentences in a paragraph usually answer questions raised by the topic sentence. **Supporting sentences** explain the topic sentence by giving specific details, facts, examples, or reasons.

As you read the following topic sentence about the eruption of Mount St. Helens, think about the questions you would want answered in the rest of the paragraph.

Topic Sentence The eruption of Mount St. Helens in May of 1980 and the ashfall that followed took an awesome toll on the region's wildlife.

The obvious question raised is, What was the toll? The supporting sentences answer that.

MODEL: Supporting Sentences

The blast itself and the superheated volcanic flows accounted for more than 67,000 deaths of birds and mammals, including 6,000 black-tailed deer, 11,000 hares, and nearly 28,000 forest and sage grouse. These numbers, unfortunately, are only the beginning. By the time the tons of ash had fallen in the area, nearly one and a half *million* creatures had died, with the greatest toll in the bird families. As the fiery hot flows reached the rivers below, even more wildlife was destroyed. Rivers became boiling hot, and about eleven million salmon and other fish were killed. A whole year of desolation passed before signs of life began, little by little, to reappear in this devastated region.

—Thomas and Virginia Aylesworth, *The Mount St. Helens Disaster*

Practice Your Skills

Writing Supporting Sentences

For each of the following topic sentences, write three supporting sentences.

1. Many adults fail to understand the pressures of being a teenager today.

2. Some of the best gifts people can give or receive are not objects that can be purchased.

3. Some of the most successful people have overcome severe disabilities or hardships to achieve their goals.

Writing Tip

Develop your paragraph with **supporting sentences** that contain facts, examples, reasons, events, or specific details.

CHAPTER 3

Concluding Sentence

Good concluding sentences are not dull summaries or repetitions of the topic sentence. They offer, instead, a fresh insight that locks the main idea in the reader's mind. These sentences are called *clinchers*.

A **concluding sentence** recalls the main idea and adds a strong ending to a paragraph.

HERE'S HOW

Strategies for Ending a Paragraph

- Restate the main idea using different words.
- Summarize the paragraph.
- Add an insight about the main idea.
- Express how you feel about the subject.

The paragraph below on famous names lacks a concluding sentence and leaves the reader expecting more.

Paragraph Lacking Concluding Sentence

Many people in show business trade the names they were born with for names with more audience appeal. Whoopie Goldberg, for example, was born Caryn Johnson. Jennifer Aniston's birth name was Jennifer Anastassakis. Cher shortened her name from Cherilyn Sarkisian. Stevie Wonder was born Stevland Morris.

The following concluding sentence brings the main idea full circle.

MODEL: Concluding Sentence

Although their families probably still call these performers by their original names, they are known throughout the world by the names they use for the stage.

Practice Your Skills

Writing Concluding Sentences

Write three more sentences that could each provide a strong conclusion to the paragraph about famous names.

PROJECT PREP *Revising* *Paragraph Structure*

Write a rough draft of a paragraph defining and giving an example of a hero. Then, discuss each person's draft. Discuss what each writer would need to do to provide clearer structure to his or her writing. After the discussion, revise your draft to improve the structure.

2 Paragraph Development

The main idea of a paragraph expressed in the topic sentence is developed through supporting details. Supporting details include any specific information that will help explain your subject. The following chart shows some types of supporting details and rhetorical devices you can use.

TYPES OF SUPPORTING DETAILS		
examples	incidents	facts/statistics
reasons	directions	steps in a process
sensory details	events	comparisons/contrasts
causes and effects	analogies	classifications

CHAPTER 3

When you choose the type of supporting details to use, keep in mind the purpose of the paragraph and the kinds of questions a reader may have about the subject.

If you are familiar with the subject you are writing about, you may already have many supporting details on hand. If not, you will have to do research by reading and talking to knowledgeable people.

You can learn more about research techniques on pages 390–465.

Writing Tip

List **details** that suit the main idea of your paragraph and explain the subject clearly.

Practice Your Skills

Listing Supporting Details

For each of the following subjects, list four supporting details that would help you explain it.

1. how to bathe a dog
2. the pleasures of dancing
3. what a sick giraffe looks like
4. the reasons behind the establishment of Arbor Day
5. the ways that every citizen can help reduce pollution
6. the importance of extra-curricular activities
7. the world's best omelette
8. caring for an injured pet

Adequate Development

The supporting sentences in a paragraph develop the main idea with specific details. These specific details can take the form of facts, examples, reasons, events, or descriptive images. Whatever their form, to ensure **adequate development,** supporting details must be numerous and specific enough to make the main idea clear, interesting, and convincing.

In the following paragraph, the writer has provided enough specific details to support the main idea adequately. The details take the form of facts and examples.

CHAPTER 3

MODEL: Adequate Paragraph Development

Digital News

In 1981, the *San Francisco Examiner* was one of eight newspapers to attempt to deliver content digitally by using a service that sent the content over phone lines via modems. At that time, only about two or three thousand people in the Bay area had home computers, yet as many as 500 signed on for the digital delivery. The newspaper did not charge for the content, but download fees were very high: the daily newspaper took two hours to download via telephone, and the service charge was $5.00 per hour. Now, some 30 years later, many Americans prefer to get their news digitally, and some major newspapers have eliminated some of their print editions altogether.

Topic Sentence: Introduces the subject

Supporting Sentences: Provide details

Concluding Sentence: Extends idea logically to present time

editing

You don't need a lot of words to get your point across. In the following sentence, eliminate the extra words that weigh down rather than build up the idea. Then write a sentence that concisely expresses the thought.

> Reading news articles online has many wonderful advantages to the reader or anyone interested in the news, such as easy access any time of the night or day and no worries about a lump of heavy newsprint flying through your front screen door at 7 a.m. in the morning.

Writing Tip

Use specific details and information to achieve **adequate development** of your main idea.

You can use a rubric like the one below to evaluate how well you have developed ideas in your writing.

Idea Rubric

4 Ideas are presented and developed in depth.	3 Most ideas are presented and developed with insight.	2 Many ideas are not well developed.	1 Most ideas are not well developed.
• I developed each idea thoroughly with specific details.	• I developed most ideas thoroughly with specific details.	• I tried to develop ideas but was more general than specific.	• I tried to develop ideas but was more general than specific.
• My presentation of ideas was original.	• My presentation of some ideas was thoughtul.	• I listed rather than developed ideas.	• I listed rather than developed ideas.
• I made meaningful connections among ideas.	• I made some connections among ideas.	• I made few connections among ideas.	• I did not make connections among ideas.
• I took some risks to make my writing come alive.	• I played it safe and did not put much of myself into the composition.	• I left a few things out but I think my meaning comes across.	• I left some important things out so my meaning wasn't clear.

CHAPTER 3

PROJECT PREP *Revising* ***Developing Ideas***

Use the rubric above to evaluate the development of your ideas in your draft. After the evaluation, make revisions to improve the development of your ideas. Share your revision with your writing group and make further improvements as needed.

The Power of Language

Dashes: Dash It All

When adding details and information to your writing, you can use the dash to call attention to especially important additions. Used sparingly, the dash creates a break between most of a sentence and something you want to emphasize, as in these examples from "In Search of Bruce Lee's Grave" by Shanlon Wu.

> The hunger is eased this gray morning in Seattle. After asking directions from a policeman—Japanese—I easily locate Bruce's grave. The headstone is red granite with a small picture etched into it. The picture is very Hollywood—Bruce wears dark glasses—and I think the calligraphy looks a bit sloppy. Two tourists stop but leave quickly after glancing at me.

> My pat response seemed to please them. It certainly pleased me. I thought I'd found a place of my own—a place where the law would insulate me from the pressure of defining my Asian maleness. I sensed the possibility of merely being myself. . . .

In the first example, Wu uses two dashes to set off information within a sentence. Rather than writing "a Japanese policeman," he emphasizes the police officer's identity by setting it between dashes. To further enhance the words "very Hollywood," Wu uses an aside that describes Bruce Lee's glasses.

In the second paragraph, Wu uses one dash to set off a thought at the end of the sentence. Here, the dash sets off a further, deeper explanation of his idea of finding a place of his own—describing what this place meant to him.

Try It Yourself

On your project topic, write two sentences similar to the ones above, with a dash preceding and emphasizing the important material. Write one sentence in which the additional material comes in the middle of the sentence and is enclosed by dashes. Write a second with the additional details at the end of the sentence.

Punctuation Tip

When you want to create a dash on the computer, be sure it is not an en-dash (–), which is shorter, or a hyphen, which is shorter still (-), but an em-dash (—), which is the longest dash and is created on some computers by using the shift, option, and hyphen keys together.

3 Unity

In a paragraph that has **unity,** all the sentences relate directly to the topic sentence. Ideas or details that stray from the main idea distract the reader and weaken the impact of the paragraph. As you write and revise, make sure that each sentence in the paragraph clearly supports and develops the topic sentence.

CHAPTER 3

MODEL: Paragraph That Lacks Unity

The aurora borealis, or northern lights, appears in many forms. Sometimes it looks like a faint green curtain in the sky, fading in and out of view. Sometimes it appears in white, yellow, or red, like a glowing arc in the sky. ~~Appearances occur more often during intense sunspot activity.~~ At other times it appears as a cloud shimmering in the far northern skies. ~~The corresponding event in the Southern Hemisphere is called the aurora australis.~~ Whatever form it takes, the aurora borealis, with its quiet mystery, is always a sight to be remembered.

The sentences that destroy the unity of the paragraph are crossed out.

Writing Tip

Achieve **unity** by making sure all the supporting sentences relate to the topic sentence.

Practice Your Skills

Checking for Unity

Write the two sentences that stray from the subject in the paragraph below.

Henry David Thoreau had a strong connection to pencils—not only because he was a prolific writer. He was also a pencil maker and inventor. Thoreau was raised in his father's pencil business. His uncle was a part of the business too. In those days, pencils were made by cutting the wood in half and filling it with graphite and a binder and gluing the pieces together. Thoreau had studied at Harvard in the 1830s. Thoreau invented a way to inject lead directly into a hollowed-out pencil, thus revolutionizing the pencil industry.

PROJECT PREP Evaluating *Unity*

In your writing group, evaluate one another's drafts by looking for any stray sentences that destroy the paragraph's unity. Make changes in your draft according to the evaluation of your peers.

4 Coherence

In a **coherent** paragraph, ideas follow logically and smoothly.

Writing Tip

Achieve **coherence** by presenting ideas in logical order and by using transitions.

Following are some methods of organization and transitions you can use to write coherent paragraphs.

CHAPTER 3

Chronological Order and Transitions

Chronological order is used with events or stories to tell what happened first, second, third, and so on.

It is also used to explain a sequence of steps in a process. Words and phrases called **transitions** are used to show the relationship of events. The following chart lists transitions that are commonly used for chronological order.

TRANSITIONS FOR CHRONOLOGICAL ORDER			
after	meanwhile	during	last night
before	next	at last	on Monday
suddenly	then	at noon	the next day
just as	immediately	while	by evening

Practice Your Skills

Using Chronological Order

Arrange the following events in chronological order.

- The second step was to find the Endnote directory under Program Files.
- Mai wanted to know how to find a certain folder in a library file.
- The first step was to go to the Toolbar Menu and click on File/Open/Open Library.
- Mai talked to her school librarian about how to find this folder.
- The librarian told her to follow four steps.
- Having clicked on the Endnote directory, Mai then found the Examples directory and opened it.
- Mai then had the folder she was looking for.
- Once she had the Endnote directory, Mai was told to click on it.

Practice Your Skills

Using Transitions

Write a paragraph using transitions to show the sequence of events in the previous practice. Give the paragraph a plot in which Mai works through the task chronologically.

Spatial Order and Transitions

CHAPTER 3

A well-organized description leads the reader from point to point until the picture is complete. This method of organization is called spatial order.

Spatial order arranges details according to their location.

When using spatial order, transitions show where each item fits into the larger picture. Readers can see clearly the object or scene that is being described. Transition words help orient the reader. The chart below shows transitions commonly used for spatial order.

TRANSITIONS FOR SPATIAL ORDER	
top to bottom (or the reverse)	higher, lower, above, below, at the base (top), in the middle, halfway
side to side	at the left (right), in the middle, next to, beside, at one end, at the other end
inside to outside (or the reverse)	within, in the center, on the outside, innermost, in the middle
near to far (or the reverse)	in front of, nearby, farther, beyond, across, to the north (etc.), in the distance

Paragraphs can also use a special spatial order in which details are described in the order in which the details strike the writer rather than in a set pattern. Transitions make this order clear.

Practice Your Skills

Recognizing Spatial Order and Transitions

Write all the transitional words and phrases in the following paragraph. Then write *top to bottom* (or the reverse), *side to side, inside out* (or the reverse), *near to far* (or the reverse), or *special* to indicate the type of spatial order.

The lagoon in the center of Lincoln Park is like a mirrored floor reflecting the alternating layers of city and country above it. On the surface of the lagoon, afternoon idlers paddle around in bright yellow boats, their laughs and splashes muted by the windy day. Overhead the trees rise and arch, rustle and sway. Above the tree line, the city skyscrapers thrust their sleek gray heads, lording over the bending trees. Still higher, though, the white clouds race and billow, reminding all who stop to notice that some heights are beyond the reach of concrete and steel.

Order of Importance and Transitions

Another common way to organize supporting details in a paragraph is to use the order of importance.

> **Order of importance** arranges supporting points in the order of least to most important or most to least important.

Writers use transitions to show the relative importance of ideas. That is, these transitions show the relationship among the supporting points. Some of the most common transitions used with order of importance are listed in the following chart.

TRANSITIONS FOR ORDER OF IMPORTANCE		
also	moreover	for this reason
another	furthermore	more important
besides	in addition	most important
finally	similarly	in the first place
first	likewise	to begin with

The following transitions are useful for showing contrast.

TRANSITIONS SHOWING CONTRAST		
but	however	nevertheless
yet	instead	in contrast
or, nor	still	on the other hand

Practice Your Skills

Using Transitions

In the following paragraph, the ideas are arranged in order of importance, but the transitions are missing. Using examples from the preceding charts, add appropriate transitions. Write the transitions on a separate piece of paper. Use commas as needed.

In Case of Fire . . .

Know in advance what you will do if a fire starts in your home. **(1)** ___ thing to do is stay calm and rational. Don't panic. **(2)** ___ you should see that all the people in the house are assembled and ready to leave right away. **(3)** ___ if you see smoke, stop, drop to the ground, and crawl to the nearest door. **(4)** ___ you open the door, feel it with your hand to be sure it isn't hot. **(5)** The ___ important things to think about are your possessions.

CHAPTER 3

Use the following rubric to evaluate the order of your ideas and your use of transitions.

Organization Rubric			
4 Ideas progress smoothly and the organization clarifies meaning.	**3 Most ideas progress smoothly and the organization is clear.**	**2 Some ideas progress smoothly but the organization is not consistent.**	**1 Few ideas progress smoothly and there is no clear organization.**
• My topic sentence states the main idea creatively and captures attention. • I used the best organization pattern to present the supporting details. • My concluding sentence helps make the paragraph feel complete. • My sentences flow smoothly. I used transitions throughout.	• I stated the main idea in the topic sentence and captured attention. • I used an appropriate organization to present the supporting details. • My conclusion helps make the composition feel complete. • Most of my sentences flow smoothly. I used some transitions.	• I stated the main idea in the topic sentence but did not capture attention. • I used an appropriate organization but had some things out of order. • My conclusion provides an ending but it does not feel strong. • I repeated some ideas unnecessarily. I could have used more transitions.	• I did not state my main idea clearly. • I did not really use an organizational pattern. • I repeated some things and also had some things out of order or not related to the topic. • I did not use many transitions so the order is hard to follow.

Practice Your Skills

Revising a Paragraph

Revise the following paragraph, which lacks a topic sentence and a concluding sentence. Add, delete, substitute, and rearrange as you improve the paragraph's development, organization, and coherence. Try to make it as clear as possible for someone about to take the driving test.

Driving Test

When you are called for your test, be confident. Before taking your driving test, try to relax by breathing deeply. Take your time getting ready. Sometimes you have to wait for 30 to 45 minutes at the Department of Motor Vehicles, just as you would at another public facility, such as a crowded post office. Adjust the mirrors and seats, buckle your seat belt, and take some more deep breaths. Do exactly what your examiner tells you. Watch for all signs, especially speed limits in school zones. Remember to use your blinker for all turns. Park correctly on a hill.

CHAPTER 3

PROJECT PREP *Revising* ***Achieving Coherence***

In your writing group, discuss the best way for each writer's ideas to be organized. Switch papers and write a few sentences of your partner's paragraph in its new organization. Be sure to include transitions. Look over the work your partner does on your paper and consider how effectively the writing achieves coherence.

Paragraph Writing Workshops

CHAPTER 3

1 Narrative Paragraphs

If you want to tell about a series of events—in an e-mail, on a social studies test, or in a short story—you will be writing narration. You can develop the skills required for narrative writing by creating paragraphs that grab and hold your reader's attention.

Narrative writing tells a real or an imaginary story with a clear beginning, middle, and ending.

A narrative paragraph has three main parts. Each part performs a specific function.

HERE'S HOW

Structuring a Narrative Paragraph

- In the **topic sentence,** capture the reader's attention and make a general statement that sets the scene.
- In the **supporting sentences,** tell the story event by event, often building suspense.
- In the **concluding sentence,** show the outcome, summarize the story, or add an insight.

The following narrative paragraph describes the surprising events of a horse race.

MODEL: Narrative Paragraph

A Long Shot

At a track in England some years ago, a mounted policeman was helping to get the race horses into their starting positions. At the cry "They're off!" the policeman's horse broke with the field, and the astonished bobby found himself desperately trying to pull in his mount. The best he could do, however, was to slow him down to third place. On the stretch the horse began to fight it out with one of the official entries. Despite the policeman's efforts to pull out of the race, he came in second, a scant neck behind a horse ridden by Freddie Archer, one of England's greatest jockeys.

—Reader's Digest

Topic Sentence: Sets the scene

Supporting Sentences: Relate events one by one

Concluding Sentence: Gives the outcome

Use a graphic organizer like the one below to organize your narrative paragraph.

Setting	
Event that begins narrative	
Next important event	
Next important event	
Next important event	
What the narrative tells us	

CHAPTER 3

QuickGuide for Writing Narrative Paragraphs

→ Use brainstorming to develop a list of details you might include in your narrative. Choose the details you will use and arrange them in chronological order. (See page 95.)

→ Include the incident or obstacle that set up the conflict in the story. Use suspense to show how it developed, and then tell how it was resolved.

→ Include enough details about the people involved so that they seem believable and interesting.

→ Use transitions such as *first, later,* and *finally* to keep the order clear.

→ Include a clear introduction and conclusion.

Create Real-World Texts

1. Write a narrative paragraph about a time when you had an experience that turned out to be different from what you had expected—either better or worse. For instance, you may recall a vacation that was more enjoyable than you had expected or worse than you had ever imagined it would be.
2. Write a narrative paragraph about an incident from real life or from your imagination in which a person developed an innovative solution to a problem.

2 Descriptive Paragraphs

You want your reader to see, feel, hear, smell, and taste the events you are describing. To help them do that, you use sensory details. Whether unusually striking or completely familiar, people, things, and places come to life through writing that appeals to the senses.

Descriptive writing paints a vivid picture of a person, an object, or a scene by stimulating the reader's senses.

CHAPTER 3

HERE'S HOW

Structuring a Descriptive Paragraph

- In the **topic sentence,** make a general statement about the subject and suggest an overall impression.
- In the **supporting sentences,** supply specific details that help readers use their five senses to bring the picture to life.
- In the **concluding sentence,** summarize the overall impression of the subject.

MODEL: Descriptive Paragraph

About 15 miles below Monterey, on the wild coast, the Torres family had their farm, a few sloping acres above a cliff that dropped to the brown reefs and to the hissing white waters of the ocean. Behind the farm the stone mountains stood up against the sky. The farm buildings huddled like the clinging aphids on the mountain skirts, crouched low to the ground as though the wind might blow them into the sea. The little shack, the rattling, rotting barn were gray-bitten with sea salt, beaten by the damp wind until they had taken on the color of the granite hills. Two horses, a red cow and a red calf, half a dozen pigs and a flock of lean, multi-colored chickens stocked the place. A little corn was raised on the sterile slope, and it grew short and thick under the wind, and all the cobs formed on the landward sides of the stalks.

—John Steinbeck, "Flight"

Topic Sentence: Sets the scene

Supporting Sentences: Give sensory details

Concluding Sentence: Reinforces overall impression

Notice that the topic sentence creates a picture of the landscape by using the words *wild coast, sloping acres above a cliff, brown reefs,* and *hissing white waters* to suggest that it is an unusual place.

You can use a graphic organizer like the one below to help you develop details for a descriptive paragraph.

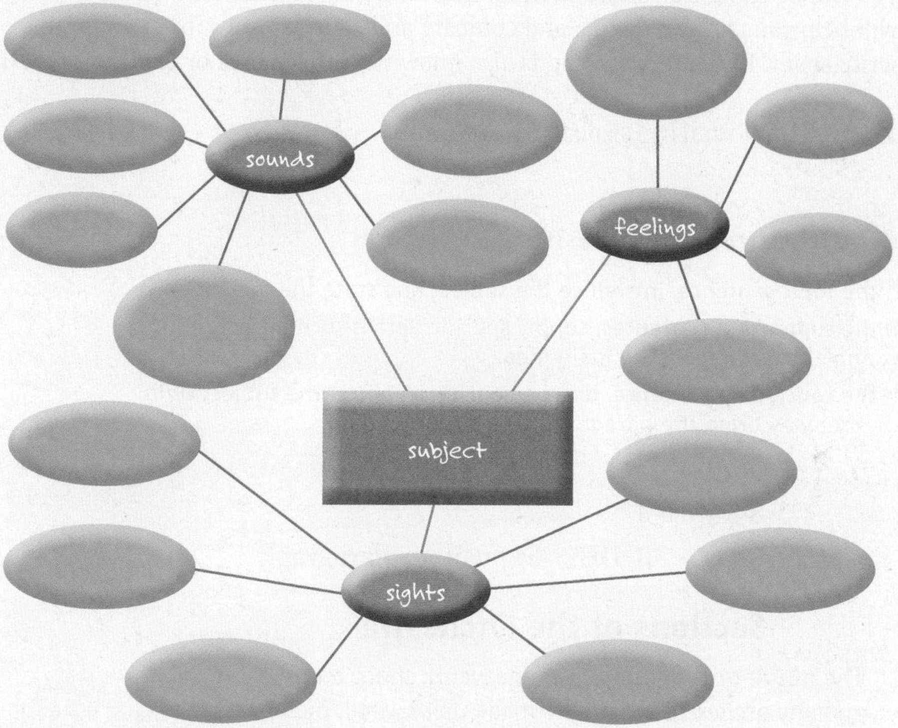

QuickGuide for Writing Descriptive Paragraphs

→ Use brainstorming, clustering, or freewriting to write down specific words and sensory details that create an overall impression of your subject.

→ Organize your details in spatial order or another logical order.

→ Write a topic sentence that expresses the overall impression of your subject.

→ Use your notes to draft the body of the paragraph.

→ Use transitions, such as *at the base, atop, next to, within,* and *nearby*, to keep the order of your details clear.

→ End your paragraph with a strong concluding sentence.

Create Real-World Texts

1. Write a paragraph describing a person after looking at his or her photograph in a book or a family album.
2. Describe one of the year's biggest fashions or fads.
3. For history class, describe the plight of farmers during the Dust Bowl days of the middle 1930s using sensory details and vivid images.

3 Expository Paragraphs

Whenever you want to provide information or explain something to your readers, you will be using expository writing. Learning how to write an expository paragraph will help you analyze, define, and compare and contrast the subject you want to write about. Expository writing is also known as **informative** or **explanatory writing.**

Expository writing explains or informs.

CHAPTER 3

HERE'S HOW

Structuring an Expository Paragraph

- In the **topic sentence,** introduce the subject and state the main idea.
- In the **supporting sentences,** supply specific details such as facts and examples that support the main idea.
- In the **concluding sentence,** draw a conclusion about the subject or in another way bring the paragraph to a strong ending.

MODEL: Expository Paragraph

Sections of the Orchestra

The music might sound like a heavenly choir, but a symphony orchestra is actually made up of wood, metal, and gifted musicians. Every symphony orchestra has four main groups of musical instruments. The first group, or section, is comprised of stringed instruments made of wood, such as violins, cellos, and basses. The musician creates a sound by drawing a bow across the strings. Woodwind instruments make up the second group and include wood or metal wind instruments, such as flutes, clarinets, and oboes. The third section of the orchestra consists of larger wind instruments made of brass. Horns, trumpets, trombones, and tubas make up this group. The fourth and final group is the percussion section. This group includes instruments such as kettle-drums, cymbals, bells, and xylophones. These instruments are generally struck with a stick or mallet or are shaken to produce sound. During an orchestral performance, each group plays an important and unique role while remaining part of the greater orchestra.

Topic Sentence: States the main idea

Supporting Sentences: Explain the four main groups

Concluding Sentence: Adds a strong ending

You can use a graphic like the one below to help you organize an expository paragraph illustrating how to do something.

Expository Paragraph

How to: ______________________________

Step One ______________________________

Step Two ______________________________

Step Three ______________________________

Conclusion: ______________________________

QuickGuide for Writing Expository Paragraphs

→ Brainstorm, cluster, or freewrite to think of possible subjects.

→ Brainstorm a list of details you will need to cover in order to explain your subject. Decide if there are any technical terms that you will need to define for your particular audience.

→ Construct a chart or outline to classify your information in a logical order.

→ Write a topic sentence that states the purpose of the paragraph and catches the reader's attention.

→ Use relevant and substantial evidence and well-chosen details to support your main idea. (See pages 90–91.)

→ Use transitions, such as *for example, in contrast,* or *however*, to show the relationships between ideas

→ Write a concluding sentence that brings the paragraph to a strong end by summarizing the important points, adding an insight, or emphasizing the importance of the subject.

Create Real-World Texts

1. Write a how-to paragraph explaining the steps needed to perform a skill or an activity that you know well to someone who is unfamiliar with it.
2. Write an expository paragraph about an event you attended recently.
3. Send an e-mail to a cousin giving driving directions to your house.

4 Persuasive Paragraphs

When you write to convince others to share your opinion or to take a certain course of action, you are writing persuasively. The kind of persuasive writing you will most commonly do in school is called **argumentative writing**.

Persuasive writing asserts an opinion or claim and uses facts, examples, and reasons to convince readers. See pages 282–321 for more on argument.

CHAPTER 3

HERE'S HOW

Structuring a Persuasive Paragraph

- In the **topic sentence,** assert an opinion or claim.
- In the **supporting sentences,** back up your assertion with facts, examples, reasons, and, if necessary, citations from experts. Appeal to the reader's reason but also engage the reader by appealing to emotion as well.
- In the **concluding sentence,** restate the assertion and draw a conclusion that follows from the supporting details.

The following model shows how each sentence in a persuasive paragraph functions. Notice how the supporting sentences back up the opinion in the topic sentence.

MODEL: Persuasive Paragraph

Flexible Work Schedules

More people should be allowed to work flexible schedules. Indeed, the number of full-time wage and salary workers who work a flexible schedule has been on the rise. In a 2006 benefits survey by the Society for Human Resource Management, 57 percent of human resource professionals reported that their organizations offered flextime options to employees. That number has more than doubled since 1991. The increase was largest for those who worked in food or beverage service and lowest for those in construction. Men are more likely to work a flexible shift than women, and private-sector employees are more likely than public sector employees to do so. In 2001, the Bureau of Labor Statistics reported that both job satisfaction and productivity increased for those working flex time. Clearly, flexible schedules are good for the economy and should be encouraged for most workers.

Topic Sentence: Asserts an opinion

Supporting Sentences: Give further evidence to support the main idea

Concluding Sentence: Drives home the main point

You can use a graphic organizer like the one below to help you develop and organize a persuasive paragraph.

I would like to persuade ____________________ **to** ____________________

Topic Sentence	
Reason 1	
Supporting Evidence	
Example/Fact	
Reason 2	
Supporting Evidence	
Example/Fact	
Conclusion	

CHAPTER 3

QuickGuide for Writing Persuasive Paragraphs

→ Explore your ideas on an issue by brainstorming, freewriting, or using another prewriting strategy and form an opinion about the issue.

→ Write a topic sentence that states your position.

→ Brainstorm a list of supporting facts, examples, and reasons you could use to develop a convincing argument.

→ Arrange your details in order of importance.

→ Use transitions such as *for example, in contrast,* and *however* to clarify the relationship between supporting details.

→ Write a strong concluding sentence that reinforces the main idea or summarizes your arguments.

Create Real-World Texts

1. Students in your school must participate in some form of volunteer community service as a requirement for graduation. Write a one-paragraph letter to the school board expressing your opinion on the graduation requirement.
2. You want to go on vacation with your friend's family during spring break. Write a paragraph to your parents suggesting reasons why you should go on vacation.
3. Think of a music group that you feel speaks to your generation. Write a critique of their music that encourages others to listen to them.

Compositions

CHAPTER 3

A paragraph is like a musical phrase—however lovely it may be, it needs further development to sound full and complete. In contrast, a good composition is like a song—in several paragraphs a worthwhile idea is introduced, developed, and wrapped up in a satisfying way. A composition is a complete unit that is interesting and can stand on its own.

A **composition** presents and develops one main idea in three or more paragraphs.

A composition can be a tool of discovery; often you cannot really know what you think about a subject until you begin to explore it in writing. Developing a written composition helps you think through your ideas and viewpoints rigorously and bring them into better focus.

1 Structure of a Composition

Carefully constructed compositions have three main parts: an introduction, a body, and a conclusion. These three parts of a composition parallel the three parts of a paragraph.

PARAGRAPH STRUCTURE	COMPOSITION STRUCTURE
Introduction	
topic sentence that introduces the subject and expresses the main idea	introductory paragraph that introduces the subject and expresses the main idea in a thesis statement
Body	
supporting sentences	supporting paragraphs
Conclusion	
concluding sentence	concluding paragraph

As you read the composition about Chico Mendes on the following page, notice how the three parts of the composition work together as a whole.

MODEL: Composition Structure

Earthkeeper Hero: Chico Mendes

Saving the planet's rain forests has become one of the world's most popular environmental causes. People from all walks of life have given selflessly of their time and money to help fund projects that teach people how to use the resources the rain forests have to offer without destroying them in the process. One person, however, has made the supreme sacrifice for this worthy cause. His name was Chico Mendes, and on December 22, 1988, he was killed while trying to save his beloved Amazon from destruction.

Introductory Paragraph with Thesis Statement

Born on December 15, 1944, in Ecuador, Mr. Mendes grew up in a family of rubber tappers (also known as *seringueiros*). Rubber tapping has been practiced by families in the Amazon for generations. It is a process whereby one harmlessly extracts sap from rubber trees which is then used in such products as car tires and Tupperware. Rubber tapping is one of the many ways in which the resources of the Amazon are exploited without permanently harming the ecosystem. It is a sustainable agricultural system, and Chico Mendes followed in his father's footsteps in becoming a *seringueiro*.

Body Paragraphs

Unfortunately, not everyone is interested in sustainable use of the Amazon. For the cattle ranchers and mining interests in Brazil, sustainable agriculture represents an impediment to profits. Much money can be made by tearing down the forest as fast as possible and replacing it with pasture land and strip mines. Sadly, what is left behind after the ranchers and miners leave with their profits is usually nothing more than a shattered wasteland, a ruined desert where once stood a forest more than 180 million years old.

Mr. Mendes fought courageously to oppose the destructive practices of such large companies and individuals. He advocated a return to sustainable agricultural systems and urged his fellow Brazilians to protest non-violently against corporations that would rob them of their livelihoods.

Not surprisingly, Mr. Mendes encountered a great deal of opposition from industrialists and corrupt government officials who were profiting from the tearing down of the Amazon. He was jailed and fined and threatened, but nothing could deter him from his mission to save his beloved jungle. And when he was killed in 1988 on the order of a rancher named Alves de Silva, the power of his grass roots movement only increased.

The international outcry against Chico Mendes' death was deafening. It marked a turning point in the fight to save the Amazon. Suddenly, a human face had been put on the cause to save the rain forests, and money and support from all over the world poured in to help complete the good work that Chico had started. The plight of the *seringueiro* has become an international *cause célèbre* and many far reaching reforms have been enacted since his death to insure the future of this eco-friendly industry.

Chico Mendes is not just a hero of the Amazon; he is a hero of the entire planet. The burning of the Amazon is a burning that impacts every forest and city and village on Earth. The fires that Chico Mendes fought to put out threatened more than just a few strange and exotic locations thousands of miles away. On a planet where the giant chain of life stretches from continent to continent, the flames of their endless burning continue to lick at the very edges of our own homes and backyards.

Concluding Paragraph

—Jeff Trussell

CHAPTER 3

Practice Your Skills

Analyzing a Composition

Answer these questions about the composition on Chico Mendes.

1. What is the main idea of the composition?

2. How do the body paragraphs support this main idea?

3. How is the conclusion of the composition different from the introduction?

PROJECT PREP *Expanding* *From Paragraph to Composition*

In your writing group, discuss each writer's paragraph with a focus on how to expand it. For example, can the topic sentence be adapted to serve as a thesis statement? Can each supporting detail become the topic of a supporting paragraph? Use an organizer like the following to map out ways the supporting points can be expanded into paragraphs of their own. Make a plan for a rewrite.

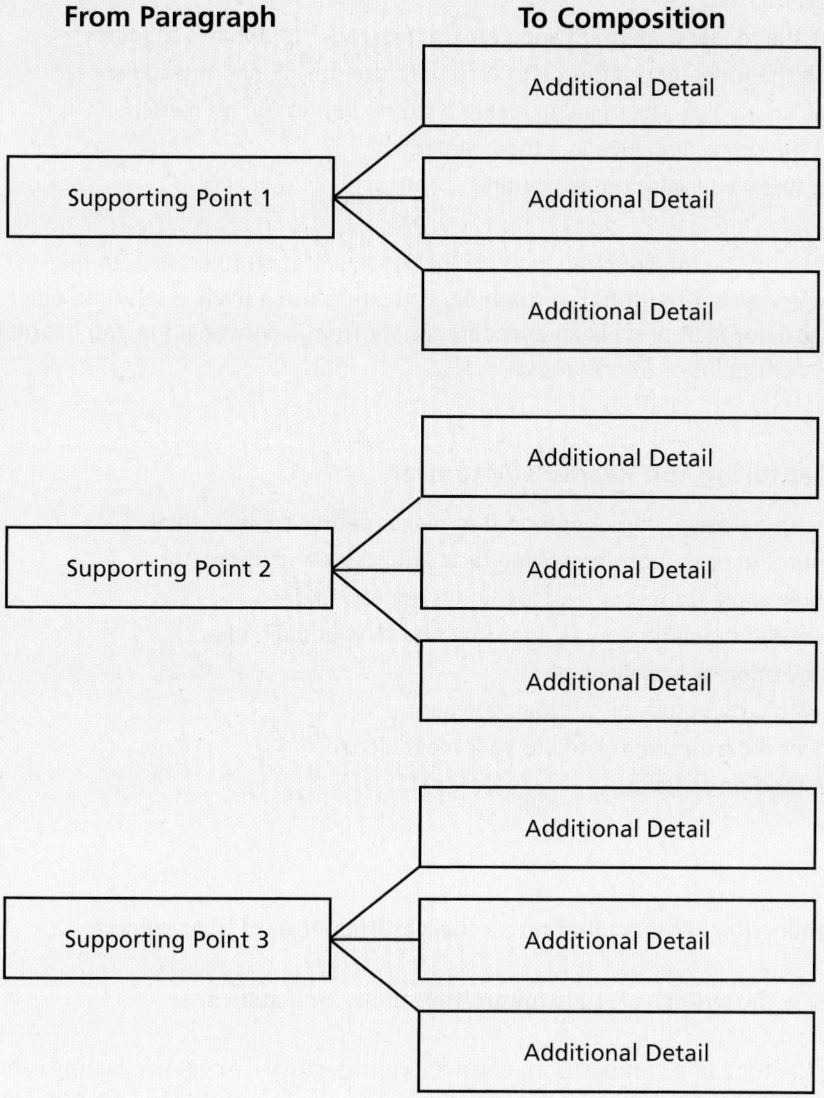

2 Introduction of a Composition

Whether it is a single paragraph or a series of inviting paragraphs, the introduction of a composition accomplishes several important purposes.

HERE'S HOW

Writing an Introduction

- Introduce the subject.
- Capture the reader's attention and prepare the reader for what is to follow.
- Establish the tone—your attitude toward both the subject and the audience.
- Establish your voice. The opening makes a strong impression on readers.
- Present the controlling idea in a thesis statement.
- State or imply your purpose for writing.

CHAPTER 3

When beginning the introduction, you might use any of a number of strategies to capture the reader's attention. For example, you could use a lively quotation, cite a little-known statistic or fact, provide an anecdote, quote from a conversation you heard, or just relate an arresting bit of information.

HERE'S HOW

Capturing the Reader's Attention

- Begin with a strong, crisp quotation that makes people smile or think.
- Cite surprising or thought-provoking facts or background information.
- Give an example from your own life, if it is appropriate.
- Relate a brief dramatic story or anecdote tied to your main idea.
- Pose a question or a challenge.
- Begin with a humorous or satirical statement.
- Paint a vivid description related to your main idea.
- Take a stand on an issue.

TONE

In the introduction, writers often reveal their attitude toward their subject.

Tone is the writer's attitude toward the subject and audience.

In setting the tone of a composition, consider your positive or negative feelings about your subject. For example, your tone may be serious or comical, admiring or critical, sympathetic or mocking. The tone of Shanlon Wu's "In Search of Bruce Lee's Grave" is serious yet friendly. In the following paragraph about Asian Americans, Connie Young Yu employs a serious tone.

MODEL: Serious Tone

In Asian America there are two kinds of history. The first is what is written about us in various old volumes on immigrants and echoed in textbooks, and the second is our own oral history, what we learn in the family chain of generations. We are writing this oral history ourselves. But as we research the factual background of our story, we face the dilemma of finding sources. Worse than burning the books is not being included in the record at all, and in American history—traditionally viewed from the white male perspective—minority women have been virtually ignored. Certainly the accomplishments and struggles of early Chinese immigrants, men as well as women, have been obscured.

—Connie Young Yu, "The World of Our Grandmothers"

In the following composition, the writer uses a very different tone—lighthearted and casual.

MODEL: Lighthearted Tone

For the sake of argument, let's say you don't know a thing about science fiction but want to. It makes sense to begin your research at your local bookstore. Toward the rear of the store, just past a sign saying WESTERNS and pressed between sections labeled MYSTERIES and THE OCCULT, you find a collection of titles labeled SCIENCE FICTION. You're standing before a rack six rows high and twenty feet long—a small galaxy of paper-back SF books from A to Z. You randomly select a few and read the publishers' blurbs hoping to get some idea of what SF is all about, hoping to see what all these books have in common. And that's where your troubles begin.

—Gary Goshgarian, "Zeroing in on Science Fiction"

Practice Your Skills

Identifying Tone

Read each opening sentence and write an adjective—such as *reflective, humorous,* or *enthusiastic*—to describe the tone of each.

1. I regard driving a car as a responsibility, not a right.

2. My first car was a used-parts shop on wheels.

3. I was thrilled when I got my first car.

4. My new car was a symbol of my deep desire for freedom.

THESIS STATEMENT

In many compositions, the introduction includes a thesis statement.

The **thesis statement** states the main idea and makes the purpose of the composition clear.

Notice how each of the following thesis statements makes the main idea and purpose of the composition clear.

CHAPTER 3

MODEL: Thesis Statements

Using a search engine effectively on the Internet is easy if you know a few simple tricks. (The purpose is to explain these simple tricks.)

To prepare students for the changing workplace, schools should offer a wider range of computer-related courses. (The purpose is to persuade decision-makers to offer a different kind of preparation for students.)

My first job was not the most thrilling experience, but it taught me several valuable lessons. (The purpose is to relate an experience and reflect on its significance.)

The thesis statement is the **controlling idea** of the composition. It should be broad enough to include the main points in the composition yet limited enough to allow you to cover your subject adequately. It usually creates the strongest impression when it is the first or last sentence of the introduction.

Practice Your Skills

Identifying Thesis Statements and Purpose

Write the thesis statement from the introductory paragraph. If the thesis statement is not contained in any one sentence, compose a sentence that expresses it. Then write a sentence telling what you think the author's purpose is.

Good evening, ladies and gentlemen. Welcome to *The Seven o'Clock News*. Nothing newsworthy happened today. Goodnight.

That's the way television *should* handle the four out of seven days every week when current events go into suspended animation or extreme trivial-overdrive. But don't grab your zapper and wait at the ready for that to happen. Because the television news, contrary to FCC disclaimers, is not really the news at all. It's just another way for the networks to sell us things we don't need and for corporate America to unwind after its collective tough day at the office.

Practice Your Skills

Writing a Thesis Statement

Use the list of details accompanying each of the following subjects to formulate a possible thesis statement.

1. Subject: family photographs

Details:
- age destroys old photographs
- pictures tend to get lost
- digital cameras are now available
- widespread Internet access lets people publish personal Web pages
- no pictures are lost or deteriorate with digital cameras
- digital cameras store an image in universal format that lets you print it out on paper, e-mail it, view it on television, or publish it on a Web page

2. Subject: what college admissions committees look for in candidates

Details:
- academic record most important
- difficulty of your classes and school's grading standards
- extracurricular activities in which you excel
- community involvement as shown by volunteering and belonging to clubs and associations
- good writing as shown in sample essay
- culture, geographic location, legacy (relatives who went to that college)
- standardized test scores

PROJECT PREP Drafting *Introduction*

Following the plan you developed with your writing group, draft an introduction to your expanded paper. Refer to the charts on page 112 to make sure your introduction accomplishes its purposes.

CHAPTER 3

In the Media

Internet Connections

In print, the reader is at the writer's mercy. For the most part, a reader must read text in the order in which it is presented. On the Internet, however, the user decides what to read and when. Here's an example of how text appears on the Web. All the blue phrases are links to other pages.

Facing an Interview

Nervous about interviewing for your next job? Here are some resources to help. First of all, you need to do some research on the company you are going to interview with. Another technique to help you prepare is to think of questions you want to ask your interviewer. Plan how to dress and how to behave with our presentation guidelines. Check out our online dictionary for unfamiliar words that might come up in your interview. Then you'll need to practice, in front of a mirror if necessary, or better yet, in front of our Online Interviewer. Most important, put your résumé online! Good luck and happy hunting!

In hypertext, transitions are not only unnecessary, but also inappropriate, since the creators cannot control where the reader will go. Instead, each section needs to be able to stand alone.

Media Activity

Experiment by designing a Web presentation for "Earthkeeper Hero: Chico Mendes" (pages 109–110). Design a top page that has links to the various sections. If necessary, rewrite each section so that it can stand alone when a user clicks on it.

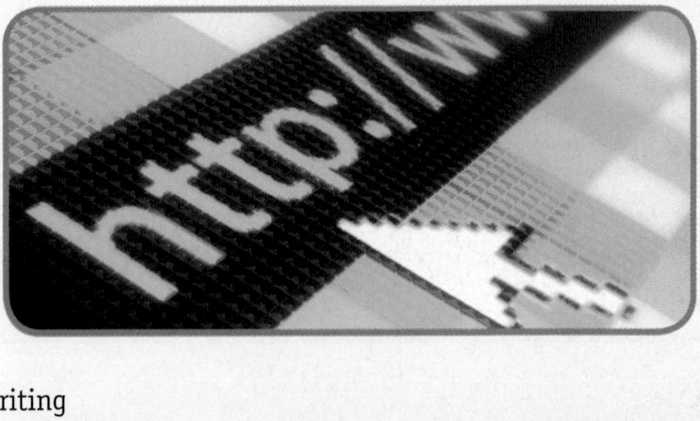

3 Body of a Composition

After the introduction gets the reader interested and ready, the body of a composition does the work of laying out the substance of your ideas, point by point.

SUPPORTING PARAGRAPHS

All the supporting paragraphs in a composition relate to the main idea. Each one, however, develops a distinct topic within that main idea, helping to support the thesis statement. In most cases, each supporting paragraph follows its own rules of good development and includes a topic sentence and a body of supporting sentences.

The **supporting paragraphs** in the body of a composition develop the thesis statement.

Following is the introduction and body of a composition. Notice how each of the supporting paragraphs develops the thesis statement (highlighted).

MODEL: Introduction and Body of a Composition

The Cowhand's Life

Thousands of books, movies, and television shows have made the American cowhand an exciting figure. For the most part, however, a cowhand's life was hard and filled with dull jobs. Riding the dusty range day after day tired even the hardiest of the hands. For weeks at a time cowhands had to catch quick naps, sleeping with their boots on and using a saddle as a pillow. Their Colt revolvers were never out of reach. And there was always the danger of a stampede. The wild longhorns, frightened by any strange noise, would scatter in all directions, crushing everything in their path.

Much of a cowhand's life was spent doing daily chores on a large Texas ranch. There were no fences between ranches, so cattle roamed freely during most of the grazing season. To keep cattle on the owner's ranch, cowhands rode all day back and forth along the property lines. Cattle drifting over the rancher's border were driven back. This job was called line driving.

Despite line driving, cattle still drifted from ranch to ranch. The herds became mixed. To return cattle to their rightful owners, ranchers held roundups—usually two a year. In the spring newborn calves would be rounded up for branding. Each ranch had its own brand, a mark that identified the owner. In the fall came the beef roundup, when the ranchers chose the cattle to be driven to market.

All the ranchers in an area joined in the roundup. Each rancher sent a group of cowhands and a chuck wagon with a cook. The cowhands would gather a huge herd of cattle. Then they would separate the cattle by brands. When one herd was separated, the process was repeated with another herd. The roundup lasted for weeks.

—Clarence Ver Steeg, *American Spirit*

The body of "The Cowhand's Life" can be presented in a simple outline that shows how the main idea of each paragraph supports the thesis statement of the entire composition.

Thesis Statement A cowhand's life was hard and filled with dull jobs.

I. There was sleep deprivation and danger.

II. They were line driving every day.

III. They had to round up and brand cattle for weeks.

Practice Your Skills

Analyzing Supporting Paragraphs

Reread the thesis statement and paragraphs that make up the body of "Earthkeeper Hero: Chico Mendes" on pages 109–110. Then develop an outline like the one above, using Roman numerals to show the main idea of each paragraph and how each supports the thesis statement.

Practice Your Skills

Developing Supporting Ideas

Under each of the following thesis statements, write three ideas that could be developed into three supporting paragraphs for the body of a composition. Write them in the form of the preceding outline.

1. The human nose is a most remarkable appendage.

2. My favorite author has some remarkable qualities.

3. Three of my favorite actors have similar acting styles.

4. Its distinctive features make rap music different from other popular music.

ADEQUATE DEVELOPMENT

When a composition has **adequate development,** readers feel the main point is well supported. They feel they have enough details to clarify any possibly confusing points, and they are not left having to guess the specifics.

The clues to adequate development often come in the form of questions that arise during writing. These questions usually help generate further topics to develop into supporting paragraphs. Examples and details that can help clarify what the writer is trying to say also serve as answers to such questions.

Writing Tip

Check your compositions for **adequate development** and, if necessary, add more information to clarify and enrich your main idea with strong, lively examples, illustrations, and other supporting details.

MODEL: Inadequately Developed Paragraph

Get Caught Recycling is a program that encourages everyone to recycle on a daily basis. Recycling is a really good thing to do. Get Caught Recycling began in 1995 and continues to this day. At the X Games, fans were rewarded for recycling and that was a good idea.

Finding new value for old objects is also recycling. Things receive a new life as useful, even treasured and valuable, objects that anyone would love to have in their home.

MODEL: Adequately Developed Paragraph

Get Caught Recycling is a program that encourages everyone to recycle on a daily basis. It began during the X Games (or Extreme Games), action sports that were first televised in 1995 and continue to this day. At the X Games, fans who were seen recycling were rewarded with tokens that they could redeem for environmentally friendly prizes. Putting a positive, and tangible, spin on recycling helped spread the word.

Finding new value for old objects is also part of the recycling movement. Things that would otherwise end up in landfills and garbage dumps now receive a new life as useful, even treasured, objects.

Practice Your Skills

Checking for Adequate Development

The following paragraph lacks adequate development. Use your own knowledge or do some research to find specific supporting details that will strengthen the paragraph. Then revise the paragraph accordingly.

Extreme Biking

To most of us, riding a bike is a pretty tame pastime. For extreme bikers, however, it's the ultimate thrill. These athletes ride on surfaces and over terrain where we wouldn't even want to walk. They risk life and limb for the thrill of it. What makes them so different from us? Why are we satisfied coasting along on two wheels while they pop a wheelie and spin along like cowboys on a bucking bronco?

Logical Development

The ideas you developed to support your thesis statement are claims. **Claims** are statements asserted to be true.

In the opening reading from "A Cowhand's Life," the claims are:

- A cowhand's life was hard.
- A cowhand's life was dull.
- A cowhand's life was dangerous.

The author develops those claims with examples.

CLAIMS	EXAMPLES
A cowhand's life was hard.	Riding the range was tiring and deprived them of sleep.
A cowhand's life was dull.	They rode day after day.
A cowhand's life was dangerous.	There was always the possibility of getting crushed in a stampede.

Simply providing examples for claims, however, does not support your assertion that they are true. You need to go further and provide a warrant, or explanation, that makes clear how the example supports the claim. Warrants often use the word *because:* Because there was always the chance of getting crushed in a stampede, a cowhand's life was dangerous.

Think Critically

Making Valid Inferences

In addition to providing warrants for your claims, you also need to make sure that your conclusions or inferences are valid. An inference is **valid** if it follows logically from the claims. For example, suppose you make these claims:

Claim: A cowhand's life was hard.

Claim: Stoney Burke was a cowhand.

Valid Inference: Stoney Burke's life was hard.

That inference is valid because the first claim asserts that all cowhands led hard lives; in that case, since Stoney Burke is a cowhand, his life must have been hard.

Suppose, though, you make these claims:

Claim: A cowhand's life was hard.

Claim: Poppy Martinelli had a hard life.

Invalid Inference: Poppy Martinelli was a cowhand.

This inference is invalid because it does not follow logically from the claims. The original claim is that a cowhand's life was hard, not that *only* a cowhand's life was hard. Because Poppy has a hard life does not logically lead to the inference that she was a cowhand.

Thinking Practice

Read each set of claims and the inference that follows them and determine if the inference is valid or invalid. If it is invalid, rewrite the set of claims to end up with a valid inference.

1. **Claim:** Surfers are thrill seekers.
   Claim: Robin is a thrill seeker.
   Inference: Robin is a surfer.
2. **Claim:** Ferrets make good pets.
   Claim: Rex is a good pet.
   Inference: Rex is a ferret.

4 Focus, Coherence, and Emphasis

A composition has **unity,** or **focus** when all the supporting paragraphs relate to the main idea in the thesis statement. No sentences or paragraphs should wander off the main point.

Compositions should also have **coherence**—the quality that makes the ideas in the paragraphs flow logically and naturally from one to the next.

CHAPTER 3

HERE'S HOW

Strategies for Achieving Coherence

- Double-check your organization to make sure each detail fits logically into your method of organization.
- Use transitional words and phrases. See charts with transitions on pages 5, 95–97, 253, and 304.
- Every now and then repeat key words.
- Use similar words or phrases in place of key words.
- Use pronouns in place of key words.

Emphasis, another important quality of a composition, helps readers recognize your most important ideas. You can show emphasis by writing more about one idea, by discussing it first, or by using transitional words and phrases to highlight it.

Writing Tip

Check your composition for the qualities of **unity, coherence,** and **emphasis.**

Jeff Trussel's composition about Chico Mendez on pages 109–110 shows all three qualities of unity, coherence, and emphasis. It has unity because all the supporting paragraphs describe the work of Chico Mendez. It has coherence because in each of the supporting paragraphs, the author uses helpful transitions such as *unfortunately* and *not surprisingly* to make the organization clear. Finally he reveals his emphasis by placing his most important idea in his first supporting paragraph.

Practice Your Skills

Analyzing Unity, Coherence, and Emphasis

Reread the introduction and body of the composition on cowhands (pages 117–118). Then write answers to the following questions.

1. How do the three body paragraphs help the composition achieve unity?
2. What transition in the second body paragraph links that paragraph to the previous one?
3. What key word is repeated in the third body paragraph to help link it back to the previous one?
4. How would you evaluate the unity, coherence, and emphasis of this composition (recognizing that it lacks a conclusion)? Evaluate each quality in a separate sentence.

CHAPTER 3

PROJECT PREP Evaluating *Reviewing Drafts*

Bring your expanded draft to your writing group. For each paper, think about how effectively the author makes claims and warrants and draws valid inferences. Also evaluate one another's latest drafts for unity, coherence, and emphasis. Note suggestions your partners make for your writing and make revisions as you see fit.

TIME OUT TO REFLECT

As you come near to the end of a writing project, stand back from it and determine the extent to which it accomplishes its purpose, addresses its audience, and suits the occasion. If you have strayed from the requirements of your purpose, audience, and occasion, make revisions now.

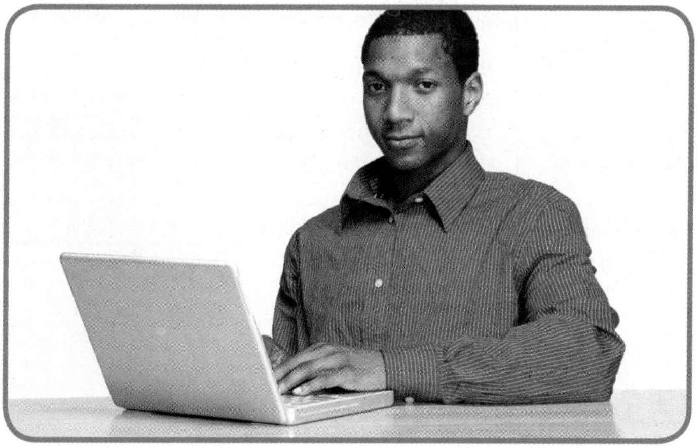

5 Conclusion of a Composition

Like the end of a song that reprises a key phrase, the conclusion of a composition often repeats a key idea or image to make the composition come full circle.

The **conclusion** completes the composition and reinforces the thesis statement.

A good conclusion also often ends with a **clincher**—a memorable phrase or statement that leaves a deep impression.

CHAPTER 3

The following paragraphs conclude the composition about the cowhands. They help bring the composition full circle by putting a face on the "exciting figure" referred to in the first paragraph. The final paragraph refers back to a memorable image in the introduction—the cowboy using his saddle as a pillow.

MODEL: Conclusion of a Composition

Though the rich rancher—the so-called cattle baron—was the ruler of cattle country, the cowhand was its hero. Most hands were young men, often in their teens. About a third of them were black or Mexican-American. Cowhands worked for room and board and about $40 a month. They carried or wore everything they needed.

Most precious of all a cowhand's belongings was the saddle. One person commented about a cowhand: "He might sell his gun or his coat or his boots, and he cares nothing how many times he changes his horse. . . . But he will never part with his saddle."

Writing Tip

The **concluding paragraph** completes the composition and reinforces the main idea.

PROJECT PREP Drafting *Conclusion*

Based on the feedback from your writing group, revise the introduction and body of your composition and add a strong conclusion. As he or she may direct, submit your draft to the teacher as well as your writing group members for review.

The Language of Power Run-on Sentences

Power Rule: Use the best conjunction and/or punctuation for the meaning when connecting two sentences. Revise run-on sentences. (See pages 728–730.)

See It in Action A run-on sentence is the incorrect joining of two complete sentences. When this mistake is made with a comma between the sentences, it is called a **comma splice.**

Comma Splice	Computers can make work easier, programs sometimes take a long time to master.

Computers can make work easier is an independent clause. It can stand alone as a sentence. The same is true for *programs sometimes take a long time to master.* One correction of the comma splice would be to write each sentence separately.

Corrected	Computers can make work easier. Programs sometimes take a long time to master.

A better, less choppy correction would be to combine the sentences using a conjunction.

Corrected	Computers can make work easier, but programs sometimes take a long time to master.

Remember It Record this rule and examples in the Power Rule section of your Personalized Editing Checklist.

Use It Read through your project and check your sentences for comma splices and other run-ons. Add the proper conjunction to correct a comma splice or separate the independent clauses. Combine sentences, when possible, by making one clause dependent on the other.

PROJECT PREP Editing *Getting Ready to Publish*

Read your composition, this time looking for possible errors in grammar, usage, and mechanics. If you find any problems, use proofreaders' marks to correct them or correct them on your word processor. Get to know your word processor's way of showing you potential errors, such as a red squiggly line under a word. Correct any errors the program may point out to you that seem in need of correcting.

Using a Six-Trait Rubric

CHAPTER 3

Ideas	**4** The text conveys an interesting idea with abundant supporting details and is well chosen for the purpose and audience.	**3** The text conveys a clear idea with ample details and suits the purpose and audience.	**2** The text conveys a main idea with some supporting details and suits the purpose and audience.	**1** The text does not convey a main idea and fails to suit the purpose and audience.
Organization	**4** The organization is clear with abundant transitions.	**3** A few ideas seem out of place or transitions are missing.	**2** Many ideas seem out of place and transitions are missing.	**1** The organization is unclear and hard to follow.
Voice	**4** The voice sounds natural, engaging, and personal.	**3** The voice sounds natural and personal.	**2** The voice sounds mostly unnatural with a few exceptions.	**1** The voice sounds mostly unnatural.
Word Choice	**4** Words are specific, powerful, and precise.	**3** Words are specific and some words are powerful and precise.	**2** Some words are overly general.	**1** Most words are overly general.
Sentence Fluency	**4** Varied sentences flow smoothly.	**3** Most sentences are varied and flow smoothly.	**2** Some sentences are varied but some are choppy.	**1** Sentences are not varied and are choppy.
Conventions	**4** Punctuation, usage, and spelling are correct. The Power Rules are all followed.	**3** Punctuation, usage, and spelling are mainly correct and Power Rules are all followed.	**2** Some punctuation, usage, and spelling are incorrect but all Power Rules are followed.	**1** There are many errors and at least one failure to follow a Power Rule.

PROJECT PREP Revising and Editing *Final Draft*

Based on the feedback from your writing group and teacher, prepare a final, polished version of your essay. You might exchange papers with a writing partner for one final critique before you consider it done. When you are satisfied with your essay, publish it to an appropriate place. For instance, you might find places on the Internet where heroes are discussed, and post your essay as part of a wider conversation.

Using a Wiki

In addition to publishing for a very specific audience (see page 84), you can share your completed work—even your work-in-progress—more broadly if you publish it on the Internet. One easy way to publish on the Web and to make the most of your community of writers is to create a **wiki**, a collection of user-generated linked Web pages focused on a theme, project, or collaboration. Wikipedia is the most famous example.

One way to learn your way around a wiki is to study and participate in Wikipedia. The excerpt below is from the Wikipedia entry on wikis.

CHAPTER 3

Characteristics

This section needs additional citations for verification. Please help improve this article by adding reliable references. Unsourced material may be challenged and removed. (December 2009)

Notes like this appear throughout Wikipedia, indicating places where reliable sources need to be included.

Ward Cunningham, and co-author Bo Leuf, in their book *The Wiki Way: Quick Collaboration on the Web* described the essence of the Wiki concept as follows:

- A wiki invites all users to edit any page or to create new pages within the wiki Web site, using only a plain-vanilla Web browser without any extra add-ons.
- Wiki promotes meaningful topic associations between different pages by making page link creation almost intuitively easy and showing whether an intended target page exists or not.
- A wiki is not a carefully crafted site for casual visitors. Instead, it seeks to involve the visitor in an ongoing process of creation and collaboration that constantly changes the Web site landscape.

Links throughout articles lead to other topics within Wikipedia. Most articles also have links at the end that lead to other Web sites.

PROJECT PREP Publishing *Wiki-ing*

1. Go to Wikipedia. In the search box, type the words *Wikipedia: Tutorial*. The tutorial will take you through the steps you need to follow to add or edit content. Follow the tutorial all the way through. Write a paragraph summarizing what you learned.
2. If your school has or participates in a wiki, with your class create a section devoted to the topic of heroes and publish your compositions there.

Writing Lab

CHAPTER 3

Project Corner

Speak and Listen Define a Hero

Engage in a class discussion based on the writing of all students. Where is there agreement on the qualities of a hero? Where is there disagreement? Is there room for more than one definition of a hero? After the discussion, write a paragraph summarizing the various definitions that may have surfaced.

Get Dramatic Act it Out

In your writing group, **write a short drama** in which a hero and non-hero are put in a situation requiring heroic action. Either act the play out in front of an audience or film it and play the recording on a screen for an audience.

Investigate Further Research and Report

Using a variety of sources, from the Internet to printed or spoken news, **research a person you consider to be a hero**. As you learn more about this person, does he or she still meet your definition of a hero? Possibly develop this investigation into a research report that you could present as a Web page, a written report, a set of slides on presentation software, a documentary film, or other form of presentation.

Get Personal Apply to Your Life

Think about your own life in relation to the heroes and non-heroes you have discussed. How can you live your own life with these heroic qualities and examples in mind? **Write a diary entry** expressing your thoughts.

In the Workplace

Narrative Report

Apply and Assess

1. You are a firefighter who recently returned from a four-alarm fire where you rescued a young boy from a burning building. Fire department policy requires that you write a report detailing actions you took during a life-saving mission. ***Write a narrative report*** to the fire chief, telling about your rescue. Use a topic sentence to set the scene, capture the reader's attention, set the story in motion, and give an overview of the events. Use the supporting sentences to develop the story. Use a concluding sentence to provide the outcome.

CHAPTER 3

In Everyday Life E-mail to Your Grandmother

2. You love your grandmother, but you do not care for her cooking. For example, she always serves meatloaf and lima beans for holiday meals. ***Write an e-mail*** to your grandmother describing the meal you volunteer to provide for the next holiday dinner. Make sure your letter has an introduction, a body, and a conclusion. Choose a light-hearted tone for your e-mail, and make sure your ideas flow naturally from one paragraph to the next.

Timed Writing Letter to the Editor

3. Strange as it may seem, there are students at your school who do not see the value in nature. They are so excited by progress and technology that they do not see the importance of parks and forests. The editor of the school paper has asked you to write an essay for publication that will inform students that trees are necessary and integral to life on Earth.

   Before You Write Consider the following questions: What is the subject? What is the occasion? Who is the audience? What is the purpose?

   Prewrite to develop your main idea in three or more paragraphs. Be sure your composition has an introduction with a thesis statement that captures the reader's attention. Establish a strong tone and organize your ideas to ensure coherence, logical progression, and support for your ideas. To expand your conclusions, be sure to elaborate fully on your ideas. You have 25 minutes to complete your work.

   After You Write Evaluate your work using the six-trait evaluation rubric on page 126.

Unit 2

Purposes of Writing

The best writing begins with a good drenching—of ideas, information, details, words. But how, exactly, do you form something meaningful from this flood? A keen understanding of both your purpose and your audience can point the way. Will you write to inform or to persuade? Will you analyze or satirize? Will you amuse your readers or soothe them? Do your readers share your views or are they skeptical? Are they knowledgeable about your subject or uninformed? In this unit you will learn that when you are thoroughly soaked with information and words, a clear purpose will allow the "proper" patterns to form, and powerful writing will follow.

One must be drenched in words, literally soaked in them, to have the right ones form themselves into the proper patterns at the right moment. — *Hart Crane*

Personal Writing

Narrative writing tells a real or imaginary story that has a clear beginning, middle, and end.

A **personal narrative,** a story based on personal experience, is one kind of narrative writing.

Here are just a few examples of personal narratives that enrich people's understanding of one another.

- **A blogger writes a memoir inspired** by his encounters with ordinary people.
- **A newspaper columnist** writes about the personal side of public issues.
- **A travel writer narrates** events in which he took part in places he has visited.
- **A friend tells humorous anecdotes** about herself, her friends, and family members.

Writing Project Personal Narrative

Cultural Connections ***Write a personal narrative that reflects your feelings about a group with which you identify and how this group has helped shaped you.***

Think Through Writing Most people see themselves as members of at least one culture—the shared traditions that perpetuate one's sense of identity, history, and belonging. This identity may involve race, ethnicity, nationality, gender, social class, political orientation, faith community, interests, or any other feature. Most people think of themselves as a part of overlapping groups. Consider, for example, a white Italian Catholic New Yorker. Write about the cultural group or groups with which you identify. How has this identity developed? What experiences as a member of this group have helped you define who you are as a person in society?

Talk About It In your writing group, discuss your group's responses. What cultures were identified? How has being part of these cultures shaped the way each writer views the world and acts in it?

Read About It The following personal narrative by Caroline Hwang expresses a young woman's thoughts and feelings about her cultural identity. Think about how she orients herself as a member of more than one culture and how that orientation affects her feelings about herself and her world.

MODEL: Personal Narrative Writing

From

The Good Daughter

Caroline Hwang

The moment I walked into the dry-cleaning store, I knew the woman behind the counter was from Korea, like my parents. To show her that we shared a heritage, and possibly get a fellow countryman's discount, I tilted my head forward, in shy imitation of a traditional bow.

By writing in the first person, Hwang invites readers to share in her experiences. These first few paragraphs set the scene for the dilemma she will soon relate.

"Name?" she asked, not noticing my attempted obeisance.

"Hwang,"[1] I answered.

"Hwang? Are you Chinese?"

Her question caught me off-guard. I was used to hearing such queries from non-Asians who think Asians all look alike, but never from one of my own people. Of course, the only Koreans I knew were my parents and their friends, people who've never asked me where I came from, since they knew better than I.

I ransacked my mind for the Korean words that would tell her who I was. It's always struck me as funny (in a mirthless sort of way) that I can more readily say "I am Korean" in Spanish, German, and even Latin than I can in the language of my ancestry. In the end, I told her in English.

The dry-cleaning woman squinted as though trying to see past the glare of my strangeness, repeating my surname under her breath. "Oh, Fxuang,"[2] she said, doubling over with laughter. "You don't know how to speak your name."

1 **Hwang:** Pronounced hwan
2 **Fxuang:** Pronounced fwon

CHAPTER 4

CHAPTER 4

I flinched. Perhaps I was particularly sensitive at the time, having just dropped out of graduate school. I had torn up my map for the future, the one that said not only where I was going but who I was. My sense of identity was already disintegrating.

When I got home, I called my parents to ask why they had never bothered to correct me. "Big deal," my mother said, sounding more flippant than I knew she intended. (Like many people who learn English in a classroom, she uses idioms that don't always fit the occasion.) "So what if you can't pronounce your name? You are American," she said.

Though I didn't challenge her explanation, it left me unsatisfied. The fact is, my cultural identity is hardly that clear-cut.

My parents immigrated to this country 30 years ago, two years before I was born. They told me often, while I was growing up, that, if I wanted to, I could be president someday, that here my grasp would be as long as my reach.

The story Hwang relates serves as a concrete example of her cultural identity confusion.

To ensure that I reaped all the advantages of this country, my parents saw to it that I became fully assimilated. So, like any Americans of my generation, I whiled away my youth strolling malls and talking on the phone, rhapsodizing over Andrew McCarthy's blue eyes or analyzing the meaning of a certain upper-classman's offer of a ride to the Homecoming football game.

To my parents, I am all American, and the sacrifices they made in leaving Korea—including my mispronounced name—pale in comparison to the opportunities those sacrifices gave me. They do not see that I straddle two cultures, nor that I feel displaced in the only country I know. I identify with Americans, but Americans do not identify with me. I've never known what it's like to belong to a community—neither one at large, nor of an extended family. I know more about Europe than the continent my ancestors unmistakably come from. I sometimes wonder, as I did that day in the dry cleaner's, if I would be a happier person had my parents stayed in Korea.

This paragraph contains the main theme of the narrative.

I first began to consider this thought around the time I decided to go to graduate school. It had been a compromise: my parents wanted me to go to law school; I wanted to skip the starched-collar track and be a writer—the hungrier the better. But after twenty-some years of following their wishes and meeting all of their expectations, I couldn't bring myself to disobey or disappoint. A writing career is riskier than law, I remember thinking. If I'm a failure and my life is a washout, then what does that make my parents' lives?

This and following paragraphs include lots of detail to help the reader understand the author's dilemma.

I know that many of my friends had to choose between pleasing their parents and being true to themselves. But for the children of immigrants, the choice seems more complicated, a happy outcome impossible. By making the biggest move of their lives for me, my parents indentured me to the largest debt imaginable—I owe them the fulfillment of their hopes for me.

It tore me up inside to suppress my dream, but I went to school for a Ph.D. in English literature, thinking I had found the perfect compromise. I would be able to write at least about books while pursuing a graduate degree. Predictably, it didn't work out. How could I labor for five years in a program I had no passion for?

When I finally left school, my parents were disappointed, but since it wasn't what they wanted me to do, they weren't devastated. I, on the other hand, felt I was staring at the bottom of the abyss. I had seen the flaw in my life of halfwayness, in my planned life of compromises. . . .

My parents didn't want their daughter to be Korean, but they don't want her fully American, either. Children of immigrants are living paradoxes. We are the first generation and the last. We are in this country for its opportunities, yet filial duty binds us. When my parents boarded the plane, they knew they were embarking on a rough trip. I don't think they imagined the rocks in the path of their daughter who can't even pronounce her own name.

The concluding sentence refers back to the first paragraph and the author's encounter with a Korean woman of her parents' generation.

Respond in Writing Respond to Caroline Hwang's essay about her uncertainty based on her mixed cultural identities. How does her experience compare to your own ideas about cultural and group identity?

CHAPTER 4

Develop Your Own Ideas Work with your classmates to develop ideas for stories about the role culture and group identity plays in your own self concept.

Small Groups: In your writing group, discuss possible stories about your cultural and group identity as you explore your own experiences and hear the thoughts of those in your group.

Whole Class: Make a master chart of all of the ideas generated by the small groups. Choose a few and discuss how each might be developed in a personal narrative. Below are a few questions each writer might ask.

- What rules, traditions, values, perspectives, actions, speech, and other factors are central to this identity?
- Do you experience multiple cultural identities that clash within yourself?
- Do you feel that your group or cultural identity comes in conflict with other cultures or groups in your social context?
- How does being a member of one or more cultures affect your sense of belonging, values, sense of social destiny, and other factors?

Write About It You will next write a focused narrative about some aspect of your cultural or group identity. You may choose from the options below.

Possible Topics and Examples	Possible Audiences	Possible Forms
• a cultural tradition that is important to you • multiple cultural identities as a confusing or clarifying force in personal development • a clash between you and someone else based on cultural or group differences • your own or another's cultural practice or tradition that you would like to explore further	• people from your own culture or cultures • people from a culture very different from your own • students who are experiencing cultural confusion • adults who insist on perpetuating cultural values	• a blog • a story for the yearbook or for the school's *Writers' Showcase* magazine • a letter to someone with whom you especially want to communicate your experience and perspective • a drama to be performed for the benefit of other students

1 Getting the Subject Right

The personal narrative is the most intimate of writing forms and therefore perhaps the most risky. Writing effectively about yourself does not involve pouring out your thoughts and experiences indiscriminately. Rather, you must thoughtfully select specific aspects of those thoughts and experiences that your audience will want to share. In the following excerpt from her personal narrative, Lai Man Lee discusses a possession that has deep significance for her.

MODEL: Subject of a Personal Narrative

When I stop to think about which possession of mine means the most to me, I find myself looking at my left wrist. Adorning my wrist is a simple solid jade bracelet. Its color is uneven, ranging from a pale green, almost-white, to a sea green, and it has a brown spot, an imperfection in the stone. There are tiny scratches on the bracelet, hardly noticeable, and a crack on one side—where the bracelet may eventually break completely. But in spite of its imperfections, the bracelet could not be any more perfect to me than it is because of the sentimental value it holds.

Thesis Statement

I will always remember the first time I saw a jade bracelet of this kind, when I was eight. It was in a museum collection of Chinese jewelry. I found it amazing that the bracelet could be a perfectly polished ring carved from one single piece of jade, and thought it must be very valuable.

Body paragraphs

I went home and told my mother, who explained to me that such bracelets were quite common among Chinese women, and varied greatly in expense and quality. Some women would get jade bracelets when they were very young and wear them until they died. Since jade is a soft stone, it can break very easily when treated roughly. My mother told me that if a bracelet did break, the woman would wrap all the fragments up in a handkerchief and save the pieces for the rest of her life, for even the pieces would bring good luck. This gave me an image of the Chinese woman, and having my bracelet will always remind me of my culture and the individual that I am.

I remember very clearly the night my parents gave me the bracelet. It was in my sophomore year of high school, and I had stayed out past my curfew of midnight. When I got home that night, my parents gave me a lecture on responsibility. I expected to be placed on restriction, but instead they gave me a jade bracelet. I was totally shocked . . . but when I went to bed that night I was supremely happy.

Conclusion

—Lai Man Lee, "My Bracelet"

CHAPTER 4

Drawing on Personal Experience

Personal narratives are based on individual experiences. Look through your journal for experiences you have written about as well as observations on people and places that are important to you. Try clustering, freewriting, and observing to generate additional ideas. Finally explore the following possible sources for appropriate subjects.

SOURCES OF SUBJECTS FOR PERSONAL NARRATIVES	
photograph albums or scrapbooks	images from newspapers and magazines
letters from friends	school newspapers
family stories	souvenirs from vacations
friends' stories	school yearbooks
special gifts	old journals

Exploring the Meaning of an Experience

A personal narrative is informal in structure but should still express a main idea to your reader. You may state this idea directly or imply it by providing clues through descriptions and incidents. Either way, the main idea should emerge. Read the student model on the next page and consider how the author expressed the meaning of the experience she wrote about—having a photograph of the three women who influenced her.

STUDENT MODEL: *Expressing the Meaning of an Experience*

{This} photo would always serve as a reminder that no matter how hard an issue may seem to be to overcome, as humans, we will always find a way to remember happiness despite the despair, and we will always be able to push through it.

—Erica Gallon, Canton South High School, Canton, Ohio

CHAPTER 4

PROJECT PREP Prewriting *Recognizing Importance*

With your group, discuss possible subjects for a personal narrative. (See pages 136 and 138 for ideas.) Choose one that seems the most compelling to you. Discuss the importance of your chosen subject.

Think Critically

Think Critically

Interpreting Experience

In planning a narrative based on personal experience, you should determine what that experience meant to you. The meaning of an experience is not always immediately clear, and you must **interpret** that experience—mentally explore it for an insight it gave you. To interpret an experience, ask yourself questions like those below.

Checklist for Interpreting Experience

Experience: At Ellis Island, I saw a computerized exhibit about my great-grandparents, who immigrated in the late 1800s.

This experience is important to me now because it

__ helped me see something in a new way.

✓ changed the way I felt about someone.

✓ changed the way I felt about myself.

I will always remember this experience because it

✓ strongly affected my emotions.

✓ gave me new knowledge or understanding.

__ had important consequences.

This experience is worth writing about because

✓ it will be familiar to many readers.

__ it is unique or extraordinary.

✓ writing will help me to understand it better.

Interpretation: The experience at Ellis Island has increased my pride in and knowledge of my family heritage.

Thinking Practice

Interpret one of the following experiences or one of your own by making a chart like the one above.

- visiting a relative whom you had not seen in a long time
- an experience that gave you an insight into a family member or friend
- helping others by using a talent or skill

2 Considering Your Audience and Purpose

When you write personal narratives, your challenge is to make that experience as understandable and significant to your audience as it is to you. Consider the age and backgrounds of your readers and ways in which your audience may have had similar experiences. Look for the universal without sacrficing the specifics of your own unique narrative.

In a personal narrative, you can reach your readers through a variety of approaches. Your overall purpose is usually to express your thoughts and feelings in a way that entertains or enlightens your readers. To achieve this purpose, you will often make use of narrative, descriptive, and expository writing. For example, if you were writing a personal narrative about participating in an outdoor survival program, you might write paragraphs for the specific purposes shown in the following box.

CHAPTER 4

PURPOSE IN PERSONAL WRITING

Overall Purpose: to express ideas and feelings about participating in an outdoor survival program

Specific Aims	Kinds of Paragraphs
to tell an anecdote in which you learned about leadership	narrative
to describe the outdoor environment in which you lived	descriptive
to explain specific outdoor survival techniques you learned	expository

You can review the different types of writing on pages 100–107.

PROJECT PREP Prewriting *Identifying Your Audience*

In your writing group, offer an interpretation of the experience you chose as the subject for your narrative. Talk about the audience you will be addressing and how best to approach that audience.

TIME OUT TO REFLECT

Now that you have chosen a subject for your personal essay, take a few minutes to reflect on your subject. Try to think of a scene that vividly depicts your feelings and ideas. Remember this scene as you gather details to use in your writing.

3 Developing and Organizing Details

Selecting Details

An important part of developing a personal narrative is using details that will flesh out your experience. If your narrative includes a description of a person, picture that person walking and talking. Ask a partner to help you brainstorm for as many details as possible. The following strategies will help you generate details for your personal narrative.

STRATEGIES FOR DEVELOPING DETAILS	
Events	Close your eyes and slowly visualize the experience you are writing about. Use your five senses. Then write down as many details as you can.
People	Visualize each person you are writing about. Start by visualizing the face of each person and then continue down to his or her feet.
Places	Visualize the place you are describing. Start at the left side of the setting and slowly visualize to the right.
Feelings	Imagine yourself once again undergoing the experience you are writing about. Focus on your feelings and reflections as you move through the experience.

After you have made a list of specific details, select those best suited for your personal narrative. The following guidelines will help you choose the most effective details to include in the first draft of your essay.

HERE'S HOW

Guidelines for Selecting Details

- Choose specific details that are appropriate for your purpose and audience.
- Use factual details to provide background information about your experience.
- Use vivid descriptive and sensory details to bring your experience to life.

In the excerpt from a personal narrative on the following page, the writer describes her father's role in teaching her to drive. Notice how she has selected details to describe her father's patience.

MODEL: Details in a Personal Narrative

Greater love hath no man for his children than to teach them how to drive. As soon as I turned 15 years and 8 months—the requisite age for obtaining a learner's permit—my father took me around our neighborhood to let me get a feel for the huge Chevrolet we owned. The quiet, tree-shaded, narrow streets of the neighborhood witnessed the blunders of yet another new driver: too-wide (or too-narrow) turns; sudden screeching halts (those power brakes take some getting used to); defoliation of low-hanging trees by the radio antenna or the car too close to the curb; driving on the wrong side of the street to avoid the parked cars on the right side.

—Ann Upperco, "Learning to Drive"

Writing Tip

Be sure to make the subject of your personal writing both understandable and significant to your audience. Provide **vivid details** that bring your experience to life for your reader.

Practice Your Skills

Identifying Vivid Details

Analyze the model paragraph above for details that are so vivid that you can visualize the scene in an instant. Make a list of the writer's carefully selected images that make the scene immediate and real. Then try to write a short paragraph of your own using equally vivid details.

Organizing Details

The overall organization of your personal narrative will probably be in **developmental order.** That is, ideas will be arranged in a progression so that one idea grows out of the previous idea and leads to the next idea. However, within this overall pattern of organization, you will usually use individual paragraphs that are narrative, descriptive, or informative. Within each paragraph, you should use an appropriate method to organize details. To help you organize the details for each specific type of writing, see the chart on the next page. You might also want to refer to the graphic organizers on pages 101–107.

WAYS TO ORGANIZE		
Kind of Writing	**Kind of Details**	**Type of Order**
Narrative	events in a story, narrated from the beginning to the end	chronological order *(first, second, next, then, finally)*
Descriptive	details to help readers visualize a person, object, or scene	spatial order *(left to right, top to bottom, far to near, etc.)*
Expository	background details and details explaining the significance of a particular experience	order of importance *(most to least important or least to most important)*

CHAPTER 4

Practice Your Skills

Revising for Adequate Development

Revise the following paragraph by adding details that would help readers visualize or understand the experience.

> Sarah looked at her aunt and said, "Is it really for me?" Aunt Sally had given her a ring. It had belonged to Gramma Sue, Sally's mother. Sarah put it on her finger and stared at it. She had never seen anything so shiny. She tried to picture her grandmother, but the image was vague.

PROJECT PREP Prewriting *Listing Details*

In your writing group, discuss the details of each event in the narrative. Are there activities, people's actions, places, or occasions that would be especially helpful in getting your message across? Are there details in the environment—a windstorm, a band playing in the background—that could help you describe the mood? Focus on the key details. Instead of writing, "It was windy," you might write: "The breeze picked up speed. My hair blew wildly, slapping my face, and my eyes were pelted with bits of debris." For each writer, focus on the details of the events of the narrative, providing suggestions for descriptions that could bring scenes to life for readers. Keep notes you can use when you draft.

The Power of Language

Fluency: Let It Flow

You have learned various ways of adding content and detail to your sentences and using grammatical options to add style and voice to your writing. In addition to these, you also have options for keeping your writing smooth. To keep your sentences and paragraphs flowing invitingly, you need to vary the structure of your sentences.

Notice how smoothly the sentences flow in this passage from "The Good Daughter."

> The moment I walked into the dry-cleaning store, I knew the woman behind the counter was from Korea, like my parents. To show her that we shared a heritage, and possibly get a fellow countryman's discount, I tilted my head forward, in shy imitation of a traditional bow.

The core sentences in this paragraph are: *I knew the woman was Korean*, and *I tilted my head.* The varied placement of additional sentence parts, however, makes the rhythm of these essentially simple sentences interesting and fluent.

Elements Added to Sentence Beginnings	The moment I walked into the dry-cleaning store (adverbial clause) To show her that we shared a heritage, and possibly get a fellow countryman's discount (adverbial phrases)
Elements Added to Sentence Endings	like my parents (adjectival phrase) in shy imitation of a traditional bow (adverbial phrase)

Try It Yourself

Write two consecutive unadorned sentences on your project topic. Then using the examples above, add an adverbial clause to the beginning of each and an adjectival or adverbial phrase to the end. Evaluate the flow. Experiment with different placement of the added elements to see which is most effective.

Punctuation Tip

Use a comma after certain introductory elements. (See pages 926–927.)

Power of Language

Personal narratives often have a less formal structure than expository or persuasive essays. Despite this informal structure, however, a personal narrative should include three basic components of any good piece of writing: a captivating introduction, a body that develops the subject in an interesting way, and a memorable conclusion.

1 Drafting the Introduction

Your personal narrative may focus on a subject that might be unfamiliar or irrelevant to your reader at first glance. Therefore, your goal in the introduction is to make an immediate impact on your reader while still maintaining focus on the attitude you are going to present. Following are some strategies for writing an interesting introduction.

HERE'S HOW

Guidelines for Drafting an Introduction

- Introduce the subject and purpose of the essay.
- Make clear the main idea of the essay.
- Set the tone to reveal the writer's point of view.
- Capture the reader's interest.

Creating a Tone

The introduction of your narrative should not only build interest but also reveal your feelings about the subject. Consequently the introduction should establish the **tone,** which is the writer's attitude toward a subject.

To choose an appropriate tone, think about the effect the subject has on you. If the subject makes you laugh, then perhaps you should use a humorous tone. If a subject saddens you, use a serious tone. Personal narratives can express a variety of tones as wide as the range of human emotions.

In the introduction that follows notice how N. Scott Momaday's description "All things in the plain are isolate" establishes a reflective tone.

MODEL: Reflective Tone

A single knoll rises out of the plain in Oklahoma, north and west of the Wichita Range. For my people, the Kiowas, it is an old landmark, and they gave it the name Rainy Mountain. The hardest weather in the world is there. Winter brings blizzards, hot tornadic winds arise in the spring, and in summer the prairie is an anvil's edge. The grass turns brittle and brown, and it cracks beneath your feet. There are green belts along the rivers and creeks, linear groves of hickory and pecan, willow and witch hazel. At a distance, in July or August the steaming foliage seems almost to writhe in fire. Great green and yellow grasshoppers are everywhere in the tall grass, popping up like corn to sting the flesh, and tortoises crawl about on the red earth, going nowhere in the plenty of time. Loneliness is an aspect of the land. All things in the plain are isolate; there is no confusion of objects in the eye, but *one* hill, or *one* tree or *one* man. To look upon that landscape in the early morning, with the sun at your back, is to lose the sense of proportion. Your imagination comes to life, and this, you think, is where Creation was begun.

—N. Scott Momaday, "A Kiowa Grandmother"

Garrison Keillor uses details and anecdotes to create a light-hearted tone in his introduction below.

MODEL: Light-Hearted Tone

I don't have many friends who have done one thing so well that they're famous for it and could sit on their laurels if they wanted to, although I do know a woman who can touch her nose with her tongue, which she is famous for among all the people who have ever seen her do it. She doesn't do it often, because she doesn't need to, having proved herself. I also know a man who wrote a forty-one-word palindrome, which is about as far as you can go in the field of writing that reads the same forwards and backwards.

—Garrison Keillor, *The New Yorker*

PROJECT PREP **Drafting** ***Writing the Introduction***

With your writing group, discuss the most appropriate tone for your personal narrative. Brainstorm an opening paragraph for each writer that expresses that tone. When you have finished your brainstorming and discussion, write a draft of the introduction of your personal narrative.

2 Drafting the Body

Once you have written an introduction that captures your reader's interest and sets the tone, you are ready to draft the body of your narrative. As you draft, include the details you selected earlier to add clarity and richness to your narrative.

The following guidelines will help you draft the body of your personal narrative.

HERE'S HOW

Guidelines for Drafting the Body

- Make sure each paragraph has a topic sentence that supports the main idea.
- Follow a logical order of ideas and details.
- Use transitions between sentences and paragraphs to give your narrative coherence.
- If you discover new ideas and details as you write, go back and make changes in those sections of the essay that are affected by your new insights.

As you draft the body of your personal essay, use narrative, descriptive, and expository writing when appropriate. In her personal essay "Eavesdropping," Eudora Welty effectively uses different types of writing. For example, in the following passage, she describes how the room made her feel like a protected observer.

MODEL: Description in Personal Writing

But I never dreamed I could learn as long as I was away from the schoolroom, and that bits of enlightenment far-reaching in my life went on as ever in their own good time. After they'd told me goodnight and tucked me in—although I knew that after I'd finally fallen asleep they'd pick me up and carry me away—my parents draped the lampshade with a sheet of the daily paper, which was tilted, like a hatbrim, so that they could sit in their rockers in a lighted part of the room and I could supposedly go to sleep in the protected dark of the bed. They sat talking. What was thus dramatically made a present of to me was the secure sense of the hidden observer. As long as I could make myself keep awake, I was free to listen to every word my parents said between them.

—Eudora Welty, "Eavesdropping"

PROJECT PREP Drafting *Writing the Body*

Draft the body of your piece, continuing in the same tone that you established in your introduction. Are your feelings about the subject clear? Get together with your group and help each writer phrase the narrative so that the intent is evident. Avoid simply stating an emotion, such as "I was enthralled." Rather, help your reader feel the emotion with words such as "The music moved me so that I felt suddenly lighter, floating on a cloud of notes."

3 Drafting the Conclusion

The conclusion of a personal narrative should give readers a sense of completion and a lasting impression of the personal experience or insight that you have written about. Following are several appropriate ways to end a personal narrative.

HERE'S HOW

Ways to End a Personal Narrative

- Summarize the body or restate the main idea in different words.
- Add a new insight about the experience.
- Add a striking new detail or memorable image.
- Refer to ideas in the introduction.
- Appeal to your readers' emotions.

CHAPTER 4

The following paragraph concludes Momaday's personal narrative. The conclusion brings the essay full circle by returning to a more immediate description of Rainy Mountain.

MODEL: Conclusion of a Personal Narrative

The next morning I awoke at dawn and went out on the dirt road to Rainy Mountain. It was already hot, and the grasshoppers began to fill the air. Still, it was early in the morning, and the birds sang out of the shadows. The long yellow grass on the mountain shone in the bright light, and a scissortail hied above the land. There, where it ought to be, at the end of a long and legendary way, was my grandmother's grave. Here and there on the dark stones were ancestral names. Looking back once, I saw the mountain and came away.

—N. Scott Momaday, "A Kiowa Grandmother"

Practice Your Skills

Analyzing a Conclusion

Reread the final paragraph of "The Good Daughter," and consult the preceding strategies to determine which technique Caroline Hwang uses to end her personal narrative. Find examples of two or more of those techniques in the selection.

PROJECT PREP Drafting *Writing the Conclusion*

Based on the introduction and body you have written, write a conclusion that uses one of the ways to end a personal narrative described above.

Personal Narrative Writing Revising

Once you have drafted your personal narrative, set it aside for a few days so that you can return to it with a fresh eye. Then to review your draft, read it aloud and imagine you are hearing it for the first time. Is the composition detailed and engaging? Do the words flow naturally? Is your tone consistent?

1 Checking for Adequate Development

After reviewing and evaluating your draft, you need to revise it so it sounds as natural and smooth as possible. The following box shows strategies for correcting common problems with first drafts of personal narratives.

STRATEGIES FOR REVISING PERSONAL NARRATIVES

Problem	Strategy
The essay is too short, general, or vague.	Revise for more adequate development. Visualize again the people, places, things, or experiences about which you are writing.
The tone is inconsistent.	Revise sentences that stray from the tone you set in the introduction.
The essay sounds too stiff and formal.	Replace any formal, technical, or unfamiliar words with more familiar, everyday vocabulary. Such words sound more natural and are, therefore, more suitable for a personal narrative.

PROJECT PREP Revising *Checking Development*

In your writing group, focus on the physical feelings of the event. For each writer, suggest ways to describe elements of the narrative vividly. Rather than simply describing a sensation, such as, "My grandad's suit was scratchy," use your imagination to say something like, "As my grandad hugged me, the fibers of his suit prickled my arm like the fur of an ancient woolly mammoth."

2 Checking for Unity, Coherence, and Clarity

Use the following checklist to help you identify areas for improvement.

Evaluation Checklist for Revising

Checking Your Narrative as a Whole

✓ Is your narrative appropriate for your audience? (page 141)
✓ Did you use an appropriate tone and stay with it throughout your narrative? (pages 146–147)
✓ Did you interpret the experience and draw meaning from it? (pages 138–140)
✓ Does your narrative have unity, coherence, and clarity? (pages 25 and 94–97)

Checking Your Sentences

✓ Did you combine related sentences to avoid too many short, choppy sentences in a row? (pages 59–63)
✓ Did you vary the length and beginnings of your sentences to achieve fluency? (pages 64–66)
✓ Did you avoid rambling sentences? (page 67)
✓ Did you avoid unnecessary repetition and empty expressions? (pages 68–69)
✓ Did you use such schemes as parallelism and repetition for emphasis? (page 75)

Checking Your Words

✓ Did you use specific words? (page 49)
✓ Did you use words that appeal to the senses? (pages 102–103 and 142)
✓ Did you use such tropes as similes and metaphors? (pages 53–54 and 168)

PROJECT PREP Revising *Using a Checklist*

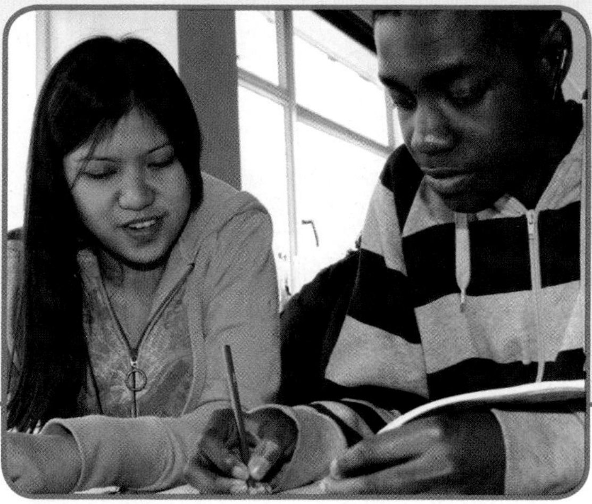

Exchange papers with a writing partner and read one another's narratives with the checklist items in mind. Make suggestions to help the author prepare the most effective version of the personal narrative possible.

When you are happy with your latest revision, you will want to spend some time polishing it. As always, pay special attention to the Power Rules.

The Language of Power *Past Tense*

Power Rule: Use mainstream past tense forms of regular and irregular verbs. (See pages 742–766.)

See It in Action The following sentence from "The Good Daughter" correctly uses past tense forms of the irregular verbs *tear* and *go* and the past perfect form of the irregular verb *find*.

> It tore me up inside to suppress my dream, but I went to school for a Ph.D. in English literature, thinking I had found the perfect compromise.

Irregular verbs form their past and past participle in a number of different ways. It is a good idea to simply recite and memorize the parts of the most common irregular verbs. For example, the principal parts of the verb *tear* are *tear* (present), *tore* (past), and *(has) torn* (past participle).

Remember It Record this rule and example in the Power Rule section of your Personalized Editing Checklist.

Use It Read through your personal narrative and look for irregular verbs. Be sure you have used the correct past tense verb form in your sentences.

PROJECT PREP Editing *Conventions*

Exchange papers with a writing partner and check one another's narratives for any problems in grammar, usage, punctuation, or spelling. Pay special attention to the Power Rules. (See pages 9–11.)

Using a Six-Trait Rubric — Personal Narratives

Use a rubric like the one below to measure a personal narrative.

Ideas	**4** The topic and details convey the experience powerfully to the intended audience and fulfill the intended purpose.	**3** The topic and details convey the experience to the intended audience and fulfill the intended purpose.	**2** The topic and details do not clearly convey the experience to the intended audience or fulfill the intended purpose.	**1** The topic and details do not convey the experience. They fail to address the audience or fulfill the purpose.
Organization	**4** The introduction, body, and conclusion fulfill their purposes.	**3** The organization is mostly clear, but a few ideas seem out of place or transitions are missing.	**2** Many ideas seem out of place and transitions are missing.	**1** The organization is unclear. The narrative does not present, develop, or interpret the experience.
Voice	**4** The voice sounds natural, engaging, and personal.	**3** The voice sounds natural and personal.	**2** The voice sounds mostly unnatural with exceptions.	**1** The voice sounds mostly unnatural.
Word Choice	**4** Words are vivid, specific, and rich in sensory images.	**3** Words are specific and some appeal to the senses.	**2** Some words are overly general.	**1** Most words are overly general.
Sentence Fluency	**4** Varied sentences flow smoothly. Devices that promote coherence are used effectively.	**3** Most of the sentences are varied and smoothly flowing. Transitions help coherence.	**2** Some sentence patterns are not varied and some sentences are choppy. Few transitions are present.	**1** Sentences are not varied and are choppy. There are very few transitions and little coherence.
Conventions	**4** Punctuation, usage, and spelling are correct.	**3** There are only a few errors in punctuation, usage, and spelling.	**2** There are some errors in punctuation, usage, and spelling	**1** There are many errors and at least one failure to follow a Power Rule.

PROJECT PREP — Editing — *Using a Rubric*

Produce a final version of your story, using correct grammar, spelling, and punctuation.

CHAPTER 4

In the Media

Blogs

Tabloid newspapers, TV newsmagazines, best-selling memoirs, and Internet home pages are all media in which the personal narrative form has flourished. In expressing reflections on your life experiences, you have the luxury of choosing from among many media. Each has its own way of presenting your thoughts to the world and each its own advantages and drawbacks, but none is easier to share with a large audience than an online blog.

Think about how you would adapt or "translate" the personal narrative you have just written into your own blog on the Web. Use the following questions to analyze how effective your narrative would be as a blog.

- Which aspects of your written narrative would translate well into this medium? Why?
- Which aspects would be more challenging to adapt into a Web site? Why?
- Which aspects might you convey more effectively online?
- How else do you think a blog's format might shape your narrative or an audience's appreciation of the experience?

Finally, given what you know of the media, do you think a blog is the best choice for adapting your personal narrative? Why?

Personal Narrative Writing — Publishing

You may decide to complete the writing process by sharing your writing with someone who was part of your experience or may have an interest in it.

PROJECT PREP Publishing *Sharing Your Work*

1. Based on the feedback from your writing partner, prepare a final draft of your narrative. If you chose one of the forms listed on page 136 for your published work, meet with others in your class to discuss the publishing conventions of that form. For example, if you chose to include your narrative in your own blog, does your finished work have all the elements necessary for publishing on a blog? If you chose to write a letter, in what ways did you need to adjust your narrative to fit the form? How might you have done that better?
2. When you are satisfied that you have polished it as well as you can, publish your work through your chosen medium. If you wrote a letter, for example, send it to the person for whom it was intended.

Writing Lab

Project Corner

Speak and Listen
Share Insights

With your classmates, **engage in a discussion of cultural values and practices.** Is adhering to cultural traditions beneficial to a person? What are the effects of culture on how a person acts, dresses, speaks, engages with others, and otherwise performs in the world? How should people act when they come into conflict with members of cultures unfamiliar to them?

Collaborate and Create Recast

In your writing group, select one narrative and **recast part of it as a dramatic scene**. Consider how the tone, details, emotions, perspective, interpretation, and other aspects of the narrative would be affected with the narrative voice removed.

Think Creatively
Create a Trio

Consider the personal narrative you wrote as one part of three in a "trio" of personal narratives that tell different experiences but that have a common theme or thread. **Write two more personal narratives** to round out the collection and publish your trio in an innovative way.

In Everyday Life
Descriptive Thank-you Note

1. For your birthday, your Aunt Belinda in Florida has sent you a giant pink flamingo for your yard. You don't love the flamingo, but you love your Aunt Belinda. ***Write a tactful note*** to Aunt Belinda thanking her for the flamingo. Describe the flamingo without revealing your true feelings about the gift. In your note focus on your relationship with Aunt Belinda and what it means to you to keep in touch with her in this way.

For Oral Communication Narrative Oral Presentation

2. You are lead singer of a successful band. Your old high school has asked you to return to deliver the annual graduation speech. You sincerely believe that you wouldn't be as successful if you had left school. How did school help prepare you for your life as a performer? ***Prepare a speech*** to give to the high school graduates. Try to enlighten and motivate the graduating seniors by giving specific details of your life and by relating stories of your school learning. Begin your speech with an interesting quote or anecdote, and conclude with reflections on the meaning of your experiences. (You can find information on writing narrative oral presentations on page 577.)

Timed Writing Presentation

3. A historian is gathering material for a book about family traditions. She is paying $150 for personal narratives on such topics as birthday celebrations and holiday traditions. Write a personal narrative describing a tradition that you or your family observe and explain why the tradition is important to you. You have 25 minutes to complete your work. (For help with budgeting time, see pages 37 and 500–501.)

   Before You Write Consider the following questions: What is the situation? What is the occasion? Who is the audience? What is the purpose?

   Introduce your subject in a way that catches your reader's interest and sets the tone for the personal narrative. Try to interweave the narration of events with the expression of your thoughts. Add a memorable conclusion that leaves your reader with the idea or feeling that you wish to convey.

   After You Write Evaluate your work using the six-trait evaluation form on page 153.

CHAPTER 5

Descriptive Writing

Descriptive writing creates a vivid picture in words of a person, an object, or a scene by stimulating the reader's senses.

Detailed, thoughtful description is the hallmark of good writing in almost any form, on almost any subject. Here are just a few of the ways in which description and observation come into play in writing.

- **Talented fiction writers describe scenes and characters** so vividly that the reader can see and hear them.
- **Conscientious police officers and fire investigators write accurate, detailed, official reports** on crimes and fires.
- **Astronauts and military officers give detailed debriefings** after completing their missions.
- **Nature writers provide readers and viewers with rich sensory descriptions** of plant and animal wildlife for nature magazines or documentaries.
- **Journalists, after taking accurate notes, include description and observation in their articles** to make news events come alive.
- **Good guidebook writers describe the conditions and prices** of hotels, restaurants, and attractions, and how people can get from one place to another.

Descriptive Writing Project

Descriptive

On the Road ***Write a description of how you get from one classroom to another.***

Think Through Writing School hallways are often crowded during the passing periods, making it difficult at times to get from one class to another on time. Describe your method for getting from one class to the next when the distance is great and the time is short. What strategies and techniques do you use to get from one place to another in heavy traffic?

Talk About It In your writing group, discuss the writing you have done. What sorts of details has each author included to help you understand how he or she negotiates hallway traffic between classes?

Read About It John Hockenberry, a journalist, observes both with his eyes and with his imagination. As someone who has used a wheelchair all of his adult life, he has had ample opportunities to observe other people's responses to him as he travels on crowded city streets. Compare his method of getting around Chicago with your experiences in navigating your school's hallways between classes. How are they similar and different?

CHAPTER 5

MODEL: Descriptive Writing

From

The Point of No Comment

John Hockenberry

It took years of being in a wheelchair before I could be truly amazed by what it could do, and what I could do with it. On a winter night in Chicago, after a light snow, I rolled across a clean stretch of pavement and felt the smooth frictionless glide of the icy surface. I made a tight turn and chanced to look around and back from where I had just come. The street lamp cast soft icicle rainbows that arched over and highlighted the white surface with bursts of color. Tracing out from where I sat I saw two beautiful lines etched in the snow. They began as parallel and curved, then they crossed in an effortless knot at the place where my wheelchair turned to look back. My chair had made those lines. The knot was the signature of every turn I had ever made, revealed by the wintry template of newly fallen snow. It was the first time I dared to believe that a wheelchair could make something, or even be associated with something, so beautiful.

The first sentence provides key background about the writer and his perspective on his wheelchair.

A simple short sentence, after a longer sentence, makes the writer's point clear and strong.

I float through forests of pedestrians on the sidewalks of New York, Chicago. A wheelchair presses its advantage on the pavement, street-smart, good with cargo, fast and smooth. While walking measures out landmarks in running shoe bounces or high heel castanets, rolling glimpses a city in pans and dolly shots . . . a pedestrian movie with a soundtrack of breathing. The spaces in the pedestrian traffic are liquid passageways that open and close. I weave my way through the people as sunlight passes through a crowd of sky divers on its way to the ground. I live in the blank spaces between the business suits and the gridlock.

On America's pavement there is a rough coexistence between wheels and legs. Between intersections, battles are lost and won every minute of every day. Scores are calculated, rules are kept and broken. It's a finesse game of bowling where speed and precision rule, but the object in this contest is never to knock down any pins. Points are acquired for continuous motion, for never having to say excuse me, for weaving from sidewalk to road and back without stopping for a light. Points are lost for causing elderly people to jump, and for running over anyone's feet. The only way to shoot a strike is to roll from point A to point B at top speed without stopping. There are at least two ways to shoot a gutter ball. You lose if you scare someone so badly that they fall down, or if someone asks if you need a push or tries to push you. This is the worst of all.

The comparison of moving in a wheelchair to bowling is a metaphor, which extends through the rest of the paragraph.

These days, more than just wheelchairs roll down the alley. Wheels are everywhere. Whether they be other wheelchairs, stroller wheels, or Rollerblades, a whole civilization inhabits the pedestrian strip. Vendors throw their nets and homeless beggars cast their palms into the current. The river yields only with difficulty. There is no simple fitting of a wheelchair into the pedestrian world. The ramped curb cuts built for wheelchairs are now clogged with mothers and governesses pushing carriages. People stand in the curb ramps, sucked intuitively to the lowest point in the channel of traffic. They yield only when a chair comes straight toward them, and only then at the last minute.

Comparing the flow of pedestrians on a sidewalk to a river helps readers visualize what the writer is saying.

It is quite difficult to get a mother with a stroller to yield a wheelchair ramp, but it can be done. Often, approaching with speed alone from the front can move the stroller back or to the side. But scaring the mother is strictly forbidden. From behind, when a stroller is present all you can do is leap the curb or say excuse me. Leaping the curb acknowledges that the ramp is shared territory. Some chairs always need the ramps, and have no option. The real pavement hogs are the Rollerbladers. They weave in and out between the people where I once rolled unchallenged. They always seek the strip of pavement at the center of a road, the smooth pavement fillet road engineers call the crown. Bladers are intruders in a ramped world. In the manifesto of crips, four wheels good, eight wheels bad. Some wheels are more equal than others.

The last two sentences paraphrase famous lines from *Animal Farm*, by George Orwell: "four legs good, two legs bad." and "All animals are equal, but some animals are more equal than others."

In Chicago, on Michigan Avenue, there is a wide sidewalk on the west side of the street. From the Chicago River to Lake Shore Drive the sidewalk descends steeply at one point. It is ramped on the west side on virtually every block. During 1987 I lived in an apartment at the bottom of that hill and worked in an office at the top. Rolling to work every morning was a character-building, hand-over-hand, rope climb. Coming home in the evenings was flat-out, downhill, and effortless.

The first sentence in the paragraph establishes the topic for the rest of the paragarph.

Though I rolled in rhythm and wove my way with precision, the presence of a wheelchair in the crowd never seemed as natural to the crowd as it did to me. Where I saw beauty and grace gliding down, others, particularly those walking toward me, saw terror, collisions and serious injury. Going up, where I saw a bracing physical challenge, others saw pain and suffering. On the uphill leg the pedestrian comment was, "Here, let me push." The downhill caption was, "Hey, watch out! You're going to get a speeding ticket." Up and down the sidewalk hill in Chicago I imagined that there was a way of rolling in the chair between fast coasting and slow climbing where people would not be compelled to remark either that I needed a push or a speeding ticket. I took the unwanted closed captioning as a physical challenge. Somewhere between fast and slow, between deliberate and headlong was this mythical point of no comment.

On the streets every day as I reach a cruising speed virtually anyone in my path will say, "Excuse me," or "Watch out," to the person next to them. Mothers who see me look around for their wandering toddlers, and scream, "Look out!" The child runs to Mommy and stares fearfully as I go by. It always seems so odd to hear it, yet to dwell on it seems neurotic too. I can steer. I truly can negotiate my way down the street. But the impulse of pedestrians is to imagine collisions, to presume that there is something wrong. The people who'd rather be safe than sorry, without realizing it, erect walls of chilly exclusions as I pass. I cannot control the impression that my physical shape and presence is foreign . . . .

Rolling isn't as different from walking as you might imagine. The speed at which I travel is a function of rhythm. Inside my paralyzed soul the pendulum of walking still swings. Beat . . . Beat . . . Step . . . Step . . . A wheelchair with standard 20-inch wheels requires a stroke in cut time. Step . . . Step . . . Step . . . becomes

Knowing that most of his audience has little experience rolling in a wheelchair, the author tries to help them understand the experience better.

Roll Roll Roll Roll RollRollRollRollRollRollRoll Roll Roll Roll.

CHAPTER 5

Because I still feel the old rhythms of walking, I have large, bicycle-sized wheels on my chair and small diameter hand rims for pushing. They slow down my stroke and flatten out the rhythm of rolling. They also allow me to go faster, but with large-diameter wheels the beat of rolling is that same centered rhythm of walking, at a speed about twice as fast as a normal walking pace.

Roll . . . Roll . . . Roll . . . Push . . . Push . . . Glide . . .

Rhythm is something that must be felt. Rhythm breaks down the menacing foreign threat of wheelchairs into the fluid motion of rolling, which anyone can see if they look. There are places where the rhythm comes through to everyone. The joggers and tourists on the wide paved trail along Lake Michigan in Chicago would watch me roll toward them, in some places for half a mile as I made my way from the hill at the Shedd Aquarium to where the path curves around Lake Point Tower. To them what I was doing looked like fun.

The final sentence, by stating how the writer thinks people might view him, provides a strong conclusion to the paragraph.

A runner might catch the rhythm of my arms and at that exact moment we would be racing. Two runner's steps to each rolling push of mine. The adrenaline would surge in each of us. We would pace each other for a while and either an uphill grade would slow me and the runner would pull ahead, or a downhill would allow me to surge forward. If we were on the flats, it was a joyous battle of physical wills. I might pass the runner or the runner might pass me. In each case, the rhythms of forward motion, legs and spokes, were intertwined. . . .

So is there a point of no comment? I found it one day on the way down the Michigan Avenue hill. It had been a long day. I was tired and I stopped worrying about speed and pedestrians: a dreamy dissolve and the walking people became moving posts in a paved slalom course. I pushed ahead, and the territory between the bodies became an ether, a river of space into which I could glide while they, like cattails in the current, could not.

Gravity pushed the chair ahead, and with the smoothness of curves etched on a lathe, I carved a trajectory around the pedestrians at a speed far above that of walking. Fingers touched the wheel rims, trimming to the right and left. I was trailing a thread on a windless slope, drifting around briefcases and suits and ankles and dress shoes. Speed became a test of the limits of the fabric of the space itself. The only appropriate speed was the fastest possible. The space between people became my space, and the whole scene unfolded as a postulate: Can this be done? Can the staccato pedestrian rhythms blend with the reedy line of effortless rolling descent? Wheel jazz.

When the fear of collision vanished, I ceased to look like a piano rolling down a hill. The chair and the legs joined for all to see in an unsolicited statement of grace. There was no suggestion that I was speeding. I glided by faster than it took to think of comments about speeding tickets, but this was no mad dash of escape; for once, I was not trying to outrun their preconceived notions. The spaces between pedestrians were made for wheelchairs, and I belonged there. Pedestrians saw it as well. On their faces was: "That looks like fun." When had they ever yearned to be in a wheelchair before?

The words "as well" mark the transition from describing how the writer's thoughts have changed to how the thoughts of others have changed.

The promise of art and revolution is that people might discard their preconceptions and truly understand what is in the mind of another. What would a world look like in which people dare to wish to know what it is like not to walk? The point of no comment exists. It has a signature. It is the smooth curve a wheelchair makes in cold snow.

The final sentence connects back to the first paragraph.

CHAPTER 5

Respond in Writing Respond to Hockenberry's essay about getting around Chicago in a wheelchair. How do you feel about his situation? How would you respond if you came across him while you were in a hurry to get somewhere?

Develop Your Own Ideas Work with your classmates to develop ideas that will help you describe your hallway navigation techniques.

Small Groups: In your writing group, use the following graphic organizer to consider the sorts of information that you might include in your writing.

The characteristics of the school hallways: width, length, surface areas	Special obstacles that stand in your way	Special circumstances of your own that slow you down	Distances traveled and particular traffic gridlocks in stairwell or crossroads	Your own physical characteristics (size, speed, for example) and how they figure into your strategies

Whole Class: Make a master chart of all of the ideas generated by the small groups, and discuss the types of features that people have included in their hallway navigation strategies.

Write About It You will next write about how you navigate crowded hallways between classes in school while traveling a long distance under the pressure of time. The following chart provides possible topics, audiences, and forms for your writing.

Possible Topics and Examples	Possible Audiences	Possible Forms
• problems that follow when some teachers don't enforce tardiness rules and their students linger in the hallway • how to solve problems of congestion at major hallway crossroads • how to schedule classes to eliminate long trips during the passing period • problems of people of different size, strength, and speed meeting the same rules for punctuality in a crowded school	• a teacher to whose class you are often late • the principal in charge of hallway etiquette • classmates who get in your way as you travel • your parents who are concerned about your tardiness to class	• a letter to an authority figure • an appeal of a disciplinary measure for being late to a class • an article for the school newspaper • a speech to be given at an all-school assembly

Elements of Descriptive Texts

As with the descriptive paragraph (pages 102–103), the descriptive essay has three main parts.

CHAPTER 5

HERE'S HOW

Structuring a Descriptive Text

- In the **introduction,** capture attention, introduce the subject, and suggest an overall impression of the subject.
- In the **body of supporting paragraphs** present details, especially sensory details, that bring the subject to life.
- In the **conclusion**, reinforce the overall impression and give a feeling of closure.

Vivid language plays an important role in each part of a descriptive text.

1 Specific Details and Sensory Words

Detailed, thoughtful description is the hallmark of good writing in almost any form, on almost any subject. Strong specific, descriptive details and words appeal to the senses. When you describe a scene, *show* it—make the reader feel that he or she is there—rather than just tell the reader about it.

Henry David Thoreau, the great American naturalist and philosopher, brought the woods of rural New England so strongly to life that reading his work can feel like taking a much-needed vacation. In the following selection from *Walden*, he is describing part of the house he built for himself.

Writing Tip

Use **specific details** and **sensory words** to bring your description to life.

MODEL: Sensory Details

I dug my cellar in the side of a hill sloping to the south, where a woodchuck had formerly dug his burrow, down through sumac and blackberry roots, and the lowest stain of vegetation, six feet square by seven feet deep, to a fine sand where potatoes would not freeze in any winter. The sides were left shelving, and not stoned; but the sun having never shone on them, the sand still keeps its place. It was but two hours' work. I took particular pleasure in this breaking of ground, for in almost all latitudes men dig into the earth for an equable temperature. Under the most splendid house in the city is still to be found the cellar where they store their roots as of old, and long after the superstructure had disappeared posterity remark its dent in the earth. The house is still but a sort of porch at the entrance of a burrow. . . .

I began to occupy my house on the 4th of July, as soon as it was boarded and roofed, for the boards were carefully feather-edged and lapped, so that it was perfectly impervious to rain, but before boarding I laid the foundation of a chimney at one end, bringing two cartloads of stones up the hill from the pond in my arms. I built the chimney after my hoeing in the fall, before a fire became necessary for warmth, doing my cooking in the meanwhile out of doors on the ground. . . . When it stormed before my bread was baked, I fixed a few boards over the fire, and sat under them to watch my loaf, and passed some pleasant hours in that way.

—Henry David Thoreau, *Walden*

One reason this passage is so richly descriptive is that Thoreau is really observing two things: his cellar and himself. His descriptions of building a cellar are interwoven with the thoughts and feelings the cellar evokes in him. The most important factor in the success of this description, however, is Thoreau's generous use of specific details and sensory words.

Practice Your Skills

Using Specific Words

With a partner, make a two-column chart. In the left column, list at least ten specific words Thoreau used in the excerpt above. In the right column, write a general word that could take the place of each specific word. Read a passage of the excerpt with the general words replacing the specific words to see how the writing becomes drained of color.

PROJECT PREP Prewriting *Specific Language*

With your writing group, make a list of general words and phrases that describe travel. Then, for each general word, list more precise words that specify or clarify aspects of it. Save your work for later use.

2 Figurative Language

A figure of speech, also called a **trope** or a play on words, can give an added dimension to descriptions. The most familiar types of tropes are imagery, similes, and metaphors. Others include personification, onomatopoeia, oxymoron, hyperbole, irony, analogy, paradox, and symbolism. (See pages 53–54 and 226.) In the following sentence from *Walden,* Thoreau makes a literal comparison that does not belong to any of the above categories of figurative language.

> There is some of the same fitness in a man's building his own house that there is in a bird's building its own nest.

Following are some examples of how that literal comparison might have been turned into other kinds of comparisons.

Simile	It is as fit for a man to build his house as it is for a bird to build its nest.
Metaphor	A man's house is his nest.
Personification	Every bird is the architect and builder of a nest.
Hyperbole	Between human house and avian nest, there is absolutely no difference in architectural skill.

Writing Tip

Use **figurative language** and **comparisons** to add color and depth to your description.

PROJECT PREP *Prewriting* *Using Tropes*

In your writing group, develop figurative language for the general words and phrases you developed in the previous activity. Create similes, metaphors, examples of personification, statements of hyperbole, or other tropes that express the concepts colorfully.

As with other types of writing, the prewriting phase in description can overlap and intermix with other phases of the process. You do not have to do all or even most of your prewriting before you physically put words on the page. You do, however, need to think as you write. Your prewriting time is for you to generate ideas, formulate questions, develop your voice, and make a plan for your writing.

1 Purpose, Subject, and Audience

Purpose

Some poems and prose sketches are entirely descriptive, but more often, description is found within the fabric of other types of writing. Fiction, which is narrative writing, usually contains description. Expository writing is often made clearer for the reader when descriptions are judiciously supplied. Descriptions can make a persuasive essay more persuasive. For example, if you are trying to win readers over to the rescue of endangered Siberian tigers, you might want to describe how these tigers look and behave, and what their environment is like. The skills of description will help you enrich virtually any kind of writing you do.

Subject

Henry David Thoreau did not describe his cellar because someone assigned him to do so. He described his cellar because he cared deeply about building his own house. For him, that act was not just a physical labor but an expression of his view of how to live; so was the act of writing.

A good subject needs to be important to you. A good subject for a descriptive essay, however, does not have to be about an earth-shaking phenomenon. Thoreau's cellar was of little importance to anyone but himself—at least until he wrote about it.

HERE'S HOW **Guidelines for Choosing a Subject**

- Choose a subject that matters to *you.* Your interest will carry over to the reader.
- Choose a subject that you can develop with descriptive details such as sensory words and figurative language.
- Choose a subject you know well enough to describe better than anyone else you know.

AUDIENCE

If Thoreau had been writing for an audience of professional architects, he probably would have used a more technical vocabulary than he did in describing his house. If you were writing a descriptive essay about your home, you might write differently depending on whether your intended reader was a friend in another state, a realtor who wanted to sell the house, or an art student assigned to draw a picture based on your written description. Try not to write down to your audience or over their heads. The following questions will help you determine a voice and style that is appropriate to your audience and your purpose.

HERE'S HOW

Questions for Analyzing an Audience

- What does my audience already know about my subject?
- What background information, if any, do I need to provide to make the description more meaningful?
- What attitude does my audience have toward my subject?
- What am I providing to my audience that is new for them? What kind of language would be best in order to present this fresh material clearly?

PROJECT PREP Prewriting The Subject

Select a subject for a descriptive essay. (See page 165 for topics on traveling through hallways between classes.) To find subjects that are meaningful to you and to readers, use the familiar techniques of brainstorming, freewriting, and clustering, as well as any other techniques you have found useful. Review your journal entries for ideas. Follow the suggestions on page 169 for thinking of subjects. Then visualize your audience. Write out answers to the **Questions for Analyzing an Audience** on this page to help you target your writing effectively. Save your work.

Finally, consider what genre or form will best help you convey your intended meaning to your audience.

2 Creating an Overall Impression

Hockenberry did not describe every single detail of his wheelchair, and Thoreau did not describe his house in enough exact detail for a reader to build a duplicate. If they had, the reader would have experienced sensory overload and, in all probability, would have been bored. Selecting the important details is one of the primary skills of writing—especially of descriptive writing.

In order to have criteria for selecting certain details and omitting others, you should be conscious of an overall impression you want to convey. You can then determine whether your words do, in fact, convey that impression or feeling.

The impression a writer wishes to convey is sometimes stated, but more often it is implied and left for the reader to infer. Different readers may carry away with them different impressions of a description, and the author's intentions may allow for a mixed impression. As a reader, you are not forced to share or agree with the feelings that constitute the author's overall impression; however, as a good reader, you should be aware of the feelings the author tries to express.

CHAPTER 5

Practice Your Skills

Determining Overall Impressions

1. What is the overall impression Hockenberry was trying to flesh out in "The Point of No Comment"?
2. What phrases or passages introduce this overall impression?
3. What is the overall impression of the passage from *Walden?*
4. Cite specific words or phrases in the *Walden* passage that convey this impression.

PROJECT PREP Prewriting *Reader's Emotions*

In your writing group, discuss the overall impression that each writer is trying to create. What should a reader feel as he or she reads each piece of writing? What images should go through a reader's mind? What emotions should a reader take away after reading the story?

3 Developing a Description

With your overall impression in mind, and with a vision of an audience, you can begin to develop the details of a description. Use these strategies for developing a description.

HERE'S HOW

Strategies for Developing a Description

- Use your memory and direct observation, if appropriate, to list the sights, sounds, smells, tastes, and feelings you associate with your subject. Making a chart like the one on page 173 may help.
- Brainstorm for a list of imaginative comparisons you might use to help readers understand your description. These could be metaphors or similes or other types of figurative language.
- Gather any factual details and information you might need to provide background for your readers or to help set the stage for your overall impression.
- If you are describing a scene, draw a picture or a map so you can clearly see the relationship of one part of the subject to another.
- Apply your filter: remember to test each detail against your desired overall impression to make sure it adds rather than detracts.

CHAPTER 5

PROJECT PREP Prewriting *Developing Details*

In your writing group, discuss the details that will give your description life. For the school hallways project, focus especially on parts of the trip where the author encounters or creates obstacles, such as making extra stops, talking with friends, being a slow walker, or creating extra distance by avoiding certain places. Help each author detail these delays with vivid language.

TIME OUT TO REFLECT

After developing details for your descriptive essay, think again about the subject you have chosen. Be open to any new ideas or feelings that come to mind as a result. Jot them down and decide whether they might be effective as additional details.

Think Critically

Observing

Film in a camera records an impression of the light that passes through the shutter. The camera makes an **objective** observation: it has no opinion about the objects at which it is pointed. The person pointing the camera, however, is **subjective.** The photographer chooses to point the camera in a certain direction, among other choices. This picture expresses the photographer's point of view.

Objective facts lay the foundation for subjective observations. The facts are there, but your writing skills affect what you do with them and thus how the reader will interpret them. The following chart shows some objective facts John Hockenberry reports about riding in a wheelchair and some of the subjective observations he developed from those facts.

OBJECTIVE DETAILS	SUBJECTIVE DETAILS
street lamp shines on the snow	street lamp casts "soft icicle rainbows"
wheel tracks are parallel lines in the snow	"beautiful," "effortless," "the signature of every turn I had ever made"
wheelchair rolls amid a crowd of pedestrians	chair "float[s]," "presses its advantage" through "liquid passageways"

If you compare the two kinds of details, you can see that the objective ones would be verified by any impartial onlooker. The subjective observations, in contrast, might vary depending on the attitudes, personality, and outlook of each person. They also happen to be the details that make Hockenberry's essay a fine, moving, and revealing piece of descriptive nonfiction.

Thinking Practice

Make a chart like the one above to record objective and subjective observations of your school. Compare your work to that of other students in your class.

4 Organizing a Description

How you organize your description depends on your writing aim and the nature of your details. The following chart shows some possible patterns of organization.

WRITING AIM	KINDS OF DETAILS	TYPE OF ORDER
to **describe** a person, place, object, or scene	sensory details	spatial (page 96)
to **re-create** an event	sensory details, events	chronological (page 95)
to **explain** a process or how something works	sensory and factual details, steps in a process, how parts work together	sequential (pages 95 and 265)
to **persuade**	sensory and factual details, examples, reasons	order of importance (page 97)
to **reflect**	sensory and factual details, interpretations	order of importance (page 97)

You may wish to use the graphic organizers on pages 101–107 to help you organize your ideas.

PROJECT PREP **Prewriting** *Sensory Details*

In your writing group, help each author improve the sensory depiction of the subject focusing on each of the five senses. For example, schools include odoriferous places, such as locker rooms, home economics classrooms, chemistry classrooms, agriculture classes, and other areas where pungent odors emanate. Which ones are walked through or past on the route? Avoid simply listing smells, as in, "The locker room is stinky." Rather, use your imagination to provide a vivid account, as in, "As I leave gym class and head to algebra, I put my gym clothes into my locker, hoping to lock in the aroma of perspiration, old socks, and body odor but always carrying its remnants with me, the stench soaking into my fresh clothes from the shower stall moisture and making me a walking advertisement for a strong deodorant." Then, on your own, organize these details using an outline or graphic organizer. (See pages 101–107 and 245–248.)

The Power of Language

Who or What? Appositives

Details that elaborate on a person, place, or thing that may be unknown to your reader will strengthen your personal narrative. As you draft, you can add such details in the form of appositive phrases. An **appositive** is a noun or pronoun phrase that identifies or adds identifying information to a preceding noun. In "The Point of No Comment," John Hockenberry uses appositives to clarify who felt frightened of seeing him come toward them. Note that the appositive is set off by commas.

> Where I saw beauty and grace gliding down, others, particularly those walking toward me, saw terror, collisions and serious injury.

He also uses a long and complex appositive to describe the limits on pedestrians:

> I pushed ahead, and the territory between the bodies became an ether, a river of space into which I could glide while they, like cattails in the current, could not.

An appositive that comes at the end of a sentence is separated from the rest of the sentence by a comma or dash.

Try It Yourself

1. Write a sentence on your project topic that imitates the structure and punctuation of the first example sentence above. Elaborate on the subject of your sentence with an appositive phrase.
2. Write a sentence on your project topic that includes an appositive for elaboration at the end of the sentence.
3. Use the resulting sentences in your draft if you can, and try creating other similar sentences. You can always add more details with appositives when you revise.

Punctuation Tip

Use **two commas** to enclose an appositive **in the middle** of a sentence.

Use **one comma or a dash** to separate an appositive from the rest of the sentence when it appears **at the end.**

During the drafting stage, concentrate on the flow of your ideas without stopping to revise. Let yourself say what you want; you can change or delete passages later if you find you have made wrong turns or misstated your observations. Keep your reader in mind as a way of aiming your draft in the direction of your desired overall impression.

HERE'S HOW

Tips for Drafting a Description

- Find a catchy way of introducing your description; try out several if necessary.
- Suggest or imply your overall impression early on so that it will carry through the entire essay.
- Follow your outline, but feel free to make improvements as they occur to you.
- Use fresh, vivid, descriptive words that appeal to readers' senses.
- Use transitions appropriate to the type of order you have chosen to help readers move easily from paragraph to paragraph and sentence to sentence.
- Conclude your essay on a strong note, perhaps referring back to an idea in the introduction or raising questions that stimulate further thought.

PROJECT PREP Drafting Sentence Structure

Write a draft of your descriptive text. Share it with your writing group. Help each author to provide sentence structure variety so that the presentation does not become predictable. Consider using sentence structures that affect a reader's sense of drama. A series of short sentences, for instance, tends to convey action, while longer sentences convey a slowing down of time.

Descriptive Writing *Revising*

Use the following checklist to help you improve your draft.

Evaluation Checklist for Revising

Checking Your Introduction

- ✓ Does your introduction seize the reader's attention? (pages 112, 166, and 176)
- ✓ Does your introduction give a sense of your subject? (pages 112, 166, and 176)
- ✓ Does your introduction set a tone that is appropriate for your subject and audience? (pages 112–113)

Checking Your Body Paragraphs

- ✓ Have you supported your overall impression with suitable details? (pages 171–172)
- ✓ Did you include specific, well-chosen sensory words and details, and have you avoided generalities? (pages 49–58)
- ✓ Is each paragraph within the body well-developed, with a clear main idea and adequate supporting details? (pages 90–99 and 172–174)
- ✓ Did you use figurative language effectively? (pages 53–54 and 168)
- ✓ Did you move logically from one paragraph to the next in a clear order and with helpful transitions? (pages 95–97 and 253–254)

Checking Your Conclusion

- ✓ Does the conclusion reinforce the overall impression? (pages 124, 166, and 176)
- ✓ Do you refer back to an idea in your introduction to give a sense of completion to your essay? (pages 166 and 176)
- ✓ Did you end with a memorable phrase or image? (pages 124 and 176)

Checking Your Overall Essay

- ✓ Is your essay adequately developed with supporting details? (pages 90–91 and 119–120)
- ✓ Does your essay have unity, coherence, and emphasis? (pages 94–97 and 122)

Checking Your Words and Sentences

- ✓ Are your words specific and lively? Do they appeal to several senses? (pages 49–58 and 166–167)
- ✓ Are your sentences varied? (pages 59–66)

PROJECT PREP *Revising* *Using Feedback*

Use the checklist above to help you prepare a new draft of your descriptive text.

In the Media

Short Documentary

Documentary skills can make you a better writer, a more critical viewer of visual media, and a valued worker in today's visual culture. The following steps will guide you in making a 7– to 10–minute descriptive documentary.

HERE'S HOW

Steps in Making a Short Documentary

- Choose a subject that can be observed nearby, such as someone's rooftop garden or the area outside your school before the morning bell rings.
- Brainstorm subjects and choose one that you could capture on video without problems. If you are videotaping people, you may need to get their permission.
- Make a list of places, objects, and people you want to include. Identify your audience and the impression you want to make. Write your ideas in a paragraph.
- Do some preliminary research. Visit the location and observe it before you start shooting. Read books and articles and view documentaries related to the subject.
- Take notes on each scene of your rough footage to help you during editing. Note details that are distant from each other on the tape but closely related in concept.
- Make a word-for-word transcript of any interviews. Decide which lines you want to use. Try to connect spoken ideas with images. You may want to spread clips of the interview throughout your documentary.
- Use notes and consider ways to shape your material into a unified, coherent presentation. You may decide to veer from your original plan.

Show your documentary in class. Encourage questions like the following.

QUESTIONS FOR ANALYZING A SHORT DOCUMENTARY

- Who is the intended audience? What effect might the film have on that audience?
- What is the denotative meaning or theme of the documentary—the obvious meaning that people would probably agree on?
- What are possible connotative meanings of the documentary—those based on interpretation, which might differ from viewer to viewer? Specifically, how did such techniques as editing, camera angles, reaction shots, and music convey messages or themes?
- How have documentaries affected your view of the world? Cite examples.
- How has making this documentary, and viewing the result, affected your view of the subject, the creative process, and yourself and your skills?

You can find more information on making videos in Electronic Publishing, *(pages 598–603).*

Descriptive Writing Editing

When you are confident about your latest revision, spend some time polishing your descriptive essay. Being a tough critic of your own work will improve your writing.

The Language of Power *Sound-Alikes*

Power Rule: For sound-alikes and certain words that sound almost alike, choose the word with your intended meaning. (See pages 860–887.)

See It in Action It is easy to confuse two words that are pronounced alike but have different meanings and spellings. The following sentence from "The Point of No Comment" uses homophones correctly.

> **There** are places **where** the rhythm comes **through** to everyone. (homophones: *there, their, they're; wear, where; threw, through)*

Some words sound almost alike and are easily misused, such as *moral/morale, advice/advise, farther/further, alter/altar, compliment/complement,* and *loose/lose*. If you are unsure about a word choice, use a dictionary to confirm a word's meaning and usage.

Remember It Record the rule and examples in the Power Rule section of your Personalized Editing Checklist. Also review **A Writer's Glossary of Usage** on pages 860–887 and record any homophones you frequently confuse.

Use It Read through your project topic and check to see that you have chosen and used the word with your intended meaning.

editing

As you edit, remember to cut out needless words and phrases. Practice by editing the following wordy sentence.

> My trip traveling from one class to my next class down the second-floor corridor that connected one room with another was slow because it took a lot of time.

Using a Six-Trait Rubric Descriptive Writing

Ideas	**4** The text conveys an overall impression with abundant vivid details and is well chosen for the purpose and audience.	**3** The text conveys an overall impression with ample details and suits the purpose and audience.	**2** The text conveys an overall impression with some vivid details and suits the purpose and audience.	**1** The text does not convey an overall impression and fails to suit the purpose and audience.
Organization	**4** The organization is clear with abundant transitions.	**3** A few ideas seem out of place or transitions are missing.	**2** Many ideas seem out of place and transitions are missing.	**1** The organization is unclear and hard to follow.
Voice	**4** The voice sounds natural, engaging, and personal.	**3** The voice sounds natural and personal.	**2** The voice sounds mostly unnatural with a few exceptions.	**1** The voice sounds mostly unnatural.
Word Choice	**4** Words are specific and powerful, rich in sensory images.	**3** Words are specific and some words appeal to the senses.	**2** Some words are overly general.	**1** Most words are overly general.
Sentence Fluency	**4** Varied sentences flow smoothly.	**3** Most sentences are varied and flow smoothly.	**2** Some sentences are varied but some are choppy.	**1** Sentences are not varied and are choppy.
Conventions	**4** Punctuation, usage, and spelling are correct. The Power Rules are all followed.	**3** Punctuation, usage, and spelling are mainly correct, and Power Rules are all followed.	**2** Some punctuation, usage, and spelling are incorrect, but all Power Rules are followed.	**1** There are many errors and at least one failure to follow a Power Rule.

PROJECT PREP Publishing *Quality and Conventions*

1. Exchange revisions with a writing partner, and read each other's writing with an eye toward correcting any grammar, usage, mechanics, or spelling errors, especially the Power Rules.
2. Make necessary corrections based on feedback from your partner. Then evaluate your work using the rubric above and make further revisions as appropriate.

Descriptive Writing Publishing

Make your writing available to interested readers by publishing it in an appropriate format of your choice. Some possible avenues of publication for a descriptive writing include the following.

HERE'S HOW **Publishing Options for Descriptive Writing**

- an e-mail message to a friend who may (or may not) know about the object or experience you describe
- a submission to a magazine or other periodical
- an oral reading in your classroom, involving a group of student readers and listeners

CHAPTER 5

PROJECT PREP Publishing *Sharing Your Work*

Using standard manuscript form, prepare a neat final copy of your description. Share your description in the format you chose for your project (see page 165) or in another way you think might be effective. Encourage your readers to give you feedback on your writing.

Writing Lab

Project Corner

Speak and Listen
Propose Traffic Patterns

Discuss with your classmates the problems of navigating hallways between classes and **develop a series of proposals** to present to your student government to improve hallway traffic. For more on listening effectively, see pages 581–585.

Collaborate and Create
Make a Game

In your writing group, combine your papers to **plan a video game** based on the hallway navigation journey. What is the game called? What genre would the game fall in? What features would it have? What is the object for players?

Map It
Show the Path

Accompany your written account with a **map** that clearly lays out the route you must take and includes symbols for all of the obstacles you face in making the journey from class to class.

Experiment
Try a Different Form

Explain your journey through another genre, such as a poem, a graphic short story, a personal narrative, or other form. What is lost and gained through explaining the journey in a different medium?

In the Workplace

Apply and Assess

Descriptive Business Letter

1. Your job as a dog groomer has given you a good understanding of how a dog thinks. The owner of your shop has decided to build a park just for dogs called "Old Yellerstone." His idea of fun for a dog, however, is a long stretch of pavement and a few park benches. He doesn't even plan to provide a place for the dogs to dig holes or chew bones. ***Write a business letter*** to your boss describing what you think would be the ideal setting for a dog. Create an overall impression of the park using specific details. Be sure to include sensory details that will describe how a dog will feel in your proposed park. (You can find information on writing business letters on pages 530–537.)

In Academic Areas Descriptive Business Proposal

2. You are an architecture professor at a large state university. The principal of your high school alma mater calls to inform you that the old high school building has burned to the ground. He asks you to submit your ideas for the design of a new high school based on your memory of what the old school was like. ***Write a business proposal*** to the school committee describing how you envision the new school. Be sure to create an overall impression of what the school will be like and to be specific in your descriptive details. (You can find information on writing business proposals on pages 560–562.)

Timed Writing Essay to Describe and Inform

3. For a class on human behavior, you are asked to write an essay describing why people do things to make themselves look a certain way. For example, why do they comb their hair the way they do? Why do some people wear make-up?

   Before You Write Consider the following questions: What is the situation? What is the occasion? Who is the audience? What is the purpose?

   You must be specific in your sensory descriptions. Use figurative language and comparison to add color to your essay. You have 25 minutes to complete your work. For help in budgeting time, see pages 37 and 500–501.

   After You Write Evaluate your work using the six-trait evaluation rubric on page 180.

CHAPTER 6

Creative Writing

You have read, viewed, and listened to many examples of creative writing throughout your lifetime. The imagined worlds of creative writers are all around us in the form of entertainment and in some other surprising places as well.

Here are just a few examples of the ways in which creative writing makes a place for itself in real life.

- **From childhood through old age, people turn to creative writing** both for recreation and in order to help them find meaning in life.
- **People read novels, listen to audiotapes, and watch plays and movies** for pleasure and as important preparation for travel.
- **Software developers create plots, characters, and settings** to give liveliness and structure to computer games.
- **Stories and plays** are the cornerstone of the film and television industries; poems in the form of song lyrics are fundamental to the popular music industry.
- **Comedians and political writers** often use satire to attack what they consider inconsistencies in an opponent's ideas.

Writing Project — Satire

Big Shot ***Write a satirical short story about a well-known public figure, such as a politician, actor, musician, or athlete.***

Think Through Writing A **satire** is a work of art that mocks human folly. A satire is designed to make people laugh at problems that are often very serious. As a result, satires rely on **irony,** which typically involves an indirect criticism. For instance, if you are wearing an ugly shirt and someone says, "Nice shirt," the person is probably being ironic. Irony goes beyond mere sarcasm in a satire, however. In this chapter, you will write a satire using specific techniques.

For now, write about a well-known public figure that you find does not live up to his or her expressed values and behaves in a way you think deserves criticism. You may write about many possible targets of satire or focus on just one. You may want to use pseudonyms, or fake names, to protect the identities of those you are satirizing. Pseudonyms make most sense when it is the actions, and not really the individual, that the writer wants to criticize.

Talk About It In your writing group, discuss which subjects might make a good focus for a satirical short story. The best targets of satire are rarely people who are already facing unusual challenges, such as poverty or illness. Rather, they tend to be people who have power, wealth, or other advantages and use them poorly because of greed, pride, sloth, or another trait.

Read About It In the following selection, author Kurt Vonnegut writes a satire set in the future. His character, Harrison Bergeron, is so talented that society gives him handicaps so that he is not superior to anyone in any way. Think about what Vonnegut is criticizing through his satire and what techniques he uses to make fun of humanity.

MODEL: Short Story

Harrison Bergeron

Kurt Vonnegut

The year was 2081, and everybody was finally equal. They weren't only equal before God and the law. They were equal every which way. Nobody was smarter than anybody else. Nobody was better looking than anybody else. Nobody was stronger or quicker than anybody else. All this equality was due to the 211th, 212th, and 213th Amendments to the Constitution, and to the unceasing vigilance of agents of the United States Handicapper General.

What might explain how the number of amendments rose from 27 (today) to 213 in 2081?

The first paragraph establishes the setting.

Some things about living still weren't quite right, though. April, for instance, still drove people crazy by not being springtime. And it was in that clammy month that the H-G men took George and Hazel Bergeron's fourteen-year-old son, Harrison, away.

The second paragraph introduces the main characters of the story.

It was tragic, all right, but George and Hazel couldn't think about it very hard. Hazel had a perfectly average intelligence, which meant she couldn't think about anything except in short bursts. And George, while his intelligence was way above normal, had a little mental handicap radio in his ear. He was required by

CHAPTER 6

law to wear it at all times. It was tuned to a government transmitter. Every twenty seconds or so, the transmitter would send out some sharp noise to keep people like George from taking unfair advantage of their brains.

George and Hazel were watching television. There were tears on Hazel's cheeks, but she'd forgotten for the moment what they were about.

On the television screen were ballerinas.

A buzzer sounded in George's head. His thoughts fled in panic, like bandits from a burglar alarm.

"That was a real pretty dance, that dance they just did," said Hazel.

"Huh?" said George.

"That dance—it was nice," said Hazel.

"Yup," said George. He tried to think a little about the ballerinas. They weren't really very good—no better than anybody else would have been, anyway. They were burdened with sash-weights and bags of birdshot, and their faces were masked, so that no one, seeing a free and graceful gesture or a pretty face, would feel like something the cat drug in. George was toying with the vague notion that maybe dancers shouldn't be handicapped. But he didn't get very far with it before another noise in his ear radio scattered his thoughts.

George winced. So did two out of the eight ballerinas.

Hazel saw him wince. Having no mental handicap herself, she had to ask George what the latest sound had been.

"Sounded like somebody hitting a milk bottle with a ball peen hammer," said George.

The descriptions of the sounds that George hears are precise and colorful.

"I'd think it would be real interesting hearing all the different sounds," said Hazel, a little envious. "All the things they think up."

"Um," said George.

"Only, if I was Handicapper General, you know what I would do?" said Hazel. Hazel, as a matter of fact, bore a strong resemblance to the Handicapper General, a woman named Diana Moon Glampers. "If I was Diana

Moon Glampers," said Hazel, "I'd have chimes on Sunday—just chimes. Kind of in honor of religion."

> The dialogue between Hazel and George demonstrates their characters and how handicaps make everyone equal.

"I could think, if it was just chimes," said George.

"Well—maybe make 'em real loud," said Hazel. "I think I'd make a good Handicapper General."

"Good as anybody else," said George.

"Who knows better'n I do what normal is?" said Hazel.

"Right," said George. He began to think glimmeringly about his abnormal son who was now in jail, about Harrison, but a twenty-one-gun salute in his head stopped that.

"Boy!" said Hazel, "that was a doozy, wasn't it?"

It was such a doozy that George was white and trembling, and tears stood on the rims of his red eyes. Two of the eight ballerinas, who had collapsed to the studio floor, were holding their temples.

"All of a sudden you look so tired," said Hazel. "Why don't you stretch out on the sofa, so's you can rest your handicap bag on the pillows, honeybunch." She was referring to the forty-seven pounds of birdshot in a canvas bag, which was padlocked around George's neck. "Go on and rest the bag for a while," she said. "I don't care if you're not equal to me for a while."

George weighed the bag with his hands. "I don't mind," he said. "I don't notice it any more. It's just a part of me."

"You've been so tired lately—kind of wore out," said Hazel. "If there was just some way we could make a little hole in the bottom of the bag, and just take out a few of them lead balls. Just a few."

> Using common phrases such as "kind of wore out" instead of the more formal and correct usage makes the dialogue sound realistic.

"Two years in prison and two thousand dollars fine for every ball I took out," said George. "I don't call that a bargain."

"If you could just take a few out when you came home from work," said Hazel. "I mean—you don't compete with anybody around here. You just sit around."

"If I tried to get away with it," said George, "then other people'd get away with it—and pretty soon we'd be back to the dark ages again, with everybody competing against everybody else. You wouldn't like that, would you?"

"I'd hate it," said Hazel.

"There you are," said George. "The minute people start cheating on laws, what do you think happens to society?"

If Hazel hadn't been able to come up with an answer to this question, George couldn't have supplied one. A siren was going off in his head.

"Reckon it'd fall all apart," said Hazel.

The society's philosophy is explained through the dialogue between Hazel and George.

"What would?" said George blankly.

"Society," said Hazel uncertainly. "Wasn't that what you just said?"

"Who knows?" said George.

The television program was suddenly interrupted for a news bulletin. It wasn't clear at first as to what the bulletin was about, since the announcer, like all announcers, had a serious speech impediment. For about half a minute, and in a state of high excitement, the announcer tried to say, "Ladies and gentlemen—"

He finally gave up, handed the bulletin to a ballerina to read.

"That's all right—" Hazel said of the announcer, "he tried. That's the big thing. He tried to do the best he could with what God gave him. He should get a nice raise for trying so hard."

"Ladies and gentlemen—" said the ballerina, reading the bulletin. She must have been extraordinarily beautiful, because the mask she wore was hideous. And it was easy to see that she was the strongest and most graceful of all the dancers, for her handicap bags were as big as those worn by two-hundred-pound men.

And she had to apologize at once for her voice, which was a very unfair voice for a woman to use. Her voice was a warm, luminous, timeless melody. "Excuse me—" she said, and she began again, making her voice absolutely uncompetitive.

The figurative description of the ballerina's voice as a "warm, luminous, timeless melody" is an example of a metaphor.

"Harrison Bergeron, age fourteen," she said in a grackle squawk, "has just escaped from jail, where he was held on suspicion of plotting to overthrow the government. He is a genius and an athlete, is underhandicapped, and should be regarded as extremely dangerous."

Hazel and George hear of their son's arrest on television, which demonstrates how disconnected from their children parents have become.

A police photograph of Harrison Bergeron was flashed on the screen—upside down, then sideways, upside down again, then right side up. The picture showed the full length of Harrison against a background calibrated in feet and inches. He was exactly seven feet tall.

This sentence provides the topic for the rest of the paragraph.

The rest of Harrison's appearance was Halloween and hardware. Nobody had ever borne heavier handicaps. He had outgrown hindrances faster than the H-G men could think them up. Instead of a little ear radio for a mental handicap, he wore a tremendous pair of earphones, and spectacles with thick wavy lenses. The spectacles were intended to make him not only half blind, but to give him whanging headaches besides.

Scrap metal was hung all over him. Ordinarily, there was a certain symmetry, a military neatness to the handicaps issued to strong people, but Harrison looked like a walking junkyard. In the race of life, Harrison carried three hundred pounds.

And to offset his good looks, the H-G men required that he wear at all times a red rubber ball for a nose, keep his eye-brows shaved off, and cover his even white teeth with black caps at snaggle-tooth random.

"If you see this boy," said the ballerina, "do not—I repeat, do not—try to reason with him."

There was the shriek of a door being torn from its hinges.

The comparison to an earthquake is another figure of speech, or trope.

Screams and barking cries of consternation came from the television set. The photograph of Harrison Bergeron on the screen jumped again and again, as though dancing to the tune of an earthquake.

George Bergeron correctly identified the earthquake, and well he might have—for many was the time his own home had danced to the same crashing tune. "My . . ." said George, "that must be Harrison!"

The realization was blasted from his mind instantly by the sound of an automobile collision in his head.

When George could open his eyes again, the photograph of Harrison was gone. A living, breathing Harrison filled the screen.

Clanking, clownish, and huge, Harrison stood in the center of the studio. The knob of the uprooted studio door was still in his hand. Ballerinas, technicians, musicians, and announcers cowered on their knees before him, expecting to die.

"I am the Emperor!" cried Harrison. "Do you hear? I am the Emperor! Everybody must do what I say at once!" He stamped his foot and the studio shook.

Harrison's statements shows the essence of his personality. He thinks he is great and wants people to see his greatness.

"Even as I stand here—" he bellowed, "crippled, hobbled, sickened—I am a greater ruler than any man who ever lived! Now watch me become what I *can* become!"

Harrison tore the straps of his handicap harness like wet tissue paper, tore straps guaranteed to support five thousand pounds.

Harrison's scrap iron handicaps crashed to the floor.

Harrison thrust his thumbs under the bar of the padlock that secured his head harness. The bar snapped like celery. Harrison smashed his headphones and spectacles against the wall.

He flung away his rubber-ball nose, revealed a man that would have awed Thor, the god of thunder.

"I shall now select my Empress!" he said, looking down on the cowering people. "Let the first woman who dares rise to her feet claim her mate and her throne!"

A moment passed, and then a ballerina arose, swaying like a willow.

Harrison plucked the mental handicap from her ear, snapped off her physical handicaps with marvellous delicacy. Last of all, he removed her mask.

She was blindingly beautiful.

A short sentence, set off in its own paragraph, makes the point about the ballerina's beauty strongly.

"Now—" said Harrison, taking her hand, "shall we show the people the meaning of the word dance? Music!" he commanded.

The musicians scrambled back into their chairs, and Harrison stripped them of their handicaps, too. "Play your best," he told them, "and I'll make you barons and dukes and earls."

The music began. It was normal at first—cheap, silly, false. But Harrison snatched two musicians from their chairs, waved them like batons as he sang the music as he wanted it played. He slammed them back into their chairs. The music began again and was much improved.

Harrison and his Empress merely listened to the music for a while—listened gravely, as though synchronizing their heartbeats with it. They shifted their weights to their toes.

Harrison placed his big hands on the girl's tiny waist, letting her sense the weightlessness that would soon be hers.

And then, in an explosion of joy and grace, into the air they sprang!

Not only were the laws of the land abandoned, but the law of gravity and the laws of motion as well.

They reeled, whirled, swiveled, flounced, capered, gamboled, and spun.

They leaped like deer on the moon.

The studio ceiling was thirty feet high, but each leap brought the dancers nearer to it.

It became their obvious intention to kiss the ceiling.

They kissed it.

And then, neutralizing gravity with love and pure will, they remained suspended in air inches below the ceiling, and they kissed each other for a long, long time.

It was then that Diana Moon Glampers, the Handicapper General, came into the studio with a double-barreled ten-gauge shotgun. She fired twice, and the Emperor and the Empress were dead before they hit the floor.

The murder happens without warning, adding to its power to shock the reader.

Diana Moon Glampers loaded the gun again. She aimed it at the musicians and told them they had ten seconds to get their handicaps back on.

It was then that the Bergerons' television tube burned out.

Hazel turned to comment about the blackout to George. But George had gone out into the kitchen for a can of beer.

George came back in with the beer, paused while a handicap signal shook him up. And then he sat down again. "You been crying?" he said to Hazel.

"Yup," she said.

"What about?" he said.

"I forget," she said. "Something real sad on television."

"What was it?" he said.

"It's all kind of mixed up in my mind," said Hazel.

"Forget sad things," said George.

"I always do," said Hazel.

"That's my girl," said George. He winced. There was the sound of a riveting gun in his head.

"Gee—I could tell that one was a doozy," said Hazel.

"You can say that again," said George.

"Gee—" said Hazel, "I could tell that one was a doozy."

The closing line repeats one of the main themes of the story–that Hazel is unable to think for herself.

CHAPTER 6

Respond in Writing Respond to "Harrison Bergeron." What and who is the target of the satire? What techniques does Vonnegut use to make fun of people? In what ways is the story ironic?

Develop Your Own Ideas Work with your classmates to develop ideas that you might incorporate into a satirical short story.

Small Groups: In small groups, use a planning guide like the following to generate ideas about what could go into an effective satire. Take into account what you have written about in response to "Harrison Bergeron," and also think about other satires you are familiar with through film, television, literature, art, and other sources. Note the variety of techniques used for satire, including irony, exaggeration, distortion, absurdity, parody, and reversal. **Reversal** is the technique of presenting the opposite of what is expected.

Satire Planning Guide	
The setting of the story	
The person or people being satirized	
What the people do to merit being the target of a satire	
The specific acts, belongings, appearance, and other traits that could be exaggerated for a satiric effect	
The specific techniques you might use for the satire and how you might use them	

Whole Class: Make a master chart of all of the ideas generated by the small groups to get a broader idea of what tools are available for satire.

Write About It You will next write a satire in which you mock the foolishness of a person or type of person, a set of people, or the whole of humanity. You may choose from any of the following topics, audiences, and forms.

Possible Topics	Possible Audiences	Possible Forms
• a person or group who take themselves very seriously • a person or people who act in opposition to how they tell others to act • a person or group of people who are greedy • leaders who are more interested in personal power than in public welfare	• the people being satirized • people who think the target of the satire is silly • people who think the target of the satire is offensive • people who are being cautioned not to act like the target of the satire	• a short story • a song • a poem • a graphic novel • an animation

A **short story** is a well-developed fictional narrative of characters resolving a conflict or problem.

The freedom of expression that makes fiction writing so exciting also makes it challenging. With no limits on the characters and story, how do you decide where to start? A practical way to begin is with one of the basic story elements—the conflict, theme, characters, point of view, setting, or plot. Sometimes you will already have a vague idea of a character, place, or theme that you can develop. At other times you will simply have to choose one of the story elements and use a technique like freewriting or clustering to see where it takes you. In any case, you should view the prewriting strategies in this section as suggestions only. Choose, adapt, and add strategies according to your own writing needs.

For information about how the elements of a short story contribute to its meaning, turn to pages 200 and 334–335.

1 Developing a Conflict or Problem

A story revolves around some conflict or problem, and the **plot** unfolds as the main character or characters go about resolving that problem. Out of conflict comes the tension, the interest, and the suspense. In a well-told story, the reader wonders, "What will happen next?" "How will the character handle that?" "Will he or she succeed?" "How will it all end?" The following chart shows examples of different types of conflicts.

TYPES OF CONFLICTS	
Between the main character and another character	a son complains to his parents about his curfew
Between the main character and a natural force	a young driver must deal with a suddenly flooded road
Between forces or feelings inside the main character	a competitor is torn between her conscience and the temptation to sabotage a rival

You do not have to stretch your imagination in your search for a conflict. A problem as ordinary as trying to catch a bus can make an exciting story if the tale is well told. To find story ideas, just open your eyes and ears to conflicts big and small that surround you. What do your friends and family talk about? What do you hear about on television or on the radio? What do you read about in newspapers, books, and online? Then think about your own life. What conflicts or problems did you face today, a few days ago, a few months ago, or a few years ago?

Start by brainstorming for conflicts. List conflicts that come to mind when you think about school, sports, family, friends, work, the past, the future, and the world. Think about seemingly small problems as well—a baseball error, a threatening rain cloud, an empty fuel tank, or an unexpected visitor. Search your journal for ideas. Then talk to people you know. What bothers them? What kinds of conflicts have they faced?

PROJECT PREP Prewriting *Possible Conflicts*

In your writing group, discuss possible conflicts to include in your story. For Harrison Bergeron, there was a conflict between Harrison and the government. What might serve as the primary conflict in the stories being developed by the authors in your writing group?

CHAPTER 6

2 Choosing a Theme

Your main purpose in writing a story is to entertain your reader. You may also want to leave the reader with some message, idea, or question. The main idea you want to plant in the reader's mind is called the **theme.** Usually you imply the theme, rather than state it directly. You arrange details and events so that your reader can **infer,** or figure out, your message. What theme might you, as a reader, infer from the following passage about a man who sees his father again after 25 years?

MODEL: Implied Theme

That day a quarter of a century later when I visited him on the plantation—he was standing against the sky, smiling toothlessly, his hair whitened, his body bent, his eyes glazed with dim recollection, his fearsome aspect of twenty-five years ago gone forever from him—I was overwhelmed to realize that he could never understand me. . . . I forgave him and pitied him as my eyes looked past him to the unpainted wooden shack.

—Richard Wright, *Black Boy*

While the author never states it, the implied theme suggests that "growing up means being able to see your parents as people." (See page 201 for more on implying.)

As you prepare to write a story, you may already have a theme. At other times you may have only a notion about an event or a character with no thought about a theme. In that case start with what you have and freewrite or cluster. After you have generated some possible themes, use the following questions to help you decide on one.

CHOOSING A STORY THEME

- Is the idea one I really care about?
- Is the idea one my audience will care about?
- Can I fit interesting characters and plot around it?

PROJECT PREP **Prewriting** *Theme*

In your writing group, discuss each author's story in terms of the theme being developed. In satire, the theme is often centered on one common type of human vice or folly. What is each author's theme, and how might he or she develop it In the story?

3 Sketching Characters

The main character of a story can be a person, a bumblebee, the wind, or a robot, but there must be someone—or something—working through a conflict. In other words, there can be no story without characters.

How do you create characters? You might start with your journal. Whom have you met or seen lately? What intriguing conversations have you heard? Make lists of people, real or fictional, that you found interesting, surprising, or curious.

To help you develop characters, learn to be a careful observer. Focus on details of how people move and stand, how they sound, and how they look and dress. Make notes in your journal for use later. You can also create a cluster of details to help you. Your objective is to use such details to develop characters.

MODEL: Character Cluster

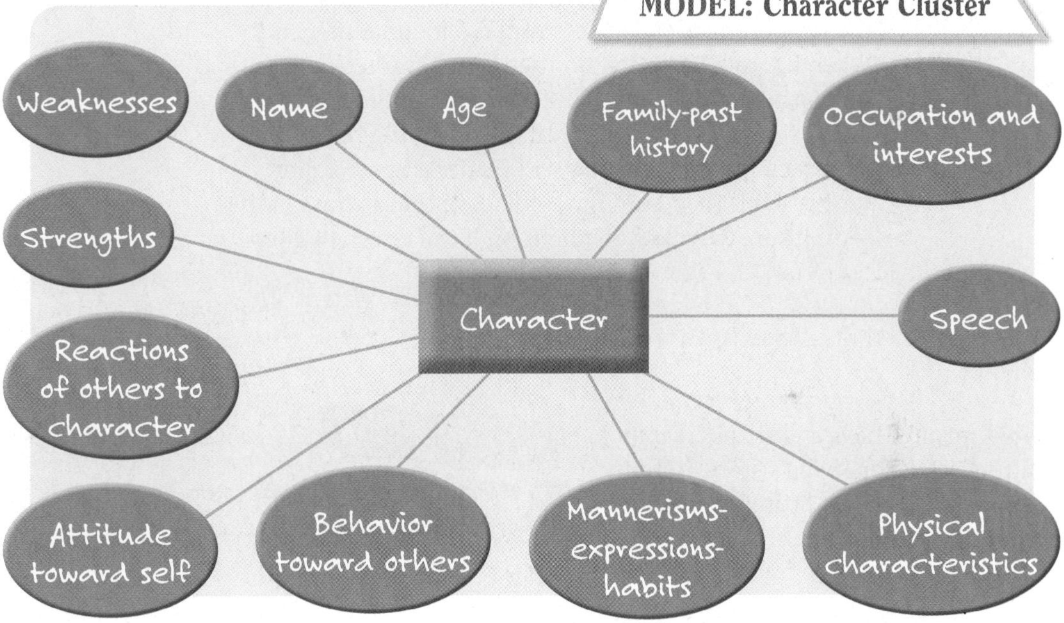

PROJECT PREP *Prewriting* ***Character Traits***

In your writing group, discuss the traits each author's main characters will have. Note that a satire does not necessarily have a sympathetic protagonist; the protagonist may be the story's most flawed and ridiculous character. Or, the protagonist may be a relatively innocent character who encounters other flawed and ridiculous characters. Also note that some authors use animals to represent people, as when the pigs take over the farm in George Orwell's *Animal Farm*. In order to mock a human folly, what sorts of characters should each author develop for the story?

4 Framing Your Story

Once you have your conflict and characters in mind, you can frame your story by creating a meaningful setting and deciding on what point of view to use.

Creating a Setting

The **setting** shows when and where a story takes place. The location sometimes creates a mood that sets up the events of the plot. For example, what events might occur in the following setting?

MODEL: Setting

Every change of season, every change of weather, indeed, every hour of the day, produces some change in the magical hues and shapes of these mountains. . . . When the weather is fair and settled, they are clothed in blue and purple, and print their bold outlines on the clear evening sky; but some-times, when the rest of the landscape is cloudless, they will gather a hood of gray vapors about their summits, which, in the last rays of the setting sun, will glow and light up like a crown of glory.

—Washington Irving, "Rip Van Winkle"

The "magical hues and shapes" set a fitting scene for Irving's story. In the same way, choose a fitting setting for your own story.

Writing Tip

Match the setting of your story to the action, mood, and characters' feelings.

Choosing a Point of View

Every story has a **narrator** who tells what happens and provides the **point of view**—the eyes through which the reader views the events. Once you choose a point of view, use it consistently throughout the story. The following chart summarizes your main choices.

POINT OF VIEW	NARRATOR'S ROLE IN THE STORY
First-Person	• Observes or participates in the action • Tells personal observations and thoughts • Uses first person pronouns such as *I, we*
Third-Person Objective	• Observes one character who participates in the action • Tells words, actions, and feelings of the character and observations about him or her • Uses third person pronouns *he, she, they*
Third-Person Omniscient ("All-Knowing")	• Observes but does not participate in the action • Tells the words, actions, and feelings as well as the observations about all characters • Uses third person pronouns *he, she, they*

CHAPTER 6

The **first-person point of view** gives your story a personal touch, for the reader can see and feel what one character sees and feels.

> As **I** dashed to the bus stop, the only thing on **my** mind was that **I** had to catch that bus!

With **third-person limited,** the tone is less personal. However you can show a bit more of what takes place around a character.

> As **Ronald** dashed to the bus stop, the only thing on **his** mind was that **he** had to catch that bus! **He** didn't even realize that **he** had dropped **his** fare as **he** ran.

Third-person omniscient is not personal in tone, but it allows you to reveal everything that takes place.

> As **Ronald** dashed to the bus stop, the only thing on **his** mind was that **he** had to catch that bus! Unfortunately, the **bus driver** had other ideas.

PROJECT PREP Prewriting *Narrator*

For each author, discuss who would be the best narrator for the story, and what that narrator should know and tell. For example, should the target of the satire tell the story and reveal his or her foolishness by what he or she says? Or should a different character, or perhaps a third-person narrator, tell the story? No matter which narrator each author selects, consider what point of view would be available and how that character would relate the story.

5 Planning Story Events

Before drafting your story, you need to have an idea of where the events lead, who is involved, and where and when it all takes place. You may decide later to change your plan, but it is helpful to list the main story elements before you begin to write.

Outlining the Story

Prepare a written sketch of the important elements of your story to make sure that the parts fit together.

Title A good **title** grabs the reader and hints at the story's theme or events.

Setting Describe the setting for your story. Remember that the setting often mirrors the feelings of the main character and relates to the central conflict.

Characters Next on your outline, describe the characters. Start with a brief description of the main character or characters, and then describe the others. (page 197)

Conflict State in a sentence the problem confronting the main character. (pages 194–195)

Plot The series of events in a story make up the **plot.** Most plots have a definite shape. The first major event triggers the conflict, which builds to a critical point, or **climax,** and is finally resolved. In your sketch, list the events in the order in which you will tell them. Ask yourself, "What will happen next?" Let the events lead you, step-by-step, to the climax of the plot. Usually you will relate events in **chronological order,** the order in which they occur. However, you may use **flashback**—that is, opening in the middle of the action and going back to the beginning. Flashback is a good way to build suspense.

Resolution The resolution is more than just an ending. It is a working out of the conflict by the character. The resolution can be either happy or sad, but it must bring together the events of the story. Complete your sketch by writing the resolution—the way the conflict is settled.

PROJECT PREP *Prewriting* **Plot**

With your setting, characters, primary conflict, and narrator selected, discuss with the members of your writing group how to structure the plot. What events will comprise your story? How will they illustrate the story's theme? Help each author to develop a plot structure that will enable readers to see what they are satirizing.

Think Critically

Implying

In "Harrison Bergeron," Vonnegut did not come out and say that society in 2081 was an affront to human potential, but he implied it. When you **imply,** you provide details and clues that hint at a theme or conclusion. These clues lead the reader to draw **inferences.**

> The next thing he remembered was Esme sitting by the bed holding his hand. . . . Behind her nurses came and went in a dizzy world of motion, their double-peaked hats like gulls in a high wind. . . .
>
> —Lawrence Thornton, *Imagining Argentina*

The reader must draw on background knowledge to conclude that the setting is a hospital. A chart like the one below can help you imply unstated facts or conclusions. On the left, list story elements. On the right, list details that imply those elements.

STORY ELEMENT	DETAILS
Character trait: kindness	soft, gentle voice; cared for the trembling, injured puppy
Setting: just before band practice	students getting to their seats, cacophony of warm-up notes, award banners on the walls
Event: a party	large crowd, blaring music, colorful balloons

Thinking Practice

Write a passage that implies a setting, event, or trait from your story or use any of the suggestions below. Make a chart like the one above to list descriptive details for your passage.

1. **Character traits:** anxiety, determination, greed
2. **Settings:** a farm, a bowling alley, a fire station
3. **Events:** end of a race, a graduation, a boat capsizing

Next try to imply the truth about a character in your satire. In a satire, exaggerating a flaw is an effective technique of implying criticism. Identify some traits of a character in your satire to distort to an absurd state so your readers can infer your real meaning.

The Power of Language

Adjectives: Come Early or Lately

Adjectives add specific details that make rich writing as they add style, voice, and content. They usually "come early," before the noun or the pronoun they modify. Sometimes, however, adjectives "come lately," following the noun or the pronoun, either in the middle or at the end of the sentence. Notice in the following sentences how Kurt Vonnegut, Jr., provides extra details in the story. The noun or pronoun that the adjectives modify is underlined.

> "Even as I stand here—" he bellowed, "crippled, hobbled, sickened—I am a greater ruler than any man who ever lived!
>
> Clanking, clownish, and huge, Harrison stood in the center of the studio.
>
> A police photograph of Harrison Bergeron was flashed on the screen—upside down, then sideways, upside down again, then right side up.

Since these adjectives are details not essential to the basic meaning of the sentence, they are separated from the rest of the sentence with a comma or a dash.

Try It Yourself

Start with the following sentence. Change the period to a comma, and add at least two adjectives describing the handicap harness.

> Because he was a genius and an athlete, Harrison wore a handicap harness.

Now write four sentences. In two, use two or more nonessential adjectives that come before the noun or pronoun they describe, as in the first two examples. In two, use adjectives that come after the noun or pronoun they describe. Try to write sentences on the topic you've chosen for your project and include them in your draft. Later, check your draft to see if you'd like to add additional adjectives.

Punctuation Tip

When modifiers "come lately" within a sentence, they are enclosed in commas or dashes.

When modifiers "come lately" at the end of a sentence, they are preceded by a comma or dash.

When modifiers do not "come lately," but instead occur at the very beginning of the sentence, they are followed by a comma.

Writing a Short Story — Drafting

As you draft your story, remember that your goal is to produce a workable narrative—one that can be shaped and polished into a solid story. You can use a variety of types of writing in different parts of your story to achieve your goal, including narration, description, and informative writing. With your story outline in hand, write your first draft. The strategies that follow will help guide your thoughts as you write the beginning, middle, and end of your story.

The Beginning

The opening of a story should engage and orient the reader by setting out a problem, situation, or observation as well as its significance. It should also establish point of view and introduce the narrator and/or characters. Following are common ways to begin a story.

STARTING A STORY

Method	Example
Introduction of the Main Character	I am Gimpel the fool. I don't think myself a fool. On the contrary. But that's what folks call me. —Isaac Bashevis Singer, "Gimpel the Fool"
Details about the Character or Setting	As Mr. John Oakhurst, gambler, stepped into the main street of Poker Flat on the morning of the twenty-third of November, 1850, he was conscious of a change in its moral atmosphere since the preceding night. —Bret Harte, "The Outcasts of Poker Flat"
General Statement	The "Red Death" had long devastated the country. No pestilence had ever been so fatal, or so hideous. —Edgar Allan Poe, "The Masque of the Red Death"
Action	The old woman and her daughter were sitting on their porch when Mr. Shiftlet came up their road for the first time. —Flannery O'Connor, "The Life You Save May Be Your Own"

Each of these story beginnings extends a hook to catch the reader's attention. Why is Gimpel a fool? What has changed in Poker Flat? What were the hideous results of the "Red Death"? Who is Mr. Shiftlet, and why will he be important to the story? Once you have hooked your readers, pull them in with additional information.

HERE'S HOW

Guidelines for Beginning a Story

- Set the time and place.
- Introduce the main character or characters.
- Provide needed background information.
- Set the plot in motion with a triggering event.
- Establish the conflict or problem.

CHAPTER 6

THE MIDDLE

As you develop your story, keep in mind that a story is made up of connected events. Each should build on the previous event and lead to the next event, right up to the climax. To show these connections and to guide your reader through the events, use transitions such as *at the same time* or *the next day.* If you choose to include flashback, be sure it is clearly marked by one of the following methods.

Showing Flashback with Spacing

Emma relaxed in the soft, plushy chair and opened the book. She tried to read, but her thoughts escaped into the rainy night.

****

It had been raining that night too—a soothing sound interrupted by the sudden shriek of the phone.

Showing Flashback with Narrative

Emma relaxed in the soft, plushy chair and opened the book. She tried to read, but her thoughts traveled back to that night over a month ago. It had been raining then too, when the soothing sound of the raindrops was interrupted by the shriek of the phone.

As you write, picture your story unfolding like a movie. Jot down the details and focus on your characters. How do they look, sound, think, and speak? Then add dialogue to give your story life and sound. Notice how dialogue livens up the following story part.

No Dialogue	Emma was annoyed at being interrupted.
Dialogue	"What is it? I'm busy!" Emma complained.

Use the following guidelines to help you write the middle of your story.

HERE'S HOW

Guidelines for Drafting the Middle of a Story

- Tell the events in a logical and dramatic way, chronologically or with flashbacks.
- Use transitions to connect the events smoothly and clearly.
- Use dialogue to make your characters vivid, to show what characters are thinking, and to advance the plot.
- Use such narrative techniques as pacing, description, reflection, and multiple plot lines to develop experiences, events, and characters.

CHAPTER 6

The Ending

When you draft the end of your story, your goal is to leave your reader feeling satisfied. The reader may be sad or touched or surprised, but he or she should feel that the story has come to a fitting conclusion.

HERE'S HOW

Guidelines for Ending a Story

- Resolve the climax and complete the action of the plot by providing a conclusion that follows from and reflects on what is experienced, observed, or resolved over the course of the narrative.
- Use dialogue, action, or description to *show* what happens.

Practice Your Skills

Analyzing a Short Story

Reread "Harrison Bergeron" and write answers to the following questions.

1. Which method of beginning a story does Vonnegut use? Is there a triggering event? Has the author established a conflict or problem?
2. Are the events described by using chronological order or flashbacks? How does the dialogue contribute to the story's plot and characterizations?
3. What is the climax of the story? How is the action completed? In what ways does the ending seem fitting?

PROJECT PREP Drafting *First Version*

Take ideas you have discussed with your writing group and draft a version of your short story. For the satire, make certain that the theme becomes clear through your target's exaggerated follies, and that a conflict amplifies the effects of these techniques. Do your best to create complex, non-stereotypical characters and use a range of literary strategies to develop the conflict and enhance the plot. End with a satisfying resolution that follows from the narrated events.

Revising comes from the Latin word *revise,* meaning "to see again." However, the key to revising is to forget about *again* and concentrate on *see.* First you should detach yourself from your work and approach it as if you have never seen it before. Only then can you really evaluate what you have written.

Improving the Plot

Although a plot is a sequence of events, you cannot just string some events together and call it a plot. Read the two sequences below and think about how they are different.

Events Leila turned on the computer. She yawned. The phone rang. She answered it. She looked at her watch. She had dinner.

Plot Leila turned on the computer. She *had* to finish! The phone rang. She ignored it. The screen went blank. The lights went out. With a candle and pen and paper, she rewrote and finished her work.

In the first sequence, the only connection is that one event follows another. In the second sequence, however, all the events relate to Leila's work and the question of whether she will finish the job. Therefore, each event builds on the one before in a coherent pattern of rising action that leads to a particular outcome and tone. Look for that pattern when you revise a story and ask the following questions as you revise your plot.

HERE'S HOW

Guidelines for Improving the Plot

- Are the events arranged chronologically, except for flashbacks?
- Are flashbacks easily recognizable?
- Are transitions used to help show the passage of time?
- Does every event revolve around the central conflict?
- Is each event clearly linked to the events before and after?
- Did you use a range of techniques to enhance the plot?
- Does each event add to the tension and build to the climax?
- Does the resolution follow from and tie up the events?

Improving Characterization

When you breathe life into your characters, they will then breathe life into your story. As you read the excerpt below, see if you can identify the techniques that bring a stranger to life.

MODEL: Characterization

Elisa saw that he was a very big man. Although his hair and beard were greying, he did not look old. His worn black suit was wrinkled and spotted with grease. The laughter had disappeared from his face and eyes the moment his laughing voice ceased. His eyes were dark, and they were full of the brooding that gets in the eyes of teamsters and of sailors. The calloused hands he rested on the wire fence were cracked, and every crack was a black line. He took off his battered hat. . . .

He leaned confidentially over the fence. "Maybe you noticed the writing on my wagon. I mend pots and sharpen knives and scissors. You got any of them things to do?"

"Oh, no," she said quickly. "Nothing like that." Her eyes hardened with resistance.

—John Steinbeck, "The Chrysanthemums"

In this brief passage, Steinbeck portrays a man who breaks down the resistance of his customers. Here are three techniques that writers, including you, can use.

HERE'S HOW

Guidelines for Improving Characterization

- Add natural-sounding dialogue that fits the personality.
- Add descriptive details about appearance and behavior.
- Show how the character acts and how others react to him or her.

Improving Style

Like every other writer, you have your own writing **style**—that is, your own way of putting words and sentences together. You can adjust your style to get the effect you want. When you review the draft of your story, ask yourself the following questions.

HERE'S HOW

Guidelines for Improving Style

- Does your style fit the theme, events, and characters?
- Is the style appropriate for your audience?
- Do all words and sentences fit the style and characters?
- Does the language fit the tone, or feeling, of the story?
- Is the tone consistent throughout the story?
- Did you use precise words and phrases and sensory language to convey vivid pictures?
- Are the length and structure of your sentences appropriate?
- Do your sentences have a smooth rhythm and flow?

As you continue to work on your draft, use the following checklist to help you evaluate what you have written.

Evaluation Checklist for Revising

- ✓ Does the beginning engage and orient the reader, start the conflict, and present the setting and main characters? (pages 203–204)
- ✓ Do you present events chronologically or through flashbacks? Do all events relate to the conflict and build to a climax? Do you use transitions to connect the events smoothly? (pages 200–205)
- ✓ Did you use such narrative techniques as pacing, description, reflection, and multiple plot lines to develop the story? (page 205)
- ✓ Does the resolution follow from and reflect on the narrated events and observations? (page 205)
- ✓ Are the dialogue and description lively? (pages 204–205)
- ✓ Is your theme clearly implied? (page 196)
- ✓ Is your point of view clear? (pages 198–199)

PROJECT PREP Revising *Plot, Character, and Style*

1. Use the guidelines above to improve the plot of your story. As you revise, think about how the sequence of events establishes a pattern of rising action.
2. Use the guidelines above to revise the scene by strengthening the characterization.
3. Revise the story once more, this time looking closely at your writing style. Use the guidelines above to enhance your style.
4. Share your completed draft with the members of your writing group. For each author, give suggestions on how to make the point of the satire more humorous. In addition, give each author feedback on the presentation, including attention to grammar, punctuation, and spelling, so that readers can clearly follow the story.

editing

Make the following wordy passages more "fuel efficient" by cutting out needless words and phrases.

> The speaker who was talking said that telling the truth was such a precious commodity that it should be used by people in their communications only when the occasion was really special.

The checklist on page 208 can help you as you edit. As always, pay special attention to the Power Rules.

The Language of Power Pronouns

Power Rule: Use subject forms of pronouns in subject position. Use object forms of pronouns in object position.(See pages 781–789.)

See It in Action In mainstream or Standard English, subject pronouns *(I, you, he, she, it, we, they)* are used in the subject position. Object pronouns *(me, you, him, her, it us, them)* are used as objects. Notice the use of pronouns in the following examples from "Harrison Bergeron."

Subject Form	They were equal every which way.
Object Form	The spectacles were intended to make him not only half blind, but to give him whanging headaches besides.

In short stories and other fiction, writers sometimes use dialect forms of pronouns to make dialogue sound realistic. For example, they might write, "Me and him are going to play football" instead of "He and I are going to play football." In formal writing, however, writers use mainstream forms.

Remember It Record this rule and example in the Power Rule section of your Personalized Editing Checklist.

Use It Read through your short story and circle each pronoun. Check each one to make sure you have used subject and object forms appropriately unless you are using non-mainstream forms to show character.

PROJECT PREP Editing *New Draft*

Based on the feedback from your writing group, produce a new draft of your story. For the satire, make revisions that will enhance your readers' enjoyment of its lessons.

Using a Six-Trait Rubric *Stories*

Ideas	**4** The plot, setting, characters, and dialogue are original and creative.	**3** The plot, setting, characters, and dialogue are effective.	**2** Most aspects of the plot, setting, characters, and dialogue are effective.	**1** Most aspects of the plot, setting, characters, and dialogue are ineffective.
Organization	**4** The organization is clear with abundant transitions.	**3** A few events or ideas seem out of place or transitions are missing.	**2** Many events seem out of place and transitions are missing.	**1** The order of events is unclear and hard to follow.
Voice	**4** The narrator's voice sounds natural and the point of view is effective.	**3** The narrator's voice sounds mostly natural and the point of view is effective.	**2** The narrator's voice sounds unnatural at times and the point of view seems forced.	**1** The narrator's voice sounds mostly unnatural and the point of view is forced and ineffective.
Word Choice	**4** Specific words and sensory images help readers picture characters and setting.	**3** Words are specific and some words appeal to the senses to help readers picture characters and setting.	**2** Some words are overly general and do not bring characters or setting into focus.	**1** Most words are overly general and do not bring characters or setting into focus.
Sentence Fluency	**4** Varied sentences flow smoothly and dialogue reflects characters.	**3** Most sentences are varied and flow smoothly, and dialogue reflects characters.	**2** Some sentences are choppy and dialogue seems forced.	**1** Sentences are choppy and not varied, and dialogue seems forced or is missing.
Conventions	**4** Conventions are correct, and Power Rules are followed except for effect.	**3** Conventions are mainly correct, and Power Rules are followed except for effect.	**2** Some conventions are incorrect, but Power Rules are followed except for effect.	**1** There are many errors and at least one accidental failure to follow a Power Rule.

PROJECT PREP *Editing* *Final Suggestions*

Exchange papers with one other student and read each other's stories. Make final suggestions in any areas in which the author might Improve the story, and then prepare a final copy of your satire.

Writing a Short Story Publishing

In the publishing stage, you make a final copy for your intended audience. You might also want to read your story aloud to one or more family members, and give them copies to read on their own afterwards. You might send your story by e-mail or regular mail to friends, pen pals, or family members who live far away. If your school has a literary magazine, consider submitting your story to it. If your school does not have such a magazine, consider starting one.

PROJECT PREP Publishing *Final Copy*

Make a final copy of your story, and publish it through the medium you chose (page 193) or some other appropriate medium. You might create an online anthology of satires, organized by themes or vices, so that others may enjoy your creative criticism of humanity.

Writing a Play

"The play's the thing," wrote William Shakespeare. When people see a stage play for the first time in their lives, they often agree that this medium has a kind of magic which no other literary form possesses.

> A **play** is a piece of writing containing action that can be presented on a stage by live actors.

What then is the difference between fiction and drama? Read the following excerpt from *Death of a Salesman* by Arthur Miller once for pleasure. As you reread, think about why a play might be more effective than a short story for portraying certain life experiences. Then you will begin to understand the unique magic that this literary form possesses.

Death of a Salesman

Willy: Pst! Pst!

Howard: Hello, Willy, come in.

Willy: Like to have a little talk with you, Howard.

Howard: Sorry to keep you waiting. I'll be with you in a minute.

Willy: What's that, Howard?

Howard: Didn't you ever see one of these? Wire recorder.

Willy: Oh. Can we talk a minute?

Howard: Records things. Just got delivery yesterday. Been driving me crazy, the most terrific machine I ever saw in my life. I was up all night with it.

Willy: What do you do with it?

Howard: I bought it for dictation, but you can do any thing with it. Listen to this. I had it home last night. Listen to what I picked up. The first one is my daughter. Get this. [*He flicks the switch and "Roll out the Barrel" is heard being whistled.*] Listen to that kid whistle.

Willy: That is lifelike, isn't it?

Howard: Seven years old. Get that tone.

Willy: Ts, ts. Like to ask a little favor if you . . .

[*The whistling breaks off, and the voice of* HOWARD's *daughter is heard.*]

His Daughter: "Now you, Daddy"

Howard: She's crazy for me! [*Again the same song is whistled.*] That's me! Ha! [*He winks.*]

Willy: You're very good!

[*The whistling breaks off again. The machine runs silent for a moment.*]

Howard: Sh! Get this now, this is my son.

His Son: "The capital of Alabama is Montgomery; the capital of Arizona is Phoenix; the capital of Arkansas is Little Rock; the capital of California is Sacramento..."[*and on, and on.*]

Howard [*holding up five fingers*]: Five years old, Willy!

Willy: He'll make an announcer some day!

His Son [*continuing*]: "The capital . . ."

Howard: Get that—alphabetical order! [*The machine breaks off suddenly.*] Wait a minute. The maid kicked the plug out.

Willy: It certainly is a—

Howard: Sh, for God's sake!

His Son: "It's nine o'clock, Bulova watch time. So I have to go to sleep."

Willy: That really is—

Howard: Wait a minute! The next is my wife. [*They wait.*]

Howard's Voice: "Go on, say something." [*Pause.*] "Well, you gonna talk?"

His Wife: "I can't think of anything."

Howard's Voice: "Well, talk—it's turning."

His Wife: [*shyly, beaten*]: "Hello." [*Silence.*] "Oh, Howard, I can't talk into this . . ."

Howard: [*snapping the machine off*]: That was my wife.

Willy: That is a wonderful machine. Can we—

Howard: I tell you, Willy, I'm gonna take my camera, and my bandsaw, and all my hobbies, and out they go. This is the most fascinating relaxation I ever found.

Willy: I think I'll get one myself.

Howard: Sure, they're only a hundred and a half. You can't do without it. Supposing you wanna hear Jack Benny, see? But you can't be at home at that hour. So you tell the maid to turn the radio on when Jack Benny comes on, and this automatically goes on with the radio . . .

Willy: And when you come home you . . .

Howard: You can come home twelve o'clock, one o'clock, any time you like, and you get yourself a Coke and sit yourself down, throw the switch, and there's Jack Benny's program in the middle of the night!

Willy: I'm definitely going to get one. Because lots of time I'm on the road, and I think to myself, what I must be missing on the radio!

Howard: Don't you have a radio in the car?

Willy: Well, yeah, but who ever thinks of turning it on?

Howard: Say, aren't you supposed to be in Boston?

Willy: That's what I want to talk to you about, Howard. You got a minute? [*He draws a chair in from the wing.*]

Howard: What happened? What're you doing here?

Willy: Well . . .

Howard: You didn't crack up again, did you?

Willy: Oh, no. No . . .

Howard: Geez, you had me worried there for a minute. What's the trouble?

Willy: Well, tell you the truth, Howard. I've come to the decision that I'd rather not travel any more.

Howard: Not travel! Well, what'll you do?

Willy: Remember, Christmas time, when you had the party here? You said you'd try to think of some spot for me here in town.

Howard: With us?

Willy: Well, sure.

Howard: Oh, yeah, yeah. I remember. Well, I couldn't think of anything for you, Willy.

Willy: I tell ya, Howard. The kids are all grown up, y'know. I don't need much any more. If I could take home—well, sixty-five dollars a week, I could swing it.

Howard: Yeah, but Willy, see I—

Willy: I tell ya why, Howard. Speaking frankly and between the two of us, y'know—I'm just a little tired.

Howard: Oh, I could understand that, Willy. But you're a road man, Willy, and we do a road business. We've only got a half–dozen salesmen on the floor here.

Willy: God knows, Howard, I never asked a favor of any man. But I was with the firm when your father used to carry you in here in his arms.

Howard: I know that, Willy, but—

Willy: Your father came to me the day you were born and asked me what I thought of the name of Howard, may he rest in peace.

Howard: I appreciate that, Willy, but there just is no spot here for you. If I had a spot I'd slam you right in, but I just don't have a single solitary spot.
[*He looks for his lighter.* Willy *has picked it up and gives it to him. Pause.*]

Willy: [*with increasing anger*]: Howard, all I need to set my table is fifty dollars a week.

Howard: But where am I going to put you, kid?

Willy: Look, it isn't a question of whether I can sell merchandise, is it?

Howard: No, but it's a business kid, and everybody's gotta pull his own weight.

Willy: [*desperately*]: Just let me tell you a story, Howard—

Howard: 'Cause you gotta admit, business is business.

Willy: [*angrily*]: Business is definitely business, but just listen for a minute. You don't understand this. When I wasa boy—eighteen, nineteen—I was already on the road. And there was a question in my mind as to whether selling had a future for me. Because in those days I had a yearning to go to Alaska. See, there were three gold strikes in one month in Alaska, and I felt like going out. Just for the ride, you might say.

Howard: [*barely interested*]: Don't say.

Willy: Oh, yeah, my father lived many years in Alaska. He was an adventurous man. We've got quite a little streak of self-reliance in our family. I thought I'd go out with my older brother and try to locate him, and maybe settle in the North with the old man. And I was almost decided to go, when I met a salesman in the Parker House. His name was Dave Singleman. And he was eighty-four years old, and he'd drummed merchandise in thirty-one states. And old Dave, he'd go up to his room, y'understand, put on his green velvet slippers—I'll never forget—and pick up his phone and call the buyers, and without ever leaving his room, at the age of eighty-four, he made his living. And when I saw that, I realized that selling was the greatest career a man could want. 'Cause what could be more satisfying than to be able to go, at the age of eighty-four, into twenty or thirty different cities, and pick up a phone, and be remembered and loved and helped by so many different people? Do you know? When he died—and by the way he died the death of a salesman, in his green velvet slippers in the smoker of the New York, New Haven, and Hartford, going into Boston—when

CHAPTER 6

he died, hundreds of salesmen and buyers were at his funeral. Things were sad on a lotta trains for months after that. [*He stands up.* Howard *has not looked at him.*] In those days there was personality in it, Howard. There was respect, and comradeship, and gratitude in it. Today, it's all cut and dried, and there's no chance for bringing friendship to bear—or personality. You see what I mean? They don't know me any more.

Howard: [*moving away, to the right*]: That's just the thing, Willy.

Willy: If I had forty dollars a week—that's all I'd need. Forty dollars, Howard.

Howard: Kid, I can't take blood from a stone, I—

Willy: [*desperation is on him now*]: Howard, the year Al Smith was nominated, your father came to me and—

Howard: [*starting to go off*]: I've got to see some people, kid . . .

Willy: [*stopping him*]: I'm talking about your father! There were promises made across this desk! You musn't tell me you've got people to see—I put thirty-four years into this firm, Howard, and now I can't pay my insurance! You can't eat the orange and throw the peel away—a man is not a piece of fruit! [*After a long pause*] Now pay attention. Your father—in 1928 I had a big year. I averaged a hundred and seventy dollars a week in commissions.

Howard: [*impatiently*]: Now Willy, you never averaged—

Willy: [*banging his hand on the desk*]: I averaged a hundred and seventy dollars a week in the year of 1928! And your father came to me—or rather, I was in the office here—it was right over this desk—and he put his hand on my shoulder—

Howard: [getting up]: You'll have to excuse me, Willy, I gotta see some people. Pull yourself together. [*Going out*] I'll be back in a little while.

Finding Ideas for a Play

When choosing a potential subject for a play or scene, remember that it must be dramatic. As in a work of fiction, a play is built on **conflict**. The characters are at a crossroads in their lives: they may be falling in or out of love, falling ill or dying, recovering, giving birth, or suffering the hardships of war or the problems of ordinary life. Whatever the specifics, the characters are faced with a problem that poses obstacles for them to try to overcome.

The scene you read from *Death of a Salesman* was only a small part of the play. In this chapter, you will be writing one scene rather than an entire play. A **scene** is a portion of a play that contains a single unified action taking place in one setting or place. Most good scenes convey a sense of ongoing drama. However, scenes are like chapters in a novel; they do not contain a complete plot. A **scene** captures one point in a plot's development, and it may lead to, or hint at, things that have happened before and things that might happen later.

To find possible subjects for a scene, you must look at the really important parts of your life, the lives of other people with whom you have come into contact, or the lives of people whom you imagine. In addition to reading and writing in your journal, you can make a cluster diagram, freewrite, or ask yourself questions to probe the drama of life.

Practice Your Skills

Finding Ideas for a Scene by Self-Questioning

Freewrite responses to each question below. Save your work.

1. Who are the most interesting people you know? Why? What would happen if two or three of them got together and interacted?
2. What events in your life have cost you the greatest struggle?
3. What public events have made you feel most deeply about the world you live in?
4. What would you be like if you lived among different people?
5. How would you change if you had to go to war, became very ill, or if you fell in love or got married?
6. What would be the most surprising thing that could happen to you or to the interesting people you named above? How would you, or they, respond, and what would be the result?

Crafting a Theme

A play, like a story, should have a **theme**—the main idea or message you want the audience to take away. A theme can be explicit and stated directly by a character, or it can be implicit, not stated directly so that the audience infers the message. In a scene from the contemporary play *West Side Story*, which is based on Shakespeare's play *Romeo and Juliet*, the theme of hate destroying all that is good is explicitly stated through Maria's dialogue: "All of you! You all killed him!... Not with bullets, or guns, with hate. Well, now I can kill, too, because now I have hate!" The theme of two star-crossed lovers in a doomed relationship that is beyond their control is inferred through action, events, and characters' dialogue. Think about the theme you want to convey in your play, and keep it in mind as you write.

Developing Characters

To create a scene, you must have more than a meaningful subject; you must have clear-cut characters and action. The action may consist largely of talk, but the talk must move the characters toward some meaningful change in their lives. The vast majority of dramatic scenes contain two to four characters; this is the most practical size group in which to stage an intense conversation that an audience can follow. Use this size group of characters in your scene.

Remember that a role in a play can be interpreted and performed in different ways by different actors. Also remember that the audience, sitting at a distance from the actors, cannot always see every detail of their features. To begin sketching out a character, therefore, you do not need to write a complete physical or psychological profile. Instead, you should write a brief, vivid outline of the character's major traits. There is no need to say, "John has a small but annoying wart on his left thumb"—a detail you might include in a short story. Nor should you specify that John has blue eyes—an actor who plays the role may have brown eyes. You might say, instead, "John, who is 17, moves awkwardly, like a boy who has grown quickly; he seems friendly and open to experience, but not naive."

Practice Your Skills

Sketching Characters

Think back to the people you mentioned as most interesting and dramatic. Write concise, vivid character sketches that would help a director find actors to play their roles.

Creating a Setting

One of the most fascinating challenges for playwrights and directors is to create action within a confined setting. Many plays only have one setting, often a room or some isolated location such as a battlefield or a ship at sea. This is simply because a play occurs in a theater—a specific, small space in which only certain things are physically possible. When a play changes settings, the scenery and set furniture are usually moved between acts or scenes; or a revolving stage may be used; or the director or playwright may be able to think of a brilliant new way to present two or more settings at once. It is also possible to stage a play without scenery, so that the bare stage can represent any and every location in turn.

Practice Your Skills

Visualizing Settings

Jot down a list of at least ten kinds of places that you think might be viable settings for dramatic scenes. Do not include a battlefield or a ship at sea. Do include at least five different kinds of rooms. For each possible setting, jot down a brief description of one or more specific dramatic actions that might take place there.

Establishing Tone and Mood

Once you have established a setting for your play, you can think about creating its tone and mood. **Tone** is the writer's attitude toward the characters and events. **Mood** is the feeling or atmosphere the audience draws from the setting and characters. Tone and mood influence one another and are often closely intertwined. The setting, props, costumes, lighting, music, and sound effects all help set the tone and mood of a play. Characters portray their moods and set the tone through dialogue and body language. For example, one character may react to a tense situation by telling a joke and laughing. Another character may react to the same situation with stony silence and folded arms. Develop the tone and mood you want in your play with dialogue and stage directions.

CHAPTER 6

Writing Dialogue

When most people think of plays, they probably think of dialogue being spoken. **Dialogue** is the medium in which the action in most plays transpires. Even more than fiction or real life, the dialogue in a play expresses emotion and conveys meaning. The **exposition** of a play—the essential information that the audience must understand about the dramatic situation and its background—is conveyed through dialogue.

An audience sitting in a darkened theater cannot read a description of a landscape or a biographical summary of a character's past. Much of this kind of information must be put into the mouths of characters. For example, a character entering the stage might say, "Whew, it sure has been a hot day out in the alfalfa field." Thus, from one line, the audience learns something about three things: (1) the character's feelings: he is hot and tired; (2) the character's occupation: he works on a farm; (3) the setting: a farmhouse.

At the same time, the dialogue must sound natural. Each character should speak in an individual voice that suits his or her role.

Practice Your Skills

Writing Dialogue

Review the scene from *Death of a Salesman* that focuses on its closing moments. Write a continuation of the conversation between Willy and Howard, which might occur immediately after the scene ends. Your conversation should contain at least two separate speeches for each character. Try to be true to the spirit of the two different characters as portrayed in the scene. Write only the dialogue; do not worry about descriptions at this point. Save your work.

Writing Stage Directions

When you read the scene from *Death of a Salesman,* you undoubtedly noticed the brief passages in italics and brackets that described the characters' actions. These are called **stage directions.** As a general rule of thumb, you should try to make the dialogue stand on its own when possible, and provide stage directions only when they will noticeably enhance a reader's or actor's understanding of the action and characters.

If you are describing scenery or a character's gesture or a **prop** (short for *property,* a physical object used in a play), describe only the details that are necessary and that the audience would notice. Here are some useful guidelines for selecting what to put into stage directions.

HERE'S HOW

Guidelines for Writing Stage Directions

- At the beginning of the scene, write a brief description of the set.
- When a new character enters the scene for the first time, provide a thumbnail description of the character's appearance and, if you want, personality.
- Indicate which character the speaker is talking to only when there is more than one possibility and the distinction is important. Indicate important breaks in dialogue—if, for instance, there is a pause or if the characters laugh.
- Indicate a speaker's emotion or tone of voice if it may not be clear from the dialogue alone—for example, "Howard [*impatiently*]".
- Indicate significant movements and gestures on the part of a character, such as "Willy [*stopping him*]".
- Do not indicate small-scale details that make no difference to the action, the characterization, the mood, or the meaning, or that would vary with each actor.
- Keep the language of stage directions clear and simple.

Practice Your Skills

Writing Stage Directions

Return to the new conversation that you wrote for the characters in *Death of a Salesman* and do the following tasks.

1. Use the guidelines above to add at least two necessary stage directions.
2. Separately, write two or more stage directions that you think would be possible for this conversation, but that you feel are not necessary.
3. Explain why the items are, in your opinion, unnecessary or necessary.

PROJECT PREP Changing Genres *From Story to Scene*

Choose a section from your story to use as the basis of a brief dramatic scene. With your writing group, discuss the different techniques you would use as a dramatist.

In the Media

Across the Media: Photography

With a few well-chosen words on paper, you can bring a whole new personality and character to life. The visual media can also create rich characters and suggest relationships. Using shape, line, color, and texture, the photograph below conveys a vivid personality inside those shoes. What kind of character do you think this man has? What do you think he does for a living?

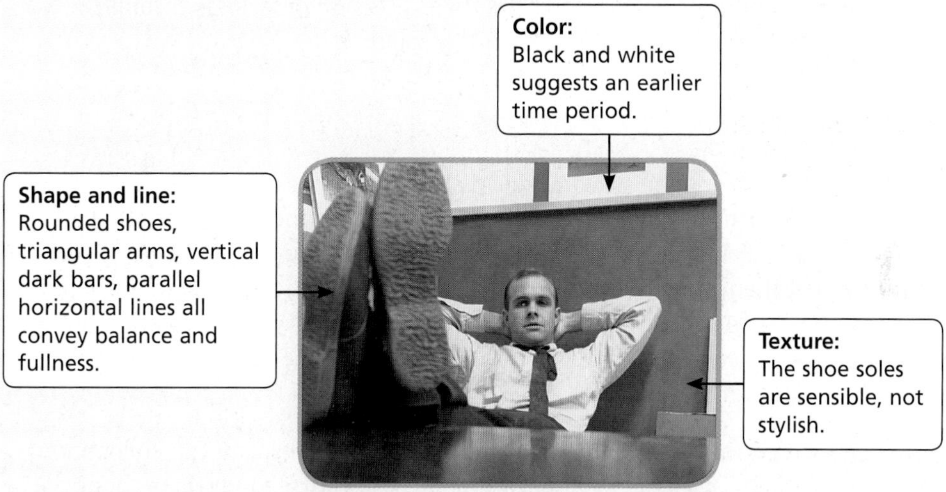
Color: Black and white suggests an earlier time period.
Shape and line: Rounded shoes, triangular arms, vertical dark bars, parallel horizontal lines all convey balance and fullness.
Texture: The shoe soles are sensible, not stylish.

Now look at the photograph below. In a paragraph, describe the relationship this picture conveys. Explain how each design element contributes to the overall effect and message.

Bring your own or a borrowed camera to class. Take photos of at least two students together. As you pose your subjects, ask yourself what relationship you wish to show. Create a classroom photo gallery of the finished work.

Writing a Poem

Even more than a short story, poetry is an outlet for our deepest emotions, insights, sensations. According to American poet Edwin Arlington Robinson, poetry allows us to say "something that cannot be said"—at least not in ordinary language. In this section you will use language to express special feelings. In other words, you will learn to write a poem.

Poetry is a form of writing that encourages the expression of feelings through sound, images, and other imaginative uses of language.

1 Finding Ideas for Poems

Time and again when you are asked to find a subject to write about, you are advised to look inside yourself. In no form of writing is this advice more appropriate than in poetry. A poem is an expression of what you feel, what you sense, and what you dream. In a way, then, you are the subject of every poem you write. A poem about a bird, for example, is not really about the bird, but it is about your impression of the bird. When you are looking for a subject, think about whether your feeling about the subject is right for a poem.

Since your poem is really about your own feelings and impressions, you can choose any subject, from a towering wave to a crawling caterpillar. Ask yourself questions about the events and scenes in your life. For example, how does it feel to miss a bus? What comes to mind when you see the color orange? To get your thoughts moving, list some general subject areas in a chart and then brainstorm examples.

IDEA CHART

Events	hockey goal, traffic jam, graduation
Scenes	moon landscape, beach in winter, football fields
Sensations: Taste	burning hot chili, too-sweet honey, lemonade

Explore ideas from your chart by brainstorming, freewriting, clustering, or questioning. Your goal is to spark your imagination and find sensations, images, and emotions you want to write about.

Practice Your Skills

Charting to Find Ideas for a Poem

Choose item 1 and four others to create an idea chart like the one above. List at least ten ideas for each subject. Then save your charts in your writing folder.

1. growing up
2. emotions
3. special objects
4. imaginary places
5. historical events
6. sensations: sounds
7. sensations: textures
8. humorous incidents
9. hopes and dreams
10. movement

Practice Your Skills

Freewriting to Find Ideas for a Poem

Freewrite a response to each of the questions that follow. Keep your notes for later use.

1. What does the word *maturity* mean to you?
2. Why do you like—or dislike—eating spaghetti?
3. What thoughts do you have about violence in the media?
4. What does a snowy day bring to mind?

Practice Your Skills

Drawing on Poetic Tradition to Find Ideas for a Poem

In addition to exploring your own feelings and experiences, explore the world of poetry to find ideas. In your writing group, brainstorm a list of your favorite poems. Discuss what forms you are familiar with, such as sonnets, ballads, limericks, haiku, or free verse. Consider what subjects are treated in each of these forms. Then freewrite a list of subjects that you might consider for different forms. Save your work.

PROJECT PREP Changing Genres ***From Story to Poem***

In your writing group, discuss how you could reduce your story or some part of it to a poem. What would you eliminate In order to make this transformation? What might you add for poetic effect? Produce a draft of a poetic version of your story based on your understanding of poetic conventions and forms.

2 Using Sound, Rhythm, and Meter

Sound

All creative writing uses the way words sound, but sound in poetry is basic. Most poems are strongest when read aloud. The chart below lists sound devices that poets use to appeal to the ear of a reader. Use these devices when you write poetry.

SOUND DEVICES	
Onomatopoeia	use of words whose sounds suggest their meaning ***belch, hum, murmur, plop, fizz, click, splash, moo, thump***
Alliteration	repetition of a consonant sound at the beginning of a series of words ***B**right **b**lack-eyed creature, **b**rushed with **b**rown* —Robert Frost, "To a Moth Seen in Winter"
Consonance	repetition of a consonant sound or sounds, used with different vowel sounds, usually in the middle or at the end of words ***clitter clatter** on the **cellar stair***
Assonance	repetition of a vowel sound within words From the m**o**lten-g**o**lden n**o**tes —Edgar Allan Poe, "The Bells"
Repetition	repetition of a word or phrase *O **Captain!** My **Captain! rise up** and hear the bells;* ***Rise up—for you** the flag is flung—**for you** the bugle trills* —Walt Whitman, "Oh Captain! My Captain!"
Rhyme	repetition of accented syllables with the same vowel and consonant sounds The woods are lovely, dark, and d**eep** But I have promises to k**eep** And miles to go before I sl**eep** —Robert Frost, "Stopping by Woods on a Snowy Evening"

To develop ideas for a poem, put together a "word pool"—a list of words and phrases to draw from as you write. Start by freewriting words and phrases. Then focus on each term separately, and list other words and phrases connected with it by sound or by meaning.

Rhythm and Meter

The rhythm of a poem is a distinct beat produced by the pattern of accented and unaccented syllables. In the lines below, / marks accented syllables and ˘ marks unaccented syllables. Read the lines and notice the strong and regular rhythm.

> Because I could not stop for Death—
> He kindly stopped for me—
>
> —Emily Dickinson, from "Because I Could Not Stop for Death"

When a poem follows a strict rhythm, it has a certain **meter,** or rhythm that can be counted. The most common meter is a line of five accented syllables called **iambic pentameter** as in the example below.

> The **sha**ttered **wa**ter **made** a **mis**ty **din.**
> Great **waves** looked **o**ver **oth**ers **com**ing **in,**
> And **thought** of **do**ing **some**thing **to** the **shore**
> That **wa**ter **ne**ver **did** to **land** bef**ore.**
>
> —Robert Frost, from "Once by the Pacific"

Poetry without a meter, or strict beat, is called **free verse.** Poems in free verse like the following example have a rhythm, but the rhythm does not follow a pattern.

> They eat beans mostly, this old yellow pair.
> Dinner is a casual affair.
> Plain chipware on a plain and creaking wood,
> Tin flatware.
>
> —Gwendolyn Brooks, from "The Bean Eaters"

Practice Your Skills

Developing Sound Devices

For each subject, make a word list to develop sound devices like those on the chart on page 224. Save your work.

1. yourself today and four years ago
2. a person or object in motion
3. a month
4. a color

PROJECT PREP Revising Using Feedback

In your writing group, discuss the poem that you drafted in terms of the poetic conventions of sound, meter, and rhythm. Help each author add elements in these areas to improve the impact of the poem.

3 Using Figurative Language

Poetry touches both the ear and the eye—the mind's eye. To help the reader "see" mental pictures, poets use vivid, imaginative language called figurative language. The following chart shows examples of figurative language in poetry.

CHAPTER 6

FIGURATIVE LANGUAGE	
Imagery	use of concrete details to create a picture or appeal to senses other than sight *And the sky went wan, and the wind came cold,* *And the sun rose dripping, a bucketful of gold.* —Edna St. Vincent Millay, "Recuerdo"
Simile	comparison of unlike things, using the word *like* or *as* *And like a thunderbolt he falls.* —Alfred, Lord Tennyson, "The Eagle"
Metaphor	implied comparison of unlike things, without *like* or *as* *Life is a broken-winged bird* *That cannot fly.* —Langston Hughes, "Dreams"
Personification	use of human qualities to describe something non-human *Shadows hold their breath.* —Emily Dickinson, "A Certain Slant of Light"
Paradox	statement containing seemingly contradictory terms or ideas *The Child is father of the Man* —William Wordsworth, "My Heart Leaps Up When I Behold"
Hyperbole	use of exaggeration or overstatement *And fired the shot heard 'round the world.* —Ralph Waldo Emerson, "Concord Hymn"
Oxymoron	use of opposite or contradictory terms such as *living death, dark snow, happy misery* *Beautiful tyrant! fiend angelical!* —William Shakespeare, *Romeo and Juliet*
Symbol	use of an object or action to stand for another, as the "ball of gold" below stands for our illusions *A man saw a ball of gold in the sky;* *He climbed for it,* *And eventually he achieved it—* *It was clay.* —Stephen Crane, "A Man Saw a Ball of Gold in the Sky"

Collect interesting images, comparisons, and other figures of speech in your journal. Then use them to enrich your poetry or to lead you to productive new ideas.

Sometimes images will pop into your mind. More often, however, you need to guide your thoughts. Directed relaxation is a good way to start. As you close your eyes, take a deep breath and relax. Direct your thoughts to the subject of your poem. Take the subject apart and focus on one part or aspect at a time, examining it from different angles, at different times, and as different people. Follow your thoughts closely, keeping all your senses alert. If something wonderful occurs to you, jot it down but try not to interrupt the flow of images. Then, after you have buried yourself in your ideas for a while, do some freewriting about what you thought, imagined, and sensed.

Practice Your Skills

Developing Figurative Language for Poems

In the activity on page 225, you developed sound devices for three poems. Now explore figurative language for each poem by using the technique of directed relaxation described above. Save your notes for later use.

PROJECT PREP Revising *Figurative Language*

In your writing group, discuss each author's satirical poem in terms of its possibilities for including figurative language. Help each author think of figurative expressions that would help the poem come alive for readers.

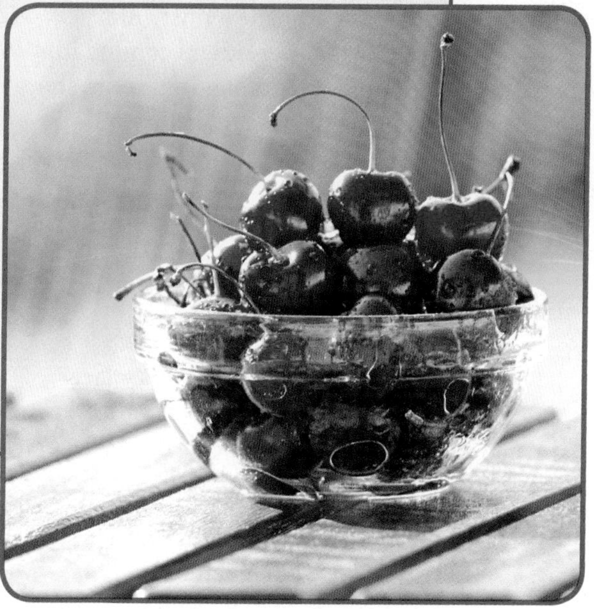

4 Choosing a Form

The patterns of rhyme, rhythm, and lines determine the form of a particular poem. For example, a poem about a train might have a strong, driving meter and a formal structure, while a poem about a cloud might have no meter and a loose structure.

You can choose a form for your poem in different ways and for different reasons. If your prewriting activities point you in a definite direction, then select a form that fits your subject, theme, sound devices, and figures of speech. Change the form, however, if you find it does not seem appropriate for your thoughts.

CHAPTER 6

Sometimes you will choose a form first. Then you can use it to set your thoughts in motion. If you want to write a structured poem, then you might write lines that fit the structure. If you want to write free verse, then you might begin with some freewriting.

Try fitting your form to your mood or tone. For example, you might choose a tightly structured poem to convey a direct, formal, or bright feeling. On the other hand, you might choose a loose structure to help you capture a brooding, thoughtful feeling.

Rhymed Poem

A rhymed poem usually has a pattern, or **rhyme scheme,** that can be shown by letters of the alphabet.

The shattered water made a misty **din.** a
Great waves looked over others coming **in,** a
And thought of doing something to the **shore** b
That water never did to land **before.** b

—Robert Frost, from "Once in the Pacific"

Does the road wind up-hill all the **way?** a
    Yes, to the very **end.** b
Will the day's journey take the whole long **day?** a
    From morn to night, my **friend.** b

But is there for the night a resting-**place?** a
    A roof for when the slow dark hours **begin.** b
May not the darkness hide it from my **face?** a
    You cannot miss that **inn.** b

Shall I meet other wayfarers at **night?** a
    Those who have gone **before.** b
Then must I knock, or call when just in **sight?** a
    They will not keep you standing at that **door.** b

—Christina Rossetti, from "Up-Hill"

The day is **ending,** a
The night is **descending;** a
The marsh is frozen,
The river **dead.** b

Through clouds like **ashes** c
The red sun **flashes** c
On village windows
That glimmer **red.** b

—Henry Wadsworth Longfellow, from "Afternoon in February"

When lines have similar rhyme schemes and rhythms, they are often grouped into stanzas. The preceding poems also have meter. The first poem has five accents per line, while the second has two.

The following poem, with three accented syllables per line, follows another rhyme scheme; some of the rhymes—such as purple/circle—are half rhymes created by assonance.

Taught Me Purple

My mother taught me **purple** a
Although she never **wore it.** b
Wash-gray was her **circle,** a
The tenement her **orbit.** b
My mother taught me **golden** c
And held me up to **see it,** d
Above the broken **molding,** c
Beyond the filthy **street.** d
My mother reached for **beauty** e
And for its lack she **died,** f
Who knew so much of **duty** e
She could not teach me **pride.** f

—Evelyn Tooley Hunt

The rhyme schemes shown—*aabb, abab, aabccb,* and *ababcdcdefef*—are common patterns, but you may choose any scheme that allows you to express your ideas in rhyme. To help you find rhymes, you might consult a rhyming dictionary, in which words are grouped by their endings.

A number of poetic forms use rhyme. The table below describes a few of the more common rhyming forms.

SELECTED RHYMED POETIC FORMS	
Ballad	Poem that tells a story; narrative poetry. Many ballads use a four-line stanza called a **quatrain** with the second and fourth lines rhyming.
Sonnet	A form with several variations. The Shakespearean sonnet is a 14-line poem consisting of three quatrains, each with alternating rhymes, and a final couplet, a pair of rhymed lines.
Limerick	A humorous five-line poem with a rhyme scheme AABBA
Ode	A poem written in tribute to an inspirational subject. John Keats's "Ode on a Grecian Urn" and "Ode to a Nightingale" are early nineteenth-century versions of a form that goes back to Roman times.

FREE VERSE

Free verse is verse without meter but not without rhythm, for it uses the natural rhythm of the spoken language. A poem in free verse may or may not be rhymed, and the lines and stanzas, if any, may vary in length. The following poem by William Carlos Williams is written in free verse.

The Great Figure

Among the rain
and lights
I saw the figure 5
in gold
on a red
fire truck
moving
tense
unheeded
to gong clangs
siren howls
and wheels rumbling
through the dark city.

—William Carlos Williams

Unrhymed poems can also have very strict forms, such as the **cinquain,** a five-line poem with two syllables in the first line, four in the second, six in the third, eight in the fourth, and a return to two in the fifth.

Practice Your Skills

Writing Poetry in a Variety of Forms

Choose one rhymed form from the chart on page 230. Find out more about it and locate some examples in a library or online. Then, using any of the ideas you have collected, try writing a poem in that form. Using the same subject, write an unrhymed poem as well so you can see the limits and possiblities of each type.

Poetry Rubric You can use the rubric below to evaluate poetry.

Poetic Techniques	**4** The rhyme scheme (if used) and sound devices create a strong effect and help express a meaningful idea.	**3** The rhyme scheme (if used) and sound devices create a strong effect and help express an idea.	**2** The rhyme scheme (if used) is inconsistent but sound devices help express meaning.	**1** The rhyme scheme (if used) is inconsistent and few if any sound devices are used.
Figurative Language	**4** The poem is enriched by a wide variety of memorable figurative language.	**3** The poem is enriched by a variety of figurative language.	**2** The poem uses figurative language once or twice.	**1** The poem uses no figurative language.
Graphic Elements	**4** The poem uses line length, capitalization, and punctuation to express ideas precisely.	**3** The poem uses line length, capitalization, and punctuation to help express ideas.	**2** The poem uses line length, capitalization, and punctuation in uninspired ways.	**1** The poem's use of line length, capitalization, and punctuation seems unintentional.

PROJECT PREP Revising *Possible Forms*

In your writing group, discuss possible forms for a poem based on your satire. Help each author determine which form will work best. Then write a final version of your satirical poem and publish it through an appropriate medium.

TIME OUT TO REFLECT

You have now written literary works in three different forms: short story, play, and poem. Which form is your favorite and why? What did you learn about creative writing from this experience, and what did you learn about your own abilities as a writer?

Writing Lab

Project Corner

Get Creative

Make a Game

Create a board game based on your story. Consider the setting as the basis of the board, the players' path as the plot line, the pieces as the characters, and the destination as the climax.

Get Dramatic

Act It Out

Using one of the satires written by a member of your writing group as the basis, **write a play,** which you may either perform live before an audience or record to project on a screen.

Speak and Listen

Create Categories

Based on all of the satires written by members of your class, **categorize** the sorts of foolish behavior exhibited by people in society. Discuss what a satire might accomplish to change these behaviors.

Investigate Further

Research and Write

Read and watch a series of satires, considering the targets they skewer, the follies they mock, the techniques they employ, and the solutions they offer to the problem of human foolishness. **Write a short essay** summarizing how effective you think satires can be in changing society for the better.

In Everyday Life Dramatic Dialogue

Apply and Assess

1. You are a writer for *The Depths of My Heart,* a soap opera set in a small-town hospital. The next episode will introduce a new character, Terrence Stern. Terrence barely survived a plane crash and has just emerged from a long coma. He cannot remember his life as a top-secret government spy, nor can he remember his love for his physician, Dr. Beatrice Hart. ***Write dialogue*** for the scene in the next episode in which Terrence awakes from his coma. Use the dialogue to make your characters as vivid and convincing as possible. (You can find information on writing dialogue on page 219.)

In the Workplace Poem for an Advertisement

2. The Beauty Sleep Pillow Company has solicited poems for an advertising campaign pitching its new product, peacock feather pillows with alarm clocks built inside. The poem they are looking for will inform people that their pillows not only ensure a good night's sleep, but also help people wake up on time the next morning. ***Write a ten-line poem*** for the Beauty Sleep Pillow Company. Use rhyme in the poem, and include at least two instances of onomatopoeia. In addition, try to use a humorous tone for the poem. (You can find information on writing poems on pages 222–231.)

Timed Writing Short Short Story

3. Use the following passage as the beginning for a short short story:

> An hour into their mountain hike, Allessa and Erin stopped in their tracks and looked at each other. The clouds had drawn tight in the sky and the trail had darkened. The wind carried leaves and pine needles across their path. Then the sky opened and the rain poured down. With each thunderclap, their bones rattled. Within minutes they were soaked. They desperately needed to find shelter.

Include additional details and vivid descriptions about the scene and the characters involved. Use figurative language and sensory words. Be sure to choose an appropriate point of view, and to set the plot in motion with a triggering event. You have 30 minutes to complete your work.

Before You Write Sketch out your story using the information on pages 194–200.

After You Write Evaluate your work using the six-trait rubric on page 210.

Expository Writing

Expository writing presents information or offers an explanation or analysis.

Writing—both inside and outside school—is a way to explore subjects and learn about the world. As a part of your formal education, you will write many essays not only to explore subjects but also to share what you have learned with others.

Communicating facts and explanations in an interesting way is one of the primary tasks of the informative writer. Here are just a few kinds of information that writers provide to the public.

- **News stories inform citizens** about what is happening in the world, the nation, and the community.
- **Scientific reports inform scientists** and the community about new scientific advances.
- **Computer manuals teach the ordinary consumer** about the skills and tips necessary to make the most of high-tech equipment.
- **Biographies and histories give information** about important people and events.
- **Encyclopedias offer basic information** on a comprehensive array of subjects arranged alphabetically and sometimes by area.
- **Guidebooks answer travelers' questions** about places of interest.
- **The Internet provides nearly instantaneous updates** on topics ranging from late-breaking news to sports highlights to changes that are influencing everyday life.

Writing Project — Analytical

Point of View* *Write an analytical essay about a change that has happened during your lifetime.

Think Through Writing Throughout history, people have had to adapt to new situations. The invention of the car changed how people thought about travel. The development of the computer changed communication, the speed and accuracy of forecasting weather, and much else. Think of a change that has come about in your lifetime. It could be a new invention, an advanced version of an old invention, a new set of beliefs, new laws, new rules in a game, or any other change that requires people to adapt. Explain what this change is and how it has required people to change in order to adapt.

Talk About It In your writing group, discuss the writing you have done. What changes did you describe? What sorts of adaptations have been required by people to adjust to the change in circumstances?

Read About It The following article from *Mass High Tech, The Journal of New England Technology,* reports on how future homes will differ from current homes.

MODEL: Expository Writing

The future home offers efficiency, entertainment and advice

By James M. Connolly

So, you're a homeowner, the boss, king of the castle. Now, suppose that your home was in control, that it knew where you were along your commute home, or that your home "persuaded" you to save energy, exercise and eat right. So much for being king or queen of that castle.

The first sentence captures attention with informal language.

The home of the future is taking shape in high-end, custom-designed homes, houses wired by gadget geeks, and labs. Proven and new technologies are being pulled together in home-area networks by system integrators and architects responding to the demands of people who love their toys, care for the environment and hate fat utility bills. However, while the owners of multimillion-dollar homes will pay tens of thousands of dollars for customized touchscreen control over lights, heat, music and more, home automation hasn't developed into a wave yet because the mass market hasn't demanded it.

Using three phrases, starting with "love their toys" makes the sentence flow smoothly.

However, researchers at MIT are working on having the technologies ready for homeowners when that tipping point occurs. One element of the future home may be that it will use "context aware and persuasive technologies," according to Kent Larson, lead investigator for MIT's House_n initiative, a research group that explores new residential designs, materials and technologies.

One example of what House_n has prototyped is a thermostat that communicates with a GPS-enabled cell phone to know when the resident is enroute home and adjusts the temperature to a pre-set comfort level. But it can go still further, detailing how much energy it helped you save, perhaps by noting how many carbon-fuel power plants won't have to be built if everyone adopts similar technology.

The words "One example" connect what follows with the previous sentence.

"Persuasion is how it shows you the implications in savings of a higher temperature setting in the summer or a lower setting in the winter," said Larson.

Another House_n project uses persuasion through software on a PDA to encourage people to get more exercise and watch less TV. "It maintains a real-time activity count based on the exercise you are getting, your goals in limiting how much TV you watch, and it suggests alternative activities," said Larson.

While what Larson discusses is still in the lab, architect Joseph L. Luna, principal of the Luna Design Group in Lynnfield, brings today's technologies into the home, albeit some pretty expensive homes. Many feature centralized control of diverse systems, such as heating and cooling, lighting, home theater and computing, in addition to leading-edge, energy-saving windows, doors and insulation.

Starting a sentence with "While" provides a smooth transition to a related but different topic.

"This originally came out as bells and whistles and bragging rights at cocktail parties. Today we're looking at not only how integrated systems work for fun stuff like lighting and audio/video but for things like heating and cooling. You can see some cost savings by tying these systems together," said Luna.

While some concepts, such as home theater, have trickled down into mid-market residences, initiatives continue at the high end, according to Luna. Today, high-end home systems aren't about a single room but about extending home theater to any space with a TV, shades or blinds that open and close in response to sunrise and sunset, the ability to control every light from a single touchscreen, and room-level control of heating and cooling.

Specific examples help the reader understand and remember the general trends.

While high-end systems managing hundreds of elements require programming and specialized installers, Luna notes that companies such as Cutting Edge

Systems Corp. of Westford are offering the midmarket basic, pre-programmed packages of its custom systems.

The desire to go "green" is a driving force in new home design. Homeowners want to save energy and be environmentally responsible. But don't link that interest in home automation to the recent spikes in fuel prices, noted IDC research manager Jonathan Gaw. A $20 bump in the electric bill "doesn't get people running out to buy these things," he said.

The first sentence of the paragraph sets the topic for the rest of the paragraph.

Gaw said one persuasive technology is ready for tests in California where utilities will use advanced electric meters to show consumers in real time how much energy they are consuming, and, potentially, warn them of price hikes during peak usage periods.

Gaw cites one of the limitations on adoption of advanced home electronics, particularly in older homes. "I don't see any major stumbling blocks in terms of the capability of the technology. I see it as more of a marketing issue. What are the business cases? How do we sell it? How do we package it?" he said.

Quotations provide informed opinions to support general statements.

One homeowner who moved to green design is Jeff Fullerton, a consultant with Acentech of Cambridge. He renovated a century-old house in Somerville and incorporated spray-in insulation and geothermal heat. "The fact that we were able to drill a well in the city would surprise some people," he said.

Fullerton also incorporated sound-absorbing materials wherever possible. That makes sense; he's a sound consultant. Costing up to $50 per square foot today, those materials will be more suited for the average home, he said.

Not only are home components and controls changing. Larson predicts a move to plumbing and electric components that snap together, and homes that are computer configurable. Working off a standard design, home buyers would customize elements such as colors to their own tastes, as people do today with cars. In most cases, the architect notes, that approach "would eliminate people like me."

A surprising quotation ends the article with a memorable statement.

Respond in Writing Respond to James A. Connolly's account of how houses are changing. What do you like about these changes? Do any of them concern you?

Develop Your Own Details Work with your classmates to develop ideas that you might use to write about changes.

Small Groups: In your small group, discuss the writing you have done. Use an organizer like the following to help think of possible details for each author's description in each of the following categories.

Questions About a Change
• The setting of the change: What were things like when the change came about? • The change itself: How did it come about in the context of the setting you have described? • The types of adaptations: What did people have to do in order to succeed in the wake of the change? • The variety of reactions: What types of people adapted, and what types had difficulty adapting? • What followed from the change: What were the benefits and the problems?

Whole Class: Make a master chart of all of the ideas generated by the small groups to aggregate all of the perspectives on changes.

Write About It You will next write an analytical essay about a change that has happened during your lifetime.

Possible Topics	Possible Audiences	Possible Forms
• a change in technology, such as the development of sophisticated cell phones • a change in the rules of a sport, such as limited use of instant replay in baseball • a change in laws, such as rules governing the sharing of music over the Internet • a change in environment, such as the reduction in rainfall in a region	• people needing advice on how to adapt • people who develop technologies • people who are in charge of the rules for a game • judges, politicians, and others who affect how laws are written	• a guide to a new product • a critical magazine article • an informative magazine article • a blog

CHAPTER 7

An effective expository essay presents a subject that the writer knows well, feels strongly about, and has thought through or researched carefully. The prewriting stage includes all of the planning that precedes the writing of the first draft. Prewriting will help you discover subjects, develop ideas, and shape those ideas into an organized plan.

1 Getting the Subject Right

The best subjects for expository essays may come from your own interests. One way to discover subjects is to identify topics that you know about from your own experiences—in school, in extra-curricular activities, in your job, or elsewhere.

Discovering and Choosing a Subject

Start by using the prewriting strategies discussed in Chapter 1, such as taking stock of your interests, freewriting, and keeping a journal. Ask yourself questions about your interests, skills, and the books and magazines you have read.

The more enthusiastic a writer is about a subject, the better the essay that writer will produce. As you choose a subject from the many ideas you discovered, consider first and foremost which subject will interest you most. The following strategies will help you.

HERE'S HOW **Strategies for Choosing Subjects for Expository Essays**

- Choose a subject with depth and complexity that you would enjoy writing about.
- Choose a subject you know enough about now or can learn enough about later to develop adequately in a short essay.
- Choose a subject that will interest your readers.

Limiting and Focusing a Subject

Limiting your subject is the next step. A subject that is too broad will probably result in a poorly organized essay. A focused subject, on the other hand, will take on a sharp, clear form as you add specifics. Limit your subject by asking the following questions.

HERE'S HOW **Strategies for Limiting a Subject**

- What aspect of my subject do I want to explain to my readers?
- Who are my readers? What do they need to know to understand my subject?
- What tone is best suited to the message I wish to express?
- What insight or understanding can I draw from my subject?
- How can I express the main idea of my essay in one sentence?

Suppose the subject you chose was one you learned about in your history class—women spies during the American Civil War. The answers to the five questions for limiting a subject might look like the following.

- I would like to explain the similarities and differences between Belle Boyd (South) and Emma Edmonds (North).
- Since my readers may not have heard of these women, they will need background information.
- A serious tone is best suited to the message I wish to express.
- People who serve causes they believe in are motivated by a variety of forces.
- In their similarities and differences, Belle Boyd and Emma Edmonds reveal a variety of motivations that led them to serve causes in which they believed.

PROJECT PREP Prewriting ***Possible Subjects***

Based on the discussions you have had with your classmates, make a list of four possible topics for your expository writing project. For each possible topic, identify the audience for your project and the genre or form it would take. Evaluate its complexity to be sure it is suitable for a meaningful composition.

2 Exploring and Refining the Subject

GATHERING INFORMATION

Once you have limited your subject, you can begin to gather information that will help you explain it in an essay of three or more paragraphs. Research primary and secondary sources in your library or media center—magazines, newspapers, the Internet, and other sources. Evaluate each source for validity, reliability, and relevance. (See pages 303 and 402–405.) Gather information on a number of relevant perspectives on your subject. Your goal is to accumulate enough well-chosen details to provide substantial evidence for your thesis and to cover your subject effectively.

The specific types of details you select will usually indicate the method of development you should use. (See pages 22, 90, and 144.) You can find information about gathering information on pages 390–433 and about methods of development on pages 90–91 and 119–120.

TYPES OF DETAILS USED IN INFORMATIVE ESSAYS		
facts	analogies	similarities/differences
examples	incidents	quotations
concrete details	extended definitions	causes and effects

The following list of details is about the limited subject of the similarities and differences between Belle Boyd and Emma Edmonds. As you read the list, notice that the details are not yet arranged in any logical order.

MODEL: List of Details

- Belle Boyd—seventeen years old
- Belle Boyd—fun-loving, adventurous, warmhearted
- Emma Edmonds became a spy when the man she loved was killed.
- Boyd was a spy for the South; Edmonds for the North.
- both young and highly independent
- both passionately committed to their causes
- Boyd became a spy after her home was attacked.
- Edmonds was a master of disguise; disguised herself as a peddler to penetrate lines at Yorktown.
- Boyd delivered messages to J.E.B. Stuart and Stonewall Jackson.
- Boyd's cheerfulness led her to sing "Maryland, My Maryland" when she was imprisoned.

- George McClellan interviewed Edmonds for her job as spy.
- Edmonds faced many hardships—enemy fire and disease.
- Both worked as nurses.
- Edmonds's best work was to identify five Confederate spies.
- Boyd was a charmer; Edmonds, a masquerader.
- Boyd was inspired by Rose O'Neal Greenhow in Washington, D.C.
- Boyd's greatest success was helping Confederates recapture Front Royal.
- Boyd was surrounded by gaiety; knew how to make people admire her.
- Edmonds helped a dying Confederate soldier.

Developing a Working Thesis

Once you have gathered the information about your subject, you are ready to formulate a **working thesis**—a preliminary statement that expresses the main idea of your essay. A working thesis will help you keep your purpose clear and guide you as you select and organize your details. However, as you plan and draft, you may modify the thesis or even change it entirely. Later you will refine it into a final thesis statement.

HERE'S HOW

Steps for Developing a Working Thesis

- Look over your prewriting notes and the questions you answered to limit your subject.
- Write down your main idea.
- Look closely at your notes to see that your working thesis takes into account all your information and ideas.

Notice that the following working thesis takes into account all the ideas listed in the prewriting notes on pages 239–242.

EXAMPLE:

Working Thesis Belle Boyd and Emma Edmonds were brave and unique in their reasons for spying and the way they spied.

PROJECT PREP Prewriting *Working Thesis*

From your list of possible topics, choose one to pursue. Write a working thesis that will guide your drafting. It might fit in a frame like this: The development of [ ] has caused changes in [ ], and people who [ ] are likely to benefit the most from this change.

Think Critically

Constructing Analogies

When writing an expository essay, you may need to explain an unfamiliar idea. In such a case, you may wish to make a comparison, or draw an analogy. An **analogy** compares something unfamiliar to something familiar.

You can begin to build an analogy by focusing on the specific concept you want to clarify. For example, when writing about the complex activity of the human brain, you should focus on familiar, visible things that are complex and always busy, such as a highway with its cloverleaf, many lanes, and constant traffic. A brain is not exactly like a highway, but the comparison is close enough to introduce your readers to the unfamiliar subject.

One useful thinking strategy for working out analogies is to make a chart like the one that follows to compare familiar and unfamiliar ideas.

ANALOGY CHART

Unfamiliar Idea: Atom	Familiar Idea: Baseball
Nucleus: the center of the atom, but extremely small compared to the rest of the atom	A pitcher on the mound: the central figure of the game, but extremely small compared to the surrounding stadium
Electron cloud: a relatively large space surrounding the nucleus	The whole stadium: the large area surrounding the pitcher

Thinking Practice

Choose one of the following subjects or one of your choice and make an analogy chart.

1. the human eye
2. democracy
3. the movement of the planets
4. maintaining physical fitness

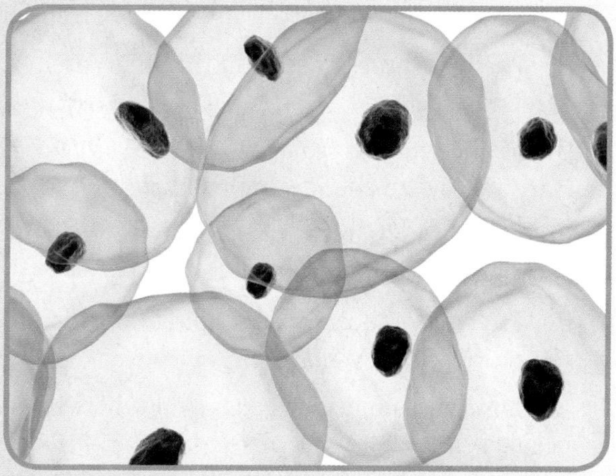

3 Organizing Your Essay

After you have gathered your details, developed a working thesis, and selected relevant details, you are ready to organize your ideas. Many writers find that the best way to organize supporting details is to outline them. The outlining process involves two steps: grouping details into meaningful categories that will help you examine and convey complex information and arranging those categories in a logical order with letters and numbers.

CHAPTER 7

Grouping Supporting Details into Categories

Group your list of supporting details into categories by asking yourself what one detail on your list has in common with some of the other details on your list. Review your list of supporting details to see what categories you can create. The following three categories were made from the list of details about Belle Boyd and Emma Edmonds on pages 241–242.

Writing Tip

Develop an **outline** that shows how you will organize the **main topics, subtopics,** and **supporting details** of your subject.

MODEL: Grouping Supporting Details

- both women young and highly independent — Similarities (Category 1)
- both worked as nurses
- both passionately committed to their causes
- at seventeen years of age, Boyd became spy after her home was attacked — Belle Boyd's Story (Category 2)
- Belle Boyd—fun-loving, adventurous, warmhearted
- Boyd delivered messages to J.E.B. Stuart and Stonewall Jackson
- Boyd's cheerfulness led her to sing "Maryland, My Maryland" when she was imprisoned
- Boyd was inspired by Rose O'Neal Greenhow in Washington, D.C.
- Boyd's greatest success was helping Confederates recapture Front Royal
- Boyd was surrounded by gaiety; knew how to make people admire her
- Boyd was a charmer

- Edmonds became a spy when the man she loved was killed
- Edmonds was a master of disguise
- disguised herself as a peddler to penetrate lines at Yorktown
- George McClellan interviewed Edmonds for her job as spy
- Edmonds faced many hardships—enemy fire and disease
- Edmonds's best work was to identify five Confederate spies
- Edmonds was a masquerader
- Edmonds helped a dying Confederate soldier

Emma Edmonds's Story (Category 3)

CHAPTER 7

Arranging Categories in Logical Order

The categories you create from your prewriting notes are the main topics you will use to support your thesis statement. The next step, then, is to arrange those topics in logical order. The following chart shows five common ways to organize ideas.

METHODS OF ORGANIZATION	
Chronological Order	Items are arranged according to when they happened in time.
Spatial Order	Items are arranged according to their location (top to bottom, side to side, inside out, near to far or the reverse).
Order of Importance	Items are arranged in order of importance, interest, or degree.
Developmental Order	Items are arranged in a logical progression, in which one idea grows out of another.
Comparison/Contrast	Items are arranged according to similarities and differences.

The categories of supporting details about Belle Boyd and Emma Edmonds address the similarities and differences between the two women. Therefore, the most logical arrangement for the categories is comparison and contrast. If a Roman numeral is assigned to each main category, a simple outline for the body of this essay would look like the one at the top of page 246.

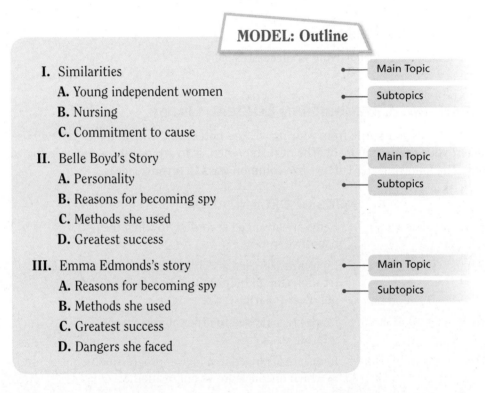

MODEL: Simple Outline

I. Similarities

II. Belle Boyd's story

III. Emma Edmonds's story

Once you have arranged your main categories logically and assigned them Roman numerals, continue the outlining process by grouping and arranging the items within each category. These items, called **subtopics,** are each assigned a capital letter.

MODEL: Outline

I. Similarities — Main Topic
- **A.** Young independent women — Subtopics
- **B.** Nursing
- **C.** Commitment to cause

II. Belle Boyd's Story — Main Topic
- **A.** Personality — Subtopics
- **B.** Reasons for becoming spy
- **C.** Methods she used
- **D.** Greatest success

III. Emma Edmonds's story — Main Topic
- **A.** Reasons for becoming spy — Subtopics
- **B.** Methods she used
- **C.** Greatest success
- **D.** Dangers she faced

The final step in outlining is to add any supporting points under the subtopics. Use only the most significant and relevant details. These points are assigned Arabic numerals. If you break them down further, use lowercase letters to show the divisions. A completed outline shows a paragraph-by-paragraph overview of an essay. The model that follows shows the correct form for an outline.

MODEL: Outline Form

I. Main topic

- **A.** Subtopic
  - **1.** Supporting point
  - **2.** Supporting point
    - **a.** Detail
    - **b.** Detail
- **B.** Subtopic
  - **1.** Supporting point
    - **a.** Detail
    - **b.** Detail
  - **2.** Supporting point

A final outline for the informative essay about Belle Boyd and Emma Edmonds might appear as follows:

MODEL: Final Outline

I. Similarities

- **A.** Young women, highly independent
- **B.** Dedication to nursing
- **C.** Commitment to cause

II. Belle Boyd's story

- **A.** Personality
  - **1.** Fun-loving nature, adventurous, warmhearted
  - **2.** Ability to charm people and make them admire her
- **B.** Reasons for becoming spy
  - **1.** Attack on home
    - **a.** How she handled attacking officers
    - **b.** How she gathered intelligence
  - **2.** Inspiration of Rose O'Neal Greenhow
- **C.** Methods she used
- **D.** Greatest success: recapture of Front Royal

III. Emma Edmonds's story

  A. Reasons for becoming a spy

  B. Methods she used

  C. Greatest success

    1. Disguise as Southern country boy

    2. Identification of five Confederate spies

  D. Dangers she faced

    1. Enemy fire

    2. Disease on scouting missions

CHAPTER 7

An outline makes it easy for you to see the arrangement of ideas in your essay without thumbing back and forth or, if you are using a word processor, scrolling up and down through the text. It also enables you to determine at a glance whether or where you need to add, cut, or move blocks of text. Use the following questions to check your outline.

HERE'S HOW

Questions for Checking an Outline

- Did you use Roman numerals for main topics?
- Did you use capital letters for subtopics?
- Did you use Arabic numerals for supporting points?
- If your supporting points can be broken down, did you use lowercase letters?
- Do you have at least two subtopics under each topic?
- If you include supporting points under subtopics, do you have at least two?
- If you break down your supporting points, do you have at least two details in the breakdown?
- Does your indentation follow the model on pages 247–248?
- Did you capitalize the first word of each entry?
- Are your main topics and each group of subtopics expressed in parallel forms?

PROJECT PREP Prewriting *Outline*

In your writing group, discuss possible ways in which to organize and present the information in your piece. Does your information conveniently fall into categories? Should you use the graphic organizer you developed in your small group to sequence the things you talk about? For each author, help to determine an effective way of presenting the information so that your readers may follow your thinking clearly and easily.

In the Media

Information Sources

The late 20th and early 21st centuries have been called the Information Age. Informational sources surround us, from the morning news feed and radio shows to the evening news. People who know what kinds of information sources are best for which purposes are ahead of the game. "They are," according to the American Library Association, "people prepared for lifelong learning, because they can always find the information for any task or decision at hand."

In primarily visual forms, information resources range from the two- to three-minute stories on the nightly news to 20-minute segments on newsmagazines or the in-depth probe in documentaries (usually 50 minutes or longer, carefully crafted and artfully edited video with multiple quotes and sources).

Similarly, coverage in newspapers tends to be fuller than on the nightly news but not as complete as in a newsmagazine. In addition, where broadcast coverage may have a camera on the scene within hours, print media take longer to cover a story.

Information resources on the Internet mix visual and print presentations. Often the basic coverage of a news story is comparable to that in a newspaper, but it is usually presented with links to related information.

Media Activity

To investigate the strengths and weaknesses of the various information resources, choose a story in the news and track its coverage in the newspaper, on television, and on the Internet. Write at least five paragraphs comparing, contrasting, and critiquing the coverage in the different media. Consider how well the different media offered multiple perspectives on the story. How do the validity and reliability of the sources compare?

Next think about how to locate information that would help you with an expository essay currently in progress. The information might come from the Internet, a book, periodicals such as magazines and newspapers, television programs, first-hand sources, or other places. Using your outline or a rough draft, identify where facts are missing and think of sources to consult in order to produce the most effective, informative, and valid writing possible.

The Power of Language

Parallelism: The Power of 3s

One way to make your writing clear and lively is to use a writing device called parallelism. **Parallelism** means using the same kind of word or group of words in a series of three or more. In his essay on future homes, Connolly uses parallel words and parallel phrases and quotes an expert who uses parallel short sentences.

> So, you're a homeowner, the boss, king of the castle.
>
> . . . architects responding to the demands of people who love their toys, care for the environment, and hate fat utility bills.
>
> "I see it as more of a marketing issue. What are the business cases? How do we sell it? How do we package it?"

Punctuation Tip

Use commas to separate items in a series. Use a comma before the final item, and the word *and*.

Try It Yourself

Write three sentences about the change that is the topic of your project or another change. Use parallelism in each sentence, and try to make each sentence the strongest it can be. If appropriate, use your sentences in your project draft. You can look for more places to add parallelism when you revise.

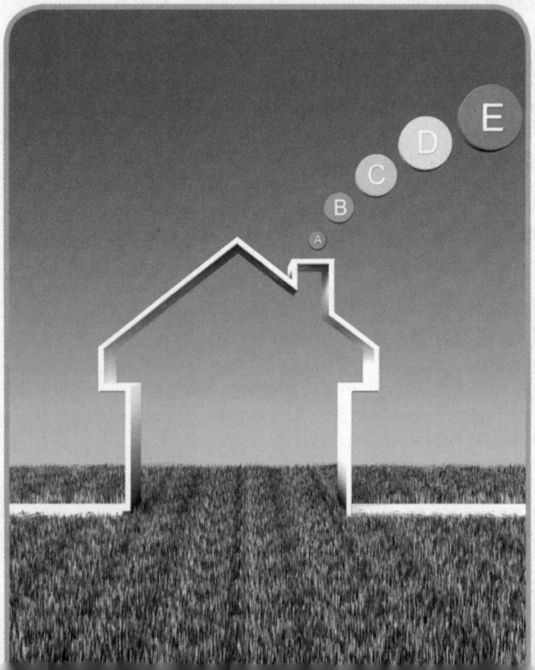

The second stage of the writing process is writing the first draft. During this stage you will use your outline and other prewriting notes to express your ideas in sentences and paragraphs. As you write, you may discover new ideas. As long as these ideas relate directly to your main idea, include them, revising your outline as needed. Remember that a first draft should not be a polished final essay, but it should include all the parts of an introduction with a thesis statement, a body of one or more supporting paragraphs, and a conclusion.

1 Drafting the Introduction

Writing the Thesis Statement

Before you start to draft your essay, refine your working thesis into a clear, polished **thesis statement.** Look over your outline and revise your working thesis so that it covers all of your main topics. As you draft your thesis statement, avoid expressions such as "In this paper I will . . ." or "This paper is about . . ." that distract the reader by focusing their attention on you or on your paper rather than on your subject.

Reread the prewriting notes and the outline on pages 241–242 and 244–248. Then examine the following weak thesis statements.

Weak Thesis Statement	Belle Boyd and Emma Edmonds used different methods in their spying missions. (too specific: does not take into account all the similarities and differences between the two women)
Weak Thesis Statement	Everyone has unique reasons for serving a cause of great importance. (too general: does not even mention the women by name)
Weak Thesis Statement	In this essay I will explain the similarities and differences between Belle Boyd and Emma Edmonds. (shifts the reader's attention from the subject to you, the writer)

The following thesis statement is appropriately specific and accounts for all the supporting details.

Strong Thesis Statement	Both Belle Boyd for the Confederacy and Emma Edmonds for the Union served their causes bravely, but their reasons for spying and their methods were entirely different.

CAPTURING ATTENTION

In many short essays, the thesis statement is the final sentence of the first paragraph. The sentences that lead up to the thesis statement capture the reader's interest and set the tone of the essay. Use any of the following strategies to help you write an effective introduction that establishes a formal style and objective tone.

HERE'S HOW

Strategies for Drafting an Introduction

- Begin with an incident that shows how you became interested in your subject.
- Begin by giving some background information.
- Begin by giving an example or an incident that catches the reader's attention.

CHAPTER 7

You may need to reword your thesis statement to fit smoothly with the other sentences. Notice how the strong thesis statement about Belle Boyd and Emma Edmonds on page 251 was revised.

MODEL: Introduction of an Expository Essay

Picture a seventeen-year-old girl, in a dark blue dress and white sun bonnet, scurrying between the cross fire of Confederates and the Union army to deliver a message to Stonewall Jackson's troops near Front Royal, Virginia. This was Belle Boyd, the most famous spy for the South during the Civil War. Next picture another young woman, her face blistered and her eyes red from the disguise she used to penetrate the Confederate lines at Yorktown, Virginia. This was Emma Edmonds, a master masquerader and a spy for the Union in the Civil War. Both young women served their causes bravely, but their reasons for spying and their methods were entirely different.

Refined Thesis Statement

PROJECT PREP Drafting *Introduction*

In your writing group, help each author determine an effective way to begin. What would best prepare readers for the information to follow? Should an author begin with a quiet and deliberate tone, or with a dramatic and provocative statement?

2 Drafting the Body

The outline you wrote is for the body of your essay. Each Roman numeral, which precedes a main topic in your outline, should correspond to at least one paragraph in the body of the essay. If you have a number of supporting details, you may need two or more paragraphs to cover each topic adequately. An outline can guide you from point to point in the order you have established.

HERE'S HOW

Guidelines for Adequately Developing an Essay

- Include enough relevant and substantial evidence to develop your thesis statement fully.
- Include information on a number of relevant perspectives.
- Include enough information to present each topic and subtopic fully.
- Use well-chosen details and precise domain-specific language to manage the complexity of the topic.
- Develop your ideas logically. For each claim you make, supply an example and a warrant. (pages 120–121 and 293)
- Make valid inferences. (pages 121 and 297)

CHAPTER 7

As you draft the body of your essay, you will need to use transitions such as the following to connect your thoughts and make your essay read smoothly.

For additional lists of transitions, see pages 5, 95–97, and 304.

COMMON TRANSITIONS

Chronological Order	Spatial Order	Order of Importance
first, second	above	first, second
then	below	more important
at first	right	most important
immediately	beyond	the least/most
as soon as	east	the largest
Developmental Order	**Comparison and Contrast**	
furthermore	also	although
besides	both	however
however	just as	by contrast
nonetheless	like	unlike

Transitions will give your essay **coherence,** the quality that makes each sentence seem connected to the one before it. Other strategies for achieving coherence are listed below.

HERE'S HOW

Strategies for Achieving Coherence

- Repeat a key word from an earlier sentence.
- Use a pronoun in place of a word used earlier.
- Use transitional words and phrases and syntax to link the major sections of the text and clarify relationships among complex ideas and concepts.

CHAPTER 7

Compare the outline on pages 246–248 to the following coherent body of an essay. Words and phrases that aid coherence are in boldface.

MODEL: Body of an Expository Essay

The similarities between the two spies emphasize some of the qualities that helped them carry out their work. **Both** were young women and, as such, aroused less suspicion than young men might have. **Both** were highly independent, driven by a belief that an individual can make a difference. **Both** served as nurses, and so they knew how to talk easily to soldiers. **Both** were also passionately committed to their cause.

From I in Outline

The two spies' differences, **however,** point out the variety of motivations that lead people to give of themselves for a **cause.** Belle Boyd, for example, was fun-loving, adventurous, and warm-hearted. When troops of the Union overtook **her** hometown of Martinsburg, Virginia, and threatened to burn down her house, Boyd appealed to the chivalry of the commanding officer. So effective were her **appeals** that the officer not only saved her house but also assigned Union soldiers to protect it! Surrounded by admiring enemy troops, **she** soon picked up valuable information and began her career as a spy. Her most useful tools were her **warmheartedness** and **charm,** which made people admire and trust her. Boyd redoubled her efforts when she learned of the glamorous Rose O'Neal Greenhow, spying for the South in Washington, D.C. Using her **charm** to obtain information and her courage to cross enemy lines, Boyd delivered secret information to General J.E.B. Stuart and General Stonewall Jackson. Her aid helped the South to recapture an important

From II in Outline

bridge near Front Royal and take 3,000 prisoners along with valuable supplies. Although the danger Boyd faced on her missions was serious, her **powers to charm** protected her from harm.

Emma Edmonds, **on the other hand,** spent her life as a spy in grueling, exacting labor. **She** first decided to become a spy when the man she loved, a Union soldier, was shot and killed. General George McClellan interviewed her and, finally, despite her slight build, enlisted her service in the Union cause. **In all** she made 11 trips through enemy lines, adopting difficult and sometimes painful disguises. Some required that she shave her head; some required that she learn different dialects. **All** required quick thinking to avoid a fatal slip that would betray her disguise. **Her last assignment** was her highest achievement. Disguised as a Southern boy wanting to become a Confederate spy, she was able to identify five spies working for the Confederacy. In the two years she served as a spy, she faced **danger** constantly—not only in the form of enemy fire but also in the form of disease and hardship.

From III in Outline

CHAPTER 7

PROJECT PREP Drafting *Body*

1. Using the guidelines on the preceding pages, draft the body of your analytical essay. Choose your supporting details carefully. Provide appropriate and varied transitions from your introduction to the body of your text and between each body paragraph. Monitor how well you are addressing your purpose and audience and evaluate the appropriateness of the tone.
2. In your writing group, read each author's account. On the topic of a change and its effects, pay attention to how the author has developed the main idea. Is the evidence relevant and substantial? Are the details well chosen? Do you get a complete picture of the nature of the change? Has the author considered multiple relevant perspectives on the subject? Has the author provided paragraph breaks appropriately so that each new topic has its own distinct presentation? Make specific suggestions to improve each author's text.

3 Drafting the Conclusion

A good conclusion makes readers feel that they have reached the end of your essay in an interesting and memorable way. It may present one last insight that you want your reader to remember, or it may contain a telling detail not used earlier in the body of the essay. The conclusion, like the introduction, is often more general than the specific ideas in the body. The following are good ways to end an essay.

HERE'S HOW

Strategies for Concluding an Essay

- Summarize the essay or restate the thesis in new words.
- Refer to ideas in the introduction to bring the essay full circle.
- Appeal to the reader's emotions.
- Draw a conclusion that follows from and supports the information presented.
- Ask a question that leaves the reader thinking.

CHAPTER 7

The following conclusion to the essay on Belle Boyd and Emma Edmonds restates the thesis. Notice that details about Boyd and Edmonds are used in the conclusion. The last sentence makes a strong ending and fixes the idea in the reader's mind.

MODEL: Conclusion of an Expository Essay

Two young women: One blazes with the spirit of adventure and on her capture and imprisonment, joyously sings "Maryland, My Maryland." The other, disguised as a peddler, takes time out from her mission against the Confederacy to lighten the final hours of a Confederate soldier. Both women deserve their place in history. Enemies in their beliefs and opposites in their methods, Belle Boyd and Emma Edmonds both demonstrate the independent spirit of American heroes.

Follows from and supports the information in the essay

Drafting a Title The final step in writing the first draft is to think of a suitable title for your essay. Your title should communicate to your reader the subject of your essay. Choose a title that will make your reader want to read the essay. For the essay on Boyd and Edmonds, for example, the title "Belle Boyd and Emma Edmonds" would be clear but not engaging. A more intriguing title, however, would be "Two Female Spies of the Civil War."

PROJECT PREP Drafting *Conclusion and Title*

In your writing group, discuss what impression each writer wants to make on readers and how to do this with the most impact. Then, discuss a good title for each essay.

Expository Writing Revising

The purpose of revising is to make your final draft as clear, smooth, and readable as possible. Do you have any new ideas you wish to include in your essay? Do you think that any paragraphs or sentences need to be rearranged? Putting your essay aside for a while will help you see it with a fresh eye when it is time to revise it. Show your essay to one of your classmates. Ask your reader to give you valuable feedback as to whether your explanations are clear and understandable. Before meeting with your partner, review the guidelines for conferencing on page 27.

Good writers keep the reader's attention focused directly on the thesis by eliminating any idea that strays from the main idea. When all the details in an essay support the main idea expressed in the thesis statement, the essay is said to have **unity.** Each element of your essay should build on what precedes it to create a unified whole.

Good writers also guide the thoughts of the reader by using logical order and clear transitional words and phrases. The essays have **coherence,** the quality that creates a tightly woven fabric of ideas.

Another characteristic of well-written informative essays is **emphasis.** In many essays, one supporting point is more important than the others. You can show the importance of this point by devoting more attention to it than to the other ideas. You can also show emphasis by organizing ideas based on order of importance and by using transitional words to make the relative importance of the points clear.

When revising, also consider how the addition of formatting, such as headings, graphics (such as charts and tables), and even multimedia might aid comprehension. (See pages 592-598.)

An evaluation checklist can help you keep track of a variety of points to check during the revision stage. Read through the essay several times, focusing on different points on the checklist each time.

Writing Tip

Check your essay for **unity** by making sure that each paragraph is directly related to the thesis statement.

Writing Tip

Check your essay for **coherence** by making sure that the ideas are logically organized and smoothly connected.

Writing Tip

Check your essay for **emphasis** by making sure that the relative importance of the supporting points is clear.

Revision Strategies

Checking Your Essay

- ✓ Does the introduction set a formal tone and introduce the topic? (pages 251–252)
- ✓ Does your thesis statement make your main idea clear? (page 251)
- ✓ Does your essay have unity? Does the topic sentence of each paragraph relate directly to the thesis statement? (pages 86, 94, and 257)
- ✓ Is your idea well developed, with substantial, relevant evidence and well-chosen facts, extended definitions, concrete details, quotations, and other information and examples appropriate to the audience's knowledge of the topic? (pages 241–242)
- ✓ Did you include information on multiple relevant perspectives? (pages 241 and 253)
- ✓ Are the paragraphs arranged in logical order? (pages 245–248)
- ✓ Did you use transitions and other techniques to achieve coherence between paragraphs, to show the relative importance of ideas, and to clarify the relationships among ideas and concepts? (pages 253–254 and 257)
- ✓ Does the amount of space allotted to the ideas reflect their relative importance? (page 257)
- ✓ Do you have a strong conclusion that follows from and supports the information or explanation presented? (page 256)
- ✓ Did you establish and maintain a formal style and objective tone throughout and adhere to the norms and conventions of the discipline in which you are writing? (pages 112–113 and 252)

Checking Your Paragraphs

- ✓ Does each paragraph have a topic sentence? (page 86)
- ✓ Is each paragraph unified and coherent? (pages 94–97, 253–254, and 257)

Checking Your Sentences and Words

- ✓ Are your sentences varied, clear, and concise? (pages 59–70)
- ✓ Did you use precise language and domain-specific vocabulary? (pages 49 and 52)
- ✓ Did you include figurative language and other tropes? (pages 53–55, 168, and 226)
- ✓ Did you use parallelism and other schemes? (pages 75 and 250)

PROJECT PREP Revising *Second Draft*

Based on the feedback from your writing group and from your teacher if you have it, write a new draft of your expository writing. In this draft, pay attention to grammar, punctuation, and spelling so that readers can follow your ideas as clearly as possible.

In the editing stage you will produce an error-free manuscript. You should comb your essay, checking it for grammatical errors, errors of punctuation, and mistaken facts.

The Language of Power Verb Tense

Power Rule: Use a consistent verb tense except when a change is clearly necessary. (See pages 753–766.)

See It in Action In verbs, **tense** helps to show when. Using the same tense throughout your story or essay will help keep your reader anchored. Examine the following sentence modified from a U.S. history textbook, *The American Pageant.* (See page 270 for an excerpt). Notice how a shift in tenses causes confusion for the reader.

Shifts in Tense	Lincoln **had** a piercing, high-pitched voice and **is** often ill at ease when he **begins** to speak. *(shifted from past tense to present tense)*

Now compare this sentence with what actually appears in *The American Pageant*.

Correct Tense: Consistent	Lincoln **had** a piercing, high-pitched voice and **was** often ill at ease when he **began** to speak. *(All verbs are in the past tense)*

If a sentence relates past actions but also refers to an ongoing, recurring action, the writer may need to shift tenses.

Correct Tense: Changing	Although the Rangers **played** badly last year, they usually **play** better.

Remember It Record this rule and example in the Power Rule section of your Personalized Editing Checklist.

Use It Read through your expository writing project and put a check mark by each verb. Check for any inappropriate shifts in tense.

Using a Six-Trait Rubric — Expository Writing

Ideas	**4** The topic, focus, and details convey information powerfully with valid inferences.	**3** The text conveys information, using valid inferences.	**2** Some aspects of the topic are not clear and/or well developed.	**1** Most aspects are not clear and/or well developed.
Organization	**4** The organization is clear and easy to follow. Transitions provide coherence.	**3** The organization is clear, but a few ideas seem out of place or disconnected.	**2** Many ideas seem out of place and transitions are missing.	**1** The organization is unclear and hard to follow.
Voice	**4** The voice sounds natural and knowledgeable and is appropriate for the audience.	**3** The voice sounds mostly natural and knowledgeable and is right for the audience.	**2** The voice sounds a bit unnatural and does not seem right for the audience.	**1** The voice sounds mostly unnatural or is inappropriate for the audience.
Word Choice	**4** Words are specific and figures of speech are used.	**3** Words are vivid and specific.	**2** Some words are overly general.	**1** Most words are overly general.
Sentence Fluency	**4** Varied sentences flow smoothly. Sentence structure and length vary.	**3** Most of the sentences are varied and smoothly flowing.	**2** Some sentences are not varied, and some are choppy.	**1** Sentences are not varied and are choppy.
Conventions	**4** Punctuation, usage, and spelling are correct, and all Power Rules are followed.	**3** There are only a few errors in punctuation, usage, and spelling, and no Power Rule errors.	**2** There are several errors in punctuation, usage, and spelling, and no Power Rule errors.	**1** There are many errors and at least one Power Rule error.

PROJECT PREP — Editing — *Peer Evaluation*

Based on the feedback from your writing partner, polish your grammar, punctuation, and spelling, and write a final, polished draft of your informative writing.

Expository Writing Publishing

After you have revised and edited the final draft of your essay, you are ready to share it with others.

HERE'S HOW **Publishing Options for Expository Writing**

- a formal essay (see pages 33–35 for proper manuscript form)
- an article (see pages 592–598 for reader-friendly formatting techniques)
- a speech (see pages 578–579 for a guide for presenting speeches)
- an electronic presentation (see pages 591–598 for using presentation software effectively)
- a video (see pages 598–603 for a guide to creating video presentations)

CHAPTER 7

PROJECT PREP Publishing *Web Sites*

Publish your writing through an appropriate medium. You might, for instance, find Web sites where your topic is discussed and upload your writing to a discussion board.

TIME OUT TO REFLECT

Your goal in writing an expository essay was to inform readers about a topic. What have you learned about yourself as a communicator of information? What have you learned about the writing process? What have you learned about your strengths and weaknesses as a researcher and writer? What have you learned about the kinds of writing you might want to pursue in the future? What have you learned about the fields of knowledge you might want to explore, possibly even the kinds of professions you might wish to enter in adulthood? Record your answers in the Learning Log section of your journal.

Writing Lab

CHAPTER 7

Project Corner

Speak and Listen
Discuss Progress

With your classmates, **discuss the notion of progress.** Do changes in technology, laws, and other aspects of life help to advance society? Why or why not? What determines whether a change is good or not? How do people adapt to change in ways that make their lives better?

Collaborate and Create
Design and Build

Create a Web site that is concerned with the change you have written about. How could you link information, pro and con, about the change and its consequences for people? What sorts of features—discussion boards, chat rooms, or blogs—would you want to include on a Web site of this type? What sort of interface would you create so that people can navigate the site easily?

Experiment
Adapt from Fact to Fiction

Using your expository writing as a starting point, **write a work of fiction** about the adaptation to change you have described. What sorts of characters would you include? How would you depict their engagement with the change and its consequences on their lives?

In Everyday Life
Informative E-mail

1. Your Uncle Buck has won the lottery and wants to share the wealth with everyone in the family. As a present, he plans to have a golden statue of you placed on your front lawn. You know your uncle means well, but you would prefer he do something different with his money. ***Write an e-mail*** to your uncle explaining your opinion, as well as informing him how you think he could spend his money more wisely. Arrange the paragraphs in your e-mail in order of importance. (You can find information on writing e-mails on pages 533, 567, and 611–615.)

In the Workplace Informative Letter

2. You work as a music programmer for a failing radio station, where the ratings and advertising revenues are at their lowest levels ever. You think a change in musical style might attract a larger listening audience. ***Write a letter*** to the board of directors identifying the changes you believe will boost sagging ratings and earn a profit for the station. Be sure your letter includes a strong introductory paragraph with a clearly stated thesis. Use a tone that suits your purpose and audience. (You can find information on writing informative letters on pages 530–537.)

Timed Writing Newsletter

3. You have decided to publish *Teens on the Town,* an Internet newsletter for teenage tourists. The newsletter features informative articles about unusual and exciting locations to visit in your hometown, especially those places older tourist writers might overlook. For your first article, you will write about a few of your favorite places in your hometown. You have 25 minutes to complete your work.

   Before You Write Consider the following questions: What is the situation? What is the occasion? Who is the audience? What is the purpose?

   Begin your article with an introductory paragraph that includes a thesis statement and expresses the main idea of the article. Develop a working thesis around which you can select and organize your details in a logical order. Decide whether the ideas should be organized in chronological order, spatial order, order of importance, or developmental order.

   After You Write Evaluate your work using the six-trait rubric on page 260.

Expository Writing Workshops

The most basic function of writing is to convey information. Information can be categorized in several ways, depending on its type. These workshops offer you information that will help you decide how best to gather and present the information you want to convey.

CHAPTER 7

1 How-To, or Procedural, Texts

A **procedural text** describes the sequence of steps in the process of making or doing something.

Generally these texts describe simple tasks or processes that almost anyone could do. No matter what process you write about, your goal is to provide a clear and simple explanation for your readers. The following is an example of a procedural text.

MODEL: How-To Text

Growing an Avocado

Growing an avocado tree is an easy way to develop your green thumb. Start by removing the pit from the avocado. Then push three toothpicks, angled slightly upward, into the pit. Fill a small bowl or wide-mouthed jar with water and rest the toothpicks on the rim, suspending the avocado pit in water. After a week or two of being submerged in water (make sure to maintain a high enough level to keep the bottom of the pit wet at all times), roots will begin to sprout. Once there are two or three roots, it is time to plant your avocado seedling. Fill a pot with soil and dig a small hole, big enough to cover just the bottom half of the pit. Place the pit in the hole, roots down. Water generously and keep the soil moist. Before you know it, leaves will begin to sprout and you will have a small avocado tree growing in your house!

You can use a graphic organizer to help you visualize the organization of a procedural text. The chain links in this organizer represent transitions between steps.

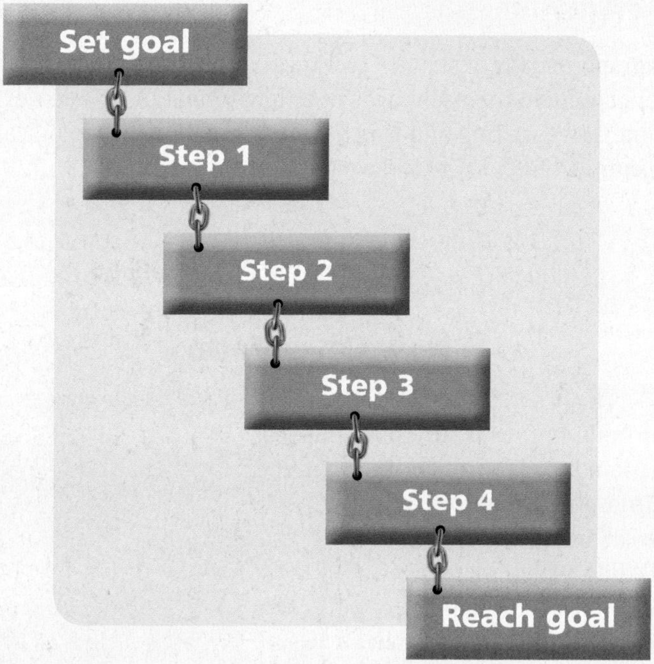

CHAPTER 7

QuickGuide for Writing Procedural Texts

- → Make a list of the steps to follow, written in sequential order.
- → Explain each of the steps, in order, as simply and clearly as possible, using transitional words and phrases to connect them.
- → Clearly state your purpose and fully support your viewpoint on the topic with facts and details.
- → Include relevant questions that engage readers and consider their needs.
- → Use appropriate formatting structures, such as bullet points, boldface heads, and illustrations if they would be helpful.
- → Make sure technical information is accurate and expressed in accessible language.
- → Include a clear introduction and conclusion.

Create Real-World Texts

1. Write a paragraph providing instructions for an adult on how to make a child's kite.
2. Compose an e-mail to a relative giving directions to your family's reunion from your house to the local park.

2 How-It-Works Texts

A **how-it-works text** describes or shows how something happens, forms, works, or is put together.

This type of paragraph usually explains a technical or abstract process, rather than something readers could do themselves, as in a how-to text. A how-it-works paragraph often resembles narrative writing and is usually arranged in chronological order. The following is an example of a how-it-works paragraph.

CHAPTER 7

MODEL: How-It-Works Text

How Caves Form

The process of caves forming in rock is very slow. As rain travels through the atmosphere, it absorbs a small amount of carbon dioxide, which increases as it moves through the soil. This mixture of water and carbon dioxide is weak carbonic acid solution. The solution drains through cracks and crevices in the ground, and in doing so dissolves soluble rock and forms pockets and channels. After thousands of years of this acidic solution flowing through rock, rooms and chambers form underground.

When you write how-it-works texts, clearly state your purpose and fully support your viewpoint on the topic with facts and details. Include relevant questions to engage readers and address their potential problems and misunderstandings. Make sure technical information is accurate and expressed in accessible language.

You can use a graphic organizer to help you visualize the organization of a how-it-works text. The arrows in this organizer represent transitions between steps.

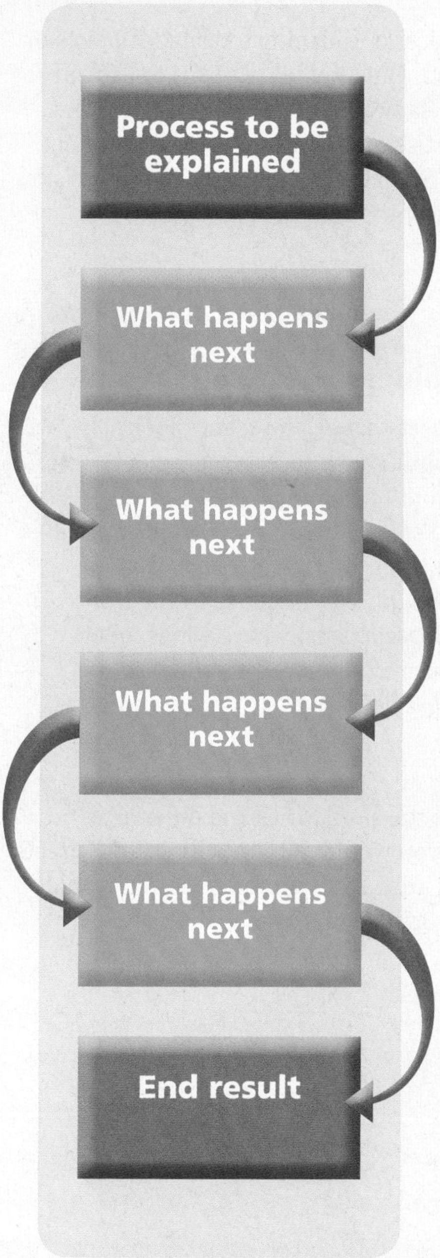

QuickGuide for Writing How-It-Works Texts

→ Make a short outline or cluster that breaks down into simple steps the process of how something works.

→ Describe the process clearly in your own words following the steps listed in your outline or cluster. Adopt a light, narrative tone that will hold your readers' interest.

→ Use transitional words and phrases to emphasize order.

→ Use appropriate formatting structures, such as bullet points, boldface heads, and illustrations, if they would be helpful.

→ Include a clear introduction with a main idea, a middle with supporting details to make the process clear, and a strong conclusion.

Create Real-World Texts

1. For the school newspaper, write out the process by which a student can try out for the annual musical production.
2. You are giving your grandmother an MP3 player for her birthday. Compose a note to include with the gift explaining how the player works.
3. For a science fair project, use a chart to explain how a balanced diet meets your nutritional needs.

3 Compare-and-Contrast Texts

A **compare-and-contrast text** examines the similarities and differences between two subjects.

This type of text will help you interpret, understand, and explain two related subjects or events (such as a film and a book on the same topic). One way to do this is to explain all the characteristics of Subject A and then, in the same order, all the characteristics of Subject B. Another way is to take the characteristics one at a time, describing them alternately as they appear in Subject A and then in Subject B until all the characteristics are covered. The following paragraph is an example of the second approach.

MODEL: Compare-and-Contrast Text

Insects and Spiders

Insects and spiders are both small creatures that at first glance look very much alike. Both have many legs, and both crawl. Insects and spiders both reproduce by laying eggs, and they both use camouflage as a natural defense. Looking closer, however, insects and spiders are quite different from one another. Insects usually have six legs (in three pairs) and a body that is divided into three parts. Spiders always have eight legs, attached to the front section of their two-sectioned bodies. Adult insects usually have wings, often two pairs. Spiders do not have wings. While people often perceive insects as being pests, spiders are seen as pest controllers because they prey on insects.

You can use a Venn diagram to help you clearly see the similarities and differences between two subjects. In the Venn diagram below, you would note the things the insects and spiders have in common in the middle (green) area. In the outer areas you would note the features that are specific to either insects or spiders.

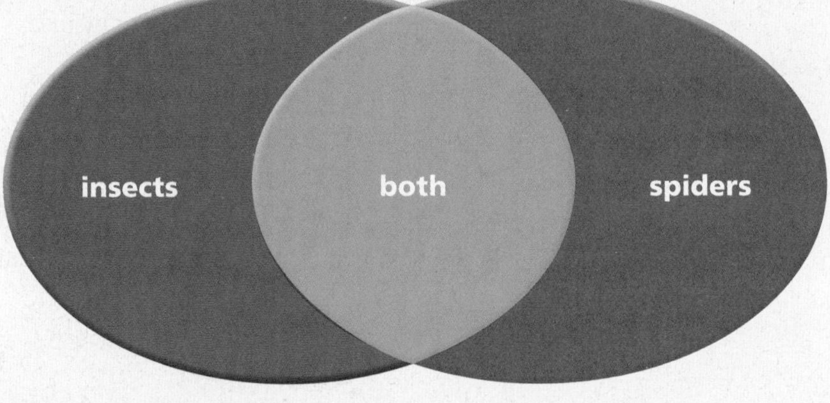

Organizing Comparison and Contrast

The outline you studied about Belle Boyd and Emma Edmonds shows one method of organizing comparison and contrast. When you write a comparison-and-contrast essay, you explain similarities and differences between two subjects. Remember that when you compare subjects, you explain how they are similar. For example, you could show how the backgrounds of two athletes are similar. On the other hand, when you contrast subjects, you emphasize differences. For instance, you could explain how those same athletes followed different career paths.

If the comparison-and-contrast method of development is appropriate for your essay, you have a choice of two patterns for organizing your information. In one pattern, which is called the **AABB pattern,** you include all that you have to say about one subject (subject A) before you discuss the other subject (subject B). You can explain subjects A and B in two halves of the same paragraph, or you can explain subject A in one paragraph and subject B in another paragraph. The following two paragraphs about Stephen Douglas and Abraham Lincoln use the AABB pattern of organization.

MODEL: AABB Pattern of Organization

Lincoln and Douglas

A very squat, bull-necked, and heavy set figure, **(A) Senator Stephen A. Douglas,** the "Little Giant," radiated the energy and breezy optimism of the self-made man. An ardent booster for the West, he longed to break the North-South deadlock over westward expansion and stretch a line of settlements across the continent. **(A) Douglas** had invested heavily in Chicago real estate and in railway stock and was eager to have the Windy City become the eastern terminus of the proposed railroad. He would thus endear himself to the voters of Illinois.

The Republicans decided to run against Douglas a rustic Springfield lawyer, **(B) Abraham Lincoln.** The candidate—6 feet 4 inches in height and 180 pounds in weight—presented an awkward but arresting figure. **(B) Lincoln's** legs, arms, and neck were unusually long; his head was crowned by coarse, black, and unruly hair. **(B) Lincoln** was born in a Kentucky log cabin to impoverished parents. He attended a frontier school for not more than a year; being an avid reader, he was mainly self-educated. After reading law, **(B) Lincoln** gradually emerged as one of the dozen or so better-known trial lawyers in Illinois.

In the second pattern of organization, called the **ABAB pattern,** instead of discussing subject **A** and subject **B** separately, you discuss them together. First you point out one similarity or difference between subject **A** and subject **B** and then you go on to another similarity or difference. For instance, if you were contrasting baseball with basketball, you might start with one difference: the number of players on a team. Then you would go on to discuss other differences between the two subjects. The following paragraph uses the **ABAB** pattern of organization.

CHAPTER 7

MODEL: ABAB Pattern of Organization

At first glance the two contestants seemed ill matched. The well-groomed and polished **(A) Douglas,** with stocky figure, presented a striking contrast to the lanky **(B) Lincoln,** with his baggy clothes and unshined shoes. Moreover, in contrast to **(A) Douglas's** bullish voice, **(B) Lincoln** had a piercing, high-pitched voice and was often ill at ease when he began to speak. However, as he threw himself into an argument, he seemed to grow in height, while his glowing eyes lighted up a rugged face.

—Thomas A. Bailey and David M. Kennedy, *The American Pageant*

You can use one of the following organizers to help you plan a compare-and-contrast text.

AABB Organizer

Subject for Compare/Contrast
Topic 1 about subject A Topic 2 about subject A Topic 3 about subject A
Transition
Topic 1 about subject B Topic 2 about subject B Topic 3 about subject B

ABAB Organizer

Subject for Compare/Contrast
Topic 1 about subject A Topic 1 about subject B
Transition
Topic 2 about subject A Topic 2 about subject B
Transition
Topic 3 about subject A Topic 3 about subject B

QuickGuide for Writing Compare-and-Contrast Texts

→ List the similarities and differences of the two subjects. Use a Venn diagram or chart to keep track of these characteristics.

→ Decide how to organize your information.

→ Use transitions such as *in contrast, on the other hand,* and *similarly* to emphasize the order.

→ Include a clear introduction and conclusion.

Create Real-World Texts

1. Create a post for an online social network comparing video game consoles.
2. Think of two career paths you could pursue upon graduation from high school. Create a chart to show your understanding of each path and the pros and cons of each.
3. Your parents are in the market for a new car. They have narrowed their choices to a fuel-efficient sedan and a smaller hybrid. Write an e-mail to your parents comparing and contrasting the cars.

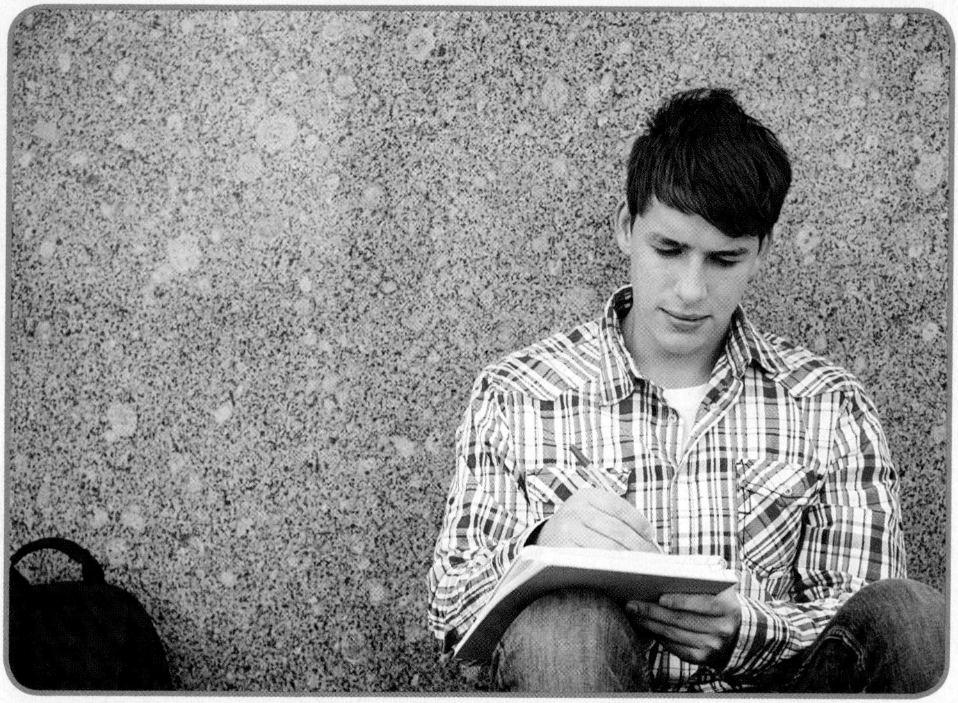

4 Cause-and-Effect Analysis Texts

A **cause-and-effect text** explains why actions or situations (causes) produce certain results (effects).

A simple cause-and-effect paragraph deals with a single cause, such as an icy sidewalk, and a single effect, such as a fall. A more complex paragraph describes a series of causes and effects, each one dependent on the one before—a chain of events. The explanation given in a cause-and-effect paragraph is supported with specific evidence that is presented in a well-organized and logical sequence. The following is an example of a cause-and-effect paragraph.

MODEL: Cause-and-Effect Text

Threatening Animals

As human populations grow and more houses are built, city limits extend farther and farther into the countryside. The immediate impact on wild animals is that they lose their natural habitat and find themselves with a choice of either sharing their space with human neighbors or moving to areas where there is still open, undeveloped space. Some animals, like coyotes, often remain in close proximity to new housing developments. Fed by well-meaning people, these coyotes become more accustomed to and less afraid of interaction with humans and, as a result, they become more aggressive. In the end, coyotes are often perceived as a menace and met with hostility.

A graphic organizer, like the ones on the next page, can help you develop and organize a cause-and-effect text. Graphic organizers can start with the cause and explain the effects or can start with the effect and explain the causes.

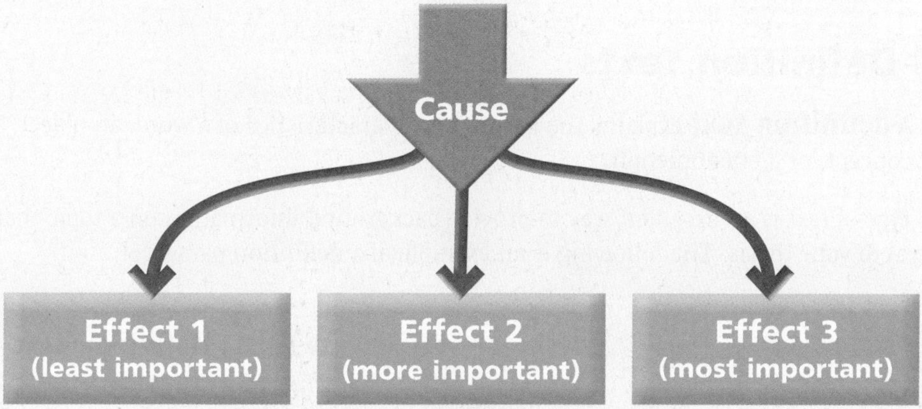

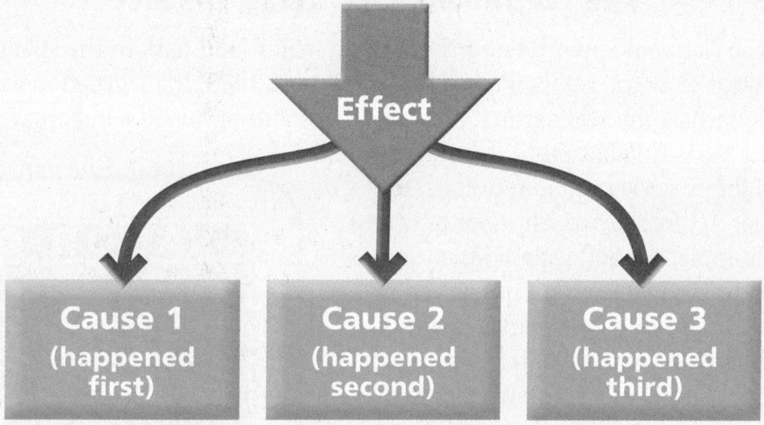

QuickGuide for Writing Cause-and-Effect Texts

→ Identify the effect(s) you want to analyze and list the causes you know.

→ Gather information to check for accuracy and add details.

→ Use logical order. Explain multiple causes in the order they occurred or by order of importance. Start with the effect and explain what caused it, or start with the cause(s) and build up to the effect.

→ Include a clear introduction and conclusion.

Create Real-World Texts

1. Use a science textbook to study a situation that depends on a chain of events, such as an earthquake or a forest fire. On a sheet of paper, make a flowchart to break down the chain into a series in which each event causes the next. Use your flowchart to explain the situation to a younger student.
2. Write a letter to the editor of your local paper explaining the causes and effects of littering in your community.

5 Definition Texts

A **definition text** explains the nature and characteristics of a word, an object, a concept, or a phenomenon.

This type of text is an excellent way to provide background information on a topic that is central to your thesis. The following is an example of a definition paragraph.

MODEL: Definition Text

The National Labor Relations Act

The National Labor Relations Act was a major landmark in the struggle to protect workers' rights. Passed by Congress in 1935, the legislation was also known as the Wagner Act, after its chief sponsor, Senator Robert Wagner of New York. In addition to upholding the right of workers to join unions, the Wagner Act forbade unfair labor practices. For example, the act declared that unions set up by companies were unfair and illegal. It also said that management must bargain "in good faith" with union leaders. Furthermore, the Wagner Act outlawed the blacklisting of workers who were union members. It also made "yellow dog" contracts—making workers agree not to join a union before giving them a job—illegal. Never before had workers' rights been so fully safeguarded by law, and one labor leader called the act "the rockbed of the modern labor movement."

A graphic organizer like the one on the following page can help you develop a definition text.

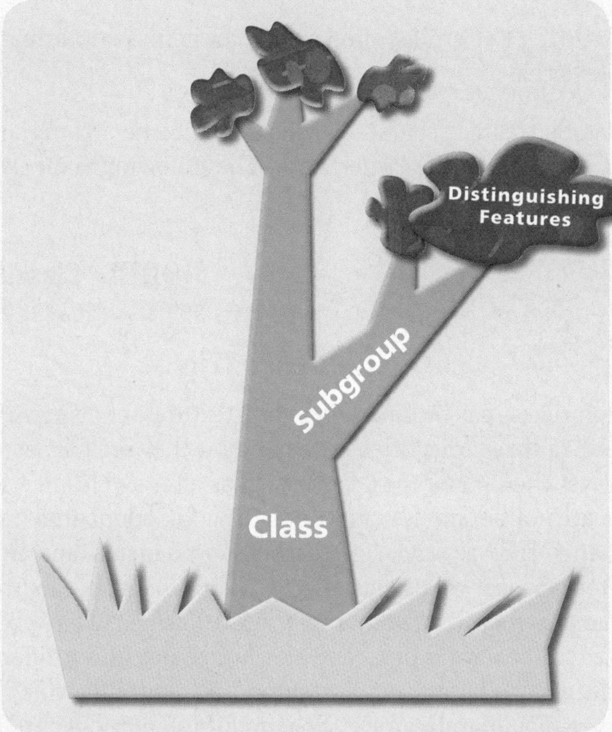

QuickGuide for Writing Definition Texts

→ Brainstorm for what you know about the nature and the characteristics of your subject. Gather information as needed and decide in which order to present the characteristics of your subject.

→ Include three basic parts: the subject you are defining, the class it belongs in, and the characteristics that make it different from other members of that class.

→ Include a clear introduction and conclusion.

→ Use clear, everyday language and avoid phrases like "a recession is when ..." or "a recession is where...."

Create Real-World Texts

1. Define the electoral college for your social studies class and create a chart to help explain it.
2. Write a definition of something special from your family's heritage, such as a recipe or a custom for a holiday celebration. Create a card with the definition inside and give it to a family member at the celebration.
3. Write a definition of a job for a help-wanted advertisement in the classified section of the newspaper.

6 Classification Texts

A **classification text** groups similar types of items or information into separate classes or categories.

Although each class is treated separately, the parts become a paragraph when they are recognized as elements of the larger work. The following is an example of a classification paragraph.

MODEL: Classification Text

The Rock Trio

Although rocks may be different colors, textures, and shapes, all rocks belong to one of three categories, based on how they are formed. 1. Igneous rock is formed when liquid rock cools, such as after a volcano erupts. Obsidian and granite are both examples of igneous rock. 2. Sedimentary rock is formed from sediment—such as sand, soil, seashells, dead plants, and animal bones—that turns to rock over thousands of years. Limestone and sandstone are both sedimentary rock. 3. Metamorphic rock is formed when a rock is heated and squeezed in the earth's crust and slowly changes into a different type of rock. Marble, which comes from limestone, and quartzite, which comes from sandstone, are metamorphic rocks. So if you think of rocks as a family, there are only three branches on this family tree.

A graphic organizer like the one below can help you develop a classification text. You might choose to organize a classification text by identifying each category and then including examples and descriptive details that help explain its characteristics.

Topic:	
Category:	
Ideas & Information	
Category:	
Ideas & Information	
Category:	
Ideas & Information	
Concluding insight	

QuickGuide for Writing Classification Texts

- → Choose a topic to write about that can be broken down into categories.
- → Arrange the information in the way that makes the most sense.
- → Arrange the supporting sentences in a logical order to explain the main groups, categories, or classes you are identifying.
- → Include a clear introduction with a topic sentence and a conclusion.

Create Real-World Texts

1. Write an article for your school newspaper on the kinds of music students download onto their portable music players.
2. Explore different methods of studying for a final exam. Make a chart and present your findings to classmates.

7 Analysis Texts

An **analysis text** examines a person, place, thing, or idea by breaking it into parts and showing how, together, they make a whole.

This kind of text is useful for explaining how the parts of an organization work together. The following is an example of an analysis text.

MODEL: Analysis Text

The United States Government

The government of the United States has three branches: the executive, the legislative, and the judicial. The executive branch includes the office of the president and all the departments and people who report to the president. The president is responsible for signing bills and enforcing the laws established by the government, and also for appointing members to the judiciary. The legislative branch consists of the Senate and the House of Representatives (together known as the Congress), who are responsible for writing and enacting laws. They must also approve appointments to the courts. The judicial branch is made up of the Supreme Court and the court of appeals, which must interpret the laws enacted by Congress. The Supreme Court has the authority to strike down any law that violates the United States Constitution. The way in which these three branches of government work together is known as a system of checks and balances, devised so that none of the branches would hold too much power. These elective and appointed bodies work together to govern our country as fairly as possible.

A graphic organizer like the one on the following page can help you develop an analysis text.

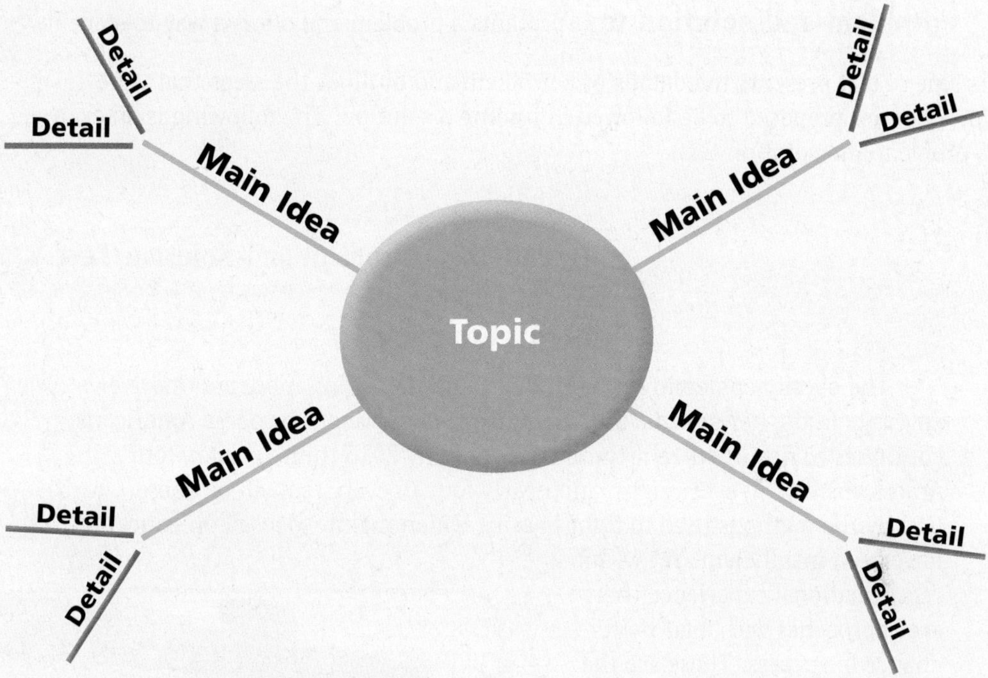

QuickGuide for Writing Analysis Texts

- → Choose a topic to write about.
- → Explore the relationship of your subject's parts to its whole.
- → Arrange the supporting sentences in a logical order and use effective transitions to guide readers comfortably through your explanation.
- → Include a clear introduction and a conclusion.

Create Real-World Texts

1. Write a few paragraphs for a student handbook that explain your school's graduation requirements.
2. Choose a profession and write a paragraph describing its attributes and functions to share with your guidance counselor.
3. Write an article for the school newspaper whose purpose is to inform students of the school's musical ensembles. Analyze the band, orchestra, or choir so students will clearly understand how it is put together.

8 Problem-and-Solution Texts

A **problem-and-solution text** presents a problem and offers a way to solve it.

This type of text presents the details of a problem and outlines the steps that were followed or are proposed to be followed in finding a solution. The following is an example of a problem-and-solution text.

MODEL: Problem-and-Solution Text

Fighting Obesity

The obesity epidemic in the United States is getting more and more coverage in the news media as the number of overweight or obese Americans continues to rise. If current trends continue, by 2015 three in every four Americans will be overweight, and nearly four in every ten will be obese. Clearly the methods used to fight obesity, which mainly focused on education, have been insufficient. Yet within recent national experience there are approaches with a far better chance of success. These are the strategies used in the anti-smoking campaign, which helped reduce the numbers of U.S. smokers from 42% of Americans in 1965 to under 20% today. Based on the strategies used in the tobacco fight, these solutions should be given urgent attention. They are: 1) impose a steep tax on fattening, non-nutritious foods; 2) require food producers to put easy-to-read nutritional labels on the fronts of packages of food; 3) require restaurants to list nutritional information next to each item on their menus; and 4) outlaw advertising of fattening foods and limit their sale. The success of these strategies in reducing smoking should encourage their use in the fight against obesity as well.

The graphic organizer on the next page shows one way to organize a problem-solution text.

Problem:	
Attempt 1 to Solve Problem	
Attempt 2 to Solve Problem	
Attempt 3 to Solve Problem	
Solution:	

QuickGuide for Problem-and-Solution Texts

- → Identify a problem.
- → Make a chart to organize ideas and arrange them in a logical order.
- → Craft detail sentences to expand upon the problem and eventually offer a solution.
- → Use transitions effectively to guide readers through the process, and maintain an evenhanded tone.
- → Define any terms that your readers may not know.
- → Include an introduction with a topic sentence that clearly identifies the problem. Include a conclusion that sends the message, *Here is the best solution to the problem.*

Create Real-World Texts

1. Write a letter to the city council identifying a problem in your community and suggesting a solution.
2. Make a flyer identifying a problem in your state, nation, or the world and suggesting what citizens can do to solve the problem.

CHAPTER 8

Writing to Persuade

Persuasive writing states an opinion on a subject and uses facts, reasons, and examples to convince readers. The kind of persuasive writing you will do most often in school is called **argumentative writing.**

CHAPTER 8

Here are some of the ways in which persuasive writing can influence people's lives and the society in which they live.

- **Speechwriters help political candidates explain, defend, and "sell"** the candidates' positions on campaign issues.
- **Business executives prepare and deliver presentations** to persuade their colleagues and clients to adopt their ideas for making or marketing goods and services.
- **Lawyers write briefs** presenting the reasons why judges and jurors should decide in favor of their clients.
- **Advertising copywriters craft ads** aimed at persuading readers, viewers, or listeners to buy products.
- **Science writers explain recent theories and discoveries** in medicine and health, urging their readers to lead healthier lifestyles.
- **News reporters write stories** that expose illegal or immoral behavior by public officials, CEOs, industrialists, and others.

Writing Project — Argumentative

Blow Your Whistle ***Write an argumentative composition that exposes a problem and suggests solutions.***

Think Through Writing You've probably heard the term "whistle-blower." A whistle-blower is a person who calls attention to wrongdoing in order put an end to it. Famous whistle-blowers have raised awareness of corruption in business, politics, education, and other important areas of life. Think of a situation in your school or community that you feel is not right and blow the whistle on it. Explain the problem so that readers agree with you and are motivated to put an end to it. Write about what the problem is and what people should do to stop it.

Talk About It In your writing group, discuss the writing you have done. What sorts of problems did the authors identify? Why have the problems not been addressed up until this point? Express your opinions freely and clearly. Ask for clarification if anyone says something you do not understand.

Read About It In the interview that follows, Randall Hayes, documentary filmmaker and environmental activist, describes the consequences of uranium mining in the American Southwest and timber production in the rain forests of the Amazon. He builds his argument on the three pillars of persuasion: appeals to reason, appeals to emotion, and appeals to ethics.

MODEL: Persuasion

Interview with Randall Hayes

Elizabeth Robinson

Elizabeth Robinson: *Let's begin with some background on how you got interested in the tropical rainforests.*

The interviewer understands the importance of background and context.

Randall Hayes: Well, in the process of getting my master's degree, I did a one-hour PBS documentary about the cultural and environmental impacts of uranium mining in the Southwest. The film is called *The Four Corners: A National Sacrifice Area?*

As he answers, Hayes establishes his credibility and ethical standards—not everyone can make a documentary for PBS (public television).

Fortunately the Southwest was not entirely sacrificed for coal and uranium, but in the early days uranium mining was done very poorly. Piles of radioactive waste were left around and the Indian children would go and play on them and ride their horses across the waste piles, and contamination started to show up in genetic defects of newborn babies.

Here Hayes appeals to the listeners' emotions by discussing the effects of the uranium mining on children.

See, the radioactive waste from processing uranium is 85 percent as radioactive as the original ore when it is mined out of the ground . . . and this waste was left lying around. The film exposed that problem and now, fortunately, a lot of these piles are being picked up.

Hayes appeals to reason when he cites a scientific fact about uranium.

ER: *How did you get from the Southwest desert to the rainforests?*

RH: While I was in the Southwest, the American Indians there told me about the problems that their

Indian friends were having in the Amazon tropical rainforest area. In 1984, after I finished this film on environmental and cultural issues in the desert, I took a trip down to the Central American rainforest. And I realized there was a *very* serious problem there.

At that time there was not much going on to alert the world about how serious this problem was. So I thought I would try to organize an information clearing house that tried to really do two things—blow the whistle on the problem and sound the alarm, but also provide avenues of action.

CHAPTER 8

Just being aware of a problem won't solve it; people want to *do* something with their awareness. Otherwise, it's rather depressing to find out we have a serious problem and not know what to do about it . . .

This comment raises the listeners' expectations that Hayes will offer specific, concrete steps people can take.

ER: *I've heard you speak about the need for educating the business community. How would you go about that?*

RH: We don't really teach ecology, and ecology—the natural processes—is really the way the world works. If our business leaders don't understand natural processes, it will be extremely difficult for them to develop businesses that are ecologically sound. If they don't know ecology, then they don't know how the world *really* works.

Industrial society needs to be transformed into a kind of post-industrial, ecologically sound society where it will still be a modern society; it will still be a technological society. It will still have modern health conveniences and transportation systems. It is just that they will be much less polluting, much more benign to the environment than they are now. But in order to make that transformation as rapid as possible, we need strong involvement from the business community.

What I would like to see very strongly is that our MBA graduates would have a dual degree, a degree in ecology and a degree in business. Nothing short of that is going to speed the transition. We don't really have *time* to go into our elementary schools and wait until the kids become chairmen of the board or the Chief Executive Officers of Chevron or Mobil or General Motors. That takes six decades and we don't have six decades. We really

Here is the first concrete step Hayes offers.

only have five or ten years to make very big changes in the way we do business in the tropical rainforests.

ER: *For example?*

RH: Well, the tropical timber industry. It is virtually impossible to have successful tropical timber plantations. We can do it in the North because our soils are better and our climate is more conducive to sustainable timber growth . . . But 99.9 percent, I mean literally 99.9 percent of the tropical timber that is harvested right now is extracted out of *virgin* rainforest. That means it is a one-time thing. It's like extracting gold out of the land. When you mine it, it's gone forever. It's not going to grow a second crop. So the tropical timber industry is going to have to essentially shut down.

Hayes appeals to both reason and emotion here. Reason says that the timber industry will put itself out of business. Words like "gone forever" stir emotions.

The forest is actually much more valuable economically by extracting different products out of it—non-timber products like Brazil nuts, like latex from naturally occurring rubber trees. See, you don't kill the rubber tree, you just extract the latex. Then there are all kinds of other plants that provide oils for lotions, essences for perfumes, that are extremely valuable but which can get driven into extinction in the logging process.

So if we leave the pristine forest alone, except to extract a small quantity of useful products out of it, it is actually economically more beneficial for the people of the Third World. By doing that, we are being more sensitive to issues of poverty and issues of economic development.

Here is a second concrete step: use the rainforest in sustainable ways.

ER: *Right, it's like the saying, if you buy a man a fish you feed him for a day, and if you teach him how to fish . . .*

RH: Exactly. I think that a lot people, when they realize that their tax dollars are funding hydroelectric dams that flood the Amazon, will want to see that that is stopped. They would rather see their tax dollars financing ecologically sound agriculture that really does provide for people's basic needs by developing these extracted reserves in a way that provides an on-going, sustainable economy . . .

Hayes appeals to the ethics of his listeners and assumes that if they were informed, they would opt for a more ecologically sound use of their tax money.

ER: *Is there anything else you would like to say to our readers?*

RH: I guess the only other point is that virtually all of the world's rainforest will be destroyed in the next 30 to 40 years. But, effectively, in the next five or ten years we have to change our policies toward the rainforest or we are really not going to have a chance to save much of it. So it is really the next five to ten years that are critical.

We need people to take this issue on as a challenge to get themselves involved in. A lot of people are involved in local community issues or even national environmental issues. But the world works as one unified system—*that* is what ecology teaches us—so we need to put a little time, energy and financial resources into this.

Hayes puts forward a third specific step: people need to get involved and "speak for nature" to the forces that have control over it, lawmakers and businesses.

If one were to think of a jaguar family in the Amazon—a mother jaguar and her cubs—and realize she has just as much right to exist and to carry on her life as we do, that the world is big enough that we ought to have enough room for both of us, for humanity to have its needs satisfied, and for there to be enough wilderness and room for the jaguar to carry on in her path of evolution, then we realize we have to change the way we perceive and deal with the rainforest.

Hayes doesn't talk generally about "animals." Instead, he focuses on a single family of jaguars. The image of the mother and cubs at our mercy stirs emotions.

Now the jaguar can't speak for herself so she retreats deeper and deeper into the forest. That's why *we* have to speak for the jaguar. And we have to speak for the Winged People and the Four Legged People and the Fish People.

What I mean by that kind of language is that these beings are alive also and they have rights, but they can't

walk into the halls of Congress and plead their case. They can't go into the grocery store and ask that the rainforest beef not be sold, and that the sustainable Brazil nuts be sold. So we have to do that on their behalf . . . *we have to speak for nature.* That is an awesome responsibility—and one that is also very exciting.

The interview ends with a strong appeal to ethics as Hayes raises awareness of humans' ethical responsibilities.

CHAPTER 8

Respond in Writing Does Randall Hayes persuade you that there is a problem to be addressed? Which of his appeals was especially persuasive for you?

Develop Your Own Ideas Work with your classmates to develop ideas that you might use in persuading readers that a problem exists that you need to expose.

Small Groups: In your small group, discuss each writer's argument based on the categories in the following graphic organizer. Make a graphic organizer of your own in which to record your groups' ideas.

Problem	
Source of the problem (who is responsible)	
Reasons why the problem came into being	
Claims	
Evidence and examples to back up claims	
Warrants to explain how evidence supports claim	
Persuasive techniques	

Whole Class: Make a master chart of all of the ideas generated by the small groups to see how different members of the class wrote about problems.

Write About It You will next write an argumentative essay in which you blow the whistle on a harmful problem that is not widely understood. You may use the topic you developed in your early writing or any of the following.

Possible Topics	Possible Audiences	Possible Forms
• a problem in a local business, such as overcharging customers or using "creative" bookkeeping to bilk investors • a problem at school, such as the violation of privacy when students use their cell phones to capture a video of someone • problem in a school sports program, such as when athletes are given grades they don't deserve to keep them on the team	• people in town who are affected by the problem • people in leadership positions who could stop the problem • people who are responsible for the problem • people in the legal system who might litigate against the problem	• a blog entry • a newspaper article • a letter exposing the problem • a speech at a press conference

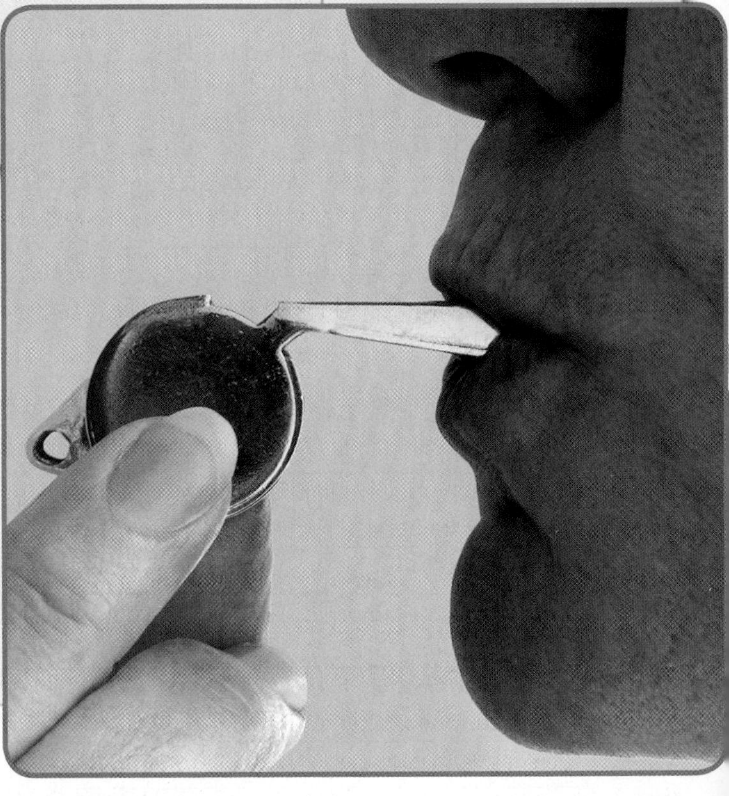

CHAPTER 8

Elements of Persuasive Texts

Analyzing

"Writing," said author and women's rights activist Gloria Steinem, "keeps me from believing everything I read." She may have meant that her attempts at trying to persuade readers to accept her views also taught her to recognize the persuasive strategies used by her fellow writers. Writing your own work and reading the work of others are two complementary activities in the process of learning how to write. Persuasive writing requires not only strong, well-constructed arguments, but also skillful presentation of your facts and opinions.

CHAPTER 8

1 Structure

While the content of argumentative essays may vary, the structure remains the same. An argumentative essay, like all essays, has three main parts: an introduction, a body, and a conclusion. The following chart shows the function of each part.

HERE'S HOW

Structuring an Argumentative Essay

- In the **introduction,** capture the audience's attention, present the issue, and introduce a precise, knowledgeable claim in a thesis statement.
- In the **body of supporting paragraphs,** logically sequence claims, counterclaims, reasons, and evidence. Clearly distinguish your claims from alternative or opposing claims.
- In the **conclusion,** present a summary or strong conclusive evidence—logically drawn from the arguments—that drives home your position.

Read the two editorials on the following pages. Both deal with the issue of global warming. The first is from the *Houston Chronicle;* the second is from the *Orange County Register* online.

Editorial: Change on the Way: Latest U.S. Global-Warming Study Predicts Sweltering Future

Thursday, June 18, 2009

Jun. 18—As southeast Texans swelter under what local National Weather Service forecasters label a "death ridge," the latest federal report on climate change indicates the abnormally high temperatures, oppressive humidity and dearth of rain may offer a taste of typical Houston summers to come. Issued as Congress debates how to reduce man-made greenhouse gas emissions that are heating the globe, the study by top government scientists, entitled "Global Climate Change Impacts in the United States," warns that Americans are already feeling the effects of global warming, which will rapidly get worse.

The opening draws readers in with its reference to the current heat wave. The writer establishes credibility by referring to a government report.

As the report states, "global warming is unequivocal and primarily human-induced." Climate-related changes are already being observed and include increases in heavy downpours, melting glaciers and lengthening growing seasons.

Quotes from authorities give the report validity.

If the current run of days in the high 90s here seems intolerable, just wait. According to projections, by the last few decades of this century the number of days over 90 degrees in southeast Texas will increase from 75 to 165 days a year, making a Houston summer that much more daunting.

These paragraphs list the many ways global warming will affect the people reading the story.

Still recovering from Hurricane Ike, Gulf Coast residents can expect rising sea levels that will endanger low-lying communities, roads, rail lines and vital oil and gas industry infrastructure. Gulf waters could rise three to four feet by 2100, pushing beaches back while bringing salt water much farther inland.

Tropical storms are likely to be more intense due to warming sea waters, while the southwest United States can look forward to prolonged droughts and water shortages in major urban areas.

Average U.S. temperatures have already risen 1.5 degrees in the past half century, and could range from two to 11 degrees more if current levels of carbon dioxide emissions are not lowered.

A bill to set up a cap-and-trade system to lower carbon output from U.S. industrial facilities is under discussion in Congress.

> The previous paragraphs dealt with the problem; in the succeeding paragraphs a possible solution is presented.

Texas Democratic lawmakers, including Houston Rep. Gene Green, have signed off on a compromise that would initially provide refiners, electric utilities and other industries with allowances to soften the economic impact of reducing emissions.

President Barack Obama's science adviser, John Holdren, hopes the latest findings "will contribute to how people think about specific legislative proposals and the need to move ahead smartly now after many years of dithering and delay."

Living in a region particularly vulnerable to the consequences of global warming, Houstonians should support congressional efforts to craft sensible measures to turn down the heat.

> This concluding paragraph is the clincher: it tells the readers what they need to do to help solve the problem.

Editorial: Global warming 'consensus' a fiction

Tuesday, January 1, 2008

Skeptics from a range of scientific disciplines get louder in their opposition to doomsday claims

AN ORANGE COUNTY REGISTER EDITORIAL

Global warming hype peaked in 2007 with calls for vast increases in government control to stifle industrial growth, eliminate fossil fuels and impose new carbon taxes.

> The word "hype" in the first sentence lets the reader know on which side of the global warming issue *The Orange County Register* stands.

We were told desperate measures are needed because there's a scientific "consensus" that man-made greenhouse gases are increasing dangerously. Former Vice President Al Gore claimed there's *no* legitimate objection to the catastrophes he and the U.N.'s Intergovernmental Panel on Climate Change predict.

All this received much media coverage and support from politicians and government bureaucrats, who stand to gain control if we heed their warnings. The problem is, there's *no* scientific consensus for doomsday claims, let alone that drastic remedies are needed.

Growing numbers of global warming science skeptics are making their opposition known. They include experts in climatology, oceanography, geology, biology, environmental sciences and physics, among others. They are affiliated with prestigious institutions worldwide, including Harvard, NASA, the National Oceanic and Atmospheric Administration and the National Center for Atmospheric Research, MIT, the International Arctic Research Center, the Royal Netherlands Meteorological Institute and many others. Many shared a portion of IPCC's 2007 Nobel Peace Prize (co-won with Mr. Gore), and others have won previous Nobel Prizes for their research.

In this paragraph the major position is stated: doubts about the reality of global warming.

A U.S. Senate report accumulated more than 400 of their views to refute Mr. Gore's claim of "consensus."

For example, physics professor emeritus Dr. Howard Hayden of the University of Connecticut said, "You think SUVs are the cause of glaciers shrinking? … Don't believe what you hear out of Hollywood and Washington, D.C. … [C]limate history proves that Gore has the relationship between carbon dioxide concentration and global warming backward. A higher concentration of carbon dioxide in the atmosphere does not cause the Earth to be warmer. Instead, a warmer Earth causes the higher carbon dioxide levels."

In the next few paragraphs, scientists are identified by name and their ideas are quoted to lend support to the editorial's position.

Climatologist Robert Durrenberger, past president of the American Association of State Climatologists, said, "because of all the misinformation that Gore and his army have been spreading about climate change I have decided that real climatologists should try to help the public understand the nature of the problem."

Read the consensus-refuting comments of these scientists online at www.epw.senate.gov (click on U.S. Senate Report: Over 400 Prominent Scientists Disputed Man-Made Global Warming Claims in 2007).

As Swedish geologist Dr. Wibjorn Karlen, professor emeritus at Stockholm University, wrote, "Newspapers should think about the damage they are doing to many persons, particularly young kids, by spreading the exaggerated views of a human impact on climate.... As far as I can see the IPCC 'Global Temperature' is wrong. Temperature is fluctuating but it is still most places cooler than in the 1930s and 1940s ... it will take about 800 years before the water level has increased by one meter."

The purpose of this editorial is not a call to action, as in the previous editorial. Instead, the goal of this persuasive writing is to change people's minds.

CHAPTER 8

PROJECT PREP *Analyzing* *Claims and Warrants*

Based on the discussions you have had with your classmates and the two opposing editorials on global warming, sketch out the kind of persuasive essay you would like to write. On the subject of blowing the whistle on wrongdoing, for example, ask yourself what argument you might try to make based on what you know about the problem. Who are the people you want to persuade, and what action, if any, would you want them to take? Organize the plan for your argument into a chart like the one below in which you make a series of claims about the problem, give examples that illustrate each claim, and assert a warrant that explains how the example illustrates the claim. (See pages 120–121 for more information on claims, examples, and warrants.)

Claims	**Examples**	**Warrants**
Child labor in China deprives children of their safety and education.	Accidents involving children are common in fireworks factories. As industry grew, high school dropout rates increased.	The number of accidents involving child workers, as well as the increased dropout rate tied to the growth of industry, shows the toll child labor practices take on child safety and education.

2 Facts and Opinions

Writers of persuasion need to be aware of the difference between facts and opinions. Facts can be proved, while opinions cannot.

A **fact** is a statement that can be proved. An **opinion** is a belief or judgment that cannot be proved.

One way to test whether a statement is factual is to look for confirmation of it within your own experience. You can, for example, test the following statement against your own experience.

CHAPTER 8

Fact	Thanksgiving falls on the fourth Thursday of November. (This can be verified by your own experience.)

The second way is to ask yourself whether you could prove it by consulting accepted authorities.

Fact	The first Thanksgiving was celebrated in the colonial settlement of Plymouth, Massachusetts. (You cannot use your experience to test this statement, but you can verify it by consulting a recognized expert or an encyclopedia.)

Opinions, unlike facts, cannot be proved. They are judgments, interpretations, predictions, or preferences that vary from person to person. Some opinions, however, are more sound than others. In any discussion or argumentative essay about issues, the soundest opinions are those that can be supported by convincing factual evidence. Claims, statements asserted to be true, are well-supported opinions.

Supported Opinion, or Claim	People should wear seat belts because they save lives. (Supporting fact: The National Safety Council estimates that thousands of lives per year could be saved if more people wore seat belts.)
Unsupported Opinion	Chocolate tastes better than vanilla. (No facts are available to back up this statement.)

Learn to recognize opinions in what you read and write, and check every opinion for facts that back it up. The following words are often used in statements of opinion.

OPINION WORDS		
should	good, better, best	probably
ought	bad, worse, worst	might
can	beautiful	perhaps
may	terrible	maybe

Practice Your Skills

Identifying Facts and Opinions

Identify each sentence as a fact or an opinion. If you are in doubt about a sentence, verify it by checking in the library or asking a reliable authority.

1. May is the most beautiful month of the year.
2. Harper Lee wrote *To Kill a Mockingbird.*
3. Mark Twain's best novel is *Tom Sawyer.*
4. Light travels faster than sound.
5. We caught fish last Saturday because we used a new bait.

Supporting Opinions with Facts

Write one fact that could be used to back up each opinion below.

1. The work week should be four days rather than five.
2. People ought to avoid eating too many sweets.
3. The city is much more interesting and exciting than the countryside.
4. There should be a law requiring people to vote.
5. Students should concentrate on learning, not socializing.

Writing Tip

Support your opinions with convincing **factual evidence** from your own observation as well as from reliable authorities.

PROJECT PREP Analyzing ***Facts and Opinions***

Share the evidence you recorded in a chart (page 293) with your writing group. For each author, focus on the kinds of examples being used. Does each have a strong factual basis? Help authors identify where facts will be needed to support assertions. Make a list of additional facts, examples, and statistics you each might use to strengthen the quality of the supporting evidence after considering whether it's based on opinion, rumor, or established fact.

3 Appeals to Reason

Once you have gathered precise and relevant factual evidence to support a claim, you need to determine how the facts fit together and what logical conclusions you can draw from them. Constructing an argument from evidence requires careful reasoning, or logic.

Generalizations

CHAPTER 8

When you state a rule or a principle based on fact and experience, you are forming a **generalization.** For example, suppose you are waiting for a bus you ride frequently. Each time you have waited for the bus, it has been late, so you assume it will be late again. You are generalizing based on past experience.

Generalizing is a useful reasoning tool. When it is not practiced carefully, however, it can cause you to overlook important exceptions, leaving you with a false or misleading conclusion.

Hasty Generalizations

Hasty generalizations are broad generalizations based on scanty evidence and are unproved. As a result, they often lead to false or misleading conclusions. To draw a sound conclusion, you need to be sure you have examined *enough* particular experiences. For example, if a bus is late only once or twice, you do not have sufficient experience to conclude that it will be late the next time. If others have caught the bus on time even though you have had to wait on a number of occasions, you cannot logically conclude the bus will be late. Similarly, if the bus is late four times but on time twice, you cannot reasonably conclude the bus will be late the next time.

A sound generalization, then, depends on three factors: (1) a sufficient and representative number of experiences, (2) verification of your generalizations by others, and (3) explainable exceptions. Hasty generalizations lack one or more of these three factors. Often they include words such as *always, never, all,* or *none.* Consider the following hasty generalizations.

Hasty Generalization	**All** dogs are loyal and obedient. (Has the writer examined enough dogs to conclude they all share these qualities?)
Hasty Generalization	Eating strawberries results in a rash. (Does everyone who eats strawberries break out in a rash?)
Hasty Generalization	**Every** younger brother imitates his older brother. (Does this statement hold true for all younger brothers?)
Hasty Generalization	Apples from Pell's Orchard are **always** the tastiest in town. (Has the writer eaten enough apples from other orchards?)

You can make the preceding hasty generalizations more sound if you limit them to *some, many,* or *most* cases instead of *all* cases.

Limited Generalization	**Many** dogs are loyal and obedient.
Limited Generalization	Eating strawberries results in a rash for **some** people.
Limited Generalization	**Some** younger brothers imitate their older brothers.
Limited Generalization	Apples from Pell's Orchard are **usually** the tastiest in town.

CHAPTER 8

Practice Your Skills

Writing Limited Generalizations

Rewrite each of the following hasty generalizations until it is a limited generalization with which you agree.

1. All adults are wiser than teenagers.
2. Life in big cities is thoroughly unbearable.
3. Life in small towns is always quiet and boring.
4. All firefighters and police officers today are courageous people.

Making Valid Inferences

To be persuasive, you also need to make sure your conclusions or inferences are valid. An inference is **valid** if it follows logically from the claims. (See page 121 for more information on valid inferences.)

Writing Tip

Avoid making **hasty generalizations** by limiting generalizations to *some, many,* or *most* cases instead of all cases. Avoid *all, total, complete, every, always, never,* and *none* in your persuasive writing.

PROJECT PREP Analyzing *Reasoning*

In your writing group, evaluate one another's claims. Decide if each writer's major claims hold up under scrutiny. Can you think of reasons not to accept the claims? Are the inferences valid? Help each author articulate additional claims that might be made in support of his or her position.

In the Media

A Political Campaign

Elected officials who are up for re-election sometimes spend more of their day campaigning and raising money than governing. Critics of our system of election say that this forces our politicians to act like advertisers, marketing an "image" through commercials and slogans. Thus, say the critics, the officials' positions on matters of substance are purposely withheld so they do not turn potential supporters away. The overwhelming use of television and, to a lesser degree, radio to conduct a campaign fosters **appeals to emotions.** Patriotic music, lofty words, and television images chosen for their ability to stir emotion take the place of the less dramatic and flashy appeals to reason. Even the critics have to agree, however, that television and radio make it possible to see and hear candidates in debates and interviews during which they are more likely to use **appeals to reason** and **appeals to ethical beliefs.**

Media Activity

Plan a campaign for one of our early presidents as if there were television and other modern media then. Study the issues he stood for and the controversies of his day. Decide what segment of the voters you will be targeting in your campaign (remember that voting rights were not universal) and which persuasive appeals you will use. Answer these questions to help you. In order to plan your campaign, ask the following questions:

- What qualities in your candidate do you want to highlight? Why?
- What events will your candidate attend? What message are you trying to convey?
- Sketch out a newspaper ad. What would the graphic be and why? What would the text say? What, if any, symbols would you use?
- Write a 15-second radio commercial and a 30-second television spot for your candidate. What stations will you play them on?
- What themes will your candidate debate with an opponent?

Use the questions to compare your campaign with those of your classmates. What do they have in common? What has this activity helped you understand about political campaigns in the media? How could political campaigns be more effective in the future?

The prewriting stage is the important planning period in the development of an argumentative essay. In this stage, you choose a subject, develop a thesis, and gather and organize factual evidence.

1 Audience, Purpose, and Subject

In a persuasive essay, your purpose is to influence the opinions and the behavior of your readers—your audience. In other words, you want to persuade your audience to adopt your point of view and to take an action that you suggest. Your first step in accomplishing this purpose is to develop a logical and reasonable argument that supports your opinion.

Audience

The better you know your audience—their likes and dislikes, their ethical beliefs, their age, gender, race, ethnic background, country of origin, artistic preferences, for example—the better you can convince them to accept what you are telling them. The better you know your audience the more able you will be to create a tone, a style, and just the right way of addressing them. The better you know your audience the more assured you will be in your choice of material to support your argument. Look over the questions below and be able to answer them (and any others pertinent to this particular group) accurately before you begin writing.

HERE'S HOW

Questions for Analyzing an Audience

- What does my audience already know about my subject?
- What is my audience's point of view about my subject?
- Do they already agree or disagree with my position?
- What are the chances of changing the attitudes and actions of my audience?
- Are there any sensitive issues of which I should be aware?

Purpose

When you write an argumentative essay, your purpose is to win readers over to your way of thinking or to persuade readers to take action. You must be very clear and very specific about what this purpose involves. Clear, logical arguments, appropriate appeals to emotions and ethical beliefs, and a strong, consistent approach to your position are your most effective tools.

Choosing a Subject

Good argumentative essays are based on views the writer feels strongly about and can support with convincing factual evidence. Brainstorming, freewriting, or clustering will help you explore controversial issues that appear in a number of places around you—in newspapers, in your school, in your community, in your home, and on television. Brainstorm or freewrite answers to questions such as "What do I care about?"

CHAPTER 8

HERE'S HOW

Guidelines for Choosing a Persuasive Essay Subject

- Choose a substantive subject with an issue that has at least two sides.
- Choose a subject you feel strongly about.
- Choose a subject you can support with facts, examples, statistics, incidents, and reasons from your own experience or from other reliable sources.
- Choose a subject for which there is an audience whose beliefs or behavior you would like to influence.

Practice Your Skills

Choosing Your Subject

Freewrite, brainstorm, or cluster for the conclusion to each of the following statements, and save your work.

1. The things I enjoy about modern progress are . . .
2. The things that concern me about modern progress are . . .
3. The things that concern other people about modern progress are . . .
4. The things I want to change in the modern world are . . .
5. If I had a million dollars to put toward an advancement in one field, I would use it to . . .

PROJECT PREP Prewriting *Reasoning*

In your writing group, discuss the audience each writer is intending to reach. Then discuss where that audience is likely to stand on the issue and how best to persuade that audience. Also help each author identify an appropriate voice and tone for the argumentative purpose.

2 Developing a Clear Thesis Statement

Once you have chosen an appropriate subject for your essay, you are ready to develop your **thesis statement,** a statement of the point of view you will argue for in your essay. Also called a **proposal,** it presents a plan for consideration related to the argument. A suitable thesis statement in an argumentative essay will express a precise and knowledgeable claim. Avoid statements of fact or mere preference, since they do not make suitable thesis statements for persuasive essays.

Fact	Much of the Brazilian rain forest has been destroyed.
Preference	Protecting the rain forest is the most important ecological problem.
Thesis Statement	People of the world must take action to stop the destruction of the Brazilian rain forest.

Use the following guidelines to develop your thesis statement.

HERE'S HOW

Guidelines for Developing a Thesis Statement

- State the thesis simply and directly in one sentence.
- Be sure the statement is a supportable claim or recommendation rather than a fact or mere preference.
- Check that the claim is debatable as you have expressed it.

Practice Your Skills

Choosing a Suitable Thesis Statement

Write whether each of the following statements would be suitable or unsuitable as a thesis statement for a persuasive essay. Use the guidelines above to evaluate each statement.

1. We should learn to be more patient with each other.
2. Responsibility for conserving energy rests with each consumer.
3. The world's population is increasing rapidly.
4. I am outraged at the condition of our city's streets.
5. The federal government should provide funds for solar power.

PROJECT PREP Prewriting *Thesis Statement*

In your writing group, help each author develop an effective thesis statement. Help each author confirm that each of the claims is in line with the paper's overall thesis and that each contributes to the essay's main purpose. Also consider whether additional material is needed to make other points that will help persuade the readers to accept the argument.

3 Developing an Argument

To develop an argument, begin by listing arguments your audience might find convincing. Anticipate the audience's knowledge level, concerns, and possible biases. Then gather and evaluate evidence to support those arguments. Your evidence will usually take the form of specific facts, examples, incidents, references to experts, and appeals to logic and reason. Look for information covering the complete range of relevant perspectives so that you can anticipate opposition and refute **counter-arguments.**

HERE'S HOW

Guidelines for Developing an Argument

- List all relevant perspectives in your prewriting notes and be prepared to represent them honestly and accurately.
- Develop claims and counterclaims fairly and thoroughly, supporting them with relevant evidence while pointing out strengths and weaknesses of each.
- Use facts and examples, but evaluate them to determine their relative value. Some data and "facts" are not as reliable as others. (For more information on evaluating sources, see pages 303 and 402–405.)
- If the opposition has a good point, admit it. Then show why the opposing point does not change your overall position. Such an admission, called **conceding a point,** will strengthen your credibility.
- Refer to well-respected experts and authorities to support your claim.
- Use the reasoning tool of generalizing to draw conclusions from your evidence.
- Use polite and reasonable language rather than words that show bias or emotions.

Practice Your Skills

Listing Pros and Cons

For each of the following thesis statements, write down three specific facts, examples, reasons, or incidents that support the thesis (pros) and three that oppose it (cons). Save your notes for later use.

1. The United States should colonize the moon as soon as possible.
2. People should not be permitted to play radios at beaches.
3. Drivers with two moving violations in a year should have their licenses revoked.

PROJECT PREP Prewriting *Counter-Arguments*

In your writing group, help each author develop at least one counter-argument in response to opposing views. Take notes so you can use this counter-argument, probably near the end of your paper, when you draft your exposé.

Think Critically

Evaluating Evidence and Sources

To make an argument in a persuasive or analytical essay as convincing as possible, use evidence consisting of facts, examples, incidents, anecdotes, statistics, or the opinions of qualified experts. However, before you include a piece of evidence, you should use the skill of **evaluating,** or critically judging, that evidence. Use the following criteria to decide whether the evidence will support your argument.

- Is the evidence precise and clearly relevant to the thesis?
- Is the source of the evidence reliable?
- Is the evidence up-to-date?
- Is the evidence unbiased and objective?

Suppose, for instance, you are arguing for greater federal support for day-care services for young children. Here is how you could evaluate evidence on this issue.

EVIDENCE	EVALUATION
More that 50 percent of parents of young children work.	Supports thesis—shows the need for day care
A study in the early 1970s showed that urban day-care centers were more expensive than rural centers.	Does not support thesis—information is out-of-date
Some businesses oppose laws allowing parents to take leave from their jobs.	Does not support thesis—evidence is not related to thesis

You also need to evaluate the validity, reliability, and relevance of the primary and secondary sources you use for your evidence. (See pages 402–405 for more on evaluating sources.) When you draft, demonstrate the consideration you gave to the validity of sources by identifying why they can be trusted or what their limitations might be.

Thinking Practice

Choose one of the following thesis statements or one based on an issue important to you. Make a chart like the previous one to evaluate the evidence for your position.

- The food in the school cafeteria should be more nutritious.
- Students should not work at a job more than 15 hours a week.
- School hours should be increased.

4 Organizing an Argument

Organize your ideas in a way that logically sequences claims, counterclaims, reasons, and evidence and that is appropriate to your purpose, audience, and context. For example, if your purpose is to convince people that your solution to a problem is the best one, you would probably follow a **problem-solution pattern** (see pages 280–281). Or maybe you want to structure your text as a **comparison-contrast,** alternating opposing views with your views and showing why yours are stronger (see pages 268–271). **Order of importance** is often the most effective tool in persuasive essays, since writers can make their emphasis clear and show how they have evaluated each piece of evidence. If your audience is policymakers deciding on funding for a new law, you might want to intersperse personal stories from citizens in with your hard evidence in support of your view. If your context is that you are responding to a magazine article you read via a letter to the editor, you would probably want to follow the structure of other letters to the editor you have read. There is no one "right" way to organize an argumentative text. The right way is the way that takes your purpose, audience, and context into account.

Remember to guide your reader with transitions that link major sections of the text, create cohesion, and clarify the relationships between claims and reasons, between reasons and evidence, and between claims and counterclaims. The following transitional words and phrases are especially useful when conceding a point or showing contrasting ideas.

TRANSITIONS FOR USE IN PERSUASIVE WRITING	
while it is true that	nonetheless
although	granting that
admittedly	still
nevertheless	of course
despite	however
on the other hand	instead

Using an Outline

An outline helps you organize your ideas. Read the tips for creating an outline below.

HERE'S HOW

Tips for Organizing and Outlining a Persuasive Text

- Review the supporting evidence you prepared. Then list the points that support your position in the order of least to most important. Leave two blank lines under each point.
- Assign each of your points a Roman numeral, as in an outline.
- Add at least two supporting points under each Roman numeral.

Your outline should look like this, though it may well have more than three main points.

MODEL: Outline

I. (Least important point)
- **A.** (Supporting point)
- **B.** (Supporting point)

II. (More important point)
- **A.** (Supporting point)
- **B.** (Supporting point)

III. (Most important point)
- **A.** (Supporting point)
- **B.** (Supporting point)

Using a Reasoning Pillar

Another way to picture a solidly built argumentative essay is to see it as a pillar, with each block strengthening the whole.

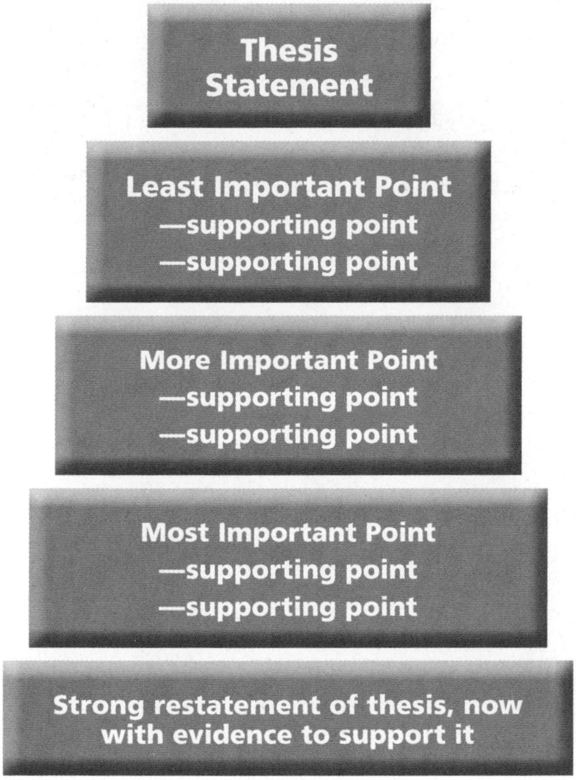

Without support, the claim expressed in the thesis statement would topple.

Each main point includes a claim, example, and warrant when appropriate.

Supporting points are presented so that each one rests on an even stronger one.

Counterclaims are addressed either point by point or all at once, often near the end.

A thesis with compelling evidence is the foundation for an effective essay.

PROJECT PREP Prewriting Organizing Ideas

In your writing group, focus your attention on the best way for each author to organize the essay. Talk through which are the most important ideas and what kind of supporting material each requires. Help each author produce a logical sequence for the body paragraphs of the exposé. You will probably include your refutation of a counter-argument at the end of your essay's body and before its conclusion.

The Power of Language

Adverbial Clauses: Tip the Scale

One important skill in argumentative writing consists of showing the flaws in your opponent's argument. Instead of ignoring the opposition, a strong persuasive argument acknowledges the opposition in order to conquer it. To signal that you intend to refute opposition, mention the opposing view in your thesis statement. One way to do this is to present your view and the opposing view in two independent clauses within the same sentence, as below. (The opposing view is highlighted.)

Two Independent Clauses	The timber industry makes a lot of money harvesting timber from virgin rainforests, but the forest is much more valuable economically when different products are extracted from it.

In the example above, independent clauses give the two viewpoints equal weight. Changing the sentence can give your side the advantage and put the opposition's opinions in a weaker light. In the following example, the subordinate, or dependent, clause is used for your opponents' views (highlighted). This construction allows you to present opposing views while "tipping the scale" in favor of your own position.

One Subordinate Clause, One Independent Clause	Although the timber industry makes a lot of money harvesting timber from virgin rainforest, the forest is much more valuable economically when different products are extracted out of it.

Putting it this way shows that you have considered both sides of the question and have rejected the opposing view. The spotlight is on your viewpoint, which is presented in the main independent clause. The use of a subordinating conjunction, such as the word *although,* tends to weaken the opposing viewpoint.

Try It Yourself

Write a sentence or sentences presenting your opponent's view in an introductory subordinate clause, followed by your own viewpoint in an independent clause. Later, you can check your draft to see if there are any other places you can "tip the scale."

Punctuation Tip

Place a comma after an introductory subordinate clause.

1 Following Your Outline

When you draft your essay, use your outline and other prewriting notes to express your ideas in sentences and paragraphs. As you write, however, you may include any new ideas or arguments that occur to you. You may also need to obtain new evidence or perhaps even alter your position slightly. Remember that your goal is not to write a polished draft, but to include all the points of your argument in a clear and logical manner.

HERE'S HOW

Guidelines for Drafting a Persuasive Essay

- Introduce your subject in a way that makes your thesis clear and that distinguishes your claim from alternate or opposing claims.
- Present precise and relevant evidence (facts, expert opinions, quotations, and/or expressions of commonly accepted beliefs).
- Represent the complete range of relevant perspectives accurately and honestly.
- Demonstrate that you considered the validity and reliability of the sources you used.
- Use carefully crafted language to move audiences who are either neutral or opposed.

Begin by writing your thesis statement. If you find it does not include all the points in your outline, refine it until it does. Then write an introductory paragraph that includes your refined thesis statement. Your paragraph should capture the reader's attention and lead up to your thesis by making the importance of your subject clear.

Next, draft the body paragraphs, devoting one paragraph to each main topic in your outline. In addition to presenting your own arguments, anticipate and refute counter-arguments. Be certain to concede a point to the opposition where appropriate and then go on to show why that point fails to change your opinion. Use transitions to guide the reader through your argument and clarify relationships among claims, counterclaims, reasons, and evidence.

Finally, draft a conclusion that follows from and supports your argument. If the purpose of your essay is to recommend a specific action, then make that request. Complete your draft by writing a title that catches the reader's attention.

PROJECT PREP Drafting *First Draft*

Write a first draft of your argumentative text and bring it to your writing group. Discuss how each draft accomplishes the tasks in the guidelines above. Offer specific suggestions for improvement, and take notes you can use when you revise.

2 Using Persuasive Rhetoric

In a persuasive essay, the introduction and conclusion often appeal to the reader's emotions or ethical beliefs. If the tone of the emotional appeal is sincere and reserved, such an approach can strengthen the force of the argument. If, on the other hand, the appeal is inflamed with loaded words and overcharged emotions, the writer may sharpen the lines that divide opinions. Establish and maintain a formal style and objective tone throughout your essay.

Inflamed	The gym in our school is a useless mess.
Reasonable	The gym in our school needs new lighting and other improvements that would make it a pleasant place to exercise and compete.

CHAPTER 8

If you choose your words carefully, you can make effective use of **persuasive rhetoric**—language with strong positive or negative connotations that appeals to the reader's emotions. Be sure to support your statements with facts.

Persuasive Rhetoric	Tens of thousands of our precious young people are massacred and maimed each year by drunk drivers.

PROJECT PREP Drafting *Persuasive Rhetoric*

In your writing group, help each author to review the language of the essay so that it does not offend or alienate a neutral or opposed audience. Play the role of the readers targeted for the essay. How do they feel about the language employed? Give each author suggestions on how to rephrase potentially inappropriate language so that the writing has the desired effect on its designated readers.

editing

The following sentence uses emotionally charged words. Write the sentence and circle the overly emotional words. Then revise the passage (you can use more than one sentence in the revision) in straightforward, forceful language.

> The greedy timber industry has carved unseemly profits by slashing and desecrating life-giving forests.

When you revise your persuasive essay, you improve your first draft by making your argument clearer and more convincing. You may need to strengthen the introduction, add new evidence, or refine your language to help the reader focus on your main point and follow your argument. You will be most successful if you read your essay several times, each time addressing a different aspect of the writing.

- Does your introduction challenge your audience?
- Is your thesis statement a strong and clear statement of your position on the issue?
- Can your evidence be strengthened by better examples?
- Have you overlooked any important points?
- Have you conceded a point? In other words, have you admitted that an opposing point has validity but is not strong enough to sway you?
- Are there words you might use that have more impact?
- Does your conclusion work?

Once you have refined your language and strengthened your argument, read your essay again to check your logic and eliminate any of the following logical fallacies.

1 Eliminating Logical Fallacies

A **fallacy** is an error in logic. You have already seen how to avoid hasty generalizations on pages 296–297. Following are several other fallacies that can creep into your reasoning and weaken your argument. As you revise your persuasive essay, test your ideas to make sure you have not fallen into one of the following traps.

Attacking the Person Instead of the Issue

The Latin name for this fallacy is *argumentum ad hominem.* It means "argument against the man." Writers who commit this fallacy sidestep the real issue and instead try to slur the character of their opponent.

Writing Tip

Eliminate logical **fallacies** in your writing.

***Ad Hominem* Fallacy**	Candidate Young's proposal for a new highway is filled with potential problems. Young does things at the last minute, and his proposal was probably thrown together too quickly. He suffered from this problem in college too, where he failed two courses. (That Mr. Young does things at the last minute and failed two college courses does not necessarily mean that his proposal is faulty.)

Using positive but equally irrelevant personal qualities as the basis for an argument is also illogical.

***Ad Hominem* Fallacy**	Because Joseph Chen is a good father and a friendly neighbor, I know he's right about the new school proposal. (Mr. Chen's goodness as a father and neighbor is no assurance that his views about the school are right.)

Fallacy of Either-Or Reasoning

Writers of persuasive essays often assume there are only two sides to any question. Between two opposite points of view, there are usually many alternative viewpoints. Notice how the following statement ignores alternatives between the two extremes.

Either-or Fallacy	Either you support the wilderness bill or you favor killing baby seals. (There may be people who want to save seals but who also want a different wilderness bill.)

Although the words *either...or* are often used in this fallacy, be ready to detect this fallacy when it is expressed in other words.

Either-or Fallacy	By refusing to be a volunteer in the hospital, you show your lack of compassion. (There are many other ways a person can show compassion.)

Fallacy of the *Non Sequitur*

Non sequitur is a phrase from Latin meaning "it does not follow." Like the either-or fallacy, the *non sequitur* omits reasonable alternatives. As a result, the conclusion drawn in a *non sequitur* does not follow logically from the evidence.

CHAPTER 8

Non Sequitur	Because David was more nervous at the auditions than Sam, David deserved to get the part. (A person's nervousness at an audition is not as important as acting ability.)
Non Sequitur	Debbie got the most votes; she must be the best-qualified candidate for the job. (Debbie may have waged the best campaign and won, but another candidate may have been better qualified.)
Non Sequitur	The less time you spend watching television, the more time you will spend studying. (There may well be other distractions.)

Confusing Chronology with Cause and Effect

This fallacy results when something that happens *after* an event is assumed to be the result of that event. In many cases the relationship between the two events is coincidental. The Latin name for this fallacy is *post hoc, ergo propter hoc.* This means "after this; therefore, because of this."

Cause-Effect Fallacy	Since Albert went to sleep right after watching the movie, the movie must have caused his nightmares. (Just because the movie came before Albert's nightmares does not mean it caused them.)
Cause-Effect Fallacy	Every time Robert attends a game, his team loses. He must have a bad effect on the team. (A likelier explanation is that Robert happens to go to the games in which the team plays poorly or is facing a tough opponent.)

False Analogies

An **analogy** is a comparison between two things that are alike in some significant ways. This useful tool can help you communicate ideas your reader might otherwise find difficult to grasp. Suppose, for example, you were trying to persuade your mayor that bicycle lanes are necessary in your city. You might help the mayor understand your view by using the following analogy.

Analogy	Depriving bicycle riders of bicycle lanes is like depriving pedestrians of sidewalks.

A **false analogy** is an attempt to compare two things that are alike in some ways but too far apart in others to be logically compared.

False Analogy	I can't complete my book report on time. After all, Rome wasn't built in a day. (Although completing a book report and building Rome both involve an effort, the size of the effort is so dramatically different that the analogy is illogical.)
False Analogy	Regina will probably make the cheerleading squad. Her sister did. (Regina and her sister, although probably similar in some ways, may have different levels of athletic ability.)

When they compare things that are truly similar, analogies can enrich and clarify writing. Avoid using analogies as proofs, however, since what is true about one thing is not necessarily true about something that is similar.

CHAPTER 8

Begging the Question

Building an argument on an unproved assumption is called **begging the question.** In the following examples, all of the assumptions offered as facts need to be proved before the argument is logical.

Begging the Question	Because students who wear uniforms perform better, uniforms should be required. (First prove that such students perform better.)
Begging the Question	The irresponsible attitudes of today's youth are the main cause of juvenile delinquency. (First prove that today's youth have irresponsible attitudes.)
Begging the Question	The government's excessive spending on weapons is a waste of taxpayers' money. (First show that the spending is excessive by proving that the government could and should spend less.)

Begging the question is a form of **circular reasoning.** In the last example, "excessive spending" and "waste of money" mean the same thing. What the sentence is actually expressing is simply this: Because the government wastes taxpayers' money on weapons, this spending is a waste of taxpayers' money. This kind of reasoning is meaningless because it goes around in circles. Notice the circular reasoning in the following example.

Circular Reasoning	My doctor must be smart because she made it through medical school. (Translation: my doctor must be smart because she is a doctor.)

PROJECT PREP Revising *Checking for Logical Fallacies*

In your writing group, read each author's essay to make sure that rules of logic are followed. Help each author eliminate fallacious reasoning and present the argument with clarity and straightforwardness.

2 Avoiding Propaganda Techniques

The purpose of **propaganda** is to get the reader or listener to accept a particular point of view or to take some action. Rather than facts, evidence, proved generalizations, and logical reasoning, however, writers who use propaganda techniques misrepresent or distort information, or they present opinions as if they were facts. Propaganda often stirs emotions through the use of emotional language, stereotypes, and exaggeration.

The best persuasive texts, however, couple the appeal to emotions and ethical beliefs with clear-headed logic and reasoning and appeal to a reader's rational side. As you revise, challenge your thinking at every stage. Watch especially for the following propaganda techniques and avoid them.

Confusion Between Fact and Opinion

See pages 294–295 for a discussion of fact as opposed to opinion. When opinions are presented as facts, confusion and misunderstanding often result. Be careful not to express an opinion, yours or anyone else's, as a fact.

Bandwagon Appeals

The **bandwagon appeal** tries to get people to do or think the same thing as everyone else. Often bandwagon appeals try to make people feel left out if they do not conform.

Bandwagon Appeal	Elect James Streeter—the People's Choice—Governor. Do as your neighbors do. Vote for a winner. Elect James Streeter.

Testimonials

A famous person's endorsement, or support, of a product, candidate, or policy is called a **testimonial.** A testimonial may be misleading if it suggests that because the famous person used the product, everyone else should use it.

Testimonial	Hi, Sports Fans! I'm Hank Hawkins, the Fairview Ferrets' fearsome quarterback. I need to have lots of pep and zip to run and throw that ball. I get all the energy I need from Grizzlies. Eat Grizzlies for breakfast; you'll be just like me—ready to go!

Supporting your ideas with the opinions of credible experts can be an excellent way to strengthen your argument. That expert opinion must be genuine, however.

Glittering Generalities

Careless thinking about general ideas can lead to a reasoning problem called **glittering generalities,** words and phrases most people associate with virtue and goodness. They are used intentionally to trick people into feeling positive about a subject. Below are some words that typically stir positive feelings in people.

VIRTUE WORDS					
democracy	family	motherhood	education	values	moral

However, what one person means by any of these words can differ greatly from what another person means. When one of these words is attached to a controversial idea, chances are the writer or speaker is trying to evoke a positive attitude toward this idea. For example, if a politician says, "We must change this law to preserve our democracy," he or she presumes you support democracy and hopes to convince you to support changing the law so that democracy will not come tumbling down.

When you recognize a glittering generality, slash through it by asking yourself the questions below, recommended by the Institute for Propaganda Analysis.

QUESTIONS FOR ANALYZING PROPAGANDA

- What does the virtue word really mean?
- Does the idea in question have any legitimate connection with the real meaning of the word?
- Is an idea that does not serve my best interests being "sold" to me merely by its being given a name that I like?
- Leaving the virtue word out of consideration, what are the merits of the idea itself?

Platitudes

Platitudes are dull, overused generalizations. A writer who uses platitudes offers a simple saying rather than a carefully reasoned solution to a problem. How many times have you heard the following platitudes?

Platitudes	Boys will be boys. Time heals all wounds.	Life is not a bed of roses. Every cloud has a silver lining.

Platitudes are a form of empty rhetoric—language meant to sound grand and important, but lacking in specific ideas. Clear thinking is specific.

PROJECT PREP Revising ***Checking for Propaganda***

In your writing group, help each author to avoid using propaganda. Give suggestions on how to improve presentations so that all arguments contain no false persuasion.

3 Using a Revision Checklist

Use the following checklist to go over your persuasive text one more time.

Evaluation Checklist for Revising

Checking Your Introduction

✓ Does your thesis statement express your claim clearly? (page 301)

✓ Does your introduction establish the significance of the claim and capture attention? (pages 289 and 308)

Checking Your Body Paragraphs

✓ Is each paragraph unified and coherent? (pages 94–97 and 257)

✓ Have you supported your main points with facts, examples, and expert views? (pages 289 and 294–295)

✓ Have you consistently used an organizing structure appropriate for your purpose, audience, and context that logically sequences claims, counterclaims, reasons, and evidence? (pages 299–300)

✓ Have you evaluated your evidence and sources and demonstrated that you have done so? (pages 302–303 and 402–405)

✓ Have you presented the whole range of relevant perspectives and accurately and honestly worded opposing views? (page 302)

✓ Have you anticipated and refuted counter-arguments? (page 302)

✓ Have you conceded a point if appropriate? (pages 302 and 310)

✓ Have you used sound reasoning and avoided logical fallacies? (pages 310–313)

Checking Your Conclusion

✓ Does your conclusion follow from and support your argument? (pages 289 and 308)

✓ Did you ask the reader to take action, if that was the purpose? (pages 299 and 308)

Checking Your Words and Sentences

✓ Are your sentences varied and concise? (pages 59–70)

✓ Are your emotional appeals, if any, sincere and restrained? (page 309)

✓ Have you used carefully crafted language to move a neutral or opposed audience? (pages 308–309)

✓ Did you use words, phrases, clauses, and varied syntax to link sections of the text, create cohesion, and clarify relationships? (page 304)

PROJECT PREP Revising *Add, Delete, Substitute, and Rearrange*

Based on the feedback from your writing group, prepare a new draft of your exposé. Using the checklist above, add, delete, substitute, or rearrange to make your argumentative text the best it can be. Be sure the final body paragraph states a potential counter-argument.

When you edit, you carefully reread your revised draft for the conventions of language and the norms and conventions of the discipline in which you are writing. Often you are so familiar with what you intended to say that you miss errors, so allow time to put your writing aside. And, as always, pay special attention to the power rules.

The Language of Power Agreement

Power Rule: Use verbs that agree with the subject. (See pages 814–839.)

See It in Action Pronouns such as *many*, *some*, and *few,* called **indefinite pronouns,** have number. Some are singular, some are plural, and some can be either singular or plural. A verb must agree with its subject in number, whether the indefinite pronoun—in this case—is singular or plural. Notice in the following sentence about global warming that the verb *have* agrees with its indefinite plural subject *others*.

> Many shared a portion of IPCC's 2007 Nobel Peace Prize (co-won with Mr. Gore), and others have won previous Nobel Prizes for their research.

In the sentence concerning problems in the Amazon tropical rainforest, the singular indefinite pronoun *much* agrees with the verb *was going on.*

> Not much was going on to alert the world about how serious this problem was.

Other singular indefinite pronouns include *another, anybody, anything, each, either, everyone, everything, much, neither, nobody, no one, one, somebody,* and *something*. *Others* and *several* are plural indefinite pronouns. *All, any, most, none,* and *some* can be either singular or plural. Often something before or after the indefinite pronoun offers a clue to its number.

> None of the trees were cut down. None of the land was damaged.

Remember It Record this rule and the examples in the Power Rule section of your Personalized Editing Checklist.

Use It Read through your persuasive essay and check that the correct verb form is used in each sentence with an indefinite pronoun.

Using a Six-Trait Rubric — Persuasive Writing

Ideas	4 The thesis statement is clear. Evidence is solid and there are no logical fallacies. Counter-arguments are effective.	3 The thesis statement is clear. Most evidence is solid and there are no logical fallacies. Some counter-arguments are effective.	2 The thesis statement could be clearer. Some evidence is solid, but there is one logical fallacy. Rebuttals are weak.	1 The thesis statement is missing. Some evidence is solid, but there are logical fallacies. No counter-arguments are offered.
Organization	4 The organization is clear with abundant transitions.	3 A few ideas seem out of place or transitions are missing.	2 Many ideas seem out of place and transitions are missing.	1 The organization is unclear and hard to follow.
Voice	4 The voice sounds natural, engaging, and appropriately persuasive.	3 The voice sounds natural and engaging.	2 The voice sounds mostly natural but is weak.	1 The voice sounds mostly unnatural and is weak.
Word Choice	4 Words are specific and powerful. Language is respectful.	3 Words are specific and language is respectful.	2 Some words are too general and/or emotional.	1 Most words are overly general and emotional.
Sentence Fluency	4 Varied sentences flow smoothly.	3 Most sentences are varied and flow smoothly.	2 Some sentence are varied but some are choppy.	1 Sentences are not varied and are choppy.
Conventions	4 Punctuation, usage, and spelling are correct. The Power Rules are all followed.	3 Punctuation, usage, and spelling are mainly correct and Power Rules are all followed.	2 Some punctuation, usage, and spelling are incorrect but all Power Rules are followed.	1 There are many errors and at least one failure to follow a Power Rule.

PROJECT PREP Editing *Checking Conventions*

In your writing group, evaluate one another's persuasive essay using the rubric above. Based on the feedback, prepare a final, polished version of your work, Pay special attention to the overall effectiveness of the argument and the author's use of proper grammar, spelling, and punctuation.

Persuasive Writing Publishing

Persuasion can be one of the most gratifying kinds of writing to undertake, for it can change the minds of others, and sometimes even change the world. In writing your essay, you have considered your purpose, audience, and occasion, and you have made revisions accordingly. The medium in which you publish your essay also has a bearing on the style and format of your work. Consider the requirements of these publications.

CHAPTER 8

CHARACTERISTICS OF ASSORTED PUBLISHING FORMATS	
Blog	• style is often more casual than printed text • may be written to invite interaction from readers in the form of comments to the blog • reader-friendly formatting techniques, such as bullet lists and a clear heading structure, assist in reading from the computer screen • graphics may be added to enhance the message • hyperlinks lead to related stories
Magazine article	• article's style and tone need to fit with the style and tone of the publication (For example, an article in a financial magazine would likely need to be somewhat formal). • in some two-column magazines paragraphs tend to be short • graphics often accompany the article
E-mail notice	• e-mails need to be concise and to the point • the text is often "chunked" in manageable amounts for ease of reading • hyperlinks are often provided
Public announcement	• generally has very neutral and formal language • may include charts and other graphics

PROJECT PREP Publishing *Final Review*

Publish your finished essay through an appropriate medium. You might send your essay to people who need to be aware of the issues you have brought to light.

TIME OUT TO REFLECT

Before you wrote this argumentative essay, how effective did you think you were at persuasive writing? How have your persuasive writing skills improved? Which skills might you want to improve even more?

Writing Lab

Project Corner

Speak and Listen
Hold a Group Discussion

With your classmates, **discuss the role of exposés** in society. Are they always welcome? What are possible consequences for whistle-blowers? Should these consequences deter someone from exposing a problem? What are appropriate ways of addressing problems of corruption in an otherwise civilized society?

Collaborate and Create Make a Collage

In your writing group, **create a large collage** that illustrates the problems of one of your exposés. Your collage should help to persuade viewers that a problem exists and that it is their responsibility to challenge it.

Further Research
Take a Closer Look

Conduct further research on one of the problems exposed by either you or a classmate. What additional issues could be raised? What other examples would contribute to a better understanding of the issues? Your research could either be focused on existing sources, such as information available on the Internet, or could follow from your own investigation into the problem through interviews and other fact-finding efforts.

In Everyday Life
Persuasive Note

Apply and Assess

1. Your family is going on vacation, and you will not be able to take your dog with you. Your best friend has taken care of Blanche many times. However, your friend's mother was frightened recently by a dog with a slight resemblance to Blanche, and she may be opposed to the idea of keeping your dog. ***Write a note*** to your friend's mother that will reassure her about taking care of Blanche. What are some pros and cons you can consider mentioning to her? It may be helpful to call attention to Blanche's many wonderful qualities, too.

CHAPTER 8

In the Workplace Business E-mail

2. You are an advertising executive representing Crispy Batch, a snack-foods company. For years, Crispy's marketing department has placed its products exclusively in grocery chains and convenience stores. You think a Web site selling all of Crispy Batch's products is a great way to improve productivity and customer satisfaction. ***Compose an e-mail*** to the president of Crispy Batch, outlining your ideas for a new marketing plan. Make sure you understand your audience, and avoid using generalizations that may weaken the logic of your argument. (You can find information on writing e-mails on pages 533, 567, and 611–615.)

Timed Writing Persuasive Letter

3. CyberDome is Eastview's new arcade with the latest virtual reality and 3-D video games. However, more than 15 Eastview High School students who spent time at CyberDome received poor grades last quarter. Concerned parents have proposed a curfew ordinance requiring students to vacate the CyberDome by 8:00 p.m. on weeknights and 10 p.m. on weekends. As someone who enjoys an occasional video game after studying, you think the parents' plan is a little rigid. Write a letter to the editor of the *Eastview Chronicle* to persuade parents and students to consider your ideas for a compromise. You have 25 minutes to complete your work.

   Before You Write Consider the following questions: What is the situation? What is the occasion? Who is the audience? What is the purpose?

   Keep your audience in mind while you organize your ideas. Use polite and reasonable language rather than words that show bias or overly charged emotions. Present pros and cons, and be sure to use facts to support your opinions.

   After You Write Evaluate your work using the six-trait evaluation rubric on page 318.

CHAPTER 9

Writing About Literature

A literary analysis presents an interpretation of a work of literature and supports that interpretation with appropriate responses, details, and quotations.

Here are some examples of how the skills of thinking, writing, and speaking about literature are used in school and in life.

- **High school students read and analyze literary passages** in standardized tests, including college admissions tests.
- **Public officials enhance their speeches** with meaningful references to literary works in order to inspire and impress the public.
- **Writers, directors, and other artists adapt literary works** into different media, such as plays, film, and dance. They rely on their critical judgment in developing finished adaptations.
- **People read literature for pleasure and for lessons about life.** Literature is a catalyst that moves people to ponder ideas and emotions. They may respond by writing in journals or discussing their ideas with others.
- **Professional critics write about books and movies.** The critic shares a personal reaction to the work based on knowledge of the genre, focusing on the characters, plot, dialogue, and stylistic elements.

Writing Project — Interpretive Response

Literary Analysis ***Write a response to a literary work that uses evidence from the text to support a thoughtful interpretation.***

Think Through Writing Think about a short story, novel, play, or poem that you like, and write about why you like it and why you think the author wrote it. What is the point of the literary work?

Talk About It In your writing group, discuss the writing you have done. What did people identify in the literature that they like?

Read About It In the short story "A Mother in Mannville" by Marjorie Kinnan Rawlings, Jerry lives in an orphanage in the North Carolina mountains. As you read about Jerry, try to identify with his experience. What does it mean to be an orphan, to live in a place where you do not feel at home, and to be misunderstood? Read the story first for enjoyment. As you read it a second time, consider how you were able to bring your own experience, whether similar or vastly different, to the story. How would you begin to write a literary analysis of this classic short story?

MODEL: Literary Text/Short Story

A Mother in Mannville

Marjorie Kinnan Rawlings

The orphanage is high in the Carolina mountains. Sometimes in winter the snowdrifts are so deep that the institution is cut off from the village below, from all the world. Fog hides the mountain peaks, the snow swirls down the valleys, and a wind blows so bitterly that the orphanage boys who take the milk twice daily to the baby cottage reach the door with fingers stiff in an agony of numbness.

"Or when we carry trays from the cookhouse for the ones that are sick," Jerry said, "we get our faces frostbit, because we can't put our hands over them. I have gloves," he added. "Some of the boys don't have any."

He liked the late springs, he said. The rhododendron was in bloom, a carpet of color, across the mountainsides, soft as the May winds that stirred the hemlocks. He called it laurel.

"It's pretty when the laurel blooms," he said. "Some of it's pink and some of it's white."

I was there in the autumn. I wanted quiet, isolation, to do some troublesome writing. I wanted mountain air to blow out the malaria from too long a time in the subtropics. I was homesick, too, for the flaming of maples in October, and for corn shocks and pumpkins and black-walnut trees and the lift of hills. I found them all, living in a cabin that belonged to the orphanage, half a mile beyond the orphanage farm. When I took the cabin, I asked for a boy or man to come and chop wood for the fireplace. The first few days were warm, I found what wood I needed about the cabin, no one came, and I forgot the order.

I looked up from my typewriter one late afternoon, a little startled. A boy stood at the door, and my pointer dog, my companion, was at his side and had not barked to warn me. The boy was probably twelve years old, but undersized. He wore overalls and a torn shirt, and was barefooted.

He said, "I can chop some wood today."

I said, "But I have a boy coming from the orphanage."

"I'm the boy."

"You? But you're small."

"Size don't matter, chopping wood," he said. "Some of the big boys don't chop good. I've been chopping wood at the orphanage a long time."

I visualized mangled and inadequate branches for my fires. I was well into my work and not inclined to conversation. I was a little blunt.

"Very well. There's the ax. Go ahead and see what you can do."

I went back to work, closing the door. At first the sound of the boy dragging brush annoyed me. Then he began to chop. The blows were rhythmic and steady, and shortly I had forgotten him, the sound no more of an interruption than a consistent rain. I suppose an hour and a half passed, for when I stopped and stretched, and heard the boy's steps on the cabin stoop, the sun was dropping behind the farthest mountain, and the valleys were purple with something deeper than the asters.

The boy said, "I have to go to supper now. I can come again tomorrow evening."

I said, "I'll pay you now for what you've done," thinking I should probably have to insist on an older boy. "Ten cents an hour?"

"Anything is all right."

We went together back of the cabin. An astonishing amount of solid wood had been cut. There were cherry logs and heavy roots of rhododendron, and blocks from the waste pine and oak left from the building of the cabin.

"But you've done as much as a man," I said. "This is a splendid pile."

I looked at him, actually, for the first time. His hair was the color of the corn shocks and his eyes, very direct, were like the mountain sky when rain is pending—gray, with a shadowing of that miraculous blue. As I spoke, a light came over him, as though the setting sun had touched him with the same suffused glory with which it touched the mountains. I gave him a quarter.

"You may come tomorrow," I said, "and thank you very much."

He looked at me, and at the coin, and seemed to want to speak, but could not, and turned away.

"I'll split kindling tomorrow," he said over his thin ragged shoulder. "You'll need kindling and medium wood and logs and backlogs."

At daylight I was half wakened by the sound of chopping. Again it was so even in texture that I went back to sleep. When I left my bed in the cool morning, the boy had come and gone, and a stack of kindling was neat against the cabin wall. He came again after school in the afternoon and worked until time to return to the orphanage. His name was Jerry; he was twelve years old, and he had been at the orphanage since he was four. I could picture him at four, with the same grave gray-blue eyes and the same—independence? No, the word that comes to me is "integrity."

The word means something very special to me, and the quality for which I use it is a rare one. My father had it—there is another of whom I am almost sure—but almost no man of my acquaintance possesses it with the clarity, the purity, the simplicity of a mountain stream. But the boy Jerry had it. It is bedded on courage, but it is more than brave. It is honest, but it is more than honesty. The ax handle broke one day. Jerry said the woodshop at the orphanage would repair it. I brought money to pay for the job and he refused it.

"I'll pay for it," he said. "I broke it. I brought the ax down careless."

"But no one hits accurately every time," I told him. "The fault was in the wood of the handle. I'll see the man from whom I bought it."

It was only then that he would take the money. He was standing back of his own carelessness. He was a free-will agent and he chose to do careful work, and if he failed, he took the responsibility without subterfuge.

And he did for me the unnecessary thing, the gracious thing, that we find done only by the great of heart. Things no training can teach, for they are done on the instant, with no predicated experience. He found a cubbyhole beside the fireplace that I had not noticed. There, of his own accord, he put kindling and "medium" wood, so that I might always have dry fire material ready in case of sudden wet weather. A stone was loose in the rough walk to the cabin. He dug a deeper hole and steadied it, although he came, himself, by a shortcut over the bank. I found that when I tried to return his thoughtfulness with such things as candy and apples, he was wordless. "Thank you" was, perhaps, an expression for which he had had no use, for his courtesy was instinctive. He only looked at the gift and at me, and a curtain lifted, so that I saw deep into the clear well of his eyes, and gratitude was there, and affection, soft over the firm granite of his character.

He made simple excuses to come and sit with me. I could no more have turned him away than if he had been physically hungry. I suggested once that the best time for us to visit was just before supper, when I left off my writing. After that, he waited always until my typewriter had been some time quiet. One day I worked until nearly dark. I went outside the cabin, having forgotten him. I saw him going up over the hill in the twilight toward the orphanage. When I sat down on my stoop, a place was warm from his body where he had been sitting.

He became intimate, of course, with my pointer, Pat. There is a strange communion between a boy and a dog. Perhaps they possess the same singleness of spirit, the same kind of wisdom. It is difficult to explain, but it exists. When I went across the state for a weekend, I left the dog in Jerry's charge. I gave him the dog whistle and the key to the cabin, and left sufficient food. He was to come two or three times a day and let out the dog, and feed and exercise him. I should return Sunday night, and Jerry would take out the dog for the last time Sunday afternoon and then leave the key under an agreed hiding place.

My return was belated and fog filled the mountain passes so treacherously that I dared not drive at night. The fog held the next morning, and it was Monday noon before I reached the cabin. The dog had been fed and cared for that morning. Jerry came early in the afternoon, anxious.

"The superintendent said nobody would drive in the fog," he said. "I came just before bedtime last night and you hadn't come. So I brought Pat some of my breakfast this morning. I wouldn't have let anything happen to him."

"I was sure of that. I didn't worry."

"When I heard about the fog, I thought you'd know."

He was needed for work at the orphanage and he had to return at once. I gave him a dollar in payment, and he looked at it and went away. But that night he came in the darkness and knocked at the door.

"Come in, Jerry," I said, "if you're allowed to be away this late."

"I told maybe a story," he said. "I told them I thought you would want to see me."

"That's true," I assured him, and I saw his relief. "I want to hear about how you managed with the dog."

He sat by the fire with me, with no other light, and told me of their two days together. The dog lay close to him, and found a comfort there that I did not have for him. And it seemed to me that being with my dog, and caring for him, had brought the boy and me, too, together, so that he felt that he belonged to me as well as to the animal.

"He stayed right with me," he told me, "except when he ran in the laurel. He likes the laurel. I took him up over the hill and we both ran fast. There was a place where the grass was high and I lay down in it and hid. I could hear Pat hunting for me. He found my trail and he barked. When he found me, he acted crazy, and he ran around and around me, in circles."

We watched the flames.

"That's an apple log," he said. "It burns the prettiest of any wood."

We were very close.

He was suddenly impelled to speak of things he had not spoken of before, nor had I cared to ask him.

"You look a little bit like my mother," he said. "Especially in the dark, by the fire."

"But you were only four, Jerry, when you came here. You have remembered how she looked, all these years?"

"My mother lives in Mannville," he said.

For a moment, finding that he had a mother shocked me as greatly as anything in my life has ever done, and I did not know why it disturbed me. Then I understood my distress. I was filled with a passionate resentment that any woman should go away and leave her son. A fresh anger added itself. A son like this one—The orphanage was a wholesome place, the executives were kind, good people, the food was more than adequate, the boys were healthy, a ragged shirt was no hardship, nor the doing of clean labor. Granted, perhaps, that the boy felt no lack, what blood fed the bowels of a woman who did not yearn over this child's lean body that had come in parturition[1] out of her own? At four he would have looked the same as now. Nothing, I thought, nothing in life could change those eyes. His quality must be apparent to an idiot, a fool. I burned with questions I could not ask. In any, I was afraid, there would be pain.

"Have you seen her, Jerry—lately?"

"I see her every summer. She sends for me."

I wanted to cry out, "Why are you not with her? How can she let you go away again."

He said, "She comes up here from Mannville whenever she can. She doesn't have a job now."

His face shone in the firelight.

"She wanted to give me a puppy, but they can't let any one boy keep a puppy. You remember the suit I had on last Sunday?" He was plainly proud. "She sent me that for Christmas. The Christmas before that"—he drew a long breath, savoring the memory—"she sent me a pair of skates."

"Roller skates?"

My mind was busy, making pictures of her, trying to understand her. She had not, then, entirely deserted or forgotten him. But why, then—I thought, "I must not condemn her without knowing."

"Roller skates. I let the other boys use them. They're always borrowing them. But they're careful of them."

What circumstance other than poverty—

1 **parturition:** The act or process of giving birth.

"I'm going to take the dollar you gave me for taking care of Pat," he said, "and buy her a pair of gloves."

I could only say, "That will be nice. Do you know her size?"

"I think it's 8½," he said.

He looked at my hands.

"Do you wear 8½?" he asked.

"No, I wear a smaller size, a 6."

"Oh! Then I guess her hands are bigger than yours."

I hated her. Poverty or no, there was other food than bread, and the soul could starve as quickly as the body. He was taking his dollar to buy gloves for her big stupid hands, and she lived away from him, in Mannville, and contented herself with sending him skates.

"She likes white gloves," he said. "Do you think I can get them for a dollar?"

"I think so," I said.

I decided that I should not leave the mountains without seeing her and knowing for myself why she had done this thing.

The human mind scatters its interests as though made of thistledown, and every wind stirs and moves it. I finished my work. It did not please me, and I gave my thoughts to another field. I should need some Mexican material.

I made arrangements to close my Florida place. Mexico immediately, and doing the writing there, if conditions were favorable. Then, Alaska with my brother. After that, heaven knew what or where.

I did not take time to go to Mannville to see Jerry's mother, nor even to talk with the orphanage officials about her. I was a trifle abstracted about the boy, because of my work and plans. And after my first fury at her—we did not speak of her again—his having a mother, any sort at all, not far away, in Mannville, relieved me of the ache I had had about him. He did not question the anomalous[2] relation. He was not lonely. It was none of my concern.

He came every day and cut my wood and did small helpful favors and stayed to talk. The days had become cold, and I often let him come inside the cabin. He would lie on the floor in front of the fire, with one arm across the pointer, and they would both doze and wait quietly for me. Other days they ran with a common ecstasy through the laurel, and since the asters were now gone, he brought me back vermilion[3] maple leaves, and chestnut boughs dripping with imperial yellow. I was ready to go.

---

2 **anomalous:** Differing from what is normal or common; abnormal.

3 **vermilion:** A vivid red to reddish orange.

I said to him, "You have been my good friend, Jerry. I shall often think of you and miss you. Pat will miss you too. I am leaving tomorrow."

He did not answer. When he went away, I remember that a new moon hung over the mountains, and I watched him go in silence up the hill. I expected him the next day, but he did not come. The details of packing my personal belongings, loading my car, arranging the bed over the seat, where the dog would ride, occupied me until late in the day. I closed the cabin and started the car, noticing that the sun was in the west and I should do well to be out of the mountains by nightfall. I stopped by the orphanage and left the cabin key and money for my light bill with Miss Clark.

"And will you call Jerry for me to say good-by to him?"

"I don't know where he is," she said. "I'm afraid he's not well. He didn't eat his dinner this noon. One of the other boys saw him going over the hill into the laurel. He was supposed to fire the boiler this afternoon. It's not like him; he's unusually reliable."

I was almost relieved, for I knew I should never see him again, and it would be easier not to say good-by to him.

I said, "I wanted to talk with you about his mother—why he's here—but I'm in more of a hurry than I expected to be. It's out of the question for me to see her now too. But here's some money I'd like to leave with you to buy things for him at Christmas and on his birthday. It will be better than for me to try to send him things. I could so easily duplicate—skates, for instance."

She blinked her honey spinster's eyes.

"There's not much use for skates here," she said.

Her stupidity annoyed me.

"What I mean," I said, "is that I don't want to duplicate things his mother sends him. I might have chosen skates if I didn't know she had already given them to him."

She stared at me.

"I don't understand," she said. "He has no mother. He has no skates."

Respond in Writing What do you think is the point of the story? What evidence in the text makes you think so?

Develop Your Own Ideas for Analysis Work with your classmates to develop ideas that you might use in writing a literary analysis—that is, an argument in which you try to persuade other people that your interpretation of a work of literature is sound.

Small Groups: In your small group, discuss the writing you have done. Use a graphic organizer like the following to help you think of possible details for each author's description in each of the categories.

Overall Meaning: What do you think is the point of the story?	
Who is the narrator in the story? Are the speaker and author the same? If not, what effect does the choice of narrator have on the story?	
How do the plot and dialogue express the point of the story?	
What is the setting of the story? How does the setting affect your understanding of the point of the story?	
How would the story be different if it were told by the boy? By the woman at the orphanage?	
How does the story's ending affect your understanding of the point of the story? Does the ending change the story's meaning to you? If so, how and why?	

Whole Class: Make a master chart of all of the ideas generated by the small groups to see how different members of the class interpreted the story's meaning and the author's craft in implying that meaning.

Write About It You will next write a literary interpretation of "A Mother in Mannville" by Marjorie Kinnan Rawlings. You may choose from any of the following possible topics, audiences, and forms.

Possible Topics	Possible Audiences	Possible Forms
• the story's meaning with a focus on the narrator's actions • the story's meaning with a focus on the boy's actions • the story's meaning with a focus on the relationship between the narrator and the boy	• university English professors • other short story authors • people who don't understand the story • your friends	• an essay • a blog • a literary magazine • a Web discussion board post

CHAPTER 9

Responding to Literature

"Beauty in things exists in the mind which contemplates them," wrote the philosopher David Hume. In terms of literature, the story, play, or poem becomes meaningful—beautiful, tragic, interesting, or humorous—when you, as the reader, connect with the work. By contemplating the work—analyzing, evaluating, and interpreting it—you determine the significance of the work for yourself and for other readers.

As the following chart shows, the basic structure of a literary analysis is the same as that of other kinds of essays.

STRUCTURE OF A LITERARY ANALYSIS

Title	Identifies which aspect of the work the writer will focus on
Introduction	Names the author and the work; contains a thesis statement expressing an interpretation of some aspect of the work
Body	Supports the thesis statement with responses, quotations from the work and from respected sources, and commentary
Conclusion	Summarizes, clarifies, or adds an insight to the thesis statement

In a sense, a literary work is created anew every time someone reads it, for every reader interprets and reacts to it uniquely. In some ways, the best place to begin exploring a piece of literature is within yourself—in the personal experience and knowledge you bring to whatever you read.

Reading, then, is a two-way process, a kind of mental conversation between the writer and a reader. The writer makes a statement on the page, and you, the reader, respond in your mind. Your responses will be different from anyone else's because each person brings individual experience, background, and knowledge into the reading process.

1 Responding from Personal Experience

Even though fiction is imaginary, it must somehow be connected to reality if it is to have any meaning. Therefore, to make sense out of a piece of literature, you must look for its roots in the world of your own experiences.

You make many of those connections automatically. Even when you are not aware of doing so, you search your memory as you read. A character, a place, an event, or a feeling will often bring to mind someone or something familiar. Use that familiar circumstance to help you understand and interpret new circumstances you encounter in your reading.

You will not always react to these connections in a positive way. Something you read may irritate, anger, or bore you. A negative response is no less responsive than a positive one—both deserve to be explored. Your personal responses give context and meaning to the work and provide the most direct way to approach it. The following strategies will help you explore your responses to a literary work.

HERE'S HOW

Personal Response Strategies

1. In your journal, freewrite answers to the questions below:
   a. Which character do you identify with most closely? Why? Do your feelings about the character change? If so, what causes them to change?
   b. What characters remind you of people you know? How are they alike?
   c. If you were the character you most identified with, would you have behaved the same way? Why or why not?
   d. Did any events in the story make you think of situations in your own life? How would you compare them? What feelings do you associate with the experiences?
   e. What feelings does the work bring out in you? What moved you the most?
2. Write a personal response statement that explains what the work means to you. Use any form that allows you to express your response comfortably.
3. In small discussion groups, share your reaction to the questions above. Listen carefully to the reactions of others; compare and contrast them with your own. Be open to other points of view that may help you see the work in a new way. Later, write freely about how and why the discussion affected your ideas.

CHAPTER 9

Practice Your Skills

Responding from Personal Experience

Review "A Mother in Mannville" on pages 323–329. Then answer the following questions.

1. Do you like the story? Why or why not?
2. Does either character remind you of yourself or someone you know?
3. Do you have trouble understanding any of the characters? Why?
4. Does the situation in the story connect to a situation in your own life? How?
5. With what feelings are you left at the story's end?

PROJECT PREP Responding *Personal Experience*

In your writing group, discuss your responses to "A Mother In Mannville." Do you agree on a point to the story? Can you resolve any difficulties you have had in understanding any of the characters' actions? Discuss the various ideas your writing group members have, and be open to changing your mind if a group member's ideas seem valid.

2 Responding from Literary Knowledge

You already know a great deal about literature. Over the years you have learned what to look for and what to expect in different literary forms. For example, when you read a story, you expect the main problem to be resolved by the end. When you read a play, you expect to learn about characters and events through the dialogue. When you read a poem, you expect to find images that awaken your imagination. You bring these expectations to every new work of literature.

From years of reading and writing, you have learned that a work of literature is made up of certain elements—such as plot, characters, dialogue, figures of speech, and sound devices. When you analyze a work, you separate it into these elements. To evaluate the work, you set standards for the elements and judge how well the standards are met.

The following chart shows the main elements of three literary genres—fiction, poetry, and drama. Since drama and fiction share many of the same elements, those listed under "drama" pertain only to the reading of a dramatic work.

ELEMENTS OF LITERATURE	
FICTION	
Plot	the events that lead up to a **climax,** or high point, and resolve the central **conflict** or explain the outcome
Setting	when and where the story takes place
Characters	the people in the story whose thoughts and actions move the events forward
Dialogue	the conversations among characters that reveal personalities, actions, and **motivations,** or reasons for behaving as they do
Tone	the author's attitude toward the events and the characters
Mood	the prevalent feeling or **atmosphere** in a piece of literature
Irony	the occurrence of the opposite of what is expected; can be verbal, dramatic, or situational
Point of View	the "voice" telling the story: first person (*I*) or third person (*she or he*), all knowing or limited in view
Theme	the main idea or message of the story

CHAPTER 9

ELEMENTS OF LITERATURE	
POETRY	
Persona	the person whose "voice" is reciting the poem
Meter	the pattern of stressed and unstressed syllables in each line
Rhyme Scheme	the pattern of rhymed sounds usually at the ends of lines
Sound Devices	techniques for playing with sounds to create certain effects, such as **alliteration** and **onomatopoeia**
Figures of Speech	imaginative language, such as **similes** and **metaphors,** which creates images by making comparisons
Images	expressions that appeal to the senses
Symbols	objects or events that stand for other things
Allusions	references to persons or events in literature or in the past
Shape	the way a poem looks on the printed page, which may contribute to the poem's overall meaning
Theme	the overall feeling or underlying meaning of the poem

ELEMENTS OF LITERATURE	
DRAMA	
Setting	the time and place of the action; lighting and stage sets, as described in the stage directions
Characters	the people who participate in the action of the play
Plot	the story of the play divided into acts and scenes and developed through the characters' words and actions
Theme	the meaning of a play, as revealed through the setting and the characters' words and actions

How Literary Elements Contribute to Meaning

In each literary genre, writers use various elements to communicate the meaning of a work. For example, in fiction a writer uses plot, setting, characters, and other stylistic and rhetorical devices to achieve certain aesthetic effects and to reveal his or her message to the reader. One way to find meaning in a work of literature is to analyze the author's use of such elements and their interrelationships.

The charts on the following page list questions you can ask as you explore the meaning of fiction, poetry, and drama. As part of a **close reading** of a literary work, plan to reread several times to get the most meaning possible out of the text.

HERE'S HOW

Questions for Finding Meaning in Fiction

Plot

- What is the impact of each main event in the development of the plot? How does each event in the plot affect the main characters?
- What details in the plot reveal the narrator's attitude toward the central conflict?
- What do the climax and the ending reveal about the theme?

Setting

- How does the setting contribute to the tone or mood of the story? How do details of the setting help define the characters?
- What details of the setting are most important in the development of the plot? How do details of the setting relate to the theme?

Characters

- How do the characters relate to their setting?
- How does each character contribute to the development of the plot? How are the characters revealed by their thoughts, actions, words, or by others' actions toward them?
- What does the dialogue reveal about the characters' personalities and motivations?
- How does the point of view of the story affect the characterizations?

Theme

- What passages and details in the story best express the main theme? What other recurring ideas contribute to the meaning?
- How does the author communicate the theme through the development of setting, characters, and plot?
- Does this theme have meaning for you? What else have you read that has a similar theme?

HERE'S HOW

Questions for Finding Meaning in Poetry

- What is the poet's persona? How does the persona relate to the subject, mood, and theme of the poem?
- How does the meter affect the rhythm of the poem? How does that rhythm express the mood?
- How does the rhyme scheme, if any, affect the expression of thoughts and feelings?
- If the poet uses sound devices like alliteration and onomatopoeia, what sounds do you hear in the poem? What images do those sound devices create in your mind?
- What images do the figures of speech create? What feelings do those images suggest?
- How does the shape of the poem relate to the subject, mood, or theme?
- What effect does the poem have on you? How does the poem achieve its effect?
- What feeling, theme, or message does the poem express? What meaning does the poem have for you?

HERE'S HOW

Questions for Finding Meaning in Drama

- What details of setting and character do the stage directions emphasize? How do those details contribute to the meaning of the play?
- What are the key relationships among the characters? How do those relationships reveal the central conflict? What changes in the relationships help resolve the central conflict?
- How does the dialogue advance the plot? What plot developments occur with each change of act and scene?
- What subject and theme are explored in the play? What in the play has meaning for you?

CHAPTER 9

EVALUATING A LITERARY WORK

Analyzing the elements in a story, play, or poem helps you make judgments about the work. You set standards for each element and judge how well those standards are met. To evaluate a work, you should ask specific questions about the construction of the work, such as "Are the characters believable?" and "How does the tension build in the story?" In the process you learn about the work and about the techniques used to create it.

Because there are many different standards of evaluation, your personal judgment will not always agree with the judgments of literary critics, historians, biographers, teachers, and classmates. You may find it helpful to know the criteria by which a **classic**, or great work of literature, is usually judged.

SOME CHARACTERISTICS OF GREAT LITERATURE

- Explores great themes in human nature and the human experience that many people can identify with—such as growing up, family life, personal struggles, or war
- Expresses universal values—such as truth or hope—to which people from many different backgrounds and cultures can relate
- Conveys a timeless message that remains true for many generations of readers
- Presents vivid impressions of characters, settings, and situations that many generations of readers can treasure

Whether or not a literary work you are reading is regarded as a classic, you can apply other standards of evaluation. When you are making judgments about a work, ask yourself the questions on the following page.

HERE'S HOW

Questions for Evaluating Literature

- How inventive and original is the work?
- How vividly and believably are the characters, settings, dialogue, actions, and feelings portrayed?
- In fiction, how well-structured is the plot? Is there a satisfying resolution of the central conflict?
- How strongly did you react to the work? Did you identify with a character, situation, or feeling?
- Did the work touch your memories and emotions?
- Did the work have meaning for you? Will you remember anything about it a year from now?

Practice Your Skills

Responding from Literary Knowledge

Answer the following questions about "A Mother in Mannville," on pages 323–329.

1. What is the central conflict? What are the key events? How is the story finally resolved?
2. Describe the main setting. How does it create a suitable backdrop for the events? What does it add to the story?
3. Describe the tone. What is the author's approach to the events and characters?
4. Describe the mood of the story. How do the characters reflect the mood?
5. Describe the main character, Jerry. How does the narrator feel about him?
6. How would you describe the narrator? What is her impact on the story?
7. From what point of view is the story told? How might it have been different if told from a different point of view?
8. What is the underlying theme of the story?
9. How well does the author convey the theme through the characters and plot?
10. What is the meaning for you?

PROJECT PREP Responding *Evaluating*

In your writing group, discuss your written responses from literary knowledge to "A Mother in Mannville." Use this discussion to further your understanding of the story so that you can write a strong interpretive essay on it.

Think Critically

Making Inferences

When you meet new people, you are usually told just a few facts about them. Their other traits are left for you to figure out, or **infer,** from their appearance, behavior, speech, and other clues. Similarly you are not told everything about the characters you meet in your reading. To learn more about them, you need to take advantage of certain clues given by the writer. As you follow the clues, you bring into play both your literary and personal responses.

The chart below shows some inferences one student made about the character of Jerry in "A Mother in Mannville" on pages 323–329. Using such a chart can help you track and refine your inferences.

INFERENCE CHART

Type of Clue	Clue	Inference
Description	He wore overalls and a torn shirt.	He is probably poor, but doesn't seem to mind his worn-out clothes.
Statement	His courtesy was instinctive.	He is deeply, naturally caring and considerate.
Character's own words	"Size don't matter . . . Some of the big boys don't chop good."	Not well-educated, but self-reliant and self-assured.
Character's actions and behavior	I expected him the next day, but he did not come.	He is probably upset about the narrator's departure.
Another character's words	"But you've done as much as a man."	She sees that Jerry is responsible and a hard worker.

Thinking Practice

Make a chart like the one above, based on the character of the narrator in "A Mother in Mannville."

1 Choosing and Limiting a Subject

Once you have explored your personal and literary responses to a work, you are ready to decide on a subject for your literary analysis. You already have a rich source of possible subjects in your written responses to the literature. The next step is to review those ideas and focus on ones that strike you as most suitable for your literary analysis.

Unless your teacher has given a specific assignment, you will probably end up with a wide range of possible subjects. To narrow that range, look for subjects that appeal to you personally. The questions below will help you target a subject for your critical essay.

HERE'S HOW

Questions for Choosing a Subject

- What parts of the work do I find moving? Surprising? Disappointing? Why do they have an effect on me?
- What images or details made a strong impression on me? What do they contribute to the overall work?
- With which character do I identify most? Why?
- What makes the characters distinct from one another? What motivates each of them?
- What parts of the work puzzle me? What would I like to understand better?
- What does the work "say" to me? What message does it convey? What insight or understanding have I gained?

Synthesizing Personal and Literary Responses

To help you zero in on a subject with both personal and literary value, try **synthesizing,** or combining, your personal and literary responses. Which of the questions on pages 332 and 335–337 struck the deepest personal chord? What ideas did you emphasize in your personal response statement?

For example, suppose that "A Mother in Mannville" reminded you of a time when you tried to reach out to someone, but then realized you had misunderstood the situation. That kind of personal response can lead you to a meaningful subject for an essay. To make a subject more specific, you can synthesize your personal response with your literary response. To do so, think about elements of the story that connect with the theme—*reaching out to someone, but misunderstanding him or her.* The following elements from "A Mother in Mannville" relate to this theme.

Characterization	Jerry is hard-working and likable, so the narrator comes to trust him.
Point of View	We see the story through the narrator's eyes, and she only knows as much about Jerry as she learns from him and others.
Setting and Plot	Jerry lives at an orphanage; when Jerry tells the narrator that he has a mother, we are fooled into thinking that this is the story's major surprise.

CHAPTER 9

These details show how the story's theme is developed through several elements, including plot, characterization, point of view, and setting. To develop your essay, you would show how each different element expresses that theme.

Finding a Subject Focus

In a literary analysis, as in any piece of informative and persuasive writing, you need to be sure you can cover your subject effectively. After you choose a subject, you may need to limit its focus so that it is manageable.

First decide on your approach. For example, you might focus on the content of the work by analyzing one or more of its elements. Alternatively, you might choose to focus on the writer's style.

Now start to limit your subject. Begin by restating the subject as a phrase rather than a word, or as a long phrase rather than a short one. Ask yourself, "What do I want to say about the subject?" Your answer will lead you to a focused, limited subject.

EXAMPLE: Focusing a Subject

Too General	The characters
Ask Yourself	What do I want to say about the characters?
Possible Answer	The narrator fails to see Jerry's need for a true family bond. When he claims to have a mother in Mannville. she believes him and is angry at the mother.
Focused Subject	The author shows that people's own self-absorption can prevent them from understanding the real problems and needs of others.

Practice Your Skills

Choosing and Limiting a Subject

Divide into five groups, one for each element of literature listed below. With your group members, think of a possible subject for a literary analysis of "A Mother in Mannville" related to your literary element. Then limit each subject by expressing it in a phrase or a sentence. Share your ideas with the rest of the class.

Example	theme
Possible Subject	what the story says about the challenge of understanding the needs of others

1. character
2. setting
3. plot
4. point of view
5. style

CHAPTER 9

PROJECT PREP — Prewriting — *Limiting a Subject*

Synthesize your personal and literary responses and use the strategies on pages 339–340 to choose and limit a subject on "A Mother in Mannville" or another work. Share your subject with your writing group and refine it further based on their feedback.

In the Media

Media Texts: From Literature to Video

When you write about literature, you share your response with others. There are many other ways to share a literature analysis, and adapting the literature into a video presentation is an excellent choice. Imagine that you will be writing and directing a scene for a video of "A Mother in Mannville." Here are some of the questions you might ask yourself.

- What do the characters look like?
- What are the details of the setting?
- Should I change the setting?
- What are the interactions between characters?
- What do they learn about one another?
- How can these feelings and changes best be shown?
- Is there a narrator?
- Is there music?

Once you have answered these questions, you can write the script, create the storyboard, gather your actors, and direct your video. Think about how to synthesize information from multiple points of view as you would when writing an essay. Refer to *Electronic Publishing,* pages 591–605, for ideas.

Media Activity

Work with a team of six classmates to choose a scene and identify your audience. Then decide who will do what. Who will write the video script (or will it be a group effort)? Who will be the director, the assistant? Who will act in which roles? Who will work the camera? Who will edit the tape? Who will be responsible for sound? Who will be responsible for costumes, sets, and props?

Before shooting the live action, have at least one rehearsal. Critique one another's contributions honestly and constructively, with the aim of improving the performance as a whole.

Arrange to show your completed video. Encourage discussion afterward about the questions above. Then answer the two reflective questions below in your Learning Log.

- How did the process of making a video help me understand the literary work better?
- How could I do a better job the next time I make a video?

2 Developing a Thesis

A literary analysis is based on a **thesis,** or proposition, that explains your interpretation of an aspect of a literary work. Your tone will be matter-of-fact and impersonal, but your interpretation will be based on your individual responses. Because you bring your own personal history to a piece of literature, your view of it may be different from anyone else's. Therefore, your task is to defend your thesis by presenting evidence that will convince the reader that your interpretation is valid. A literary analysis, then, is not just a collection of reactions to a work; it is a carefully reasoned set of arguments.

If you have done a good job of limiting your subject, you may already know the thesis of your literary analysis. Simply rephrase your limited subject as a statement, and decide whether you can defend it effectively. If you need to narrow it further, repeat the technique you used to limit your subject by asking, "What exactly do I want to say about the subject?"

The thesis you develop at this stage should be precise enough to guide your writing, but you should regard it as a **working thesis** only. You may want to adjust it or even replace it as you move further along in your writing process. A writer working on a literary analysis about "A Mother in Mannville" proceeded from a limited subject to a thesis in the following way.

EXAMPLE: Developing a Thesis

Limited Subject	The author's message about gaining insight into another human being
Thesis	Through the characters in "A Mother in Mannville," the author illustrates how a person's own interpretations can prevent him or her from seeing someone else's true needs—even someone for whom he or she cares deeply.

As you think about your subject, take a moment to ask yourself what personal experiences may be influencing your response to the literature. This will help you discover your thesis.

PROJECT PREP *Prewriting* ***Thesis and Introduction***

Develop a thesis statement and share it with your writing group. For each author, offer suggestions for sharpening the thesis statement so that it provides a clear focus for the essay. Then draft an introductory paragraph for your essay. You might begin by stating your thesis and then explaining it briefly.

3 Gathering Evidence

As you read, you automatically pick out important details and combine them with information already stored in your mind. Then you organize those details into a unified view of that work of literature. For example, the first time you read "A Mother in Mannville," whether or not you were aware of it, you were already gathering details that eventually led you to your thesis.

Once you have determined your thesis, return to the short story and collect your supporting evidence more systematically. Reread the work carefully with your thesis in mind, and search for supporting details. Look for descriptive passages, specific events, and characters' dialogue and thoughts. Notice the stylistic or rhetorical devices that create certain aesthetic effects that may be related to your thesis. The more evidence you can offer in support of your thesis, the stronger your literary analysis is likely to be.

For additional support of your thesis, you may choose to consult outside sources. Reference works such as literary histories, author biographies, and collections of critical reviews can provide useful information. Be sure to refer to recognized and respected sources only, and to credit each source in your literary analysis. Always use quotation marks when you quote a source directly.

The following basic steps will help you gather evidence for a literary analysis.

HERE'S HOW

Gathering Details for a Literary Analysis

- Scan the work of literature, looking for quotations and any other details that support your interpretation. You can include events, descriptions, and any other elements of the work.
- Write each detail on a note card. If it is a quotation, indicate who said it and write the page number on which it appears. If it is from a reference work, write the title and author of the source, as well as the page number from which the information was taken.
- Add a note telling how the detail supports your interpretation.
- Use a separate commentary card for each detail you find.

Using Commentary Cards

The following commentary cards show some of the evidence collected by a writer for a literary analysis of "A Mother in Mannville." On the left are portions of the story from which the notes were made. The details were chosen by the writer to support the thesis that "A Mother in Mannville" showed how a person's own needs can blind him or her to the needs of others.

As you study the model, notice how the writer follows the guidelines above in gathering details for the literary analysis.

MODEL: Gathering Evidence

"Or when we carry trays from the cookhouse for the ones that are sick" Jerry said, "we get our faces frostbit, because we can't put our hands over them. I have gloves," he added. "Some of the boys don't have any."

1. "I have gloves," he added. "Some of the boys don't have any." (Jerry, p. 323)
—Shows Jerry's pride; because he wants to be different from others, special.

I looked up from my typewriter one late afternoon, a little startled. A boy stood at the door, and my pointer dog, my companion, was at his side and had not barked to warn me. The boy was probably twelve years old, but undersized. He wore overalls and a torn shirt, and was barefooted.

2. First sight of Jerry: "undersized," "overalls and a torn shirt," "barefooted." (Narrator, p. 323)
—First impression is of small, poor, needy boy; his neediness important—affects the narrator. Narrator's point of view.

"But you've done as much as a man," I said. "This is a splendid pile."

3a. — Shows boy's pride in his work and need for approval. Also shows tie to the narrator.

I looked at him, actually, for the first time. His hair was the color of the corn shocks and his eyes, very direct, were like the mountain sky when rain is pending—gray, with a shadowing of that miraculous blue. As I spoke, light came over him, as though the setting sun had touched him with the same suffused glory with which it touched the mountain. I gave him a quarter.

3b. "As I spoke, a light came over him, as though the setting sun had touched him with the same suffused glory with which it touched the mountains." (Narrator, p. 324)

"You may come tomorrow," I said, "and thank you very much."

I could picture him at four, with the same grave gray-blue eyes and the same—independence? No, the word that comes to me is "integrity."

4. In Jerry's "grave, gray blue eyes," narrator sees a rare kind of "integrity." (Narrator, p. 325)

The word means something very special to me, and the quality for which I use it is a rare one. My father had it—there is another of whom I am almost sure—but almost no man of my acquaintance possesses it with the clarity, the purity, the simplicity of a mountain stream. But the boy Jerry had it.

5. Jerry's integrity reminds narrator of her father. (p. 325)

CHAPTER 9

CHAPTER 9

He made simple excuses to come sit with me.

I suggested once that the best time for us to visit was just before supper, when I left off my writing. After that, he waited always until my typewriter had been some time quiet.

6. "He made simple excuses to sit with me." (Narrator describes how Jerry waits for her to finish work each day so they can talk.) (p. 325) —Shows Jerry's deepening bond with narrator.

One day I worked until nearly dark. I went outside the cabin, having forgotten him.

7. "I went outside the cabin, having forgotten him." (Narrator, p. 325) —Shows narrator's dedication to her work—makes her forget even Jerry.

But that night he came in the darkness and knocked at the door.

"Come in, Jerry," I said, "if you're allowed to be away this late."

"I told maybe a story," he said. "I told them I thought you would want to see me."

8. "I told maybe a story," he said. (Jerry, p. 326) —Shows Jerry's willingness to stretch truth when friendship with narrator is involved. Could have been clue to his later story about his mother.

PROJECT PREP *Prewriting* *Evidence*

In your writing group, discuss the details of the story that have suggested to you the meaning of the story. Identify ambiguities, nuances, and complexities that you may wish to explore further. Use a graphic organizer like the one below to help you sort the details into categories. These categories will then serve as the basis for the body paragraphs of your essay.

Category	Details from the text	Possible meaning of details in light of the thesis statement	Reason that this example fits in this category
Sample category: The narrator's view of the boy at different points in the story			

4 Organizing Details into an Outline

After gathering your supporting details, organize them in a way that makes sense. As the following chart shows, your method of organization will often depend on the nature of your thesis.

PRIMARY METHODS OF ORGANIZATION

Thesis	Method
changes in a character over time	chronological order (page 95)
reasons why a character behaves in a certain way	order of importance or cause and effect (page 97)
differences between two characters	comparison and contrast, using AABB or ABAB pattern of development (pages 269–270)
analysis of a friendship between two characters	developmental order (pages 143–144)

Using Comparison and Contrast

Comparing and contrasting different characters, settings, or works is a common approach to writing a literary analysis. When you compare and contrast, you examine both the similarities and differences between two subjects.

In a comparison and contrast literary analysis, you can organize the details in several ways. In one pattern of organization, called **AABB** or **whole by whole,** you can show how subjects are similar and different by discussing all the points about the first subject (A), and then all the points about the second subject (B).

In a second pattern, called **ABAB** or **point by point** organization, you discuss each point and show how your subjects are similar and different with regard to that point. Experiment with these different arrangements when you are comparing and contrasting. Choose the one that helps you present your argument in the most effective way.

For example, suppose that you were comparing and contrasting Jerry in "A Mother in Mannville" with the narrator of that story. Using their motivations and personalities as a basis, you could arrange details in either pattern of organization.

CHAPTER 9

METHODS OF ORGANIZATION IN COMPARISON AND CONTRAST	
AABB Pattern	**ABAB Pattern**
Jerry (subject A)	Motivations (point 1)
Motivation (point 1)	Jerry (subject A)
Integrity (point 2)	Narrator (subject B)
Narrator (subject B)	Integrity (point 2)
Motivation (point 1)	Jerry (subject A)
Integrity (point 2)	Narrator (subject B)

Making an Outline

After choosing a method of organization for your literary analysis, arrange your supporting details in an outline to guide your writing. The outline for your literary analysis can be informal, with just major groups of your ideas; or it can be formal, with several levels of topics.

The formal outline below was prepared for the body of a literary analysis of the short story "A Mother in Mannville." As you study the outline, notice how the main ideas are arranged in developmental order, with one idea growing out of another in a logical progression.

Thesis Through the characters in "A Mother in Mannville," the author portrays how a person's own interpretations can prevent him or her from seeing someone else's true needs—even someone for whom he or she cares deeply.

MODEL: Outline

I. Character of narrator — Main Topic
- **A.** Devotes most of her time to writing — Subtopics
- **B.** Travels extensively
- **C.** Has a brother, but does not mention a husband or child

II. Character of Jerry (external features) — Main Topic
- **A.** Undersized — Subtopics
- **B.** Poor appearance
- **C.** Uneducated

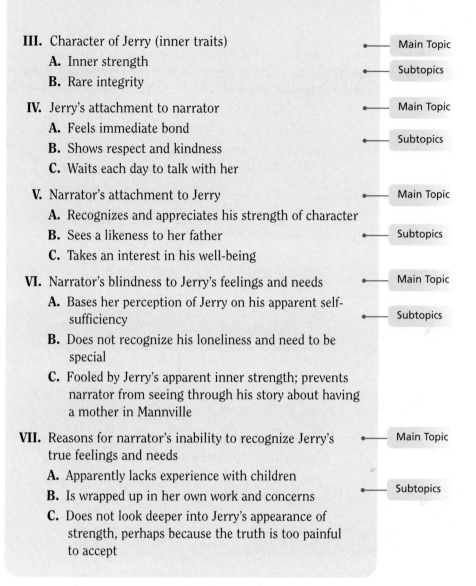

III. Character of Jerry (inner traits) — Main Topic
   A. Inner strength — Subtopics
   B. Rare integrity

IV. Jerry's attachment to narrator — Main Topic
   A. Feels immediate bond — Subtopics
   B. Shows respect and kindness
   C. Waits each day to talk with her

V. Narrator's attachment to Jerry — Main Topic
   A. Recognizes and appreciates his strength of character — Subtopics
   B. Sees a likeness to her father
   C. Takes an interest in his well-being

VI. Narrator's blindness to Jerry's feelings and needs — Main Topic
   A. Bases her perception of Jerry on his apparent self-sufficiency — Subtopics
   B. Does not recognize his loneliness and need to be special
   C. Fooled by Jerry's apparent inner strength; prevents narrator from seeing through his story about having a mother in Mannville

VII. Reasons for narrator's inability to recognize Jerry's true feelings and needs — Main Topic
   A. Apparently lacks experience with children — Subtopics
   B. Is wrapped up in her own work and concerns
   C. Does not look deeper into Jerry's appearance of strength, perhaps because the truth is too painful to accept

Conclusion

The narrator's ending indicates that she will regret having misunderstood Jerry. Because she cares deeply for him, the narrator may see her mistake in hindsight and wish that she had paid closer attention. She has missed the chance to really know Jerry and perhaps help him more.

CHAPTER 9

If you have taken notes on a story but have difficulty fitting those notes into an outline, mapping the story's meaning can be a helpful intermediate step. A **meaning map** plots a story's main events in sequence, along with other major elements such as setting and characters.

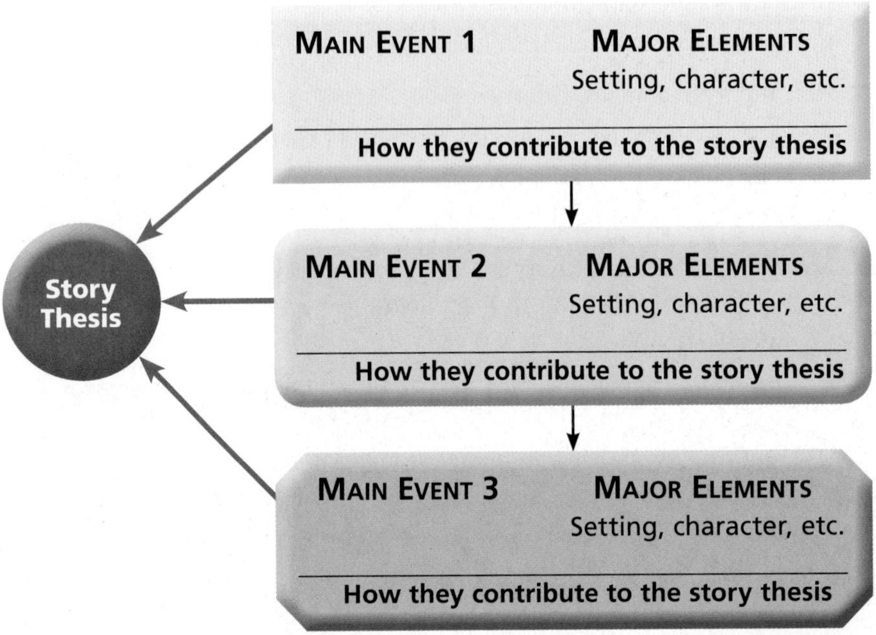

PROJECT PREP *Prewriting* *Outline*

In your writing group, make a **meaning map** for "A Mother in Mannville" or another story you are analyzing. Group the major details into categories or main topics, and decide on an appropriate topic order. Develop an outline for your literary analysis of the story based on the graphic organizer (pages 330 and 346) and meaning map you have constructed.

The Power of Language

Participial Phrases: Getting Into the Action

You've learned that a participle with its modifiers becomes a **participial phrase.** Present participial phrases, the ones ending in *–ing,* add physical and/or mental action to a sentence. By adding variety to sentences, they can eliminate choppiness and help make your paragraphs flow.

Some participial phrases add detail necessary for us to understand who or what is being described.

Essential Participial Phrase	The boy **chopping wood** became a familiar sight outside my cabin.

In other instances, such as the example from "A Mother in Mannville" below, the participial phrase may add an important detail that is set off by a comma or commas, making it technically nonessential from a grammatical viewpoint, despite its importance.

Nonessential Participial Phrase at the End	I went back to work, **closing the door.**

Such modifiers often occur at the end of a sentence, as in the example above, or at the beginning, followed by a comma.

Nonessential Participial Phrase at the Beginning	**Driving away from the orphanage,** I thought of Jerry and his broken heart.

Such modifiers are set off by a comma because of their location, and because the writer wants to signal a pause between the participial phrase and what it modifies.

Punctuation Tip

When a nonessential participial phrase comes at the beginning or end of the sentence, it is set off by a comma. In the middle of a sentence, it is enclosed by a comma before and after.

1 The First Draft

As you write your first draft of a literary analysis, consult your notes and fill in details, using your outline as a guide. The guidelines below will help you.

HERE'S HOW

Guidelines for Drafting a Literary Analysis

- In the introduction, identify the title and the author of the work you are analyzing.
- Do not retell the story. You can assume your readers have read the work you are analyzing.
- Keep yourself and your feelings out of the analysis. Use the third person point of view, and do not use *I*.
- Use present tense to discuss the work. For example, write, "The character **seems** needy at first . . . " or "In the third stanza, the speaker **describes**. . . ."
- Work your thesis statement into the introduction as smoothly as possible. Revise it if necessary as you develop your draft.
- In the body of your literary analysis, present your supporting details in a clearly organized form.
- Put each main topic into its own paragraph. Use transitions to show how one detail relates to another.
- Throughout your literary analysis, use direct quotations from the work to strengthen the points you want to make. Be sure you document any citations.
- In the conclusion, draw together your details to reinforce the main idea of your literary analysis. Restate the thesis in a slightly different form.
- Add a title that suggests the focus of your literary analysis.

Using Quotations

Use **direct quotations** from the work to support your points and provide evidence that strengthens your position.

As you gathered evidence to support the thesis of your literary analysis, you took notes from the work itself. These notes may have included descriptive passages, lines of dialogue, narrative, and other kinds of details. In drafting your analysis, you should include this evidence in a way that will convince the reader of your thesis.

Strengthen your arguments by using relevant quotations that support a point. Do not drop in quotes randomly. Work them smoothly into your writing and punctuate them correctly. The guidelines that follow will help you.

HERE'S HOW

Guidelines for Writing Direct Quotations

- Always enclose direct quotations in quotation marks.
- Follow the examples below when writing quotations in different positions in the sentence. Notice that quotations in the middle or at the end of a sentence are not ordinarily capitalized.

Begins Sentence	"He wore overalls and a torn shirt," observes the narrator (323).
Interrupts Sentence	In his "grave gray-blue eyes," the narrator sees a rare and precious quality (325).
Ends Sentence	The narrator feels that Jerry's integrity makes him "more than brave" (325).

- Use ellipses—a series of three dots (. . .)—to show that words have been left out of a quotation.

  "For a moment, finding that he had a mother shocked me . . . and I did not know why it disturbed me" (327).

- If the quotation is five lines or longer, set it off by itself, without quotation marks. Indent one inch from the left margin and leave space above and below it.

> And after my first fury at her—we did not speak of
> her again—his having a mother, any sort at all,
> not far away, in Mannville, relieved me of the ache I
> had had about him. . . . He was not lonely. It was none
> of my concern. (328)

- After each quotation cite the page number of the source in parentheses. The citation should precede punctuation marks such as periods, commas, colons, and semicolons. For plays or long poems, also give main divisions, such as the act and scene of the play or the part of the poem, plus line numbers.

In addition to using quotations, you should include commentary on them to make sure that readers understand why the quotation supports a particular point.

On the next page is a model of a literary analysis. Since it has already been revised and edited, it is more polished than your first draft will be. As you read, notice how each point has its own paragraph and is backed up with appropriate quotations from the story.

Writing Tip

Use direct quotations from the work to support your points and to provide evidence that strengthens your position.

CHAPTER 9

MODEL: A Literary Analysis

The Roots of Misunderstanding in "A Mother in Mannville"

Title: Identifies Focus

"A Mother in Mannville," by Marjorie Kinnan Rawlings, tells a story about the friendship between a writer and a boy from an orphanage. At first the story may seem simple and direct, but a closer look at the characters and theme reveals that there is an important message for the modern reader. The author shows how a person's own interpretations can prevent him or her from seeing someone else's true needs—even someone for whom the person cares deeply.

Introduction: Identifies author and title

Thesis Statement: Identifies the main point of the analysis

What are the two characters like? The narrator of the story is a writer, but she does not say much about her own life. She seems to be mature and well-traveled, and she devotes most of her time to her writing. Furthermore, since she moves from place to place and mentions only a brother, she probably does not have a husband or child.

First Body Paragraph: Describes the narrator of the story

The narrator paints a much clearer picture of the boy, Jerry. He first appears as an "undersized" twelve-year-old. "He wore overalls and a torn shirt, and was barefooted" (323). He has a "thin ragged shoulder" and shows his ignorance of grammar in statements such as, "Some of the big boys don't chop good" (324). In addition, he is left speechless and awkward when the woman pays him a quarter for his work. At the beginning, then, the reader sees Jerry as a poor, needy boy.

Second Body Paragraph: Describes the external features of the boy, Jerry

There is much more to Jerry, however. It soon becomes obvious that he has an unusual strength in his "thin ragged" body, a strength that comes from the inside. In his "direct" and "grave gray-blue eyes," the narrator sees a rare and precious "integrity" (325). He works hard to chop astonishing amounts of wood, shows up for work faithfully each day, and takes care of the dog when fog keeps the writer away from her cabin. In fact, this combination of neediness and strength is exactly what makes Jerry so appealing to the writer.

Jerry feels a tie to the woman almost immediately. When she first compliments him on the "splendid" pile of wood he has cut, "a light came over him, as though the setting sun had touched him with the same suffused glory with which it touched the mountains" (324). When she tries to thank him for his efforts with candy or apples, she sees in his eyes not only "gratitude" but

Fourth Body Paragraph: Describes Jerry on a more internal level

CHAPTER 9

"affection" as well (325). Furthermore, "he made simple excuses to come and sit" (325) and waits each day until she finishes her work so they can talk. After Jerry cares for the woman's dog, the woman observes that "he belonged to me as well as to the animal" (326).

Fifth Body Paragraph: Analyzes the narrator's attachment to Jerry

The writer too begins to feel closer to Jerry. She is touched by his need for her friendship, on the one hand, and the "firm granite of his character" (325) on the other. His pure, simple integrity reminds her of her father. When the boy sits with her, she says, "I could no more have turned him away than if he had been physically hungry" (325). By the time they sit near the fire and talk about Jerry's two days with the dog, she admits, "We were very close" (326).

Sixth Body Paragraph: Analyzes the narrator's blindness to Jerry's real needs

Despite this closeness, however, the writer does not manage to see through Jerry's story about his mother. Should she have realized that he was making it up? After all, she is a mature woman who has been to many places and met many people. As a writer, furthermore, she should have been sensitive to others and able to pick up important clues about them. For example, in spite of his honesty, Jerry admits that he "told maybe a story" (326) when he informed the orphanage people that the woman wanted to see him after her trip through the fog. She knows, then, that the boy is capable of stretching the truth for the sake of their friendship. Even more important, she knows that he has a very strong sense of pride. This quality is made clear right at the beginning of the story, when the boy declares, "I have gloves. . . . Some of the boys don't have any" (323). The boys in the orphanage do not have mothers either. Therefore, having a mother who cares and sends gifts would certainly be something to be proud of, something worth making up a story about. Why does the writer not make this connection? Why does she not even wonder about the truth of the boy's unlikely story? Why does she not guess that he might have made it up to make himself special in her eyes?

Seventh Body Paragraph: Analyzes the reasons for the narrator's blindness to Jerry's needs

The answer lies in the character of the writer herself. Everything we know about her shows her devotion to her work. She comes to the isolated cabin to concentrate, and that is exactly what she does. The first time she sees Jerry, in fact, she is sitting at her typewriter, "well into work and not inclined to conversation" (324). A short time after the boy has started to chop wood, she says, "I had forgotten

CHAPTER 9

him" (324). The woman's ability to push Jerry out of her thoughts does not mean that she does not care about him. On the contrary, she seems to care about him very much, and is touched by his affection for her. Perhaps she is afraid that she is becoming too close to Jerry, and even beginning to think of him as a son. Perhaps she feels guilty because she does not want to adopt him and give up her freedom to work and travel whenever and wherever she likes.

> And after my first fury at her—we did not speak of her again—his having a mother, any sort at all, not far away, in Mannville, relieved me of the ache I had had about him. . . . He was not lonely. It was none of my concern. (328)

CHAPTER 9

The narrator believes the story about Jerry's mother because she wants to believe it. She believes he is not lonely because she wants to believe it. Her own need to remain free and independent keeps her from seeing, or at least admitting, that Jerry is needy.

Conclusion: Reinforces the thesis statement

There are few orphanages anymore. There are probably no twelve-year-olds as innocent as Jerry anymore. There are, however, many people who care about each other but never really communicate their feelings because their own needs get in the way. Thus, the characters and theme of "A Mother in Mannville" remind the reader that to see others clearly, people must first turn their eyes on themselves.

PROJECT PREP Drafting *First Draft*

1. Draft the body paragraphs of your essay. Each body paragraph and its topic sentence should be built on one of the categories from your graphic organizer or outline. This focus should serve as your topic sentence for the paragraph.
2. The details you have gathered will serve as the supporting evidence with which you will develop each paragraph and the essay as a whole.
3. For each body paragraph, state an interpretive claim in the form of a topic sentence, give examples that support this claim, and show the examples' support of the claim by means of an explanatory warrant. (See pages 120 and 293.) For example, "These details show that. . . ." Then write a concluding paragraph in which you show how the evidence provided supports the essay's thesis stastement.

2 The Second Draft

When you have your first draft completed, you have the basics in place for an interpretive essay. Now you can begin the process of "stepping it up," of taking it to a new level of analysis and criticism.

HERE'S HOW

Guidelines for a Close Critical Analysis

- Look even more closely at the aesthetic effects of an author's use of **stylistic or rhetorical devices.**
- Identify and analyze **ambiguities, nuances,** and **complexities** within the text.
- Anticipate and respond to **readers' questions** and **contradictory interpretations.**

CHAPTER 9

In the following passage from an analysis of F. Scott Fitzgerald's *The Great Gatsby*, student Morgan Nicholls recognizes the ambiguities, nuances, and complexities within the text as she interprets the novel's theme.

STUDENT MODEL: *Close Critical Analysis*

The Corrupted Dream of Jay Gatsby

The dominant theme in F. Scott Fitzgerald's *The Great Gatsby* is the corruption of the ideal of the American Dream. Fitzgerald seems to believe that the dream that created America, the search for freedom and happiness through hard work and hope, has been contorted into a quest for money and power. In support of this message, Fitzgerald brings to light what the American Dream once meant to Americans and what it has come to represent in the present.

The ethic of hard work is apparent in the young James Gatz, whose focus on becoming a great man is documented in his journal. His father declares, "Jimmy was bound to get ahead" (182). Gatsby's journal reflects the goal of many early Americans who worked hard and sought a better life, and his need to win Daisy's affection reflects this goal. But along the way, Gatsby's search for this dream has led him onto a path of corruption and dishonesty.

Nicholls addresses the ambiguities of the American dream in this paragraph.

Fitzgerald attributes the corruption of the dream to the drive for wealth and privilege, which creates a void in the human spirit. Money is clearly identified as the central reason for the dream's demise; it becomes easily enmeshed with hope and success but, in the end, usurps them with materialism. This is apparent in Gatsby's use of illegal practices and unsavory connections to acquire his dream.

Gatsby is first seen staring at a green light in the evening, "out to determine what share [is] his of our local heavens" (25). Gatsby's goal gives him a purpose in life and sets him apart from the upper class. He is constantly striving to reach Daisy, from the moment he is seen reaching towards her house in East Egg to his last days. But Gatsby is a man who has long ago traded his soul for money. He is a man who may once have embodied traits idealized in the American Dream, but he dispenses with them when he takes on the dream's ugly, twentieth-century face.

—Morgan Nicholls, Evanston Township High School, Evanston, Illinois

Nuances of the text are examined here as they relate to the theme.

CHAPTER 9

ADDRESSING CONFLICTING INTERPRETATIONS

As in any argument, anticipating questions and challenges is an important part of presenting a convincing case. When you write your literary analysis, be sure to confront any strong opposing interpretation to your analysis. For example, when writing her second draft, the author of "The Corruption of Jay Gatsby" decided to rework a paragraph to include reference to another possible interpretation of the novel's theme.

First Draft For Jay Gatsby, the drive to live his dream at any cost proves to be his downfall.

Second Draft While it is true that society and class play a large part in corrupting the morals of many of the characters in *The Great Gatsby,* for Gatsby himself it is the drive to live his dream at any cost that proves his downfall.

PROJECT PREP Drafting *Second Draft*

1. Read the relevant portions of the work you are analyzing again. Look closely for stylistic and rhetorical techniques that support your interpretation. Look for and explain in the framework of your interpretation any nuances, ambiguities, and complexities you see.
2. Ask members of your writing group to challenge your interpretation. Note their questions and concerns with your approach and analysis. Prepare a second draft of your critical essay that addresses the closer look you took as well as your partners' concerns.

Writing a Literary Analysis Revising

When you are reasonably satisfied with your draft, do not look at it for a day or two. By taking a break, you can return to it with a fresh, critical eye. Meanwhile, if possible, share the draft with at least one peer to read and comment on. Then use those comments, any suggestions from your teacher, and the checklists that follow to make your revisions.

CHAPTER 9

Evaluation Checklist for Revising: Whole Essay

- ✓ Do you have a strong introduction that identifies the author and the work you will discuss? (pages 331 and 352)
- ✓ Does your introduction contain a clearly worded thesis? (pages 343 and 352)
- ✓ Does the body of your essay provide ample details from the work and commentary on them to support your thesis? (pages 331 and 352)
- ✓ Does your essay examine the aesthetic effects of an author's use of stylistic or rhetorical devices? (pages 344 and 357–358)
- ✓ Does your essay identify and analyze ambiguities, nuances, and complexities within the text? (pages 346 and 357–358)
- ✓ Does your essay anticipate and respond to readers' questions and contradictory interpretations? (page 357)
- ✓ Have you quoted from the work to strengthen your points? (pages 352–353)
- ✓ Are your major points organized in a clear, appropriate way? (pages 347–350)
- ✓ Does your conclusion synthesize the details in the body of the essay and reinforce the thesis statement? (pages 331 and 352)
- ✓ As a whole, does your essay show unity and coherence? (pages 94–97)
- ✓ Would any part of your essay be improved if you **elaborated** by adding details, **deleted** unnecessary or irrelevant parts, **substituted** better examples or details, or **rearranged** any parts? (pages 25 and 316)
- ✓ Do you have an interesting, appropriate title? (pages 331 and 352)

editing

As you revise, watch for and eliminate wordiness. How would you improve the sentence below?

> The narrator gives us clues all along as to her relationship with Jerry, that relationship being one that seems rather one-sided.

CHAPTER 9

Evaluation Checklist for Revising: Paragraphs, Sentences, and Words

Checking Your Paragraphs

✓ Does each paragraph have a topic sentence? (page 86)

✓ Is each paragraph unified and coherent? (pages 94–97 and 257)

Checking Your Sentences and Words

✓ Are your sentences varied and concise? (pages 59–70)

✓ Are your words specific and lively? (page 49)

✓ Have you used language precisely to express subtle shades of meaning? (pages 7 and 52–57)

Checking Your Tropes and Schemes

✓ Have you correctly used such tropes as metaphors, similes, analogies, hyperbole, understatement, rhetorical questions, and irony to express complex thoughts clearly? (pages 53–54, 168, and 226)

✓ Have you used such schemes as parallelism, antithesis, inverted word order, repetition, and reversed structure to add emphasis and clarity? (page 75)

PROJECT PREP Revising *Alone and with Peers*

1. When you have completed your draft of your essay, share it with your writing group. Help each author provide as clear a thesis statement as possible in the introduction and a series of body paragraphs that are guided by a topic sentence and supported with warranted evidence. Also aid each author in writing a conclusion that explains how the examples demonstrate the plausibility of the thesis statement. Finally, help each author analyze the aesthetic effects of the text's use of stylistic or rhetorical devices; identify and analyze nuances, ambiguities, and complexities in the text; and anticipate and respond to readers' questions or conflicting interpretations, if this hasn't already been done.
2. Based on the feedback from your writing group, revise your second draft. In addition to attending to suggestions from your writing partners, make every effort to use proper grammar, punctuation, and spelling.

Writing a Literary Analysis Editing

Now that you have revised your composition for clarity and strength of evidence, you can focus on editing for final changes. At this stage, proofread for mechanics and usage. To add some variety to your writing style, pay attention to participial phrases. Make sure you have used participial phrases appropriately and have punctuated them correctly.

CHAPTER 9

The Language of Power *Negatives*

Power Rule: Use only one negative form for a single negative idea. (See page 853.)

See It in Action A sentence that contains a double negative has two negative words in it. Notice in the following dialogue from "A Mother in Mannville," Jerry correctly avoids using a double negative when he uses the word *any*.

Correct Negative	Some of the boys don't have any.
Double Negative	Some of the boys don't have none.

Contractions containing the word *not* are negative words. Do not use them with other negatives. The adverbs *barely, hardly,* and *scarcely* are also negatives and should not be used with other negative words.

Double Negative	Jerry couldn't barely say thank you for the coin.
Correct Negative	Jerry could barely say thank you for the coin.

Remember It Record this rule and the examples in the Power Rule section of your Personalized Editing Checklist.

Use It As you edit your paper, look for negative words. Check to make sure your sentences do not contain double negatives.

PROJECT PREP Editing *Checking for Conventions*

Read aloud your revised literary analysis to hear whether your words and ideas flow smoothly. Make sure you have punctuated all phrases correctly. Listen for sentences that sound too short or abrupt. Use the rubric on the next page for a final evaluation.

Using a Six-Trait Rubric — Literary Analysis

Ideas	**4** The thesis statement is clear. Evidence and inferences are solid. The analysis goes beyond mere summary.	**3** The thesis statement is clear. Most evidence and inferences are solid. The analysis goes beyond mere summary.	**2** The thesis statement could be clearer. Some evidence and inferences are solid, but there is too much simple summary.	**1** The thesis statement is missing or unclear. There is little evidence and few inferences, and the ideas rarely go beyond summary.
Organization	**4** The organization is clear with abundant transitions.	**3** A few ideas seem out of place or transitions are missing.	**2** Many ideas seem out of place and transitions are missing.	**1** The organization is unclear and hard to follow.
Voice	**4** The voice sounds natural, engaging, and forceful.	**3** The voice sounds natural and engaging.	**2** The voice sounds mostly natural but is weak.	**1** The voice sounds mostly unnatural and is weak.
Word Choice	**4** Words are specific and powerful. Language is appropriate.	**3** Words are specific and language is appropriate.	**2** Some words are too general and/or inappropriate.	**1** Most words are overly general and inappropriate for the purpose and audience.
Sentence Fluency	**4** Varied sentences flow smoothly.	**3** Most sentences are varied and flow smoothly.	**2** Some sentence are varied but some are choppy.	**1** Sentences are not varied and are choppy.
Conventions	**4** Punctuation, usage, and spelling are correct. Quotes are handled correctly. The Power Rules are all followed.	**3** Punctuation, usage, and spelling are mainly correct and Power Rules are all followed.	**2** Some punctuation, usage, and spelling are incorrect but all Power Rules are followed.	**1** There are many errors and at least one failure to follow a Power Rule.

PROJECT PREP — Evaluating — *Final Version*

Prepare a polished version of your essay. Get feedback from a writing partner and teacher before declaring your essay done.

Writing a Literary Analysis Publishing

Publishing a literary analysis is a way of continuing the mental conversation you began when you read the work. You are inviting your readers to join in the conversation by reacting to your analysis. Find out whether your school's newspaper or literary magazine publishes reviews or other types of analyses. If so, submit yours for publication and invite other students to respond to your ideas.

CHAPTER 9

PROJECT PREP Publishing *Connecting with Readers*

1. For your chapter project, you were free to choose among four possible types of publications for your literary analysis: an essay (the most common medium for writing of this type), a blog (an increasingly popular way to share ideas about literature), a literary magazine (these can be found in print form and on the Web), and a Web board post (many literary scholars and aficionados use the Web to share their insights and theories). In your writing group, discuss ways in which an essay and a blog would require different treatment from a writer. After the discussion with your writing group, make any changes that would be fitting for the medium you chose and make an effort to connect your literary analysis with one or more readers.
2. Entering your literary analysis in a competition is one great way to share your work with others. For information on literary contests, write to the National Council of Teachers of English, 1111 Kenyon Road, Urbana, IL 61801. Be sure to follow standard manuscript form and follow any specific entry rules for the competition.
3. You may also want to have a literary conference, an interactive way to share opinions and discuss responses. With other interested students and teachers, find a suitable room in which to gather and read aloud your works of literary analysis. Follow each reading with questions and discussion. If you cannot meet in person, meet via Internet in a safe space you can create for a private conference. Distribute e-mail addresses of all participants, and begin the conference by e-mailing a paper to everyone on the list. A lively discussion is likely to follow.

TIME OUT TO REFLECT

This experience in writing about literature has involved reading a short story, thinking and taking notes about it, and writing about it in depth. Has your process with this story affected your feelings about reading fiction, and if so, how? How has writing about "A Mother in Mannville" affected your understanding and appreciation of that story? Has it affected your view of literary criticism? Finally, do you feel this experience has strengthened your skills of analysis and evaluation for areas beyond literature? If so, how, and if not, why not?

Writing Lab

Project Corner

Speak and Listen
Debate

Hold a debate with your classmates on the question of why an author would choose to write a short story rather than a novel. What does one offer that the other doesn't? Is one considered more "serious" than the other? Who are your favorite short story writers? Whose novels do you enjoy? Why? Form teams and develop arguments arranged on both sides of any of these issues. Research debate formats, collectively decide how to organize your debate, and hold a debate in your class.

Think Creatively
Change Point of View

Rewrite "A Mother in Mannville" from the perspective of a different narrator. How would telling the story from the boy's point of view affect the story's meaning, for example?

Get Artistic
Interpret in a Different Genre

Interpret the story "A Mother in Mannville" through art rather than writing: draw, sculpt, dramatize, choreograph, animate, or create a video that reflects your understanding of the story. Then write a reflection answering these questions: How does this form of interpretation influence your understanding of the story's meaning? How is it similar to, and different from, writing a formal literary analysis?

Apply and Assess

In Everyday Life

Analytical Note

1. On the school bus this morning you finished reading a classic literary work. At school you notice that the interesting classmate you've been trying to impress all semester is sitting two rows in front of you reading the same book you just finished. ***Write a note*** to your classmate in which you analyze what you liked most about the book. Then impress your classmate by comparing the classic to another book that you have read in the past. To narrow your subject, compare a specific element from each book, such as a character, setting, or scene. Use informal language; be conversational in tone but keep your ideas clear. (You can find information on responding to literature on pages 331–338.)

CHAPTER 9

For Oral Communication Analytical Oral Review

2. You are a music reviewer for newspapers and magazines known for your witty critiques. The *Up Before Dawn* radio show has asked you to appear as a special guest. You have been asked to talk about a recording by the band "Only a Mother Could Love." ***Prepare a review*** for the show's audience. Use concrete examples to back up your reasons—for example, the message of song lyrics, the musical arrangement, the instruments used, and the vocal performance if any. You can choose to limit your subject to a particular song or album. (You can find information on oral presentations on pages 575–581.)

Timed Writing Grant Request

3. You are the director of a theater company that is planning to adapt a literary work for the stage. You would like to obtain a grant, due to the high literary quality of the work you are adapting. Write a letter to the Arts Council persuading its members to fund the performance. Your letter must provide a detailed literary analysis and point out specific strengths in the plot, conflict, setting, characters, and dialogue. Choose a familiar novel or short story as the work to be adapted. You have 30 minutes to complete your work.

   Before You Write Consider the following questions: What is the situation? What is the occasion? Who is the audience? What is the purpose? Include a clearly worded thesis statement that presents a supportable idea.

   After You Write Evaluate your work using the six-trait evaluation rubric on page 362.

Unit 3

Research and Report Writing

The best research question is the one that takes root in your mind, urging you onto a path toward an answer. The chapters in this unit will help you germinate a meaningful question. They will then help you clear a path through the tangle of sources and ideas you might find as you seek to answer that question. But when you are finished with your research, don't be surprised if your most important discovery is that your one question wasn't answered with a single, definitive answer. Along the way you just may have planted a few seeds—a few new questions—in your mind and in the minds of others.

The outcome of any serious research can only be to make two questions grow where only one grew before. — *Thorstein Veblen*

CHAPTER 10

Summaries and Abstracts

A **summary** is a concise condensation of a longer piece of writing, covering only the main points of the original.

Here are some examples of how the skills of summarizing are used in school, in the workplace, and in everyday life.

- **A student summarizes a chapter of his history book** to prepare for a test.
- **A novelist jots down brief summaries of experiences and ideas** that she may wish to explore in her writing later on.
- **An assistant summarizes a long report** to save her boss and other readers time.
- **A reporter writes a summary of a news story** to present to his executive editor in hopes of getting an assignment for a front-page article.
- **A friend summarizes the events of last night's party** in an e-mail to you because you were unable to attend the function.
- **A friend summarizes a movie** he has seen or a book he has read and wants to encourage you to see or read also.

Writing Project: Summary

Back to Basics ***Write a summary of an article or editorial.***

Think Through Writing Read or reread the article on future homes on pages 235–237 and the editorials on climate change on pages 290–293. After reading each one, write a summary of it.

Talk About It In your writing group, discuss the summaries. What information did each author include in the summary? What else might be included, without including too much? In what ways were the summaries alike, and in what ways were they different?

Read About It In the following passage, Edward Edelson explains the ways in which animals have been used in film. Following that passage is a summary of it. As you read the summary, think about the quick summary you wrote and the discussion you had with your group about what to include in a summary.

MODEL: Original Passage and Summary

Great Animals of the Movies

Edward Edelson

Original

From the beginning Hollywood has been fascinated by wild beasts—elephants, tigers, lions, apes, rhinos, and any other species that could be worked into a film. Few Hollywood adventures with wildlife have had much connection with the real thing, however. Filmmakers generally swing to one extreme or to another: Either they make wild animals seem tamer than they are, or they make them seem wilder than they are.

The last sentence of the first paragraph states the main idea for the essay.

Two species that have gotten bad reputations because of the latter habit are the gorilla and the wolf. Until recently, the movies have pictured both as villains of the worst dye. It is part of movie folklore that gorillas are vicious animals, dangerous when they are encountered, always ready to attack humans, and consistently displaying a mean streak. As for wolves, it is an equally old movie tradition that they are utterly savage killers who have no redeeming qualities and who destroy other animals and attack humans out of sheer blood lust.

The second paragraph focuses on two specific examples.

Hollywood can hardly be blamed for these attitudes, since they reflect an old, established image of both species. It is only in relatively recent years that ethologists—scientists who study animals in their native environments—have made a concerted effort to change the old images because of observations in the wild.

Those observations have shown that the gorilla is a gentle animal that eats only vegetation, avoids contact with humans whenever possible, and poses no threat unless it is attacked. The breast-beating and roaring that

Repeating the word *observations* provides a transition from the last paragraph to this one.

CHAPTER 10

seem so ferocious are actually just an effort by the gorilla to scare possible attackers away by a bluff. In addition, the gorilla is one of the most intelligent animals known; a captive gorilla named Koko has been taught dozens of words (which are "spoken" by sign language) and is said to have an intelligence quotient of 60 to 90.

As for the wolf, observers describe it as an animal that is no more vicious than any other predator, that does not attack humans unless provoked, and that has strong family ties. Rather than being a totally destructive killer, the wolf is described by scientists who have studied its behavior as a useful creature who helps to maintain the strength of the species on which it preys because it kills only the animals that are least equipped to survive.

CHAPTER 10

Summary

Hollywood movie makers tend to represent wild animals as either more gentle or more ferocious than they actually are. The gorilla and the wolf are usually shown as vicious animals that are ready to attack humans unprovoked. This view reflects long-held attitudes that have only recently been discovered to be false. Scientists studying the gorilla in the wild have found that they are gentle, plant-eating creatures that avoid attack whenever possible. Studies have also shown the gorilla to be an intelligent animal. The wolf, according to observers, is no more violent than any other predator, and it does not attack humans without cause. Because it attacks the weakest members of its prey, the wolf strengthens the species it preys upon and serves a useful purpose.

The summary includes one or two sentences for each paragraph in the original text but keeps the sense of a beginning, middle, and ending.

Respond in Writing Make a comparison chart of the original passage and the summary. What information is in the original that is not in the summary? How might you generalize about information to include in a summary?

Develop Your Own Data Work with your classmates to develop ideas that you might incorporate into a movie summary.

Small Groups: In your small group, discuss the writing you have done so far. Use a graphic organizer like the one below to help you clarify your thoughts. The characteristics of the original text are listed in the first box. With your group, decide what characteristics should be listed in the second box.

Original	Summary
• Has beginning, middle, and end	•
• Has main ideas	•
• Has ample supporting details	•
• Uses author's language	•
• Is as long as necessary to present the topic in a well-developed way	•
• Uses a flowing, engaging style	•

Whole Class: Make a master chart of all of the ideas generated by the small groups about the characteristics of summaries. You can refer to this chart as you work on improving your summary.

Write About It You will next write a well-developed summary of the article on homes of the future on pages 235–237, of either editorial on climate change on pages 290–293, or on an article or editorial of your choice, with your teacher's permission. You may use any of the following possible topics, audiences, and forms.

Possible Topics	Possible Audiences	Possible Forms
• article on homes of the future (pages 235–237) • editorial on climate change (pages 290–293) • an article or editorial of your choice	• other teenagers • adults you are trying to persuade • the general public • an editor for an online magazine	• an entry in your blog • an article in the magazine *Green Digest* • contribution to the "In Short" section of the science corner of your school newspaper

CHAPTER 10

Understanding Summaries

The formal summary, sometimes called a **précis,** is a very practical form of writing. It condenses writing from a longer piece into a much shorter, easily readable piece that contains only essential information and saves reading time. It is usually no more than one-third the length of the original work. Its brevity and concise style make the summary a valuable aid for professionals and students alike.

Unlike an essay, a summary does not include personal comments, interpretations, or insights. It is a straightforward reworking—in condensed form—of the original piece of writing. The challenge of writing a good summary is to be true to the original and at the same time use your own words in a smooth, easy-to-follow style.

HERE'S HOW

Features of a Summary

- A summary is usually no more than one-third the length of the original.
- A summary states the main ideas of the original, including only the most vital details.
- A summary presents the main ideas in the same order as the original.
- A summary states the main ideas of the original in the summary writer's own words.

Practice Your Skills

Analyzing a Summary

Review "Great Animals of the Movies" and the summary that follows the essay. Then answer the following questions.

1. About how long is the summary as compared to the original?
2. To how many sentences are the first three paragraphs in the original reduced in the summary?
3. What two details about gorillas are not in the summary?
4. What adjective in the summary replaces the clause "that eats only vegetation" in the original?
5. What detail about wolves is omitted in the summary?
6. In what order does the summary present the main ideas of the original?

PROJECT PREP Analyzing Key Points

Review the summary you wrote and check it against the chart above, **Features of a Summary.** Share your summary with your writing group and discuss what each author needs to do to write a summary with all the expected features.

Writing a Summary Prewriting

During the prewriting stage, your main goal is to make sure you thoroughly understand the main ideas of the original work.

Preparing to Write a Summary

When you write a paragraph or an essay, your task is to develop your main idea or thesis statement into a full composition. When you write a summary, however, your task is to break the material down to its main ideas. You need to retrace the author's steps, locating the most important information. The following steps will help you.

CHAPTER 10

HERE'S HOW **Preparing to Write a Summary**

- Read the original work to get the main idea.
- Read the work again, writing down unfamiliar words.
- Write a synonym or a simple definition for each unfamiliar word.
- Write down the main ideas in the order in which they are presented.
- Determine the length of the original, in words, lines, or pages.

Recognizing Main Ideas

The most important skill in summarizing is distinguishing between main ideas and supporting ideas. To help you identify the main ideas, ask yourself, "Which idea is more general than all the others?" In some cases the answer to this question will be the thesis statement of an essay or the topic sentence of a paragraph. In other cases, however, a main idea may be implied rather than stated directly. If a main idea is implied, phrase a statement that expresses it. Look for the main ideas in the following examples.

MODEL: Main Idea Stated

The Brain

Your brain is constantly guarded by a complicated mechanism known as the blood-brain barrier. This is a system that protects the central nervous system from harmful chemicals by blocking their entry into the brain. Much remains to be learned about the blood-brain barrier, but some scientists hope that they may learn enough about it to help in the treatment of brain disorders and to influence sleep, learning, emotions, and other processes that are controlled by the brain. If scientists can alter the chemicals that enter and are rejected by the brain, they will have a powerful tool, indeed.

—Margaret Hyde, Edward Marks, James Wells, *Mysteries of the Mind*

The main idea of this paragraph is stated directly in the first sentence, which is the topic sentence. The other sentences provide supporting details, including a description of what the barrier does and how scientists hope to use what they learn about it to treat brain disorders.

MODEL: Main Idea Implied

Sizing Up the Moon

The surface area of the moon is about 1/14 that of Earth, and just about the size of the continent of Africa. The diameter of Earth is a little less than 4 times the diameter of the moon, and its volume is about 49 times that of the moon. If Earth and the moon had the same density, Earth would weigh about 49 times its satellite. However, the moon is somewhat less dense and weighs only 1/81 as much as Earth. Lest we underestimate this weight, it amounts to about 70 million trillion tons. Actually, *mass* is the correct word, instead of *weight*. Because of its smaller mass, the moon has a surface gravity only 1/6 that of Earth. On the moon a 180-pound astronaut will thus weigh only 30 pounds, although his mass will be the same as on Earth.

—D. S. Halacy, Jr., *Colonization of the Moon*

In this paragraph all of the sentences are equally specific. The general idea is implied: By all significant measurements, the moon is much smaller than Earth. All the sentences contain supporting details that expand on this implied main idea.

Writing Tip

Find the **main ideas** in a passage by identifying the most general statements or by expressing an **implied main idea** in your own words.

Practice Your Skills

Recognizing Main Ideas

Write the main idea of each paragraph. If the main idea is implied, write a sentence that expresses the main idea.

1. The Saxons have left their name in many parts of the south of England. Essex, Sussex, and Middlesex were lands of the East, South, and Middle Saxons. The great King Alfred, who lived in the ninth century, was King of Wessex (the West Saxons), but he spoke of his people as the "Anglekin," or English folk. In his lifetime both Angles and Saxons began to call all their land England.

2. When Julius Caesar came to Britain in 55 B.C., the Thames River already had its name. It means "dark" and so also do the river names *Tame, Teme,* and *Tamar,* all coming from the same origin. The river name *Wye* means "winding," and *Wey* means the same. *Trent* means "wandering" or "flooding"; *Stour* (probably) means "strong." *Darwen, Derwent, Darent,* and *Dart* all come from a Celtic word meaning "oak trees" and tell of the forests through which these rivers flowed.

3. Wherever the British have settled all around the world, they have often longed for the sights and sounds of home. These they could not have, but a familiar name could be had at once, and this was often their choice. There is hardly a town in Britain without a namesake overseas. The Pilgrims in America began this naming, but Canadians, Australians, and New Zealanders have all done it too. There are at least 16 towns outside Britain called Cambridge, 20 called Oxford, 20 called Chester, and over 30 called Richmond.

—C. M. Mathews, *How Place Names Began*

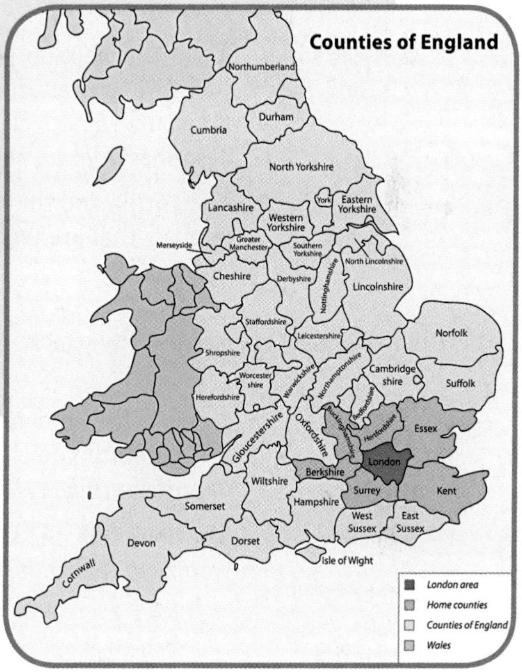

PROJECT PREP *Prewriting* ***Main Ideas***

Make a list of the main ideas in the text you are summarizing. Bring your list to your writing group for feedback and comparison with others' writing on the same text.

The Power of Language

Adjectival Clauses: Which One? What Kind?

When you write a summary or abstract, you condense and paraphrase the author's ideas. One of the best ways to condense information is to combine sentences by making one into a subordinate clause.

A subordinate clause that modifies a noun or pronoun is an **adjectival clause.** It usually answers one of two questions: Which one? or What kind?

Notice Edward Edelson's use of adjectival clauses in the following sentences.

What Kind?

As for the wolf, observers describe it as an animal that is no more vicious than any other predator. (The subordinate clause is an adjectival clause that describes *animal.* What kind of animal?)

The gorilla and the wolf are usually shown as vicious animals that are ready to attack humans unprovoked.

Other adjectival clauses identify which one.

Which One?

Jackie is the student who is wearing the green coat. (The subordinate clause is an adjectival clause that describes *student.* Which student is she?)

The book tells the story of entertainers whose parents were also their business managers.

Punctuation Tip

If the clause is an adjectival clause, first determine whether the clause is **essential** or **nonessential.** No punctuation is used with an adjectival clause that contains information that is essential to identifying a person, place, or thing in the sentence. Commas are always used, however, to set off nonessential adjectival clauses. An adjectival clause is nonessential if it can be removed without changing the basic meaning of the sentence.

Writing a Summary Drafting

Once you identify the main ideas of a selection, you are ready to write the first draft of your summary. Rewrite the original by condensing it into your own words.

CONDENSING

One way to **condense,** or shorten, a passage is to omit repetition and such details as examples, incidents, and descriptions. Another way is to reduce wordy clauses and long phrases to short phrases or even single words. You can often combine two or more sentences into one concise sentence.

Read the following model. Then use the chart that follows it to study the various methods used to condense the original. The sentences are numbered for easy reference.

MODEL: Condensing

TADPOLES

Original

(1) One might assume that if few tadpoles can survive in small puddles, frogs should deposit their eggs in larger bodies of water such as lakes. **(2)** Lakes are certainly more stable than puddles in the road; they rarely dry up. **(3)** In large, permanent bodies of water, however, tadpoles may have to compete with many species for the organic food on which they depend. **(4)** Also, large lakes are often nutrient-poor, since sunlight cannot penetrate to their bottoms, permitting photosynthesis and plant growth. **(5)** Finally, lakes usually support fish that would prey on relatively defenseless tadpoles. **(6)** Indeed, tadpoles and fish very rarely occur together. **(7)** To escape aquatic predators, some tadpoles that live in tropical streams actually crawl up wet rocks and out of the water, or they burrow into leaf matter at the edge of streams. **(8)** Clearly, large bodies of water are not a preferred habitat.

—Richard Wassersug, "Why Tadpoles Love Fast Foods"

Summary

(1) Puddles make better homes for tadpoles than do large, more stable lakes. **(2)** In lakes tadpoles might have to compete with other species for food. **(3)** Lakes are also poor in nutritious plants because of the way they block the sunlight. **(4)** Lakes are home to many fish that could prey on tadpoles or force them to find shelter on rocks or under leaves.

The following chart shows how information from the original paragraph is recast in the summary by using various methods of condensing. Notice also that the summary states the main idea in the first sentence and then presents the important supporting ideas in the same order as the original.

ORIGINAL SENTENCE		SUMMARY SENTENCE
1	→	omitted: unnecessary detail
2 and 8	→	1 (main idea)
3	→	2
4	→	3
5 and 7	→	4
6	→	omitted: unnecessary detail

Writing Tip

Condense information from the original by omitting repetition and unnecessary details, by replacing long phrases and wordy clauses with short phrases or single words, and by combining ideas from two or more sentences into one sentence. Present the main ideas and the important supporting ideas in the same order as the original.

Practice Your Skills

Condensing

Condense each paragraph in the following passage to one or two sentences. Write your sentences next to the proper number.

1. You can develop a sense of humor. You may never turn into a wit—the kind of person who can crack jokes all day—but that isn't necessary. It is more important for you to learn to be an appreciative audience and to learn to see the humor in various situations.

2. Perhaps the first thing you need to do is to begin looking for things that are funny in yourself and in the people and things around you. If you have a sour outlook on life, very little will ever seem funny to you. You have to shake yourself up a bit and say, "Look, let's take off these dark glasses and see what there is around here that is funny." Then you may see or hear something that will give you a great big laugh. Looking for humor and being alert to instances where it is likely to be present will help you detect it more readily, even if it is a joke on you.

3. Second, it will help you a great deal to be around people who have a good sense of humor. You will notice what they think is funny. You will hear them say funny things, which you might even apply yourself in a similar situation. You will also begin to pick up their attitude toward things in general. They will teach you to see the funny side of things.

4. Third, you might want to make a little study of just what it is that makes people laugh. Even if you apply this only to your own friends, you will discover this interesting fact: Different kinds of humor appeal to different people. What seems funny to one will not seem funny to another. One reason for this is difference in background and vocabulary. For instance, someone who has been reared on a farm might tell a joke about farm animals, which would mean absolutely nothing to someone who had been reared in the city and knew nothing about farm animals and their habits. Certainly, city people tell jokes about things that require a city background to understand.

5. Fourth, you can study the cartoons or jokes that are printed in some of the leading magazines. Why are they considered funny? What is humorous about them? You will soon find that the element of surprise is likely to be present. Often a person or an animal is pictured as doing something ridiculous or unusual. Frequently you find everyday situations exaggerated to such an extent that they become funny. After you have analyzed these cartoons and jokes, be on the lookout for incidents that you think might make good cartoons, or for a conversation that might make a good joke. It will be an interesting experiment, and it will help to make you humor-conscious.

—Virginia Bailard and Ruth Strang, *Ways to Improve Your Personality*

CHAPTER 10

Paraphrasing

When you condense, you need to rephrase ideas from the original work in your own words. Putting a writer's ideas in your own words is called **paraphrasing.** One technique for paraphrasing is to replace words in the original with synonyms. A second technique is to vary the structure of the original sentences.

Original	When Nelson Mandela won the vote to become president on April 27, 1994, nearly fifty years of apartheid came to an end for the country of South Africa.
Paraphrase	Nelson Mandela's election as president of South Africa on April 27, 1994, marked the end of almost fifty years of apartheid.

CHAPTER 10

Writing Tip

Paraphrase the original work by using synonyms and varying sentence structure.

Practice Your Skills

Paraphrasing

Paraphrase each sentence in the following paragraph.

(1) Nature provides a process to remove practically every known pollutant from its atmosphere. **(2)** As contaminants are discharged, wind causes all materials to disperse; gravity brings the heavier substances to the ground. **(3)** As lighter particles, which remain afloat, collide and coagulate with each other, they increase in size and then fall. **(4)** Oxygen in the air reacts with many pollutants, changing them to a form that is more readily removed. **(5)** Rain and snow absorb and carry down many substances; trees and grasses act like large filters that collect particles and some gases. **(6)** Sunlight causes some gases to react chemically and form particulate matter that can settle down. **(7)** Nature can provide the cleansing function as long as the natural process can keep up with the quantities of material discharged. **(8)** Air becomes polluted when excess quantities of material are discharged and exceed nature's cleansing capabilities. **(9)** To prevent air-pollution conditions, people can assist by abating the contaminants prior to their discharge into the atmosphere. **(10)** This can be accomplished by separating the pollutants from exhaust prior to emission, or by converting them to innocuous products that may then be discharged.

—Richard T. Sheahan, *Fueling the Future: An Environment and Energy Primer*

Think Critically

Making Evaluations

When you decide which ideas and details to include in a summary, you are **evaluating**. To evaluate which ideas should be part of the summary and which should be left out, you need to use a set of standards, or criteria, that your summary must meet. One set of criteria can be applied to the main ideas.

HERE'S HOW

Criteria for Evaluating Main Ideas

1. Is each stated or implied main idea included in the summary?
2. Does your wording include necessary supporting details?
3. Is your summary understandable without additional detail?
4. Does each idea lead logically to the next?

If the answer to every question is yes, then your summary may be complete. Otherwise, you may need to include additional supporting details to make your summary complete and readable. The following set of criteria can be applied to supporting details.

HERE'S HOW

Criteria for Evaluating Details

1. Is the information necessary for an understanding of the content?
2. Has redundant information been omitted?
3. Can a term or phrase replace a list?

Thinking Practice

Use the criteria in the charts above to help you write and evaluate a short summary from an article of your choosing.

PROJECT PREP Drafting *First Draft*

Using feedback from your group and the instruction on pages 373–378, write a first draft of your summary. Condense, paraphrase, and evaluate the main ideas and details to determine their usefulness to include in the summary. Share your draft with your writing group and ask for feedback.

Writing a Summary Revising

The main goals of revising are to check the accuracy of your summary against the original and to reduce your first draft to the most concise version possible. The following checklist will help.

Evaluation Checklist for Revising

- ✓ Compare your summary to the original. Are the ideas presented accurately? (pages 372–378)
- ✓ Are the ideas in your summary presented in the same order as they appear in the original? (pages 372–373 and 378)
- ✓ Is your summary no more than one-third the length of the original? (page 372)
- ✓ Did you use your own words and vary the sentence structure of the original? (page 380)
- ✓ Did you use transitions and other connecting devices to make your summary flow smoothly? (pages 95–97 and 122)

PROJECT PREP Revising *New Draft*

1. Based on the feedback you have gotten from your writing group, write a new draft of your summary.
2. Consider your chosen audience and format. Is your summary appropriate for those? If not, make necessary revisions.
3. Share your new draft with your writing group for feedback.

In the Media

News Summaries

Summaries and abstracts serve different communications purposes in different media and different settings. No doubt you recognize the following "tease" from radio and television.

> *Citizens protest decision on the new downtown development.*
> *Full story at 10.*

The purpose is to give you the gist of a story with enough drama to make you want to hear the full story. Although the purpose of the story may be informative, the purpose of the tease is both persuasive and entertaining.

Some newspapers offer front page summaries of each story covered. These summaries serve as a table of contents, as well as teasing readers to buy the paper. Newsmagazines often summarize articles in the table of contents.

Other print summaries have a simpler purpose: to save readers' time. Business reports, for example, often include an **executive summary**—a one-page summary of the main ideas and conclusions of the report. Academic and scientific journals also include abstracts. These save readers time by letting them decide quickly whether the article interests them. They are also used in online databases as a search aid.

Media Activity

Use pieces from your writing portfolio to create summaries for different purposes, as follows.

1. Write a television news tease for a personal narrative you have written.
2. Write a newsmagazine table-of-contents summary for one of your informative essays.
3. Write a summary of one of your research reports.
4. Write an abstract of a literary analysis you have written.

In the editing stage, pay special attention to the Power Rules, as always.

The Language of Power Fragments

Power Rule: Use sentence fragments only the way professional writers do, after the sentence they refer to and usually to emphasize a point. Fix all sentence fragments that occur before the sentence they refer to and ones that occur in the middle of a sentence. (See pages 663–664.)

See It in Action The writer of the piece on a sense of humor could have added a fragment to deepen and emphasize a point.

An Effective Fragment	It is more important for you to learn to be an appreciative audience and to learn to see the humor in various situations. Yes, even in yourself.

Contrast that with the following ineffective fragment. Instead of deepening and emphasizing a point, as in the previous example, it simply adds completely new information. Following it are two ways to fix the fragment.

An Ineffective Fragment	Oxygen in the air reacts with many pollutants. Changing them to a form that is more readily removed.
Fixing a Fragment with a Comma	Oxygen in the air reacts with many pollutants, changing them to a form that is more readily removed.
Fixing a Fragment by Adding a Subject	Oxygen in the air reacts with many pollutants. The oxygen changes them to a form that is more readily removed.

Remember It Record this rule and the examples in the Power Rule section of your Personalized Editing Checklist.

Use It As you edit your paper, look for sentence fragments. Use them effectively.

PROJECT PREP Editing and Publishing *Polishing Your Work*

Evaluate one another's summaries, paying close attention to grammar, spelling, and punctuation. Prepare a final, polished version of your summary.

Writing an Abstract

When you must make your way through vast seas of information, abstracts can serve as helpful guides. Whether you are looking for a good book to read for a research paper or simply making plans for the weekend, abstracts can save time and prevent wild-goose chases.

> An **abstract** is a very condensed summary that communicates the essential content of a work in as few words as possible.

Writing Tip

Read **abstracts** when compiling a list of sources to read for a research project.

CHAPTER 10

Abstracts appear in several formats and serve many purposes. A typical scientific or scholarly abstract tells the purpose of a study, the procedures of investigation, the findings, and the conclusions. Abstracts in various fields of study compile volumes of print and electronic information. Such **informative abstracts** seldom exceed 350 words, but contain enough detail for the reader to grasp the essential information without reading the full article.

You are probably more familiar with **indicative abstracts,** which give a general summary of an article, book, play, or movie in no more than two or three sentences. The entries that you find in annotated bibliographies, the content descriptions that appear in Internet search results, the synopses that appear in the table of contents of a journal, as well as the one- to two-line book and movie reviews from a newspaper or magazine are examples of indicative abstracts. Both informative and indicative abstracts usually include the title, the author's name, a general statement of content, and publication information.

Learning Tip

Developing the skills of writing summaries and abstracts will help you throughout school and even in the workplace. In school you will use the skill as you work on research reports or literary analyses. It will also help you on statewide exams. Outside of school, you will use the skill of summarizing in writing proposals and other work-related documents. (See pages 549–567.)

The following is an example of an abstract entry from an online database. The abstract precedes the full text version of the article.

CHAPTER 10

MODEL: Abstract

Ancient World's Great Database in Alexandria to Get a Successor
Houston Chronicle; Houston, Tex.; Nov 21, 1999; DOUGLAS JEHL;

Sub Title:	[2 STAR Edition]
Start Page:	29
Dateline:	ALEXANDRIA, Egypt
Personal Names:	Zahran, Mohsen

Abstract

At its glorious peak, Alexandria was the center of science and commerce in the ancient world. And at its center—before fires, earthquakes and conquest sent this Mediterranean port city into its long decline—stood an extraordinary library. It was a center of scholarship that attracted the likes of Euclid and Archimedes and may well have achieved its goal of amassing a copy of every known book under a single roof.

Now, after years of planning, a spectacular successor is to open soon, the product in part of a worldwide appeal to "efface the disaster" caused by the old library's loss. Even in the dirt and decay of modern Alexandria, some see in the new institution a way that Alexandria may regain its place as a cultural crossroad.

Full Text

ALEXANDRIA, Egypt – This city is trying hard to recapture the luster it lost 2,000 years ago.

At its glorious peak, Alexandria was the center of science and commerce in the ancient world. And at its center—before fires, earthquakes and conquest sent this Mediterranean port city into its long decline—stood an extraordinary library. It was a center of scholarship that attracted the likes of Euclid and Archimedes and may well have achieved its goal of amassing a copy of every known book under a single roof.

Now, after years of planning, a spectacular successor is to open soon, the product in part of a worldwide appeal to "efface the disaster" caused by the old library's loss. Even in the dirt and decay of modern Alexandria, some see in the new institution a way that Alexandria may regain its place as a cultural crossroad.

"Its revival will benefit humanity," Mohsen Zahran, an MIT-educated architect who is the project manager, said of the new library. In a bow to the past, the new structure, like the old one, is to be christened the Bibliotheca Alexandrina.

The planned opening, expected early next year after more than 10 years of construction, comes at a time when politicians, businessmen and archeologists have thrown themselves into efforts to recapture some of Alexandria's old glory.

A 20-mile road that skirts the Mediterranean has been widened, horn honking forbidden and dilapidated buildings torn down, all to open a fresh window to a sea that has always fed Alexandria's cosmopolitan spirit.

And just offshore, underwater beneath the city's historic harbor, archeologists from France and Egypt are uncovering remnants of much that disappeared long ago, having toppled into the sea. If the claims are accurate, they include remnants from Cleopatra's palace, and from the fabled lighthouse that was one of the seven wonders of the ancient world.

There is talk of one day transforming the waters into an underwater park. The highly popular governor, Muhammad Abdel al-Mahgoud, has taken a big step in that direction by halting sewage flow that rendered the waters of the city's harbor a kind of translucent muck.

PROJECT PREP *Analyzing* ***Abstracts***

With a partner, compare this abstract with the summary you wrote or with another one in this chapter. In what ways are they similar? In what ways are they different? Share your findings with the rest of the class.

TIME OUT TO REFLECT

Through most of the writing instruction in this program, you have been asked to elaborate, expand, and develop ideas, the opposite process of what is required when summarizing. Write a few sentences in your Learning Log about why both types of skills—elaborating with details on the one hand and getting back to the basics of main ideas on the other—go hand in hand.

Writing Lab

Project Corner

CHAPTER 10

Extend It
Lengthen Your Summary

Write a more extended summary of the text you chose, including extra information for readers who want a more comprehensive understanding of the subject.

Create Multimedia
Use Software

Use computer software to **embellish your summary.** Add features such as images, Web-based clips, links to other reviews, and additional content. Consider what information your readers might want.

Get Technical
Tweet

With its strict limit of 140 characters, a tweet is almost automatically a summary. **In a series of 5 tweets, summarize the article or editorial you chose for your project.** When you have finished, compare the tweets to your formal summary. With a partner, discuss why tweeting may have become so popular. Also consider whether or not it contributes to superficiality of communication.

In Everyday Life

Paraphrase for Test Preparation

1. You have a final exam in your favorite subject in two days. You hope to do well on the test, but there are so many ideas and terms to remember that you're afraid you will confuse many of them. ***Paraphrase*** four of the ideas or terms you need to remember and understand for the exam. State them in your own words. Use synonyms and varying sentence structures in your paraphrases. (You can find information on paraphrasing on page 380.)

In the Workplace

Summary of Investment Risks

2. You are a staff researcher for a manufacturing company that is considering opening a new factory in Latin America. Your boss has asked for information on the political conditions in each country. ***Prepare a summary*** of a newspaper or magazine article about the political conditions in one country in Latin America. Keep the summary concise and interesting. Avoid repetition and unnecessary details. Combine like ideas into one sentence or paragraph. (You can find information on preparing summaries on pages 372–384.)

Timed Writing

Summary of a Literary Work

3. In an effort to encourage students to read more, your local library is creating a booklet of summaries of short stories and novels that students have read and enjoyed. Write a summary of a short story or novel to submit to the booklet. Choose a work that you know well enough to be able to write about without additional research. You have 25 minutes to complete your work.

   Before You Write Consider the following questions: What is the situation? What is the occasion? Who is the audience? What is the purpose?

   Be sure to include all the important points in the plot, staying true to the original yet using your own words in a smooth and easy-to-follow style. Keep the summary concise and interesting to attract potential readers.

   After You Write Check your summary to be sure you included only the most important points and only necessary details.

CHAPTER 11

CHAPTER 11

Research: Planning and Gathering Information

Research reports are compositions based on research drawn from books, periodicals, online sources, interviews with experts, and other authoritative media.

Developing the skills to write effective research reports will help you in your present and future schooling. It will also help you in the business world, where reports are widely used to convey the information needed for important decisions. Here are just a few of the ways that research reports are used in everyday life.

- **Research assistants provide information on issues** to public officials in order to help the officials make policies.
- **Statisticians provide data** on an athlete's accomplishments for game broadcasts and for books and magazines.
- **Genealogists do research on family histories** and write reports for clients wanting to know more about their ancestors.
- **Agricultural advisory services give expert advice** to farmers on ways to increase crop yields.
- **Meteorologists do research on historical weather patterns** as part of preparing long-range forecasts.

Create your own research report by completing the project below.

Writing Project Research Report

Finding the Answer ***Plan and gather information for a research report on a question that you would like to answer.***

Think Through Writing Think of a question that you would like answered through research. It could be a long-standing question, such as "Who shot JFK?" or it could be an everyday question, such as "What's the best way to grow tomatoes?" It could be a question regarding taste, such as "Who is the greatest guitar player ever?" Think of a question that you would like to answer by conducting research to find evidence. Brainstorm about this question and why it intrigues you by writing down everything you know about it.

Talk About It In a group of three to five students, discuss the questions you have identified to explore through research. What topics did you consider? What do these interests tell you about your curiosity about the world around you?

Read About It The following passage from the *Unsolved Mysteries* Web site explores the question of whether there is life on Mars. Think about the evidence consulted to inquire into this question.

MODEL: Research Report

LIFE ON MARS

Does a meteorite found in the Antarctic hold evidence of life on Mars?

Asking a provocative question is one way to raise readers' interest.

CASE DETAILS

Deep Space is the last great frontier. Each new image captured by telescopes brings up the age-old question: Is there life somewhere else in the universe?

Some imagined the answer would come from a spaceship carrying aliens from a faraway civilization. But, in fact, the truth might be hidden in this ordinary-looking piece of meteorite known as Rock 84-001. It came from the planet Mars and traveled millions of miles over millions of years until it slammed into Earth. Richard Berendzen, professor of astronomy at American University, says it may forever change the way we view the universe:

Thesis Statement

Credentials of expert are established. Each time a new expert is introduced, the credentials are made clear.

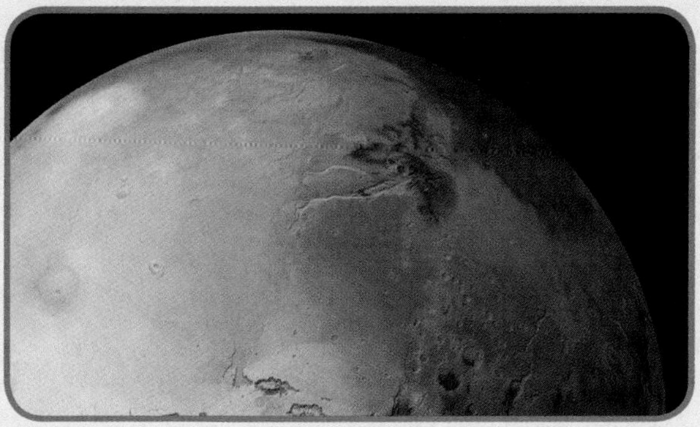

CHAPTER 11

"This meteorite, if it should prove true, would be literally one of the turning points, one of the defining epochs in all of human exploration and discovery. I think it'd be almost an icon for the twentieth century."

Kathie Thomas-Keprta is a planetary geologist with Lockheed Martin:

"It still shocks me that we have found what we've found, and we're able to present it. I would have never dreamed anything like this in a million years."

CHAPTER 11

Some scientists theorized that the seeds for life on Earth were planted by microorganisms from Mars. Ironically, what may prove to be the most remarkable discovery in the history of [humankind] began with a completely unremarkable event. In December of 1984, Dr. Robert Score was among a team of American scientists on a geological expedition searching for meteorites in Antarctica. Dr. Score picked up the rock now known as 84-001. It weighed only 4.2 pounds and was the size of a large potato. No one paid much attention to it. For eight years, it sat on a shelf gathering dust. Donald W. Goldsmith is the author of "The Hunt For Life On Mars":

Narrative passages help fill in background information.

"This meteorite was essentially misclassified, or not very carefully classified, as an ordinary Earth meteorite. And only later, when a geologist named David Middlefeld looked at it more carefully, did he realize, no, this is characteristic of a Martian meteorite. It has just the precise ratio of certain isotopes that make it clear that it came from Mars."

In an unconventional presentation, the quotes of experts are presented in italics. In a formal research report, they would be in quotation marks, or paraphrased, and in both instances would be accompanied by a reference to their source.

As it turned out, 84-001 was only the 12th Martian meteorite ever found. It is 4.5 billion years old, almost as old as our solar system, and existed at least one billion years before life on Earth began. A team of NASA scientists finally analyzed the rock. Deep within were what appeared to be signs of life: the fossilized remains of dozens of incredibly tiny microorganisms. Dr. Everett K. Gibson is senior planetary scientist with NASA:

"It's not a smoking gun, as we said in our paper. We have not found proof of living biogenic activity in this Martian sample. But we have a trail of evidence."

For a scientist, "a trail of evidence" is like a map to buried treasure. However, this map goes back in time as well as taking us to a different place. It suggests a remarkable journey that began on Mars, four and a half billion years ago, when our solar system was just taking shape. At the same time that 84-001 was being formed, Mars was being bombarded by a catastrophic meteor storm. Its surface was left covered with craters and crevices. Dr. Everett K. Gibson:

"Early in the history of Mars, we feel it was warmer and it was wetter. There was an abundance of water on the surface of the planet. The atmosphere was more dense, liquid water moved across the surface of the planet, it also percolated down through the cracks."

Over the next 500 million years, chemical reactions in this "primeval soup" apparently produced a primitive life form. As the water evaporated, the microscopic life forms were enclosed in rock and became fossilized. According to Everett Gibson, one such rock may have been 84-001:

"Then it sat on the surface of the planet for a period of time, up until 16 million years ago, when a large meteorite, or comet possibly, slammed into the surface of Mars, with enough energy that it caused it to be lifted off the surface of Mars and escaped the gravitational field of the planet. It traveled through space for 16 million years, and 13,000 years ago, fell on the ice fields of the Antarctic. It lay on the ice fields until in 1984, Robbie Score picked it up, and the rest is history."

While the organisms in 84-001 were fossilized, it's quite possible that other meteorites carried living organisms all the way to Earth. These organisms could have been the source of all life on our planet. Author Donald Goldsmith says that the origin of the human race may, in fact, be Mars:

"There's no doubt that life could have originated on Mars and come to Earth billions of years ago. This kind of process, where something hits Mars and knocks pieces loose, it's just as possible more or less that life could have originated on Earth, and gone to Mars."

The possibilities are enough to excite even the most skeptical scientist. But they warn that 84-001 is not definitive proof of life on Mars. Richard Berendzen says a follow up mission is needed:

"What we really need to do is to send a sample return mission, dig up Martian soil, dig up a rock, ideally from a meter or two beneath the soil, bring it back, chemically analyze it in a pristine lab, find a cell, it's done."

Research reports often suggest directions for future research.

On December 4th, 1996, the unmanned Pathfinder spacecraft took off for Mars. During its nine month visit to the "Red Planet," Pathfinder collected more than 17,000 images and performed more than a dozen chemical studies of rocks, soil and weather data. But to look for signs of life, says David McKay, we'll have to dig:

"We're really intrigued by the possibility that life may still exist on Mars. And if it does exist, it almost has to exist underneath the surface."

Geologist Dr. Robert C. Anderson with JPL:

"Now that doesn't mean little green men or UFOs, or anything like that. But it does mean that scientists

really do believe that life does exist in other places, and we just have to find it."

NASA scientist Everett Gibson:

"I never dreamed that I would have the opportunity to work on a problem of this magnitude. This is a tremendous awakening to mankind that, hey, we might not be alone in this vast universe in which we reside. Perhaps there are people out there on these other bodies that are also searching for life."

During its Phoenix Mission in 2008, NASA landed a robotic spacecraft on the surface of the planet and tested for [and found] traces of water in the soil and atmosphere. Scientists still hope to get one step closer to answering the age-old question: Are we alone or is there any other life out there?

Respond in Writing Respond to the various kinds of evidence provided to answer the question regarding life on Mars and elsewhere in the universe. What, if anything, are you now convinced of? What has influenced your belief?

Develop Your Own Research Questions Brainstorm with your classmates to come up with your own ideas on topics that would be interesting to investigate.

Small Groups: Use a chart like the following to help each author identify the information you might need to solve a mystery or investigate a question.

Research Question:	
Why does this topic interest you?	
What do you know about the topic already?	
What do you need or want to know about the topic?	
What kinds of evidence do you need to answer your questions?	
Where can you find this evidence?	

Whole Class: Make a master chart of all of the kinds and locations of needed evidence identified in the small groups to get a broader idea of how each author might go about researching his or her topic.

Write About It You will next write a research report in which you inquire into a question that requires detective work to find evidence in support of an answer or interpretation. Your report should be of sufficient length and complexity to address the topic. You may choose from any of the following topics, audiences, and forms.

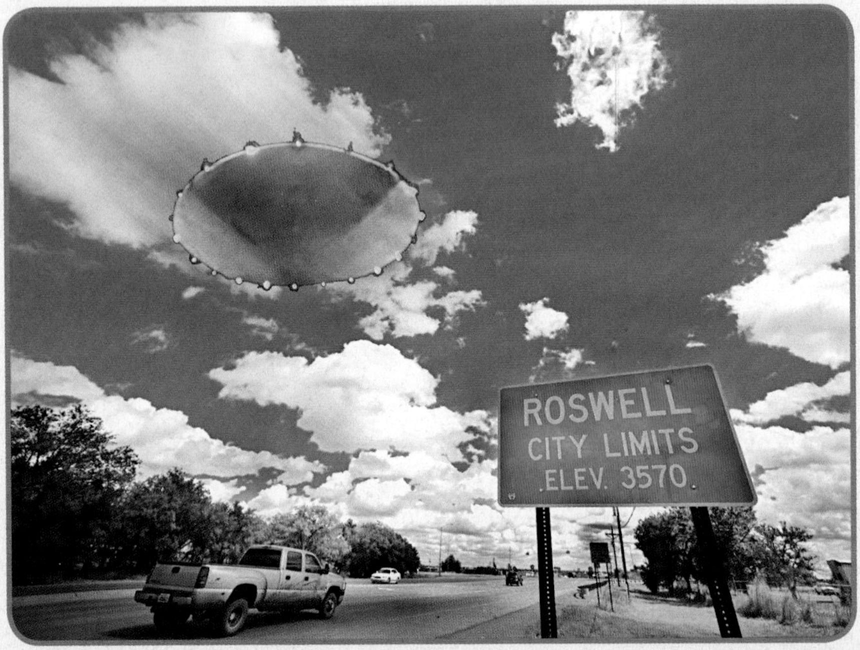

Possible Topics	Possible Audiences	Possible Forms
• an enduring mystery, such as what happened in Roswell, NM, in 1947 • an evaluation, such as who has been the greatest president in U.S. history • a search for causes, such as what factors resulted in the U.S. Civil War • a scientific inquiry, such as what conditions produce the juiciest blueberries	• people who are interested in your topic • people who are unfamiliar with your topic • people who would like to educate others about your topic • people in a doctor's office waiting room looking to kill time	• a blog entry • a post to a Web-based discussion board • a formal report • a letter

When you write research reports, you draw on many different skills. Since the main purpose of a research report is to convey information, you use the skills and techniques of informative writing. In the course of taking notes from a variety of sources, you will also draw upon the skills of summarizing and paraphrasing.

Since you must collect pieces of information from a number of different sources, keeping good track of all the pieces becomes very important. If you are not working on a computer, use a folder with pockets, index cards, paper clips, and rubber bands to keep your work organized. If you are working on a computer, especially one that is not your own, store your work on a flash drive, in a secure spot on the hard drive, or in a wiki (page 127) or some other online application. On your own computer, keep track of any Internet sources you consult by creating a bookmark folder for your report topic.

1 Choosing and Limiting a Subject

Your teacher may assign a topic for a research report, provide a list for you to choose from, or leave the decision up to you. If you are to decide, there are two fundamental places to look for research topics. One is inside you—your interests and desires. The other is outside—classes or books you enjoy, news stories online or in print that you find interesting. Brainstorm with others and consult with your teachers to explore possible research topics. (See page 19 for more on brainstorming.) The following chart has tips to help you choose one idea as a subject.

HERE'S HOW

Guidelines for Choosing a Research Subject

- Choose a subject you would like to know more about.
- Choose a subject that will interest your audience.
- Choose a subject that can be adequately covered in a research report of approximately eight double-spaced pages.
- Choose a subject for which you can find a variety of information in the library or media center.

You may want to make a preliminary search of the library's computer catalog or online databases for some subject ideas. If you do not find at least two books and two magazine articles on your subject, you should probably choose a different one.

Some very broad research topics require a whole book to cover them adequately. Within these broad subjects, however, are specific areas that could be covered in a shorter research paper. Even a complex, multi-faceted topic must be focused so that it can be covered adequately in a certain amount of space. The subject of oceans, for example, is too broad for a short paper. Contained within that subject, though, are such specific topics as "mining the ocean for gold," or "how a tidal wave forms." Any of these would be a suitable subject.

One good way to limit and focus a major research topic is to ask yourself a series of "what about" questions. The following model shows how one writer limited the subject of a research paper by asking questions.

MODEL: Limiting a Research Subject

Broad Subject	the lost city of Atlantis
First Question	*What about* Atlantis?
More Limited	myth versus reality
Second Question	*What about* myth versus reality?
More Limited	theories that attempt to explain Atlantis as a real place
Third Question	*What about* these theories?
Suitably Limited	the strengths and weaknesses of the theory that places Atlantis on the Aegean island of Thera

You will need more than one or two words to express the focus of most suitably limited subjects. Continue limiting your subject until you can express the focus of your report in a phrase or partial sentence. Asking "what about" questions is the first step toward developing a major research question.

Writing Tip

Limit your subject by asking, "What about [the subject]?" until you can express the focus of your research report in a phrase or partial sentence.

Practice Your Skills

Limiting a Research Subject

Study each of the following broad subjects for a research report. For each subject write a series of "what about" questions until you have arrived at a suitably limited subject. Use the preceding model as a guide for limiting each subject.

1. earthquakes
2. the Internet
3. baseball
4. American writers

Practice Your Skills

Using an Idea Tree

Ask "what about" questions to help you limit a single broad topic and find several alternatives for limiting the subject. Notice that, at any level, a "what about" question may generate more than one answer.

The following idea tree shows how you might organize ideas for creating a commercial Web site. Copy and complete the idea tree for this subject, or, if you prefer, fill out a similar tree for one of the other broad topics given in the previous activity: earthquakes, baseball, or American writers.

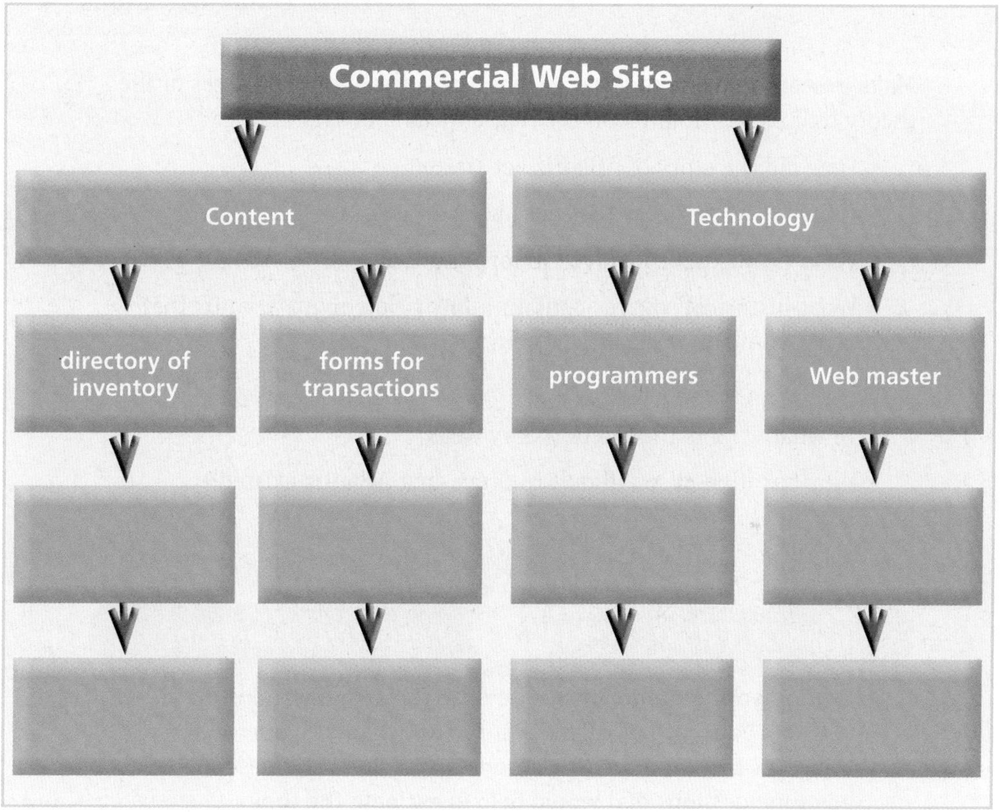

PROJECT PREP **Prewriting** ***Limiting a Topic***

In your writing group, brainstorm ideas and discuss your topic. Talk about your interest in the topic and what you want to learn. Help each author to limit the topic so that the research inquiry is manageable in a research report that is of sufficient length and complexity to adequately address the topic.

2 Developing Research Questions

Once you have a limited subject clearly in mind, you can start planning your research. A good first step is to write a list of five to ten open-ended guide questions that will help you find specific information. If you decided to write a paper on the theory that the lost city of Atlantis was on the island of Thera, your guide questions might include the following. As you gather your research based on these questions, be prepared to narrow or broaden your inquiry when appropriate.

MODEL: Guide Questions

Major research question: What are the strengths and weaknesses of the theory that places Atlantis on the Aegean island of Thera?

- How did the story of Atlantis get started?
- What are some other theories about Atlantis?
- What people were involved in forming theories?
- What historical sources contain information about Atlantis that could confirm or deny the Thera theory?
- On what evidence does the Thera theory rest?
- In what ways is the Thera theory weak?
- Why has it been so difficult to prove that Atlantis existed?

PROJECT PREP *Prewriting* *Research Questions*

1. In your writing group, discuss possible research questions that will help you learn what you want to know about your limited topic. For each author, develop one major research question and any sub-questions that would help investigate the topic.
2. Write your major research question clearly, since that is what will guide your research. Evaluate your question to make sure it represents a complex, multi-faceted topic worth the time and effort you will spend on it.
3. Formulate a plan for your in-depth research on your multi-faceted topic question and sketch it out. Remember, you can modify your question as needed.

1 Finding Relevant Sources

With your subject and research questions on hand, formulate a plan to gather relevant and substantial evidence from experts on your topic and from texts written for informed audiences in the field. Use the following steps as a guide.

HERE'S HOW

Strategies for Gathering Information

- Use a general reference work such as an encyclopedia, either in print or online, to get an overview of your subject. (pages 420–433)
- Use the online catalog or other database in the library or media center to find books on your subject. (pages 416–418)
- Use a variety of primary sources (firsthand accounts), and secondary sources (information about primary sources) to explore your topic, especially if the subject is about a historical figure or event. (pages 420–433)
- Consult online databases or indexes in the library or media center to find magazine and newspaper articles on your subject. (pages 420–422)
- Use a search engine to do a keyword search on the Internet for your topic. Make note of any Web sites you find that you think would be useful. (pages 430–433)
- Make a list of all your sources. For each book or video write the author, title, copyright year, publisher's name and location, and call number (if available). For each periodical, also include the full date, the volume and issue numbers, and pages. For each Web site, include the exact address and the site author, if available. If you found a source through a library database, note the name of the database with the other information.
- Assign each source on your list a number for later note-taking.

Practice Your Skills

Gathering Information

Use the library or media center to compile a list of five sources for each of the following subjects. At least two sources for each subject should be magazine articles, and one should be an online source. Assign an identifying number to each source and use the guidelines above to note your sources.

1. special effects in science-fiction movies

2. recent underwater discoveries

3. adult illiteracy in the United States

4. sightings of meteorites since 1980

PROJECT PREP Prewriting *Sources*

Follow the research plan to gather relevant and substantial evidence on your topic from experts and from texts written for informed audiences in the field.

2 Evaluating Sources

Before you can begin using your sources effectively, you should review each one for its reliability and relevance. Look for relevant and substantial evidence from experts on the topic and texts written for informed audiences in the field that represent multiple perspectives. Avoid sources that represent only one narrow view.

CHAPTER 11

Evaluating Print Sources

As you begin your research process, you may find bibliography references or other citations that lead you to possible print sources. Just because someone else cited a particular source or because it is in your library catalog or database doesn't mean that it's appropriate for your project. You still need to decide if it's relevant to your subject and whether the information is valid, accurate, up-to-date, and appropriate to the kind of report you are writing. The following checklists can help you evaluate books and articles.

Checklist for Evaluating Books

✓ Check the table of contents and the index. Is there information on your limited subject in the book?

✓ Who is the author? What are the author's credentials? You can find this information by reading the notes on the book jacket or by looking up the author's name in a biographical reference work.

✓ Is there anything in the author's background or associations that might suggest that the source has a biased viewpoint?

✓ What is the publication date? (If your subject requires the most up-to-date information, such as recent medical findings or current economic data, then avoid books that are more than a few years old.)

✓ Who is the publisher? Major publishers such as university presses and government agencies are likely to be reputable sources.

Checklist for Evaluating Articles

✓ Does the article contain specific information on your limited subject?

✓ Who is the author? What are his or her credentials? (You can usually find these in a note at the bottom of the first or last page of the article.)

✓ Does the magazine or newspaper appeal to a special interest group that may have a biased viewpoint on your subject? (For example, a magazine called *Saving the Planet* might have a bias toward preserving and protecting the environment at all costs. On the other hand, a magazine called *Industrial Progress* might have a bias toward serving the needs of business and industry rather than serving the needs of the environment.)

✓ When was the article published? (If your subject requires the most up-to-date information, then avoid publications that are more than a few years old.)

Evaluating Online Sources

When you check out a book from the library, a librarian or a committee of educators has already evaluated the book to make sure it's a reliable source of information, but remember, no one owns or regulates the Internet. Just because you read something online doesn't mean it's true. How can you tell the difference? This checklist will help you evaluate an online source.

Checklist for Evaluating Internet Sources

- ✓ Start by identifying the top-level domain name. Is the site maintained by a for-profit company (.com) that might be trying to sell something? Is it an educational institution (.edu) which tends to be more reliable, or an independent organization (.org)? If it is an organization, is it one whose name you recognize or is it one that you have never heard of before? Be aware that ".org" sites are often owned by nonprofit organizations that may support a particular cause.
- ✓ If the Web site contains an article, who wrote the article? Is it signed? If it is not signed, you should be skeptical of its credibility. If it is signed, see if the author is an acknowledged expert. If you do not recognize the author's name, you can send a question to a newsgroup or e-mail list server asking if anyone else knows something about this person. You can also do a Web search using the author's name as the keyword to get more information.
- ✓ Is the text well written? Does it use reasonable and sufficient facts and examples to make its points? Is it free from obvious errors?
- ✓ Is the site well designed and organized? Do the language and graphics avoid sensationalism?
- ✓ Has the site been recently updated? Is the information still current? Look for a date on the main Web page indicating the last time it was updated.
- ✓ Is the site rated by a reputable group for the quality of its content? You can find recommendations for reliable Web sites at ipl2, the Internet Public Library <http://www.ipl.org/>.

You can learn more about using the Internet for research on pages 430–433.

After you have screened your primary and secondary sources, you may find that only a few of them are valid, reliable, and relevant. As you evaluate your sources, remember that four to six good sources are better than ten or more questionable ones. Quality, not quantity, is the key.

Practice Your Skills

Evaluating Sources

Each of these sources on automobile safety suffers from one of the weaknesses listed below. Write the weakness of each source.

probably outdated	lacks strong author credentials
probably biased	does not relate to subject

1. *Paving the Way to Safety,* a book published in 1974 by Winston S. Martinsberg, director of Consumer Safety for the city of Atlanta, Georgia.

2. "Airbags Not the Answer," an article in *Auto Executives,* published in 2002, written by William O'Donnely, vice president of Zephyr Motors, Inc.

3. "Passenger Safety on Public Transportation," an article in *City News* written by Caroline Levy, executive director of the Federal Safety Commission, published in 2008.

4. "Tips for Safe Driving," an article published in *Modern Family* magazine, written in 2005 by Randolph Sutton, a freelance writer with a varied background in science, sports, and law.

5. *Building a Safe Car,* a book by Gregory Francis, professor of engineering at State University, published in 1982.

6. "On Rear Seat Lap Belts," sponsored by M. Gillick and W. Prachthauser law offices, The Safety Forum, 2009. <http://www.safetyforum.com/>

PROJECT PREP Prewriting *Analyzing Sources*

Compare the information you have found on the same topic from two or more sources. Do you get the same facts and opinions from both sources? If not, how can you decide which source to trust when assembling information for your research? Plan to incorporate complexities and discrepancies in information from multiple sources by anticipating and refuting counter-arguments in your report. (See page 446.) Continue to collect information and take notes, making sure to evaluate each source to determine how valid, reliable, and relevant it is before including its information in your report.

Think Critically

Evaluating Sources for Accuracy

The authors of books, magazine articles, and Web sites are not perfect. Even with care, factual errors in the material occasionally occur. The best way to confirm the accuracy of a source is to check it against another source. If at least two sources contain the same basic facts, you can probably rely on their accuracy.

HERE'S HOW

Guidelines for Using Sources

- Locate at least two sources that contain the same basic facts.
- Skim each source for specific details, such as dates, locations, and statistics.
- If the specific details in both sources agree, you can probably rely on the accuracy of both. As you take notes, be alert for discrepancies in broader concepts such as in the sequence of events or in the relationship between cause and effect. If necessary, confirm this information against another source.
- If you discover discrepancies, use a third source to determine which source is likely to be more accurate.
- Address these complexities and discrepancies in information from multiple sources by anticipating and refuting counter-arguments in your report.

Thinking Practice

The following paragraph contains three errors. Find two library sources and one online source to check the information. Then rewrite the paragraph with the correct information.

Jeanette Rankin was a crusader for women's rights and for world peace. She was born in Montana in 1808, and after attending college, she decided to devote her life to public service. For six years she traveled around the country speaking on behalf of women's rights. In her home state of Montana, women won the right to vote in 1916, in large part because of Rankin's efforts. Rankin soon went on to national politics and became the second woman ever elected to Congress. Throughout her career she stood for human rights and peace at all costs.

Before you begin studying your evaluated sources and taking notes, review the research questions you wrote at the beginning of your research. At this point, you may want to modify your research question to refocus your research plan. These questions will direct you to the information you need in each source. As you take notes, keep the goals of note-taking in mind.

Writing Tip

The goals of note taking are to paraphrase the information you gather, summarize the main points in your own words, and record quotations that you might use in your research report.

Once you are ready to start taking notes, bring out the index cards from your folder. As you use each card, write the identifying number of the source in the upper right-hand corner. In the upper left-hand corner, identify the key aspect of your subject. This heading should correspond in most cases to one of your guide questions. For example, notes taken to answer the guide question "How did the story of Atlantis get started?" might be labeled *Source of the Atlantis story.*

Avoid taking notes on unrelated information. Do your best to take notes on material written by experts in the field for informed audiences in that field. If you find information that is unrelated to your questions but you think is still relevant to your research, identify the new aspect on a note card and add a question to your guide questions.

The following paragraphs are from page 19 of *Unearthing Atlantis,* by Charles Pellegrino. The source has been assigned the identifying number 4. Read the excerpt and compare it with the sample note card that follows.

MODEL: Taking Notes on a Source

Thera is now a ring-shaped string of islets whose central lagoon drops vertically, hundreds of feet, to life-giving hot water springs. The largest of the islets looks from the air like a curl of broken rib. Almost nothing grows on it, and there is a lost city under it, with canals and drainage systems and apartments that look for all the world like present-day ocean-front condos. Plato, when he wrote about the sinking of Atlantis (*Timaeus,* 112), described "a land carried round in a circle and disappeared in the depths below. By comparison to what then was, there are remaining in small islets only the bones of the wasted body, as they may be called, all the richer and softer parts of the soil having fallen away, and the mere skeleton of the country being left."

The island, like Plato's Atlantis, is a broken skeleton of its former self. Its whole center is missing and flooded with sea water, and near its southern coast you will find one of the world's most hauntingly beautiful archaeological sites.

Sample Note Card

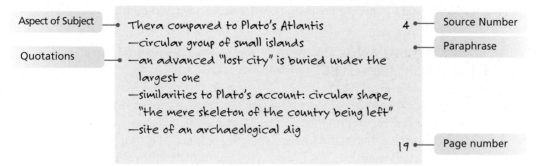

Aspect of Subject → Thera compared to Plato's Atlantis — 4 ← Source Number

—circular group of small islands ← Paraphrase

Quotations → —an advanced "lost city" is buried under the largest one

—similarities to Plato's account: circular shape, "the mere skeleton of the country being left"

—site of an archaeological dig

19 ← Page number

If you include more than one note on a card, be sure that all of the notes are closely related and are on a single aspect of your subject. Writing unrelated notes on one card will make it difficult to sort your cards later. For print sources, be sure to record the number of the page from which the note was taken. If you have been browsing the Internet, be sure to record, or bookmark, the locations of useful sites. Later, when you write citations to give credit to your sources, you will need to identify the exact page on which you found the borrowed material.

As you finish with each source, clip all the note cards from that source together with a paper clip. Be sure that each card carries the identifying number in the upper right-hand corner.

PROJECT PREP Prewriting *Note Taking*

Continue to follow your research plan and gather evidence in reliable sources that will help you answer your research questions. Paraphrase, summarize, and quote from your sources as you take notes when you find information you can use in your report. Focus your efforts on gathering relevant and substantial evidence from texts written by experts for informed audiences in the field. Share your ideas with your teacher and peers.

Practice Your Skills

Taking Notes

Assume the source below has been assigned the identifying number 2, and make a note card for it. Identify the aspect of the subject. Then paraphrase the information and summarize the main points. Record any good quotations.

ASSATEAGUE ISLAND, Md.–What do you do when one of your natural treasures starts eating all the others?

That's the National Park Service's dilemma on this storied barrier island. Proof of its problem can be found on a spongy stretch of salt marsh, where one section is fenced off by barbed wire.

Inside the fence, the island's native smooth cordgrass is growing thickly, a foot tall. Outside it, the grass is cropped nearly to the roots.

"Inside. Outside. A lot different," said Mark Sturm, a Park Service ecologist, gesturing at the denuded muck. The culprit is obvious: There's only one animal on Assateague that can't get through the fence.

"This is all horses," Sturm said.

Yes. Those horses. About 140 wild ponies live on the Maryland half of the island—less famous than their cousins in Virginia, who star in the annual Chincoteague pony penning, but still a major part of the Assateague mystique.

Now, Park Service officials say, the horse population is eating away at the plants that underpin rare coastal ecosystems here. They're considering a radical solution: selling or relocating as much as a third of the Maryland herd.

"There is no doubt in my mind," Sturm said, "that in the absence of action, things are only going to get worse."

Assateague Island stretches 37 miles along the Atlantic Coast of the Eastern Shore, from Chincoteague, Va., almost to Ocean City, Md. In between, officials say, is the kind of wilderness that has become rare on the East Coast: nearly pristine sand dunes, salt marshes and coastal forests.

But much as scientists treasure the island's rare birds and flora, it is neither the piping plover nor the sea beach amaranth plant that has imbedded Assateague in childhood memories and young-adult fiction.

It's the ponies.

—David A. Farenthold, "A Gnawing Problem on Assateague Island"

CHAPTER 11

You can learn more about the use of direct quotations on pages 352–353, 452, and 966–973.

In the Media

The Library of Congress Online

There are critical questions you must ask before relying too much on Internet sites for accurate information. One site, however, is well known for its high standards—and its fascinating content. That is the site of the Library of Congress, physically located in Washington, D.C., but virtually located at <http://www.loc.gov/index.html>. Especially if you are studying American history, this online resource will provide you with countless treasures. Among them:

- *The American Memory Historical Collections,* a major component of the Library's National Digital Library Program, consisting of digitized documents, photographs, recorded sound, moving pictures, and text from the Library's Americana collections.
- *Today in History,* which reports a significant event from history that happened on the current date
- *Using the Library of Congress,* a guide to the library's catalogs, collections, and research services
- *Thomas,* Congress at work, an up-to-date searchable database of bills currently before the House and Senate

Media Activity

Put your pencil-and-paper research aside and visit the Library of Congress online. Take your time and browse through the site, following your interests. Then write a paragraph comparing your online browsing to a browse through a real world library.

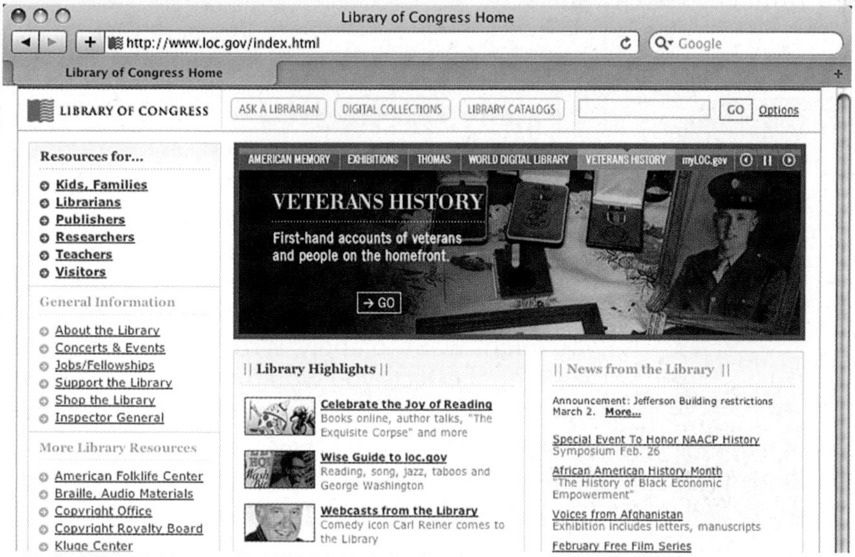

Writing Lab

Project Corner

Speak and Listen
Class Discussion

You know that the Web is an excellent source for up-to the-minute information, but that spelling and grammar need checking for correctness. You also look at the bibliography accompanying any given site for relevance, validity, and reliability. Beyond that, how do you ascertain the real qualifications of a Web page? **Discuss with your classmates their most successful use of search engines** and domain extensions when authenticating the validity and reliability of various Web sites. (See pages 586–588 for help with group discussions.)

Think Critically Predict

At this point in your academic career, research in high school is accomplished primarily by using the sources discussed in this chapter. You've learned how to find topics, limit a subject, gather information, take notes, and structure your research. **With three partners, brainstorm** ways people in the year 2050 will be conducting research and writing research papers.

Think Critically
Recast Your Research

Look over the work you have done on your research report. Suppose you were asked to present this information as a television special with you as the host and any type of audiovisual bells and whistles you might want to apply. **Write a short list** of all the special effects you would require and a brief explanation of how you would use each one. Also write an overview of the approach you would take as the host of the one-hour presentation.

Apply and Assess

In Everyday Life
Note to Self

1. You want to spend the summer exploring a field you'd like to study in college or work you might want to do after high school graduation. ***Develop a research plan*** that details how you would look for information on possible jobs. You may look for paid work, internships, or volunteer opportunities. Include sources that provide background information on the type of work and the outlook for future employment in the field. Take notes on the information you find.

CHAPTER 11

In the Workplace Memo

2. You work as an assistant manager at a local mall. Your job is to recommend kiosk vendors for the upcoming holiday shopping season. Your boss is particularly interested in sellers whose stands feature unique and affordable gifts for different kinds of shoppers—senior citizens, young families, singles, and teenagers. ***Write a memo*** to your boss outlining a plan to research the latest trends in gift ideas that will appeal to shoppers in your community. Consider interviewing classmates and family members along with researching online and in the library.

Timed Writing Research Plan

3. As Student Events Coordinator at your high school, you are in charge of coming up with an event that will promote school spirit as safely as possible. Human pyramids are banned, and the fire marshal says that the gymnasium does not have the capacity to fit all of the students at once for an indoor rally. Develop a research plan that would help you find examples of possible events in the library, online, or in interviews. Be as specific as you can in your plan, and feel free to consult the *Research Companion* on pages 412–433 for ideas on specific sources to consult. You have 25 minutes to complete your work.

   Before You Write Consider the following questions: What is the subject? What is the occasion? Who is the audience? What is the purpose?

   After You Write Evaluate your plan to be sure it is as thorough and realistic as possible and is likely to gain you the information you require.

Research Companion

Finding information for a research report can feel like climbing a mountain—the goal seems very far away, and you are not sure what you will find along the way. Like the mountain climber, however, you have tools to help you reach the top. These tools are reference skills. Developing and using your reference skills will make you a better researcher and make this challenging process more enjoyable, too.

CHAPTER 11

Using the Library or Media Center

Today, most libraries and media centers have much more than books. You will also find magazines, newspapers, and a wide range of reference materials in print, online, or in electronic formats. In addition to printed materials, libraries and media centers also carry nonprint materials, such as audio recordings, video documentaries, downloadable audio books and electronic books, photographic archives, and computers that provide access to the Internet, online databases, and the World Wide Web. All of these references are arranged so that you can locate them easily.

Library or Media Center Arrangement

Libraries use two systems of organization to arrange the thousands of books in their stacks. Most school and smaller libraries use the Dewey decimal classification system. This system can organize up to 30,000 titles. Larger libraries, including those at most colleges and universities, use the Library of Congress system, which has the capacity to organize millions of books.

Dewey Decimal System In the Dewey decimal classification system, works of fiction and nonfiction are shelved in separate sections. Works of fiction, such as short stories and novels, are arranged by the authors' last names. In some libraries and media centers they are also marked with the letters *F* or *Fic*. The following rules will help you locate works of fiction.

HERE'S HOW

Guidelines for Finding Fiction

- Two-part last names are alphabetized by the first part of the name. (**Mac**Namara, **O'**Hara, **Van** Buren)
- Names beginning with **Mc** or **St.** are alphabetized as if they began with **Mac** or **Saint.**
- Books by authors with the same last name are further alphabetized by the authors' first names.
- Books by the same author are alphabetized by the first important word in the title, not including the words *a, an,* and *the.*
- Numbers in titles are alphabetized as if they were written out. (1001 = one thousand and one)

CHAPTER 11

In the Dewey decimal classification system, nonfiction books are assigned a number according to their subject.

DEWEY DECIMAL SYSTEM	
000–099	General Works (reference books)
100–199	Philosophy and Psychology
200–299	Religion
300–399	Social Sciences (law, education, economics)
400–499	Languages
500–599	Natural Sciences (math, biology, chemistry)
600–699	Technology (medicine, inventions)
700–799	Arts (painting, music, theater)
800–899	Literature
900–999	Geography and History (including biography and travel)

Each main subject area has ten subdivisions. For example, the subdivisions for science are as follows.

500–599 NATURAL SCIENCES			
500–509	Pure Sciences	**550–559**	Earth Sciences
510–519	Mathematics	**560–569**	Paleontology
520–529	Astronomy	**570–579**	Life Sciences
530–539	Physics	**580–589**	Botany
540–549	Chemistry	**590–599**	Zoology

These subdivisions can be broken down even further with the use of decimal points and other identifying symbols.

The numbers identifying a book form the **call number.** In addition to the call number, some nonfiction works carry a special label to show the section of the library or media center where they are shelved. *B* or *92* (short for 920 in the Dewey decimal system), for example, indicates that a work is a biography or an autobiography.

Biographies and Autobiographies Biographies and autobiographies are usually found in a section of their own. They are arranged in alphabetical order according to the subject of the book, not the author. Books about the same person are arranged according to the author's last name. Other books that have special labels are in the following chart.

CATEGORIES	SPECIAL LABELS
Easy Reading	E
Juvenile Books	J or X
Young Adult	YA
Reference Works	R or REF

Develop Research Skills

Using the Dewey Decimal System

Using the list of classifications on the previous page, write the subject number of each book. If the title is marked with an asterisk (*), also write the science subdivision listed on the previous page.

Example *Basic Concepts of Chemistry**

Answer 500–599, 540–549

1. *Exploring the Milky Way**
2. *Doctor in the Zoo*
3. *Spanish Step-by-Step*
4. *Berlin: A Handbook for Travelers*
5. *Painting Sharp-Focus Still Lifes*
6. *Earthquakes and Tornadoes**
7. *Physics for Nonscientists**
8. *United States Foreign Policy*
9. *Gateway to Judaism*
10. *An Introduction to Philosophy*

The Library of Congress System This system uses letters instead of numbers and has 20 main categories. Unlike the Dewey decimal system, the Library of Congress system does not separate fiction and biography from other kinds of works. A book about Mark Twain, for example, would be shelved with novels by Mark Twain. The chart below outlines the 20 subject categories found in the Library of Congress system.

LIBRARY OF CONGRESS SYSTEM

A	General works	M	Music
B	Philosophy, religion	N	Fine Arts
C	Sciences of history	P	Language and literature
D	Non-American history and travel	Q	Science
E	American history	R	Medicine
F	U.S. local history	S	Agriculture
G	Geography, anthropology	T	Technology
H	Social sciences	U	Military science
J	Political science	V	Naval science
L	Education	Z	Library science

These 20 main categories can be further divided by using a second letter. QB, for example, refers to the general category of science, with a focus on astronomy. Further subdivisions are made by using numbers and letters.

Develop Research Skills

Using the Library of Congress System

Using the classifications for the Library of Congress system, write the first letter of the call number for each of the books listed in the previous Develop Research Skills activity on page 414.

Example *Basic Concepts of Chemistry*

Answer Q

The Library Catalog

Most libraries and media centers store records of their holdings in an **online catalog.** Computer systems can vary from library to library, but generally the search methods are the same. To search the listings in an online catalog, you select a category to search—author, title, or subject. Authors' names are written last name first; for most titles, the words *A, An,* and *The* are omitted at the beginning of a title; and for subjects, searchers must enter the exact words for each category.

CHAPTER 11

On some systems, you can execute a keyword search, just as you would on an Internet search engine. A keyword search can sort through the library's collections by both title and subject headings simultaneously. The computer can tell you whether the book you seek is available or—if it has been checked out—when it is due back. By using the Web to search other library databases, the librarian can also tell you if the book is available elsewhere.

If your book is in the catalog, the computer displays an entry similar to that in the following example. Hypertext links enable you to move back and forth between sections of the catalog.

ONLINE CATALOG RECORD

Asimov's chronology of science and discovery
Asimov, Isaac, 1920–1992

Personal Author:	Asimov, Isaac, 1920–1992
Uniform title:	[Chronology of science and discovery]
Title:	Asimov's chronology of science and discovery/Isaac Asimov.
Edition:	1st ed.
Publication info:	New York : Harper & Row, c1989.
Physical descrip:	707 p. : col. ill. ; 25 cm.
General Note:	Includes indexes.
Subject term:	Science—History.
Subject term:	Science—Social aspects.
Subject term:	Inventions—History.
Added title:	Chronology of science and discovery.

You may also find a simpler record of the book that may appear as follows. This type of catalog entry tells you where you can find the book in the library. It may also include a brief summary of the book.

ITEM INFORMATION ENTRY

Asimov's chronology of science and discovery
Asimov, Isaac, 1920–1992

Combining world history with scientific discoveries and inventions, Asimov illustrates, in chronological order, how science and cultural, social, and political events have affected each other. A good reference for the general reader. No bibliography. Annotation copyrighted by Book News, Inc., Portland, OR

Publisher:	Harper & Row,
Pub date:	c1989.
Pages:	707 p. :
ISBN:	0060156120
Item info:	2 copies available at Columbia Public Library and Callaway County Public Library in Fulton.

A Look Inside:

Holdings

Columbia Public Library	Copies	Material	Location
509 ASI	1	Book	Non-Fiction
Callaway County Public Library in Fulton	Copies	Material	Location
R509 ASI	1	Reference book	Reference

HERE'S HOW

Strategies for Using an Online Catalog

Think about what you already know that can limit your search. A title or author search will always give you more focused results than a subject search. If you are doing a subject search, find a way to limit the category, either by year or by subcategory.

Searching by Author's Name

- If the last name is common, type the author's complete last name followed by a comma and a space and the author's first initial or complete first name.
- Omit all accent and punctuation marks in the author's name.
- For compound names, try variations in placement of the parts: **von stubin karl** or **stubin karl von**

CHAPTER 11

Searching by Title

- If the title is long, type only the first few words. Omit capitalization, punctuation, accent marks, and articles.

  manual of sty (you need not include the full title)

  great escape (omit initial article words)

  up up and away (omit punctuation)

- If you are unsure of the correct form of a word, try variations such as spelling out or inserting spaces between initials and abbreviations; entering numbers as words; using an ampersand (&) for *and;* spelling hyphenated words as one or two words.

Searching by Subject

- Omit commas, parentheses, and capitalization.
- Broad categories can be divided into subcategories to make your search more specific.
- If you don't know the correct subject heading, find at least one source relevant to your topic by doing a title or keyword search. Use one or more of the subject headings listed there for additional searches.

Searching by Keyword

- Searching with a single word such as *inventions* will find that word anywhere in the entry: in the title, author, subject, or descriptive notes.
- A phrase such as *public transportation* finds entries containing the words *public* and *transportation*. To search for *public transportation* as a phrase, type *public and transportation*, or *public adj transportation* (adj = adjacent).
- An open search will look anywhere in the entry for your word. You can limit your keyword searches to specific search fields (author, title, or subject) by doing an advanced search and selecting the appropriate field.

Develop Research Skills

Searching Online Catalogs

Write the category you would select for a search on the following items. Then write the words that you would enter to find each item.

1. the life of Daniel Boone
2. the books of Ernest Hemingway
3. the art of ceramics
4. *The End of Time*
5. the Grand Canyon
6. *The Elements of Style*
7. air travel safety
8. classical music
9. the works of Maya Angelou
10. healthcare funding

Parts of a Book

Once you find several sources, you need to determine whether they have any information that you can use. Finding this information is easier if you know how to use the parts of a book effectively.

INFORMATION FOUND IN PARTS OF A BOOK

PART	INFORMATION
Title Page	shows the full title, author's name, publisher, place of publication
Copyright Page	gives the date of first publication and of any revised editions
Table of Contents	lists chapter or section titles in the book and their starting page numbers
Introduction	gives an overview of the author's ideas in each chapter and in relation to the work that other writers have done on the subject
Appendix	gives additional information on subjects in the book; charts, graphs, maps, and glossaries are sometimes included here
Bibliography	lists sources that the author used to write the book, including title and copyright information on related topics
Index	lists topics that are mentioned in the book and gives the page numbers where these topics can be found

CHAPTER 11

Develop Research Skills

Using the Parts of a Book

Write the part of the book you would use to find each of the following items of information.

1. the title of a specific chapter
2. a specific topic or person mentioned in the book
3. the year of publication
4. definition of a difficult or technical word
5. the name and publication information for a source used by the author
6. the author's explanation of the book's contents
7. the name and location of the publisher
8. a chart or graph with additional information

Using Print and Nonprint Reference Materials

Most libraries have a separate room or section for reference materials. Since these materials cannot be taken from the library or media center, most reference rooms also provide a study area.

Now libraries and media centers are also often the best way to find the most authoritative online reference sources. Most libraries subscribe to **online databases** that can be accessed through computers in the library. Often, anyone with a library card may use a home computer to search the databases through the library's Web site. These databases provide a wealth of reliable information that is not usually available for free just by searching on the Internet. Some databases are especially designed for high school students. Following are some of the reference materials you may find most helpful in the reference section.

PRINT AND ELECTRONIC REFERENCES

- general and specialized encyclopedias
- general and specialized dictionaries
- atlases, almanacs, and yearbooks
- specialized biographical and literary references
- online databases and indexes of periodicals (including magazines, newspapers, and journals)
- microfilm and microfiche files of periodicals and government documents
- computers with access to the Internet and World Wide Web
- audio recordings and video documentaries
- vertical file of print material

Periodicals—Magazines and Newspapers

Periodicals, including magazines and journals, are excellent sources for current information. The periodical reading room in the library or media center should have the most recent print issues of all the periodicals to which the library subscribes. You can usually search for periodical titles in the library's online catalog but you cannot search for individual articles. The entry will describe the extent of the library's holdings. For example, a library may keep two months of a daily newspaper and two years of weekly or monthly magazines.

By subscribing to online databases, libraries can now offer people access to a wider variety of periodicals than they would have space for in the library. Databases may cover general interest periodicals, scholarly journals, or periodicals covering specialized fields such as business or health. A librarian or media specialist can help you determine which databases are best for your particular research project. You can search in a database using keywords as you would with an Internet search engine. Database entries provide an abstract or short summary of the article so you can decide if it is useful to read the full text. Full text is available for many articles from the 1990s onward. These full text articles can be downloaded or printed. Many databases allow you to save your search results in folders for future reference.

You can learn more about searching with keywords on pages 431–432.

CHAPTER 11

Newspapers

Newspapers are valuable sources of current and historical information. Some online databases contain only newspapers and others combine newspapers and magazines. Some even include radio and television news transcripts. Many databases allow you to limit your search to specific dates or even specific periodical titles. While most databases focus on articles from the 1990s to the present, some include references to articles from earlier periods. The *Historical New York Times* database offers full text articles back to the newspaper's first issue in 1851.

Most major newspapers now have Web sites and electronic databases where you can view current issues and search for archived articles. The following examples are only a few of the many available online.

The Chicago Tribune	http://www.chicago.tribune.com
The Dallas Morning News	http://www.dallasnews.com
The Los Angeles Tmes	http://www.latimes.com
The Miami Herald	http://www.herald.com
The New York Times	http://www.nytimes.com

By going directly to the Web, you can also search databases that locate and access the home pages of newspapers from every state in the United States and many countries around the world. Both of the following sites list hundreds of newspapers by location (country and state) and by subject (business, arts and entertainment, trade journals, or college papers).

ipl2 (The Internet Public Library)	http://www.ipl.org/div/news
Newspapers Online!	http://www.newspapers.com

Remember: always read the guidelines at the home page for each newspaper. Recent articles are usually available free of charge, but you may have to pay a fee to download and print an archived article.

Older Periodicals

To save space, many libraries store older issues of some magazines and newspapers as photographic reproductions of print pages on rolls and sheets of film. **Microform** holdings may be included in the library's online catalog or may have a separate catalog or list in the microform area of the library or media center. **Microfilm** (rolls) or **microfiche** (sheets) are stored in filing cabinets and can be viewed easily on special projectors. Newspapers, for example, are arranged in file drawers alphabetically by keywords in their titles. The holdings for each newspaper are then filed chronologically by date. For example, if you wanted to know what happened in Houston, Texas, on New Year's Eve in the year you were born, you could go to the file cabinets and get the roll of film for the *Houston Chronicle* on that day in that year. Check with a librarian to see if there are indexes for any of the newspapers to help you locate articles on specific topics.

Researchers looking for older magazine articles not covered in online databases may use *The Readers' Guide to Periodical Literature,* an index of articles, short stories, and poems published in a large number of magazines and journals. Articles are indexed by date, author, and subject. Libraries may subscribe to print or online versions of the *Readers' Guide*. A search of the library's catalog will tell you which issues of the guide are available in your library and whether they are in print or electronic form. Once you know the name of the magazine or journal you want, you will need to check the library's catalog to see if that specific periodical is available.

Develop Research Skills

Locating Articles in Online Databases or Indexes

Using your library's online databases or periodicals index, list two recent magazine articles on four of the following subjects. List the title of the article, the name of the magazine in which each article can be found, the date of publication, the pages on which the article can be found, and the database or index.

1. genius grants
2. world music
3. Bluetooth technology
4. solar energy
5. NASCAR
6. space travel
7. video games
8. high fashion

ENCYCLOPEDIAS

Encyclopedias provide basic information on a wide variety of subjects. These subjects are arranged alphabetically in a number of volumes. An encyclopedia is a good reference to start with when you begin to collect information for a report.

Online encyclopedias are arranged in the same manner as printed encyclopedias—alphabetically, but there are no guide words or indexes. Instead, in order to find information on a particular subject, you enter the subject in a search box. The best online encyclopedias are the ones available through your library's databases. Beware of open source encyclopedias that have unsigned articles that can be changed without being reviewed by an expert.

Print and Online	Through libraries and media centers:
	Compton's by Encyclopaedia Britannica
	World Book Encyclopedia
	Encyclopedia Americana
	Grolier Multimedia Encyclopedia
Online	Reliable free encyclopedia:
	Columbia Encyclopedia http://www.bartleby.com/65/

These sites provide links to online dictionaries, thesauruses, and other reference materials as well.

Specialized Encyclopedias Specialized encyclopedias contain detailed information that is concentrated on a specific subject or discipline, such as art or animals. Specialized encyclopedias provide more detailed information on a subject than you will find in a general encyclopedia. These can also be found in the reference section of the library. Specialized encyclopedias online let you search for information by subject and connect to other Web sites on your topic through hyperlinks. The online *Encyclopedia Smithsonian,* for example, covers topics in physical sciences, social sciences, and U.S. and natural history.

Following are some specialized encyclopedias.

Print	*World Sports Encyclopedia*
	Encyclopedia of Mythology
	International Wildlife Encyclopedia
	Encyclopedia of American Facts and Dates
	The International Encyclopedia of the Social Sciences
Online	*Encyclopedia Smithsonian* http://www.si.edu/Encyclopedia_SI/default.htm
	A collection of almost 50 different encyclopedias http://www.encyclopedia.com

CHAPTER 11

Biographical References

Information about famous people of the past and of the present may be found in biographical reference books. Some biographical references contain only a paragraph of facts about each person, such as date of birth, education, occupation, and the person's accomplishments. Others, such as *Current Biography* and *Who's Who in America,* contain long articles. Some biographical references may have longer entries describing the person's life in more detail, depending on their focus.

Many libraries subscribe to one or more biographical databases that contain information from a variety of published sources including books and magazine articles and that may have links to reliable Web sites with information on the person. Some biographical resources focus on the lives of women and African Americans in U.S. history, and some multimedia or online resources contain film clips and audio recordings of important historical events.

Print	*Current Biography*
	Who's Who and *Who's Who in America*
	Merriam-Webster's Biographical Dictionary
	Dictionary of American Biography
	American Men and Women of Science
Online	*Distinguished Women of Past and Present* http://www.distinguishedwomen.com
	Encyclopaedia Britannica Guide to Black History http://search.eb.com/blackhistory/

REFERENCES ABOUT LANGUAGE AND LITERATURE

Sometimes in your English courses you may need to use reference works, such as the following ones, that focus specifically on the subjects of language and literature.

Specialized Dictionaries	*Dictionary of Literary Terms* *Brewer's Dictionary of Phrase and Fable*
Specialized Encyclopedias	*Reader's Encyclopedia of American Literature* *Encyclopedia of American-Indian Literature*
Biographical References	*Contemporary Authors* *American Authors 1600–1900* *Contemporary Poets* *Notable African American Writers*

Handbooks, or companions, are another kind of literary reference. Some handbooks give plot summaries or describe characters. Others explain literary terms or give information about authors.

Handbooks	*The Oxford Companion to American Literature* *The Oxford Companion to English Literature*

Books of quotations tell you the source of a particular quotation. These books also list complete quotations as well as other quotations on the same subject.

Books of Quotations	*Bartlett's Familiar Quotations* *The Oxford Dictionary of Quotations*

Indexes are useful for finding a particular poem, short story, or play. An index such as *Granger's Index to Poetry* lists the books that contain the particular selection you are looking for. The *Gale Literary Index* contains information about authors and their major works.

Indexes	*Short Story Index* *Ottemiller's Index to Plays in Collections*

Comprehensive online databases combine many of these literary references into a convenient resource that you can search by author, title, subject, or keyword. You may find complete works along with biographical information and literary criticism. A database likely contains information from hundreds of sources on thousands of authors. Ask your librarian what your library provides.

Online

About.com: Classic Literature http://classiclit.about.com/
Gale Literary Index http://www.galenet.com/servlet/LitIndex
Bartlett's Familiar Quotations http://www.bartleby.com/100
The Quotations Page http://www.quotationspage.com/

CHAPTER 11

Develop Research Skills

Using Literary References

Write the name of one source listed on page 425 that you could use to answer each question.

1. What does the term *stream of consciousness* mean?
2. Where could you find a short story by Tillie Olson titled "I Stand Here Ironing"?
3. Which American writer wrote the words "Simplify, simplify"?
4. In what year was the American writer Dorothy Parker born?
5. Where could you find the title of a publication that includes the play *Rosencrantz and Guildenstern Are Dead?*

Atlases

These books of maps present information about the regions of the world, including a region's physical geography, cities, population, climate, industries, natural resources, and systems of transportation. Historical atlases show maps of the world during different periods of history. In addition, some specialized atlases focus on the geography and history of a specific country or state. Some online resources from the United States Geological Survey incorporate satellite imagery to let you examine the geography of the United States by state and by region.

Print	*Goode's World Atlas*
	The Times Atlas of the World
	Rand McNally International World Atlas
	The National Geographic Atlas of the World
	Rand McNally Atlas of World History
Online	*National Atlas of the United States* http://www-atlas.usgs.gov/

Almanacs and Yearbooks

Almanacs and yearbooks published once a year are reliable sources for current information on a wide range of subjects, including information about famous people, unusual achievements, and sports. Almanacs also provide historical facts and geographic information, and some, such as *The Old Farmer's Almanac,* focus on weather-related and seasonal information.

Print	*Information Please Almanac*
	World Almanac and Book of Facts
	Guinness Book of World Records
Online	*The Old Farmer's Almanac* http://www.almanac.com *Infoplease* http://www.infoplease.com/

Specialized Dictionaries

Specialized dictionaries contain words used in particular disciplines or subjects. Some online dictionary sites include dictionaries in several languages and even excerpts from guidebooks on writing style.

Print	*Harvard Dictionary of Music*
	Concise Dictionary of American History
	Merriam-Webster's Geographical Dictionary
Online	Medical, legal, and multilingual dictionaries and a style guide http://dictionary.reference.com/ *Strunk's Elements of Style* http://www.bartleby.com/141/

Books of Synonyms

Another type of dictionary, called a **thesaurus,** features synonyms (different words with the same meanings) and antonyms (words with opposite meanings). This resource is especially helpful if you are looking for a specific word or if you want to vary your word usage and build your vocabulary. Many Web browsers, online databases, and word processing software programs include dictionary and thesaurus features.

Print	*Roget's 21st Century Thesaurus in Dictionary Form*
	Merriam-Webster Dictionary of Synonyms and Antonyms
	Oxford American Writer's Thesaurus
Online	*Roget's Thesaurus* http://thesaurus.reference.com/
	Merriam-Webster Dictionary and Thesaurus http://www.merriam-webster.com/

Other Reference Materials

Most libraries and media centers have a variety of printed materials that are not found in bound form. They also have other nonprint resources such as audio recordings and video documentaries that contain information that cannot be conveyed in print form.

Vertical Files Libraries often store pamphlets, catalogs, and newspaper clippings alphabetically in a filing cabinet called the vertical file. Materials are stored in folders in file cabinets and arranged alphabetically by subject.

Government Documents and Historical Records Many libraries and media centers save storage space by storing some documents and back issues of periodicals on microfilm and microfiche—photographic reproductions of printed material that are stored on rolls or sheets of film. References stored on microforms may include government documents from state and federal agencies and original, historic records and papers. These rolls and sheets of film are stored in filing cabinets in another part of the library or media center and can be viewed easily on special projectors. Libraries may also subscribe to databases that provide access to some government documents or historical records. Many government Web sites also provide access to such documents. Two useful sites for federal government documents are <http://usasearch.gov/> and <http://www.gpoaccess.gov/>.

Audiovisual Materials Audiovisual materials can be valuable sources of information and are often available through your library or media center. Audiovisual materials may include recordings of interviews and speeches, and DVDs of documentaries and educational programs. If you cannot check out these materials to view in the classroom, listening and viewing equipment is usually available in the library. CD-ROMs have largely been replaced by online databases and other online or electronic resources. Some libraries may still have specialized indexes, databases, encyclopedias, or dictionaries such as the complete *Oxford English Dictionary* on CD-ROM. Check with the media specialist to see which resources are available in these forms.

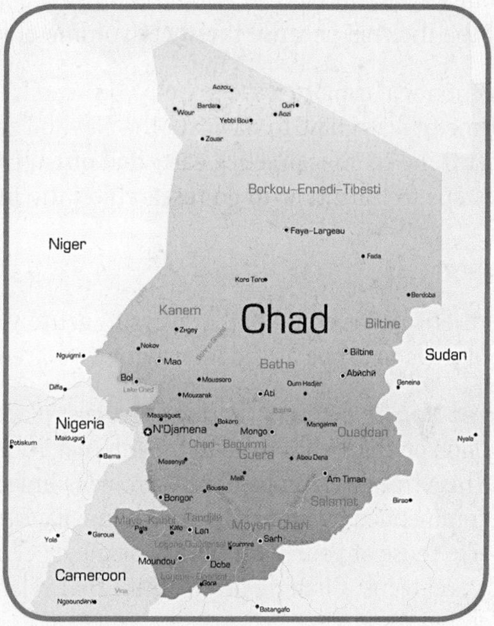

Develop Research Skills

Using Specialized References

Write one kind of reference work, other than a general encyclopedia, which would contain information about each of the following.

1. the life of news commentator Edward R. Murrow

2. the population of the African country of Chad

3. a pamphlet explaining the meanings of road signs

4. the names of the Academy Award winners from last year

5. catalogs of museum art exhibits

6. the birthplace of the author Toni Morrison

7. the location of the highest mountain range in Asia

8. information about Hinduism

9. a synonym for the word *accurate*

10. information about an earthquake that occurred one month ago

Using the Internet for Research

The Information Superhighway could be the best research partner you've ever had. It's fast, vast, and always available. But like any other highway, if you don't know your way around, it can also be confusing and frustrating. This is particularly true of the Internet because the sheer volume of information can be intimidating.

This section will explore ways to help you search the Web effectively. Be patient. It takes time to learn how to navigate the Net and zero in on the information you need. The best thing to do is practice early and often. Don't wait until the night before your paper is due to learn how to do research on the Internet!

Getting Started

Just as there are several different ways to get to your home or school, there are many different ways to arrive at the information you're looking for on the Internet.

Internet Public Library Perhaps the best place to start your search for reliable information on the Web is to go to the Internet Public Library (ipl2) site <http://www.ipl.org/>. This virtual reference library provides links to Web sites that have been reviewed and recommended by librarians. The home page is organized with links to sections much like those at your local library or media center. There are even special sections for kids and teens. Clicking on the links that relate to your topic will take you to a list of suggested resources.

Search Bar Another good first step is your browser's search bar. You can usually customize your browser by adding the search tools you use most often to the drop down menu.

Search Tools There are several different free search services available that will help you find topics of interest by entering words and phrases that describe what you are searching for. Some of the most popular **search engines** include:

AltaVista	http://www.altavista.com/
Ask	http://www.ask.com/
Bing	http://www.bing.com/
Google	http://www.google.com/
Lycos	http://www.lycos.com/
Yahoo!	http://www.yahoo.com/

Metasearch engines search and organize results from several search engines at one time. Following are a few examples:

Clusty	http://clusty.com/
Dogpile	http://www.dogpile.com/
Ixquick Metasearch	http://ixquick.com/

Search services usually list broad categories of subjects, plus they may offer other features such as "Random Links" or "Top 25 Sites," and customization options. Each one also has a search field. Type in a **keyword,** a word or short phrase that describes your area of interest. Then click Search or press the Enter key on your keyboard. Seconds later a list of Web sites known as "hits" will be displayed containing the word you specified in the search field. Scroll through the list and click the page you wish to view.

So far this sounds simple, doesn't it? The tricky part about doing a search on the Internet is that a single keyword may yield a hundred or more sites. Plus, you may find many topics you don't need.

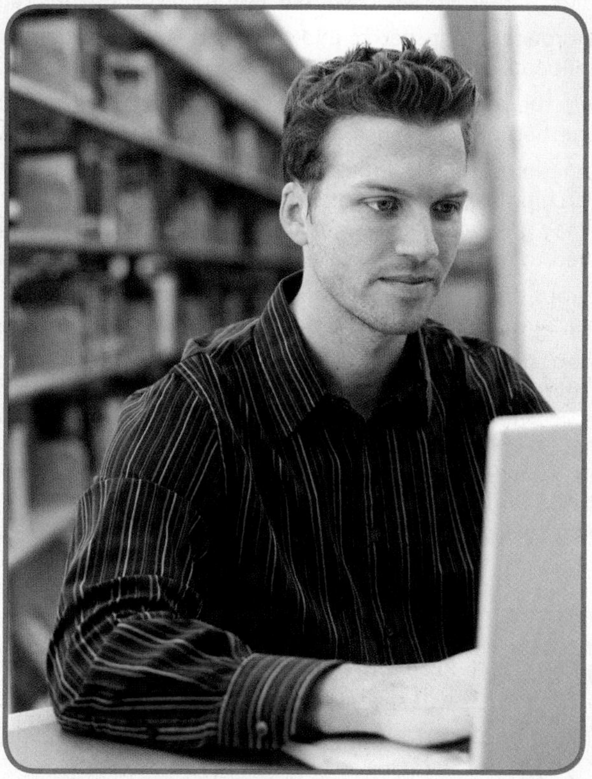

For example, suppose you are writing a science paper about the planet Saturn. If you type the word *Saturn* into the search field, you'll turn up some articles about the planet, but you'll also get articles about NASA's Saturn rockets and Saturn, the automobile company.

Search Smart

Listed below are a few pointers on how to narrow your search, save time, and search smart on the Net. Not all strategies work in all search engines, however.

HERE'S HOW

Guidelines for Smart Searching

- The keyword or words that you enter have a lot to do with the accuracy of your search. Focus your search by adding the word "and" or the + sign followed by another descriptive word. For example, try "Saturn" again, but this time, add "Saturn + space." Adding a third word, "Saturn + space + rings" will narrow the field even more.
- On the other hand, in some online databases you can limit unwanted results by specifying information that you do *not* want the search engine to find. If you type "dolphins not football," you will get Web sites about the animal that lives in the ocean rather than the football team that uses Miami as its home base.
- Specify geographical areas using the word "near" between keywords as in "islands near Florida." This lets you focus on specific regions.
- To broaden your search, add the word "or" between keywords. For example, "sailboats or catamarans."
- Help the search engine recognize familiar phrases by putting words that go together in quotes such as "Tom and Jerry" or "bacon and eggs."
- Sometimes the site you come up with is in the ballpark of what you are searching for, but it is not exactly what you need. Skim the text quickly anyway. It may give you ideas for more accurate keywords. There might also be links listed to other sites that are just the right resource you need.
- Try out different search engines. Each service uses slightly different methods of searching, so you may get different results using the same keywords.
- Check the spelling of the keywords you are using. A misspelled word can send a search engine in the wrong direction. Also, be careful how you use capital letters. By typing the word *Gold,* some search services will only bring up articles that include the word with a capital *G.*

You can learn more about evaluating online sources on pages 403–405.

Saving a Site for Later

You may want to keep a list handy of favorite Web sites or sites you are currently using in a project. This will save you time because you can just click on the name of the site in your list and return to that page without having to retype the URL.

Different browsers have different names for this feature. For example, AOL's Netscape® calls it **My Links,** Mozilla's Firefox® calls it **Bookmarks,** while Microsoft's Internet Explorer® calls it **Favorites.**

Internet + Media Center = Information Powerhouse

Although the Internet is a limitless treasure chest of information, remember that it's not cataloged. It can be tricky to locate the information you need, and sometimes that information is not reliable. The library is a well-organized storehouse of knowledge, but it has more limited resources. If you use the Internet *and* your local media center, you've got everything you need to create well-researched articles, reports, and papers.

HERE'S HOW

Using the Internet and Media Center

Use the Internet to

- get great ideas for topics to write about;
- gather information about your topic from companies, colleges and universities, and professional organizations;
- connect with recognized experts in your field of interest;
- connect with other people who are interested in the same subject and who can put you in touch with other sources.

Use the Media Center to

- find reliable sources of information either in print or online;
- get background information on your topic;
- cross-check the accuracy and credibility of online information and authors.

TIME OUT TO **REFLECT**

How does the Internet compare to some of the print resources you have used in terms of access, quality, and reliability? Why might one resource—print or online—be better than another? What strategies have you learned that will make researching easier in the future? What notes would you make to improve your reference skills for the future? Record your thoughts in your Learning Log.

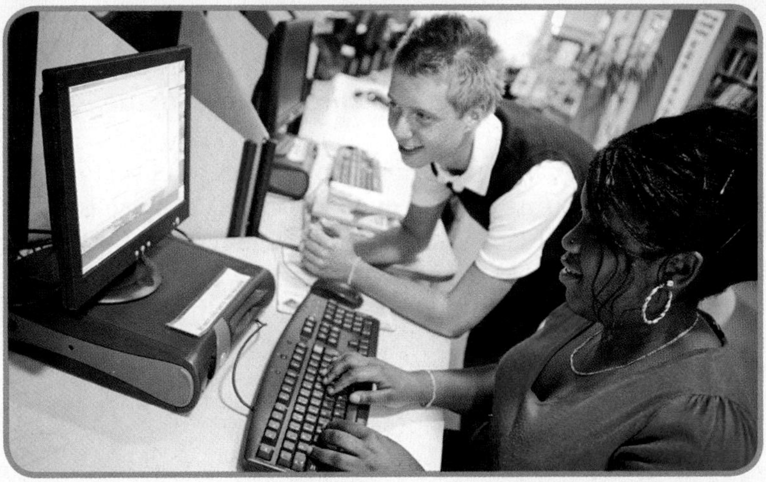

CHAPTER 11

CHAPTER 12

Research: Synthesizing, Organizing, and Presenting

CHAPTER 12

Like a quilter, when you are putting together a research report you need to plan your design and gather your materials and supplies before starting to sew the pieces together. In the previous chapter you have done just that. You have

- chosen and limited a subject
- posed a major research question
- formulated a research plan
- followed the plan to find sources in your library and media center
- evaluated those sources
- taken notes

The activities in this chapter will take you through the rest of the process of preparing a research report.

Writing Project Research Report

Finding the Answer ***Complete a research report on the open-ended question you chose to investigate.***

Review Now that you have followed your reseach plan to gather information you need, you are ready to draft, revise, edit, and publish your report on a question you sought to answer through research. As you work on and complete your research report, you may wish to modify or revise your major research question so that it is aligned with the emphasis of your inquiry.

Writing a Research Report *Synthesizing*

To prevent your report from being a mere collection of facts, you need to synthesize what you have learned to develop your own insights. To **synthesize** means to merge together information from different sources and your own experience and understanding. The following diagram shows the steps you can take to synthesize information.

SYNTHESIZING INFORMATION FROM DIFFERENT SOURCES

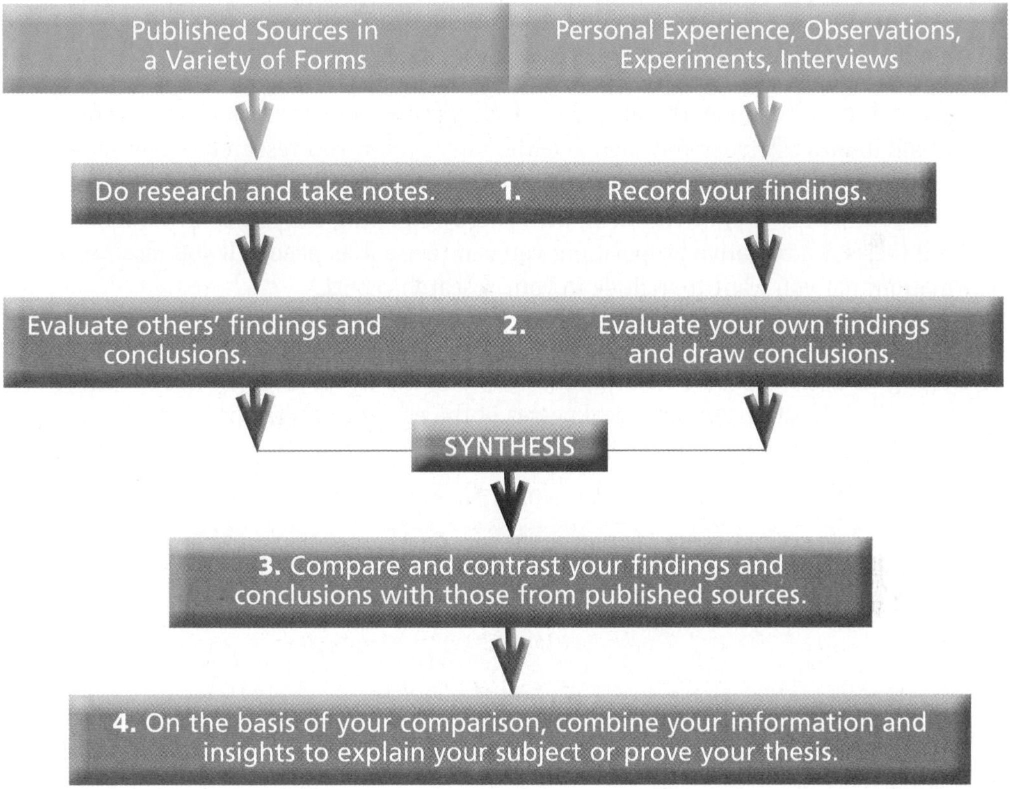
Published Sources in a Variety of Forms
Personal Experience, Observations, Experiments, Interviews
Do research and take notes.
1.
Record your findings.
Evaluate others' findings and conclusions.
2.
Evaluate your own findings and draw conclusions.
SYNTHESIS
3. Compare and contrast your findings and conclusions with those from published sources.
4. On the basis of your comparison, combine your information and insights to explain your subject or prove your thesis.

PROJECT PREP *Prewriting* *Synthesis*

Review your research question and all the notes you took as you conducted research. Follow the steps in the diagram above to synthesize the information, beginning with step 2. Write a brief paragraph evaluating the findings and conclusions of others. Write a second brief paragraph evaluating your own views on the subject. Then complete steps 3 and 4. Write a few sentences explaining how you combined the various sources of information to build the understanding you now have.

1 Developing a Working Thesis

After you have taken notes on your subject, you should have enough information to write a rough draft of your thesis statement. This **working thesis** statement establishes the purpose and the main idea of your research report and helps you to organize the information that you have collected. Before you formulate your working thesis, review your major research question and notes. See if you have modified the question or want to refocus your report.

In a research paper, as in a critical essay, you may frame your thesis as a statement that you intend to prove is true. You then give the information you researched as evidence to support your thesis. In such a paper it is necessary to develop a cogent argument that supports your personal opinion rather than simply restating existing information. A working thesis is a tentative proposition; you can revise it as needed if you discover more information that you want to include in your research report.

The following is a working thesis statement for the research report on Atlantis. In developing an argument based on this thesis, the writer needs to differentiate between the theory and the strengths and weaknesses of the evidence that supports it.

MODEL: Working Thesis Statement

The theory that places the lost city of Atlantis on the island of Thera has strengths and weaknesses.

When you write the first draft of your research report, you can revise your working thesis statement to fit more smoothly into your opening paragraph.

PROJECT PREP Prewriting *Working Thesis*

In your writing group, help each author develop a working thesis statement. You should each use your major research question as the guide for a thesis statement, which you will include in your introductory paragraph. Discard statements that are too broad or obvious or so narrow you will have trouble finding supportive arguments. These arguments would need to be backed up by precise and relevant evidence, including facts, expert opinions, quotations, and/or commonly accepted beliefs.

2 Organizing Your Notes

With your working thesis statement in mind, you can use your guiding questions to organize your note cards containing relevant and accurate information into categories of information. These categories should reflect the central ideas, concepts, and themes of your report. In Chapter 11, research centered on the lost city of Atlantis. Notice how the following categories on the subject of Atlantis are related to the questions that guided the research.

Category 1	General information: the nature of the problem and various attempts at explaining Atlantis
Category 2	Plato's story of Atlantis
Category 3	Strong evidence for the Thera theory
Category 4	Weak evidence for the Thera theory
Category 5	The difficulties in proving that Atlantis existed

CHAPTER 12

After determining the appropriate categories for your research, sort your note cards into these categories and clip each group together. Check to see that the categories reflect the central ideas, concepts, and themes of your planned report. If some of your cards do not fit into your categories, clip them separately. You may find a use for these notes when you write the introduction or conclusion of your research paper.

Writing Tip

Group your notes into three or more main categories of information.

PROJECT PREP **Prewriting** ***Organizing Notes Electronically***

Many students write their notes on 3 x 5 or 4 x 6 note cards, but you may prefer to use a computer. To retain your notes electronically, decide how you want to set them up for easy access. Unless you have a computer program that organizes notes, it is best to put all your notes into one file so that you can search them with one search. Be sure to save your information every two or three minutes, and back it all up when you are finished. In your word processor's menu bar, you will see "Edit"; click that and then go to "Find" to search your notes for a particular word or phrase. To further organize your notes, you may want to assign a code to each source. Whatever method you use to organize your notes, include only relevant and accurate information that supports the central ideas, concepts, and themes of the report.

3 Outlining

The final step in the prewriting stage is to organize your notes into an **outline** of your research report. The categories you made for your note cards will be the basis for your outline. Look over the categories and your working thesis statement and decide which type of order is most appropriate for your subject. **Chronological order,** for example, is the best type of order for a research paper on a historical subject or on the steps in a process. **Comparison/contrast** is best for exploring similarities and differences between two things. **Spatial order** is sometimes useful for a research report that describes or analyzes something. **Order of importance** and **developmental order** are perhaps the most common types of organization for research reports.

Once you have chosen the best method of organization, you can begin outlining. Before you develop a formal outline you may want to outline your ideas using conceptual maps or timelines. Timelines are especially useful for papers using chronological order. Various conceptual maps such as Venn diagrams or cluster diagrams may help you visualize how your ideas are related.

The categories for the research report on the lost city of Atlantis were arranged in developmental order. Notice that the categories are assigned Roman numerals and are phrased in parallel form.

Writing Tip

Begin the outline of your research report by deciding on a method of organization and assigning Roman numerals to your categories accordingly.

MODEL: Categories in Developmental Order

I. Plato's story of Atlantis

II. Strong evidence for the Thera theory

III. Weak evidence for the Thera theory

An outline organizes the material for the body of a research report. It should show how you intend to support central ideas, concepts, and themes. You may choose, therefore, to save one or two of your main categories for the introduction and the conclusion. The person writing on Atlantis, for example, outlined three of the categories above and saved the other two categories for the introduction and conclusion of the report. As you review your categories, decide which ones you might want to save for your introduction and your conclusion.

After you establish your main topics, the next step is to go back over your notes and add **subtopics** (indicated by capital letters) and **supporting points** (indicated by Arabic numerals) to fill out the outline. Below is an outline for the research report on Atlantis. Notice that, like main topics, each group of subtopics and supporting points is phrased in parallel form.

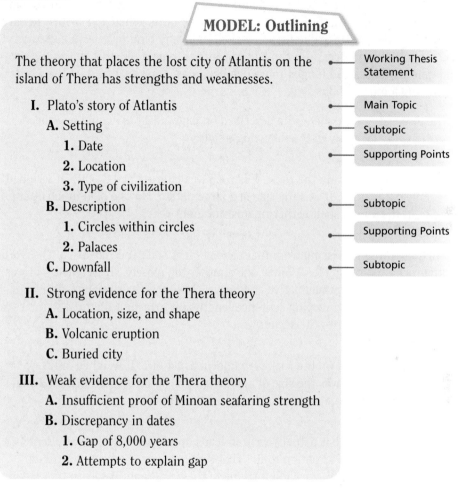

MODEL: Outlining

The theory that places the lost city of Atlantis on the island of Thera has strengths and weaknesses. — Working Thesis Statement

- **I.** Plato's story of Atlantis — Main Topic
  - **A.** Setting — Subtopic
    - **1.** Date — Supporting Points
    - **2.** Location
    - **3.** Type of civilization
  - **B.** Description — Subtopic
    - **1.** Circles within circles — Supporting Points
    - **2.** Palaces
  - **C.** Downfall — Subtopic
- **II.** Strong evidence for the Thera theory
  - **A.** Location, size, and shape
  - **B.** Volcanic eruption
  - **C.** Buried city
- **III.** Weak evidence for the Thera theory
  - **A.** Insufficient proof of Minoan seafaring strength
  - **B.** Discrepancy in dates
    - **1.** Gap of 8,000 years
    - **2.** Attempts to explain gap

You may wish to use the outline above as a model when writing your research report outline.

PROJECT PREP Prewriting *Outline*

With your writing group, write an outline for the body of your research report. Write the working thesis statement at the top of your paper. Next, use a conceptual map or timeline to outline your ideas. Develop the outline based on the categories you created. As you fill in subtopics and details from your notes, check the form of your outline. Save your work.

The Power of Language

Fluency: Let It Flow

You have learned how to add content and detail to your sentences, and style and voice to your writing. But fluency involves still more. When you write a research report about a complicated topic, you will naturally tend to have longer, more complicated sentences. You can add variety to a report like this by varying short, simple sentences and longer, more detailed ones. Your goal is to let the words flow, avoiding a monotonous style.

The discovery of the meteorite described on pages 391–395 could have been written very factually in the following manner:

> Dr. Score picked up the rock. This rock was later named 84-001. It weighed only 4.2 pounds. It was the size of a large potato. No one paid much attention to it. It sat on a shelf gathering dust for eight years.

But something is missing from that passage. It is stale and repetitive. The words "the rock" and "This rock" follow one another too closely. "It weighed," "It was," and "It sat" seem unimaginative and heavy. Now read the actual passage from "Life on Mars" to see how varying sentence length and inverting the final sentence add fluidity and interest to the account.

> Dr. Score picked up the rock now known as 84-001. It weighed only 4.2 pounds and was the size of a large potato. No one paid much attention to it. For eight years, it sat on a shelf gathering dust.

The way the passage is actually written leads up to the most dramatic sentence, "No one paid much attention to it." That sentence and the next contribute significantly to the fluency and intrigue of the paragraph. We learn that eight years went by until something happened to that rock. It is a passage that invites the reader to keep reading to learn more.

Try It Yourself

Write a passage of about five sentences on your project topic. Include sentences of varying length and structure.

Punctuation Tip

Use a comma after an introductory prepositional phrase. (See pages 926–927.)

1 Revising a Working Thesis

As you write the first draft of your research report, begin fitting the pieces of your research quilt into a well-formed whole. Your goal at this stage is to present your ideas by working the information from your sources smoothly into the outline of your research paper.

The thesis statement expresses the main idea and organizes the entire research report. It is helpful, therefore, to begin writing the first draft by revising your working thesis statement. When you write your introduction, you can easily work your thesis statement into the appropriate spot. The following guidelines will help you revise your working thesis statement.

HERE'S HOW

Guidelines for Revising a Thesis Statement

- The thesis statement should make the main point of your research paper clear to the reader.
- The thesis statement should be broad enough to cover all the main topics listed in your outline and narrow enough to cover only those topics.
- The thesis statement should fit smoothly into your introduction.

The following main topics relate to a research paper on becoming a master craftsman in eighteenth-century America.

Apprenticeships in Eighteenth-Century America

I. Acquiring an apprenticeship

II. Serving as an apprentice

III. Becoming a master: independence

Based on these topics, you might write the following working thesis statement.

MODEL: Working Thesis Statement

Serving as an apprentice in eighteenth-century America meant placing your life in the hands of the master.

This working thesis statement is weak because it is too narrow. It does not cover all of the main topics listed in the outline. The following thesis statement would be better.

MODEL: Revised Thesis Statement

Becoming a master craftsman in eighteenth-century America involved acquiring and serving an apprenticeship, which was often difficult for the apprentice.

Northwind Picture Archives

PROJECT PREP *Drafting* ***Refining Thesis Statement***

Use the guidelines on page 441 to evaluate your working thesis statement. If necessary, modify, refocus, or revise the working thesis statement to align with any changes that your inquiry has produced in your topic. Using this refined thesis, then, each author should draft an introductory paragraph that states and briefly develops the statement. This paragraph will provide the focus for the body paragraphs that follow.

2 Using Sources

Whether you quote the exact words or paraphrase the information, you are required by law to give credit to any author whose ideas or words you use. Failure to give credit is called **plagiarism,** a serious offense. In a research report, all borrowed material must be indicated with citations within the paper. These citations are then keyed to a list of your sources at the end of the paper. Work the borrowed material smoothly into your own writing. Following are five good strategies.

HERE'S HOW

Tips for Using Sources

- Use a quotation to finish a sentence you have started.

Example Photographs taken in 1977 of underwater stones are believed to "bear the mark of human handiwork" (Whitney).

- Quote a whole sentence. If you omit words from a quoted sentence, indicate the omission with an ellipsis (. . .).

Example "He suggests that the structures match the description in Plato's dialogue Critias . . . and that the high mountains of Atlantis are actually those of the Sierra Morena and Sierra Nevada" (Shermer).

- Quote five or more lines from your source. For a quotation of this length, skip two lines and set the quotation off as a block indented one inch on the left. You do not need quotation marks for such an extended quotation.

Example Here is how Plato describes the downfall of Atlantis in the dialogue called *Timaeus:*

> Some time later excessively violent earthquakes and floods occurred, and after the onset of an unbearable day and a night, your entire warrior force sank below the earth all at once, and the Isle of Atlantis likewise sank below the sea and disappeared. (1232)

- Quote just a few words.

Example According to Plato, in an "unbearable day and a night" Atlantis was destroyed (*Timaeus* 1232).

- Paraphrase information from a source.

Example "Although many have dismissed Atlantis as a myth, some 50,000 volumes have been written trying to describe and locate it." [original]
Curiosity about Atlantis and efforts to locate it gave rise to some 50,000 books on the subject ("Greek Backs Plato Theory"). [paraphrase]

As you took notes from the relevant sources on your major research topic, you probably encountered both factual information and complex inferences made by the experts. Perhaps you began to make such inferences yourself. Separate facts and inferences as you organize the information from your sources so that you can accurately include the material in your report. You must give citations for borrowed facts and inferences.

Practice Your Skills

Using Sources

The excerpt below is about the origin and development of the parachute. Read it carefully. Then use it as a source to complete the exercises that follow.

Parachutes Past and Present

The principle and construction of the parachute might seem pretty elementary in these days of advanced aerodynamic technology. Early experiments with the devices, however, were feats of considerable daring, usually performed before breathless crowds at country fairs. Louis Sébastien Lenormand of France was the first to demonstrate his rustic canopy parachute in action. In 1783, he leaped from a high tower to a safe landing. Fourteen years later an excited crowd of Parisians gathered in the Parc Monceau to watch André Jacques Garnerin rise to an altitude of 3,000 feet in the basket of a balloon, abruptly cut the suspension cord, and descend gracefully to Earth with a parachute resembling an oversized umbrella. Garnerin went on to exhibit his jumps at ever increasing heights in various countries, leaping 8,000 feet in England in 1802.

The first parachutes were of canvas, later replaced by silk, and then nylon, which is used today. An important development, undoubtedly not considered in the early parachutes, is the use of numerous different pieces of fabric. These are cut, sewn, and arranged to confine a possible tear to the section in which it starts. The apparatus (parachute and suspension lines) is assembled in a pack. The rip cord that releases the parachute may be operated manually, or automatically via a timing device, or by a line attached to an aircraft.

The first man to jump from a plane was Captain Albert Berry of the U.S. Army in 1912. Enormous parachutes helped the Apollo 14 space capsule land in 1971. Perhaps the most extraordinary parachute is that used for getting out of an aircraft moving at supersonic speeds. In this case, the entire seat goes along—pilot, seat, and parachute are ejected by a rocket charge. Eventually, the seat is left behind and the parachute opens automatically, cutting the pilot's speed as he or she descends.

—Caroline Sutton, *How Did They Do That?*

1. Write a sentence about early experiments with parachutes. End your sentence with a quotation from the excerpt.
2. Write three sentences about Lenormand and Garnerin. One sentence should be a direct quotation.
3. Write a paragraph about modern parachutes that includes an extended quotation of five lines or more.
4. Write a sentence describing Garnerin's parachute that quotes just a few words from the source.
5. Write two sentences paraphrasing the information about parachutes used to leave supersonic aircraft.

CHAPTER 12

PROJECT PREP Drafting *Using Sources*

Practice paraphrasing and using quotations from your note cards for your research report. Clearly indicate inferences made by other authors and jot down your own inferences next to quoted or paraphrased material. Share your work with your partner and exchange suggestions.

Think Critically

Anticipating and Refuting Counter-Arguments

When you research varying points of view on a topic, there are likely to be complexities and discrepancies in information from multiple sources. In developing a strong argument to support your thesis statement, you should incorporate these complexities and discrepancies in your report. To do this, anticipate the possible counter-arguments or objections to your thesis and related claims. Then think of a way to refute or answer each counter-argument. To try this strategy, create a two-column chart showing a list of counter-arguments and possible refutations.

Thesis: The most believable explanation of Atlantis is that it was a Minoan city.

COUNTER-ARGUMENTS	REFUTATIONS
1. The Minoans were never really a powerful enough seagoing empire to fit the Atlantis description.	1. Plato might have been embellishing the strength of the Atlanteans to teach the moral that warlike people will get their punishment.
2. The date of the volcanic eruption found on Thera was 8,000 years later than Plato's Atlantis.	2. In the long process of transmitting the Atlantis story, all the dates got multiplied by 10.

Thinking Practice

With a partner, discuss the complexities and discrepancies you have found in your research. Talk through the various positions until both you and your partner understand them well. Then construct a chart of the counter-arguments, and try to develop a refutation to answer each one.

3 Studying a Model Research Report

The model below is a final draft, so it is more polished than your first draft will be. It is presented here in revised and edited form to show you how each element in the structure of a research report contributes to the whole.

Notice that whenever a fact, opinion, or quotation is borrowed from outside sources, a parenthetical citation refers the reader to the source listed on the works-cited page at the end of the report. Also note that the writer used a variety of sources written for informed audiences rather than relying too heavily on one source. When you prepare your rough draft, indicate borrowed material by writing the title, author, and page number of the source in parentheses after the borrowed material. In the next draft, you will put your citations and works-cited page in the correct form.

Your report may be more complex than this brief model or have a different purpose. But you too will need to differentiate between theories and the evidence that supports them. You will need to analyze which evidence is strong and which is weak and use that analysis to create a cogent argument, as this report does. The analysis reflects the writer's opinion about the evidence in the conclusion of the paper. This report only briefly summarizes the complex information and discrepancies found in a variety of sources. You may be asked to do a more detailed analysis of different perspectives and to explicitly anticipate and refute counter-arguments. In writing such a research report you would use the formats and strategies of persuasive writing to argue for your thesis. (See pages 106–107 and 282–321.)

MODEL: Research Report

Atlantis Rediscovered?

Title

For hundreds of years, people have wondered whether the sunken city of Atlantis was myth or reality. Speculations about Atlantis and efforts to locate it have given rise to some 50,000 books on the subject ("Greek Backs Plato Theory"). Over the centuries, theorists have placed the lost city in virtually all parts of the world, even in highly unlikely areas. These include "the Canaries, the Azores, the Caribbean, Tunisia, West Africa, Sweden, Iceland and even South America" (Shermer). Evidence used to support these various theories includes ruins found by digging, strange migration patterns of eels (Muck 88), and photographs of underwater stones that are believed to "bear the mark of human handiwork" (Whitney). Since the 1960s, the theory that has received the most attention links the lost city of Atlantis to the real-life ancient Minoan culture on the Aegean islands of Crete and Thera.

Introduction: Background Information

Thesis Statement

The original and only written source of the Atlantis story is in writings of the Greek philosopher Plato, who lived between 427 and 347 B.C. He relates the story of a powerful, seagoing civilization that lived about 9500 B.C. on a continent called Atlantis in front of the Strait of Gibraltar. With their mighty power, the Atlanteans began conquering nearby peoples, including Athenians and Egyptians, and their might continued to grow (*Timaeus* 1231–32). Plato describes in specific detail the island home of these people, painting a picture of a kingdom built in circles within circles, each separated by a canal. He also describes palaces of unbelievable beauty housing temples to the god Poseidon (*Critias* 1299–1306). Plato says that in the height of their glory, the Atlanteans' island home was swept by sudden floods and earthquakes and in an "unbearable day and a night" sank into the depths of the sea (*Timaeus* 1232).

Body: Main Topic I

Borrowed words are in quotation marks

Some evidence about the Minoans and their island home fits Plato's descriptions. Although the center of the empire was on Crete, other Minoans lived on Thera. Thera is part of a circular group of islands about 75 miles north of Crete (Pellegrino 112). The location, size, and shape of this island group match those same features of Plato's Atlantis (Pellegrino 19). Perhaps the most significant evidence is that scientists now know that a volcano that erupted on Thera threw more than twice as much pumice and cinders into the atmosphere as Krakatoa did in 1883 (Leadbeater).

Body: Main Topic II

In 1967, diggings on the island of Thera uncovered a prehistoric Minoan city buried in the layers of volcanic ash (Pellegrino 20). The cataclysmic explosion created killer waves that reached nearby Crete and weakened or destroyed the Minoans' all-important harbors. With their naval strength cut off, the Minoan empire faded (Lilley).

Borrowed interpretation cited with note

Many important details in the story of the Minoans, however, do not even come close to matching Plato's story of Atlantis. Some scholars, for example, do not believe that the Minoan culture was ever a very powerful seagoing empire. The most glaring difference between the stories, however, is the date of the volcanic eruption, which scientists place at about 1450 B.C. Plato's version relates a catastrophe that happened 8,000 years earlier. Atlantis expert A. G. Galanopoulous explains this disagreement by arguing that in the centuries-long process of transmitting the Atlantis story, all the numbers were mistakenly multiplied by ten (Ramage 41). Most scientists, whether they believe in the reality

Body: Main Topic III

of Atlantis or accept it as a myth, agree that no advanced civilization could have existed as early as 9500 B.C.

Conclusion

The Thera-Crete theory about Atlantis suffers from the same fundamental problem as all the others. The problem is Plato's original account, with its own perplexing contradictions. Many people believe that Plato made up the story of Atlantis as a fable to show how warlike peoples are punished for their deeds (Shermer). So conceived, the Atlantis myth has had an enduring influence on Utopian literature and, in our own century, in science fiction films (Dirks). As far as people know, no other written source besides Plato's relates the Atlantis story, even though extensive written accounts of other ancient happenings do exist. After more than 40 years, the theory that identifies Atlantis with Thera remains the "most popular," even though attempts to explain the difference in dates are far from satisfactory (Greer 109). Although the evidence is not conclusive, it is clear from the many books and articles that continue to be published about Atlantis that interest in this sunken city endures.

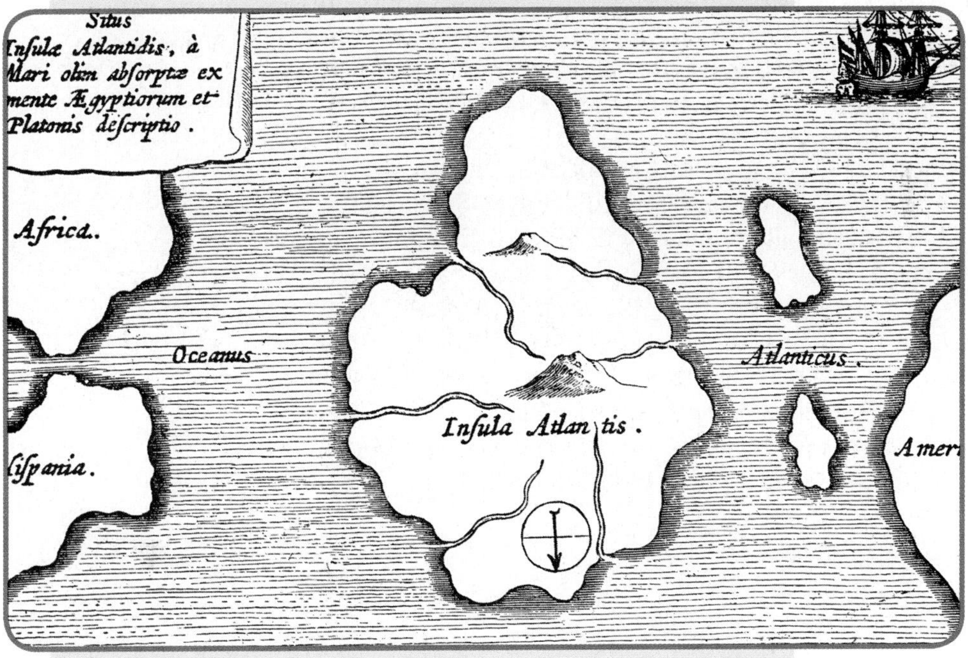

CHAPTER 12

Works Cited

Dirks, Tim. "Science Fiction Films: Verne and Wells Derivatives." *Filmsite.org*. American Movie Classics, 2009. Web. 17 Mar. 2009.

"Greek Backs Plato Theory on Where to Find Atlantis." *New York Times* 29 Aug. 1979: A4. *ProQuest Historical Newspapers The New York Times (1851–2005)*. Web. 17 Mar. 2009.

Greer, John Michael. *Atlantis: Ancient Legacy, Hidden Prophecy*. Woodbury: Llewellyn, 2007. Print.

Leadbeater, Elli. "Thera Eruption Was Bigger Still." *BBC News*. BBC, 27 Aug. 2006. Web. 17 Mar. 2009.

Lilley, Harvey. "The Wave That Destroyed Atlantis." *BBC Timewatch*. BBC, 20 Apr. 2007. Web. 17 Mar. 2009.

Muck, Otto. *The Secret of Atlantis.* Trans. Fred Bradley. New York: Times, 1978. Print.

Pellegrino, Charles R. *Unearthing Atlantis: An Archaeological Odyssey*. New York: Random House, 1991. Print.

Plato. *Critias.* Trans. Diskin Clay. *Plato: The Complete Works*. Ed. John M. Cooper. Indianapolis: Hackett, 1997. 1292–1306. Print.

---. *Timaeus.* Trans. Donald J. Zeyl. *Plato: The Complete Works*. Ed. John M. Cooper. Indianapolis: Hackett, 1997. 1224–91. Print.

Ramage, Edwin S. "Perspectives Ancient and Modern." *Atlantis: Fact or Fiction?* Ed. Edwin S. Ramage. Bloomington: Indiana U P, 1978. 3–45. Print.

Shermer, Michael. "The Myth Is the Message." *Scientific American* Oct. 2004: 42. *Health Source — Consumer Edition*. Web. 17 Mar. 2009.

Whitney, Craig R. "Soviet Scientist Says Ocean Site May Be Atlantis." *New York Times* 21 May 1979: A14. *ProQuest Historical Newspapers The New York Times (1851–2005)*. Web. 17 Mar. 2009.

Three hyphens show work by same author as above

As You Write

Begin drafting by reviewing your organized notes, your outline, and your revised thesis statement. As you draft your introduction, rework your thesis statement to make it fit in smoothly. Then follow your outline to draft the body. Use **transitional words and phrases** such as *first, second, most important,* and *finally* to help achieve a smooth and logical progression of ideas.

As you write, use a variety of rhetorical strategies to argue for your thesis, and anticipate and refute counter-arguments. Differentiate between theories and the evidence that supports them. Analyze your evidence to determine how strong it is. Use the evidence you have gathered to create a cogent argument that your readers will understand.

When you finish the body, draft your conclusion. Your conclusion should consider how you have answered your major research question in the body paragraphs of your paper. The conclusion is a good place to go beyond restating information by providing personal opinions that your research and analysis support.

PROJECT PREP Drafting *First Draft*

Using the model and the instruction above, write a first draft of your research report. Don't worry about using the correct form for citations just yet. For now identify the source and page number in parentheses.

4 Citing Sources

Notes that indicate the source of a quote or borrowed ideas are called **citations.** To determine whether or not you need to use citations, look carefully at the information you have used. The following guidelines will help you determine what information requires a citation.

HERE'S HOW

Guidelines for Citing Sources

- Cite the source of a direct quotation. Use direct quotations only when the author's original wording makes the point more strongly or interestingly than you could by using your own words.
- Cite the source of any paraphrased fact or idea that your readers might otherwise assume is your own.
- Do not cite facts or ideas that are considered to be common knowledge.

The type of citation you will use is often determined by your subject matter. Standards are set by professional organizations, such as the Modern Language Association (MLA) in the language arts and humanities or the American Psychological Association (APA) in the sciences and social sciences. Scholars in many fields often refer to *The Chicago Manual of Style (CMS)* for guidelines. The MLA and the APA both use parenthetical citations. However, the APA style manual is now focused on professionals writing articles for publication. The *CMS* reference-list style of citation uses parenthetical citations that are similar to the APA style. A useful guide to *CMS* for students is Kate Turabian, *A Manual for Writers of Research Papers, Theses, and Dissertations*.

Parenthetical citations, as shown in the model research report on pages 447–450, identify the source briefly in parentheses directly following the borrowed material. This textbook uses the MLA guidelines for parenthetical citations—the preferred way to give credit to your sources. For most literary research papers, you will use the MLA style. Turabian *(CMS)* uses a slightly different style of parenthetical citation that includes the date of publication. (See page 453.)

> **Writing Tip**
>
> Cite the sources of information you include in your research report by using **parenthetical citations, footnotes,** or **endnotes.**

The *CMS* notes-bibliography style cites sources with endnotes or footnotes. This style calls for a number to be placed directly after the borrowed material. The number refers the reader to the source listed at the bottom, or foot, of the page or at the end of the report.

Parenthetical Citations

The following guidelines and examples will help you use parenthetical citations correctly. Keep in mind that the citations in parentheses are intentionally brief. Their purpose is to provide the reader with only enough information to identify the source of the borrowed material. Readers then refer to the list of works cited at the end of the research paper for complete information on each source. The following examples show two different styles of parenthetical citations.

MLA STYLE GUIDELINES	
Book by One Author	Give author's last name and a page reference: (Pellegrino 112).
Book by Two or More Authors	Give both authors' last names and a page reference: (Zapp and Erikson 56).
Article; Author Named	Give author's last name and a page reference; omit page number if the article is only one page long: (Powell 50).
Author Already Named Most Recently in the Text	Give only a page number from the source being used (106).
Article; Author Unnamed	Give title of article (full or shortened; omit initial *A, An,* or *The*) and page reference; omit page number if the article is only one page long: ("Findings").
Article in a Referene Work; Author Unnamed	Give title (full or shortened) and page number, unless title is entered alphabetically in an encyclopedia: ("Atlantis").
Online Article; Author Named	Give author's last name; include a page or paragraph number only if the online source includes them; do not use page references from a print version of the article: (Shermer).
Online Article or Web Page; Author Unnamed	Give title of article or Web page, as used on the works-cited page: ("Atlantis Myth").

TURABIAN (*Chicago Manual of Style*) GUIDELINES	
Book or Article by One Author	Give author's last name and date of publication, then a page reference separated by a comma: (Pellegrino 1991, 112).
Book or Artlce by Two Authors	Give both authors' names and date of publication, then a page reference (Zapp and Erikson 1998, 56).
Author Most Recently Named in the Text	Give only the date of the source being used and a page reference (2007, 109).
Article; Author Unnamed	Use the name of the publication in place of the author, then give the date of publication and page reference; omit page number if the article is on a single page: (*Harper's* 2009).

No matter which style you use, parenthetical citations should be placed as close to the words or ideas being credited as possible. To avoid interrupting the natural flow of the sentence, place them at the end of a phrase, a clause, or a sentence. The following guidelines will tell you where to place the citation in relation to punctuation marks.

HERE'S HOW

The Correct Placement of Parenthetical Citations

- If the citation falls next to a comma or end mark, place the citation before the punctuation mark.
- If the citation accompanies an extended quotation that is set off and indented, place the citation after the end mark.
- If the citation falls next to a closing quotation mark, place the citation after the quotation mark but before any comma or end mark.

CHAPTER 12

*You can learn more about using citations by looking at the model research paper on pages 447–450 and in the **Tips for Using Sources** on page 443.*

Footnotes and Endnotes

Your teacher may ask you to cite your sources in footnotes or endnotes, rather than in parenthetical citations. The form for footnotes and endnotes is the same. In the research paper itself, you place a small number, called a **superscript,** halfway above the line and immediately after the borrowed material. The number refers readers to the footnote or the endnote with the same number. As shown in the following examples, the footnote or endnote entry itself does not begin with a superscript. **Footnotes** are placed at the foot of the page containing the borrowed material. **Endnotes,** however, are placed together on a separate page after the conclusion of the report but before the list of works cited. The following examples will help you write footnotes or endnotes correctly.

The Turabian *Manual* is also a useful guide for footnotes or endnotes. This notes-bibliography style of citations is used primarily in the humanities and some social sciences.

EXAMPLES: Turabian (*Chicago Manual of Style*) Footnotes and Endnotes

General Reference Works	1. C. Scott Littleton, "Atlantis," in *World Book Encyclopedia,* 2009 ed. 2. *World Book Encyclopedia,* 2009 ed., s.v. "Atlantic States." [s.v. = "under the word"]
Books by One Author	3. Charles R. Pellegrino, *Unearthing Atlantis: An Archaeological Odyssey* (New York: Random House, 1991), 112.
Books by Two or More Authors	4. Ivar Zapp and George Erikson, *Atlantis in America: Navigators of the Ancient World* (Kempton, IL: Adventures Unlimited Press, 1998), 56.

Articles in Magazines	5. Eric A. Powell, "Arise Atlantis!" *Archaeology*, March 2009, 50.
Articles in Newspapers	6. Henry Fountain, "Scientists Document Bustling Community Far Below Ocean Floor," *New York Times*, May 27, 2008.
Articles from Online Databases	7. Michael Shermer, "The Myth Is the Message," *Scientific American*, October 2004, 42, http://search.ebscohost.com/login.aspx?direct=true&db=hxh&AN=14394127&site=src-live (accessed March 17, 2009).
Articles from Web Sites	8. Harvey Lilley, "The Wave That Destroyed Atlantis," BBC Timewatch, April 20, 2007, http://news.bbc.co.uk/2/hi/science/nature/6568053.stm (accessed March 17, 2009).
Interviews	9. Stan Harrison, telephone interview by author, March 18, 2009.

For repeated references to a work already cited, you can use a shortened form of footnote. The author's last name and the page number are enough to refer to a work already fully cited. If you have cited more than one work by the author, include the title, if brief, or a shortened form of the title after the author's last name.

Repeated References	10. Pellegrino, 19.
	11. Plato, *Timaeus*, 1232.

Works-Cited Page

All of the sources cited or mentioned in the report are listed in the works-cited section.

A **works-cited page** is an alphabetical list of sources used in a research paper. It appears at the end of the report.

In addition to the citations within your research report, a complete list of all of the sources you have cited should appear on a works-cited page, which is similar to a bibliography. The entries in a list of works cited differ from footnotes and endnotes in three main ways. (1) The first line is not indented, but the other lines are indented. (2) The author's last name is listed first. (3) Periods are used in place of commas, and parentheses are deleted. The following examples show the correct form for the entries in a list of works cited.

Writing Tip

A **works-cited page** is an alphabetical list of all the sources cited in a research paper. It appears on a separate page at the end of the research paper.

EXAMPLES: MLA Guide to Works-Cited Page

General Reference Works	Littleton, C. Scott. "Atlantis." *World Book Encyclopedia.* 2009 ed. Print. "Atlantic States." *World Book Encyclopedia.* 2009 ed. Print.
Books by One Author	Pellegrino, Charles R. *Unearthing Atlantis: An Archaeological Odyssey.* New York: Random, 1991. Print.
Books by Two or More Authors	Zapp, Ivar, and George Erikson. *Atlantis in America: Navigators of the Ancient World*. Kempton: Adventures Unlimited, 1998. Print.
Articles; Author Named	Powell, Eric A. "Arise Atlantis!" *Archaeology* Mar. 2009: 49–54. Print.
Articles; Author Unnamed	"Findings." *Harper's* May 2009: 84. Print.
Articles in Newspapers	Fountain, Henry. "Scientists Document Bustling Community Far Below Ocean Floor." *New York Times* 27 May 2008: 3. Print.
Interview	Harrison, Stan. Telephone interview. 18 Mar. 2009.
Articles from Online Databases	Shermer, Michael. "The Myth Is the Message." *Scientific American* Oct. 2004: 42. *Health Source – Consumer Edition.* Web. 17 Mar. 2009.
Articles from Web Sites	Lilley, Harvey. "The Wave That Destroyed Atlantis." *BBC Timewatch.* BBC, 20 Apr. 2007. Web. 17 Mar. 2009.

These entries follow the style recommended in the *MLA Handbook for Writers of Research Papers* (7th ed.). The MLA no longer recommends including URLs for most online sources because they change so frequently. If your teacher requires you to include a URL, enclose it in angle brackets (< >), as the last entry in the citation.

The Turabian (*The Chicago Manual of Style*) recommends including URLs for most electronic sources. Following are examples for a works-cited page using different citation styles.

EXAMPLES: Turabian (*Chicago Manual of Style*) Bibliography Style for Works-Cited Page

Books by One Author	Pellegrino, Charles R. *Unearthing Atlantis: An Archaeological Odyssey.* New York: Random House, 1991.
Books by Two or More Authors	Zapp, Ivar, and George Erikson. *Atlantis in America: Navigators of the Ancient World*. Kempton, IL: Adventures Unlimited Press, 1998.
Magazine Articles	Powell, Eric A. "Arise Atlantis!" *Archaeology*, March 2009.
Articles from Online Databases	Shermer, Michael. "The Myth Is the Message." *Scientific American,* October 2004. http://search.ebscohost.com/login.aspx?direct=true&db=hxh&AN=14394127&site=src-live (accessed March 17, 2009).
Articles from Web Sites	Lilley, Harvey. "The Wave That Destroyed Atlantis." *BBC Timewatch,* April 20, 2007. http://news.bbc.co.uk/2/hi/science/nature/6568053.stm (accessed March 17, 2009).

EXAMPLES: Turabian *(Chicago Manual of Style)* Reference-List Style for Works-Cited Page

Books by One Author	Pellegrino, Charles R. *Unearthing Atlantis: An Archaeological Odyssey.* New York: Random House, 1991.
Books by Two or More Authors	Zapp, Ivar, and George Erikson. *Atlantis in America: Navigators of the Ancient World*. Kempton, IL: Adventures Unlimited Press, 1998.
Magazine Articles	Powell, Eric A. "Arise Atlantis!" *Archaeology*, March 2009.
Articles from Online Databases	Shermer, Michael. "The Myth Is the Message." *Scientific American,* October 2004. http://search.ebscohost.com/login.aspx?direct=true&db=hxh&AN=14394127&site=src-live (accessed March 17, 2009).

Articles from Web Sites Lilley, Harvey. “The Wave That Destroyed Atlantis.” BBC Timewatch, April 20, 2007. http://news.bbc.co.uk/2/hi/science/nature/6568053.stm (accessed March 17, 2009).

Use the Turabian bibliography style with footnotes or endnotes; use the reference-list style with parenthetical citations based on the Turabian style. Whatever style you use, use it consistently for all the citations in your paper.

CHAPTER 12

Your teacher may ask you to include a **bibliography** or a list of works consulted. These lists of sources include all of the sources that you used to research your subject, regardless of whether you cited them in the research report. Your teacher may also ask you to separate primary and secondary sources on your works-cited page or bibliography. Entries would then be alphabetized within each section. Primary sources might include statistics; autobiographies or interviews; historical documents such as letters, diaries, speeches, photographs, or newspaper articles; or works of literature or art. Secondary sources include books and articles written by experts who have analyzed a particular subject. Consult one of the style manuals for correct citation forms.

Apply the following rules when you write titles in your research report.

Capitalization and Punctuation of Titles

- Capitalize the first word, the last word, and all important words in the titles of books, newspapers, magazines, online references and sources, stories, poems, movies, plays, and other works of art. In Turabian reference-list style only the first word and proper names are capitalized in most titles.
- Italicize the titles of long written or musical works that are published as a single unit—such as books, newspapers, magazines, full-length plays, and long poems—as well as the names of Web sites and online databases.
- Use quotation marks to enclose the titles of chapters, articles, stories, one-act plays, short poems, songs, pages in Web sites, and entries in encyclopedia references either in print or online. Turabian reference-list style does not use quotation marks.

Titles “Cultural Differences within a Country” is an article in the magazine *Learning about Peoples and Cultures*.

PROJECT PREP Drafting *Citations*

Prepare the works-cited list for your research report. Alphabetize the entries and follow a format on pages 456–457. If necessary, distinguish between primary and secondary sources. Then refer to page 453 to put your citations in the correct form. Refer to the *MLA Handbook for Writers of Research Papers* or another manual for sources not included here.

In the Media

Media Purposes

By now you have enough experience researching to have a good idea of which reference materials are sources of reliable, accurate information, especially in your library or media center. You have learned to ask the critical questions: "Who wrote this, why, and when? Is the article's main purpose to inform, to entertain, or to advertise? Does the author have any biases or associations that might taint his or her reliability?"

The same questions apply when evaluating a piece in the visual media. If you are careful to distinguish the purpose behind the presentation, you will not mistake fact for hype.

Evaluating information sources on the Internet, both print and visual, is a special challenge. Unlike encyclopedia publishers, for example, people who publish materials on the Internet do not necessarily have a publishing reputation to protect. In fact, their business might be trying to sell another product, and the "information" they publish on the Internet might be just a fancy advertisement for their product, rather than a rigorous, fact-based study. Many articles on the Internet are written by people who provide little information about themselves and about their reasons for writing. They may, in fact, be experts, but there are no credentials listed to verify their professional expertise. For a very good overview of how to identify writing purposes and sift through the 50 million Web pages available to you for research, visit this page hosted by University of California Berkeley: http://www.lib.berkeley.edu/TeachingLib/Guides/Internet/Evaluate.html.

Media Activity

Find what you believe to be a high-quality Web site on the subject of your research report or a related subject. Then write an evaluation of the graphics and text using the criteria outlined on the Berkeley site. Did your site hold up to scrutiny?

Writing a Research Report *Revising*

Once you have completed a draft of your research report, step back and take a critical look at your creation. Have you achieved the purpose of your research paper? Then ask yourself: Does the report inform or persuade the audience as fully and accurately as possible? The checklist below will help you revise your research report.

CHAPTER 12

✓ Evaluation Checklist for Revising Your Research Paper

✓ Does your introduction contain a thesis statement that makes the main point of your research report clear? (pages 436 and 441)

✓ Does the body of your research report support the thesis statement and create a cogent argument? (pages 446–447 and 451)

✓ Is your report organized to support central ideas, concepts, and themes? (pages 437–439)

✓ Is your research report long enough to address a complex topic? (page 447)

✓ Does your research report differentiate between theories and the evidence that supports them? (pages 447 and 451)

✓ Have you evaluated the strength and weakness of that evidence in developing your argument? (pages 303, 405, and 446–447)

✓ Does your analysis support and develop your personal opinions on the topic? (pages 436 and 447)

✓ Does your research report use a variety of formats and rhetorical strategies to argue for the thesis? (page 451)

✓ Does the argument in your research report address different perspectives from multiple sources and anticipate and refute counter-arguments? (pages 446–447, 451)

✓ Does your research report have unity, coherence, and emphasis? (pages 94–97 and 122)

✓ Does your conclusion add a strong ending? (page 451)

✓ Did you use and cite sources correctly? (pages 452–458)

✓ Does your research report have a title?

✓ Did you use a style manual to format written materials? (pages 453–458)

PROJECT PREP *Revising* *Strategies*

Use the checklist above to revise your research report. When you have finished making changes, exchange papers with a classmate and refer to the checklist as you review each other's work. If necessary, revise your report with your partner's comments. If appropriate, use feedback from your teacher to revise your draft further.

Your final draft should be a document that others can use as a reference. Check your work for spelling, punctuation, grammar, or usage errors that could weaken its impact.

The Language of Power Past Tense

Power Rules: Use mainstream past tense forms of regular and irregular verbs. (See pages 742–766.)

See It in Action In the first draft, the writer of the report on Atlantis wrote this:

> Perhaps the most significant evidence is that scientists now know that a volcano that erupted on Thera throwed more than twice as much pumice and cinders into the atmosphere as Krakatoa did in 1883.

When editing, the writer caught the mistake. *Throw* is an irregular verb; its past tense form is *threw,* not *throwed.* Other irregular past-tense verbs in the report include *built* (not *builded*), *swept* (not *sweeped*), and *sank* (not *sinked*).

Remember It Record this rule in the Power Rule section of your Personalized Editing Checklist. You may also want to memorize the past-tense forms of some commonly used or easily mistaken verbs.

Use It Read through your research report to make sure you have used the correct past-tense forms of verbs.

PROJECT PREP Editing *Using a Checklist and Rubric*

Check your work for grammar, usage, mechanics, and spelling. As you edit, refer to your Personalized Editing Checklist. Also refer to page 454 to check the correct placement of parenthetical citations. When you are finished, use the rubric on the following page to measure the strength of each of the six traits in your writing. Discuss your evaluation with your writing group members and ask for final feedback.

Using a Six-Trait Rubric — Research Reports

Ideas	**4** The text conveys a clear, original thesis statement with abundant supporting details drawn from reliable sources.	**3** The text conveys a thesis statement with ample details from suitable sources.	**2** The text conveys a thesis statement with some supporting details from acceptable sources.	**1** The text does not convey a thesis statement and fails to offer support from research.
Organization	**4** The organization is clear with abundant transitions.	**3** A few ideas seem out of place or transitions are missing.	**2** Many ideas seem out of place and transitions are missing.	**1** The organization is unclear and hard to follow.
Voice	**4** The voice sounds engaging and is appropriate for purpose and audience.	**3** The voice sounds natural and is appropriate for purpose and audience.	**2** The voice sounds mostly unnatural with some exceptions.	**1** The voice sounds mostly unnatural.
Word Choice	**4** Words are specific. All terms are explained or defined.	**3** Words are specific and some terms are explained or defined.	**2** Some words are overly general and some technical terms are not explained.	**1** Most words are overly general.
Sentence Fluency	**4** Varied sentences flow smoothly.	**3** Most sentences are varied and flow smoothly.	**2** Some sentences are varied but some are choppy.	**1** Sentences are not varied and are choppy.
Conventions	**4** Punctuation, usage, and spelling are correct. The Power Rules are all followed. Citations are correct.	**3** Punctuation, usage, and spelling are mainly correct and Power Rules are all followed. Citations are correct.	**2** Some punctuation, usage, and spelling are incorrect but all Power Rules are followed. Some citations are incorrect.	**1** There are many errors and at least one failure to follow a Power Rule. Most citations are incorrect or there are no citations.

The writing process is not complete until you are ready to share your work with others. There are many ways that you can publish your work, and several different media you can use to do so.

HERE'S HOW

Publishing Options for Research Reports

- Submit a copy of your report to a Web site that would be interested in the results of your research.
- Present a talk to a group that is interested in the same type of research that you have conducted.

PROJECT PREP Publishing

Make a neat and final copy of your report using a manual of style to format it. In addition to sharing your work with your teacher, you might want to share it with someone interested in your subject—either a classmate or family member.

You can learn more in the section of the book called Electronic Publishing *on pages 591–605.*

TIME OUT TO **REFLECT**

In the future, you will likely have many opportunities to use your research skills and write reports either in the workplace or as a concerned citizen. What have you learned so far? What tips do you want to remember that will help you to write reports in the future? Also, what mistakes would you like to avoid so your work will be easier next time?

Writing Lab

Project Corner

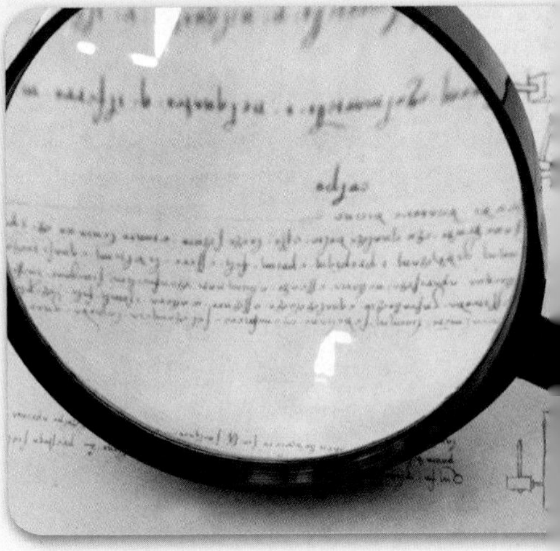

Speak and Listen
Discuss the Research Process

With your classmates, **discuss the process** of conducting research. How is research conducted in a responsible way? What shortcuts produce sloppy work? How do you evaluate someone else's research as valid and reliable? (See pages 397–433 for information on conducting research.)

Collaborate and Create Write a Summary

Work with two other students who wrote on the same topic as you did to **create a summary** of your projects. Figure out the process you will follow to complete the summary, and assign each group member a task. In the summary, use transitions to connect the various parts, and include direct quotes from each paper. (See pages 372–384 for help with summarizing.)

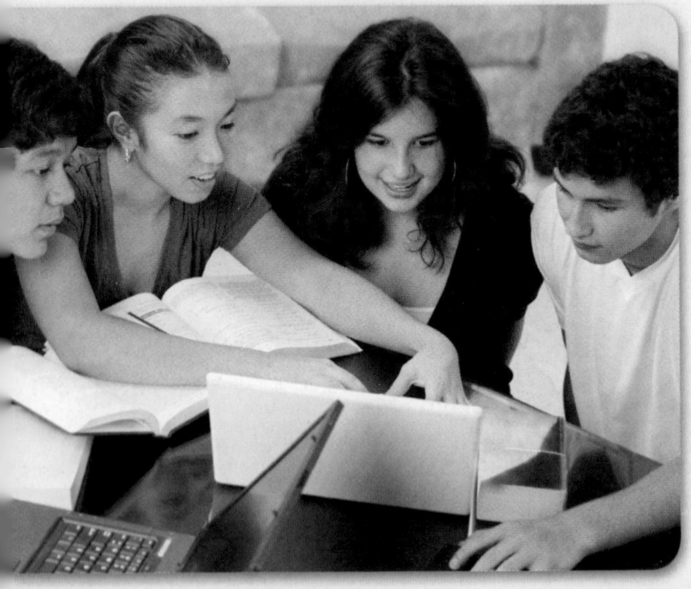

Experiment
Try a Different Form

Review the suggested project forms on page 396. Think about how your project would be different if it were in one of those forms you didn't use or another that you can think of. Choose a part of your project and **recast it in that new form.** What changes would you need to make? Write a brief paragraph explaining those changes.

In Everyday Life
Persuasive E-mail

1. Return to the information you found about summer work opportunities (see page 411). Decide whether you want to spend your summer working, volunteering, or traveling. ***Write an e-mail*** to your parents offering arguments that defend your choice. Use information from a variety of sources to develop your argument. Anticipate and refute possible counter-arguments your parents might make. Use the most appropriate rhetorical strategies to argue for your position. (See pages 533, 567, and 611–615 for more on writing e-mails.)

In the Workplace Marketing Proposal

2. Build on the information you found about gift trends for the upcoming holiday shopping season (see page 411). ***Write a proposal*** to your boss that presents your recommendations for new vendors for kiosks at the mall. Before you start to write, outline your ideas into a conceptual map using a graphic organizer. Organize your information so that it effectively supports your recommendation. Your analysis should reflect your opinion, not just restate the information you discovered in your research. Anticipate and refute possible counter-arguments your boss might make. (See pages 560–561 for more on writing proposals.)

Timed Writing Research Report

3. Return to the research you did about an event to promote school spirit safely (see page 411). Write a report to the school board that summarizes your research and recommends the most appropriate event. Use a variety of sources and determine whether the evidence you find is strong or weak as you create your argument. Organize your ideas so they systematically support your central ideas. Your report should be long enough to cover the topic effectively. Once you have your sources gathered, you have 30 minutes to complete your work. (For help budgeting time, see pages 37 and 500–501.)

   Before You Write Consider the following questions: What is the subject? What is the occasion? Who is the audience? What is the purpose?

   After You Write Evaluate your work using the Six-Trait Rubric on page 462.

Guide to 21st Century

School and Workplace Skills

Do not go where the path may lead; go instead where there is no path and leave a trail.
— *Ralph Waldo Emerson*

The challenges of the 21st century call for communication, collaboration, and leadership. The skills you learn in school will help prepare you for a rewarding adult life in a global society.

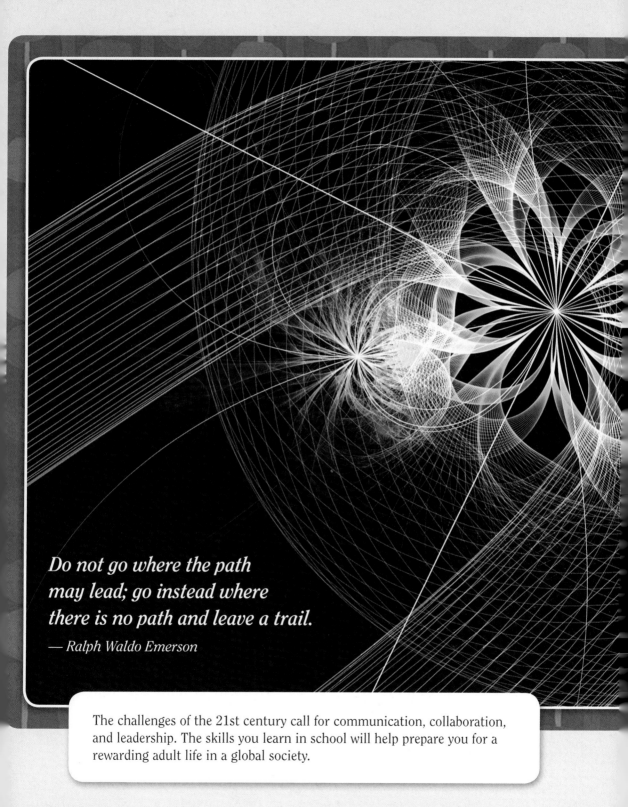

PART I

Critical Thinking and Problem Solving for Academic Success

21ST CENTURY

Part I	Critical Thinking and Problem Solving for Academic Success
Part II	Communication and Collaboration
Part III	Media and Technology

Essential Skills

In Part I of this guide, you will learn how to apply your **critical thinking** and **problem-solving skills** in order to achieve academic success. These skills will also help you succeed in the workplace.

1 Critical Thinking

Using Reasoning

Sound reasoning is essential for every task you perform in school and in the workplace. You frequently use two basic types of reasoning: deductive and inductive. When you use the **deductive** method, you start with a general concept or theory and support it with or apply it to specifics. For instance, you use deductive reasoning when you defend your thesis on an essay test. When you use the **inductive** method, you start with specifics and build to a general point. You use inductive reasoning, for example, when you draw a conclusion based on close reading. Make sure the type of reasoning you use suits the task, and always check for flaws in your logic. (See pages 294–306 and 310–313.)

Analyzing Outcomes

In your science class, you may be asked to examine how parts of an ecosystem work together. Your history class may examine the economic system, focusing on the factors that led to the global economic decline in 2009. Understanding relationships—among events, factors, or parts of a system—is essential for analyzing outcomes, both their causes and their significance. By analyzing interactions and cause-and-effect relationships, you will gain insight into how systems work.

Evaluating and Drawing Conclusions

To think critically, you must do much more than simply comprehend information. You need to analyze and evaluate evidence, claims, and different points of view. (See pages 120–121, 303, and 446.) You need to infer, interpret, make connections, and synthesize information. (See page 435.) Then you must draw conclusions. You should also reflect on your learning in order to evaluate your progress, skills, and methods. Learning how to evaluate information effectively (see pages 402-405) and draw logical conclusions will help you make sound judgments and decisions in school and in the workplace.

You can learn more about specific critical thinking skills on the following pages:

- *Comparing, page 55*
- *Making Valid Inferences, page 121*
- *Interpreting Experience, page 140*
- *Observing, page 173*
- *Implying, page 201*
- *Constructing Analogies, page 243*
- *Evaluating Evidence and Sources, page 303*
- *Making Inferences, page 338*
- *Making Evaluations, page 381*
- *Evaluating Sources for Accuracy, page 405*
- *Anticipating and Refuting Counter-Arguments, page 446*

2 Developing Solutions

Solving Problems

Your critical thinking skills—using sound reasoning, analyzing outcomes, evaluating and drawing conclusions—will help you solve problems effectively. Faced with a problem on a test, for example, look for connections between it and other problems you have solved in the past to see if the solution should follow certain conventions. Use reasoning and draw conclusions to determine the correct solution. To solve complex problems, ask questions. Then synthesize and evaluate information and different viewpoints to produce strong, creative solutions. Developing and applying your problem-solving skills in school will prepare you for resolving various types of problems in the workplace.

A. Learning Study Skills

Apply Critical Thinking Skills

How can you expand your knowledge and understanding and become an independent, creative thinker? The key is to develop your critical thinking skills.

Thinking critically means thinking actively about what you read and hear. It involves asking questions, making connections, analyzing, interpreting, evaluating, and drawing conclusions. When you compare documents from different historical periods or evaluate an author's style, you are using your critical thinking skills.

Thinking critically also involves reflecting on your learning. Evaluating the methods you use to study and prepare for assignments and tests will help you identify your strengths. It will also help you determine how you can learn more effectively.

In this chapter, you will develop your study skills. Improving these skills will help you become a better critical thinker and help you succeed academically.

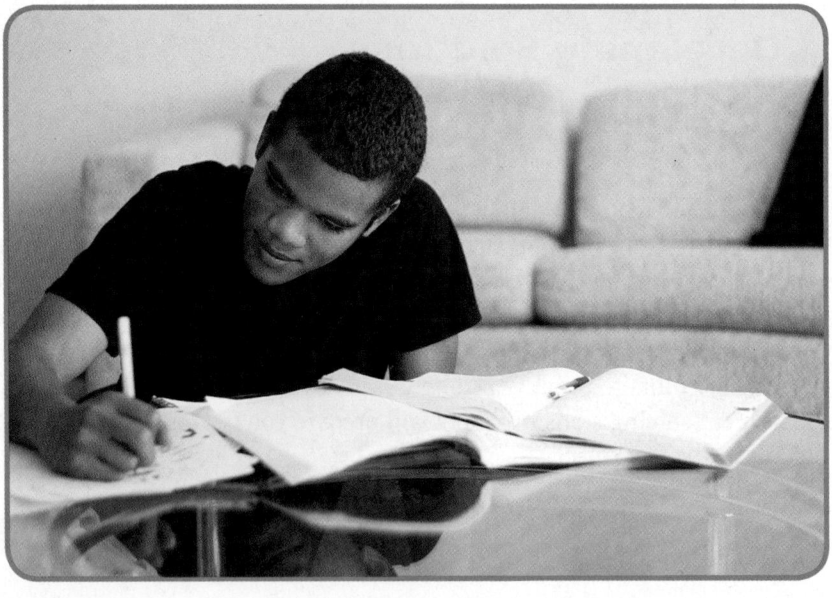

Developing Effective Study Skills

Good study habits will help you do well on all your daily classroom assignments. The following strategies will help you study more effectively.

HERE'S HOW **Strategies for Effective Studying**

- Choose a study area that is well lit and free from noise and other distractions.
- Equip your study area with everything you need for reading and writing. You can easily access a dictionary and thesaurus online, but you may want to have print versions of these resources on hand.
- Keep a journal for recording assignments and due dates.
- Allow plenty of time for studying. Begin your assignments early.

21ST CENTURY

1 Adjusting Reading Rate to Purpose

When you read, keep your purpose in mind. If you are reading a magazine or a story solely for entertainment, you may read at any rate that is comfortable and that allows you to comprehend the material. When you are reading for school assignments or preparing to take a test, however, you need to read more carefully and purposefully. The following techniques will help you match your reading rate to your purpose.

Scanning

Scanning is reading to get a general impression and to prepare for learning about a subject. To scan, read the title, headings, subheadings, picture captions, words and phrases in boldface or italics, and any focus questions to determine the topic of the reading and the questions to keep in mind.

Skimming

After scanning a chapter, section, or article, quickly skim the introduction, topic sentence and summary sentence of each paragraph, and conclusion. **Skimming** is reading quickly to identify the purpose, thesis, main ideas, and supporting details of a selection.

Close Reading

Close reading is used for locating specific information, following the logic of an argument, and for comprehending the meaning and significance of information. It is an essential step for critical thinking. After scanning a selection, you should read it more slowly and carefully. Then apply your critical thinking skills to analyze and interpret information and ideas. Be sure to evaluate points and draw conclusions in order to make judgments and decisions. Pose questions based on your close reading to help you solve problems.

Practice Your Skills

Choosing a Reading Rate

With a partner, discuss the benefits and drawbacks of skimming, scanning, and close reading. Then, for each technique, think of two specific situations when you would use it. Present your examples to the rest of the class. Be sure to explain why the particular technique would be effective in the given situation.

2 Taking Notes

Note taking is an important skill for helping you remember what you read in a textbook or hear in a class. It will also prepare you to engage in critical thinking. Focusing on and recording key information will help you to make connections, evaluate points, and draw conclusions. Three methods for taking notes are the informal outline, the graphic organizer, and the summary.

In an **informal outline,** you use words and phrases to record main ideas and important details. When you study for an objective test, an informal outline will help you easily see important facts and details.

In a **graphic organizer,** words and phrases are arranged in a visual pattern to indicate the relationships between main ideas and supporting details. This is an excellent tool for studying information for an objective test, for preparing an open-ended assessment, or for writing an essay. The visual organizer allows you to see important information and its relationship to other ideas instantly.

In a **summary,** you use sentences to express important ideas in your own words. Summaries are useful in preparing for an essay test because you must think about the information, see relationships among ideas, and state conclusions.

In the following passage from a textbook, the essential information is underlined. Following the passage are examples of notes in the form of an informal outline, a graphic organizer, and a summary.

MODEL: Essential Information

Computer Printers

The laser printer and the ink jet printer are the most commonly used non-impact computer printers. The choice between them depends on the kind of output one needs and the amount one can afford to spend on a printer.

Laser printers output a full page at a time by using a laser—hence, the name—and the electrophotographic method. Laser printers offer features like color printing, collating, stapling, and three-hole punching. While the higher quality laser printers, generally used by businesses, can cost more than $300,000, the lower quality printers, designed for home use, cost under $300.

Ink jet printers—the best-selling printers on the market—drop ink onto the page by using either the continuous ink method or the drop-on-demand method. The continuous ink method is the earlier technique and is quickly being replaced by the more effective drop-on-demand method. Ink jet printers are lower in cost—ranging in price from $400 to $3,000—than laser printers and more commonly used. However, the quality of both the color and the text resolution of ink jet printers is lower.

Informal Outline

A. Computer Printers

Non-impact printers

1. Laser printers
    - a. Print a page at a time using a laser
    - b. Special features
    - c. High quality for business use—expensive
    - d. Lower quality for home use—inexpensive
2. Ink jet printers
    - a. Drop ink on the page
    - b. Lower quality
    - c. Less expensive
    - d. More popular

21ST CENTURY

Graphic Organizer

Computer Printers

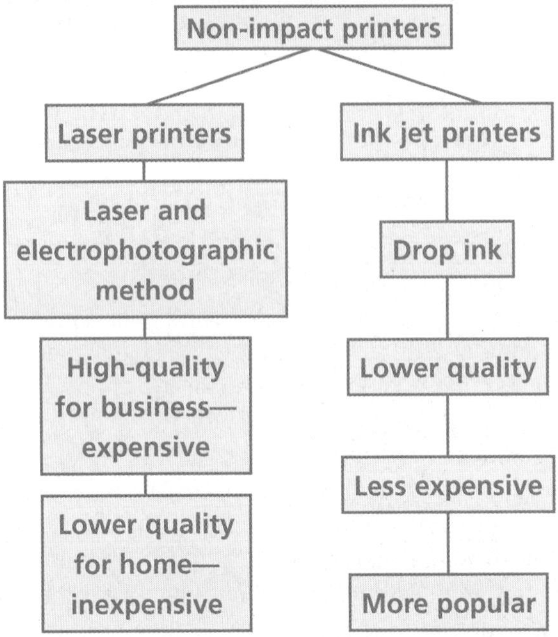

Summary

Computer Printers

Laser printers and ink jet printers are both non-impact printers. Laser printers use a laser and offer high-quality printing and features convenient for businesses. Laser printers can be extremely expensive.

Ink jet printers use ink and print at a lower quality than laser printers. Ink jet printers are more affordable and more popular than laser printers.

The following guidelines will help you take well-organized notes.

HERE'S HOW **Strategies for Taking Notes**

- Label your notes with the title and page numbers of the chapter or section or with the topic and date of the class.
- Record only the main ideas and important details.
- Use the titles, headings, subheadings, and words in special type or color to help you select the most important information.
- Use your own words; do not copy word for word.
- Use as few words as possible.

Informal Outline

- Use words and phrases.
- Use main ideas for headings.
- List any supporting details under each heading.

Graphic Organizer

- Draw a visual.
- Use words and phrases.
- Include main ideas.
- Show relationships among ideas.

Summary

- Write complete sentences, using your own words.
- Show the relationships among ideas, being careful to use only the facts stated in the textbook or in the class.
- Include only essential information.
- Organize ideas logically.

Practice Your Skills

Taking Notes

Form a small group with three to five classmates. Choose one reading assignment for a class that you all take. On your own, you and the other members should each decide what form of note taking to use and then take notes on the reading. As a group, compare your notes and discuss the choices you made. Did you use the same form of notes? Did you record similar or different information? Write a paragraph in which you reflect on what you learned about note-taking from this activity.

3 Preparing Subject-Area Assignments

The strategies you have learned for reading textbooks and reference books and taking notes can be applied to assignments in any subject area.

Mathematics and science textbooks often list rules, formulas, equations, or models. Many of your assignments in math and science will require you to apply these rules or models to solve particular problems—that is, to use your analytical and computational skills along with sound reasoning and problem-solving strategies.

History, government, and economics classes may emphasize analyzing and interpreting maps, charts, graphs, chronologies, time lines, documents, and statistical data. In preparing for assignments or tests in these subjects, you should pay special attention to information provided in these formats. Remember to use your critical thinking skills to analyze outcomes and understand how systems work. Analyze and connect the information presented in different formats and draw conclusions based on this information.

Use the following tips to help you study and prepare assignments.

HERE'S HOW

Tips for Preparing Subject-Area Assignments

- Carefully read all directions before beginning any assignment.
- Adjust your reading rate to suit your purpose.
- Take notes on your reading as well as in your classes. If you can write in your copy of the reading material, use the technique of highlighting to help you identify and remember important information.
- Be organized. For example, in a notebook, keep together your reading notes and class notes on the same topic. Label your notes with the date, pages, and subject of the assignment or the date and the class or teacher.
- For review purposes, keep a separate list of vocabulary words, key terms and concepts, and rules and equations.
- Keep a running list of questions that arise as you read, listen, or review. Seek answers promptly. If there is anything you do not understand, get help.
- Participate in study groups to prepare long-term assignments or to review for tests.
- In preparing for tests, leave ample time for studying. Focus on anticipating and answering questions that might appear on the test.
- Practice applying what you have learned. Also practice using the specialized learning aids and skills for a subject area.

B. Taking Standardized Tests

Applying Your Critical Thinking and Problem-Solving Skills

Applying your critical thinking skills is essential for success. Standardized test questions, such as analogies, require you to use reasoning to arrive at the correct answer. Other types, such as reading comprehension questions, ask you to analyze, infer, interpret, make connections, and draw conclusions. An essay test may ask you to evaluate ideas and give your opinion about a subject.

All types of test questions demand that you use problem-solving skills. You must determine what a question is asking and how you should arrive at the correct answer. You should decide if a particular question is a familiar type and therefore if the answer should match certain conventions.

Learning to apply your critical thinking and problem-solving skills effectively will help you not only when taking tests but also when completing your daily classroom assignments. It will also prove essential in areas beyond the classroom—in all aspects of your daily life and career.

This section will help you succeed on standardized tests. It will help you become familiar with the kinds of questions you will encounter. Learning test-taking strategies will help you become a better test taker as well.

Strategies for Taking Standardized Tests

Standardized tests measure your skills, progress, and achievement in such a way that the results can be compared with those of other students in the same grade. Standardized tests that measure your verbal or language skills are divided into two broad categories: analogy tests and tests of reading and writing ability. Your best preparation for any standardized test is to work conscientiously in all your school courses, to read widely, and to learn test-taking strategies.

HERE'S HOW

Strategies for Taking Standardized Tests

- Relax. Concentrate on doing the best you can.
- Read the test questions carefully. Take time to answer sample questions at the beginning of the test to be sure you understand what the test requires.
- Preview the whole test by quickly skimming it. This quick look will give you an overview of the kinds of questions you will be asked and will help you plan your time.
- Plan your time carefully, allotting a certain amount of time for each part of the test. Pace yourself so that you complete sections within the given time frame.
- Answer first the questions you find easiest. Skip those you find hard, and come back to them if you have time.
- Read all choices before you answer. If you are not sure of the answer, eliminate choices that are obviously wrong. Making an educated guess is usually wise, but check the test directions to find out if you will be penalized for guessing. If so, determine when an educated guess is helpful.
- If you have time, check your answers. Look for omissions and careless errors on your answer sheet.

1 Analogies

Analogy questions test your skill at figuring out relationships between words. To complete an analogy, you need to use reasoning. The first step is to determine how the two words in the first pair are related. (These words usually appear in capital letters.) The next step is to find the pair of words among the choices with the same relationship.

The colon (:) in an analogy question stands for *is to*; the double-colon (::) stands for *as*. The analogy HAMMER : CARPENTER :: rolling pin : baker would read as follows: a *hammer* **is to** a *carpenter* **as** a *rolling pin* **is to** a *baker*. A hammer is a tool that a carpenter uses; a rolling pin is a tool that a baker uses.

In the following example, try to make a sentence that explains the relationship between the two words in capital letters. You might say, "a tree is part of a forest." Then choose the correct answer.

TREE : FOREST ::

(A) common : unusual (B) page : book

(C) halibut : fish (D) flood : destruction

(E) flower : petal

(The answer is *(B) page : book.* It is the only choice among those given that contains a part-to-whole relationship.)

In the analogy TREE : FOREST, the relationship of the two words is part-to-whole. A tree is a part of a forest (the whole). The order of the words must be the same in the answer as in the given pair. If the given pair is in a cause-to-effect order, the words in the answer must also be in a cause-to-effect order.

Knowing some of the common types of analogies, such as those in the following chart, will help you figure out word relationships. In the first step for completing an analogy, determining whether the relationship between the words is one of the familiar, conventional types will make it easier to select the correct answer.

COMMON TYPES OF ANALOGIES

Analogy	Example
word : synonym	legal : lawful
word : antonym	ruthless : merciful
part : whole	carburetor : engine
cause : effect	overproduction : glut
worker : tool	electrician : pliers
worker : product	playwright : drama
item : purpose	fence : enclose
item : category	lobster : crustacean

Practice Your Skills

Recognizing Analogies

Using the chart above, write the relationship of the words in each pair in capital letters. Then write the letter of the word pair that has the same relationship.

1. CHEF : OVEN ::
(A) drill : dentist
(B) patient : doctor
(C) job : typist
(D) potter : kiln
(E) pump : gasoline

2. FARMER : CROPS ::
(A) wet : rain
(B) tent : camper
(C) bus : driver
(D) metal : welder
(E) contractor : building

3. BALLAD : SONG ::
(A) haiku : poem
(B) scene : drama
(C) flight : bird
(D) desert : dry
(E) novel : plot

4. HARD DRIVE : COMPUTER ::

(A) brake : bike
(B) arm : hand
(C) cup : saucer
(D) parrot : mimic
(E) leather : wallet

5. RIVALRY : COMPETITION ::

(A) mystery : clue
(B) secret : covert
(C) victory : team
(D) general : specific
(E) glittering : gem

21ST CENTURY

Practice Your Skills

Recognizing Analogies

Use the chart on page 479 to determine the relationship of the first set of words in italics. Then complete the analogy by writing the letter of the word that best completes the sentence.

1. *Writer* is to *pencil* as *carpenter* is to ▒.

(A) construction
(B) hammer
(C) electricity
(D) house
(E) wrecker

2. *Generous* is to *miserly* as *trustworthy* is to ▒.

(A) uncomfortable
(B) boring
(C) ridiculous
(D) serious
(E) undependable

3. *Hull* is to *ship* as *chassis* is to ▒.

(A) automobile
(B) wheel
(C) accelerator
(D) framework
(E) building

4. *Consensus* is to *agreement* as *narrative* is to ▒.

(A) argument
(B) story
(C) bookbinding
(D) patriotism
(E) athletics

5. *Painter* is to *art* as *journalist* is to ▒.

(A) typewriter
(B) press box
(C) news
(D) steel
(E) columnist

2 Sentence-Completion Tests

Sentence-completion tests measure your ability to comprehend what you read and to use context correctly. Each item consists of a sentence with one or more words missing. First read the entire sentence. Then read the answer choices. Use logical reasoning to select the answer that completes the sentence in a way that makes sense.

The two state representatives have little in common either personally or politically; they are about as ___ as two officeholders can be.

(A) dissimilar
(B) far-fetched
(C) moderate
(D) philosophical
(E) commendable

(The answer is *(A) dissimilar*. The key words that provide a clue to the answer are *little in common*. The other choices do not make sense in the context of the sentence.)

Some sentence-completion questions have two blanks in the same sentence, with each answer choice listing two words. Find the correct answer in this example.

After the ___ of a strong rally late in the ball game, we were doubly ___ that our team had lost.

(A) lack . . . surprised
(B) threat . . . amused
(C) dispute . . . annoyed
(D) excitement . . . disappointed
(E) skill . . . doubtful

(The answer is (D) excitement . . . disappointed. The key words that help you determine the answer are *strong, rally*, and *lost*. *(A) lack . . . surprised* would make sense only if the team had won. In *(B) threat . . . amused,* the word *threat* seems reasonable, but the word *amused* does not make sense in the context. In *(C) dispute . . . annoyed* and *(E) skill . . . doubtful,* the meanings are incorrect in the context of the sentence.)

Practice Your Skills

Completing Sentences

Write the letter of the word that best completes each of the following sentences.

1. While the history of the Aztecs can be reconstructed largely from written records, Toltec history is a curious mixture of fact and ▒.

(A) reality (B) fossil
(C) legend (D) conflict
(E) history

2. Boats returning to the harbor from open water use buoys as ▒; they must keep red—or even-numbered—buoys on the right and black—or odd-numbered—buoys on the left.

(A) sails (B) anchors
(C) targets (D) guides
(E) docks

3. Preserving historical buildings often extends to the ▒ of other structures, such as covered bridges.

(A) building (B) restoration
(C) photographing (D) dilapidation
(E) purchase

4. The proliferation of computers has introduced Americans to a whole ▒ of terms to describe the new technology.

(A) word (B) printing
(C) mirage (D) perimeter
(E) array

5. Even good keyboarders may ▒ letters in certain words, such as the *he* in *the (teh)* and the *an* in *can (cna).*

(A) delete (B) repeat
(C) obscure (D) erase
(E) transpose

21ST CENTURY

Practice Your Skills

Completing Sentences with Two Blanks

Write the letter of the pair of words that best completes each of the following sentences.

1. There is nothing quite so ▒ as assembling a complicated model airplane or car and having two parts ▒ left over.
(A) humorous . . . vaguely (B) gruesome . . . simply
(C) burdensome . . . dismally (D) neat . . . cleverly
(E) frustrating . . . unaccountably

2. Across the road stood a ▒ house, its frame sagging, its shingles loose, its chimney crumbling, and its windows ▒.
(A) cheerful . . . sparkling (B) new . . . cobwebbed
(C) rambling . . . intact (D) Victorian . . . insulated
(E) deserted . . . broken

3. The last rays of the sun ▒, and darkness ▒ the land.
(A) glared . . . swallowed (B) disappeared . . . lighted
(C) faded . . . enveloped (D) sparkled . . . abandoned
(E) disengaged . . . pacified

4. Most of the ▒ cities in the United States are not state capitals, but Phoenix—among the most populous—is an ▒.
(A) larger . . . exception (B) oldest . . . original
(C) growing . . . example (D) common . . . oddity
(E) urban . . . ideal

5. Many of the most ▒ architects since the 1930s have ▒ buildings for the city of Columbus, Indiana.
(A) eager . . . built (B) moody . . . criticized
(C) imaginative . . . razed (D) renowned . . . designed
(E) argumentative . . . defended

3 Reading Comprehension Tests

Reading comprehension tests assess your ability to understand and analyze written passages. The information you need to answer the test questions may be either directly stated or implied in the passage. You must use your critical thinking skills to make inferences as you read, analyze, and interpret the passage, and then draw conclusions in order to answer the questions. The strategies on the next page will help you answer questions on reading comprehension tests.

HERE'S HOW

Strategies for Answering Reading Comprehension Questions

- Begin by skimming the questions that follow the passage so you know what to focus on as you read.
- Read the passage carefully and closely. Notice the main ideas, organization, style, and key words.
- Study all possible answers. Avoid choosing one answer the moment you think it is a reasonable choice.
- Use only the information in the passage when you answer the questions. Do not rely on your own knowledge or ideas on this kind of test.

Most reading comprehension questions focus on one or more of the following characteristics of a written passage.

- **Main Idea** At least one question will usually focus on the central idea of the passage. Remember that the main idea of a passage covers all sections of the passage—not just one section or paragraph.
- **Supporting Details** Questions about supporting details test your ability to identify the statements in the passage that back up the main idea.
- **Implied Meanings** In some passages not all information is directly stated. Some questions ask you to infer or interpret in order to answer questions about points that the author has merely implied.
- **Tone** Questions on tone require that you interpret or analyze the author's attitude toward the subject.

Practice Your Skills

Reading for Comprehension

Read the following passage. Then write the letter of the correct answer to each question.

One of the most fascinating institutions in American history was the short-lived Pony Express, established in 1860. The plan seemed brilliant at the time. A relay system of horseback riders would carry mail between Missouri and California in the breathtaking time of just 10 days. The feat required the building of 190 way stations at 10-mile intervals between St. Joseph, Missouri, and San Francisco, California. As work on the way stations progressed, 500 horses were chosen, and a group of adventurous, experienced, rough-and-ready riders was hired.

On April 3, 1860, this new, lightning-fast mail service began operation. Cheering crowds in St. Joseph and San Francisco sped the first two riders on their way. Each rider raced at full gallop for 10 miles and then thundered into a way station where another mount was saddled and waiting. The rider leaped onto the fresh horse and dashed off again. Each rider put in 70 miles of this grueling work at breakneck speed before turning his mail over to the next rider.

The Pony Express made Americans proud. It cut a full 10 days off the usual stagecoach schedule, and it was the stuff of romance. Eighty riders were always traveling, day and night, winter and summer, rain or shine, 40 of them racing east, 40 flying west.

Alas, the glory of the Pony Express exceeded its profits, and technology soon made it obsolete. Despite rates of $4 to $10 per ounce and a steady increase in letters carried, each piece of mail cost the company $38 to transport. The venture was already losing money when, on October 24, 1861, an unbeatable competitor entered the field. On that date the wires of a new transcontinental telegraph company were joined, and communication time between the coasts dropped from 10 days to a fraction of a second. Then, if not earlier, the Pony Express was doomed.

1. The best title for this passage is
(A) A Dangerous Gamble.
(B) How the Pony Express Operated.
(C) Early Communication.
(D) The Ill-fated Pony Express.
(E) Technology and the Pony Express.

2. The Pony Express failed because
   (A) its rates were too high.
   (B) the telegraph was invented.
   (C) the trip was too dangerous.
   (D) service was too slow.
   (E) operating costs and competition made it unprofitable.

3. It seems to be true that the Pony Express
   (A) made money at first but not later on.
   (B) experienced many disasters on the trail.
   (C) appealed to the Americans of that time.
   (D) might have succeeded with better management.
   (E) was an unworkable scheme because of its organization.

THE DOUBLE PASSAGE

You may also be asked to read a pair of passages and answer questions about each passage individually and about the way the two passages relate to each other. The two passages may present similar or opposing views or may complement each other in other ways. A brief introduction preceding the passages may help you anticipate the relationship between them. Questions about double passages require you to use your critical thinking skills in order to make connections and synthesize information.

Practice Your Skills

Reading for Double-Passage Comprehension

The following passages present the childhood memories of two writers, particularly of the physical environment in which each writer grew up. The first passage is by Dylan Thomas, a Welsh poet. The second is by Alfred Kazin, American critic, editor, and teacher, who grew up in a Jewish immigrant community in east Brooklyn. Read the passages and write the letter of the correct answer to each question.

Passage 1

I was born in a large Welsh town at the beginning of the Great War—an ugly, lovely town (or so it was and is to me), crawling, sprawling by a long and splendid curving shore where truant boys and sandfield boys and old men from nowhere, beachcombed, idled and paddled, watched the dockbound-ships or the ships steaming away into wonder and India, magic and China, countries bright with oranges and loud with lions; threw stones into the sea for the barking outcast dogs; made castles and forts and harbors and race tracks in the sand; and on Saturday summer afternoons listened to the brass band, watched the

Punch and Judy, or hung about on the fringes of the crowd to hear the fierce religious speakers who shouted at the sea, as though it were wicked and wrong to roll in and out like that, white-horsed and full of fishes. . . .

This sea-town was my world; outside a strange Wales, coal-pitted, mountained, river-run, full, so far as I knew, of choirs and football teams and sheep and storybook tall hats and red flannel petticoats, moved about its business which was none of mine.

Passage 2

The block: *my* block. It was on the Chester Street side of our house, between the grocery and the back wall of the old drugstore, that I was hammered into the shape of the streets. Everything beginning at Blake Avenue would always wear for me some delightful strangeness and mildness, simply because it was not my block, *the* block, where the clang of your head sounded against the pavement when you fell in a fist fight, and the rows of storelights on each side were pitiless, watching you. Anything away from the block was good: even a school you never went to, two blocks away: there were vegetable gardens in the park across the street. Returning from "New York," I would take the longest routes home from the subway, get off a station ahead of our own, only for the unexpectedness of walking through Betsy Head Park and hearing the gravel crunch under my feet as I went beyond the vegetable gardens, smelling the sweaty sweet dampness from the pool in summer and the dust on the leaves as I passed under the ailanthus trees. On the block itself everything rose up only to test me.

1. In Passage 1, the description of India and China as "bright with oranges and loud with lions" serves mainly to
(A) show a similarity to the Welsh sea town.
(B) suggest the climate of these countries.
(C) suggest the distance of these countries.
(D) provide a contrast to the Welsh sea town.
(E) contrast the wonder of India with the magic of China.

2. The style of Passage 1 is
(A) scholarly.
(B) formal.
(C) poetic.
(D) humorous.
(E) concise.

21ST CENTURY

3. In Passage 2, the author probably put "New York" in quotation marks to suggest
   (A) the importance of the big city.
   (B) sarcasm and criticism of the city.
   (C) the strangeness of Manhattan compared with his Brooklyn neighborhood.
   (D) his confusion about where he had been.
   (E) the city and not the state of the same name.

4. In Passage 2, the sensory details used to describe the author's block all contribute to a sense of
   (A) comfortable familiarity.
   (B) close-knit community life.
   (C) the immigrant experience.
   (D) hardness.
   (E) longing.

5. With which of the following statements would the authors of Passages 1 and 2 probably agree?
   (A) My own neighborhood was rich and interesting, but it felt cut off from the rest of the world.
   (B) My neighborhood was full of eccentric people and unusual activities, and I longed for the outside world.
   (C) Everything outside my neighborhood felt exotic.
   (D) My neighborhood shaped my personality and prepared me for the outside world.
   (E) My neighborhood was both lovely and ugly.

4 Tests of Standard Written English

Objective tests of Standard written English assess your knowledge of the language skills used for writing. They contain sentences with underlined words, phrases, and punctuation. The underlined parts contain errors in grammar, usage, mechanics, vocabulary, or spelling. These tests ask you to use your problem-solving skills to find the error in each sentence or to identify the best way to revise a sentence or passage.

Error Recognition

The most familiar way to test knowledge of grammar, usage, capitalization, punctuation, word choice, and spelling is through error-recognition questions. A typical test item is a sentence with five underlined choices. Four of the choices suggest possible errors in the sentence. The fifth choice states that there is no error. Read the following sentence and identify the error, if there is one.

> Thomas Jeffersons’ (A) design for (B) Monticello included the first dome to be built (C) on an American (D) house. No error (E)
>
> (The answer is *A*. The possessive form is *Jefferson’s,* not *Jeffersons’*.)

Sometimes you will find a sentence that contains no error. Be careful, however, before you choose *E (No error)* as the answer. It is easy to overlook a mistake, since common errors are the kind generally included on this type of test.

The parts of a sentence that are not underlined are presumed to be correct. You can use clues in the correct parts of the sentence to help you search for errors in the underlined parts.

Practice Your Skills

Recognizing Errors in Writing

Write the letter of the underlined word or punctuation mark that is incorrect. If the sentence contains no error, write ***E***.

(1) In the year 1835, Nathaniel Currier, (A) a lithographer, (B) begun (C) producing black-and-white (D) and colored prints. **(2)** These prints, (A) which often had sentimental, sports, (B) or humorous (C) subjects, were popular in alot (D) of homes. **(3)** James M. Ives joined the company in 1857, (A) and the firm Currier and Ives became (B) famous throughout (C) america. (D) **(4)** It offered more then (A) 7,000 pictures; several (B) were (C) hand- (D) colored. **(5)** Irregardless (A) of the unusual (B) quality, (C) small prints sold for the incredible (D) price of fifteen cents each. **(6)** By the time Ives died in 1895, (A) photographs had (B) caused Currier and Ives prints to become (C) a rareity. (D) **(7)** Within a few years, (A) in fact, the prints had become collectors’ items, (B) and prices of the unique (C) prints rose (D) rapidly.

Sentence-Correction Questions

Sentence-correction questions assess your ability to recognize appropriate phrasing. Instead of locating an error in a sentence, you must use your problem-solving skills to select the most appropriate and effective way to write the sentence.

In this kind of question, a part of the sentence is underlined. The sentence is then followed by five different ways of writing the underlined part. The first way shown, *(A)*, simply repeats the original underlined portion. The other four choices present alternative ways of writing the underlined part. The choices may differ in grammar, usage, capitalization, punctuation, or word choice. Consider all answer choices carefully. If there is an error in the original underlined portion, make sure the answer you choose solves the problem. Be sure that the answer you select does not introduce a new error and does not change the meaning of the original sentence. Look at the following example.

Tiny St. John's College in Annapolis, Maryland, is the third oldest college in the United States it was founded in 1696.

(A) States it was founded in 1696.
(B) States that was founded in 1696.
(C) States; it was founded in 1696.
(D) States, once founded in 1696.
(E) States, it was founded in 1696.

(The answer is *(C)*. As written, the sentence is a run-on. Choices *(B)* and *(D)* change the meaning of the sentence in illogical ways. Choice *(E)* does not correct the run-on.)

Practice Your Skills

Correcting Sentences

Write the letter of the best way of phrasing the underlined part of each sentence.

1. Is it true that Abraham Lincoln wrote the Gettysburg Address while riding to Gettysburg on a scrap of paper?
(A) while riding to Gettysburg on a scrap of paper?
(B) as he rode to Gettysburg on a scrap of paper?
(C) riding to Gettysburg on a train?
(D) on a scrap of paper and he rode to Gettysburg?
(E) on a scrap of paper as he rode to Gettysburg?

2. Walking though the unfamiliar park at noon, a statue of Thoreau was visible to me.
   (A) a statue of Thoreau was visible to me.
   (B) a statue of Thoreau caught my eye.
   (C) I saw a statue of Thoreau.
   (D) Thoreau's statue became visible.
   (E) my eyes caught a glimpse of a statue of Thoreau.

3. If a person wishes to leave the room, they should obtain a permission slip.
   (A) , they should obtain
   (B) he should obtain
   (C) , you should obtain
   (D) he or she should obtain
   (E) they would obtain

4. As the miner descended down into the pit, he whistled.
   (A) descended down into the pit,
   (B) ascended down into the pit,
   (C) descended into the pit,
   (D) descended down in the pit,
   (E) descended, into the pit,

5. The report that thousands of unexpected voters had cast ballots was confirmed.
   (A) had cast ballots was confirmed.
   (B) has cast ballots was confirmed.
   (C) had cast ballots were confirmed.
   (D) having cast ballots, was confirmed.
   (E) had cast ballots, was confirmed.

Revision-in-Context

Revision-in-context questions are based on a short reading and assess your reading comprehension skills, your writing skills, and your understanding of the conventions of standard written English. The questions ask you to choose the best revision of a sentence, a group of sentences, or the essay as a whole. To select the correct answer, use your critical thinking skills to evaluate the relative merits of each choice. You may also be asked to identify the writer's intention. To do so, you will need to analyze the text carefully to determine the writer's purpose.

21st Century

Practice Your Skills

Correcting Sentences

Carefully read the following passage, which is an early draft of an essay about ***The Old Man and the Sea.*** Write the letter of the correct answer to each question.

> **(1)** In Ernest Hemingway's novel *The Old Man and the Sea,* the main character is Santiago. **(2)** He endures severe physical hardships. **(3)** The hardships come mainly in his fight with the great fish. **(4)** A painful loss is also suffered by him when sharks eat most of the great fish on the long journey back to shore. **(5)** Despite the suffering and loss, however, the novel is affirmative and hopeful, stressing the power of humans to reach for greatness and to inspire greatness in others.

1. Which of the following best describes the writer's intention in sentence 5 in relation to the rest of the passage?

(A) to restate the opening sentence
(B) to present an interpretation
(C) to provide examples
(D) to summarize the paragraph
(E) to offer contradictory evidence

2. Which of the following is the best revision of the underlined portion of sentence 4?

(A) A painful loss is also suffered by Santiago
(B) A loss that is painful is also suffered by him
(C) A painful loss that is suffered by him
(D) He also suffers a painful loss
(E) He alone suffers a painful loss

3. Which of the following is the best way to combine sentences 1, 2, and 3?

(A) Santiago is the main character in *The Old Man and the Sea,* and he endures severe hardships in his fight with the great fish.

(B) Santiago, the main character in *The Old Man and the Sea,* a novel by Ernest Hemingway, fights a great fish, a severe hardship for Santiago.

(C) In Ernest Hemingway's novel *The Old Man and the Sea,* the main character, Santiago, endures severe physical hardships in his fight with the great fish.

(D) In Ernest Hemingway's novel *The Old Man and the Sea,* the main character, Santiago, enduring severe physical hardships in his fight with the great fish.

(E) Enduring severe physical hardships, Santiago in *The Old Man and the Sea* fights a great fish and is the main character.

C. Taking Essay Tests

21ST CENTURY

Apply Critical Thinking Skills

Essay tests are designed to assess both your understanding of important ideas and your critical thinking skills. You will be expected to analyze, connect, and evaluate information and draw conclusions. You may be asked to examine cause-and-effect relationships and analyze outcomes. Some questions may address problems and solutions. Regardless of the type of question you are asked, your essay should show sound reasoning. You must be able to organize your thoughts quickly and express them logically and clearly.

Doing Your Best on Essay Tests

1 Kinds of Essay Questions

Always begin an essay test by carefully reading the instructions for all the questions. Then, as you reread the instructions for your first question, look for key words.

Narrative, Descriptive, and Persuasive Prompts

Following are some sample essay prompts and strategies for responding to them.

Narrative Writing Prompt

Think of a time when you were called upon to teach something to someone else, such as taking care of equipment for your sports team or helping a younger sibling through a problem. Tell about what happened to call for your teaching, how you prepared for and did your teaching, and the outcome of the teaching for both you and your "student."

Analyze the Question The key words in this question are "tell what happened." That is your cue that you will be relating a story.

Sketch Out the Key Parts You may want to make a chart like the following to be sure that you include all the necessary parts. Refer to the question for the headings in the chart.

STORY PLANNING SKETCH	
Item	
What happened to the item	
How you decided to handle it	
The outcome	

Use What You Know About Narrative Writing Think of other narratives you have written and remember their key features: an attention-getting beginning that introduces a conflict; a plot that unfolds chronologically and often includes dialogue; a resolution to the conflict. Draft accordingly.

Save Time to Revise and Edit Read over your essay and look for any spots where adding, deleting, rearranging, or substituting would improve your essay. Edit it for correct conventions. Pay special attention to punctuation with dialogue.

Descriptive Writing Prompt

Describe the hottest day you have ever experienced. Be sure to use details that appeal to all the senses, and use figurative language to paint strong images.

Analyze the Question The key words in this question are "detailed description." The directions to use "words that appeal to the senses" is another important item. It sets forth the expectation that you will include vivid sights, sounds, smells, tastes, and feelings.

Sketch Out the Key Parts You may want to make a chart like the following to be sure that you include all the necessary parts. Refer to the question for the headings in the chart.

DESCRIPTION PLANNING SKETCH	
Identification of place	
Vivid sights	
Vivid sounds	
Vivid smells, tastes, and feelings	

Use What You Know About Descriptive Writing Call to mind the key features of descriptive writing: a main idea that represents an overall attitude toward the subject; sensory details that support that overall feeling, often organized spatially; a conclusion that reinforces the main impression of the place. Draft accordingly.

Save Time to Revise and Edit Read over your essay and look for any spots where adding, deleting, rearranging, or substituting would improve your essay. Edit it for correct conventions.

Persuasive Writing Prompt

Your class has received funding from the parents' organization to take a trip somewhere in your state. Write an essay expressing your opinion on which place would make the best destination.

Analyze the Question The key words in this question are "expressing your opinion." These words tell you that you will be writing a persuasive text to convince people that your opinion is worthwhile.

Sketch Out the Key Parts You may want to make a chart like the following to be sure that you include all the necessary parts. Refer to the question for the headings in the chart.

PERSUASIVE PLANNING SKETCH	
Your choice of place	
Reason #1	
Reason #2	
Reason #3	
Why other choices aren't as good	

Use What You Know About Persuasive Writing Call to mind the key features of persuasive writing: a main idea that expresses an opinion; facts, examples, reasons, and other supporting details arranged in logical order, often order of importance; a look at why other opinions are not as sound; a conclusion that reinforces your opinion.

Save Time to Revise and Edit Read over your essay and look for any spots where adding, deleting, rearranging, or substituting would improve your essay. Edit it for correct conventions.

Expository Writing Prompts

Most of the essay tests you will take will probably ask you to address an expository writing prompt. Look for the key words listed in the chart on the next page.

KINDS OF ESSAY QUESTIONS	
Analyze	Separate into parts and examine each part.
Compare	Point out similarities.
Contrast	Point out differences.
Define	Clarify meaning.
Discuss	Examine in detail.
Evaluate	Give your opinion.
Explain	Tell how, what, or why.
Illustrate	Give examples.
Summarize	Briefly review main points.
Trace	Show development or progress.

As you read the instructions, jot down everything that is required in your answer. Circle key words and underline key phrases in the instructions, as in the following example.

> As the nineteenth century drew to a close, the main railroad lines and the five great transcontinental lines were completed, and branch lines were built to connect them. Analyze three ways in which this great expanse of railroad lines drastically changed American life. Give specific examples to support your points.

Practice Your Skills

Interpreting Essay Test Questions

Write the key word(s) in each essay question. Then write one sentence that explains what the question asks you to do.

Example	Trace the development of a glacier.
Possible Answer	Trace—Show the development of a glacier by describing, in order, each stage in its formation.

1. Summarize the plot of William Faulkner's short story "The Bear."

2. How does the appearance of a reptile egg compare with that of an amphibian egg?

3. From your study of literature, explain and illustrate one of the following: a simile, a metaphor, or personification.

4. Abraham Lincoln wrote, "Human action can be modified to some extent, but human nature cannot be changed." Do you agree? Discuss his idea.

2 Writing an Effective Essay Answer

Prewriting

Because of the limited time in a test situation, you must carefully plan your essay before you write a single word. You should first brainstorm for ideas. Then decide what type of reasoning and organization would be most appropriate. For example, you may want to use deductive reasoning when providing analysis in support of your thesis. You may decide to use developmental order to present your ideas or to arrange them in the order of importance. To help you organize your answer, create an informal outline or a graphic organizer. This plan will give structure to your essay and help you avoid omitting important points.

21ST CENTURY

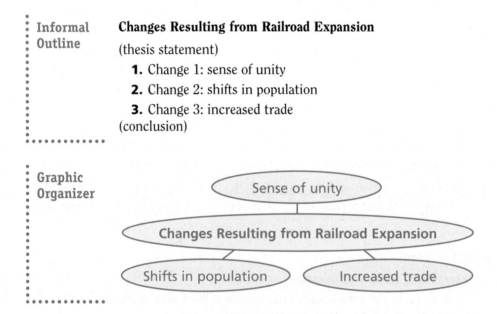

Informal Outline

Changes Resulting from Railroad Expansion

(thesis statement)

1. Change 1: sense of unity
2. Change 2: shifts in population
3. Change 3: increased trade

(conclusion)

Graphic Organizer

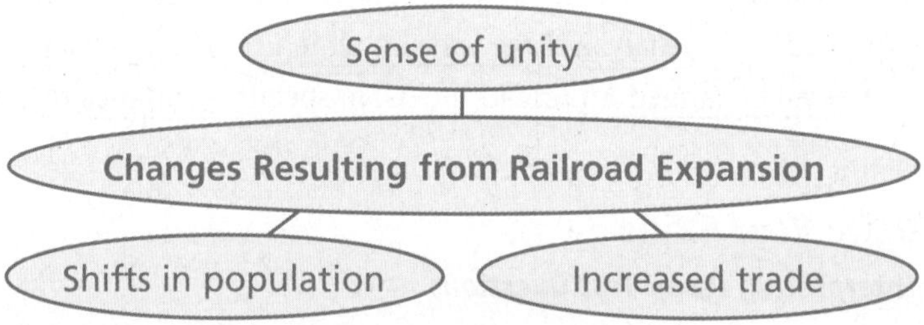

Your next step is to write a thesis statement that expresses the main idea of your essay and covers all of your supporting ideas. It is often possible to reword the test question to create a thesis statement.

Essay Question

As the nineteenth century drew to a close, the main railroad lines and the five great trans-continental lines were completed, and branch lines were built to connect them. Analyze three ways in which this great expanse of railroad lines drastically changed American life. Give specific examples to support each of your points.

Thesis Statement

The completion of the railroad system drastically changed American life by bringing unity, mobility, and increased trade to American society.

DRAFTING

As you write your essay answer, use the following strategies.

HERE'S HOW **Strategies for Writing an Essay Answer**

- Write an introduction that includes a thesis statement.
- Follow the order of your outline, writing one paragraph for each main point.
- Provide adequate support for each main point by using specific facts, examples, and/or other supporting details.
- Use transitions to connect your ideas and examples.
- End with a strong concluding statement that summarizes your main ideas.
- Write clearly and legibly.

21ST CENTURY

MODEL: Essay Test Answer

By the end of the nineteenth century, railroad lines connected all of the United States for the first time. The completion of the railroad system drastically changed American life by bringing unity, mobility, and increased trade to American society.

Thesis Statement

Being linked by the railroad, people all across the country began to get a new feeling, a feeling of unity. The railroad made fellow Americans of a silversmith in New England and a farmer in Florida and united a family in Indiana with a family in Vermont.

The railroads also began to move people from one place to another. For the first time, the United States became a mobile society. People everywhere enjoyed a new sense of freedom as they traveled from the outskirts of civilization to large, populated cities. Others, looking for land at bargain prices, filled the trains as they headed for the less populated states.

In addition to moving people, railroads also began to move everything from fuel to food. People in New York found themselves eating fresh beef from Chicago and ripe fruits from California. As a result, companies employing many people sprang up across the United States in order to buy products in one place and sell them in another.

The great metal arms of the railroad reached across America and pulled people together in such a way that they would never be the same again.

Concluding Statement

Revising

Always leave a few minutes to revise your essay answer. As you revise, consider the following questions.

Checklist for Revising an Essay Answer

- ✓ Did you thoroughly follow the instructions?
- ✓ Did you begin with a thesis statement?
- ✓ Did you include facts, examples, and/or other supporting details?
- ✓ Did you use transitions to connect ideas and examples?
- ✓ Did you end with a strong concluding statement that summarized your essay?
- ✓ Did you stick to the topic?

Editing

Once you have made any necessary revisions, quickly read your essay to check for mistakes in spelling, usage, or punctuation. To keep your paper as neat as possible, use proofreading symbols to make any corrections. As you edit, check for the following:

Check your work for:

- ✓ agreement between subjects and verbs (pages 814–839)
- ✓ agreement of antecedent and indefinite pronouns (pages 801–805)
- ✓ avoidance of tense shift (pages 753–766)
- ✓ correct capitalization of proper nouns and proper adjectives (pages 895–904)
- ✓ correct use of apostrophes (pages 944–954)
- ✓ correct division of words at the end of lines (pages 979–980)

3 Timed Writing

To help you feel confident and well prepared when you take an essay test, you should practice writing about a given topic in a limited amount of time.

Time limits can vary from 20 to 60 to 90 minutes, depending upon the purpose and complexity of the task. You might organize your time for a 20-minute essay in the following way:

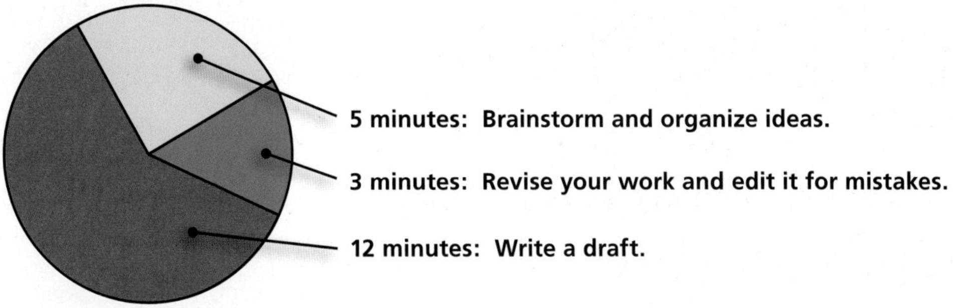
5 minutes: Brainstorm and organize ideas.
3 minutes: Revise your work and edit it for mistakes.
12 minutes: Write a draft.

HERE'S HOW

Strategies for Timed Tests

- Listen carefully to instructions. Find out if you may write notes or an outline on your paper or in the examination book.
- Find out if you should erase mistakes or cross them out by neatly drawing a line through them.
- Plan your time, keeping in mind your time limit.

The more you practice writing under time constraints, the better prepared you will be for tests. You will find timed writing prompts on all of the following pages.

	Timed Writing Prompts
Chapter 2	Memo, page 79
Chapter 3	Letter to Editor, page 129
Chapter 4	Presentation, page 157
Chapter 5	Essay to Describe and Inform, page 183
Chapter 6	Short Short Story, page 233
Chapter 7	Newsletter, page 263
Chapter 8	Persuasive Letter, page 321
Chapter 9	Grant Request, page 365
Chapter 10	Summary of a Literary Work, page 389
Chapter 11	Research Plan, page 411
Chapter 12	Research Report, page 465

Practice Your Skills

Completing a Timed Writing Assignment

You will have twenty minutes to write an essay on the following topic.

Discuss an important problem facing teenagers in your community. Explain why this problem is important and how you think it can be solved.

Plan time for each stage of the writing process, set a timer, and write your essay.

PART II

Communication and Collaboration

21ST CENTURY

Part I	Critical Thinking and Problem Solving for Academic Success
Part II	Communication and Collaboration
Part III	Media and Technology

Essential Skills

In the 21st century, you live and work in a dynamic, global community. In Part II of this guide you will learn effective communication and collaboration skills. These skills are essential for success, both in school and in the workplace.

1 Communication

The Purpose of Communication

In all areas of your life, you communicate for a variety of purposes—to inform, instruct, motivate, and persuade, for example. In school, you might motivate other students to reuse and recycle, or you might persuade them to elect you class president. At work, you might inform your boss about your research findings or instruct your colleagues on how to use new software. Having a clear purpose is essential for communicating your ideas successfully in both speech and writing.

Expressing Ideas Effectively

Regardless of the form you are using to communicate (e-mail, a speech) or the context (a group discussion, a college interview), your goal is to express your thoughts and ideas as effectively as possible. Use words precisely and correctly, and articulate your ideas in a specific, concise manner. Suit your tone to your purpose and audience. Provide valid, relevant support for your ideas, and present information in a logical order. In a speech or presentation, use nonverbal communication skills to help convey your message.

USING MEDIA AND TECHNOLOGY EFFECTIVELY

Multiple forms of media and technology now exist to help you communicate. You can e-mail, text message, or "tweet" a friend, and apply for a job online. To prepare a speech, you can look up technical terms in an online dictionary and research your subject on the Internet. You can use software to make a power presentation. To use media and technology effectively, make sure they suit the purpose and context of your communication. They should also help you make a positive impact on your audience by enhancing or facilitating your message.

LISTENING EFFECTIVELY

To listen effectively, you need to do much more than understand what words mean. Your goal is to gain knowledge and determine the speaker's purpose, values, and attitudes. Skillful listeners then evaluate and reflect on the speaker's message, views, and intentions. Listening effectively means listening actively—critically, reflectively, and appreciatively—and remembering what you have heard.

COMMUNICATING IN A DIVERSE WORLD

You probably attend school or work with people from diverse social and cultural backgrounds whose lifestyle, religion, and first language may be different from your own. To communicate effectively in these environments, listen actively in order to understand different traditions, values, and perspectives. Be sure to respect these differences when you express your thoughts and ideas.

2 Collaboration

Respecting Diversity

In school and in the workplace, you often collaborate with others on diverse teams. Open-mindedness is essential for being an effective team member. Make sure that all team members have an equal opportunity to be heard, and respect and value differences. By doing so, you will help create an environment in which ideas and opinions are freely shared. As a result, team members will benefit from each other's expertise, and you will produce sound, creative solutions.

Achieving a Common Goal

As a member of a team, you need to cooperate. Often, you may need to resolve conflicting opinions in order to achieve a common goal, whether it is completing a particular task or reaching a decision. Remember to maintain a positive attitude and put the group's needs before your own. Appreciate the merits of diverse viewpoints, and help the group work toward a compromise that all members can accept. Flexibility and openness are essential for successful collaboration.

Sharing Responsibility

For true collaboration to take place, all team members must do their fair share. Complete your assigned tasks, come to meetings prepared, and remain actively engaged in the team's work. Respect the skills, expertise, and efforts of other team members, and provide constructive feedback as necessary. A sense of shared responsibility will lead to a successful collaborative process.

A. Vocabulary

Apply Communication Skills

The study of English is the study of words. Whether you are writing an essay, reading Shakespeare's *Macbeth*, or carrying on a conversation, you are dealing with words. It is obvious that the more words you know, the more likely you are to write well and express yourself clearly; however, consider some of the other benefits of having a large vocabulary: many studies have shown that possessing an extensive vocabulary is important to achieving success on standardized tests, in college, and in the workplace.

In this chapter you will see how English developed into a language that is rich and varied. You will also learn strategies for expanding your storehouse of words. Developing your vocabulary will help you become a more effective communicator and a more skillful reader and listener in school and in the workplace.

Understanding the Development of the English Language

1 English in the Past

Old English

Throughout the world more than 300 million people speak English as their native language. English is the national language of the United States, the British Isles, Canada, Australia, New Zealand, and many countries in Southern Africa. The language that all of these people speak today began more than 1,500 years ago, in about A.D. 450.

It was about that time that England was invaded by three Germanic tribes—the Angles, the Saxons, and the Jutes. Coming from the shores of the North Sea, these warring tribes conquered the Celts, who occupied England. The invading Germanic tribes, known as the Anglo-Saxons, settled on the land, and their leaders soon discarded the Celtic and Roman cultures and languages that they found there.

Instead, they spoke their own language—Old English. As you probably discovered if you've read parts of *Beowulf,* Old English is like a foreign language to English speakers today. Even though very little has survived from Old English, this early language provided modern English with such common words as *wife, child, house, meat, eat, sleep,* and *fight*. In addition, Old English supplied most of our modern English pronouns: the articles *a, an,* and *the*; and prepositions such as *in, out, at, by,* and *under.*

Middle English

In 1066, a pivotal event in English history occurred when William of Normandy—better known as William the Conqueror—invaded England, defeated the Anglo-Saxon army, and became the ruler of England. William had been raised in an area that is now northwest France; therefore he declared French the official language of England.

Despite William's declaration, the common people of England continued to speak English. Many French words, particularly words from law and government, made their way into the English language. These words include *accuse, jail, judge, state,* and *treaty*. Gradually Old English and Latin combined with French, resulting in the language we now call Middle English.

In 1362, the English parliament, which had conducted its business in French for three centuries, began to use Middle English. Around the same time, the famous writer Geoffrey Chaucer began writing poems in Middle English. The theologian John Wycliffe translated the Latin Bible into English, and a century later William Caxton began printing books in English. These major developments permanently secured the future of the English language.

As clearly as you can, read aloud this passage from "The General Prologue" of Geoffrey Chaucer's classic, written in Middle English, *The Canterbury Tales.*

MODEL: Middle English

Here bygynneth the Book of the Tales of Caunterbury.
Whan that Aprille with his shoures soote
The droghte of March hath perced to the roote,
And bathed every veyne in swich licour
Of which vertu engendred is the flour;
Whan Zephirus eek with his sweete breeth
Inspired hath in every holt and heeth
The tendre croppes, and the yonge sonne
Hath in the Ram his halve cours yronne,
And smale foweles maken melodye,
That slepen al the nyght with open ye
(So priketh hem nature in hir corages);
Thanne longen folk to goon on pilgrimages,
And palmeres for to seken straunge strondes,
To ferne halwes, kowthe in sondry londes;
And specially from every shires ende
Of Engelond to Caunterbury they wende,
The hooly blisful martir for to seke,
That hem hath holpen whan that they were seeke.

—Geoffrey Chaucer, *The Canterbury Tales*

Here is the same passage in a recent translation.

MODEL: Modern Translation

Here begins the Book of the Tales of Canterbury.
When April with his showers sweet with fruit
The drought of March has pierced unto the root
And bathed each vein with liquor that has power
To generate therein and sire the flower;
When Zephyr also has, with his sweet breath,
Quickened again, in every holt and heath,
The tender shoots and buds, and the young sun
Into the Ram one half his course has run,
And many little birds make melody

That sleep through all the night with open eye
(So Nature pricks them on to ramp and rage)—
Then do folk long to go on pilgrimage,
And palmers to go seeking out strange strands,
To distant shrines well known in sundry lands.
And specially from every shire's end
Of England they to Canterbury wend,
The holy blessed martyr there to seek
Who helped them when they lay so ill and weak.

Practice Your Skills

Analyzing Language

With a partner, describe the differences you discover in the two passages from *The Canterbury Tales*. Be specific, citing particular words and phrases as examples. Describe also the similarities you observe. Be aware that both examples consist of rhymed couplets that are ten syllables per line. Note, too, that the writer's attention to form helps clarify how certain words are pronounced. When it is your partner's turn to speak, listen carefully and attentively. Summarize your findings and report back to the class.

2 English in the Present and Future

Modern English

Beginning around the middle of the fifteenth century, Modern English evolved out of Middle English. For the next century, writers and scholars added many words to English from Latin. Today many Latin words, such as *educate, genius, drama,* and *vacuum*, are still part of everyday conversation. By the time Shakespeare was writing—in the last half of the sixteenth century—English was a rich, versatile language that is recognizable to today's speaker of English.

Read aloud the first scene from the play *Romeo and Juliet* by William Shakespeare, as it appeared in 1599. Compare the language with Old or Middle English, and notice how much closer this passage is to the English that you are used to speaking.

MODEL: Modern English

The Most Excellent and Lamentable Tragedie, of Romeo and Juliet

Enter Sampion and Gregorie, with Swords and Bucklers, of the houfe of Capulet.

Samp: Gregorie, on my word weele not carrie Coles.
Greg: No, for then we fhould be Collyers.
Samp: I meane, and we be in choller, weele draw.
Greg: I while you hue, draw your necke out of choller.
Samp: I ftrike quickly being moued.
Greg: But thou art not quickly moued to ftrike.
Samp: A dog of the houfe of Mountague moues me.
Greg: To moue is to ftirre, and to be valiant, is to ftand: Therfore if thou art moued thou runft away.
Samp: A dog of that houfe fhall moue me to ftand: I will take the wall of any man or maide of Mountagues.
Greg: That fhewes thee a weake flaue, for the weakeft goes to the wall.
Samp: 'Tis true, & therfore women being the weaker veffels are euer thruft to the wall: therfore I wil pufh Mountagues men from the wall, and thruft his maides to the wall.
Greg: The quarell is betweene our maifters, and vs their men.
Samp: 'Tis all one. I will fhew my felfe a tyrant, when I haue fought with the men, I will be ciuil with the maides, I will cut off their heads.

—William Shakespeare, *Romeo and Juliet*

21ST CENTURY

Practice Your Skills

Analyzing Language

With a partner, describe how this language is different from Old English and the English you speak today. What words are unfamiliar? Are there any spellings that are not what you expect? Be specific, citing particular words and phrases as needed. Support your findings with specific examples. Summarize what you discover and report your findings to the class.

American English

The English language underwent a huge change when North America was settled. Separated from Europe, settlers clung to their language while at the same time drawing on a variety of sources and influences. For example, a quick look at a map of North America reveals the tremendous influence Native American languages have had on the landscape of the United States. Geographical entities such as *Massachusetts, Manhattan, Huron, Michigan, Chicago, Minnesota,* and *Alabama* are all of Native American origin.

The following two selections come from different periods in American history. As you read, think about how the language of each selection is different, and how it is similar. The first selection is from Paul Revere's etching of the Boston Massacre. In the text to his etching, Revere offers his interpretation of the events in Boston.

MODEL: Early American English

Unhappy Boston! see thy Sons deplore
Thy hallow'd Walks besmear'd with guiltles's Gore.
While Faithlefs P—n and his savage Bands,
With murd'rous Rancour stretch their bloody Hands;
Like fierce Barbarians grinning o'er their Brey.
Approve the Carnage and enjoy the Day.
If fealding drops from Rage from Anguish Wrung
If fpoechles's Sorrows lab'ring for a Tongue.
Or if a woeping World can ought appease
The plaintive Ghosts of Victims such as these;
The Patriot's copious Tears for each are fhed,
A glorious Tribute which embalms the Dead.
But know Eatz summons to that awful Goal.
Where Justice ftrips the Murd'rer of his Soul.
Should venal C—ts the fcandal of the Land.
Snatch the relentless Villain from her Hand.
Keen Execrations on this Plate infcrib'd,
Shall reach a Judge who never can be brib'd.

—John Freely, *The Blue Guide of Boston*

The second selection was written over two hundred years later. It is a description of the events surrounding the Boston Massacre, as written in a tourist guidebook. As you read, note how much the language has changed, and also note how much it has stayed the same.

MODEL: Modern American English

[Captain Thomas] Preston formed his men into a tight arc facing the crowd, which pressed in so close to him and his men that those in front were face to face with the soldiers. Preston tried to calm and disperse the crowd, telling those nearest to him that he would not let his men harm anyone. Nevertheless, he ordered his troops to load and prime their weapons and present arms, as the crowd shouted insults at the redcoats, daring them to open fire. So matters stood for a moment, until someone in the crowd threw a stick that hit one of the soldiers, causing him to lose his balance on the icy ground and accidentally discharge his gun. This led the other soldiers to fire point-blank into the crowd, after which they reloaded and fired a second round. . . .

—John Freely, *The Blue Guide of Boston*

Practice Your Skills

Analyzing Language

Write a summary of the similarities and differences you observe between the two passages above. Be specific, citing particular words and phrases to support your findings.

WORD ALERT

The Algonquian people once inhabited eastern North America from Quebec to the Carolinas. Their presence can still be found in many common words, such as *squash, caribou, terrapin, toboggan, papoose, hominy,* and *Podunk.*

English in the Future

H. L. Mencken wrote, "But as English spreads, will it be able to maintain its present form? Probably not. But why should it?" It is impossible to know what English will be like in the future. One thing is certain: the language will change. As technology erases cultural and geographic borders, English will surely reflect the diversity of influences with which it comes in contact.

WORD ALERT

The widespread adoption of Internet communication continues to influence the English language. For example, people on social networking sites use the word *friend* as a verb, as well as the related new term *unfriend.* Wireless handheld devices have also spawned widespread adoption of shorthand, such as IMHO (in my humble opinion), F2F (face-to-face), and I 1-D-R (I wonder).

Using the Dictionary

Ever since Noah Webster published the *American Dictionary of the English Language* in 1828, the dictionary has gone through numerous changes. Dictionaries now appear in a variety of sizes and cover a wide range of subject areas.

A dictionary is used mainly to check the spelling, meaning, or pronunciation of words. Dictionaries, however, contain much more information about each word. They show how the word is correctly divided into syllables, the parts of speech, other forms of the word, the history of the word, and often synonyms and antonyms. Together, this information for each word is known as a **main entry.** The word itself is called an **entry word.** The following list shows some of the different types of entry words and how they would be listed in alphabetical order in the dictionary.

21ST CENTURY

Abbreviation	a.m.
Single Word	answer
Suffix	–ant
Prefix	anti–
Compound Word	apron string

Preferred and Variant Spellings The entry word, printed in heavy type, shows the correct spelling of the word. Some words have more than one correct spelling. The **preferred spelling** is listed first. It is followed by the less common spelling called the **variant spelling.** Always use the preferred spelling of any word in your writing.

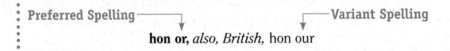

Preferred Spelling → **hon or,** *also, British,* hon our ← **Variant Spelling**

Practice Your Skills

Finding Preferred Spellings

Find each of the variant spellings in the dictionary. Then write the preferred spelling.

1. aeroplane
2. esthetic
3. copeck
4. tsar
5. practise

Division of Words into Syllables When dividing a word at the end of a line, you will need to know how the word breaks into syllables. Most dictionaries use dots or empty spaces in the entry word to show these breaks, but writers must use hyphens.

op • po • nent **pa • rab • o • la** **qual • i • fy**

Pronunciation The phonetic spelling, which directly follows the entry word, tells you how to pronounce the word. A **pronunciation key** at the front of the dictionary shows what sound each phonetic symbol stands for. Most dictionaries also place an abbreviated pronunciation key at the bottom of every other page.

To learn to pronounce a word, compare the phonetic spelling to the symbols in the key. Note that marks over vowels, called **diacritical marks,** indicate different vowel sounds. The key will tell you how to pronounce a vowel with a diacritical mark. For example, the phonetic spelling for *graduation* tells you that the *u* should be pronounced like *oo* in the word *boot.*

graj' o͞o ā' shən

Phonetic spellings also contain accent marks to show which syllables are stressed. A heavy accent mark, called a **primary stress,** indicates which syllable receives the greater emphasis. A **secondary stress** is marked with a lighter accent. This is how the word *graduation* is written phonetically, with stress marks.

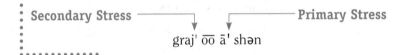

Secondary Stress → graj' o͞o ā' shən ← Primary Stress

Practice Your Skills

Using a Pronunciation Key

Use the pronunciation key below to sound out each phonetic spelling in the first column. Then write the word represented by each phonetic spelling.

1. kə–lăm' ĭ–tē
2. kăl´ sē–əm
3. kăl´ kyə–ləs
4. kən–kûr´
5. kûl´ chər
6. kûr´ tē–əs

\ă\ pat \ā\ pay \ē\ be \ĭ\ pit \û\ cut \ə\ about, item

Parts-of-Speech Labels Entries also contain one of the following abbreviations to show what part of speech a word is. The most common usage will usually be listed first.

Part-of-Speech Labels:				
	n. = noun		*v.* = verb
	pron. = pronoun		*prep.* = preposition
	adj. = adjective		*conj.* = conjunction
	adv = adverb		*interj.* = interjection

21ST CENTURY

Multiple Meanings If a word has more than one meaning, most dictionaries will list the most common meaning first. The meanings may be in historical order, however, with the oldest meaning first.

Practice Your Skills

Recognizing Multiple Meanings

Use the dictionary entry below to write the part of speech and the number of the definition that suits the use of the word *project* in each sentence.

> **proj·ect** (prŏj′ĕkt′, -ĭkt) *n.* **1.** A plan or proposal; a scheme. See Synonyms at **plan.** **2.** An undertaking requiring concerted effort: *a community cleanup project; a government-funded irrigation project.* **3.** An extensive task undertaken by a student or group of students to apply, illustrate, or supplement classroom lessons. **4.** A housing project. — **pro·ject** (prə-jĕkt′) *v.* **-ject·ed, -ject·ing, -jects.** —*tr.* **1.** To thrust outward or forward: *project one's jaw in defiance.* **2.** To throw forward; hurl: *project an arrow.* **3.** To send out into space; cast: *project a light beam.* **4.** To cause (an image) to appear on a surface: *projected the slide onto a screen.* **5.** *Mathematics.* To produce (a projection). **6.** To direct (one's voice) so as to be heard clearly at a distance. **7.** *Psychology.* To externalize and attribute (an emotion, for example) to someone or something else. **8.** To convey an impression of to an audience or to others: *a posture that projects defeat; projected a positive corporate image.* **9.** To form a plan or an intention for: *project a new business enterprise.* **10.** To calculate, estimate, or predict (something in the future), based on present data or trends: *projecting next year's expenses and income.* —*intr.* **1.** To extend forward or out; jut out: *beams that project beyond the eaves.* See Synonyms at **bulge.** **2.** To direct one's voice so as to be heard clearly at a distance. [Middle English *projecte,* from Latin *prōiectum,* projecting structure, from neuter past participle of *prōicere,* to throw out : *prō-,* forth; see PRO–[1] + *iacere,* to throw; see **yē-** in Appendix.] **—pro·ject′a·ble** *adj.*

Example The committee proposed plans for a new project.

Answer noun, 2

1. Our science project was awarded first prize at the science fair.

2. After looking over last year's budget, our class treasurer projected the expenses for next year.

3. The city's housing projects need renovation.

4. As we projected the slides on the screen, Melissa started the story.
5. The lifeguard station projects far above the water so that nothing can obstruct the view of the swimming area.

Inflected Forms and Derived Words

The dictionary shows endings, or **inflections,** that change the form of the word but not its part of speech. Verbs, for example, can be inflected with *–ed* or *–ing* to change the principal part of the verb. Adjectives can be inflected with *–er* or *–est* to show comparative and superlative degrees. Nouns have plural forms, but most dictionaries show only those plural forms that are formed irregularly.

Derived words are made by adding endings that change the part of speech of a word. For example, by adding the suffix *–ment* to the verb *resent,* the noun *resentment* is formed. Most dictionaries list derived words at the end of a main entry.

21ST CENTURY

Etymologies

A dictionary gives the **etymology,** or history, of a word. The etymology is usually explained in an entry through the use of abbreviations and symbols, or with the word *from.* The abbreviations stand for languages from which the word developed. The symbol <, or the word *from,* stands for such phrases as *derived from,* and the symbol = stands for *equivalent to.* A chart at the beginning of the dictionary lists all the abbreviations and symbols used in showing the etymology of a word. In an etymology, the most recent source of the word is listed first.

Expanding Your Vocabulary

Words are very loyal friends: once you have used a word correctly, it is yours forever. Sometimes words can appear intimidating and unapproachable, but there are several ways to befriend them. The remainder of this chapter shows you several ways to discover and remember word meanings. These methods will be invaluable to you when you speak, read, write, and take standardized tests.

1 Context Clues

The **context** of a word is the sentence, surrounding words, or situation in which the word is used. Generally the context of a word gives clues to that word's meaning rather than an outright definition.

Restatement	During the storm, travelers took a detour because the isthmus, **a narrow strip of land connecting two larger landmasses,** was flooded. (The word *isthmus* is defined within the sentence.)
Example	You may find a fossil here, perhaps **like the one in our science lab that has an imprint of a leaf.** (The word *fossil* is followed by an example that is known to readers or listeners.)
Comparison	The mayor said that tax revenues, **like personal income,** should be spent wisely. (The word *like* compares revenues to its synonym *income.*)
Contrast	Contemporary students learn more about computers **than students did a few years ago.** (A contrast is drawn between today's students [contemporary students] and students of the past.)
Parallelism	She will interrogate the suspect; I will question the witness. (The parallel structure provides a clue that *interrogate* is synonymous with *question.*)

21ST CENTURY

Practice Your Skills

Using Context Clues

Write the letter of the word or group of words closest in meaning to the underlined word. Use context clues to help you.

1. The winners of the game were exuberant, while the losers were very downcast.
(A) wealthy (B) enthusiastic (C) generous
(D) heartbroken (E) intelligent

2. Lions are carnivorous; they prey on other animals.
(A) handsome (B) trainable (C) endangered
(D) flesh-eating (E) jungle-dwelling

3. The old downtown area of the city has experienced a renaissance, a revival of the grandeur of the past.
(A) rebirth (B) catastrophe (C) new name
(D) decline (E) holiday

4. My cousin looked so <u>gaunt</u> that he reminded me of the bony Ichabod Crane in *The Legend of Sleepy Hollow.*

(A) heavyset (B) dangerous (C) thin
(D) self-confident (E) athletic

5. The decision was thoughtful and <u>judicious</u>, the kind of wise conclusion expected of the Supreme Court.

(A) grand (B) sensible (C) whimsical
(D) fast-paced (E) cruel

Practice Your Skills

Practicing Pronunciation

Use a print or online dictionary to look up the pronunciation of the words in the previous activity. Then in pairs, take turns pronouncing them. Keep practicing until you have the pronunciation just right.

2 Prefixes, Suffixes, and Roots

Many English words are made up of smaller word parts: prefixes, suffixes, and roots. You will recall that a **base word** carries the basic meaning and can stand alone as a word. It is built from the **root word.** A **prefix** is one or more syllables placed in front of the base to modify the meaning of the base word or to form a new word. A **suffix** is one or more syllables after the base word to help shape its meaning and often to determine its part of speech.

Many prefixes and suffixes come from Latin or Greek. If you know even a few roots, prefixes, and suffixes, you can increase your vocabulary. Knowing, for instance, that the root word *man* or *manu* means "hand" will help you figure out the definitions of such words as *manipulate* and *manicure*.

Using Word Parts to Determine Meanings

The following examples illustrate how the meaning of each word part contributes to the meaning of the word as a whole.

WORDS WITH LATIN ORIGINS

Word	Prefix	Root	Suffix
collinear	col– (with)	line (narrow, elongated mark)	–ar (of, relating to)
discreditable	dis– (not)	credit (worthy of belief or praise)	–able (capable of)

WORDS WITH GREEK ORIGINS			
Word	**Prefix**	**Root**	**Suffix**
hypothermia	hypo– (less)	therm (heat)	–ia (disease, condition)
sympathy	sym– (with)	path (suffering)	–y (state of)

Word parts do not usually provide the kind of exact definitions found in the dictionary; however, they do give you clues about a word's meaning. Look at the dictionary definitions below of the previous examples.

collinear	lying on or passing through the same straight line
discreditable	giving injury to one's reputation
hypothermia	subnormal body temperature
sympathy	act of sharing the feelings of another

By learning the prefixes, suffixes, and roots in the lists that follow, you will be able to determine the meaning of a number of unfamiliar words.

PREFIXES

A prefix may have more than one meaning and more than one spelling. For example, the prefix *il*– may mean "not," "in," or "into." This prefix may also be spelled *im*– (*im*mature) or *ir*– (*ir*regular), depending upon the first letter of the root word.

PREFIXES FROM LATIN		
Prefix	**Meaning**	**Example**
ab–	from, away, off	ab + normal: differing from the average or the normal
bi–	two, occurring every two	bi + monthly: occurring every two months
circum–	around	circum + spect: careful to consider all of the consequences
com–, col–, con–	with, together	com + passion: sympathy with another's distress col + lect: bringing together into one body or place
contra–	against	contra + dict: resist or oppose in argument
dis–	do the opposite	dis + engage: release from something that holds
ex–	out of, outside	ex + patriate: one who moves to a foreign country

21ST CENTURY

in–, il–, im–, ir–	not, in, into	in + human: lacking pity or mercy il + legible: not able to be read
non–	not	non + entity: something that does not exist or exists in imagination
ob–	in the way of, against	ob + noxious: offensive or very irritating
semi–	half in quantity or value	semi + annual: occurring twice a year
ultra–	beyond range or limit of	ultra + sonic: having frequency the human ear cannot hear

PREFIXES FROM GREEK

Prefix	Meaning	Example
a–, an–	not, without	a + symmetrical: lacking balanced proportions
dia–	through, across	dia + logue: conversation between two or more persons
dys–	impaired, bad	dys + function: impaired or abnormal functioning
hemi–	half	hemi + sphere: one of two half spheres
hyper–	excessively	hyper + critical: finding excessive fault with
meta–	beyond, change	meta + morphosis: change in appearance or character
para–	beside, acting as assistant	para + professional: trained aide assisting a professional
peri–	all around, surrounding	peri + scope: optical instrument for seeing around obstructed views
syn–, sym–	with, together	syn + onym: word with same or similar meaning to another word

SUFFIXES

There are two kinds of suffixes. One kind, called an **inflectional suffix** (or grammatical suffix), does not change either the essential meaning of the word or its part of speech. Instead, an inflectional suffix changes the number of nouns (*office, offices),* the form of comparison or modifiers (*simple, simpler, simplest*), and the tense of the verbs (*question, questioned, questioning*).

More important to vocabulary study, however, is the second kind of suffix. This kind, called a **derivative suffix,** changes the meaning and very often the part of speech of the word to which it is added. Consider the word *agree*.

With No Suffix	*agree*: verb
With –ment	*agreement*: noun
With –able	*agreeable*: adjective
With –ly	*agreeably*: adverb (–ly added to the *adjective* form)

As this example shows, some suffixes form nouns, some form adjectives, and some form verb forms. The only common adverb-forming suffix is *–ly*. The charts below indicate a number of suffixes and the part of speech formed by each one.

21ST CENTURY

NOUN SUFFIXES

Suffix	Meaning	Example
–ance, –ence	act, process, instance of	further + ance: act of advancing
–cy	act, state, quality	normal + cy: the state of being normal
–er	one that is, does, makes	reform + er: one that works for improvement by change
–ion	act, process, result, state	validate + ion: act or process of making legal
–ism	act, state, characteristic	colloquial + ism: the characteristic of informal conversation
–ity	quality, state, degree	objective + ity: stating of facts without distortion by emotions

ADJECTIVE SUFFIXES

Suffix	Meaning	Example
–able, –ible	capable of, fit for, tending to	perish + able: tending to spoil or decay
–ful	full of, having the quality of	event + ful: full of occurrences
–ish	characteristic of, inclined to	book + ish: inclined to rely on book learning
–less	not having, unable to act	defense + less: not having the means to protect oneself
–ous	full of, having the qualities of	advantage + ous: having superiority of position or condition
–some	characterized by action or quality	cumber + some: characterized by being unwieldy because of size and weight

VERB SUFFIXES		
Suffix	**Meaning**	**Example**
–ate	act on, cause to become	motive + ate: cause a person to act because of need or desire
–en	cause to be or have	length + en: cause to have longer dimension
–fy, –ify	make, form into, invest with	just + ify: show to be right or reasonable
–ize	become like, cause to be	crystal + ize: cause to become crystal

Roots

A root carries the basic meaning of a word; therefore, you can benefit from knowing common roots of English words. Many of these roots originally came from Latin or Greek.

A root may stand alone, as in the word *self.* A root may also be combined with a prefix (un*do*), a suffix (*free*dom), or even another root (*manuscript*). The following charts contain some common Latin and Greek roots that form the basis of many English words.

LATIN ROOTS		
Root	**Meaning**	**Examples**
–cred–	believe	credulous, credible, incredible
–fid–	faith	fidelity, confide
–frag–, –fract–	break	fragile, fragment, fracture, infraction
–grat–	thankful, pleasing	gratitude, congratulate
–mort–	death	mortuary, immortal
–omni–	all	omniscient, omnivorous
–ped–	foot	pedal, pedestrian
–port–	carry	portable, transport
–scrib–, –script–	write	scribble, inscribe, transcript, inscription
–vert–, –vers–	turn	divert, vertebra
–viv–, –vit–	live, life	vivid, revive, vitality

GREEK ROOTS		
Root	**Meaning**	**Examples**
–arch–	rule	monarch, matriarch
–bio–, –bi–	life	autobiography, biodiversity
–chron–	time	synchronize, chronology
–geo–	earth	geology, geometry
–graph–	write	graphic, photograph
–log– –logy–	speech, reason, science	prologue, logic, ecology, meteorology
–mono–	alone, single	monotonous, monosyllable
–morph–	form	amorphous, metamorphic
–ortho–	straight, correct	orthodox, orthopedic
–poly–	many	polygon, polysyllabic
–soph–	wise	philosopher, sophisticated

Practice Your Skills

Using Word Parts

Using what you have learned in this chapter, write the letter of the phrase closest in meaning to the word in capital letters.

1. OMNIPRESENT
(A) able to be carried anywhere (B) present in all places at all times
(C) ruling all

2. ADVISABLE
(A) fit to be done (B) full of suggestions
(C) having realistic stands

3. CONTROVERSY
(A) discussion of opposing views (B) expression of hostility
(C) ability to turn around in narrow places

4. SYSTEMIZE
(A) cause to be in order (B) rank in importance
(C) give rules

5. INSEPARABLE
(A) consisting of layers (B) broken into two parts
(C) not capable of being kept apart

6. MONOGRAPH

(A) written account of a single thing

(B) one handwritten name (C) unified program

7. IDEALISM

(A) state of perfection (B) act of forming standards

(C) one who seeks to make things better

8. HYPODERMAL

(A) full of energy (B) able to triumph over odds

(C) lying beneath an outer skin

Practice Your Skills

Practicing Pronunciation

Use a print or online dictionary to look up the pronunciation of the words in the previous activity. Then in pairs, take turns pronouncing them. Keep practicing until you have the pronunciation just right.

3 Synonyms and Antonyms

A thorough understanding of synonyms and antonyms is guaranteed to help you expand your vocabulary. A **synonym** is a word that has the same or nearly the same meaning as another word. An **antonym** is a word that has the opposite or nearly the opposite meaning as another word.

You may be familiar with the specialized dictionary for synonyms called a *thesaurus*. A thesaurus can be helpful in expanding your vocabulary and giving your writing variety when you find yourself repeating certain words or phrases. For further variety, use antonyms and change your sentence structure.

Practice Your Skills

Recognizing Synonyms

Decide which word is the best synonym of the word in capital letters. Check your answers in a dictionary.

1. PREMONITION

(A) payment (B) ghost (C) forewarning

(D) reward (E) greeting

2. DECREE

(A) quantity (B) loss (C) challenge

(D) order (E) joke

3. RELINQUISH
(A) release (B) conquer (C) discourage
(D) excite (E) bother

4. IMMATERIAL
(A) untidy (B) false (C) unimportant
(D) wicked (E) substantial

5. INTERVENE
(A) meddle (B) withdraw (C) contact
(D) construct (E) require

6. CONTOUR
(A) journey (B) outline (C) gathering
(D) agency (E) photograph

7. THESIS
(A) guess (B) hypothesis (C) debate
(D) example (E) definition

8. HABITAT
(A) sleep (B) custom (C) yarn
(D) promise (E) home

9. ASPHYXIATION
(A) suffocation (B) extension (C) loss
(D) delivery (E) breathing

10. ANTIDOTE
(A) poison (B) story (C) opponent
(D) cure (E) predecessor

Practice Your Skills

Using New Vocabulary

Use five of the capitalized words in the previous activity in a paragraph. Share your sentences with a partner and determine if you have used the words correctly.

Practice Your Skills

Recognizing Antonyms

Decide which word is the best antonym of the word in capital letters. Check your answers in a dictionary.

1. INTRICATE
(A) local (B) complex (C) required
(D) simple (E) flower

2. PAUPER
(A) artist (B) doctor (C) millionaire
(D) athlete (E) genius

3. RAUCOUS
(A) loud (B) entertaining (C) unusual
(D) gleaming (E) reserved

4. DISCRETION
(A) carelessness (B) caution (C) argument
(D) familiarity (E) accuracy

5. FERVENT
(A) noisy (B) inverted (C) savage
(D) unemotional (E) forgotten

6. MANDATORY
(A) mass-produced (B) critical (C) hazardous
(D) illegal (E) unnecessary

7. POSTERITY
(A) descendants (B) ancestors (C) fortune
(D) encounter (E) relatives

8. PRELUDE
(A) symphony (B) postlude (C) soprano
(D) permit (E) drama

9. LENIENT
(A) forgotten (B) casual (C) strict
(D) upright (E) sly

10. REVERENCE
(A) nonfiction (B) simplicity (C) love
(D) disrespect (E) glory

Practice Your Skills

Using New Vocabulary

Use five of the capitalized words in the previous activity in a short paragraph. Share your paragraph with a partner and determine if you have used the words correctly.

21ST CENTURY

4 Analogies

One type of standardized test question that often requires you to be able to recognize synonyms and antonyms is the analogy. **Analogy questions** ask you to identify relationships between pairs of words. The following example shows the standard format for an analogy.

LEAVE : DEPART ::

(A) inside : outside (B) house : residence

(C) smooth : rough

Start answering an analogy item by deciding how the first two words are related. In the above example, *leave* and *depart* are synonyms. Your task is to find the pair of words that have the same relationship. The answer is *B* because *house* and *residence* are also synonyms. The other two answers are incorrect because the word pairs *inside* and *outside* are antonyms, as are *smooth* and *rough*.

Practice Your Skills

Recognizing Analogies

Choose the pair of words that have the same relationship as the word pair in capital letters. Then identify the relationship as either *synonym* or *antonym.*

Example TRUST : SUSPECT ::

(A) lock : bolt (B) erupt : burst (C) distant : close

Answer (C)—antonym

1. DEVELOP : EVOLVE ::

(A) invade : withdrawal (B) pale : colorful

(C) perpetual : everlasting

2. TRANQUIL : AGITATED ::

(A) continuation : extension (B) smooth : rough

(C) depart : leave

3. FEARLESS : BRAVE ::

(A) deprive : return
(B) favorite : preference
(C) deduct : add

4. DECEIVE : FOOL ::

(A) solemn : cheerful
(B) exacting : easygoing
(C) declare : announce

5. ACQUIRE : LOSE ::

(A) partial : complete
(B) linger : stay
(C) parson : reverend

6. ENTHUSIASTIC : INDIFFERENT ::

(A) jittery : nervous
(B) promote : advance
(C) expected : unpredicted

7. TRAIT : CHARACTERISTIC ::

(A) mania : craze
(B) numbness : sensitivity
(C) disorganize : classify

8. NEGLECTED : DISREGARDED ::

(A) occupy : vacate
(B) resist : comply
(C) marvelous : wondrous

9. CONCEAL : DISCLOSE ::

(A) condemnation : forgiveness
(B) placid : quiet
(C) motivation : incentive

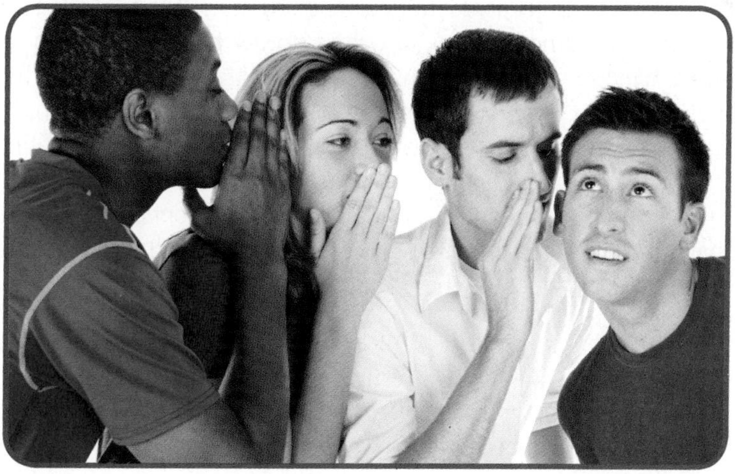

B. Communication for Careers, Business, and College

Apply 21st Century Communication Skills

As a student, a consumer, and an employee in the 21st century, you can communicate and share information in a number of ways. To communicate effectively, always have a clear purpose in mind and use technology wisely.

Real-World Communication

1 Communicating for a Purpose

Whether you are writing or speaking, communicating and sharing information can serve a variety of purposes: to inform, instruct, motivate, or persuade, for example. As a consumer, you might write an order letter to inform a company about merchandise you want to buy. As a prospective employee, you have two purposes when you interview for a job—to inform the employer about your skills and experience and to persuade the employer that you are qualified for the position. As a student applying to college, you must complete an application to inform a college about your interests, accomplishments, activities, and personal qualities. Your ultimate purpose is to persuade the school that you have the qualities to succeed there and will make a contribution to the school community.

Whether you are writing a letter or a résumé, filling out an application, or interviewing, you should always keep your purpose in mind. Your goal is to communicate in a clear, concise, focused manner because you want your audience to respond in a positive manner.

2 Using Technology to Communicate

Perhaps in the future, people in business will communicate exclusively via e-mail and other forms of electronic communication. Until that time, however, the business letter will remain an effective way to communicate. Writing a letter can be more appropriate than sending an e-mail in certain circumstances. Use these guidelines to determine whether to send a letter or an e-mail.

Send a letter in the following circumstances:

- You want to introduce yourself formally or make an impact on your audience by using impressive stationery, for example.
- You are including private, confidential information. E-mail is not a private form of communication; therefore, you should never include confidential information in an e-mail. A recipient can forward an e-mail to others without your knowledge. Also, hackers can break into e-mail systems and steal information.
- You need to have formal documentation of your communication, or you are sending authentic documents.

Send an e-mail in the following circumstances:

- You want to communicate quickly with someone.
- You want to send a message, perhaps with accompanying documents, to several people at once.
- You are instructed by a business or an organization to communicate via e-mail.

3 Characteristics of Effective Real-World Writing

Each situation and each audience requires its unique considerations when you write in everyday life, just as it does when you write in school. Effective real-world writing typically has the characteristics shown in the chart below.

CHARACTERISTICS OF EFFECTIVE EVERYDAY WRITING

- a clearly stated purpose and viewpoint supported by appropriate details
- a formatting structure that enhances readability, including the use of headings, graphics, and white space
- questions that draw readers in and that address their needs
- when necessary, accurate technical information in understandable language
- suitable and clear organizational structure with good supporting details and any necessary documentation

Strive for the above characteristics in your own writing.

Communication for Careers and Business

Whatever career you decide to pursue, a letter or résumé will often be your first opportunity to communicate information about yourself to a prospective employer. In fact, your letter or résumé may be an important factor in the employer's decision to consider you for the job. To get a favorable response from the receiver, your letter or résumé should state information clearly, purposefully, and thoroughly and should follow an appropriate format. To achieve their purpose, business letters that you write as a consumer should have these qualities as well. In this section, you will learn strategies for writing business letters for a variety of purposes. You will also learn strategies for preparing a résumé and interviewing for a job.

1 Writing Business Letters

A business letter is a formal type of communication. When you write a business letter, your goal is to present yourself in a positive, professional light. Your letter should include a clearly stated purpose, an appropriate organizational structure, and accurate information. Anticipate your reader's questions and needs, and provide relevant facts and details while excluding extraneous information. Check that your vocabulary, tone, and style are appropriate for business communication.

A business letter should be written in an appropriate, customary format that is user-friendly. A commonly used format for a business letter is called the **modified block style.** The heading, closing, and signature are positioned at the right, and the paragraphs are indented. The combination of headings and white space makes this an easy format to read.

Neatness is also essential in a business letter. Whenever possible, use a word-processing program to write your letter. Use white paper 8½ by 11 inches in size. Leave margins at least 1-inch wide.

The following model uses the modified block style. All other sample letters in this chapter use this style. The chart that follows the model explains how to write each part of a business letter.

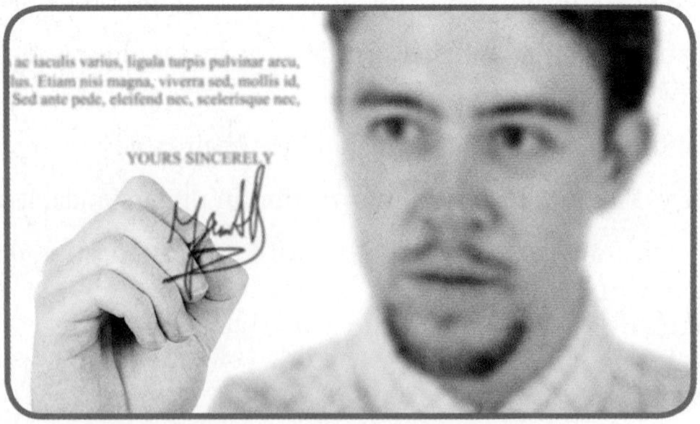

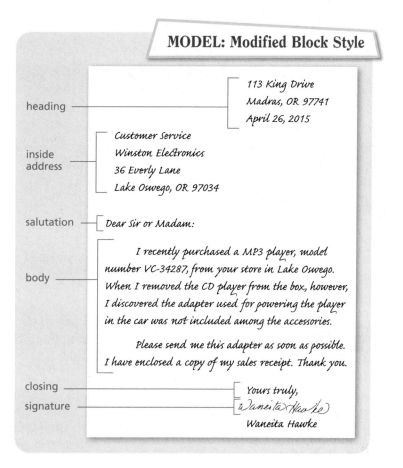

MODEL: Modified Block Style

heading — 113 King Drive
Madras, OR 97741
April 26, 2015

inside address — Customer Service
Winston Electronics
36 Everly Lane
Lake Oswego, OR 97034

salutation — Dear Sir or Madam:

body —

I recently purchased a MP3 player, model number VC-34287, from your store in Lake Oswego. When I removed the CD player from the box, however, I discovered the adapter used for powering the player in the car was not included among the accessories.

Please send me this adapter as soon as possible. I have enclosed a copy of my sales receipt. Thank you.

closing — Yours truly,

signature — Waneita Hawke

Waneita Hawke

HERE'S HOW

Parts of a Business Letter

Heading

- Write your full address, including the ZIP code.
- Use the two-letter postal abbreviation for your state.
- Write the date.

Inside Address

- Write the receiver's address below the heading.
- Include the name of the person if you know it, using *Mr., Mrs., Ms., Dr.,* or some other title.
- If the person has a business title, write it on the next line.
- Use the two-letter postal abbreviation for the state.

Salutation

- Start two lines below the inside address.
- Use *Sir or Madam* if you do not know the person's name. Otherwise, use the person's last name preceded by *Mr., Mrs., Ms.,* or some other title.
- Use a colon after the salutation.

Body

- Start two lines below the salutation.
- If the body is only a single paragraph, type it double-spaced. For longer letters, single-space each paragraph, skipping a line between paragraphs.

Closing

- Start two lines below the body.
- Line up the closing with the left-hand edge of the heading.
- Use a formal closing such as *Sincerely yours* or *Yours truly* followed by a comma. Capitalize only the first word.

Signature

- Type (or print, if your letter is handwritten) your full name four or five lines below the closing.
- Sign your full name in the space between the closing and your typed name.

Business Envelopes

If you use a word-processing program to write your business letter, you should do the same for the envelope. Fold your letter neatly in thirds to fit into a business-sized envelope. Use the format shown below for business letter envelopes.

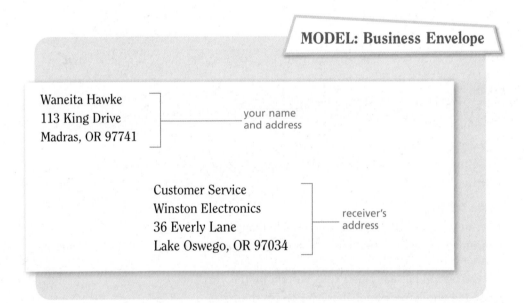

MODEL: Business Envelope

Waneita Hawke
113 King Drive
Madras, OR 97741

(your name and address)

Customer Service
Winston Electronics
36 Everly Lane
Lake Oswego, OR 97034

(receiver's address)

Business E-mails

A business letter sent via e-mail should be just as formal as a letter sent by mail. Follow these guidelines when sending a business e-mail.

HERE'S HOW **Guidelines for Writing a Business E-mail**

- Include a formal salutation and closing. Format the body of the letter correctly.
- Use proper grammar and punctuation.
- Check your spelling. (Some e-mail programs have their own spell-check function. Use it!)
- Double-check the person's e-mail address to be sure you have typed it correctly.
- In the subject line of the e-mail, remember to specify the topic you are writing about.

Letters About Employment

When you apply for a job, you may write a letter to your prospective employer. Your letter should clearly state the job for which you are applying. Anticipate what the employer wants to know about you, and provide relevant and accurate information about your qualifications and experience. Use the appropriate format for a business letter, and be sure your letter is grammatically correct and neat. If the employer requests that you submit a letter by e-mail or via a Web site, make sure that your letter is still formal and professional.

Include the following information in a letter about employment.

INFORMATION IN A LETTER ABOUT EMPLOYMENT	
Position Sought	First, state the job you are seeking and where you learned about the opening.
Education	Include both your age and your grade in school. Emphasize courses you have taken that apply directly to the job you are seeking.
Experience	State the kinds of work you have done. Although you may not have work experience that relates to the open position, any positions of responsibility you have held, whether paid or unpaid, are valuable work experiences.
References	Include at least two references, such as a teacher or a former employer, with a mailing address, an e-mail address, or a phone number for each. You should obtain permission in advance from the people you name as references.
Request for an interview	The last paragraph of your letter should ask for an interview. Indicate where and when you can be reached to make an appointment.

The following is a letter written by a student seeking employment. Note that the letter uses the modified block style. In addition, it includes information about the position sought and the applicant's education and experience, anticipating questions the employer might ask. The letter provides references and ends by requesting an interview.

MODEL: Employment Letter

4173 Hartford Road
Nashville, TN 37206
May 4, 2015

Ms. Florence Vega
Jeans for Teens
772 Route 45
Nashville, TN 37206

Dear Ms. Vega:

I would like to apply for the summer position as a sales clerk advertised in this morning's Courier Advocate. I am a high school junior. My electives at Nimitz High School have included courses in business, math, and retailing.

I have worked part-time for the past two years as a stock clerk at Renfrew's Bookstore. I have also done childcare for Mrs. Alice Schofield. Mr. Renfrew and Mrs. Schofield have agreed to act as references. The business number of Renfrew's Bookstore is (555) 337-8902. Mrs. Schofield can be reached at (555) 227-2216.

I would be pleased to come in for an interview at your convenience. My telephone number is (555) 337-3884. I am home after 3:00 p.m. on weekdays.

Sincerely yours,

Janice Patton

Janice Patton

Practice Your Skills

Applying for Employment

Write an employment letter for the following position, which has been posted in your school's guidance office. Use your own address and today's date.

POSITION AVAILABLE

Job title:	Cashier
Place:	Harvest Market, 1500 Main Street, Garland, NM 88005
Duties:	Interact with customers, learn pricing system, operate cash register, handle money
Hours:	4:00 p.m. to 6:00 p.m. Monday through Friday
Salary:	$7.00/hour
Requirements:	Punctuality, responsibility, pleasant manner
Apply to:	Mrs. Ravendiez

ORDER LETTERS

Some catalogs and advertisements include an order blank. If none is available, write a business letter to place an order. Include the order number, price, quantity, and size of the item you want. Organize the information in your letter appropriately. If you include a check or money order (never send cash), identify the amount enclosed in the letter.

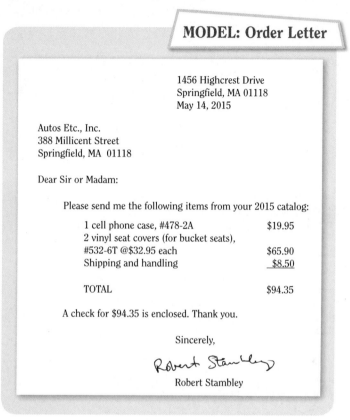

MODEL: Order Letter

1456 Highcrest Drive
Springfield, MA 01118
May 14, 2015

Autos Etc., Inc.
388 Millicent Street
Springfield, MA 01118

Dear Sir or Madam:

Please send me the following items from your 2015 catalog:

1 cell phone case, #478-2A	$19.95
2 vinyl seat covers (for bucket seats), #532-6T @$32.95 each	$65.90
Shipping and handling	$8.50
TOTAL	$94.35

A check for $94.35 is enclosed. Thank you.

Sincerely,

Robert Stambley

Robert Stambley

Practice Your Skills

Placing an Order

Use the modified block style to write a letter ordering the following merchandise. Unscramble the information below for the inside address. Use your own name and address and today's date. Be sure to organize the merchandise information appropriately, as in the model above.

Inside Address	Order Department, Menasha, Wisconsin, Wilson's Farm Stand, 11 Milford Road, 54952
Merchandise	2 lbs. country cheddar cheese, #3745, $4.79/lb.; 2 lbs. smoked summer sausage, #4351, $3.00/lb.; 2 cheese gift packs, #3398, @ $10.00 each
Shipping	$7.50

Letters of Complaint

Most companies are ready to help you if you have a problem with their service or products. Writing a polite letter explaining the problem and offering a reasonable solution will probably bring about the desired results. Write a letter of complaint as soon as you are aware of a problem. Try to anticipate the company's questions, and provide relevant facts and details. Use appropriate vocabulary and a courteous, but firm tone. Include such documents as receipts and e-mails with confirmation numbers.

MODEL: Letter of Complaint

333 Meadow Lane
Lake Hiawatha, NJ 07034
May 17, 2015

Customer Adjustment Department
Sports Togs, Ltd.
1264 Hogan Avenue
Chicago, IL 60601

Dear Sir or Madam:

I ordered and received a sweat suit from your company last week. I washed it according to the laundering instructions on the label. When I took it out of the dryer, however, I found that the stitching around the waist of the pants had unraveled. I believe I must have received a defective pair of pants, for the sweatshirt was as good as new after the washing and drying.

I have enclosed the sweat pants along with a copy of the invoice and canceled check. Please send me a new pair of pants in the same size (medium) and color (blue).

Thank you for your attention.

Yours truly,

Ty Gunnison

Ty Gunnison

Practice Your Skills

Making a Complaint

Use the following information to write a letter of complaint. Unscramble the information in the inside address. Use your own name and address and today's date. Remember to recommend a solution and to use a polite tone.

Inside Address	Portraits Incorporated, Middletown, Rhode Island, 164 South Main Street, 02842
Situation	You sent Portraits Incorporated three negatives with an order for an 8-by-10-inch enlargement of each. The receipt number of your order was 53-76891. Two days ago, you received a package of photographs of a child's birthday party in an envelope with the order number 53-76819. You are enclosing the photographs of the birthday party and a copy of the check for $11.85 that you sent with the negatives.

2 Writing a Résumé

A résumé is a summary of your work experience, education, and interests. The purpose of a résumé is to give a prospective employer a brief overview of your qualifications for a job. You will want to update your résumé whenever there is a significant change in your work or school experience. The following guidelines will help you write your own résumé.

HERE'S HOW

How to Write a Résumé

General Form

- Use one sheet of white 8½ by 11 inch paper.
- Use even margins, and leave space between sections.
- Center your name, address, telephone number, and e-mail address at the top of the page.

Work Experience

- List your most recent job first.
- Include part-time, summer, and volunteer jobs.
- For each job, include the dates you worked, your employer's name, your title, and your primary responsibilities.

Education

- List the name and address of each school and the years you attended.
- List any special courses you have taken that would help make you a valuable employee.

Skills, Activities, Awards, Interests

- List skills, such as computer literacy or fluency in a foreign language, that relate to the position you are applying for.
- List school or community activities in which you have participated, such as music lessons, volunteer work, or scouting.
- List awards or certificates of merit you have earned.
- Include any relevant hobbies or special interests.

Read the following résumé. Notice how it uses appropriate formatting structures, such as headings and white space, to present information in a clear, well-organized manner.

MODEL: Résumé

DAVID GILBERT
1782 La Habra Boulevard
Los Angeles, CA 90034
(213) 426-7135
E-mail: davidgil@myemail.com

WORK EXPERIENCE	
2012 to present	Apogee Computer Center, Inc. South Turnbull Mall, Los Angeles, CA 90034 Position: Clerk Responsibilities: Wait on customers, stock shelves, keep display area clean
2011 to 2012	Burger Delight, Olinda Road at Brea, Glendale, CA 92020 Position: Cook Responsibilities: Prepared food for serving
EDUCATION	
2010 to present	Alvarado High School, 3777 Las Altas Way, Los Angeles, CA 90034 Special Courses: computer graphics, Intro to Windows
2008 to 2010	Box Canyon Middle School, Route 71, Sierra, CA 90368
SPECIAL SKILLS	Speak Spanish and German, Proficient in Windows and Adobe Photoshop
ACTIVITIES	Math Club, varsity tennis player
AWARDS	National Honor Society, Kasner Math Award
SPECIAL INTERESTS	Computer science and software technology

3 Interviewing for Employment

After you submit your application letter for a job and your résumé, an employer may ask you to come to a formal interview. The interview provides an opportunity for both you and the employer to learn more about whether you are well suited for the job—and vice versa. You will feel more confident during an interview if you prepare for it ahead of time.

One way to prepare for an interview is to learn as much as possible about the employer. The more you know about what the employer does and how the business operates, the better you will be able to discuss the job and your qualifications for it. To obtain information about the business, you might talk with people you know who are employed there. If the company has a Web site, review it carefully, and use the Internet to search for other information about the business. In addition, many large companies publish annual reports, which may be available in the library or from the company itself. Information about companies may also be available in business-oriented magazines.

The manner in which you present yourself during an interview may determine whether the employer considers you further for the position. The following strategies will help you interview successfully.

HERE'S HOW

Strategies for Interviewing

- Prepare a list of questions that you would like to ask the interviewer. Ask questions about the job that display your interest in the business. See the chart on the next page for specific suggestions.
- Be on time for the interview. In fact, show up a few minutes early in case you need to fill out any paperwork beforehand.
- Present a neat, clean appearance.
- Be polite and make eye contact with the interviewer as you speak.
- Speak clearly and distinctly, and use proper grammar.
- Answer all questions thoroughly and honestly.
- Thank the interviewer for his or her time when the interview is finished.
- Follow up the interview with a letter thanking the interviewer and expressing your interest in the position. Summarize the reasons that you think make you a good candidate for the job.

In most interviews, the interviewer wants you to "fill in" information that may be missing from your job application, letter, or résumé. He or she also wants to get a sense of what kind of person you are—how you speak, how you handle yourself in a conversation, and how clearly you can present information about yourself. Here are some questions you may be asked.

21ST CENTURY

HERE'S HOW

Questions an Interviewer May Ask You

- How did you find out about this job opening?
- Why did you apply for this job?
- How do your previous experience and education help qualify you for this position?
- What do you study in school and what are your plans for the future?
- What activities do you enjoy in your leisure time?
- What do you expect to earn at this job?
- How many hours can you work a week?
- When can you begin to work?
- Do you have any questions before you leave?

Your answer to the last question should be "Yes." It is important to seem interested enough in the position to ask some questions about the job. Remember, you need to find out if the job suits you as much as the interviewer needs to find out if you suit the job. Here are a few suggestions for questions to ask during an interview.

HERE'S HOW

Questions to Ask an Interviewer

- What exactly would my duties be?
- Who would be my direct supervisor?
- How many hours a week would I be expected to work?
- Are the hours variable? If they are variable, who decides when I would work?
- How much does the job pay and how often are employees paid?
- Are there any benefits that come with this position, such as health insurance, sick pay, or employee discounts?
- Is there room for advancement in this job?
- When will you make a decision about whom you will hire?
- Is there any other information you need?

Practice Your Skills

Drafting Interview Questions and Responses

Pair up with another student to role-play a job interview. Decide who will play the interviewer and who will be the applicant. The applicant is interviewing for a part-time job at a local bookstore that involves checking inventory, shelving new books, serving as a cashier, helping customers, and record-keeping. Draft five to ten questions for the interview. Then, spend about 15 minutes role-playing the interview. When you are finished, discuss what you learned from this activity.

Communication for College

The communication skills you have developed for careers and business will be useful when you communicate with colleges. You should have a clearly stated purpose, and information should be precise, accurate, and concise. In written communication, you should use appropriate formatting and organizational structures. Whether you are writing or speaking, your vocabulary, tone, and style should be appropriate for the context and your audience.

In this section, you will learn strategies for writing letters of request to colleges and for completing college applications. Remember to apply these strategies even if you communicate electronically with colleges and submit applications online. You will also learn strategies for interviewing for college admissions.

21ST CENTURY

1 Writing Letters to Colleges

There are two kinds of letters you should know how to write when you correspond with colleges. The first is a short request for information or a catalog from a professional school or college. If you want specific material, be sure to ask for it. Remember to use the appropriate format for a business letter.

MODEL: Letter for Information

225 Chestnut Street
Austin, TX 78705
May 22, 2015

Admissions Office
Bucknell University
Lewisburg, PA 17837

Dear Sir or Madam:

Please send me your catalog and an application for admission to Bucknell University. I am a junior at Sedgwick High School. I am interested in majoring in business administration. Thank you.

Very truly yours,

Bernard Schwartz

Bernard Schwartz

The second kind of letter you may write to a college is one requesting an interview. Your letter should express your interest in the college and should suggest a convenient time for your visit to the campus or your meeting with an interviewer. From the response to your first letter, you may already know the name of the director of admissions. If not, you can obtain it from a college reference book or on the Internet.

MODEL: Letter Requesting a College Interview

76 Harrison Avenue
San Luis, AZ 85349
March 4, 2015

Ms. June A. Yoder
Director of Admissions
Goshen College
Goshen, IN 46526

Dear Ms. Yoder:

Having read the materials you sent me, I have decided that I would like to find out more about Goshen College. If it can be arranged, I would like to visit your campus and talk with someone from the admissions office. I will be on vacation the week of April 3–7. Since your college classes will be in session that week, I believe it would be an ideal time to visit. Would this be convenient for you? I can come any day and at any time you suggest.

Please let me know if this interview can be arranged. I look forward to seeing Goshen College and learning more about it.

Sincerely,

Marie Aiello

Marie Aiello

Practice Your Skills

Requesting College Information

Find out the name and address of a college, university, or professional school near you. Draft a letter requesting a catalog and an application, following the model on page 541. Use your own name, address, and today's date.

Practice Your Skills

Requesting an Interview

Find out the name and address of a college, university, or professional school near you. If possible, find out the name of the admissions director. Use the information to draft a letter requesting an interview, following the model on page 542. Use your own name, address, and today's date.

2 Completing College Applications

Applications are one tool used by college admissions officers to learn about your qualifications as a prospective student. To give the admissions officers a clear and accurate account of your experiences and accomplishments, you should complete the application carefully and thoroughly. The following strategies may help you.

HERE'S HOW

Strategies for Completing Applications

- Read each application thoroughly, including all the directions, before you begin to answer any questions.
- Follow the instructions for submitting an online application carefully. If you are completing a paper application, type or print neatly in dark blue or black ink. Make one or two copies of the application to practice on before you make your final copy.
- Make your responses to questions about work, travel, and awards as concise as possible.
- Do not be modest about your accomplishments, but do be selective. Stress your most important activities—those you have contributed the most to or learned the most from—instead of simply listing everything you have ever done.
- Make sure to answer every question. Do not leave any blanks. If a question asks about employment experiences and you have not had any, describe volunteer work you have done. If there are questions for which you have no answers, write "N/A" (not applicable).

Many colleges and universities use a common application for undergraduate admission. The common application makes it easier for those who are applying to several colleges at once and ensures that each school will receive the information it needs to review an applicant's qualifications. The first part of this application asks you to provide personal data. You need to read these factual questions carefully and answer them completely and accurately. The following model shows one page of the application.

MODEL: College Application

THE COMMON APPLICATION
For Undergraduate College Admission

2009-10 FIRST-YEAR APPLICATION

For Spring 2010 or Fall 2010 Enrollment

APPLICANT

Legal name ____________________
*Last/Family/Sur (Enter name **exactly** as it appears on official documents.)* — *First/Given* — *Middle (complete)* — *Jr., etc.*

Preferred name, if not first name (choose only one) __________

Former last name(s), if any __________

Birth date __________ *mm/dd/yyyy* ○ Female ○ Male

US Social Security Number, if any __________ *Optional, unless applying for US Federal financial aid with the FAFSA form*

E-mail address __________

IM address __________

Permanent home address __________
Number & Street — *Apartment #*

____
City/Town — *State/Province* — *Country* — *ZIP/Postal Code*

Permanent home phone (______) __________ *Area Code*

Cell phone (______) __________ *Area Code*

If different from above, please give your current mailing address for all admission correspondence.

Current mailing address __________
Number & Street — *Apartment #*

____
City/Town — *State/Province* — *Country* — *ZIP/Postal Code*

If your current mailing address is a boarding school, include name of school here: __________

Phone at current mailing address (______) __________ *Area Code* (from ______ to ______) *(mm/dd/yyyy)* *(mm/dd/yyyy)*

FUTURE PLANS

Your answers to these questions will vary for different colleges. If the online system did not ask you to answer some of the questions you see in this section, this college chose not to ask that question of its applicants.

College: __________

Deadline: __________ *mm/dd/yyyy*

Entry Term: ○ Fall (Jul-Dec) ○ Spring (Jan-Jun)

Decision Plan: ○ Regular Decision ○ Early Decision ○ Early Action ○ Restrictive Early Action ○ Rolling Admission ○ Early Decision II ○ Early Action II ○ Early Admission *juniors only*

Career Interest: __________

Do you intend to apply for need-based financial aid? ○ Yes ○ No
Do you intend to apply for merit-based scholarships? ○ Yes ○ No
Do you intend to be a full-time student? ○ Yes ○ No
Do you intend to enroll in a degree program your first year? ○ Yes ○ No
Do you intend to live in college housing? __________
Academic Interests: __________

DEMOGRAPHICS

○ US citizen
○ Dual US citizen
○ US permanent resident visa (Alien registration # __________)
○ Other citizenship (Visa type __________)

List any non-US countries of citizenship __________

How many years have you lived in the United States? __________

Place of birth __________
City/Town — *State/Province* — *Country*

First language __________

Primary language spoken at home __________

Optional The items with a gray background are optional. No information you provide will be used in a discriminatory manner.

Marital status: __________

US Armed Services veteran? ○ Yes ○ No

1. Are you Hispanic/Latino?
○ Yes, Hispanic or Latino (including Spain) ○ No
Please describe your background __________

2. Regardless of your answer to the prior question, please select one or more of the following ethnicities that best describe you:

○ American Indian or Alaska Native (including all Original Peoples of the Americas)
Are you Enrolled? ○ Yes ○ No If yes, please enter Tribal Enrollment Number __________
Please describe your background __________

○ Asian (including Indian subcontinent and Philippines)
Please describe your background __________

○ Black or African American (including Africa and Caribbean)
Please describe your background __________

○ Native Hawaiian or Other Pacific Islander (Original Peoples)
Please describe your background __________

○ White (including Middle Eastern)
Please describe your background __________

AP-1/**2009-10**

The application also asks you to write a short essay on one of several topics. This essay gives you an opportunity to demonstrate your ability to organize your thoughts and to express yourself effectively.

WRITING

Short Answer Please briefly elaborate on one of your extracurricular activities or work experiences in the space below or on an attached sheet (150 words or fewer).

Personal Essay Please write an essay (250 words minimum) on a topic of your choice or on one of the options listed below, and attach it to your application before submission. **Please indicate your topic by checking the appropriate box.** This personal essay helps us become acquainted with you as a person and student, apart from courses, grades, test scores, and other objective data. It will also demonstrate your ability to organize your thoughts and express yourself.

○ ❶ Evaluate a significant experience, achievement, risk you have taken, or ethical dilemma you have faced and its impact on you.
○ ❷ Discuss some issue of personal, local, national, or international concern and its importance to you.
○ ❸ Indicate a person who has had a significant influence on you, and describe that influence.
○ ❹ Describe a character in fiction, a historical figure, or a creative work (as in art, music, science, etc.) that has had an influence on you, and explain that influence.
○ ❺ A range of academic interests, personal perspectives, and life experiences adds much to the educational mix. Given your personal background, describe an experience that illustrates what you would bring to the diversity in a college community, or an encounter that demonstrated the importance of diversity to you.
○ ❻ Topic of your choice.

Disciplinary History

① Have you ever been found responsible for a disciplinary violation at any educational institution you have attended from 9th grade (or the international equivalent) forward, whether related to academic misconduct or behavioral misconduct, that resulted in your probation, suspension, removal, dismissal, or expulsion from the institution? ○ Yes ○ No

② Have you ever been convicted of a misdemeanor, felony, or other crime? ○ Yes ○ No

If you answered yes to either or both questions, please attach a separate sheet of paper that gives the approximate date of each incident, explains the circumstances, and reflects on what you learned from the experience.

Additional Information If there is any additional information you'd like to provide regarding special circumstances, additional qualifications, etc., please do so in the space below or on an attached sheet.

SIGNATURE

Application Fee Payment If this college requires an application fee, how will you be paying it?

○ Online Payment ○ Will Mail Payment ○ Online Fee Waiver Request ○ Will Mail Fee Waiver Request

Required Signature

○ *I certify that all information submitted in the admission process—including the application, the personal essay, any supplements, and any other supporting materials—is my own work, factually true, and honestly presented. I authorize all schools attended to release all requested records covered under the FERPA act, and authorize review of my application for the admission program indicated on this form. I understand that I may be subject to a range of possible disciplinary actions, including admission revocation or expulsion, should the information I've certified be false.*

○ *I acknowledge that I have reviewed the application instructions for each college receiving this application. I understand that all offers of admission are conditional, pending receipt of final transcripts showing work comparable in quality to that upon which the offer was based, as well as honorable dismissal from the school. I also affirm that I will send an enrollment deposit (or the equivalent) to only one institution; sending multiple deposits (or the equivalent) may result in the withdrawal of my admission offers from all institutions. [Note: students may send an enrollment deposit (or equivalent) to a second institution where they have been admitted from the waitlist, provided that they inform the first institution that they will no longer be enrolling.]*

Signature ✎ ____________________ Date ____________
mm/dd/yyyy

The Common Application, Inc., and its member institutions are committed to fulfilling their mission without discrimination on the basis of race, color, national origin, religion, age, sex, gender, sexual orientation, disability, or veteran status.

The complete Common Application is available online at the following Web address: <https://www.commonapp.org/CommonApp/DownloadForms.aspx>

The Essay

When you write essays for college applications, you should apply all that you have learned about effective communication and the writing process. Use the following strategies to help you write an application essay.

HERE'S HOW

Guidelines for Writing a College Application Essay

- Read the directions carefully. Pay special attention to key words that will help you define your purpose and structure your essay.
- Note any requirements for the length of the essay. Some instructions may specify that you write a 250-word or a 500-word essay. Bear in mind that a 250-word essay will be about one and one-half typed, double-spaced pages. A 500-word essay will be about three typed, double-spaced pages.
- Begin by brainstorming or freewriting to generate ideas about the topic. Then decide on your focus, write a thesis statement, and brainstorm for supporting details.
- Organize your details in an informal or a modified outline.
- Draft your essay, being sure to include an introduction that states the main idea of your essay, supporting details organized in a logical order and connected by transitions, and a strong conclusion.
- Read your draft and look for ways to improve it. You might ask a teacher, parent, or friend to read your draft and make suggestions, too.
- Make a final draft of your essay, using the form specified in the directions or standard manuscript form.

21ST CENTURY

Practice Your Skills

Writing a College Application Essay

Use the previous set of guidelines to draft a 250-word essay on the following topic frequently used in college applications: Identify a person who has had a significant influence on you, and describe that influence. You may want to work with a partner to find ways to improve your draft.

3 Interviewing for College Admission

Some colleges may request or even require an interview. An interview gives a college admissions officer an opportunity to evaluate you firsthand, and it also gives you an opportunity to learn more about the college. As you prepare for an interview, think about what questions you might be asked and how you would answer them. The following are some typical interview questions.

HERE'S HOW

Questions an Interviewer May Ask

- How has high school been a worthwhile educational experience? How might the experience have been improved?
- What have been your best or favorite subjects in school? Which have given you the most difficulty or been your least favorite?
- How do you spend your time outside of school?
- What was the last book you read that was not required reading in school? Did you enjoy it? Why or why not?
- Have you picked a college major yet? If so, what will it be? Why did you choose it?
- How do you expect to benefit from your college experience?
- How do you imagine your living situation at college? What do you look forward to? What are your concerns?

Besides answering questions, you should also be ready to ask some during an interview. In an evaluative interview (as opposed to an informational one), avoid asking questions that cover basic facts about the college. For example, do not ask, "When must a student declare a major?" Since the answers to such questions can be readily found in the college's publications or on its Web site, these questions may point to a lack of real interest in the school and a lack of initiative.

To ask good questions, prepare for a college interview as you would for a job interview—by doing research. Learn as much as you can about the college by reviewing school brochures, the course catalog, and the college's Web site. Talk to current students or recent graduates whom you know.

Then think of questions that go beyond the basic facts you have learned from your research. Ask specific questions that will give you an in-depth look at an academic department or a campus activity that interests you. Ask qualitative types of questions. For example, you might ask, "What is the atmosphere on campus like?" "How would you describe the relationship between the college and the surrounding community?" "What do you think sets the college apart from other schools with similar profiles?"

Keep in mind that the interviewer will evaluate you not only on the basis of your answers to his or her questions, but also on the types of questions you ask. You want your questions to show that you are a thoughtful, well-prepared, interested applicant.

Practice Your Skills

Drafting Interview Questions and Responses

Pair up with another student to role-play a college interview. First, each of you should draft five to ten questions that you want to ask. Then, take turns playing the role of the admissions officer, and spend about 15 minutes role-playing each interview. When you are finished, discuss what you learned from this activity.

C. Communication in the World of Work

Apply 21st Century Communication Skills

Communicating effectively has always been an important skill in the world of work. Now that technology has made the 21st century workforce more mobile as well as more global, good communication skills are even more valuable. You might work at home writing reports and proposals and telecommute to the office each day. You might have to send progress reports to your boss who works in the main office in a different state. You might even use videoconferencing to meet with colleagues in a different country. Expressing ideas clearly, directly, and purposefully is essential for making communication effective in all these instances.

In this section you will develop your business communication skills. No matter what you do for a living, it will pay to be a skillful communicator. Communicating well in the workplace will increase your overall effectiveness, make you more valuable to your employers and fellow workers, and often bring you a better salary and position.

Written Communication at Work

The ability to write effectively is a highly desirable skill in the workplace. In a survey, businesses reported that writing was the most valued skill an employee could have and that a large percentage of employees—at all levels—needed to improve their writing skills. Other surveys have concluded that business writing suffers from a lack of clarity and simplicity.

In the world of work, people write for a variety of purposes. They write narrative reports to inform, create proposals to persuade, and draw up procedures to instruct. Business writing is often read in a hurried, deadline-driven environment. More than other writing, business writing needs to achieve clarity almost instantly.

1 Writing Reports

One of the most common forms of writing in the world of work is the report. There are many different kinds of reports. For example, a report might describe the results of an advertising campaign or measure an employee's job performance. All reports should have a clearly stated purpose and share key information using formatting and organizational structures appropriate to the purpose, audience, and context.

Informational Reports

Informational reports require writers to research, interpret, and present accurate information. This information can be indispensable since management may use it to make decisions. The following steps outline the process for writing an informational report.

HERE'S HOW **Steps for Writing Informational Business Reports**

- Begin by answering three questions:
  1. What are the purpose and objectives of this report?
  2. Who is my audience?
  3. How much time can I realistically spend on preparing the report?
- Gather, evaluate, and synthesize information from a wide variety of sources. Maintain records of your information and sources to ensure that your material is current and accurate.
- Interpret the information to address the specific objectives for the audience and present a clear viewpoint expressed by a main idea statement. Make sure that your viewpoint on the topic is well supported by facts and details.
- Try to anticipate your audience's questions, needs, and possible misunderstandings, and address these issues in your report.
- Identify relevant questions to pose in your report as you seek collaboration with your fellow employees in finding answers.
- Choose an appropriate organizational structure that will enhance the clarity of your report.

- Convert information from one form to another—from written text to graphics, for example—when this will enhance clarity.
- Present technical information in accessible language. Wikipedia includes the following ways to accomplish this in its guide to contributors: 1) present the easiest parts to understand first, 2) use charts, graphs, or other illustrations, 3) avoid jargon (see pages 46–47), 4) provide clear and concrete examples, and 5) write short sentences with few adjectives but with clear, strong verbs.
- When preparing your first draft, use technology to create appropriate formatting structures, such as headings and white space, that will make your report user-friendly.
- Evaluate your report against the initial purpose and objectives. Check that all information is relevant. Cut any extraneous details. Proofread the report for errors in mechanics, grammar, and spelling. Make any necessary revisions.
- Prepare the final report. It should be neat, concise, and uncluttered.

The following case study shows how an employee of a musical instrument shop puts together an informational report.

Case Study: Saxophone Rentals

Vontrel wants to be a music major in college, so she was very glad to get a summer job at Sharps and Flats, a local music store. The store rents musical instruments to school-aged children so they can take part in extracurricular music programs.

The rental business at Sharps and Flats has been increasing each year for most instruments, but for some reason the rental of saxophones has been waning. Vontrel's boss was curious about the possible reason, so she asked Vontrel to do a report on the problem. She gave Vontrel only a few simple guidelines. "Find out what other stores charge for their rentals and if there's a reason people prefer to rent their saxophones somewhere else." She gave Vontrel two weeks to complete the report. In those remarks, Vontrel's boss spelled out the report's **objectives** and **timeline.** She also made it clear that the **audience** for the report was the boss herself.

Vontrel knew her first task was to **gather the necessary information.** She called the competing music stores in the area. Some told her over the phone what the rental prices were; others sent her a price list. She went online and gathered information from the stores that had Web sites. She also thought it would be useful to talk to the band directors at some of the local schools, so she called several and asked about their recommending the saxophone to their students.

Before long, Vontrel had a big stack of information on the subject—price lists, printouts from Web sites, notes from phone calls. Her next job was to **organize the information into file folders.** Thus, when she received an updated price list in the mail from one competitor, she could easily replace the previous year's list in that file and feel confident that she was working with up-to-date information. As she organized the materials, she also began thinking about what her report might look like. She was beginning to feel she had a good idea of what might be behind the problem.

Finally, Vontrel was ready to begin writing her report. Using a **word-processing application,** she began to draft the written part of her report. After her first draft, however, she realized that there were too many dull paragraphs that only listed prices. She decided to use the **graphics features** of her word processor to transform this information into a chart and graphs. Once she felt the report was thorough, she **proofread it for errors in spelling and grammar.** Vontrel knew that the presentation would determine how useful the report would be to her boss. She **submitted the final report in a clear folder** to protect it. This allowed her boss to carry it between home and work and easily access the information. After carefully laying out the pages, Vontrel handed her boss the report.

MODEL: Informational Business Report

Saxophone Rentals: How Sharps and Flats Compares

While rentals of all our other instruments have been steadily climbing, saxophone rentals over the past two years are down about 5 percent. This report will compare pricing as well as examine other factors that may contribute to the decline.

Scope

The competitors reviewed here include the four shops within a ten-mile radius of our shop. One additional online rental source was included in the study.

Pricing

Sharps and Flats has not raised the rental price for saxophones for four years. It remains at $35 a month. The following table and graphs show how our competitors' monthly prices compare.

Different Drummer	$32.00
Allegro con Brio	$35.00
Catch the Wave (online)	$35.00
McCarthy Band and Orchestra	$37.50
Music City	$40.00

As the following graph shows, we are near the middle range of our competitors, if only the monthly rental rates are considered.

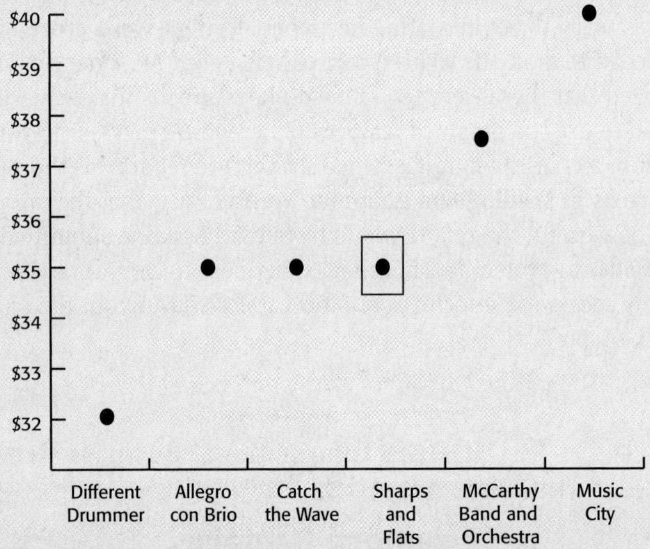

The monthly rate does not tell the whole story, however. Some of the shops have special rates for the first few back-to-school months; some give the first month free; one (McCarthy) even rebates money at the end of the rental agreement if the instrument passes inspection. When you figure all of these specials into the pricing and calculate the total for the nine months of the school year, we are by far the most expensive.

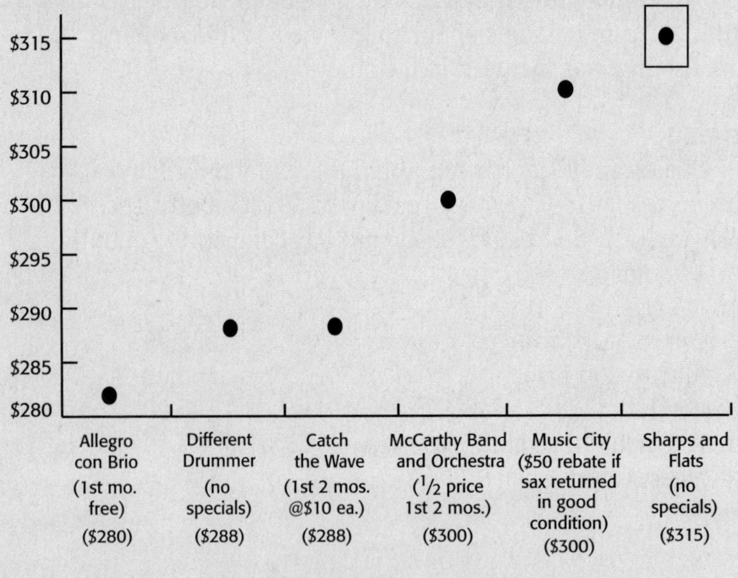

Other Considerations

It may be that other factors also influence people's rental decisions. For example, Different Drummer runs an ad in the school newspaper announcing that it will pay transportation expenses for any woodwind ensemble that qualifies for the state competition. The band director I spoke with told me that he thought some parents liked giving Different Drummer the rental business because of its community support.

Also, the online rental, Catch the Wave, gives away a "premium" with each rental. This year the premium was a music stand. Perhaps that incentive, as well as the free delivery, lures some renters to the Web.

Vontrel's report was concise, easy-to-read, and to the point. It included the following features that all good reports should have.

HERE'S HOW

Features of an Informational Business Report

- The purpose is plainly stated in the introduction.
- The scope is precisely outlined.
- The report suits the needs of the intended audience.
- Accurate and timely information is presented in a well-organized, logical way.
- Information is conveyed with graphics when they provide greater clarity than text.
- Formatting structures, such as headings, and the page layout simplify quick scanning.
- Ideas are expressed succinctly. (See pages 549–550.)
- The language is accessible and direct. (See page 550.)
- There are no errors in spelling, grammar, and punctuation.

Practice Your Skills

Drafting a Business Report

According to Shelly Field in *100 Best Careers for the 21st Century*, the job of an environmentalist is to "prevent and control pollution, solve environmental problems, and conduct research." Imagine that you are the environmentalist for your county. After several rabid raccoons had been trapped, the county council has mandated that all wild raccoons should be destroyed rather than relocated. Your supervisor has asked you to draft a report explaining the new policy to concerned citizens.

Write a brief explanation of the process you would follow to draft the report. State the scope, objectives, and audience for your report. Specify the types of sources you would consult for information. Design at least one graphic that would improve your presentation.

Using Graphics

In her informational report (pages 551–553), Vontrel uses graphics to make important points readily apparent. Using graphics can help you present information clearly and simply. Some of the more common types of graphics are tables, charts, graphs, illustrations, and maps.

HERE'S HOW **Purpose of Graphics**

- To support an idea in the written text—to prove a point
- To clarify or simplify a complex relationship
- To emphasize an important idea
- To make a report more interesting

Charts An **organizational chart** shows the hierarchy, or levels of authority, of a business or other organization.

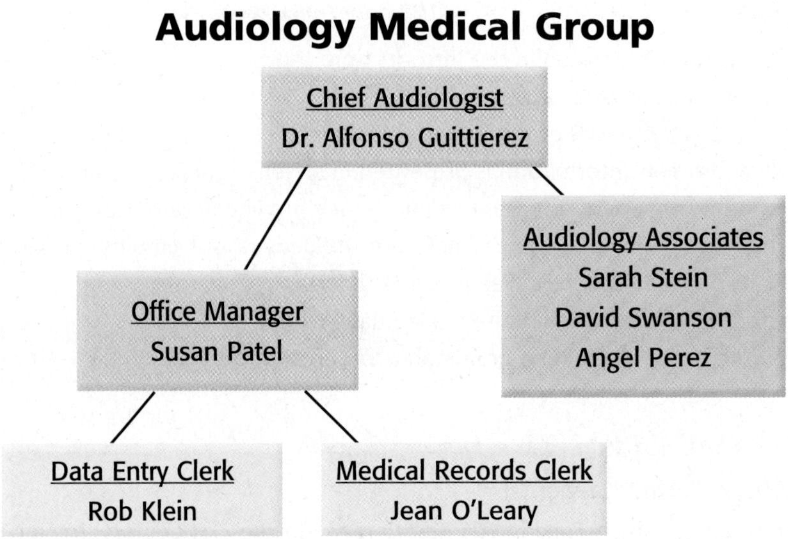

The **flow chart** is widely used to show how a process works. The following chart shows the procedure that a documentary film team will follow to produce their film.

THE PRODUCTION AND POSTPRODUCTION PROCESS FOR A DOCUMENTARY FILM

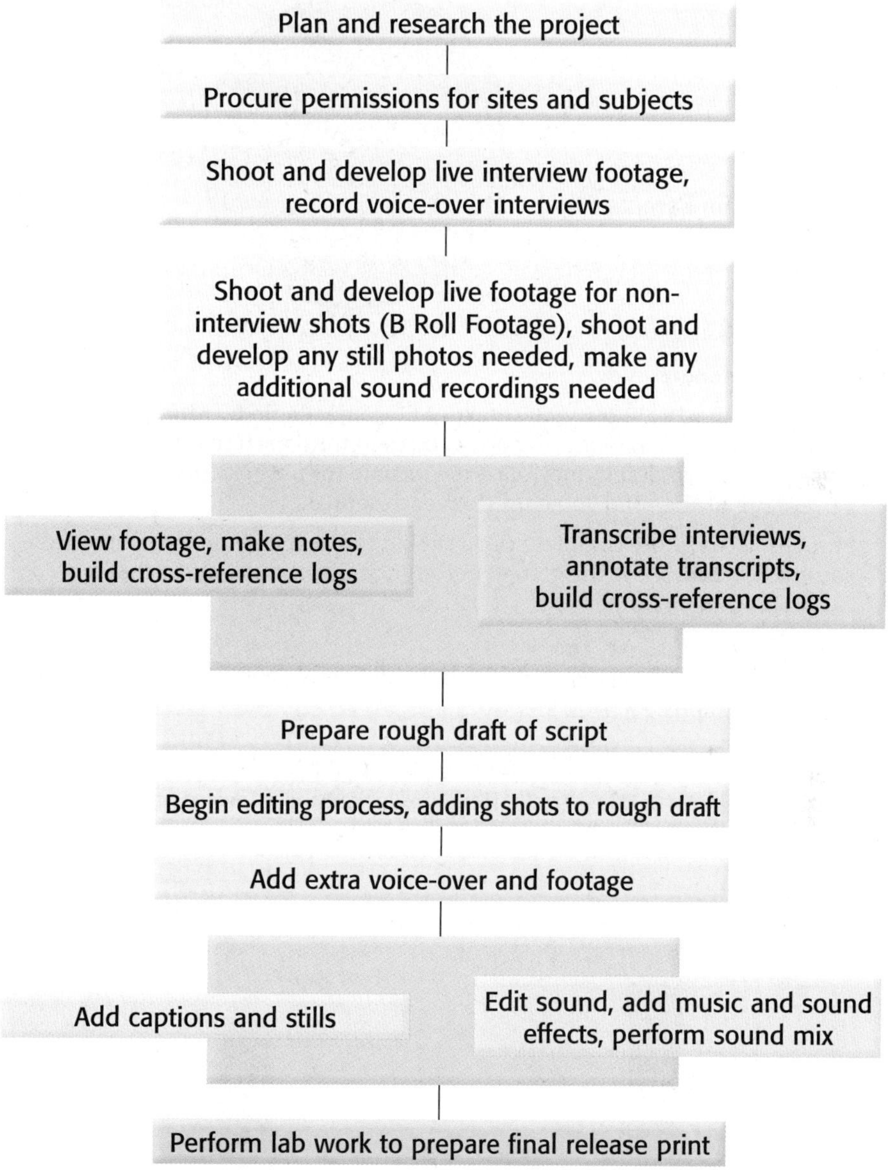

Plan and research the project
Procure permissions for sites and subjects
Shoot and develop live interview footage, record voice-over interviews
Shoot and develop live footage for non-interview shots (B Roll Footage), shoot and develop any still photos needed, make any additional sound recordings needed
View footage, make notes, build cross-reference logs
Transcribe interviews, annotate transcripts, build cross-reference logs
Prepare rough draft of script
Begin editing process, adding shots to rough draft
Add extra voice-over and footage
Add captions and stills
Edit sound, add music and sound effects, perform sound mix
Perform lab work to prepare final release print

Practice Your Skills

Creating a Flow Chart

Create a flow chart showing your writing process. Include checkpoints at which your peers (or your teacher) can provide feedback.

A **pie chart** provides an effective way to show how a total amount breaks down into categories, as in the following example of the sources of income for teenagers, ages 16 to 17. You can see at a glance how much more money teenagers get from their jobs than from any other source.

Jobs 75%

Allowance 12%

Chores 5%

Asking for Money from Parents 6%

Gifts 2%

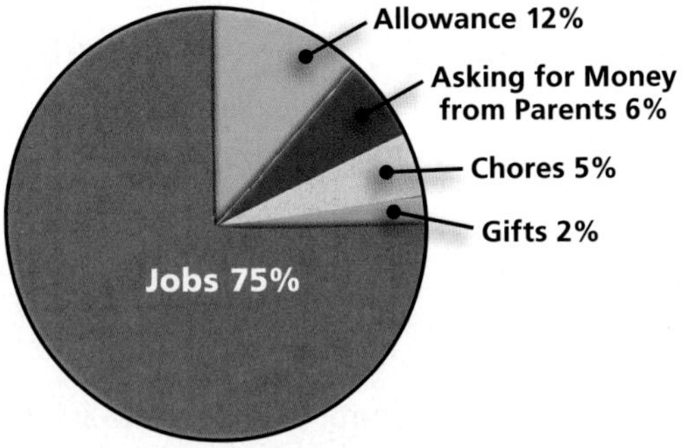

21ST CENTURY

Practice Your Skills

Creating a Pie Chart

Make a pie chart to show your sources of income. Begin by listing your sources of income and the amount of money you gain from each source in a week. Add these amounts to determine your total income for a week. Then calculate the percentage of the total you earn from each source.

In your pie chart, the complete circle should equal 100 percent of your income. Each slice should show the correct percentage of your income in that area.

Graphs Graphs come in a variety of forms. The following examples show effective ways to use bar and line graphs.

Bar graphs are especially useful for showing comparisons. The following bar graph displays—and visually contrasts—the pattern of worker absenteeism at the Dunlap-Lee factory.

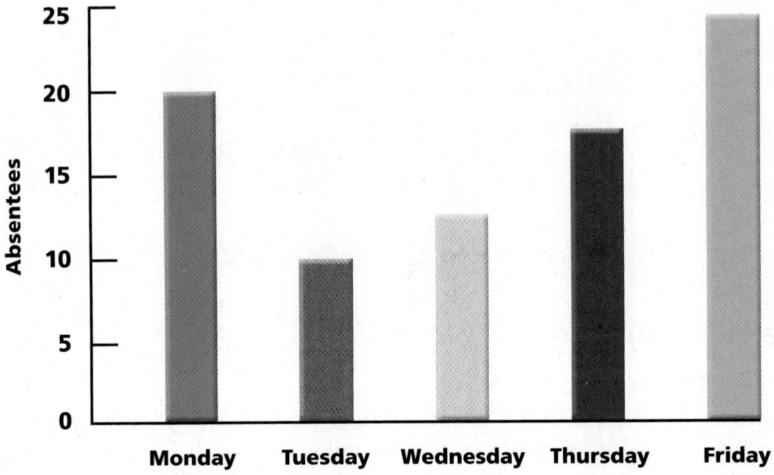

Practice Your Skills

Creating a Bar Graph

Use the following percentages to create a bar graph that compares the populations of developing and industrialized countries.

Indicators	Developing	Industrialized
Access to safe water	84	100
Access to adequate sanitation	53	100
Living in cities	44	76

(Source: UNICEF, State of the World's Children, 2009.)

Line graphs are effective for showing changes over time. The following line graph shows how sales of a breakfast cereal rose and fell over a ten-year period.

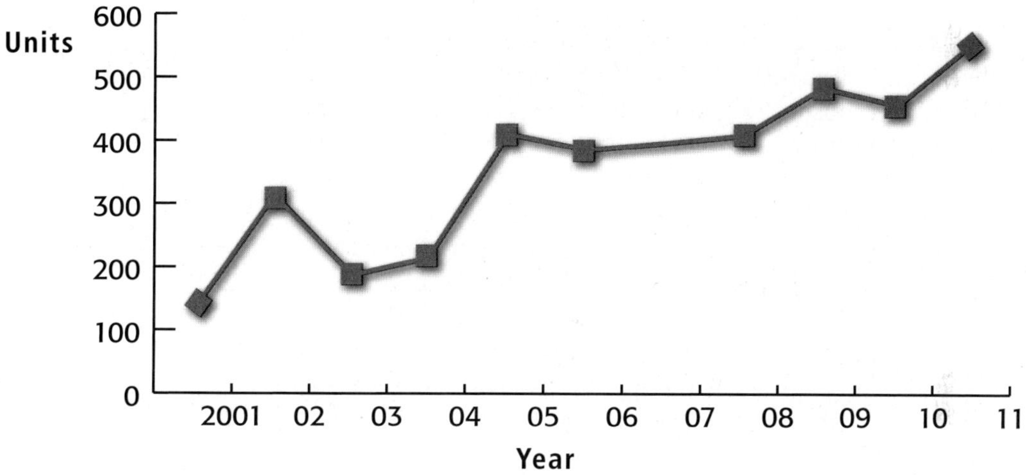

Practice Your Skills

Creating a Line Graph

Use the following ACT test scores from a school district to create a line graph showing the changes over time.

2001	27	2006	30
2002	26	2007	31
2003	28	2008	26
2004	24	2009	27
2005	29	2010	29

Narrative Reports

Like its counterpart in school, the business **narrative** tells what happened during a certain event or in a particular situation. The basic questions of all narratives are *Who? What? When? Where? Why?* and *How?* The **narrative report** answers these questions in chronological order using accessible language, facts, and a straightforward style. It is used to report accidents, incidents, and special events.

The food services manager for a hotel wrote this narrative report about an incident in the kitchen. Notice how detailed the report is and how carefully the manager documents the safety and response procedures that were followed.

MODEL: Incident Report

On Friday, April 14, 2009, at 7:35 p.m., a small fire broke out in the main kitchen. The fire started when hot olive oil in a sauté pan on the back burner splashed onto another lighted burner. This occurred after Ray Carlson, a cook on duty, stirred mushrooms in the pan. The oil caught fire and flared for a moment, just high enough to reach a potholder that was hanging on the wall above the stove. The potholder caught fire and began to burn slowly. Carlson activated the fire extinguisher hanging on the east wall and put out the fire immediately. No one was injured; the potholder has been replaced.

Following the incident, the kitchen team held a meeting to review safety procedures. We agreed to move the potholder rack; it is now mounted above the sink. We expect these changes will guard against any similar problems in the future.

Practice Your Skills

Writing a Narrative Report

Write an account of an event in a form and style suitable for a business report. Your subject might be a special event in your school or community or a minor accident you were involved in or witnessed.

Progress Reports

How do you know if you're doing a good job at work? How do your supervisors know? How do project leaders keep track of complex assignments and products? A key part of the answer to these questions is the **progress report,** which measures your performance against previously set goals and expectations.

The following progress report shows how one computer programmer monitored and evaluated his achievements. His employer requires progress reports every week.

MODEL: Progress Report

Progress Report: 6/17–6/24

This week I met the goal I set to complete testing the changes to the security measures on the company's Intranet. Testing showed that all the changes are working fine. The changes will make it almost impossible for non-authorized users to log on.

I also completed my portion of the information sheet that will be used in the employee instruction manual to show new employees how to secure their desktops.

I have still not received the patches I requested from Zanzibar Systems, so I have not been able to update the internal e-mail system.

Goals for next week

- Get firm date from Zanzibar on when patch will be ready.
- Review report from accounting, and write first-draft response on changing software needs.
- Train new programmer to update Web site.

Setting Effective Performance Goals Without carefully crafted goals, no progress report can be effective. Successful workers set goals that are measurable and achievable, monitor their time accurately, and assess their progress realistically.

Measurable goals are ones that can be tested against an easy-to-see outcome.

Measurable Goal	I will draft the first two sections of my report by Friday, October 12. (If the draft of the first two sections is complete by October 12, you met your goal. The outcome is easy to measure.)
Nonmeasurable Goal	I will learn all I can about the competing products by Friday, October 12. (It is hard to determine if you were able to "learn all" that you could; there's no way to measure your learning.)

Achievable goals are those with a realistic possibility of being accomplished. Unrealistic goals lead to failure. If you know that it truly takes two days to prepare a sample advertisement for a client, don't promise yourself or the client that you will do it in less time than that. Only you will be able to know for sure what is achievable, given your workload. Effective goals should make you reach somewhat beyond your comfort zone, but unrealistic goals are inappropriate.

Practice Your Skills

Measuring Your Progress

Think of one of your projects. It could be learning how to play the piano, training for the swim team, working on college admissions, maintaining your friendships, or earning money at a part-time job. Write three measurable, achievable goals related to this project that you plan to accomplish within the next week. At the end of the week, write a progress report measuring your progress against the goals you set.

2 Writing Proposals

Although having accurate, clear information is essential for pursuing any project, the real test of business creativity is the way that information is used. A **proposal** takes the business report one step further by recommending a course of action. It presents a clearly stated purpose and viewpoint on a topic and supports this viewpoint with logical reasons, facts, and details.

Saxophone Rentals Revisited

After writing her report on saxophone rentals (see pages 551–553), Vontrel couldn't stop thinking about the problem. She thought of ways to improve rentals and decided to write up her ideas in a proposal for her boss. Besides wanting to share her good ideas, Vontrel wished to demonstrate her capability to her boss. She hoped that showing initiative would help her to move out of her clerical position into one with more responsibility.

MODEL: Proposal

Introduction

As you know, I collected much useful information about our competitors' rental policies when I prepared the report on saxophone rentals. I have continued to think about how we might increase our rentals in light of what we learned and would now like to make some recommendations.

Two factors seemed very clear as I studied the saxophone rental options in our community. One is our comparatively high rental fees (as you recall, when the cost is averaged over the school year, our rental fee is the highest); the other is our "name recognition" in the community. This proposal will address both factors.

Pricing

I recommend that we keep our monthly rental fee at $35 but add either a half-price month at the beginning or a half-month's rebate at the end of the rental agreement if the instrument is returned in good condition. Either of these options would place us in the middle of the pricing range. (Being the lowest might make people think we do not have quality instruments; being the highest might make people think we are overcharging.) The rebate offers the most protection for us, since we would not be required to return the money if the instrument is damaged during the rental period. On the other hand, the half-price first month may be more attractive to customers.

Community Involvement

Even more important than pricing is developing community goodwill. Perhaps the best way to begin is to host a breakfast, lunch, or dinner for all the band teachers in the district. The meal would provide us with a great opportunity to improve our relationships with these key leaders, who may make recommendations to the parents about good rental sources. After the meal, we might have either a focus group or an informal brainstorming session and ask band teachers how we can improve our position in the community. We can then take their ideas, determine how much the ideas would cost to implement, and see if any plan is financially sound. When we have found an approach that we believe will boost our rentals enough to offset the costs, we should advertise it in the local papers and announce it in a letter that will accompany rental bills.

If you are interested in pursuing these ideas, I will commit to developing them along with working on my other responsibilities at the store. I believe they would lead to improved saxophone rentals and—quite possibly—a boost in the rental of other instruments as well. Please let me know what you think.

Vontrel's proposal has all of the following features of a good proposal.

HERE'S HOW

Features of a Good Proposal

- The proposed actions are clearly stated.
- Supporting facts and details are accurate and up-to-date.
- The proposal includes a way to measure the cost against the potential benefits.
- The writer uses an appropriate organizational structure. (See page 529.)
- Formatting structures, such as headings, enhance the clarity of the presentation.
- The proposal is written in accessible language and uses an appropriate style and tone.
- The proposal is addressed to the appropriate audience. It considers the reader's needs and anticipates his or her questions.
- The reader understands what he or she is called on to do.

Practice Your Skills

Writing a Proposal

There are many possible creative solutions to the saxophone rental problem besides those suggested by Vontrel. Reread Vontrel's informational report. Then write a counterproposal—a proposal that addresses the same problem but recommends different solutions. Evaluate your first draft by checking if it has the qualities listed in Features of a Good Proposal. Revise accordingly.

3 Writing Procedures and Instructions

Procedures and instructions are two other common forms of business writing. (You have already come across this kind of writing when you practiced writing how-to paragraphs, specifically when you were asked to describe a process or write a set of instructions on pages 264–265.) **Procedures** explain which steps and tasks are required to complete a job. **Instructions** tell you how to complete all the necessary steps.

A key difference between procedures and instructions is the scope of the task being described. Procedures can involve several different departments or a number of different employees. Instructions, on the other hand, are more focused. They involve smaller tasks that can be performed by one employee.

You have already seen an example of a procedure represented in a flow chart (page 555). A flow chart is often the simplest, most direct way to show a procedure. However, a clearly written procedure can present the details of a process with absolute clarity to avoid any confusion on the part of employees. In fact, many companies provide a procedures manual to all employees to make sure that everyone knows and follows the same procedures.

The following model is taken from Southern Missouri State University's online Student Employment Guide and describes the process a student employee must take to resolve an on-the-job problem, or grievance.

MODEL: Procedure

Student Employee Grievance Procedure

This grievance procedure is designed to address complaints and disputes between student employees and the departments in which they work, including working relationships, working conditions, employment practices, or differences in interpretation of policies. Student employees who believe they have a legitimate grievance may undertake the following procedure in order to rectify the matter.

Step 1 Immediate Supervisor

Discussion of the problem with the immediate supervisor is encouraged as a first step in resolving the matter informally, and resolution of the complaint can often occur at this point. Student employees should bring their grievances to the attention of the supervisor in a timely manner—generally within ten (10) days of occurrence—in order to resolve them as quickly as possible. In situations that student employees feel cannot be discussed with their immediate supervisor, a request should be made to meet with the department head or administrator.

Step 2 Appeal to the Department Head or Major Administrator

If the problem is not resolved within a short period of time after discussion with the supervisor, then the student employee may formalize the grievance in writing and present it to the department head or administrator within ten (10) days after presentation of the grievance to the supervisor. The department head or administrator will consider the facts, conduct an investigation, and may give the student employee the opportunity to present the case orally. The department head or administrator may affirm, reverse, or modify the supervisor's decision, and will notify the student employee of the decision in writing within ten (10) days after receiving the appeal.

Step 3 Appeal to the Vice President

If a student employee is not satisfied with the decision of the department head or administrator, he/she may appeal to the appropriate vice president within five (5) working days after receiving that decision. The appeal must be in writing and include all of the information included in the initial grievance and subsequent appeals, all the decisions related thereto, and any other pertinent information the student employee may wish to submit. The appeal must be signed and dated. The vice president will investigate the grievance and will give the student employee the right to present the case orally. The vice president has the option of appointing a three-member panel from the university community to hear the case and review the actions to ensure that university procedures have been followed and due process afforded to the student employee. The vice president may affirm, reverse, or modify the previous decision in writing within ten (10) working days after receiving the appeal.

Step 4 Appeal to the President

If a student employee is not satisfied with the decision rendered at Step 3 of the grievance procedure, he/she may appeal to the president within five (5) working days after receiving that decision. The appeal must be in writing, and include all of the information included in the initial grievance and subsequent appeals, all decisions related thereto, and any other pertinent information the student employee may wish to submit. The appeal must be signed and dated.

The president will initiate an investigation into the matter and may give the student employee the right to present his or her case orally. The president may affirm, reverse, or modify the previous decision and must, within a reasonable time, notify the employee of the decision in writing.

For a routine task, written instructions are usually provided to employees. An experienced worker may draft the instructions in order to help other workers who have never performed the task before. Supervisors sometimes write instructions to introduce a new technology or system to the staff. The following instructions tell employees how to record their voice mail message.

MODEL: Instructions

Instructions for Recording Voice Mail Messages

On February 19 all employees will have voice mail on their extensions. Please read these instructions ahead of time. Follow these steps to personalize your recorded message.

1) Dial 1113 followed by the pound sign ("#"—lower right-hand key). You will hear a prompt that gives you two choices of how to set up your voice mailbox. Press 1, as that is the option the entire office will use. This choice will be to use a prerecorded message with only your name added.

2) After choosing 1, you will be prompted to say your name out loud and then press the pound key. Be sure to speak clearly when you record. Your message will be: "[Your name in your voice] is not available. To leave a message, wait for the beep."

   All but your name will be heard in the voice mail prerecorded voice.

3) If you make a mistake along the way, you can press the star key (*—lower left-hand key) to start over at any time.

4) A red light at the base of your phone will go on if you have voice mail. To check your voice mail messages, dial #55 from your own extension. To check your messages from a remote phone, dial into the company and then enter your extension followed by *55.

Well-written instructions and procedures share the following features.

Features of Good Procedures and Instructions

- They provide all the information necessary to complete a task or procedure.
- They anticipate the reader's questions, problems, and mistakes, and they address these issues.
- They explain unfamiliar terms or describe unfamiliar items.
- They present the steps in their sequential order.
- They use numbering systems, when appropriate, to separate the steps in the process. They may use other formatting structures, such as headings, to make the document user-friendly.
- They describe the task in accessible, concise language.

Practice Your Skills

Writing Instructions

Think of a four- to five-step computer task that you know how to perform well. It might be hooking up a modem, logging on to the Internet, formatting a page, or manipulating graphics, for example. Write instructions for performing the task. Have a classmate evaluate the instructions by checking for the qualities listed in **Features of Good Procedures and Instructions.** If possible, ask your classmate to perform the task step-by-step to see if your instructions are easy to follow. Revise your instructions as necessary, based on your classmate's feedback.

4 Writing Memos

A **memo** (short for memorandum) is a brief, somewhat informal communication. It is often used for interoffice communication among employees. It typically begins with the same four headings (shown in boldface type in the model below).

MODEL: Memo

Date: 6/14/15
To: All members of the secretarial staff
From: *CW Cara Wong, Technical Support Director*
Subject: Training for new software

Please plan to attend a training workshop on our newly adopted word-processing program, FlashWord, on Friday, 6/23, at 1:00 in the large conference room. The session will last until 3:00 and will include interactive lessons.

Business memos are meant to be concise, usually running no longer than a single page, but they often contain complex information. The information should be well organized so that it is conveyed clearly to recipients who cannot spend much time reading the memo.

HERE'S HOW

Guidelines for Writing Clear Memos

- Begin by writing a rough draft, an outline, notes, or a list of ideas.
- Refine these ideas to create a concise document with a clearly stated purpose.
- Use an organizational structure that is appropriate for your purpose and subject. Generally, put the most important information first. Divide complex information into small sections.
- Make the relationship among ideas explicit by using formatting structures such as headings, bullets, and numbers.
- Make sure the sentences in your final draft are short and focused. Phrasing in memos should be succinct and clear.
- Use accessible, direct language. Use jargon or technical terms specific to the subject when they suit your audience and the context.
- Maintain a polite, respectful, professional tone. This encourages others to adopt the same attitude when reading the memo.

Memos are used for all of the following purposes:

HERE'S HOW

Common Purposes for Memos

1. To serve as notices or reminders of meetings. (See the model on page 565.)
2. To serve as transmittal sheets accompanying other materials. A transmittal memo should identify the materials being passed along (transmitted) and specify requests for action.

   Attached is my report on how saxophone rental at Sharps and Flats compares in pricing and in other areas to rentals at other shops. Please let me know if there is any additional information that you would like to have.
3. To provide a written summary of a conversation in order to document specific agreements.

   Thank you for working through the scheduling problem. We agreed that we will add a week to the schedule for the graphic arts department to complete its initial design, but we will shorten the turnaround time for page layout by one day per chapter. This change will keep our overall schedule on track.
4. To make a request.

   I would like to take my vacation from July 15–July 22. Please let me know if these dates are acceptable so that I can make my travel plans. Thank you.
5. To transfer information about a project, either to fellow workers within a company or to a client or employee working outside the company.

Although a memo can serve many purposes, there are times when a phone call or face-to-face conversation is preferable. Everything you put into writing can be read by anyone, whether or not the information is labeled "confidential." If you want to convey privileged information, either use the phone or meet with the person face-to-face. Also use the personal approach to resolve differences whenever possible. Human contact often promotes resolution.

E-mail versus Paper Memos

If you are sending a memo via e-mail, you should follow the same guidelines you would use for writing a paper memo. Since employees tend to receive many e-mails in the course of the day and often have to read them quickly, it is particularly important that you express your ideas clearly, directly, and concisely and present well-organized information. Remember to use a formal, professional style when writing a business e-mail.

21ST CENTURY

In memos sent via e-mail, "To," "From," and "Subject" are built into the e-mail format. You can send the same memo to many people, either by adding their e-mail addresses to the "To" entry field or by adding them to the "CC" (carbon or courtesy copy) field.

Practice Your Skills

Using an Appropriate E-mail Style

Rewrite the following e-mail message to make it suitable for a business communication.

Hey Ralph!! Sorry I couldn't make the meeting. :> I'd really like a copy of your report, though. That whole incident really bummed me. IMHO, nobody's really to blame (although Lisa sure fouled up ;>). Gotta run. TTFN

Practice Your Skills

Using Content-Area Vocabulary

Select one of the terms from this chapter listed below. Write a description of the term along with a scenario in which you might use the form of written communication.

- case study
- organizational chart
- flow chart
- line graph
- narrative report
- instructions
- memo

Nonwritten Communication at Work

In the 21st century, technology provides an increasing number of options for nonwritten communication in the workplace. Whether you are participating in a teleconference, a videoconference, or a meeting with colleagues in your office, the basic skills required for speaking and listening effectively are the same.

1 Telephone Etiquette

Often a customer's first impression of a company is formed during a telephone conversation. Here are some tips for ensuring that the impression is a good one.

HERE'S HOW

Tips for Telephone Calls in the Workplace

- Speak slowly and clearly. Keep the phone about one-and-one-half inches from your mouth.
- Use a pleasant tone. Vary the pitch of your voice throughout the conversation.
- Listen carefully to the caller's points or questions.
- If you don't know an answer, say something like "That's a good question; let me try to find out the answer for you."
- If the caller has a complaint, apologize for the problem and find some way to provide him or her satisfaction.
- Even if the caller is emotional, remain polite.
- Whenever possible, let the caller end the call. Say, "Thank you for calling," and replace the receiver gently when you hang up.
- Try to answer your calls by the second or third ring.
- Keep writing materials near the phone so you can take a message if you have to. Each message should include the name of the person called, the name and phone number of the caller, the time of the call, a brief summary of the message, and a good time to call back.

Practice Your Skills

Writing a Telephone Comedy

Several comedians have earned their fame by doing routines based on telephone conversations. Write a telephone dialogue between a caller and an employee that shows the worker doing everything wrong. Note each guideline in Tips for Telephone Calls in the Workplace that is violated in your dialogue. Pair off with a classmate, rehearse your dialogues, and perform them for the class.

2 Informal Meetings

A quick conversation by the vending machines, a discussion about a process over lunch, a problem-solving debate in a colleague's office—all are examples of informal meetings that take place at work. Every time you interact with another employee, you are "in a meeting." Your interactions will be productive if you remember the importance of acting as a team member.

The team approach helps companies achieve their goals by encouraging employees to collaborate constructively and respectfully. Workplace teams have the following traits.

HERE'S HOW **Traits of the Team Approach**

- All team members understand the goal.
- The structure is flexible enough to permit creative problem solving.
- Mutual respect creates a positive working environment.
- Belonging to a team gives members a sense of identity.
- Team members learn from one another and develop a shared understanding.

Adopting a team approach when you meet informally with your co-workers will help you interact constructively. Sometimes you may have to lead the way; other times you may have to follow another's lead. When you disagree with the ideas of other members, remember that all of you are working toward the same goal. Express your thoughts respectfully and work toward a compromise. A sense of shared responsibility will lead to successful teamwork.

3 Formal Meetings

The team approach is also used for formal meetings. The biggest differences between informal and formal meetings are that formal meetings are structured and have a designated leader.

Leading a Meeting

The most important tasks of a meeting's leader are to be well prepared and to follow a plan. To lead a meeting effectively, follow these steps.

HERE'S HOW **Guidelines for Leading a Meeting**

- Carefully think through the purpose of the meeting. Decide what you want to accomplish, and create an agenda (a list of topics to be discussed in order) to ensure that your purpose is met. Include as your final item something like "Next Steps." This item is a call for action on the issues that you will have just discussed. Estimate the time needed to discuss each topic.

- Send an advance copy of the agenda to all the people who are expected to attend the meeting. At the top, include a reminder of the meeting's scheduled time and place. You may invite people to propose changes to the agenda. However, you, as the leader, should retain the final authority over the agenda so that the meeting does not become disorganized.
- When the meeting begins, plan to get the discussion started yourself, if necessary. As your co-workers begin participating, make sure that one or two voices do not take over. Call on people who do not volunteer to guarantee that all points of view are expressed. Listen to everyone respectfully, but feel free to politely ask those who are rambling to get to the point. Make sure that participants respond respectfully to each other as well.
- Stick to your time schedule. Move the discussion from point to point even if you have not exhausted the topic.
- Wrap up the meeting with a brief summary of what it accomplished and a preview of next steps. Thank the participants.

Participating in a Meeting

Meetings at which participants feel like members of a well-functioning team can be very stimulating—even fun. Although you should contribute to the meeting by asserting your point of view, remember to be open to the diverse ideas of others. Successful participation in workplace meetings requires fine listening skills, flexibility, an open mind, and a genuine commitment to reaching a shared goal.

HERE'S HOW

Guidelines for Participating in a Meeting

- Think through the issues listed on the meeting agenda ahead of time.
- Bring useful information or documents to the meeting to share with others.
- Respect the time constraints of the meeting, and speak as succinctly as possible.
- Listen carefully and respectfully to the ideas of others.
- Appreciate the diverse viewpoints that people from different backgrounds bring to a problem.
- Compromise when appropriate.

Recording (Taking Notes or Minutes)

Accurate records must be kept of all business meetings so that the ideas, decisions, and resolutions can be put to use and widely understood. If you are in charge of taking notes (called *minutes* if they are from a very formal meeting), consider using an audio recorder as a back up to your written notes. You can then replay the audiotape to determine if any information is missing from your written notes.

Two skills are critical when recording a meeting. One is careful listening (see pages 581–585). The other is the ability to summarize (see pages 372–384 and 472). Those skills, along with the following guidelines, will help you take reliable notes. Formal minutes must sometimes follow special guidelines, but these general points still apply.

HERE'S HOW

Guidelines for Recording a Meeting

- Be thorough.
- Write down word-for-word any formal decisions, votes, resolutions, and so forth.
- Record the name of each speaker as well as the ideas he or she put forward.
- Record only what was said or what happened. Don't add any of your own opinions or observations that were not actually expressed at the meeting.
- Use an icon (perhaps a star or a check) next to items that need action.
- Create a final copy of your notes as soon after the meeting as possible so the ideas are still fresh in your mind.
- In the beginning of the notes, be sure to include the date of the meeting and a list of all attendees.
- Distribute the notes to everyone who attended the meeting.

TELECONFERENCES AND VIDEOCONFERENCES

Today many formal business meetings are held using technology so that people in remote sites can attend. A **teleconference** is a meeting in which attendees in different locations participate by using telecommunications equipment. The term often refers to meetings conducted via the telephone. In a **videoconference,** attendees use video technology to "meet" and communicate. When you lead or participate in such a meeting, you should follow the same guidelines you would use if all the attendees were on site. In addition, you may find these tips helpful.

HERE'S HOW

Guidelines for Teleconferences and Videoconferences

- Before the meeting, check that the telecommunications equipment is working properly. Make sure that all attendees have the information they need to use the technology, such as access codes.
- At the beginning of the meeting, all attendees should be introduced.
- Speak loudly and clearly. If only audio equipment is being used, say your name before you speak, unless the group is small and all attendees can recognize each other's voices.
- At all times, remember that you are communicating with people in remote sites. Make sure that all attendees are engaged in the meeting and have the opportunity to participate. Avoid side conversations with the people sitting next to you.
- Keep background noise to a minimum. For example, avoid rustling papers near speaker phones.
- If documents will be given out at the meeting, make sure these materials are sent in advance to all attendees at remote sites.

Focus Groups

One specific kind of formal meeting is the **focus group,** which involves people outside the workplace. Their job is to evaluate products or services or to test new ideas. In fact, many of the television shows you watch, jeans you wear, shampoos you use, and foods you eat were developed with input from focus groups at which participants answered questions about their preferences and tastes.

HERE'S HOW

Guidelines for Focus Groups

Planning

- Identify the purpose of the focus group. What problem are you seeking to solve? What questions do you want answered?
- Invite participants who are qualified to help you achieve your purpose. For example, if you are testing a new line of soccer balls, invite soccer players and coaches to the focus group.
- Devote time to the logistics, or the coordination of the details of the project, such as setting the time and place for the focus group and gathering materials. If possible, arrange to have an audio or video recording made of the event.
- Carefully craft the questions you will ask. Be sure the questions are worded to avoid bias. Also, make sure the questions are worded in an open-ended way to generate discussion.
- Focus group meetings should last about an hour and a half. Send a reminder about the meeting to all the participants a few days ahead of time.

Conducting the Meeting

- Introduce yourself and the others conducting the focus group to the participants. Thank everyone for coming. Review the purpose of the meeting, explain that it is being recorded, and ask those present (ideally, six to ten people) to briefly introduce themselves.
- Ask each question. Follow the general guidelines for running a good meeting by making sure that everyone participates. Keep your own comments brief.
- After all the questions have been addressed, briefly summarize the meeting to make sure you understand the points that have been made. Thank everyone for coming, and end the meeting on time.

Following Up

- Having listened objectively to what the participants said, process the data honestly, even if your favorite idea was unpopular.
- Share the results with the rest of your team, and treat the outcome as one more piece of information to help you shape your business decision.

Practice Your Skills

Developing Focus Group Questions

Reread the proposal you wrote about increasing saxophone rentals (pages 551–553). Imagine that your boss has asked you to test your ideas in a focus group. Copy the following focus group form onto a sheet of paper and complete it.

FOCUS GROUP MEETING

Date: ____________________

Time: ____________________

Place: ____________________

Purpose: ____________________

Kinds of Participants: ____________________

Questions

1.

2.

3.

Practice Your Skills

Using Content-Area Vocabulary

Select one of the terms from this chapter listed below. Write a description of the term along with a scenario in which you might use the form of nonwritten communication.

- informal meeting
- formal meeting
- teleconference
- videoconference
- focus group

D. Speeches, Presentations, and Discussions

Apply 21st Century Communication and Collaboration Skills

Communication and collaboration are powerful processes that can expand people's knowledge and bring about change. To communicate successfully, you must express your ideas clearly and forcefully so that your listeners understand and respond to your message. To collaborate constructively, you must freely exchange ideas and share responsibility to achieve a common goal.

For communication and collaboration to be truly effective, they must be based on respect. In the diverse world of the 21st century, you will learn and work with people from various social and cultural backgrounds who will have different perspectives. Whether you are making a speech, participating in a group discussion, or collaborating with a team to complete a task, respecting varied opinions and values will enrich your understanding and make you a more successful communicator and collaborator.

In this chapter, you will learn effective strategies for speaking, listening, and collaborating that will help you succeed in school and in the workplace.

Developing Public Speaking and Presentation Skills

In the course of your academic and professional career, you may often be asked to prepare and deliver a speech. In school you might give a speech to a class, a team, or a group of parents. In the workplace you might address an audience at a meeting or a large convention. Learning to express your ideas well and use media and technology effectively will help you deliver a successful speech.

1 Preparing Your Speech

When you prepare a speech, you should follow steps similar to those you use when preparing a report or a persuasive essay. In speaking, as in writing, thoughtful, careful preparation will make your final product a success.

Choosing a Subject to Suit Your Audience and Purpose

Every speech has a main purpose—to inform, instruct, motivate, persuade, or entertain. Most speeches, however, have more than one purpose. In an oral book report, for instance, you can inform audience members about the book, entertain them with an account of your favorite passage, and persuade them to read it.

21ST CENTURY

To deliver a successful speech, you need to match your subject to your purpose and audience. Use these strategies to help you choose a subject that suits your audience and purpose.

HERE'S HOW

Strategies for Considering Audience and Purpose

- Determine your main purpose. Is it to inform, instruct, motivate, persuade, or entertain? Decide, as well, whether you have more than one purpose.
- Find out the interests of your audience. Then choose a subject that matches your audience's interests and your purpose. Consider, for example, what subject you might choose if your purpose is to persuade your younger brother to attend the sleep-away camp you went to for three summers. You might discuss the freedom he would have. However, if your purpose is to persuade your parents to let your brother attend the camp, your subject might be the high-quality supervision campers receive.
- You want your audience to have confidence in you, so choose a subject that you know well or can research thoroughly.

You can learn more about specific purposes for written and oral essays on pages 5 and 16.

Practice Your Skills

Determining a Subject That Suits an Audience and Purpose

Write an example of a subject for a speech you might give for each of three purposes—to inform, to persuade, and to entertain. Choose a different audience for each speech. To show why your subject is suitable, jot down some notes in your journal about why you want to make each speech and what you know about your audience.

Limiting a Subject

After choosing an interesting subject, you should limit it so that you can cover it effectively within a given amount of time. Keep in mind that it takes about as much time to give a 20-minute speech as it does to read aloud an eight-page essay that is typed double-space. The following strategies will help you limit your subject.

HERE'S HOW **Strategies for Limiting a Subject**

- Limit your subject by choosing one aspect of it. For example, for a 20-minute speech about space exploration, you could limit the subject to the International Space Station.
- Identify what your audience already knows about your subject, and consider what your audience may expect to hear. Then limit your subject to suit your listeners' expectations.
- Limit your subject to suit your purpose.

21ST CENTURY

The following examples illustrate three ways to limit a subject according to the purpose of your speech. The main topic is driving a car.

LIMITING A SUBJECT

Purpose	Example
to inform	Explain what to do in case of a flat tire.
to persuade	Convince people not to drive after drinking alcohol.
to entertain	Tell a story about the things you did wrong during your first driving test.

Practice Your Skills

Limiting a Subject

Choose a purpose and an audience. Then limit each subject to be suitable for a 20-minute speech.

1. television
2. American poets
3. civil rights
4. technology
5. careers
6. the American presidency

Gathering and Organizing Information

After you have chosen and limited your subject, begin to gather information. List everything you already know about the subject. Then consult useful sources of information, including encyclopedias, books, periodicals, and online materials in the library or media center. You might also consider interviewing people who are knowledgeable about the subject.

Taking Notes Take notes on note cards as you do your research. Note cards are best for recording ideas because later you can easily organize the cards into categories as you prepare to outline your speech. If you interview someone, take notes or use an audio recorder. You should write down any words from the interview you intend to quote, put them in quotation marks, and get permission from the speaker to use the quotations.

Collecting Audiovisual Aids Audiovisual aids, such as maps, pictures, PowerPoint® slides, CDs, and DVDs, can add to the impact of your speech. Choose aids that suit the purpose and context of your speech. Make sure the aids will help you communicate your message effectively and will not be distracting. Once you decide which of your main points to enhance with the use of audiovisual aids, gather or create these materials as you prepare your speech.

HERE'S HOW

Strategies for Organizing a Speech

- Arrange your note cards by topic and subtopics.
- Use your note cards to make a detailed outline of your speech.
- Draft an introduction. To capture the interest of your audience, begin your speech with an anecdote, an unusual fact, a question, an interesting quotation, or some other attention-getting device. Present a clear thesis in your introduction. (See pages 112–115.)
- Arrange your ideas in a logical order, and think of the transitions you will use to connect the ideas. (See pages 95–97 and 245–248.)
- Support your points in the body of your speech with valid evidence from reliable sources. Use appropriate appeals to support your claims and argument.
- When defending a point of view, use precise language and appropriate detail.
- Write a conclusion for your speech that summarizes your main ideas. Try to conclude your speech with a memorable sentence or phrase. (See page 124.)

A good speaker presents information, findings, and supporting evidence in a clear and distinct perspective, addressing alternative or opposing perspectives. Listeners should be able to clearly follow the speaker's line of reasoning. In a good speech, the development, style, and substance are well tailored to the purpose, audience, and task.

Practice Your Skills

Gathering and Organizing Information

Choose and limit a subject for a 20-minute speech in which the purpose is to inform. Write what you know about the subject on note cards. Next, visit the library or media center, and use print and electronic resources to find additional information for at least ten more note cards. Then organize your cards, outline your speech, and draft an introduction and a conclusion. Prepare any audiovisual aids you will use.

Practicing Your Speech

To deliver your speech with as much expression and confidence as possible, you should practice it several times. In practicing the speech, however, do not try to memorize it. Memorized speeches usually sound stiff and awkward. Instead, use your outline to deliver your speech, or create a set of cue cards from your outline and note cards to remind you of the important points you wish to make. Prepare one cue card for each topic and subtopic in your outline. Write key words and phrases as well as quotations on the cards. In addition, create cards to help you present your introduction and conclusion smoothly. Remember to put your cue cards in the order in which you will use them. Use the following strategies when practicing your speech.

21ST CENTURY

HERE'S HOW **Strategies for Practicing a Speech**

- Practice in front of a long mirror so that you will be aware of your gestures, posture, and facial expressions. Use natural gestures. Rehearsed gestures may look false.
- Practice looking around the room at an imaginary audience as you talk.
- Practice using your cue cards and any audiovisual aids that are part of your presentation.
- Time your speech. If necessary, add or cut information.
- Practice over a period of several days. Your confidence will grow each time you practice, and your nervousness will decrease.

Make revisions to your speech as you practice. You can do this by experimenting with your word choice and by adding or deleting information to clarify your main points. Strategically use digital media to enhance understanding and add interest. In addition, if you practice your speech with a classmate or friend, you can use your listener's comments to improve your speech before you deliver it.

Practice Your Skills

Practicing and Revising Your Informative Speech

Make cue cards for your informative speech. Then, using the strategies above, practice your speech before relatives, friends, or classmates. Monitor their responses. Are they fidgeting in their seats or staring out the window? Are they nodding in agreement or nodding off into dreamland? Explore different ways of keeping your audience's attention.

2 Delivering Your Speech

All the time you spent researching, organizing, and practicing your speech will pay off when you deliver it. Just before starting your speech, remind yourself that you are now an expert on your subject and probably know more about it than anyone in your audience. Keep in mind these additional strategies for delivering a speech.

HERE'S HOW

Strategies for Delivering a Speech

- Have ready all the materials you need, such as your outline or cue cards and audiovisual aids or equipment.
- Make sure that your computer presentation equipment is assembled and running properly.
- Wait until your audience is quiet and settled.
- Relax and breathe deeply before you begin your introduction.
- Stand with good posture, your weight evenly divided between both feet. Avoid swaying back and forth.
- Look directly at the members of your audience, not over their heads. Try to make eye contact.
- During your speech, make sure you talk to the audience, not to a particular visual or display.
- Speak slowly, clearly, and loudly enough to be heard.
- Use good, clear diction.
- Adjust the volume, pitch, and tone of your voice to enhance the communication of your message.
- Use correct grammar and well-formed sentences.
- Use informal, technical, or standard language appropriate to the purpose, audience, occasion, and subject. Be sure to use respectful language when presenting opposing views.
- Use rhetorical strategies appropriate to the message, whether your purpose is to inform or persuade.
- Use appropriate gestures and facial expressions to emphasize your main points.
- Make sure that everyone in your audience can see your audiovisual aids, such as charts and power presentation slides.
- After finishing your conclusion, take your seat without making comments to people in the audience.

3 Evaluating an Oral Presentation

The ability to evaluate an oral presentation will help you and your classmates improve your future speeches. The following Oral Presentation Evaluation Form may be useful. When evaluating a classmate's speech and completing the form, be honest but remember to make your comments positive, respectful, and helpful. Make your comments specific in order to help the speaker understand your suggestions. Apply your listeners' suggestions to future speeches.

21ST CENTURY

ORAL PRESENTATION EVALUATION FORM

Subject: ____

Speaker: ________________________________ **Date:** __________

Content:

Were the subject and purpose of the speech appropriate for the audience?
What was the speaker's point of view?
Was the main point clear?
Were there enough details and examples?
Did all the ideas clearly relate to the subject?
Were the speaker's reasoning and use of evidence sound?
Were the speaker's stance, premises, and links among ideas reasonable and sound?
Were the speaker's word choice, points of emphasis, and tone appropriate and effective?
Was the length appropriate (not too long or too short)?

Organization:

Did the speech begin with an interesting introduction?
Did the ideas in the body follow a logical order?
Were transitions used between ideas?
Did the conclusion summarize the main points?

Presentation:

Did the speaker choose appropriate words?
Was the speech sufficiently loud and clear?
Was the rate appropriate (not too fast or too slow)?
Did the speaker make eye contact with the audience?
Did the speaker use gestures and pauses effectively?
Were cue cards or an outline used effectively?
Were audiovisual aids used effectively?

Comments: ____

____

____

____

Practice Your Skills

Delivering and Evaluating an Informative Speech

Present your informative speech to your classmates. Afterward, complete the Oral Presentation Evaluation Form for your speech at the same time that your classmates are evaluating your presentation. In addition, complete evaluation forms for your classmates' speeches. Use your listeners' suggestions to note ways that you can improve your future speeches.

Delivering and Evaluating a Persuasive Speech

Imagine that you are the publicity agent for the band Pale Thin Lizards, and it is your job to speak to executives at Zillionaire Records, a company currently showing interest in the band. Prepare a speech to persuade the executives to sign the band. Choose an organizing structure for your speech that is appropriate for your purpose, audience, and the context. Use language, including rhetorical devices, that is crafted to move your audience. Be sure that your assertions are based on logical reasons supported by relevant evidence. Use audiovisual aids to enhance your message. Present your speech to your classmates. Have them evaluate whether you used effective techniques to make your speech persuasive.

Delivering and Evaluating an Entertaining Speech

For your junior class trip, you went to Jungleland, a theme park that is not only fun, but also a learning experience—every ride, game, and show at the park provides geographical and cultural details about a specific area in the world. Prepare a speech about the trip to be delivered to the sophomore class. Your main purpose is to entertain the students, but you also want to inform them about the trip, which they will take next year. Be sure to include vivid, humorous anecdotes and details, along with informative facts and examples. Consider how you could use audiovisual aids to make your speech more entertaining. Practice your speech before a friend or family member, and then present it to your classmates. Write a brief assessment of your performance. Were the strategies you used to entertain your audience effective? Why or why not?

Developing Your Critical Listening Skills

Skillful listening requires you to pay close attention to what you hear. You must comprehend, evaluate, and remember the information. Good listeners engage in critical, appreciative, and reflective listening. They also engage in empathic listening, or listening with feeling. Skills that you have practiced while preparing and presenting a speech will be invaluable to you as you work to develop your critical listening skills.

1 Listening Appreciatively

You may have occasion to attend a public reading or an oral interpretation of a written work, such as an essay, a poem, a play, a chapter of a novel, or an excerpt from a memoir. **Oral interpretation** is the performance or expressive reading of a written work. An oral interpreter may read a script or manuscript or may present a memorized text. The following strategies will help you listen appreciatively to oral presentations and performances.

21ST CENTURY

HERE'S HOW

Strategies for Listening Appreciatively

- Be alert to the expressive power of a pause.
- Observe the use of gestures, voice, and facial expressions to enhance the message.
- Listen for changes in volume, intonation, and pitch used to emphasize important ideas.
- Listen for rhymes, repeated words, and alliteration.
- Listen for rhetorical strategies and other expressive uses of language.
- Take time to reflect upon the message, and try to experience with empathy the thoughts and feelings being expressed.

You can find many opportunities to practice listening appreciatively. Consider attending readings by authors at a nearby bookstore. A theater group might be performing a dramatic work that you have read for school. You may also have occasion to attend original artistic performances by your peers. You will get the most out of the experience by developing a listening strategy suited to the speaker's subject and purpose.

Practice Your Skills

Listening to Presentations and Performances

Develop your own strategies for listening to and evaluating the following oral presentations. Identify what you would listen for in each case.

1. an actor reading a monologue from a play
2. a poet reciting two poems
3. an author reading an excerpt from a memoir
4. a classmate reading Lincoln's *Gettysburg Address*

Practice Your Skills

Presenting an Oral Interpretation

Perform a reading of a scene for your class. Form a small group and choose a scene from a play, such as Arthur Miller's *Death of a Salesman,* that you have read for school. Then follow these steps to prepare and present your oral interpretation.

1. Sit in a circle and read through the scene. Discuss the most important ideas in the scene. Using the five *Ws* and *H,* analyze the scene for an understanding of character, purpose, and situation.
2. Prepare a brief introduction to the scene. Then prepare a script of the scene. Highlight the lines that you are to perform. Mark key words that you want to emphasize through gestures, tone, or facial expressions.
3. Rehearse the scene. Try out different readings of your lines until you arrive at the best interpretation. Listen to the other characters as they speak, and respond to them as though you were conducting a real conversation. Use the techniques that you have learned to evaluate your performance and those of your peers.
4. Perform the reading for your classmates. Have them critique your performance, and use their feedback to determine whether you successfully conveyed the meaning of the scene.

2 Listening to Directions

During a typical day, you probably follow many directions, such as those for taking a test or for getting to a friend's house. Always listen carefully to directions from beginning to end. Do not assume you know what the speaker is going to say before he or she finishes giving directions. In addition, follow these strategies.

HERE'S HOW

Strategies for Listening to Directions

- Write down the directions as the speaker gives them.
- If any part of the directions is unclear, ask specific questions.
- When you finish an assignment, review the directions to make sure you have followed them correctly.

Practice Your Skills

Following Directions

For the rest of the week, follow the previous strategies as you are given directions, whether in or outside of school. Include, for example, directions given by family members, friends, salespeople, or your employer. Explain in your journal why you think the strategies helped or did not help you to follow directions more accurately. Are there other strategies you would use in the future to help you follow directions correctly?

3 Listening for Information

You frequently listen for information—when you listen to news reports on television or to lectures in school, for instance. When you **listen for information,** you first need to comprehend what you hear so that you can evaluate the information and apply it. The following strategies will help you get the most out of informative presentations.

HERE'S HOW **Strategies for Listening for Information**

- Sit comfortably but stay alert. Try to focus your attention on what the speaker is saying without being distracted by people and noises.
- Determine the speaker's purpose, whether it is to inform, instruct, motivate, or persuade.
- Listen for verbal clues to identify the speaker's main ideas. Often, for example, a speaker emphasizes important points by using such words and phrases as *first, finally, also consider, most important, remember that,* or *in conclusion.*
- Watch for nonverbal clues, such as gestures, pauses, or changes in the speaking pace. Such clues often signal important points.
- Determine the speaker's values and point of view about the subject. For example, is the speaker expressing positive or negative attitudes or arguing for or against an issue?
- Take notes to organize your thoughts and to help you remember details. Your notes provide a basis for further discussion. You may also want to use your notes to outline the speech or write a summary of it. If the speech is a course lecture, notes will help you study for a test on the subject.
- Ask clear and relevant questions to monitor and clarify your understanding of ideas.
- Take time to reflect upon what you have heard.

Practice Your Skills

Listening and Taking Notes

Form a small group with three or four classmates. Choose a particular television news report to watch. Each member of the group should listen carefully to the broadcast and take notes. Afterward, compare the notes each of you took. Try to determine why all members recorded certain points and not others.

Listening Critically

Critical listeners carefully evaluate the information in a speech. They judge whether the information and ideas are valid. Be on the lookout for the following propaganda techniques, which a speaker may use to mislead or manipulate you.

TECHNIQUE	DEFINITION	FURTHER INFORMATION
Confusing Fact and Opinion	an opinion presented as a fact	To learn more, see page 314.
Bandwagon Appeal	an invitation to do or think the same thing as everyone else	To learn more, see page 314.
Testimonial	a statement, usually given by a famous person, that supports a product, candidate, or policy	To learn more, see page 314.
Unproved Generalization	a generalization based on only one or two facts or examples	To learn more, see pages 296–297.

Practice Your Skills

Using Content-Area Vocabulary

Watch an hour or two of commercial television and keep a log of the commercials, labelling them according to the propaganda techniques listed above.

Developing Your Group Discussion Skills

Group discussions are a way of communicating ideas, exchanging opinions, solving problems, and reaching decisions. Discussions may be formal or informal. You have informal discussions with your friends, family, and teachers every day. Formal discussions, on the other hand, may have formats and rules that must be followed, and you may have to present information you researched or use evidence to support your opinion. Developing your group discussion skills will help you to present your ideas effectively and to listen thoughtfully to others' ideas.

21ST CENTURY

1 Participating in Group Discussions

Discussions have many practical uses. You have probably participated in group discussions while brainstorming during the prewriting stage of the writing process. In the same way, you might use discussion skills to prepare an oral report. In addition, participating in a discussion group can be an effective way to study for a test. Each student in the group can take responsibility for reviewing a particular aspect of the material for the group.

For a group discussion to be successful, each member must agree with the group's goals. To make a discussion as effective as possible, follow these strategies.

HERE'S HOW

Strategies for Participating in Group Discussions

- Come to discussions well prepared, and draw on your preparation as you make comments to stimulate a thoughtful, well-reasoned exchange of ideas.
- Listen and respond respectfully to others' views.
- Keep an open mind and appreciate diverse perspectives as you promote civil, democratic discussions, setting clear goals and guidelines. Establish individual roles as needed.
- Ask questions to make sure you understand information and others' views.
- Express your ideas clearly. Present examples or evidence to support your ideas.
- Propel conversations by posing and responding to questions that probe reasoning and evidence.
- Clarify, verify, or challenge conclusions.
- Respond thoughtfully to diverse views, and synthesize comments, claims, and evidence from all perspectives.
- Keep in mind that everyone in the group should have an equal opportunity to speak.
- Give effective verbal and nonverbal feedback to other members.
- Be flexible and help your group determine what further information or research is needed to draw a conclusion or reach a consensus.

2 Leading Group Discussions

Sometimes your teacher will lead the discussion and make sure that it does not stray from the agenda. Other times a group appoints its own leader to focus the discussion and keep it on track. Such discussions are called **directed discussions.** If you are chosen to be the leader, or moderator, of a directed discussion group, use the following strategies to help you conduct the discussion.

HERE'S HOW

Strategies for Leading a Discussion

- With the group's help, state the purpose or goal of the discussion.
- Keep the discussion on track to help the group achieve its goals.
- Encourage everyone to participate and establish a tone of respect. Make sure that everyone has an equal opportunity and equal time to speak.
- Keep a record of the group's main points and decisions, or assign this task to a group member.
- At the end of the discussion, summarize the main points, and restate any conclusions or decisions the group has reached.

21ST CENTURY

Practice Your Skills

Conducting a Directed Discussion

Conduct a directed discussion. With a group select a topic relating to an issue in your community. Then establish a goal, and choose a group leader. Set a time limit for the discussion. Afterward, evaluate your participation in the group based on the **Strategies for Participating in Group Discussions.** If you were the leader, evaluate your performance based on the **Strategies for Leading a Discussion.**

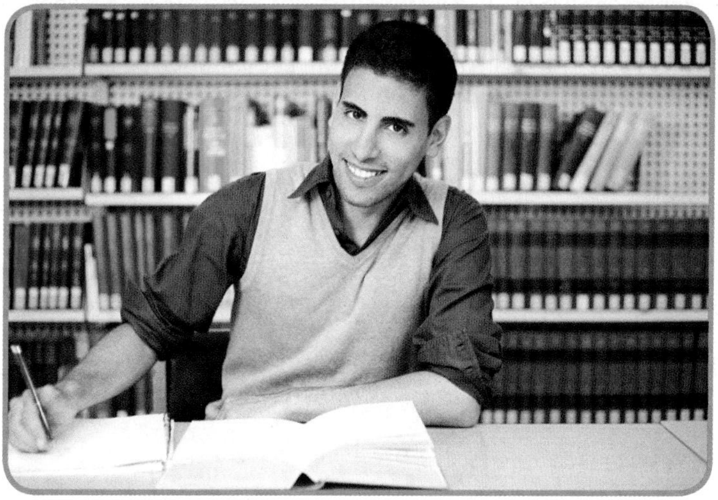

3 Cooperative Learning

Cooperative learning involves working in a group to achieve a learning goal. Each group member takes on a particular task. For example, in a cooperative learning group assigned to deliver a report on France during the Napoleonic era, one student might research Napoleon's rise to power, another might provide information about the French society of the day, and still another might prepare maps and other graphics.

Once the members have fulfilled their individual responsibilities, they coordinate their work to achieve the overall goal of the group. The success of the project depends on the effective collaboration of group members.

21ST CENTURY

HERE'S HOW

Strategies for Cooperative Learning

- Use the **Strategies for Participating in Group Discussions** (page 586).
- Participate in planning the project and in assigning tasks.
- When you have been given a task, do not let your group down by coming to meetings unprepared.
- Value the contributions of other team members.
- Cooperate with others in the group to resolve conflicts, solve problems, draw conclusions, reach a consensus, and make decisions.
- Help your group achieve its goals by taking your fair share of responsibility for the group's success.

Practice Your Skills

Organizing a Cooperative Learning Group

Form a cooperative learning group of three to five members, and plan an oral presentation about a particular current event. First, choose a leader, discuss your goal, and assign tasks. Then gather the necessary information, and coordinate the group members' work. Finally, deliver your presentation to the class, remembering to follow the steps for preparing and delivering an oral presentation.

PART III

Media and Technology

Part I	Critical Thinking and Problem Solving for Academic Success
Part II	Communication and Collaboration
Part III	Media and Technology

Essential Skills

You already understand the importance of literacy, or the ability to read and write. In the 21st century, literacy—knowledge of a particular subject or field—in the areas of information, media, and technology is also essential. Part III of this guide will help you develop literacy in these three areas. This knowledge will help you succeed in school and in your future jobs.

1 Information Literacy

Today, a tremendous amount of information is available at your fingertips. To acquire information literacy, you must know how to access, manage, evaluate, and use this wealth of information. Learning advanced search strategies will help you locate information efficiently and effectively from a range of relevant print and electronic sources. Evaluating the reliability and validity of sources will help you assess their usefulness. Then you can synthesize information in order to draw conclusions or to solve a problem creatively. Understanding the difference between paraphrasing and plagiarism and knowing how to record bibliographic information will ensure that you use information in an ethical, legal manner. Part III of this guide will help you build your information literacy skills by showing you how to use the Internet to access information.

21ST CENTURY

2 Media Literacy

Media messages serve a variety of purposes. They can have a powerful influence on your opinions, values, beliefs, and actions. Part III of this guide will help you develop your media literacy skills by showing you how to use both print and nonprint media to communicate your message. You will learn how to use these media to create effective messages that suit your audience and purpose. You will also learn about the types of tools available for creating media products.

3 Technology Literacy

In the 21st century, knowing how to use technology to research, evaluate, and communicate information is essential. You must also know how to use different forms of technology, such as computers and audio and video recorders, to integrate information and create products. Part III of this guide will show you how to use technology effectively to access information and to publish and present your ideas in different media.

A. Electronic Publishing

21ST CENTURY

Apply Media and Technology Literacy

Everything you may ever have to say or write requires some medium through which you express it and share it with others. The ability to use available media and technology to their fullest potential will enable you to communicate your ideas effectively and to a widespread audience. For now, most academic and workplace communication still depends on print technology. By using that to its full capability, you will prepare yourself for the inevitable improvements and upgrades that will be a feature of communication in the future.

In this section, you will develop your skills in using available technology in your communication.

Digital Publishing

The computer is a powerful tool that gives you the ability to create everything from digital newsletters to multimedia reports. Many software programs deliver word-processing and graphic arts capabilities that once belonged only to professional printers and designers. Armed with the knowledge of how to operate your software, you simply need to add some sound research and a healthy helping of creativity to create an exciting paper.

Word Processing

Using a standard word-processing program, such as Microsoft Word®, makes all aspects of the writing process easier. Use a word-processing program to

- create an outline
- save multiple versions of your work
- revise your manuscript
- proof your spelling, grammar, and punctuation
- produce a polished final draft document

Using a Spell Checker

You can use your computer to help you catch spelling errors. One way is to set your Preferences for a wavy red line to appear under words that are misspelled as you type. You can also set your Preferences to correct spelling errors automatically.

A second way to check your spelling is to choose Spelling and Grammar from the Tools menu. Select the text you want to check and let the spell checker run through it looking for errors. While a spell checker can find many errors, it cannot tell you if a correctly spelled word is used correctly. For example, you might have written *The books were over their.* The spell checker will not identify an error here, even though the correct word is *there*, not *their*.

Fascinating Fonts

Once your written material is revised and proofed, you can experiment with type as a way to enhance the content of your written message and present it in a reader-friendly format. Different styles of type are called **fonts** or **typefaces**. Most word-processing programs feature more than 30 different choices. You'll find them listed in the Format menu under Font.

Or they may be located on the toolbar at the top left of your screen.

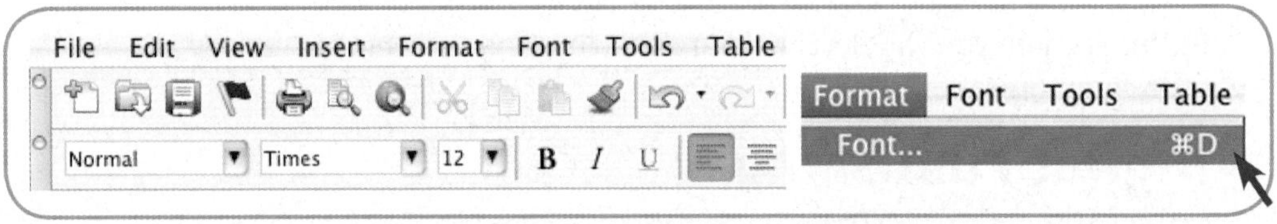

Most fonts fall into one of two categories: **serif** typefaces or **sans serif** typefaces. A serif is a small curve or line added to the end of some of the letter strokes. A typeface that includes these small added curves is called a serif typeface. A font without them is referred to as sans serif, or in other words, without serifs.

Times New Roman is a serif typeface.

Arial is a sans serif typeface.

In general, sans serif fonts have a sharp look and are better for shorter pieces of writing, such as headings and titles. Serif typefaces work well for body copy.

Each typeface, whether serif or sans serif, has a personality of its own and makes a different impression on the reader. Specialized fonts, like the examples in the second paragraph on the next page, are great for unique projects (posters, invitations, and personal correspondence) but less appropriate for writing assignments for school or business.

Since most school writing is considered formal, good font choices include Times New Roman, Arial, Helvetica, or Bookman Antiqua. These type styles are fairly plain. They allow the reader to focus on the meaning of your words instead of being distracted by the way they appear on the page.

With so many fonts to choose from, you may be tempted to include a dozen or so in your document. Be careful! Text printed in multiple fonts can be EXTREMELY confusing to read. Remember that the whole idea of using different typefaces is to enhance and clarify your message, not muddle it!

A Sizable Choice

Another way to add emphasis to your writing and make it reader-friendly is to adjust the size of the type. Type size is measured in points. One inch is equal to 72 points. Therefore, 72-point type would have letters that measure one inch high. To change the point size of your type, open the Format menu and click Font.

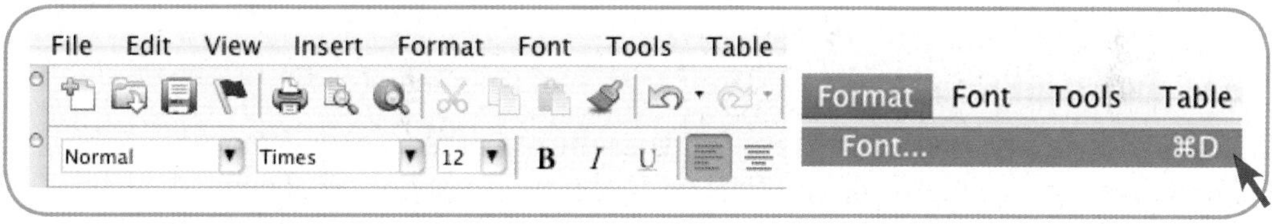

Or use the small number box on the toolbar at the top left side of your screen.

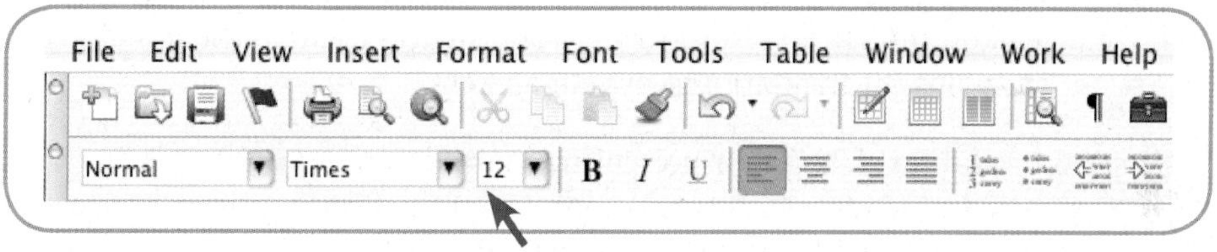

For most school and business writing projects, 10 or 12 points is the best size of type for the main body copy of your text. However, it's very effective to increase the type size for titles, headings, and subheadings to highlight how your information is organized. Another way to add emphasis is to apply a style to the type, such as **bold,** *italics,* or underline. Styles are also found in the Format menu under Font.

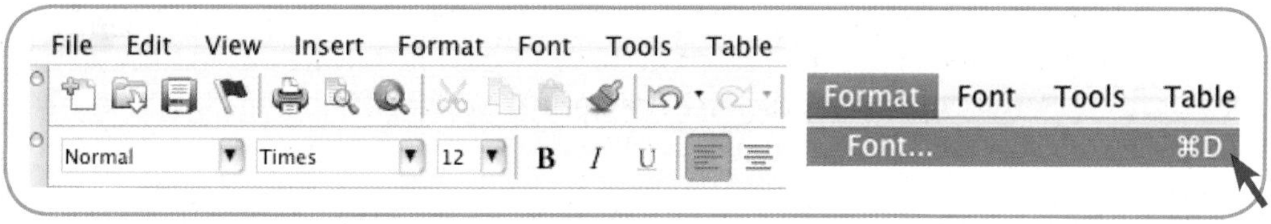

Or look for them—abbreviated as **B** for bold, *I* for italics, and U for underline—in the top center section of the toolbar on your screen.

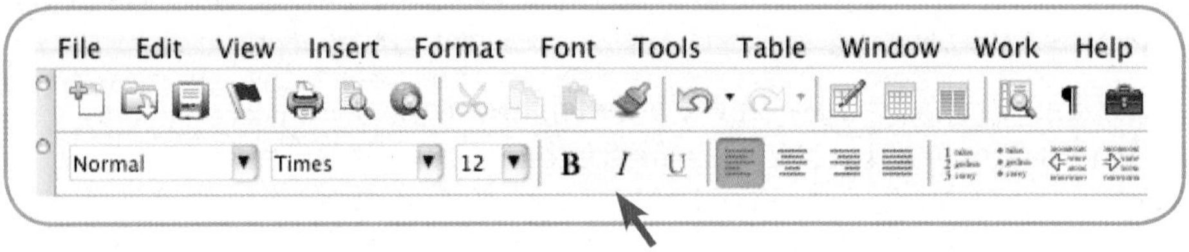

If you have access to a color printer, you may want to consider using colored type to set your heading apart from the rest of the body copy. Red, blue, or other dark colors work best. Avoid yellow or other light shades that might fade out and be difficult to read.

Use different type sizes, styles, and colors sparingly and consistently throughout your work. In other words, all the body copy should be in one style of type. All the headings should be in another, and so on. Doing so will give your work a unified, polished appearance.

Text Features

Text features such as **bulleted lists** and **numbered lists** are useful ways to organize information and give it a reader-friendly format. If you create pages of text in which information isn't broken up in any way, your readers may lose focus or have trouble identifying your main points. Instead, use bulleted or numbered lists to highlight important information and present it clearly and simply. To create these lists, open the Format menu and click on Bullets and Numbering. You can also click on the numbered or bulleted list on the toolbar at the top right of your screen.

A sidebar is another useful text feature for presenting information. A **sidebar** is a section of text that is placed alongside the main copy. Often the text in a sidebar appears in a box. Use sidebars to present additional, interesting information that relates to your main topic but doesn't belong in the body of your report or paper.

Layout Help from Your Computer

One way to organize the information in your document is to use one of the preset page layouts provided by your word-processing program. All you have to do is write your document using capital letters for main headings and uppercase and lowercase letters for subheadings. Set the headings apart from the body copy by hitting the "return" key. Then open the Format menu and click the Autoformat heading. Your copy will probably look like the illustration on the next page.

You can probably use this automatic, preset format for most of the writing you do in school. You'll also find other options available in the File menu under Page Setup.

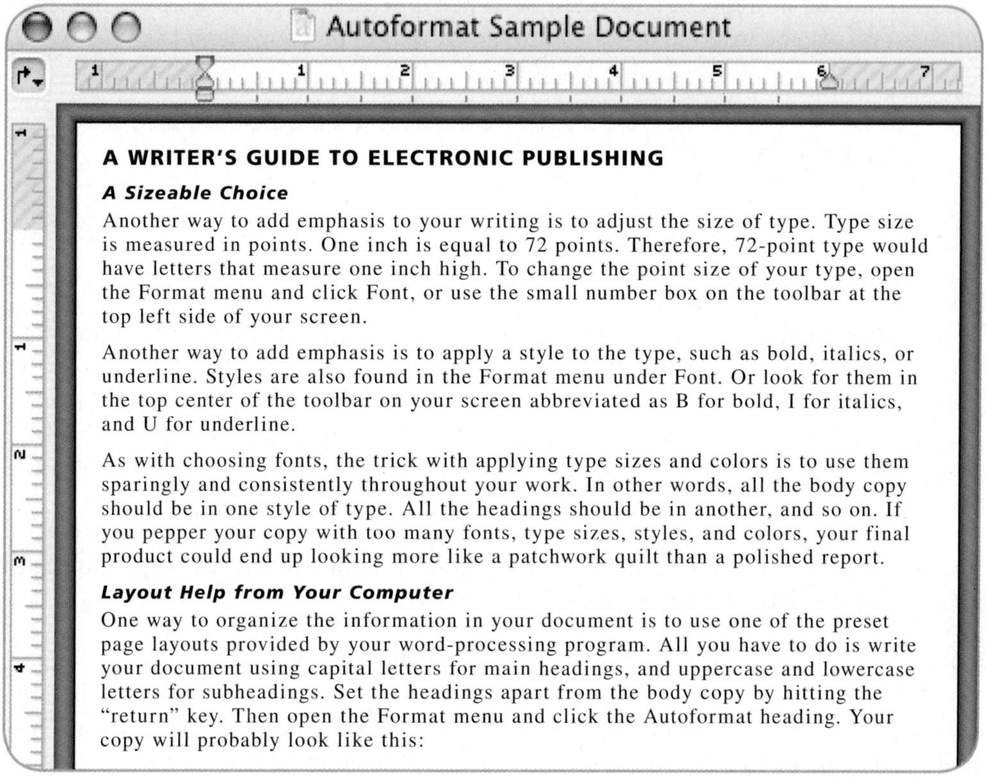

A WRITER'S GUIDE TO ELECTRONIC PUBLISHING

A Sizeable Choice

Another way to add emphasis to your writing is to adjust the size of type. Type size is measured in points. One inch is equal to 72 points. Therefore, 72-point type would have letters that measure one inch high. To change the point size of your type, open the Format menu and click Font, or use the small number box on the toolbar at the top left side of your screen.

Another way to add emphasis is to apply a style to the type, such as bold, italics, or underline. Styles are also found in the Format menu under Font. Or look for them in the top center of the toolbar on your screen abbreviated as B for bold, I for italics, and U for underline.

As with choosing fonts, the trick with applying type sizes and colors is to use them sparingly and consistently throughout your work. In other words, all the body copy should be in one style of type. All the headings should be in another, and so on. If you pepper your copy with too many fonts, type sizes, styles, and colors, your final product could end up looking more like a patchwork quilt than a polished report.

Layout Help from Your Computer

One way to organize the information in your document is to use one of the preset page layouts provided by your word-processing program. All you have to do is write your document using capital letters for main headings, and uppercase and lowercase letters for subheadings. Set the headings apart from the body copy by hitting the "return" key. Then open the Format menu and click the Autoformat heading. Your copy will probably look like this:

Here you can change the margins and add headers, footers, and page numbers. Headers and footers are descriptive titles that automatically appear at the top or bottom of each page without your having to retype them each time. For example, you may wish to add the title of your project and the date as a header or footer to each page.

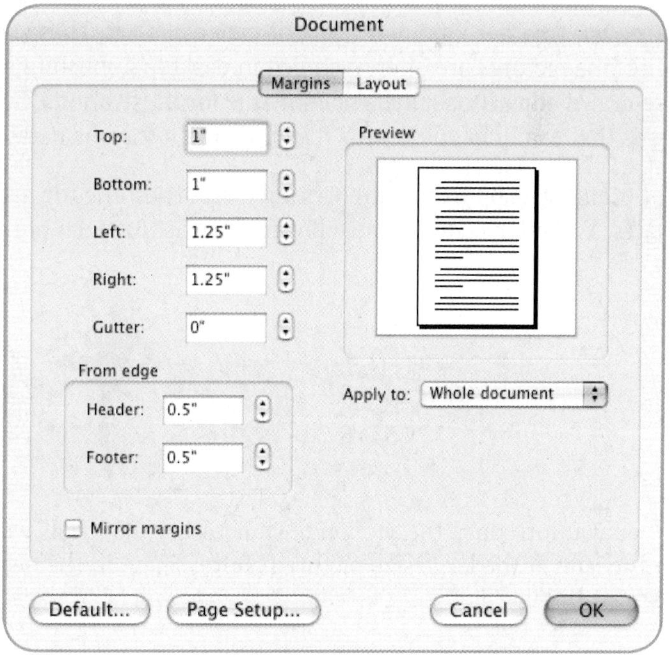

To insert a header or a footer, go to View and click on Header and Footer. Note that page numbers may also be inserted by way of the Insert option on your menu bar.

Let's Get Graphic

The old saying "A picture is worth a thousand words" is particularly true when it comes to spicing up papers and reports. Publishing and presentation software programs (such as Macromedia® FreeHand® and Microsoft PowerPoint®) give you the ability to include photographs, illustrations, and charts in your work that can express your ideas more clearly and succinctly than words alone.

The key to using graphics effectively is to make sure each one conveys a message of importance. Don't use them just for decoration. Be sure they add something meaningful, or you'll actually detract from your written message.

Drawings Many paint and draw programs allow you to create an illustration or **import** (bring in from another program) one into your document. Drawings can help illustrate concepts that are difficult to describe, such as mechanical parts or procedures. Cartoons can also add a nice touch. If you use them sparingly, they can lighten up an otherwise dry, technical report.

Clip Art Another kind of drawing is called clip art. These simple, black-and-white or color line pictures are often included in desktop publishing or word-processing programs. Pre-drawn clip art usually is not suitable for illustrations, but it does work well as graphic icons that can help guide your reader through various parts of a long report.

For example, suppose you are writing a report on the top arts programs in the United States. You might choose the following clip art for each of the sections:

When you introduce the section of your report that deals with music, you might use the music icon at the large size pictured above. Then, in the headings of all the following sections that deal with music, you might use a smaller version of the icon that looks like this:

Using clip art as icons in this manner lets your readers know at a glance which part of the report they are reading.

Charts and Graphs One of the best ways to communicate information about numbers and statistics is by using charts and graphs. Several software programs allow you to create bar graphs, pie charts, and line graphs that can communicate fractions, figures, and comparative measurements much more powerfully than written descriptions.

Photographs With the widespread availability of digital cameras and scanners, adding photos to your project is an easy and effective way to enhance your content. Using a digital camera or a scanner, you can load photos directly into your computer. Another option is to shoot photographs with a regular camera, but when you have them developed, specify that they be returned to you as "pictures on disc," which you can open on your computer screen. Photographic images are stored as bits of data in an electronic file. Once you have the photos in your computer, you can use a graphics program to manipulate the images in a variety of ways and create amazing visual effects. You can crop elements out of the photo, add special filters and colors, combine elements of two different pictures into one—the possibilities are endless.

After you have inserted the edited photo into your document, be careful when you print out your final draft. Standard printers often don't reproduce photographs well. You may want to take your document on disc to a professional printing company and have it printed out on a high-resolution printer to make sure you get the best quality.

Captions and Titles While it's true that a single photo can say a great deal, some pictures still need a little explanation in order to have the strongest impact on your reader. Whenever you include an illustration or photograph in a document, also include a simple caption or title for each image.

Add captions in a slightly smaller type size than the body copy and preferably in a sans serif typeface. Use the caption to add information that isn't immediately apparent in the photo. If there are people in the picture, tell readers who they are. If the photo features an odd-looking structure, explain what it is. Be smart with your captions. Don't tell readers the obvious. Give them a reason to read your caption.

Stand-Alone Graphics Occasionally you may include well-known graphics or logos in a report. These graphics convey powerful messages on their own and don't require captions. Examples of these logos or symbols include:

Nonprint Media—Audio and Video

The world we live in is becoming increasingly more multimedia-savvy. Many businesses rely extensively on multimedia presentations to market their products or convey messages to consumers and employees. Exciting opportunities exist for people who can produce clear, concise messages in audio and visual formats.

Pre-Production—Put It on Paper First

Although the final presentation of your subject material may be an audio recording or a video, your project needs to begin on paper first. When you write down your ideas, you do four things:

- Organize your thoughts.
- Narrow your focus.
- Isolate the main messages.
- Identify possible production problems.

Resist the urge to grab an audio recorder or camera and run off to record your project. That's a sure-fire way to create an unorganized mess. Take the time to plan your production.

Concept Outline The first task in the writing process is a short, one-page document that describes the basic idea of the project. Ideally this should be three paragraphs—one paragraph each describing the beginning, the middle, and the end. Do not go forward until you have clearly identified these three important parts of your project.

Brief Next write one to two pages that describe in detail the point of your project: how it will be used, who the intended audience is, what the purpose is, and what you hope to achieve with the presentation. Do you want your audience to be informed about something? Motivated to do something? Emotionally moved in some way?

Treatment The next phase of the writing process fleshes out the ideas you expressed in your outline and brief. The treatment is several pages long. It contains descriptions of the characters, dialogue, and settings and describes the presentation scene by scene. Include in your treatment descriptions of the mood and the tone of your piece. If your project is a video, set the stage by describing the overall look and feel of the production.

Script Once you've completed the first three steps, you are ready to go to script. Everything that is mentioned in the script will wind up in the audio recording or on the screen. Conversely, anything that is left out of the script will likely be overlooked and omitted from the final production. So write this document carefully.

For an audio recording, the script contains all narration, dialogue, music, and sound effects. For a video, it contains all of these elements plus descriptions of the characters, any sets, props, or costumes, plus all camera shots and movements, special visual effects, and onscreen titles or graphic elements. In short the audio script encompasses everything that is heard, and the video script covers everything that is seen and heard.

Storyboard Last, for video productions, it's also helpful to create storyboards—simple frame-by-frame sketches with explanatory notes jotted underneath—that paint a visual picture of what the video will look like from start to finish.

Pre-production Tasks The final stages of pre-production include assembling all the elements you will need before you begin producing your audio recording or video. Here's a general checklist.

Pre-Production Checklist

Audio Tasks

- ✓ Arrange for audio recording equipment
- ✓ Cast narrator/actors
- ✓ Find music (secure permission)
- ✓ Arrange for sound effects
- ✓ Set up recording schedule
- ✓ Coordinate all cast and crew
- ✓ Arrange for transportation if needed
- ✓ Rehearse all voice talent

Video Tasks

- ✓ Arrange for video equipment (including lighting and sound recording equipment)
- ✓ Cast narrator/host/actors
- ✓ Find music (secure permission)
- ✓ Arrange for sound/visual effects
- ✓ Set up shooting schedule
- ✓ Coordinate all cast and crew
- ✓ Arrange for transportation if needed
- ✓ Set up shooting locations (secure permission)
- ✓ Arrange for costumes, props, sets
- ✓ Arrange for make-up if needed
- ✓ Rehearse all on-camera talent

Video Production Schedule Tucked into the list of pre-production tasks is "Set up recording/shooting schedule." For a video, this means much more than just deciding what day and time you will begin shooting.

During the video production phase of your project, the idea is to shoot everything that your script calls for in the final production. Often the most efficient way to do this is what is called "out-of-sequence" filming. This means that, rather than shooting scenes sequentially (that is, in the order that they appear in the script), you shoot them in the order that is most convenient. Later you will edit them together in the correct order in post-production.

For example, your video might begin and end in the main character's office. Rather than shoot the first office scene, then move the cast and crew to the next location, then later at the end of the day return to the office, it might be easier to shoot both office scenes back-to-back. This will save a great deal of time and effort involved in moving people, lights, and props back and forth.

Lighting may be a factor in the order in which you shoot your scenes. For example, scenes 3, 4, and 7 may take place in the daytime, and scenes 1, 2, 5, and 6 may take place at night.

To accommodate all of these factors, you will need to plan your shooting schedule carefully. The difference between a smooth shoot day and chaos is a well thought-out shooting schedule.

Last, for video or audio recording, it's also a good idea to assemble your team for a pre-production meeting before you begin. This is your chance to read through the script together, go over time schedules, review responsibilities of each person involved, and answer any questions or discuss potential problems before you begin the production process.

Production

At last, it's production time! There are a number of different formats you can use for audio and video recording. Talk to the AV expert in your school or check with the media center for help in selecting the best format to use. Get tips, as well, for how to use the audio or video equipment to achieve the best results and produce a polished, professional project.

Next, if you are producing a video, think carefully about how you will shoot it. Consider the kinds of camera shots, camera moves, and special effects you will use.

Camera Shots To hold the interest of your audience, use a variety of camera shots and angles. Check your local library or media center for good books on camera techniques that describe when and how to use various shots—from long shots to close-ups, from low angles to overhead shots. As a rule, every time you change camera shots, change your angle slightly as well. This way, when the shots are edited together, you can avoid accidentally putting two nearly identical shots side-by-side, which creates an unnerving jarring motion called a "jump cut."

Do some research on framing techniques as well to make sure you frame your subjects properly and avoid cutting people's heads off on the screen.

Camera Moves Learn about ways to move the camera in order to keep your audience interested. Three common but effective camera moves are panning, tracking, and zooming. **Panning** means moving the camera smoothly from one side of the scene to another. Panning works well in an establishing shot to help orient your audience to the setting where the action takes place.

Tracking means moving the camera from one place to another in a smooth action as well, but in tracking, the camera parallels the action, such as moving alongside a character as he or she walks down the street. It's called tracking because in professional filmmaking, the camera and the operator are rolled forward or backward on a small set of train tracks alongside the actor or actress.

Zooming means moving the camera forward or back, but zooming actually involves moving the lens, rather than the camera. By touching the zoom button, you can focus in on a small detail that you would like to emphasize, or you can pull back to reveal something in the background.

The important factor in any kind of camera move is to keep the action fluid and, in most cases, slow and steady. Also, use camera movement sparingly. You want to keep your audience eager and interested, not dizzy and sick!

Cuts Another good way to keep your presentation moving is to use frequent cuts. While the actual cuts will be done during post-production, you need to plan for them in production. Professional filmmakers use the word *coverage* for making sure they have ample choices for shots. You can create coverage for your production by planning shots such as those on the following pages.

Here are three kinds of video shots:

establishing shot	This shot sets up where the action of the story will take place. For example, if your story takes place inside an operating room, you might begin with an establishing shot of the outside of the hospital.
reaction shot	It's a good idea to get shots of all on-camera talent even if one person does not have any dialogue but is listening to, or reacting to, another character. This gives you the chance to break away from the character who is speaking to show how his or her words are affecting other people in the scene.
cutaway shot	The cutaway shot is a shot of something that is not included in the original scene, but is somehow related to it. Cutaways are used to connect two subjects. For example, the first shot may be of a person falling off a boat. The second shot could be a cutaway of a shark swimming deep below the water.

Special Effects If you are adventurous, you may want to try some simple special effects. For instance, dry ice can create smoke effects. You can also have your actors freeze; then stop the camera, remove an object from the set, and restart the camera. This technique will make objects seem to disappear as if by magic. Other effects can be achieved by using false backdrops, colored lights, and filters.

Technology Tip

You may already have video editing tools on your computer or your school's computer. New Apple® computers and Windows®-based PCs come equipped with free video editing software. These programs are simple to use and can produce very effective videos or slide shows that are coordinated with music and narration and that feature interesting transitional elements like fades and dissolves. (See next page.) These programs also allow you to edit your video in a way that makes for easy uploading to video file-sharing sites. There are also free video editing tools online. Check out the computer you use most often to see what video tools it may have on it, and follow a tutorial to learn how to use the tool.

Post-Production—The Magic of Editing

Once all of your video recording is complete, it's time to create the final cut—that is, your choice of the shots you wish to keep and the shots you wish to discard. Be choosy and select the footage with only the best composition, lighting, focus, and performances to tell your story.

There are three basic editing techniques:

in-camera editing	In this process you edit as you shoot. In other words, you need to shoot all your scenes in the correct sequence and in the proper length that you want them to appear. This is the most difficult editing process because it leaves no margin for error.
insert editing	In insert editing you transfer all your footage to a new video. Then you record over any scenes that you don't want with scenes that you do want in the final version.
assemble editing	This process involves electronically copying your shots from the original source in your camera onto a new blank source, called the edited master, in the order that you want the shots to appear. This method provides the most creative control.

Consider including effects such as a dissolve from one shot to another instead of an abrupt cut. A *dissolve* is the soft fading of one shot into another. Dissolves are useful when you wish to give the impression that time has passed between two scenes. A long, slow dissolve that comes up from black into a shot, or from a shot down to black, is called a *fade* and is used to open or close a show.

In addition to assembling the program, post-production is the time to add titles to the opening of your program and credits to the end of the show. Computer programs, such as Adobe Premiere®, can help you do this. Some cameras are also equipped to generate titles. If you don't have any electronic means to produce titles, you can always mount your camera on a high tripod and focus it downward on well-lit pages of text and graphics placed on the floor. Then edit the text frames into the program.

Post-production is also the time to add voiceover narration and music. Voiceovers and background music should be recorded separately and then edited into the program on a separate sound track once the entire show is edited together. Video editing programs for your computer, such as Adobe Premiere®, allow you to mix music and voices with your edited video.

After post-production editing, your video production is ready to present to your audience or upload to a video file-sharing site.

Publishing on the Web

You can become a part of the Web community by building and publishing a Web site of your own. In fact, you may already have a Web presence with your account on a social network such as Facebook, which provides a medium for publishing your thoughts and linking to the sites of those you have designated as your "friends." Maybe you have even created your own social network through Ning or communicated with other members of your school on Twitter. Many businesses now have a presence in one or more social networks, appreciating the opportunity to interact with customers and collaborators.

If you are going to create a Web site, take advantage of all of these features. Your goal should be to make your site interesting enough that visitors will want to stay, explore, and come back to your site again—and that takes thought and planning.

PLANNING YOUR SITE

First you need to capture your thoughts and ideas on paper before you publish anything. Start with a one-page summary that states the purpose of your Web site and the audience you hope to attract. Describe in a paragraph the look and feel you think your site will need in order to accomplish this purpose and hold your audience's attention.

Make a list of the content you plan to include in your Web site. Don't forget to consider any graphics, animation, video, or sound you may want to include.

Next go on a Web field trip. Ask your friends and teachers for the URLs of their favorite Web sites. (URL stands for Universal Resource Locator.) Visit these sites, and ask yourself, "Do I like this site? Why or why not?" Determine which sites are visually appealing to you and why. Which sites are easy to navigate and why? Chances are the sites you like best will have clean, easy-to-read layouts, be well written, contain visually stimulating graphic elements, and have intuitive **interfaces** that make it simple to find your way around.

One sure drawback in any Web site is long, uninterrupted blocks of text. Decide how to break up long passages of information into manageable sections. Will there be separate sections for editorial content? News? Humor? Feedback? Which sections will be updated periodically and how often?

Make a few rough sketches for your site. How do you envision the home page of your site? What will the icons and buttons look like? Then give careful thought to how the pages will connect to each other, starting with the home page. Your plan for connecting the pages is called a **site map**.

Because the Web is an interactive medium, navigation is critical. Decide how users will get from one page to another. Will you put in a navigation bar across the top of the page or down the side? Will there be a top or home page at the beginning of each section?

Once you have planned the content, organized your material into sections, and designed your navigation system, you are ready to begin creating Web pages.

Putting It All Together

Writing for the Web is different from writing for print. The Web is a fast medium. Keep your messages succinct and to the point. Use short, punchy sentences. Break up your copy with clever subheads. Try not to exceed 500 to 600 words in any single article on any one page.

In order to turn text into Web pages, you need to translate the text into a special language that Web browsers can read. This language code is called HTML—HyperText Markup Language. There are three methods available:

- You can use the Save As Web Page feature in the File menu of most word-processing programs.
- You can import your text into a Web-building software program and add the code yourself if you know how.
- You can easily find free software programs online that will do the work for you. Web-building software programs are referred to as WYSIWYG (pronounced "Wiz-E-Wig"), which stands for "What You See Is What You Get."

Web-building software also allows you to create links to other Web pages using a simple process called **drag and drop**. Be sure to read the directions that come with your software package for complete instructions.

Blogs

Blogs (short for weblogs) are a type of Web page. In many ways, they are like online diaries or journals, where "bloggers" post the latest events of their lives and their thoughts and feelings on a wide range of subjects. Some blogs have other purposes, such as to promote community among speakers of certain languages or to influence politics. Among the most popular blogs are those devoted to celebrity news and to animal photos with funny captions. The most popular blog software is free and easy enough to use so that anyone with Web space can build one.

B. Using the Internet

Apply Information and Technology Literacy

The "age of information" dawned in the last haf of the 20th century. Success in the 21st century requires the ability to access, evaluate, and wisely use the abundance of information made available by advances in technology. Developing an understanding of the changing technologies and skill in putting them to work for your purposes are key competencies for the rest of your schooling and for your adult life ahead.

In this section, you will develop your skills for understanding and making the most of what the Internet has to offer.

How Does the Internet Work?

The Internet is made up of thousands of networks all linked together around the globe. Each network consists of a group of computers that are connected to one another to exchange information. If one of these computers or networks fails, the information simply bypasses the disabled system and takes another route through a different network. This rerouting is why the Internet is so valuable to agencies such as the U.S. Department of Defense.

No one "owns" the Internet, nor is it managed in a central place. No agency regulates or censors the information on the Internet. Anyone can publish information on the Internet as he or she wishes.

In fact, the Internet offers such a vast wealth of information and experiences that sometimes it is described as the Information Superhighway. So how do you "get on" this highway? It's easy. Once you have a computer, a modem, and a telephone or cable line, all you need is a connection to the Internet.

The Cyberspace Connection

A company called an Internet Service Provider (ISP) connects your computer to the Internet. Examples of ISPs that provide direct access are Microsoft

Network, Earthlink, Comcast, and AT&T. You can also get on the Internet indirectly through companies such as America Online (AOL).

ISPs charge a flat monthly fee for their service. Unlike the telephone company, once you pay the monthly ISP fee, there are no long-distance charges for sending or receiving information on the Internet—no matter where your information is coming from, or going to, around the world.

Alphabet Soup—Making Sense of All Those Letters

Like physical highways, the Information Superhighway has road signs that help you find your way around. Each specific group of information on the World Wide Web is called a **Web site** and has its own unique address. Think of it as a separate street address of a house in your neighborhood. This address is called the URL, which stands for Uniform Resource Locator. It's a kind of shorthand for where the information is located on the Web.

Here's a typical URL: **http://www.perfectionlearning.com.**

All addresses, or URLs, for the World Wide Web begin with **http://.** This stands for HyperText Transfer Protocol and is a programming description of how the information is exchanged.

The next three letters—**www**—let you know you are on the World Wide Web. The next part of the URL—**perfectionlearning**—is the name of the site you want to visit. The last three letters, in this case **com**, indicate that this Web site is sponsored by a **com**mercial company. Here are other common endings of URLs you will find:

- "org" is short for **org**anization, as in http://www.ipl.org, which is the URL of the Web site for the Internet Public Library, ipl2: Information You Can Trust.
- "edu" stands for **edu**cation, as in the Web address for the Virtual Reference Desk, http://thorplus.lib.purdue.edu/reference/index.html, featuring online telephone books, dictionaries, and other reference guides.
- "gov" represents **gov**ernment-sponsored Web sites, such as http://www.whitehouse.gov, the Web site for the White House in Washington, D.C.

To get to a Web site, you use an interface called a **browser**. Two popular browsers are Microsoft Internet Explorer® and Mozilla Firefox®. A browser is like a blank form where you fill in the information you are looking for. If you know the URL of the Web site you want to explore, all you have to do is type it in the field marked Location, click Enter on your keyboard, and wait for the information to be delivered to your computer screen.

BASIC INTERNET TERMINOLOGY

Here are some of the most frequently used words you will hear associated with the Internet.

address The unique code given to information on the Internet. This may also refer to an e-mail address.

bookmark A tool that lets you store your favorite URL addresses, allowing you one-click access to your favorite Web pages without retyping the URL each time.

browser Application software that supplies a graphical interactive interface for searching, finding, viewing, and managing information on the Internet.

chat Real-time conferencing over the Internet.

cookies A general mechanism that some Web sites use both to store and to retrieve information on the visitor's hard drive. Users have the option to refuse or accept cookies.

cyberspace The collective realm of computer-aided communication.

download The transfer of programs or data stored on a remote computer, usually from a server, to a storage device on your personal computer.

e-mail Electronic mail that can be sent all over the world from one computer to another.

FAQs The abbreviation for Frequently Asked Questions. This is usually a great resource to get information when visiting a new Web site.

flaming Using mean or abusive language in cyberspace. Flaming is considered to be in extremely poor taste and may be reported to your ISP.

FTP The abbreviation for File Transfer Protocol. A method of transferring files to and from a computer connected to the Internet.

home page The start-up page of a Web site.

HTML The abbreviation for HyperText Markup Language—a "tag" language used to create most Web pages, which your browser interprets to display those pages. Often the last set of letters found at the end of a Web address.

http The abbreviation for HyperText Transfer Protocol. This is how documents are transferred from the Web site or server to the browsers of individual personal computers.

ISP The abbreviation for Internet Service Provider—a company that, for a fee, connects a user's computer to the Internet.

keyword A simplified term that serves as subject reference when doing a search.

link Short for hyperlink. A link is a connection between one piece of information and another.

network A system of interconnected computers.

online To "be online" means to be connected to the Internet via a live modem connection.

plug-in Free application that can be downloaded off the Internet to enhance your browser's capabilities.

podcast An audio or video file on the Internet that is available for downloading to a personal media device.

real time Information received and processed (or displayed) as it happens.

RSS A format for distributing content to people or Web sites. It stands for "Really Simple Syndication." With an RSS "feed," users can get updates from sites of interest without having to go to the sites for the information.

search engine A computer program that locates documents based on keywords that the user enters.

server A provider of resources, such as a file server.

site A specific place on the Internet, usually a set of pages on the World Wide Web.

social network An online community of people who share interests and activities, usually based on the Web.

spam Electronic junk mail.

surf A casual reference to browsing on the Internet. To "surf the Web" means to spend time discovering and exploring new Web sites.

upload The transfer of programs or data from a storage device on your personal computer to another remote computer.

URL The abbreviation for Uniform Resource Locator. This is the address for an Internet resource, such as a World Wide Web page. Each Web page has its own unique URL.

Web 2.0 The so-called second generation of the World Wide Web, which promotes programming that encourages interaction and collaboration.

Web site A page of information or a collection of pages that is being electronically published from one of the computers in the World Wide Web.

wiki Technology that holds together a number of user-generated web pages focused on a theme, project, or collaboration. Wikipedia is the most famous example. The word *wiki* means "quick" in Hawaiian.

WWW The abbreviation for the World Wide Web. A network of computers within the Internet capable of delivering multimedia content (images, audio, video, and animation) as well as text over communication lines into personal computers all over the globe.

Communicating on the Internet

E-mail, mailing lists, and newsgroups are all great ways of exchanging information with other people on the Internet. Here's how to use these useful forms of communication, step-by-step.

1 Using E-mail

Any writer who has ever used e-mail in his or her work will agree that sending and receiving electronic messages is one of the most useful ways of gathering information and contacts for writing projects.

Once you open your e-mail program, click on the command that says Compose Mail or New Message. This will open a new blank e-mail similar to the one pictured below. Next, fill in the blanks.

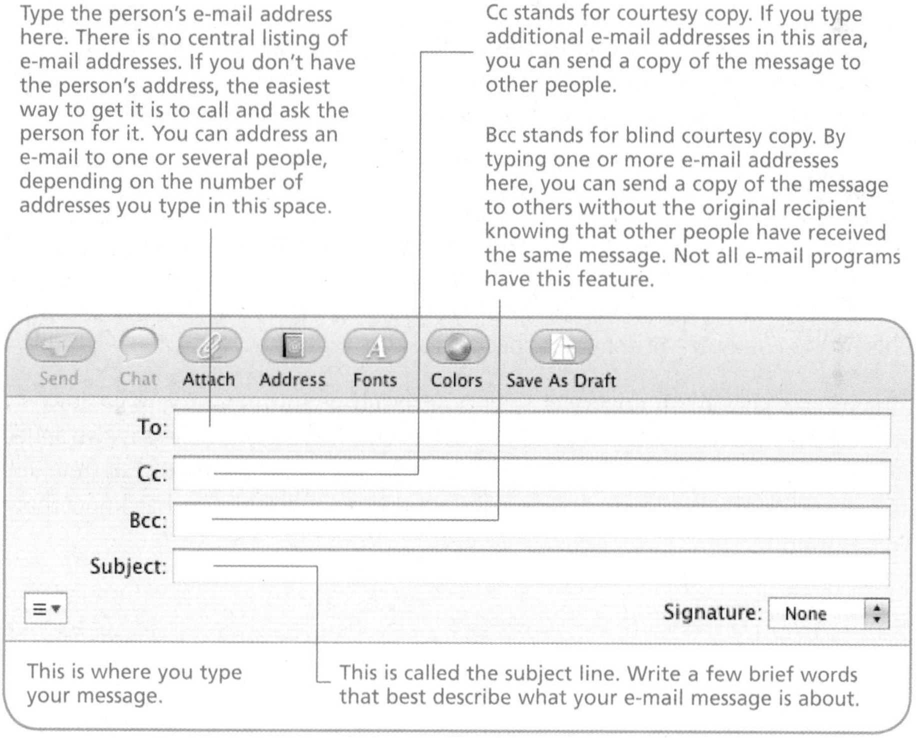
Type the person's e-mail address here. There is no central listing of e-mail addresses. If you don't have the person's address, the easiest way to get it is to call and ask the person for it. You can address an e-mail to one or several people, depending on the number of addresses you type in this space.
Cc stands for courtesy copy. If you type additional e-mail addresses in this area, you can send a copy of the message to other people.
Bcc stands for blind courtesy copy. By typing one or more e-mail addresses here, you can send a copy of the message to others without the original recipient knowing that other people have received the same message. Not all e-mail programs have this feature.
Send
Chat
Attach
Address
Fonts
Colors
Save As Draft
To:
Cc:
Bcc:
Subject:
Signature:
None
This is where you type your message.
This is called the subject line. Write a few brief words that best describe what your e-mail message is about.

Say It with Style

Like regular letters, e-mail can assume different tones and styles, depending on to whom you are writing. Usually informal e-mails and instant messages (IMs) to close friends are light, brief, and to the point. In the case of more formal e-mails, such as a request for information from an expert or a museum, keep the following guidelines in mind.

HERE'S HOW **Guidelines for Writing E-mails**

- Make sure your message is clear and concise.
- Use proper grammar and punctuation.
- Check your spelling. (Some e-mail programs have their own spell-check function—use it!)
- Double-check the person's e-mail address to be sure you've typed it correctly.

Attach a Little Something Extra

When you send e-mail, you can also send other information along with your message. These are called **attachments**. Depending on your e-mail program's capabilities, you can attach documents, photos, illustrations—even sound and video files. Click Attach, and then find and double-click on the document or file on your computer that you wish to send.

After you have composed your message and added any attachments you want to include, click the Send button. Your message arrives in the other person's mailbox seconds later, regardless of whether that person lives right next door or on the other side of the world.

Follow Up

Just because you have sent a message, you shouldn't automatically assume that the other person has received it. Internet Service Providers (ISPs) keep all messages that are sent until the recipient requests them. The person you sent your e-mail to might be away from his or her computer or may not check messages regularly.

Also, the Internet is still an imperfect science. From time to time, servers go down or other "hiccups" in electronic transmissions can occur, leaving your message stranded somewhere in cyberspace. If you don't get a reply in a reasonable amount of time, either resend your original e-mail message or call the person and let him or her know that your message is waiting.

You've Got Mail

When someone sends you an e-mail message, you have several options:

Reply Click Reply, and you can automatically send back a new message without having to retype the person's e-mail address. (Be sure you keep a copy of the sender's e-mail address in your Address Book for future use.)

Forward Suppose you receive a message that you would like to share with someone else. Click Forward, and you can send a copy of the message, plus include a few of your own comments, to another person.

Print In some instances, you may need to have a paper copy of the e-mail message. For example, if someone e-mails you directions to a party, click Print to take a hard copy of the instructions with you.

Store Do you want to keep a message to refer to later? Some e-mail programs allow you to create folders to organize stored messages.

Delete You can discard a message you no longer need just by clicking Delete. It's a good idea to throw messages away regularly to keep them from accumulating in your mailbox.

2 Other Online Communication

Another way to communicate online is Internet Relay Chat (IRC), or "chat rooms" for short. Chat rooms focus on a large variety of topics, so it's possible you'll be able to find a chat room where people are discussing the subject you are writing about.

"Chat" is similar to talking on the telephone except, instead of speaking, the people in the chat room type their responses back and forth to each other. As soon as you type your comment, it immediately appears on the computer screen of every person involved in the "conversation." There are also more advanced forms of chat available on the Net, such as video chat and voice chat.

One-to-one chatting, or instant messaging, is probably something you do frequently. With instant messaging, you need to "accept" as a buddy or contact each person you will communicate with. In contrast, anyone in a chat room can talk to you, and the anonymous nature of a chat room can make people less inhibited than they might otherwise be in person. If you sense that one of the participants in your chat room is responding inappropriately, ask your parents or teacher to step in, or simply sign off.

Join the Group

Mailing lists and newsgroups are larger discussion forums that can help you get even more information about a specific subject.

Mailing Lists To find a directory of available mailing lists, enter "mailing list directory" in a search engine. If you find a mailing list that interests you and wish to subscribe to it, just send a message to the administrative address. You will start to receive messages from the mailing list within a few days.

Remember, mailing lists use e-mail to communicate, so be sure to check your e-mail often because once you subscribe to a list, it's possible to receive dozens of messages in a matter of days.

Another good idea is to read the messages in your new mailing list for a week or so before submitting a message of your own. This will give you a good idea of what has already been discussed so you can be considerate about resubmitting old information.

You can reply to a message any time you wish. However, it doesn't do anyone any good to respond by saying "Yes, I agree." Get in the habit of replying to messages only when you have something important to add. Also, be sure to repeat the original question in your reply so that people understand which message you are responding to.

Be sure that you really want to belong to a mailing list before you subscribe. Unwanted e-mail can be a nuisance. Fortunately, if you change your mind, you can always unsubscribe to mailing lists at any time.

Newsgroups To join a newsgroup, check with your ISP. Service providers frequently list available topics under the heading "Newsgroups." Newsgroups are named with two or more words separated by a period. For example, there is a newsgroup named rec.sport.baseball.college. The first three letters—"rec"—defines the main subject, in this case recreation. Each word that follows—sport, baseball, and college—narrows the scope of the subject to an increasingly more specific area of interest. As with mailing lists, you can always unsubscribe to newsgroups at any time.

As in any social setting, there are a few guidelines to follow when you are talking to people online—via e-mail, in a chat room, or in a newsgroup. This conduct is called **netiquette.** Netiquette requires that you refrain from harsh or insulting language and from writing in all uppercase letters, which can feel like shouting. It requires you to respect other people's privacy, ideas, and work. Don't forward a message or attach documents written by someone else without first asking the author's permission. Don't send spam, unwanted messages for the purpose of selling something.

Online Collaboration and Web 2.0

The Web is always changing. One big change from its earliest days is the ease with which people can collaborate online. For example, your writing group could use Google Docs (http://docs.google.com) to work together on writing projects: to share drafts, to edit your peers' work, and to set schedules and guidelines. Through Google Docs, everyone who is invited to do so can have access to documents and edit them online.

Another useful tool for collaboration is the **wiki**, a platform for creating linked pages on a common theme or for a common project. Wikipedia is the best known example. You can start your own free wiki at wiki.com and explore how you can use it in your learning.

Cyberbullying

More than half of teenagers recently surveyed reported that they have been the victim of online bullying, also called cyberbullying, or known someone who has been. **Cyberbullying** is the use of such technology as the Internet and cell phones to deliberately hurt or embarrass someone. Cyberbullies often assume fake identities to trick people. They also knowingly spread lies and often post pictures of someone without his or her permission. Cyberbullies can trick their victims into revealing personal information which is then abused.

Victims react in different ways. Some take such reasonable measures as blocking an offending user or refusing to read comments that might be hurtful and deleting them as soon as they arrive. Some seek help from adults, who sometimes help the victim report the problem to the appropriate authorities. Other teens have a more negative and painful reaction. They might withdraw from their usual pastimes and suffer from problems with self-esteem. Or they might get caught up in the negative swirl and try to bully back.

The National Crime Prevention Council (NCPC) makes these suggestions to teens to stop cyberbullying.

- Refuse to pass along cyberbullying messages.
- Tell friends to stop cyberbullying.
- Block communication with cyberbullies.
- Report cyberbullying to a trusted adult.

The NCPC developed a slogan to summarize what to do: "Delete cyberbullying. Don't write it. Don't forward it."

Unit 4

Grammar

In this unit you will explore the bones of the English language. Just like the skeletal structure of any living thing, a language's grammar lies beneath the surface, silently providing essential support. As a child, you learned about grammatical structures simply by imitating the people around you. Everyone used verbs to set nouns in motion, modifiers to add details, conjunctions to connect ideas, and prepositions to show relationships. You naturally did the same. This unit will expand that knowledge and help you perfect the skills you've already acquired. You will examine the parts of a sentence and explore the many ways to fit those parts together. As Anthony Burgess suggests, the more acquainted you become with the structure of your language, the easier it is to help it "walk the earth."

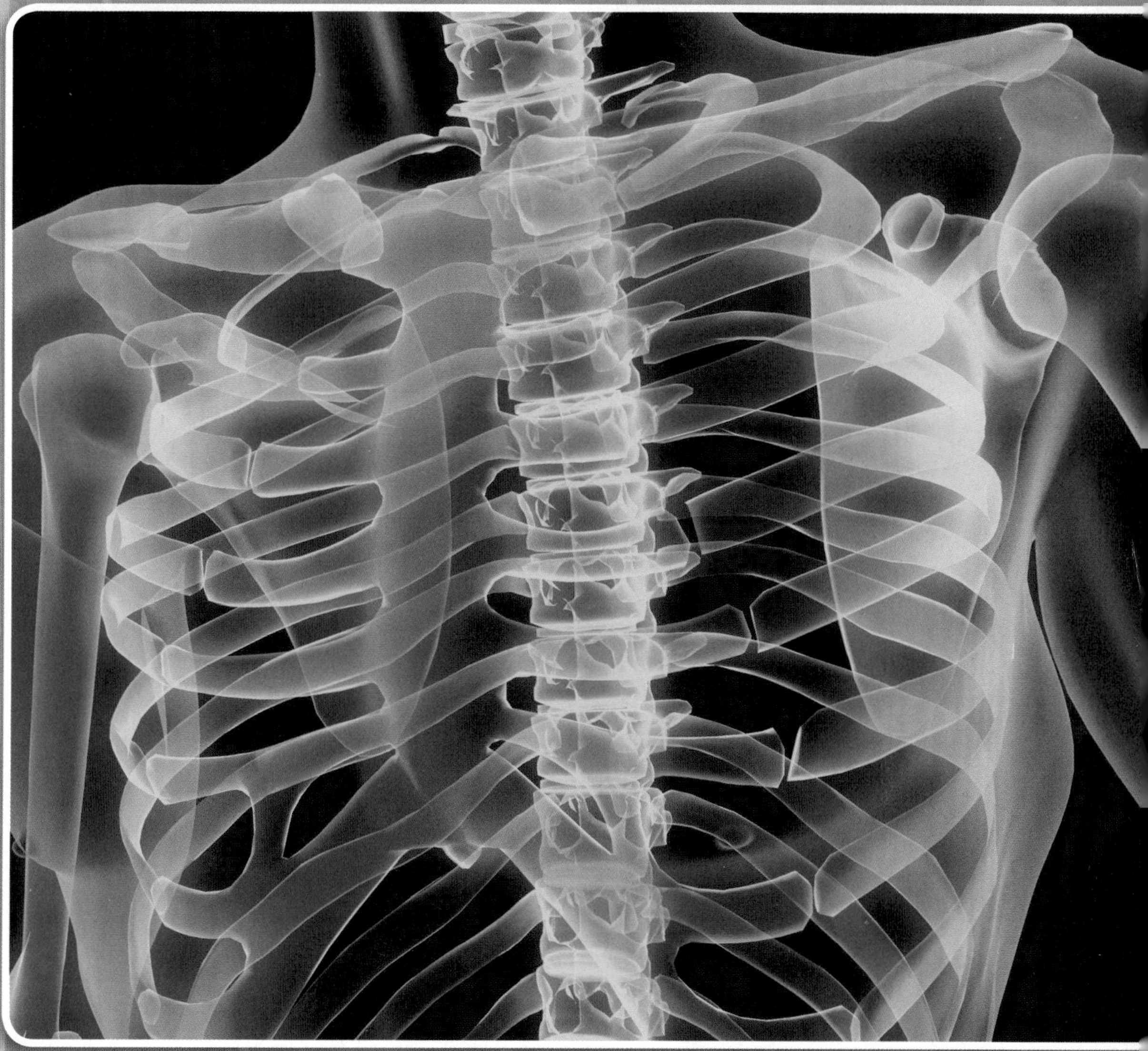

There is a satisfactory boniness about grammar which the flesh of sheer vocabulary requires before it can become a vertebrate and walk the earth. —*Anthony Burgess*

CHAPTER 13

The Parts of Speech

How can you combine the parts of speech to create vivid and exact sentences?

The Parts of Speech: Pretest 1

The following draft paragraph about bird migrations is hard to read because it contains several errors. Revise the paragraph so that it reads correctly. One error has been corrected as an example.

The migratory patterns of birds might ~~of~~ *have* seemed mysterious to early bird watchers. Scientists has a lot more answers. For why birds flies south. snow geese, for example, fly 5,000 miles roundtrip from the arctic to states on America's south but southwest. geese fly in V- and U-shapely formation because it help they to fly greater distances. These flying formations also allows. Snow geese to see each other. Snow-geese fly in flocks. Because snow goose are social animals. Flying together help make the long journey more enjoyable. The flocks often stop on familiar resting areas. Some of these frequent spots are visited by thousands of geese over the same time.

The Parts of Speech: Pretest 2

Directions

Write the letter of the term that correctly identifies the underlined word in each sentence.

Mongolia

(1) Mongolia is bordered by China on the south. **(2)** It is a vast and remote country. **(3)** The Great Wall was originally designed to protect the Chinese from Mongolian invasion. **(4)** Today a large number of Mongolians still live as nomadic herders. **(5)** They often herd sheep, goats, camels, and yaks. **(6)** Nomads travel enormous distances on horseback with their herds. **(7)** These rugged wanderers live in circular felt or canvas tents. **(8)** Here yaks thrive in Mongolia's cold mountain air. **(9)** The nomads themselves are well adapted to the climate. **(10)** Goodness! Mongolians are astonishing horsemen!

1. **A** adjective
B adverb
C preposition
D noun

2. **A** noun
B conjunction
C verb
D adverb

3. **A** noun
B pronoun
C verb
D adverb

4. **A** adjective
B adverb
C preposition
D noun

5. **A** adjective
B adverb
C preposition
D verb

6. **A** adjective
B adverb
C preposition
D noun

7. **A** conjunction
B interjection
C preposition
D adjective

8. **A** adjective
B adverb
C preposition
D noun

9. **A** noun
B pronoun
C verb
D adverb

10. **A** conjunction
B interjection
C preposition
D adjective

Nouns Lesson 1

Each word listed in a dictionary is labeled according to its *part of speech. Nouns* are one of the eight parts of speech, which are listed below. As you read the list, keep in mind that a word's part of speech is determined by its use in a sentence. The same word may be labeled as two, three, or even four different parts of speech in a dictionary.

THE EIGHT PARTS OF SPEECH	
noun (names)	**adverb** (describes, limits)
pronoun (replaces a noun)	**preposition** (relates)
verb (states action or being)	**conjunction** (connects)
adjective (describes, limits)	**interjection** (expresses strong feeling)

CHAPTER 13

This chapter will cover each part of speech, beginning with nouns.

13 A A **noun** is the name of a person, place, thing, or idea.

My **friend Jack** dreams of **success** as an **astronaut.**

Stephanie watched the solar **eclipse** from a **cabin** in **Minnesota.**

Ana has taken a **tour** around the **Kennedy Space Center.**

Types of Nouns

Nouns are often classified in several ways: **concrete** and **abstract nouns, common** and **proper nouns, compound nouns,** and **collective nouns.**

You can learn about plural nouns on pages 1002–1009 and possessive nouns on pages 944–946.

Concrete and Abstract Nouns

13 A.1 **Concrete nouns** name people, places, or things. **Abstract nouns** name ideas and qualities.

CONCRETE AND ABSTRACT NOUNS	
Concrete Nouns	hat, fur, newspaper, children, bell
Abstract Nouns	love, anger, liberty, success, hope

Common and Proper Nouns

13 A.2 **Common nouns** name any person, place, or thing. **Proper nouns** name a particular person, place, or thing.

COMMON AND PROPER NOUNS	
Common Nouns	worker, state, document
Proper Nouns	Rob Warner, Michigan, Bill of Rights

Some proper nouns, such as *Bill of Rights,* include more than one word but are still considered one noun.

Compound Nouns

13 A.3 **Compound nouns** are nouns that include more than one word.

When you are not sure which form a particular compound noun takes, check a dictionary.

COMPOUND NOUNS	
One Word	viewpoint, stagecoach, airstrip
Hyphenated Words	double-talk, brother-in-law
Two Words	living room, golf course

You can learn about the plurals of compound nouns on page 1007.

Collective Nouns

13 A.4 **Collective nouns** name a group of people or things.

COMMON COLLECTIVE NOUNS			
band	congregation	flock	nation
class	crew	group	orchestra
colony	crowd	herd	swarm
committee	family	league	team

CHAPTER 13

When You Write

Using specific nouns will help clarify your meaning and add real interest to your writing. Note the difference between these sentences:

General	The **dog** next door barked, scaring me.
Specific	The **German shepherd** next door barked, scaring me.

Practice Your Skills

Identifying Nouns

Write the nouns in each of the following sentences. A date is considered a noun. (You should find 40 nouns.)

(1) Somewhere in interstellar space, where Earth is a mere pinpoint of light, *Pioneer 10* cruises on and on. **(2)** Launched in 1972 from Cape Canaveral, the tiny spacecraft was expected to have only a 21-month life span. **(3)** It withstood radiation from Jupiter and bombardments of micrometeoroids. **(4)** Eleven years later, still sending back faint messages, it left most known planets behind.

(5) With its antennae and instruments still functioning, *Pioneer 10* continues to send back information from its eight-watt transmitter. **(6)** Communication may continue to a distance of five billion miles. **(7)** About every million years, the craft could come close to another star system. **(8)** It might then be found by other intelligent beings. **(9)** With that idea in mind, scientists attached a plaque with pictures of a man and a woman, the location of Earth, and some points of basic science. **(10)** This could be its most important message.

Connect to Writing: Revising

Using Proper Nouns

Rewrite each sentence, replacing at least one common noun with a proper noun. (You may need to make other changes, too.)

1. The astronaut left an American flag on the moon.
2. The space shuttle launches from a southern state.
3. Our galaxy contains approximately 100 billion stars.
4. The space agency displays photographs from space.
5. Our world lies 93 million miles from the sun.

Pronouns Lesson 2

13 B **A pronoun is a word that takes the place of one or more nouns.**

By taking the place of a noun, a pronoun can eliminate unnecessary repetition and awkwardness in your writing. The word that the pronoun replaces or refers to is called its **antecedent.** In the following examples, an arrow has been drawn from the pronoun to its antecedent or antecedents.

Dan, did **you** win the leading role in the play?

Joseph and Audrey said **they** would be coming later.

"Did Lisa say **she** would join **us?**" Seth asked Charlene.

Although pronouns usually follow their antecedents in a sentence, a few do not. In the preceding example, for instance, *Seth* and *Charlene* follow *us.*

You can learn more about pronouns and antecedents on pages 801–805.

CHAPTER 13

Personal Pronouns

13 B.1 **Personal pronouns** are the most common kind of pronoun and can be divided into three groups: first person, second person, and third person.

PERSONAL PRONOUNS	
First Person	(the person speaking)
Singular	I, me, my, mine
Plural	we, us, our, ours
Second Person	(the person spoken to)
Singular	you, your, yours
Plural	you, your, yours
Third Person	(the person or thing spoken about)
Singular	he, him, his, she, her, hers, it, its
Plural	they, them, their, theirs

First Person	**I** can't wait to see **my** costume.
Second Person	Why aren't **you** taking **your** script with **you?**
Third Person	**They** asked **her** to wait for **him** backstage.

Reflexive and Intensive Pronouns

A **reflexive** or an **intensive pronoun** is formed by adding the ending *–self* or *–selves* to a personal pronoun.

REFLEXIVE AND INTENSIVE PRONOUNS	
Singular	myself, yourself, himself, herself, itself
Plural	ourselves, yourselves, themselves

CHAPTER 13

13 B.2 A **reflexive pronoun** refers to the noun or the pronoun that is the subject of the sentence. It is needed to make the meaning of the sentence clear.

13 B.3 An **intensive pronoun** is not a necessary part of a sentence. It is included to add emphasis—or intensity—to a noun or another pronoun in the sentence.

Dropping an intensive pronoun from a sentence will not change the meaning of the sentence.

Reflexive Pronoun	Did Matthew make **himself** a costume? (*Himself* cannot be dropped from the sentence without changing its meaning.)
Intensive Pronoun	The mayor **herself** will be present at opening night. (*Herself* can be dropped from the sentence. The mayor will be present at opening night.)

Practice Your Skills

Identifying Pronouns and Their Antecedents

Write the personal, reflexive, or intensive pronouns in each sentence. Then, beside each pronoun, write its antecedent.

1. Jessica, where have you put your wig?

2. "I hope we can memorize our parts this weekend," Ann said to Bob.

3. Alice and Fred will sing their duet before the play's intermission.

4. Mr. and Mrs. Chin themselves said that they would help build the scenery.
5. "That costume is lovely, but I think its sleeves are a little long," said Irene.
6. "Our parents will be clapping their hands wildly," Nancy told Charles.
7. "If these props are yours, Kim, why leave them here?" Ms. Davis asked.
8. "The janitor found my script and left it near your locker," Daniel told Pepe.
9. Charlotte asked Linda if she had seen their director.
10. Rosa gave herself ten minutes for a costume change.

Connect to Writing: Revising

Using Personal Pronouns

Rewrite each sentence, replacing unnecessary nouns with pronouns.

1. "Jason told Sherry's parents that the play started at 7:00, but Jason was wrong," Sherry explained.
2. "If Heather forgets her lines," said Amy, "Heather will need to improvise."
3. Robert must project Robert's voice if Robert wants to be heard.
4. "Steve, the lighting director, checked Steve's settings during the cast's rehearsal," Liz told the cast members.
5. Jack, Tyler, and Greg practiced the lines assigned to Jack, Tyler, and Greg.

Indefinite Pronouns

13 B.4 **Indefinite pronouns** often refer to unnamed people or things.

Indefinite pronouns usually do not have specific antecedents.

COMMON INDEFINITE PRONOUNS	
Singular	another, anybody, anyone, anything, each, either, everybody, everyone, everything, much, neither, nobody, no one, nothing, one, somebody, someone, something
Plural	both, few, many, others, several
Singular/Plural	all, any, more, most, none, some

We have **many** left over, for **everyone** brought **some.**

Both of the reporters may speak with **anyone** in the cast.

You can learn about indefinite pronouns as antecedents on page 804.

Demonstrative Pronouns

13 B.5 A **demonstrative pronoun** is used to point out a specific person, place, or object.

DEMONSTRATIVE PRONOUNS	
Singular	this (points out an object close by)
	that (points out an object in the distance)
Plural	these (points out objects close by)
	those (points out objects in the distance)

This is the play I need to read.

Do you really want to wear **those?**

CHAPTER 13

Interrogative Pronouns

13 B.6 An **interrogative pronoun** is used to ask a question.

INTERROGATIVE PRONOUNS				
what	which	who	whom	whose

Which is the shortest scene in the play?

Who is going to play her part tomorrow night?

Another kind of pronoun is a relative pronoun, which is used to introduce adjectival clauses. You can learn more about relative pronouns on pages 62 and 715–719.

Practice Your Skills

Identifying Pronouns

Write each pronoun in the following sentences.

1. Take these and give them to someone in the audience.
2. Who can drive both of us to the rehearsal?
3. This must belong to somebody.
4. The tickets themselves cost only five dollars.
5. I haven't noticed anyone volunteering for the clean-up crew.

6. Those are the songs everyone should memorize.
7. Robin made herself a rehearsal schedule to follow.
8. Which is the one he wants to learn?
9. Neither of my friends has seen that yet.
10. No one would watch anything like that!

Connect to Writing: Drafting Sentences

Using Pronouns

Write five sentences about a school activity, using two of the following pronouns in each sentence.

which	he	my	one
these	us	them	anyone
herself	their	its	we

Check Point: Mixed Practice

Make two columns on your paper. Label one column *Nouns* and the other column *Pronouns.* Write each noun and pronoun in the appropriate column.

1. The director himself made casting assignments.
2. Her family members jumped to their feet for the curtain call.
3. "Jesse and I nearly forgot our cue," Katie said, "but the director signaled us."
4. Which is the cue you nearly forgot?
5. This is saved for somebody.
6. Everyone wants to play the starring role!
7. "Your mother," Lisa told Ben, "wants to sew our costumes herself."
8. She or her twin sister will play the role of Sarah.
9. This is a production everyone should see.
10. All of us took a bow at the end, and the audience cheered loudly.

Connect to Writing: Informal Speech

Using Nouns and Pronouns

You are trying out for the school production of *Romeo and Juliet*. Prepare a brief speech for your theater director, explaining why you would fit the role of either star-crossed lover. Use nouns and pronouns to compare yourself to either character.

13 C **A verb is a word that expresses action or a state of being.**

A verb is an essential part of a sentence because a group of words without a verb is a fragment, not a sentence.

Action Verbs

13 C.1 An **action verb** tells what action a subject is performing.

Action verbs are the most commonly used verbs in speech and in writing. An action verb can show physical action, mental action, or ownership.

ACTION VERBS	
Physical Action	run, pull, stir, dive, shout, yawn, bounce
Mental Action	think, wish, believe, understand, imagine
Ownership	have, possess, keep, own, control, occupy

Transitive and Intransitive Verbs

All action verbs fall within two general classes: **transitive** and **intransitive.**

13 C.2 An action verb that has an object is **transitive.** An action verb that has no object is **intransitive.**

You can find an object by asking the question *What?* or *Whom?* after the verb.

Transitive	I **left** my running shoes in my locker today. (*Left* what? *Shoes* is the object.)
Intransitive	Frank **exercised** in the gym last night. (*Exercised* what? *Exercised* has no object.)

You can learn more about objects on pages 785–789.

Some action verbs can be transitive in one sentence and intransitive in another sentence.

Transitive	April **practiced** drills before the soccer game. (*Practiced* what? *Drills* is the object.)
Intransitive	The band **practiced** after lunch. (*Practiced* what? *Practiced* has no object.)

Practice Your Skills

Identifying Transitive and Intransitive Verbs

Write the action verb in each sentence. Then label it as transitive or intransitive.

1. Ice hockey began in Canada.
2. Before 1859, baseball umpires sat in padded rocking chairs behind the catcher.
3. Wilma Rudolph won the 100-meter dash in the Olympic Games in 1960.
4. Modern gymnastics originated in Germany in the early nineteenth century.
5. At home games, the Boston Red Sox play in Fenway Park.
6. In baseball, home plate has five sides.
7. The ancient Egyptians bowled on alleys with stone balls and stone pins.
8. Johnny Vander Meer pitched two straight no-hitters in 1938.
9. The game of soccer probably first occurred in Roman Britain in A.D. 217.
10. In 1979, ice skater Beth Heiden captured four gold medals in the women's World Championships.

Connect to Writing: Revising

Using Specific Verbs

Write each sentence, replacing each verb with a more specific verb.

1. Karen ran to the finish line in record time.
2. The coach instructed his athletes with his pre-game speeches.
3. Late in the basketball game, Michael made a three-pointer.
4. The team called loudly from the sidelines.
5. Mark made a school record in the pole vault.

Verb Phrases

13 C.3 A **verb phrase** is a main verb plus one or more helping verbs.

The verb of a sentence is often more than one word. **Helping verbs,** or auxiliary verbs, can be added to the main verb to form a verb phrase.

COMMON HELPING VERBS	
be	am, is, are, was, were, be, being, been
have	has, have, had
do	do, does, did
Others	may, might, must, can, could, shall, should, will, would

In the following examples, the verb phrase is underlined and the helping verbs are in **bold** type.

> Breakfast **is being** prepared for the team.
>
> The bus **should have** arrived before now.

Often a verb phrase is interrupted by other words.

> Pauline **has** already notified her coach.
>
> The bus driver **should** never **have** left so late.
>
> She **did**n't know the final tournament schedule.

Throughout the rest of this book, the term verb *will refer to the whole verb phrase.*

CHAPTER 13

When You Write

The word *not* and its contraction *n't* often interrupt verb phrases. Neither is part of the verb.

The coach **does** not **reveal** her game strategy.

The star of the team **is**n't **giving** up yet.

When you are composing a piece of formal writing, you should spell out the word *not*. You should use the contraction *n't* only in speaking and informal writing situations.

Practice Your Skills

Identifying Verb Phrases

Write the verb in each sentence.

1. Some avid sports fans can recite game statistics.
2. My favorite baseball player will be pitching in tonight's game.
3. He might have broken his rival's record.
4. Some accomplished athletes were not considered athletic as children.
5. Stephanie will wear white during the tennis tournament.
6. I should never have eaten that greasy burger before the race.
7. The official did not see the foul until afterward.
8. Our team must have scored another point!

Connect to Writing: Revising

Using Verb Phrases

The verb phrases in these sentences do not make sense. Rewrite the sentences, correcting the verb phrases.

1. The snowboarders will wearing baggy pants on the slopes.
2. Wrestlers should have practicing in the early mornings before school.

Connect to Writing: Description

Using Verbs

As a local television reporter, you have been assigned to cover today's track meet. Describe the scene to your viewers, using compelling verbs. Include at least five helping verbs.

Linking Verbs

13 C.4 A **linking verb** links the subject with another word in the sentence. The other word either renames or describes the subject.

Chris **was** a judge at the annual chili cook-off.
(*Was* links *judge* with the subject *Chris*. *Judge* renames the subject.)

That fudge **is** too rich for me.
(*Is* links *rich* with the subject *fudge*. *Rich* describes the subject.)

The most common linking verbs are the various forms of *be*.

COMMON FORMS OF *BE*		
be	shall be	have been
being	will be	has been
is	can be	could have been
am	could be	should have been
are	should be	will have been
was	would be	would have been
were	may be	might have been
been	had been	must have been

CHAPTER 13

The forms of the verb *be* are not always linking verbs. To be a linking verb, a verb must link the subject with another word in the sentence that renames or describes that subject. In the following examples, the verbs simply make a statement. They do not link the subject to another word.

They **were** here earlier.

Ida **is** in the kitchen.

The following verbs can also be used as linking verbs.

ADDITIONAL LINKING VERBS			
appear	grow	seem	stay
become	look	smell	taste
feel	remain	sound	turn

Luisa **became** the head chef of the cooking school.
(*Chef* renames the subject.)

Kenneth **seems** hungry today.
(*Hungry* describes the subject.)

Most of the additional linking verbs listed in the preceding box can also be used as action verbs.

Linking Verb	Ryan **looked** handsome in his chef's apron.
Action Verb	Jed **looked** cautiously into the oven.

You can learn about complements of linking verbs on pages 668–669.

Practice Your Skills

Identifying Linking Verbs

Write the linking verb in each sentence. If a sentence does not have a linking verb, write *none.*

1. Sugar, flour, eggs, and water are the first four ingredients.
2. I smell smoke in the kitchen.
3. Pat has been the cook for two years.
4. The recipe appeared out of nowhere.
5. America's chocolate wizard was Milton Hershey.
6. Milk often turns sour in warm temperatures.
7. The pasta seemed soggy.
8. Miguel grows hungrier by the minute.
9. The jalapeño pepper is one of the most popular spices in Texas.
10. My older brother grows many different kinds of vegetables in his garden.

Check Point: Mixed Practice

Write the verbs in the following sentences. Then label each one ***A*** for action or ***L*** for linking.

1. Many spices have contributed to the flavor of the soup.
2. Mr. Wilson became a student again at cooking school.
3. He served the next course on beautiful dessert plates.
4. Even veteran chefs have sometimes burned their breakfast toast.
5. The barbecued spareribs tasted delicious.
6. Frank always clears the table for his guests.
7. Her favorite dish for special occasions is swordfish and vegetables.
8. These coffee beans smell very fragrant.
9. The dinner party must have been a success.
10. Every hour he looks inside the oven at the turkey.

Connect to Writing: Narration

Using Linking Verbs

Have you had much cooking experience? Do you prefer to eat a meal rather than prepare it? Write a narrative about a memorable adventure in the kitchen or a mouth-watering feast. Use some linking verbs to tell your story to your classmates.

Adjectives and Adverbs Lesson 4

13 D **Adjectives** and **adverbs** are words that modify, or describe, other parts of speech.

Adjectives and adverbs add clarity to sentences by creating vividness and exactness.

Adjectives

13 D.1 An **adjective** is a word that modifies a noun or pronoun.

Adjectives make the meaning of nouns and pronouns more precise. An adjective answers one of the following questions: *What kind? Which one(s)? How many? How much?*

ADJECTIVES		
What Kind?	**cold** feet	**portable** tents
Which One(s)?	**this** one	**blue** backpack
How Many?	**two** boots	**many** steps
How Much?	**infinite** beauty	**more** experience

Most often adjectives come before the noun or the pronoun they modify. Sometimes, however, they follow the noun or the pronoun. They may also follow a linking verb.

Before a Noun	The **clear, brilliant** lake shimmered below us.
After a Noun	The lake, **clear** and **brilliant,** shimmered below us.
After a Linking Verb	The lake was **clear** and **brilliant** as it shimmered below us.

You can learn more about adjectives that follow linking verbs on page 669.

CHAPTER 13

PUNCTUATION WITH TWO ADJECTIVES

Sometimes you will write two adjectives before the noun or pronoun they describe. If those adjectives are not connected by a conjunction—such as *and* or *or*—you might need to put a comma between them.

To decide if a comma belongs, read the adjectives and add the word *and* between them.

- If the adjectives sound natural, put a comma in to replace *and.*
- If the adjectives do not sound natural, do not add a comma.

Comma Needed	The bush had sharp, prickly leaves. (*Sharp and prickly leaves* reads well.)
No Comma Needed	Fluffy white clouds filled the sky. (*Fluffy and white clouds* does not read well.)

You can learn more about using commas with adjectives before nouns on pages 923–924.

CHAPTER 13

Proper Adjectives

13 D.2 A **proper adjective** is a special kind of adjective. It is formed from a proper noun and begins with a capital letter.

Proper Adjectives	Some **French** people live along the **Atlantic** coastline.

You can learn about capitalization of proper adjectives on page 903.

Compound Adjectives

13 D.3 **Compound adjectives** are adjectives that are made up of more than one word.

Compound Adjectives	**Downhill** skiing was done by an **all-star** team.

Articles

13 D.4 The words *a, an,* and *the* form a special group of adjectives called **articles.**

The article *a* comes before a word that begins with a consonant sound; the article *an* comes before a word that begins with a vowel sound.

ARTICLES		
a stream	**an** ice chest	**the** campfire
a horse	**an** hour	**the** eraser

You will not usually be asked to list the articles in the exercises in this book.

Practice Your Skills

Identifying Adjectives

Write each adjective in the following sentences. Do not include articles.

1. The fearless swimmers dove into the frigid water.
2. Some friends watched from the warm, dry dock.
3. Jerry, wet and cold, emerged with a big, toothy grin.
4. With Herculean strength, Sarah pulled the rowboat onto the sandy shore.
5. She paddled across the glassy waters in an old-fashioned canoe.

CHAPTER 13

Connect to Writing: Revising

Using Colorful Adjectives

Rewrite the following sentences, adding adjectives or replacing ordinary adjectives with more colorful ones.

1. My dog fetches big sticks out in the small pond.
2. Then she chases the loud ducks around the shore.
3. An old fisherman grumbles at the crowd.
4. Four large boys piled onto the raft.
5. Then the boys fell into the cold water.

Connect to Writing: Editing

Using Adjectives and Articles

Identify the errors in the following sentences, and then rewrite the sentences correctly.

1. That fish was a amazing sight!
2. She is preparing for an transatlantic sailing expedition.
3. An Italian swimming coaches are very competent.
4. A shoreline waters, shallow and clear, reveal underwater treasures.
5. An childhood friend taught me to do a backflip.

Other Parts of Speech Used as Adjectives

As you know, a word's part of speech is determined by how it is used in a sentence. For this reason, a word can be a noun in one sentence and an adjective in another sentence.

NOUNS USED AS ADJECTIVES	
Nouns	mountain, boat, bear
Adjectives	mountain goat, boat dock, bear claw

The same word can be a pronoun in one sentence and an adjective in another sentence. The following words are adjectives when they come before a noun or a pronoun and modify that noun or pronoun. They are pronouns when they stand alone.

CHAPTER 13

WORDS USED AS ADJECTIVES OR PRONOUNS

Demonstrative	**Interrogative**	**Indefinite**	
this	what	all	many
these	which	another	more
that	whose	any	most
those		both	neither
		each	other
		either	several
		few	some

Adjective	**This** hat is mine.
Pronoun	**This** is mine.
Adjective	**Many** students will be needed to help.
Pronoun	**Many** of the students will be needed to help.

The possessive pronouns *my, your, his, her, its, our,* and *their* are sometimes called **pronominal adjectives** because they answer the adjective question *Which one(s)?* Throughout this book, however, these words will be considered pronouns.

Practice Your Skills

Identifying Adjectives

Write the adjectives in each sentence of the following paragraphs. Beside each adjective, write the word it modifies. Do not include articles.

(1) For many years, curious visitors to Alaska have admired the grand terrain and raw beauty of the state. **(2)** The U.S. purchased the harsh land from Russia in 1867 for a genuine bargain: less than two cents per acre. **(3)** Alaska's Russian neighbors lie only 55 miles to the west.

(4) Three cold and furious seas surround the state's splendid coastlines. **(5)** Alaska's Mount Denali, majestic and bold, rises to 20,320 feet above sea level. **(6)** The area is inhabited by Kodiak, grizzly, and polar bears. **(7)** The king salmon that swim in the brisk waters can weigh up to 100 pounds, and the Kodiak bears can grow to 11 feet.

Connect to Writing: Descriptive Paragraph

Using Adjectives

The U.S. has just purchased Alaska from the Russians, and as an official surveyor, you must report your findings to the government. Describe the scenery and animals you observed today near Mt. Denali. Include at least ten adjectives.

Adverbs

13 D.5 An **adverb** is a word that modifies a verb, an adjective, or another adverb.

An **adverb** makes the meaning of a verb, an adjective, or another adverb more precise. Although many adverbs end in *–ly,* some do not.

COMMON ADVERBS					
afterward	down	late	now	so	there
again	even	long	nowhere	sometimes	today
almost	ever	low	often	somewhat	tomorrow
alone	far	more	outside	somewhere	too
already	fast	near	perhaps	soon	very
also	hard	never	quite	still	well
always	here	next	rather	straight	yesterday
away	just	not (n't)	seldom	then	yet

Adverbs That Modify Verbs

Most adverbs modify verbs. To find an adverb, ask the questions *Where? When? How?* or *To what extent?* Notice in the following examples that adverbs that modify verbs modify the whole verb phrase.

Where?	The guitarist jumped **down** from the stage.
When?	I was singing with my band **yesterday.**
How?	He had played the piece **quickly.**

Adverbs That Modify Adjectives and Other Adverbs

Occasionally adverbs will modify adjectives or other adverbs. These adverbs usually answer the question *To what extent?*

Modifying an Adjective	The music drills were **very** easy.
Modifying an Adverb	My rock group sang **too** loudly.

Notice in the preceding examples that the adverbs that modify adjectives and other adverbs usually come before the word they modify.

Although many adverbs end in *–ly,* a few adjectives also end in *–ly*. Be careful that you do not confuse them.

Adverb	He performs *nightly* from six to eleven.
Adjective	Do you watch the *nightly* concert?

Nouns Used as Adverbs

The same word can be used as a noun in one sentence and an adverb in another sentence.

Noun	**Yesterday** was very hectic.
Adverb	I had a rehearsal **yesterday.** (When?)
Noun	The musician and her family moved into their new **home.**
Adverb	Go **home** after the concert. (Where?)

When You Write and Speak

Using strong adverbs can make your sentences come alive, whether you are speaking or writing. Choosing an exact adverb gives your sentences different shades of meaning.

She **slowly** put away her flute.

She **wearily** put away her flute.

She **carefully** put away her flute.

Revise a recent composition by adding exact adverbs.

CHAPTER 13

Practice Your Skills

Identifying Adverbs

Write each adverb. Then beside each one, write the word or words it modifies.

1. The voices suddenly dropped down to a low whisper.
2. Our rock group sings quite professionally.
3. They did not rehearse very hard.
4. Are you still waiting for the keyboard player?
5. The lead singer spoke too rapidly.
6. That extremely small drum can be quite noisy.
7. The audience cheered uproariously.
8. I talked briefly with the musicians today.
9. Far away the marquee sign gleamed brightly.
10. An unusually hot spotlight was shining directly overhead.

Connect to Writing: Revising

Using Adverbs

Rewrite each sentence, replacing each adverb with another one to change the meaning of the sentence.

1. That fiddle player can move his fingers rapidly.

2. Fame was quite overwhelming for the young star.

3. I hope my favorite band stops here during their tour.

4. May we rehearse again tomorrow?

5. The audience was surprisingly happy with the concert.

CHAPTER 13

Check Point: Mixed Practice

Write the adjectives and adverbs in each sentence of the following paragraphs. Then label each one *adjective* or *adverb.*

(1) In 1816, there was no summer. **(2)** Across northern Europe and the eastern United States, the daytime temperatures rarely reached 50°F. **(3)** In June an extremely severe blizzard actually dumped many inches of snow on parts of New England. **(4)** What caused these unusual weather conditions? **(5)** A volcano that had erupted violently on the other side of the world on April 5, 1815, may have been the cause. **(6)** As a result of the eruption, a massive cloud of volcanic dust slowly worked its way around the world. **(7)** By 1816, the cloud became temporarily suspended over the Northern Hemisphere, deflecting the radiation of the sun. **(8)** During the night the mercury often registered below freezing temperatures. **(9)** On July 4, the high temperature in normally hot Georgia was in the forties. **(10)** It was one summer when the living was hardly easy.

Connect to Writing: Descriptive Paragraph

Using Adverbs

Write a descriptive paragraph about your favorite song. Your audience is someone who is unfamiliar with the song and the musicians. Include at least eight adverbs to characterize the band and its music.

Other Parts of Speech — Lesson 5

13 E **The three remaining parts of speech are prepositions, conjunctions, and interjections.**

Prepositions

13 E.1 A **preposition** shows the relationship between a noun or a pronoun and another word in the sentence.

On, under, and *behind,* for example, change the relationship between the dog and the couch in the following examples.

The dog **on** the couch is Betsy's.

The dog **under** the couch is Betsy's.

The dog **behind** the couch is Betsy's.

Following is a list of common prepositions.

COMMON PREPOSITIONS

aboard	before	down	off	till
about	behind	during	on	to
above	below	except	onto	toward
across	beneath	for	opposite	under
after	beside	from	out	underneath
against	besides	in	outside	until
along	between	inside	over	up
among	beyond	into	past	upon
around	but ("except")	like	since	with
as	by	near	through	within
at	despite	of	throughout	without

Many common prepositions are compounds made up of several words.

COMPOUND PREPOSITIONS		
according to	by means of	instead of
ahead of	in addition to	in view of
apart from	in back of	next to
aside from	in front of	on account of
as of	in place of	out of
because of	in spite of	prior to

A preposition is always a part of a group of words called a **prepositional phrase.**

13 E.2 A **prepositional phrase** begins with a preposition and ends with a noun or a pronoun called the **object of a preposition.**

CHAPTER 13

The prepositional phrases in the following examples are in **bold** type.

By the second hour, many **of the people** were drenched.

In place of Hank, Philip will go out **into the storm with you.**

In the following sentence, the words *store* and *bank* form a compound object of the preposition *to.*

Maria ran **to the grocery store and the bank.**

Preposition or Adverb?

A word can be a preposition in one sentence and an adverb in another. A word is a preposition if it is part of a prepositional phrase. It is an adverb if it stands alone.

Preposition	Did you look ***inside*** *the garage?*
Adverb	Did you look **inside?**
Preposition	Walk carefully ***up*** *the wet steps.*
Adverb	Turn the radio **up!**

You can learn more about prepositional phrases on pages 682–685.

Practice Your Skills

Finding Prepositional Phrases

Write all the prepositional phrases in the following sentences. (There are 20 prepositional phrases in all.)

1. Throughout the world nearly 100 lightning flashes occur each second.
2. Despite popular opinion, lightning can strike twice in the same place.
3. The average lightning bolt strikes with millions of volts behind it.
4. According to scientific investigations, lightning bolts do not move at the speed of light.
5. Spectacular color photographs of lightning can be obtained by radar.
6. Benjamin Franklin discovered the connection between electricity and lightning.
7. In 1752, Franklin built the lightning rod.
8. This device protects homes and other buildings from damage by lightning.
9. If lightning is striking near you, stay away from any tall objects.
10. In spite of contrary advice, stay inside a car but don't touch any of the metal parts.

CHAPTER 13

Conjunctions

13 E.3 A **conjunction** connects words or groups of words. **Coordinating conjunctions** are single connecting words; **correlative conjunctions** are pairs of connecting words.

CONJUNCTIONS

Coordinating				**Correlative**		
and	for	or	yet	both/and	neither/nor	whether/or
but	nor	so		either/or	not only/but also	

Did you buy the *monitor* **and** the *keyboard?* (connects nouns)

Either *type* **or** *handwrite* your reports. (connects verbs)

The programs were **both** *educational* **and** *fun.* (connects adjectives)

The computer was on, **yet** the screen was blank. (connects sentences)

13 E.4 **Subordinating conjunctions** are used to introduce adverbial clauses.

You can learn about subordinating conjunctions on pages 62 and 713.

Practice Your Skills

Identifying Conjunctions

Write each conjunction in the following sentences.

1. The Internet can reach people in the next house or around the globe.
2. Some devious hackers may break into top-secret files or private e-mail.
3. The programmer not only created but also used the software.
4. Electronic bulletin boards appear on many Web sites but are underused.
5. A browser program can both navigate the Web and store your e-mail.

Connect to Writing: Drafting

Using Conjunctions

Write three sentences that follow the directions below.

1. Use *neither/nor* to connect two nouns.
2. Use *but* to connect two verbs.
3. Use *both/and* to connect two adjectives.

Interjections

13 E.5 An **interjection** is a word that expresses strong feeling or emotion.

An **interjection** expresses an emotion but has no grammatical connection with the rest of the sentence. An interjection is followed by an exclamation point or a comma.

Wow! I can't imagine that he believes that Elvis is alive.

Oh, he believes it all right!

Practice Your Skills

Identifying Interjections

Write the interjection in each sentence.

1. Indeed, Elvis Presley was once a truck driver.
2. Wow! Who would have guessed?
3. Thank goodness, he never gave up his early dream of stardom.
4. Imagine! Elvis had fans around the world!
5. Incredible! Fifty-two-million people viewed one of his TV performances.

Parts of Speech Review

Words are extremely versatile. *Inside,* for example, can be used as four different parts of speech. Its use in a particular sentence determines its part of speech.

Noun	The **inside** of the bird's nest was lined with newspaper.
Adjective	We received some **inside** information on bird-watching.
Adverb	Let's go **inside** and get ready.
Preposition	The lights are on **inside** the house.

Asking the right question will help you determine how a word is used in a sentence.

Noun — Is the word naming a person, a place, a thing, or an idea?

After careful **thought Janet** drove to **New York** and was fortunate to find a **veterinarian** in a **matter** of **days.**

Pronoun — Is the word taking the place of a noun?

Anything you tell **her** will certainly be helpful to **us.**

Verb — Is the word showing action or linking the subject with another word?

They **are** attractive birds, but they **cost** too much.

Adjective — Is the word modifying a noun or a pronoun? Does it answer the question *What kind? Which one(s)? How many?* or *How much?*

The **bright yellow** feathers were very **pretty.**

Adverb — Is the word modifying a verb, an adjective, or another adverb? Does it answer the question *How? When? Where?* or *To what extent?*

The pigeons hopped **very quickly** around the **extremely** busy crowds.

Preposition — Is the word showing a relationship between a noun or a pronoun and another word in the sentence? Is it part of a phrase?

According to the experts, a flock **of** geese is approaching **from** the north.

Conjunction Is the word connecting two or more words or groups of words?

Neither Kim **nor** Lee can watch with us, **for** they have to work.

Interjection Is the word expressing strong feeling?

Oops! I left my binoculars at home.

Practice Your Skills

Identifying Parts of Speech

Write the underlined words in each sentence. Then beside each word, write its part of speech, using the following abbreviations:

noun = *n.*	adjective = *adj.*	conjunction = *conj.*
pronoun = *pron.*	adverb = *adv.*	interjection = *interj.*
verb = *v.*	preposition = *prep.*	

1. <u>Bird</u> migration has <u>never</u> been completely explained.
2. Flying south, birds <u>supposedly</u> seek a <u>food</u> supply.
3. Some birds, <u>like</u> the blue jay, do not migrate; <u>yet</u> they still find food throughout the winter months.
4. How do birds find their way <u>from</u> their <u>winter</u> home to their summer home?
5. <u>Alas</u>! Many theories exist, <u>but</u> no one is sure.
6. Migration patterns for birds have remained <u>relatively</u> the same <u>over</u> the years.
7. <u>Their</u> arrival and departure times <u>vary</u> by mere days.
8. For example, swans, geese, <u>and</u> ducks usually pass Point Pelee National Park in Ontario, <u>Canada</u>, on April 10.
9. Most birds <u>fly</u> at night, guiding <u>themselves</u> by stars.

Assess Your Learning

Determining Parts of Speech

Write each underlined word in the following sentences. Then beside each word, write its part of speech, using the following abbreviations:

noun = *n.*	pronoun = *pron.*	verb = *v.*
adjective = *adj.*	adverb = *adv.*	preposition = *prep.*
conjunction = *conj.*		

Edgar Allan Poe is known around the world as the master of Gothic tales of gloom and terror. His poems and stories take readers to a realm of nightmares. Half-mad characters often act out fiendish schemes of revenge, and bereaved people crazed with grief yearn for things that cannot be.

Poe himself did not have a happy life. Born in Boston in 1809, he lost both of his actor parents before he was two years old. He was then raised in the home of John Allan, a wealthy merchant. Because he was never officially adopted, Poe was very insecure and often quarreled with his foster father.

Poe became both a writer and a reviewer for several magazines in New York and Philadelphia, but his success lasted for only a short while. At the relatively young age of forty, Poe died in poverty. His influence as a writer, nevertheless, is still felt throughout the literary world today.

Determining Parts of Speech

Write the underlined word in each sentence. Then beside each word, write its part of speech, using the following abbreviations:

noun = *n.*	pronoun = *pron.*	verb = *v.*
adjective = *adj.*	adverb = *adv.*	preposition = *prep.*
conjunction = *conj.*	interjection = *interj.*	

1. Were you outside?
2. I'll take those.
3. He sings quite well.
4. Birds eat insects.
5. Those books are mine.
6. We walked away.

7. Those are for us.
8. That was made for me!
9. The lawnmower uses oil.
10. Either pen will do.

Understanding Parts of Speech

Write sentences that use the following words as the different parts of speech. Then underline each word and label its use in the sentence.

1. Use *many* as a pronoun and an adjective.
2. Use *like* as a verb and a preposition.
3. Use *both* as a pronoun, an adjective, and a conjunction.
4. Use *on* as an adverb and a preposition.

Using Parts of Speech

Write a paragraph in which you use each of the eight parts of speech at least once. Write about one of the following topics or one of your choice: something you do well, something you would like to do, or something exceptional that you have already achieved. Then underline one use of each part of speech and label it.

The Parts of Speech: Posttest

Directions

Write the letter of the term that correctly identifies the underlined word in each sentence.

Alain Locke

(1) Alain Locke, a philosopher and critic, is often regarded as the father of the Harlem Renaissance. **(2)** He urged African Americans to celebrate their culture and to identify with Africa. **(3)** He published an anthology of new writers. **(4)** These writers wrote of the beauty and energy of life in Harlem. **(5)** Alienated from society, they were struggling to forge a new identity as Americans. **(6)** Among the most important writers of the Harlem Renaissance were Langston Hughes and Zora Neale Hurston. **(7)** Langston Hughes spent his early years in the Midwest. **(8)** Zora Neale Hurston was born and raised in an all-black town in Florida. **(9)** Both moved to New York in young adulthood. **(10)** My, Hughes has written some powerful poetry!

1. **A** adjective
B adverb
C preposition
D noun

2. **A** adjective
B adverb
C preposition
D noun

3. **A** adjective
B adverb
C preposition
D pronoun

4. **A** noun
B pronoun
C verb
D adverb

5. **A** noun
B pronoun
C verb
D adverb

6. **A** conjunction
B interjection
C preposition
D adjective

7. **A** adjective
B adverb
C verb
D noun

8. **A** conjunction
B interjection
C preposition
D adjective

9. **A** noun
B pronoun
C verb
D adverb

10. **A** conjunction
B interjection
C preposition
D adjective

Writer's Corner

Snapshot

13 A A **noun** is the name of a person, place, thing, or idea. (pages 620–622)

13 B A **pronoun** is a word that takes the place of one or more nouns. (pages 623–627)

13 C A **verb** is a word that expresses action or a state of being. (pages 628–634)

13 D An **adjective** is a word that modifies a noun or pronoun. (pages 635–639) An **adverb** is a word that modifies a verb, an adjective, or another adverb. (pages 639–642)

13 E A **preposition** shows the relationship between a noun or a pronoun and another word in the sentence. (pages 643–645) A **conjunction** connects words or groups of words. (pages 645–646) An **interjection** is a word that expresses strong feeling or emotion. (page 646)

CHAPTER 13

Power Rules

When you use a **noun to show ownership,** add an *'s* to singular nouns and plural nouns that don't end in an *s*. Add only an apostrophe to plural nouns ending in an *s*. (pages 944–946)

Before Editing	After Editing
This is *Kris* notebook.	This is *Kris's* notebook.
Did you see the *boys* new bikes?	Did you see the *boys'* new bikes?

Use the contraction ***'ve*** (not *of*) when the full word is *have,* or use the whole word *have.* (page 872)

Before Editing	After Editing
The game *could of* gone either way.	The game *could've* gone either way.

Editing Checklist ✓

Use this checklist when editing your writing.

- ✓ Did I capitalize proper nouns? (See pages 621 and 895–902.)
- ✓ Did I use the correct pronoun to replace or refer to a noun? (See pages 623–627.)
- ✓ Did I use action verbs to make my writing more lively? (See pages 628–631.)
- ✓ Did I use adjectives and adverbs to make my sentences more vivid and exact? (See pages 635–642.)
- ✓ Did I use prepositions and prepositional phrases to show relatonships? (See pages 643–645.)
- ✓ Did I use conjunctions correctly to connect words or groups of words? (See pages 645–646.)
- ✓ Did I use interjections when appropriate to express strong feelings or emotions? (See page 646.)

CHAPTER 13

Use the Power

RECIPE FOR A SENTENCE

Ingredients	Directions
nouns pronouns verbs adjectives adverbs **conjunction** **prepositions** **interjections**	To form the basic sentence, blend one or more nouns and pronouns with one or more action verbs or linking verbs. Combine words or groups of words with conjunctions, and fold in prepositions to show relationships. Flavor with adjectives and adverbs. If desired, add an interjection to show emotion or strong feelings.

Oops! I baked my apple pie too long **in** the oven **and** burned the crust.

The Sentence Base

How can you use sentences to paint powerful images and tell interesting stories?

The Sentence Base: Pretest 1

The following draft paragraph about Mount Rushmore is hard to read because it contains sentence fragments and other sentence errors. Revise the paragraph so that it reads correctly. The first error has been corrected as an example.

The four men honored on Mount Rushmore. ~~Each~~ did much for this country. Washington served as our first official leader. Jefferson wrote. The Declaration of Independence, and was an important founding father. Lincoln kept the United States from becoming two separate nations Roosevelt revolutionized trade. By beginning construction on the Panama Canal. Do you think there should be another face on Mount Rushmore? Some people think the monument is perfect. As it is. They fear. That changing it would somehow ruin it. Others would add another face to the illustrious mountain. But whom? Would that be? What criteria would be used? To decide who would join the four men currently honored? What do you think?

The Sentence Base: Pretest 2

Directions

Write the letter of the term that correctly identifies the underlined word or words in each sentence.

Diet and Exercise

(1) Body fat cannot readily be converted into energy. **(2)** Weight reduction occurs through a combination of exercise and nutrition. **(3)** Even moderate exercise can be a step toward good health. **(4)** Given a low carbohydrate intake, you will burn more fat through exercise. **(5)** Too many exercises on an empty stomach can be harmful to your health. **(6)** Eat healthful snacks, do not skip meals, and avoid diet pills. **(7)** Increase your protein intake for better results. **(8)** Not all activities and sports burn a lot of calories. **(9)** A good exercise program develops the heart and lungs. **(10)** Aerobic exercise such as running will give you more energy.

1. **A** simple subject
B simple predicate
C complete subject
D complete predicate

2. **A** simple subject
B simple predicate
C complete subject
D complete predicate

3. **A** simple subject
B simple predicate
C complete subject
D complete predicate

4. **A** direct object
B indirect object
C predicate nominative
D predicate adjective

5. **A** simple subject
B simple predicate
C complete subject
D complete predicate

6. **A** compound subject
B compound verb
C compound direct object
D compound predicate nominative

7. **A** simple subject
B simple predicate
C complete subject
D complete predicate

8. **A** compound subject
B compound verb
C compound direct object
D compound predicate nominative

9. **A** compound subject
B compound verb
C compound direct object
D compound predicate nominative

10. **A** direct object
B indirect object
C predicate nominative
D predicate adjective

Subjects and Predicates Lesson 1

A **sentence** is formed by combining two essential elements: a subject and a verb. Sometimes a third element is also needed—a complement. Once you know what these elements are and how to put them together, the results you can achieve will be limitless. You can create everything from simple sentences to compound-complex sentences.

14 A **A sentence is a group of words that expresses a complete thought.**

To express a complete thought, a sentence must have a subject and a predicate. The **subject** tells the reader whom or what the sentence is about. The **predicate** completes the thought by telling something about the subject. If both are present, the reader should understand the writer's intention.

14 A.1 A **subject** names the person, place, thing, or idea the sentence is about. A **predicate** tells something about the subject.

CHAPTER 14

Sometimes a group of words is punctuated as a sentence, but it isn't a sentence because it is missing a subject, a verb, or both. These incomplete thoughts, called **fragments,** often leave the reader bewildered.

You can learn about fragments on pages 663–664, 698–699, and 726–727.

Complete Subject	**Complete Predicate**
My cousin Pedro	drove us to South Dakota.
The capital of South Dakota	is Pierre.
The 40th state in the union	borders six other states.
The pasque flower	became South Dakota's state flower.

Simple Subjects and Predicates

14 A.2 A **simple subject** is the main word in the complete subject. A **simple predicate,** or **verb,** is the main word or phrase in the complete predicate.

Within each complete subject is a simple subject; and within each complete predicate is a simple predicate, or verb. In the examples on the next page, the simple subjects and the verbs are in **bold** type.

complete subject / complete predicate

A **tourist** at the history museum **poses** for a photograph.

complete subject / complete predicate

Our **drive** across the grassy plains **was** an enjoyable trip for the entire family.

complete subject / complete predicate

Badlands National Park in southwest South Dakota **is welcoming** hikers.

In the last example, *Badlands National Park* is a single proper noun; therefore, all three words are the simple subject. Notice also that the verb phrase *is welcoming* is considered the verb of the sentence.

Throughout the rest of this book, the term *subject* will refer to the simple subject. The term *verb* will refer to the simple predicate, which may be a single verb or a verb phrase.

You can learn more about verb phrases on pages 630–631.

Finding Subjects and Verbs

To find the subject of a sentence, first find the action verb or the linking verb in the sentence. If the verb is an action verb, ask yourself *Who?* or *What?* before the verb. The answer to either of these questions will be the subject of the sentence. In the following examples, each subject is underlined once, and each verb is underlined twice.

Grandfather has traveled through South Dakota often.
(The action verb is *has traveled.* Who has traveled? *Grandfather* is the subject.)

The audiotape was explaining the monument's history.
(The action verb is *was explaining.* What was explaining? *Audiotape* is the subject.)

If the verb is a linking verb, ask yourself *About whom or what is some statement being made?* The answer will be the subject.

Craig will become a world traveler someday.
(The linking verb is *will become.* About whom is some statement being made? *Craig* is the subject.)

The immense and pristine prairie was spectacular.
(The linking verb is *was.* About what is some statement being made? *Prairie* is the subject.)

When you look for a subject and a verb, first eliminate all modifiers and prepositional phrases from the sentence. A subject is never part of a prepositional phrase.

You can learn more about verbs on pages 628–634 and 740–777 and prepositional phrases on pages 644 and 682–685.

Practice Your Skills

Identifying Subjects and Verbs

Write the subject and the verb in each sentence.

1. A huge carving is located on the side of the mountain in South Dakota.
2. This magnificent sculpture honors Washington, Lincoln, Jefferson, and Theodore Roosevelt.
3. The carved faces of the presidents average 60 feet, from the top of the head to the chin.
4. This is proportionate to men 456 feet tall!
5. The ambitious creator of these colossal figures was Gutzon Borglum.
6. In 1927, he began his work.
7. Fourteen years later his work came to an end with his death.
8. His son, however, continued the project.
9. Within a year the project was completed.
10. Today the sculptures comprise the Mount Rushmore National Memorial.

Connect to Writing: Revising

Writing Complete Subjects and Predicates

Every sentence has a simple subject and a simple predicate. Make the following sentences more interesting by adding words to create a complete subject and a complete predicate. Then underline the subject once and the predicate twice.

1. Tourists visit.
2. Trees thrive.
3. The Memorial inspires.
4. A monster appeared.
5. An actor climbed.

Different Position of Subjects

In sentences in **natural order,** the subject precedes the verb. In sentences in **inverted order,** the verb comes before the subject.

14 A.3 **Inverted order** means that the verb or part of a verb phrase comes before the subject.

In the examples below, the subject is underlined once and the verb is underlined twice.

Questions are usually written in inverted order. To find the subject and the verb in a question, recast the sentence in natural order.

Question	Have you heard the story of Sacagawea?
Statement	You have heard the story of Sacagawea.

There* and *here sometimes begin inverted sentences. To find the subject and the verb, put the sentence in its natural order. (*There* or *here* can be dropped in some cases.)

Inverted	Here are some facts of her life.
Natural Order	Some facts of her life are here.
Inverted	There is no consensus among the historians.
Natural Order	No consensus is among the historians.

Emphasis and variety are other reasons for inverted sentences. To find the subject and the verb, put the sentence into its natural order.

Inverted	Through the rough terrain traveled Sacagawea.
Natural Order	Sacagawea traveled through the rough terrain.

14 A.4 **Understood *you*** occurs when the subject does not appear in the sentence.

In a command or a request, the subject *you* usually does not appear in the sentence; it is understood to be there. *You* is the understood subject of each of the following sentences.

Read about the Lewis and Clark expedition. (*You* is the understood subject; *read* is the verb.)

CHAPTER 14

Ben, describe the harsh conditions of the explorers. (*You* is the understood subject—even though the person receiving the command is named. *Describe* is the verb.)

You can learn more about subject/verb agreement on pages 814–839.

When You Read and Write

Professional writers use sentences in both natural and inverted order. Changing the normal subject-verb order creates sentence variety and adds interest. Inverted sentences are often found in poetry. Notice the position of the subject in the second line of Henry Wadsworth Longfellow's "The Tide Rises, the Tide Falls."

The day returns, but nevermore
Returns the traveler to the shore,
  And the tide rises, the tide falls.

Revise a recent composition by adding three sentences in inverted order.

CHAPTER 14

Practice Your Skills

Identifying Subjects and Verbs

Write the subject and the verb in each sentence. If the subject is an understood *you,* write *(you).*

1. Be careful on your trip.
2. Where does the trail cross the Continental Divide?
3. There were many unexpected hardships along the journey.
4. Was the Lewis and Clark expedition a success?
5. Here in Nebraska are remnants of the trek.

Connect to Writing: Revising

Using Natural and Inverted Order

Revise the following sentences. If the sentence is written in inverted order, write it using natural order. If the sentence is already in natural order, invert the order.

1. Sacagawea was born in the Shoshone nation near Idaho.
2. At the Pacific Ocean ended the explorers' journey.
3. There was no food found for weeks.

Compound Subjects and Verbs

14 A.5 A **compound subject** is two or more subjects in one sentence that have the same verb and are joined by a conjunction.

Karen and Robert are visiting all fifty state capitals.

My sister and her friend are going with them.

14 A.6 A **compound verb** is two or more verbs that have the same subject and are joined by a conjunction.

Bill bought a guidebook of the capitol but gave it to Phyllicia.

The gold dome of Colorado's state capitol shines and brightens the downtown area.

A sentence can have both a compound subject and a compound verb.

The balloons and streamers decorated the capitol and added to the festive spirit.

You can learn more about conjunctions on pages 645–646 and compound subject/verb agreement on pages 821–823.

Practice Your Skills

Identifying Compound Subjects and Verbs

Write the subjects and verbs in the following sentences.

1. We rode the bus into Jackson, Mississippi, and walked to the museum.
2. State capitals and large cities are often named after founding fathers.
3. Boston visitors either walk along the historic path or ride on a tour bus.
4. The Denver climate appears cold but often is mild and sunny.
5. Jack caught a cold during his visit to Atlanta and returned to the hotel.
6. Both Mia and I went to Austin, Texas, and toured many different places.
7. The Arizona state flag bears a setting sun and flies over the capitol in Phoenix.
8. We drove to Montpelier, Vermont, and fished for freshwater trout.
9. My aunt and my cousin are living in Olympia, Washington.
10. Miami, Ft. Lauderdale, and Orlando are popular spots for tourists.

Connect to Writing: Revising

Combining Sentences

Combine the following sentences using compound subjects or compound verbs.

1. Harrisburg is rich in historical attractions. Richmond and Columbia are also rich in historical attractions.
2. Lola drove to Juneau, Alaska. She lived there for two years.
3. Nashville is the capital of Tennessee. Nashville draws to many musicians.
4. The state flag of New Jersey is yellow. It flies over the capitol in Trenton.
5. New York is the financial capital of the world. It does not serve as the capital of New York State.

Check Point: Mixed Practice

Write the subjects and verbs in the following sentences. If the subject is an understood ***you,*** write ***(you).***

1. The trip from Honolulu, Hawaii, to Sacramento, California, took several hours by plane.
2. Did the tour guide explain the history of Montgomery?
3. The capital of Texas was temporarily moved to Houston in the 1840s.
4. I drove, walked, and rode all over Salt Lake City, Utah.
5. There are some fascinating people in Helena, Montana.
6. On the flag pole flew the majestic state symbol.
7. The cardinal, the mockingbird, and the wren are some official state birds.
8. Show me the governor's office.
9. Do you know your state's motto?
10. The citizens and the legislators met and discussed plans for the new capitol.

Connect to Writing: Revising

Writing Complete Subjects and Predicates

Do you think there should be another face on Mount Rushmore? Write a paragraph explaining whom you would add and why. If you think the monument is perfect as is, explain why. Then review your paragraph and underline each subject once. Underline each predicate, or verb, twice.

the Texas State Capitol in Austin

Sentence Fragments

The main purpose for almost all writing is to communicate. The more completely you express your thoughts, the more likely your writing will communicate. Read your work aloud and listen for complete sentences. Edit your formal writing to make sure you have avoided ineffective sentence fragments.

14 B **A sentence fragment is a group of words that does not express a complete thought.**

Fragments due to incomplete thoughts are probably the most common kind.

No Subject	Went to the mall on Saturday.
No Verb	The perfect afternoon for shopping.

Fragments due to incorrect punctuation can also occur in writing.

Part of a Compound Verb	David bought a new CD for his music collection. **And ran straight home with it.**
Items in a Series	She found everything she wanted. **A new black purse, some running shoes, and a birthday card for Grandma.**

You can find out about other kinds of fragments on pages 698–699 and 726–727.

Ways to Correct Sentence Fragments

You can correct a sentence fragment in one of two ways. You can add words to make the fragment a complete sentence. You can also attach a fragment to a sentence next to it, adding or dropping words as necessary.

Sentence and Fragment	David bought a new CD for his music collection. **And ran straight home with it.**
Separate Sentences	David bought a new CD for his music collection. **He ran straight home with it.**
Attached	David bought a new CD for his music collection **and ran straight home with it.**

Sentence and Fragment	She found everything she wanted. **A new black purse, some running shoes, and a birthday card for Grandma.**
Separate Sentences	She found everything she wanted. **She bought a new black purse, some running shoes, and a birthday card for Grandma.**
Attached	She found everything she wanted: **a new black purse, some running shoes, and a birthday card for Grandma.**

When You Write and Speak

Fragments are routinely used in informal conversation as well as in fiction and drama. Intonation and context help give a spoken sentence a sense of completeness—even when the sentence is incomplete. Sentences in expository writing, however, lack these vocal or contextual cues. Therefore, sentences in formal writing must be grammatically complete. Look at these fragments:

Exclamation	"What a beautiful sweater!"
Request	"Size eight, please."
Question and Answer	"When?" "Tomorrow."

Add a sense of realism to a piece of fiction or drama by adding fragments to dialogue.

CHAPTER 14

Practice Your Skills

Identifying Sentence Fragments

Label each group of words ***S*** for sentence or ***F*** for fragment.

1. A small boutique one mile from the downtown shopping center.
2. A small woman carried several large bags across the parking lot.
3. Walked together around the mall.
4. Found the new jeans on sale at his favorite store.
5. The clerk in the shoe department of the gigantic store in Houston.
6. Girls in the fashion show were strolling down the brightly lit runway.

Connect to Reading: Writing Matters

Keep a log of sentence fragments you encounter while reading fiction or drama. Record the effect the fragments have on you as a reader.

Complements Lesson 3

14 C **A complement finishes the meaning of a sentence.**

Neither of the following sentences would be complete without the complements—*poster* and *confident.*

> Keith held the campaign **poster.**
>
> Jason seemed **confident.**

There are five kinds of complements. **Direct objects, indirect objects,** and **objective complements** complete the meaning of action verbs. **Predicate nominatives** and **predicate adjectives** complete the meaning of linking verbs.

CHAPTER 14

Direct Objects

14 C.1 A **direct object** is a noun or a pronoun that receives the action of the verb.

A **direct object** follows an action verb and completes the meaning of the sentence by naming the receiver of the action. Only a sentence with an action verb will have a direct object. To find a direct object, ask *What?* or *Whom?* after an action verb. Notice in the third example that a direct object can be compound.

> d.o.
> David hung the **signs** in the hallway.
> (David hung what? *Signs* is the direct object.)
>
> d.o.
> Did you see **Gretchen** at the voting booths?
> (You did see whom? *Gretchen* is the direct object.)
>
> d.o. d.o.
> Ingrid brought **posters** and marking **pens** to the rally.
> (Ingrid brought what? *Posters* and *pens* are the compound direct object.)

A complement is never part of a prepositional phrase.

> Jimmy rode with us to the campaign meeting. (The words *us* and *meeting* are objects of prepositions. They cannot be direct objects.)

You can learn more about action verbs and transitive verbs on pages 628–631 and prepositional phrases on pages 644 and 682–685.

Indirect Objects

14 C.2 An **indirect object** answers the questions *To or for whom?* or *To or for what?* after an action verb.

If a sentence has a direct object, it also can have another complement called an **indirect object.** To find an indirect object, first find the direct object. Then ask yourself, *To or for whom?* or *To or for what?* after the direct object.

An indirect object always comes before a direct object in a sentence. Notice in the third example that an indirect object can be compound.

Mr. Gorman gave **them** (i.o.) two **suggestions** (d.o.) about the campaign.
(*Suggestions* is the direct object. Mr. Gorman gave suggestions to whom? *Them* is the indirect object.)

I gave the **podium** (i.o.) a new **coat** (d.o.) of paint.
(*Coat* is the direct object. *Paint* is the object of the preposition *of.* I gave a coat of paint to what? *Podium* is the indirect object.)

Sue told **Kate** (i.o.) and **Lara** (i.o.) the **details** (d.o.) of her campaign strategy.
(*Details* is the direct object. Sue told the details to whom? *Kate* and *Lara* are the compound indirect object.)

Like a direct object, an indirect object cannot be part of a prepositional phrase.

My aunt brought **me** (i.o.) some **flowers** (d.o.) after the election.
(*Me* is the indirect object. It comes before the direct object *flowers* and is not part of a prepositional phrase.)

My aunt brought some **flowers** (d.o.) to me after the election.
(*Me* is not the indirect object because it follows the direct object *flowers* and is the object of the preposition *to*.)

CHAPTER 14

Practice Your Skills

Identifying Direct Objects and Indirect Objects

Write each direct object and indirect object. Then label each one *direct object* or *indirect object.*

1. The principal told Jerry the news about the election.
2. The election coordinator offered each candidate ten minutes to speak.
3. Mom gave the speech a quick glance.
4. Leroy distributed fliers to the students in the hallway.
5. Did you give Cathy and Carlos your votes?
6. Sign your name on the ballot.
7. Mr. Green gave us the ballot at the door.
8. Please send me the election results as soon as possible.
9. I gave my speech a thorough edit.
10. Did you offer Jeff and Kim compliments on their election success?

Connect to Reading: Speech

Using Direct and Indirect Objects

How would you improve your school? Imagine you are running for a school officer position. Suggest two or three changes and explain their significance in a brief speech to fellow students. Support your ideas with examples and facts. Create sentence variety by using different sentence patterns with complements. Be prepared to identify direct and indirect objects in your speech.

CHAPTER 14

Objective Complements

14 C.3 An **objective complement** is a noun or an adjective that renames or describes the direct object.

If a sentence has a direct object, it can also have another object called an **objective complement.** To find an objective complement, first find the direct object. Then ask the question *What?* after the direct object.

An objective complement will always follow the direct object. Notice in the second example that an objective complement can be compound.

The juniors elected Jessie class **president.**
(*Jessie* is the direct object. The juniors elected Jessie what? *President* is the objective complement. It follows the object and renames it.)

Patrick painted his campaign signs **blue** and **green.**
(*Signs* is the direct object. Patrick painted his signs what? *Blue* and *green* are the compound objective complement. These words follow the direct object and describe it.)

Practice Your Skills

Identifying Complements

Write each complement in the following sentences. Then label each one *direct object, indirect object,* or *objective complement.*

1. The impending speech made me nervous.
2. Mr. LaMar gave us some last-minute advice.
3. After the speeches, the students elected Sarah secretary of the senior class.
4. Many people consider Becky the most qualified candidate.
5. Carrie gave Will her vote for vice president.

CHAPTER 14

Subject Complements

14 C.4 **Subject complements** complete the meaning of linking verbs.

There are two kinds of subject complements—**predicate nominatives** and **predicate adjectives.**

A **predicate nominative** is a noun or a pronoun that follows a linking verb and identifies, renames, or explains the subject. To find a predicate nominative, first find the subject and the linking verb. Then find the noun or the pronoun that follows the verb and that identifies, renames, or explains the subject.

Notice in the second example that a predicate nominative can be compound.

The rural countryside (s.) is his **home** (p.n.). (home = countryside)

The country farmer (s.) is both the **boss** (p.n.) and the main **employee** (p.n.) of his business.
(boss, employee = farmer)

A predicate nominative is never part of a prepositional phrase.

s. p.n.
Harold is only **one** of the ranchers in the community.
(*One* is the predicate nominative. *Ranchers* is the object of a preposition.)

A **predicate adjective** is an adjective that follows a linking verb and modifies the subject. To find a predicate adjective, first find the subject and the linking verb. Then find an adjective that follows the verb and describes the subject.

Notice in the second example that a predicate adjective can be compound.

s. p.a.
That ranch hand is **strong.**
(*Strong* describes the subject *hand.*)

s. p.a. p.a.
The cattle were **large** but extremely **docile.**
(*Large* and *docile* both describe the subject *cattle.*)

Be careful not to confuse a regular adjective with a predicate adjective. A predicate adjective follows a linking verb and describes the subject.

You can learn more about linking verbs on pages 632–633.

CHAPTER 14

Practice Your Skills

Identifying Subject Complements

Write each subject complement in the following sentences. Then label each one *predicate nominative* or *predicate adjective.*

1. Four of the five farmers were Texans.

2. The rooms in the new barn are spacious.

3. The cattle dog is small but energetic.

4. Upon his sixteenth birthday, Cole became a ranch hand.

5. All horses are distinctive.

6. The morning chores are some of my least favorite tasks.

7. During the evening the cattle remained calm and docile.

8. Mr. Wells was the founder of the ranch.

9. The dirt road toward the gate is bumpy.

Creating Variety with Sentence Patterns

From the three primary colors of red, blue, and yellow, every conceivable color can be made. From the six basic sentence patterns, nearly every conceivable sentence can be written. Once you know these sentence patterns, you can create an endless number of fresh, original sentences by simply adding prepositional phrases and other modifiers.

Pattern 1: **S-V** (subject-verb)

S V
Rain fell.

S V
The light rain fell continuously throughout the day.

Pattern 2: **S-V-O** (subject-verb-direct object)

S V O
Grandmother knits sweaters.

S V O
My grandmother in Toledo expertly knits warm ski sweaters.

Pattern 3: **S-V-I-O** (subject-verb-indirect object-direct object)

S V I O
Signs gave hikers directions.

S V I O
The signs at the fork in the road gave the two weary hikers adequate directions.

Pattern 4: **S-V-N** (subject-verb-predicate nominative)

S V N
Graduates become engineers.

S V N
College graduates sometimes become engineers for large computer companies.

Pattern 5: **S-V-A** (subject-verb-predicate adjective)

S V A
Flowers are beautiful.

S V A
The flowers in the centerpiece are exceptionally beautiful.

Pattern 6: **S-V-O-C** (subject-verb-direct object-objective complement)

S V O C
Most elected Paul captain.

S V O C
Most of the players enthusiastically elected Paul captain.

Practice Your Skills

Determining Sentence Patterns

Write the sentence pattern that each sentence follows.

1. My aunt gave us tickets to a porpoise show at the aquarium.
2. The intelligence of porpoises is exceptional.
3. As a result, they are spectacular performers.
4. Trainers throw balls to the porpoises.
5. The porpoises also jump through hoops.
6. The secret in training porpoises is hard work.
7. Trainers give porpoises fish as a reward.
8. The porpoise, of course, is a type of sea mammal.
9. Common porpoises make the ocean their home.
10. Many of them live in the North Atlantic Ocean.

Connect to Speaking and Writing: Vocabulary Review

Using the Vocabulary of Grammar

With a partner, review the grammar terms introduced in this chapter. (Hint: Important terms are in purple type.) Then quiz each other on the terms until you have them memorized.

Sentence Diagraming

Diagraming the Sentence Base

A diagram is a picture or a blueprint of a sentence. By arranging the sentence in diagram form, you can often see the relationship among the parts of a sentence more easily.

Subjects and Verbs The subject and the verb of a sentence go on a baseline and are separated by a vertical line. Capital letters are included in diagrams, but punctuation is not included. Notice in the second and third examples that compound subjects and verbs are placed on parallel lines. The conjunction is placed on a broken line between the subjects or verbs.

Everyone has arrived.

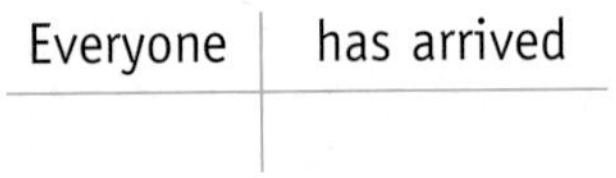

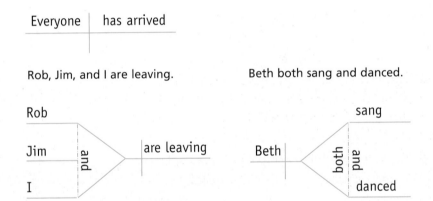

Rob, Jim, and I are leaving.

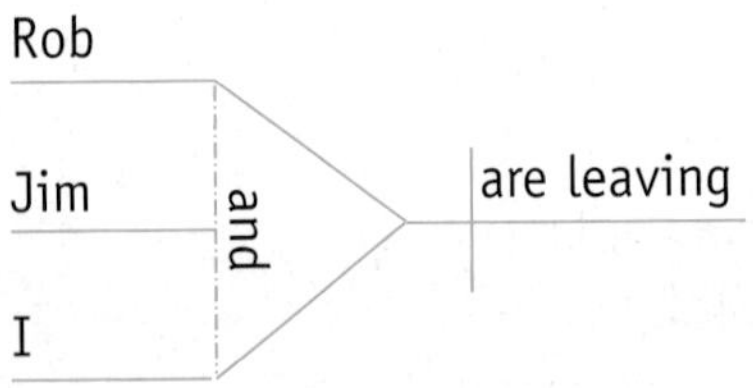

Beth both sang and danced.

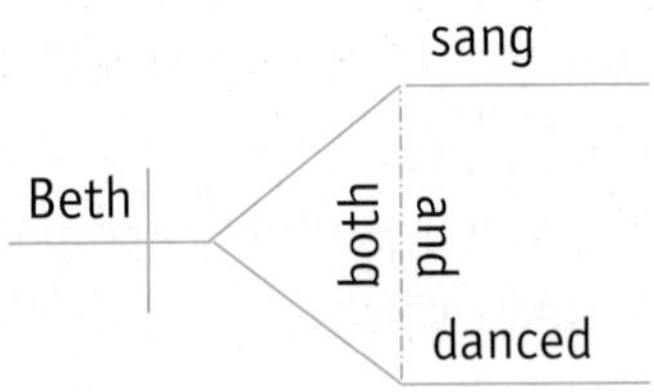

Inverted Order and Understood Subjects A sentence in inverted order is diagramed like a sentence in natural order. When a subject is an understood *you,* put parentheses around *you* in the subject position.

Are you finished?

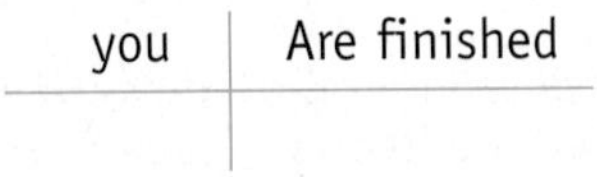

Wait!

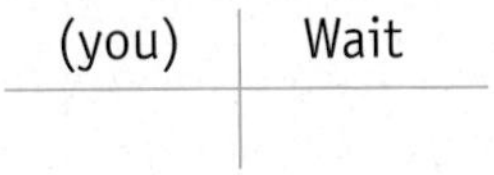

Adjectives and Adverbs are diagramed on a slanted line below the words they modify. (So are possessive pronouns.) A conjunction joining two modifiers is placed on a broken line between them.

Our small truck rides quietly and efficiently.

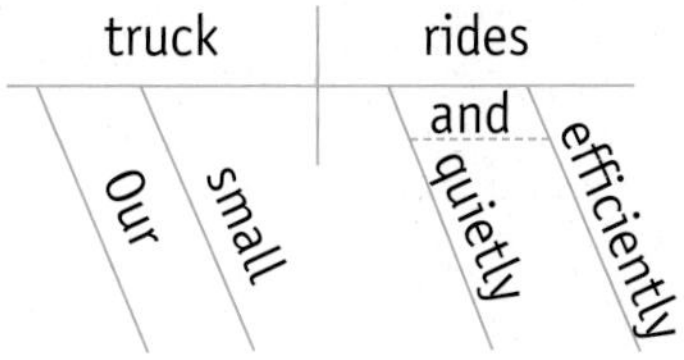

Adverbs That Modify Adjectives or Other Adverbs This kind of adverb is connected to the word it modifies. It is written on a line parallel to the word it modifies.

The unusually eager runner started too quickly.

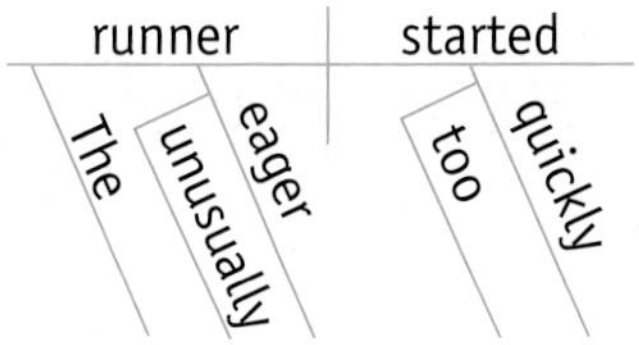

Complements All complements except indirect objects are diagramed on the baseline. A **direct object** is separated from the verb by a vertical line that stops at the baseline. The parts of a compound direct object are placed on parallel lines. The conjunction is placed on a broken line between the direct objects.

We hid her presents.

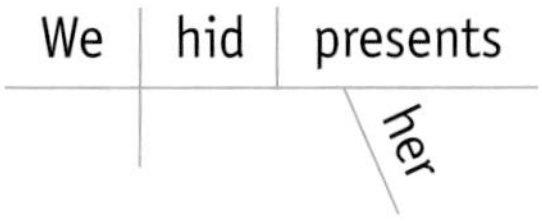

I need a black pen and a red pencil.

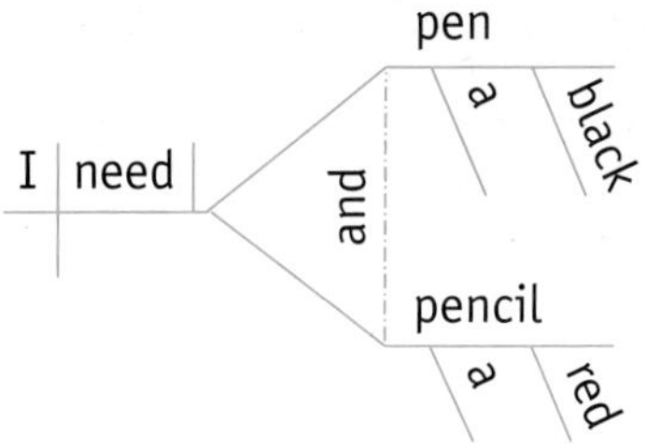

An **indirect object** is diagramed on a horizontal line connected to the verb. The parts of a compound indirect object are diagramed on separate parallel lines, with the conjunction placed on a broken line connecting the indirect objects.

Give me an answer.

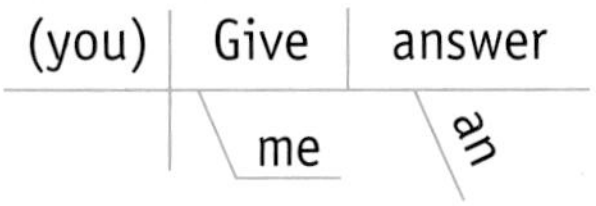

He lent Patty and me his new CD player.

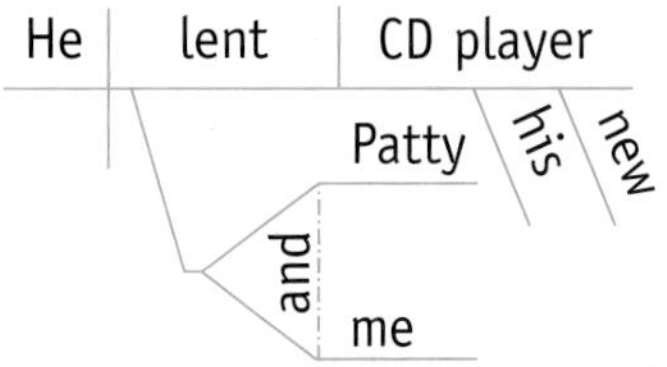

Objective Complements An objective complement is placed to the right of the direct object. The two complements are separated by a slanted line that points back toward the direct object. A compound objective complement is diagramed on parallel lines.

The team elected Betsy captain.

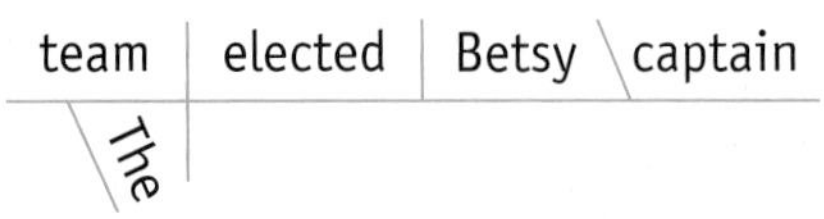

We consider her capable and dependable.

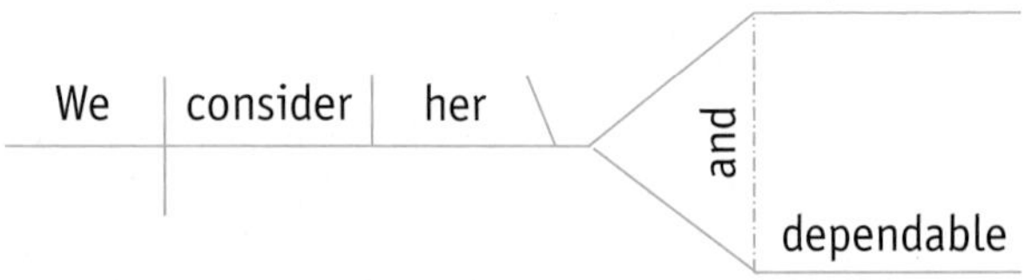

Subject Complements A predicate nominative and a predicate adjective are diagramed in the same way. They are placed on the baseline after the verb. They are separated from the verb by a slanted line that points back toward the subject. A compound subject complement is diagramed on parallel lines like a compound direct object.

Lamb is my favorite meat.

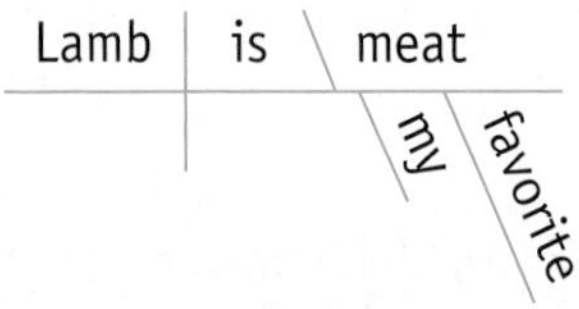

That movie was very scary.

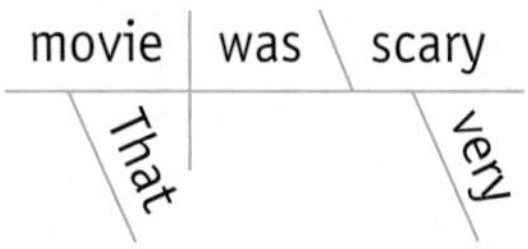

Practice Your Skills

Diagraming Sentences

Diagram the following sentences or copy them. If you copy them, draw one line under each subject and two lines under each verb. Then label each complement using the following abbreviations:

direct object = *d.o.*
indirect object = *i.o.*
objective complement = *o.c.*
predicate nominative = *p.n.*
predicate adjective = *p.a.*

1. Do you like bugs?
2. You can visit a very unusual zoo.
3. Insects, bugs, and spiders live there.
4. A guide gave Luke and me a long tour.
5. We considered the guide unusual but brave.
6. The kitchen contained 30,000 roaches!
7. Some roaches were huge and ugly.
8. Watch out!
9. We walked away very quickly.
10. The best exhibits were the ant farm and the termite colony.

Assess Your Learning

Identifying Subjects and Verbs

Write each subject and verb. If the subject is an understood *you,* write *you* in parentheses.

1. Look at this map of the state of Washington.
2. There in the northwest corner of the state is Mount Rainier National Park.
3. Tacoma and Seattle are the two largest cities near the towers of Mount Rainier.
4. In the continental U.S., there are only four taller peaks.
5. Until 1970, no one had successfully climbed to the top of the mountain.
6. Today climbers regularly make their way along the rough trails and reach the top.
7. This magnificent mountain is part of the Cascade Range.
8. The mountains and peaks of the Cascade Range belong to a series of dormant volcanoes.
9. Mount Rainier itself was built and formed by successive volcanic eruptions.
10. On the higher slopes are many glaciers.
11. Hemlocks and other evergreens cover the lower slopes.
12. Mount Rainier National Park also contains one of North America's only rain forests.
13. Rich soil, ferns, and mushrooms are abundant throughout.
14. Captain George Vancouver of the British Navy named Mount Rainier after a friend.

Identifying Complements

Write each complement. Then label each one, using the following abbreviations:

direct object = *d.o.*
indirect object = *i.o.*
objective complement = *o.c.*
predicate nominative = *p.n.*
predicate adjective = *p.a.*

1. Pat gave me this book of curious facts about U.S. presidents.
2. The author considers our presidents fascinating people.
3. The public offered Washington a third term, but he declined.
4. At his death, Thomas Jefferson was very poor.
5. James Buchanan was the only bachelor.
6. During his speech at Gettysburg, Lincoln was sick with a mild case of smallpox.
7. Woodrow Wilson gave sheep the White House lawn for grazing.
8. Franklin Roosevelt first gave a woman a cabinet position.
9. Voters elected Kennedy president at the age of only 44.
10. Before his term as president, Ronald Reagan made 54 movies in Hollywood.

Using the Sentence Base

Write five sentences that follow the directions below. (The sentences may come in any order.) Write about this topic or a topic of your choice: why you would or would not want to be president one day.

Write a sentence that . . .

1. includes a direct object.
2. includes an indirect object.
3. includes a predicate nominative.
4. includes a predicate adjective.
5. includes an objective complement.

Underline each subject once and each verb twice, and label each complement.

The Sentence Base: Posttest

Directions

Write the letter of the term that correctly identifies the underlined word or words in each sentence.

The League of Nations

(1) The Treaty of Versailles contained the basis for the League of Nations. **(2)** The goal of this international organization was world peace. **(3)** It was relatively unsuccessful in attaining the goal, especially in the 1930s. **(4)** Military forces in Japan occupied Manchuria despite the League's opposition. **(5)** Germany's seizure of Austria also took place under the League's watchful eye. **(6)** The United States did not ratify the Treaty of Versailles and never became a member of the League. **(7)** President Woodrow Wilson's disappointment was great. **(8)** The League of Nations did settle several minor disputes and problems. **(9)** Historians label the League of Nations a failure. **(10)** The League of Nations did furnish the world a sense of unity, however short-lived.

1. **A** simple subject
B simple predicate
C complete subject
D complete predicate

2. **A** simple subject
B simple predicate
C complete subject
D complete predicate

3. **A** simple subject
B simple predicate
C complete subject
D complete predicate

4. **A** simple subject
B simple predicate
C complete subject
D complete predicate

5. **A** simple subject
B simple predicate
C complete subject
D complete predicate

6. **A** compound subject
B compound verb
C compound direct object
D compound predicate nominative

7. **A** direct object
B predicate nominative
C predicate adjective
D objective complement

8. **A** compound subject
B compound verb
C compound direct object
D compound predicate nominative

9. **A** direct object
B indirect object
C objective complement
D predicate adjective

10. **A** direct object
B indirect object
C predicate nominative
D predicate adjective

Writer's Corner

Snapshot

14 A To express a complete thought, a **sentence** must have a **subject** and a **predicate.** (pages 656–662)

14 B A **sentence fragment** is a group of words that does not express a complete thought and may be missing a subject or a verb. (pages 663–664)

14 C A **complement** is a word or group of words that completes the meaning of a subject or verb. (pages 665–669)

Power Rules

CHAPTER 14

Be sure that every sentence has a subject and predicate and that **the subject and verb agree.** (pages 656–662 and 814–839)

Before Editing	**After Editing**
The pile of towels *need* to be washed.	The pile of towels *needs* to be washed.
She and Tina *plans* on dancing.	She and Tina *plan* on dancing.

Fix sentence fragments by adding the missing subject or verb. (pages 663–664)

Before Editing	**After Editing**
Arranged the flowers in the vase.	*Dora* arranged the flowers in the vase.
Traveling to Peru.	*I will be* traveling to Peru.

Check for **run-on sentences** and separate them by adding a conjunction and/or punctuation. You can also fix a run-on by writing it as two sentences. (pages 728–730)

Before Editing	**After Editing**
Sylvia made popcorn for us, I wanted grapes.	Sylvia made popcorn for us*, but I wanted grapes.*
Sam wants to run on the beach, he likes to hear the sound of the waves early in the morning.	Sam wants to run on beach. *He likes to hear the sound of the waves early in the morning.*

Editing Checklist

Use this checklist when editing your writing.

- ✓ Did I write sentences that express complete thoughts? (See pages 656–662.)
- ✓ Did I correct any sentence fragments? (See pages 663–664.)
- ✓ Did I put the subject in the correct place in questions and sentences starting with *there* or *here?* (See pages 659 and 825.)
- ✓ Did I make my writing more interesting by varying the pattern of my sentences and by using inverted sentences? (See pages 659, 670–671, and 825.)
- ✓ Did I use direct objects and indirect objects to complete the meaning of action verbs? (See pages 665–667.)
- ✓ Did I use predicate adjectives and predicate nominatives to complete the meaning of linking verbs? (See pages 668–669.)

CHAPTER 14

Use the Power

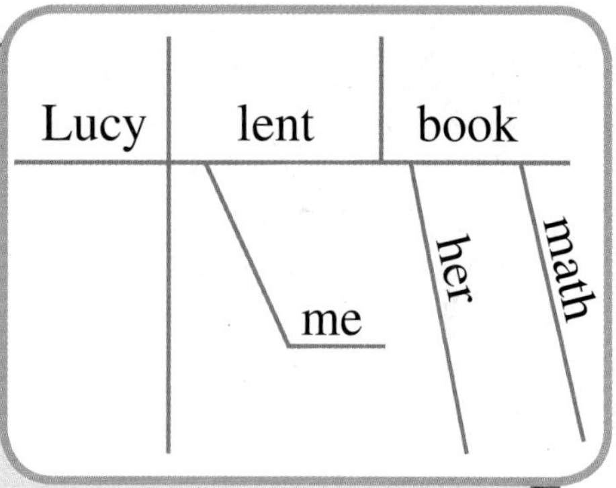

Discuss with a classmate what you have learned about the sentence base in this chapter. Summarize the most important points, including the six sentence patterns.

Study the diagram to the right. It shows the correct way to diagram this sentence:

Lucy lent me her math book.

Now diagram this nonsense sentence.

Friata salped me her sippy sant.

Create two nonsense or imaginative sentence for your partner to diagram. (Use one of the sentence patterns listed on pages 670–671.) Go over each other's diagrams and share them with your teacher and classmates.

Edit a composition you are working on for fluency. Does it contain a variety of sentence types and sentences of varying lengths?

CHAPTER 15

Phrases

How can you use phrases to add variety and clarity to your writing?

Phrases: Pretest 1

The following draft paragraph about the photographer Ansel Adams is hard to read because it contains misplaced phrases and phrase fragments. Revise the paragraph so that it reads correctly. The first phrase fragment has been edited as an example.

During the great San Francisco earthquake of 1906, four-year-old Ansel Adams was injured. The earthquake's tremors. Breaking his nose, knocked him to the ground. This early experience marked his future. And marked his face. Adams enjoyed the outdoors and often went to Yosemite National Park. Hiking, exploring, and photographing. He gained a measure of self-confidence as a teen that he had been missing, in Yosemite. He later joined the Sierra Club. Popular with the other members. In 1922 in the Sierra Club's bulletin appeared his photographs. Adams embraced the club's conservation efforts. To the Sierra Club's board of directors. He would later be elected.

Phrases: Pretest 2

Directions

Write the letter of the term that correctly identifies the underlined phrase in each sentence.

(1) About 40 years ago, all tasks related to word processing were done on typewriters. **(2)** Computers, programmable machines that store and process data, radically changed the world of work. **(3)** The CPU is generally considered the brain inside the computer. **(4)** The size of a computer's memory is given in bytes. **(5)** Starting up the computer is referred to as "booting." **(6)** Storing digitized text, images, and sound, CDs have proved invaluable to office workers. **(7)** A hard drive eliminates the need to use floppy disks. **(8)** All manuals, however, recommend saving your files on backup disks. **(9)** Mainframes are used in businesses to store huge databases of information. **(10)** Processing millions of bytes very fast, mainframe computers manipulate enormous quantities of data.

CHAPTER 15

1. **A** prepositional
B participial
C gerund
D infinitive

2. **A** participial
B prepositional
C appositive
D gerund

3. **A** prepositional
B participial
C gerund
D infinitive

4. **A** participial
B appositive
C prepositional
D gerund

5. **A** prepositional
B participial
C gerund
D infinitive

6. **A** prepositional
B participial
C appositive
D gerund

7. **A** prepositional
B participial
C gerund
D infinitive

8. **A** prepositional
B infinitive
C appositive
D gerund

9. **A** prepositional
B infinitive
C gerund
D participial

10. **A** participial
B prepositional
C appositive
D gerund

Prepositional Phrases Lesson 1

In this chapter you will review prepositional phrases and appositive phrases, as well as the three kinds of verbal phrases: participial phrases, gerund phrases, and infinitive phrases. All these kinds of phrases share two things in common. First, the words in a phrase work together as a single part of speech. Second, a phrase does not include a subject or a verb.

15 A **A phrase is a group of related words that function as a single part of speech. A phrase does not have a subject or a verb.**

Once you can recognize and use the different kinds of phrases—even a simple prepositional phrase—you can add variety and interest to your writing style. As you know, a prepositional phrase begins with a **preposition** and ends with a noun or a pronoun called the **object of a preposition.**

CHAPTER 15

The prepositional phrases in the following examples are in **bold** type.

The outside ***of* the boat** was splashed ***with* saltwater.**

***Instead* of that fishing pole,** use the one ***in* the boat.**

Prepositional phrases are used as adjectives and adverbs.

You can find a list of prepositions on pages 643–644.

Adjectival Phrases

15 A.1 An **adjectival phrase** is a prepositional phrase that is used to modify a noun or a pronoun.

An **adjectival phrase** is used like a single adjective. A single adjective and an adjectival phrase answer the same questions: *Which one(s)?* and *What kind(s)?*

Which One(s)?	Hand me the bait ***on* the boat dock.**
What Kind(s)?	That catch was an opportunity ***of* a lifetime.**

An adjectival phrase usually modifies the noun or the pronoun directly in front of it. Occasionally that word is the object of a preposition in another prepositional phrase.

The woman ***on* the dock** is the mother ***of* my best friend.**

The reflection ***from* the light *on* the water** is distracting.

Occasionally, two adjectival phrases will modify the same noun or pronoun.

The carton ***of* bait *in* the refrigerator** is mine.

Adverbial Phrases

15 A.2 An **adverbial phrase** is a prepositional phrase that is used to modify a verb, an adjective, or an adverb.

An **adverbial phrase** is used like a single adverb. A single adverb and an adverbial phrase answer the same questions: *Where? When? How? To what extent?* and *To what degree?* Occasionally an adverbial phrase will also answer the question *Why?*

Where?	Park ***inside* the marina's garage.**
When?	The boat leaves ***in* ten minutes.**
How?	Jim will catch the fish ***without* me.**
Why?	No one left the marina ***on account of* the storm.**

Notice that an adverbial phrase does not always come next to the word it modifies. Also note that adverbial phrases modify the entire verb phrase, as in the third example.

Two or more adverbial phrases sometimes modify the same verb, as in this example.

The fishing reels are stored ***in* the cabinet *on* the top shelf.**

Although most adverbial phrases modify a verb, some modify adjectives or adverbs.

Modifying an Adjective	Eddie was nervous ***about* the fishing trip.**
Modifying an Adverb	Sea sickness occurs frequently ***for* new sailors.**

CHAPTER 15

PUNCTUATION WITH ADVERBIAL PHRASES

Do not place a comma after a short introductory adverbial phrase unless it is needed for clarity or the phrase ends with a date. You should, however, place a comma after an adverbial phrase of four or more words or after several introductory phrases.

No Comma	From the marina I can see their boat.
Comma	From the marina on the bay, I can see their boat.

Practice Your Skills

Recognizing Prepositional Phrases as Modifiers

Write the prepositional phrases in the following sentences. Then beside each phrase, write the word or words it modifies.

1. The shark swims faster than any other fish in the ocean.
2. The skin of the shark contains scales like little thumbtacks.
3. The shark's mouth is on the underside of its body.
4. The mouth contains several rows of sharp, triangular teeth.
5. The teeth of a shark are very hard but frequently break off while the shark is feeding.
6. Mysterious antibodies in a shark's system eliminate many types of illnesses.
7. Shark meat is high in nutrition and is eaten in many parts of the world.
8. The liver oil of some sharks contains large amounts of vitamin A.
9. Sharks are found in most seas but are most abundant in warm waters.
10. Despite their reputation sharks rarely attack humans.

Practice Your Skills

Identifying Uses of Prepositional Phrases

Write the prepositional phrases in the following sentences. Then label each phrase ***adj.*** for adjectival or ***adv.*** for adverbial.

1. My aunt gave us tickets to a porpoise show at the aquarium.
2. Before the show I knew nothing about a porpoise's intelligence.
3. You should see the trainers with the porpoises in the tank next to the arena.
4. One rather animated porpoise jumps through hoops in midair.
5. Another rings a bell 25 feet above the surface of the water.

Connect to Writing: Editing

Using Commas with Adverbial Phrases

Write the following sentences, inserting commas where necessary. If no commas are needed, write **C** for correct.

1. Along the edge of the bay I spot shells of clams and mussels.
2. On the sand near the shore crabs sidle along.
3. By the dock is our boat.
4. On the boat look for your life jacket.
5. Under the seats in the cabin I found several orange life jackets.
6. In the water I notice some gray humps.
7. From the top of the boat I identify some huge creatures in the distance.
8. With these binoculars I can see several whales.
9. Above the whales some seagulls screech.
10. To the naked eye these sea mammals are still imposing creatures.

Connect to Writing: Editing

Using Prepositional Phrases

Write a short narrative about a sea creature. Use prepositional phrases to add variety and interest to your writing.

Appositives and Appositive Phrases

Lesson 2

15 B **An appositive is a noun or a pronoun that identifies or explains another noun or pronoun next to it in the sentence.**

Sometimes you need to identify a noun or a pronoun in a sentence so your reader knows exactly whom or what you are talking about. This identifying word is called an **appositive.** An appositive usually follows the word it identifies or explains.

My cousin **Susan** will travel to Washington, D.C.

She will visit one important landmark, **the White House.**

15 B.1 An appositive together with its modifiers is called an **appositive phrase.**

Notice in the second sentence of the following examples that one or more prepositional phrases can be part of an appositive phrase.

We walked along Pennsylvania Avenue, **a historical street.**

The group toured the Lincoln Memorial, **a tribute to our sixteenth president.**

PUNCTUATION WITH APPOSITIVES AND APPOSITIVE PHRASES

If an appositive contains information essential to the meaning of a sentence, no punctuation is needed. Information is essential if it identifies a person, place, or thing.

If an appositive contains nonessential information, a comma or commas should be used to separate it from the rest of the sentence. Information is nonessential if it can be removed without changing the basic meaning of the sentence. An appositive that follows a proper noun is usually nonessential.

Essential The United States president **Zachary Taylor** was born in 1784. (No commas are used because *Zachary Taylor* is needed to identify which president.)

Nonessential Zachary Taylor, **the twelfth president of the United States,** was born in 1784. (Commas are used because the appositive could be removed from the sentence.)

Practice Your Skills

Recognizing Appositives and Appositive Phrases

Write each sentence and underline the appositive or appositive phrase. If there is no appositive, write *none.*

1. In a letter to her husband John, Abigail Adams demanded representation for women in the new government.
2. Eleanor Roosevelt, a future delegate to the United Nations, wrote a regular column for a newspaper.
3. Louisa Adams, wife of John Quincy Adams, read the *Dialogues of Plato* to her sons in the original Greek.
4. At the insistence of Abigail Fillmore, the White House installed a new room, a library.
5. Jacqueline Kennedy once worked for a newspaper and covered Capitol Hill.

Connect to Writing: Editing

Punctuating Appositives and Appositive Phrases

Write the following sentences, adding commas where needed.

1. James Madison Randolph Thomas Jefferson's grandson was the first child born in the White House.
2. Andrew Jackson once a Tennessee Superior Court judge was the only president ever to pay off the final installment of the national debt.
3. John Quincy Adams son of President John Adams served as president from 1825 to 1829.

Connect to Writing: Speech

Using Appositive Phrases

Imagine that your best friend has decided to run for class president. He or she has asked you to write a compelling campaign speech, explaining to the voters his or her qualifications and positive attributes. To add sentence variety to the speech, use at least two appositives or appositive phrases.

Verbals and Verbal Phrases

Lesson 3

15 C **A verbal is a verb form used as another part of speech.**

A **verbal** often has the action or movement of a verb and can thus create a sense of vitality in your writing. There are three kinds of verbals: **participles, gerunds,** and **infinitives.**

Participles and Participial Phrases

15 C.1 A **participle** is a verb form that is used as an adjective.

Like an adjective, a **participle** modifies a noun or a pronoun. The participles in the following examples are in bold type.

A **flying** eagle soared past our **hidden** cabin.

There are two kinds of participles: present and past.

15 C.2 A **present participle** ends in *–ing;* a **past participle** has a regular ending of *–ed* or an irregular ending such as *–n, –t,* or *–en.*

Present Participles	act**ing,** fly**ing,** read**ing,** trott**ing**
Past Participles	discard**ed,** tor**n,** los**t,** writt**en**

Do not confuse a participle with the actual verb of a sentence, which may be in the past tense or part of a verb phrase.

Participles	The **calling** bird awakened my **tired** aunt.
Past Tense	My aunt **tired** easily.
Verb Phrase	The bird **was calling** its mate.

Participial Phrases

Since a participle is a verb form, it can have modifiers and complements. Together these form a **participial phrase.**

15 C.3 A **participial phrase** is a participle with its modifiers and complements—all working together as an adjective.

The examples below show three variations of a participial phrase.

With an Adverb	The bird's nest **located nearby** held three eggs.
With a Prepositional Phrase	After sunset we saw a bird **gliding across the sky.**
With a Complement	**Forgetting the park rules,** we peeked into the nest.

The present participle *having* may be followed by a past participle.

Having seen the baby birds, we quickly left the site.

PUNCTUATION WITH PARTICIPIAL PHRASES

Always place a comma after an introductory participial phrase.

Having studied American eagles, Jill was particularly interested in the discovery.

Participial phrases that come elsewhere in a sentence may or may not need commas.

- If the information in a phrase is essential to identify the noun or the pronoun it describes, no commas are needed.
- If the information is nonessential, commas are needed to separate it from the rest of the sentence.

Essential	The bird **flying above the deep canyon** is an eagle. (No commas are used because the participial phrase is needed to identify which bird.)
Nonessential	The eagle, **flying above the deep canyon,** is a noble sight. (Commas are used because the participial phrase can be removed.)
Nonessential	Jill, **shading her eyes for a better view,** pointed out the eagle's large wing span. (Commas are used because the participial phrase that follows a proper noun is usually nonessential.)

Power Your Writing: Getting into the Action

Participial phrases give energy to writing by showing an extra layer of action. The participial phrase in the example below is from "A Mother in Mannville" by Marjorie Kinnan Rawlings (pages 323–329).

Participial Phrase	I went back to work, **closing the door.**
Compound Verb	I went back to work and closed the door.

The main action is "I went back to work." In the revision of the sentence with a compound verb, the action continues in the past. The *-ing* construction of the participle puts the action in the present, adding vitality.

Revise a recent composition by adding at least three participial phrases.

Practice Your Skills

Recognizing Participial Phrases as Modifiers

Write each participial phrase. Then beside each one, write the word it modifies.

1. We saw the eagle soaring effortlessly above us.
2. The eagle, long known as a majestic bird, has an interesting history.
3. The Romans, considering the eagle a symbol of strength, made it their chief military emblem.
4. Replacing the lion, the eagle became the favorite design on the shields.
5. The bald eagle, pictured on the seal of the United States, is the national bird.

Connect to Writing: Editing

Punctuating Participial Phrases

Rewrite the following sentences, adding commas where necessary. If no commas are needed, write **C** for correct.

1. Being a solitary bird the eagle keeps the same mate for life.
2. Its nest built on a tree or on a cliff is a lifelong home.
3. The eagle collecting sticks and leaves enlarges its nest.

Connect to Writing: Drafting

Distinguishing Between Verbs and Participles

Write two sentences for each of the following words. Use the word as part of a verb in one sentence and as a participle in the other.

1. written **2.** blazing **3.** known **4.** hiding

CHAPTER 15

Gerunds and Gerund Phrases

15 C.4 A **gerund** is a verb form that is used as a noun.

A **gerund,** another kind of verbal, looks like a present participle because it ends in *–ing,* but it is used as a noun. The gerunds in the examples are in **bold** type.

Smiling is the usual expression for class pictures. (subject)

A less common pose is **frowning.** (predicate nominative)

Gerund Phrases

Gerunds, like participles, can be combined with modifiers and complements to form a **gerund phrase.**

15 C.5 A **gerund phrase** is a gerund with its modifiers and complements all working together as a noun.

A gerund or a gerund phrase can be used in all the ways a noun can be used.

Subject	**Talking loudly** usually distracts the photographer.
Direct Object	Everyone in my house enjoys **taking pictures of our dogs.**
Indirect Object	He gave **shooting the photo** careful thought.
Object of a Preposition	She photographed for eight hours without **taking a break.**
Predicate Nominative	A great thrill for her was **winning the photography contest.**
Appositive	Dad's hobby, **shooting outdoor scenery,** has taught him much about nature.

As you see from the previous examples, a gerund in a gerund phrase can be followed by a modifier, a complement, or a prepositional phrase.

The possessive form of a noun or a pronoun is sometimes used before a gerund and is considered part of the gerund phrase.

Mrs. Lambert insists on ***our*** **developing our own photos for the semester course.**

Jane's **adjusting the light meter** made the picture turn out too dark.

You can learn more about possessive nouns and pronouns on pages 944–951.

CHAPTER 15

Practice Your Skills

Identifying Gerund Phrases

Write the gerund phrases in the following sentences. Then underline each gerund.

1. Novice photographers sharpen their skills by taking many pictures of the same scene.
2. Mrs. Emerson encourages our using different types of film.
3. Photographers can create unusual angles by lying on their stomachs.
4. Pepe's family objects to his spending too much money on film.
5. A meter can often be used for measuring the amount of light near the photographed object.
6. Fun with cameras often includes shooting pictures of friends and family.
7. Did you know that even simple cameras are sufficient for taking interesting photos?
8. Ansel Adams's using black-and-white film won him many accolades.
9. She tried shooting the action very fast.
10. My parents were thrilled about John's finding a talent for photography.

Practice Your Skills

Determining Uses of Gerund Phrases

Write each gerund phrase. Then label the use of each one, using the following abbreviations.

subject = *subj.*	direct object = *d.o.*
indirect object = *i.o.*	object of a preposition = *o.p.*
appositive = *appos.*	predicate nominative = *p.n.*

1. A photographer focuses his or her camera by twisting the lens.
2. Kim's favorite rainy-day pastime is sorting through old photos.
3. Collecting old photographs is one way to learn about family history.
4. The award for excellence gave my taking photographs real meaning.
5. Mom and Dad approve of your purchasing the new camera for your class.
6. Do you enjoy diving and swimming with an underwater camera?
7. Carrying the large camera bag and the tripod is not difficult for me.
8. Roberto thoroughly enjoys his new interest, studying photographers' techniques.
9. Mr. Fitzgerald suggested using a telephoto lens for the landscape shot.
10. You can change the outcome of a photo by developing the film differently.

Infinitives and Infinitive Phrases

15 C.6 An **infinitive** is a verb form that usually begins with *to.* It is used as a noun, an adjective, or an adverb.

The **infinitive** looks entirely different from a participle or a gerund because it usually begins with the word *to.* An infinitive can take several forms; for example, the infinitives of *plan* are *to plan, to be planning, to have planned, to be planned, to have been planning,* and *to have been planned.*

The infinitives in the following examples are in **bold** type.

That is the kind of pet **to adopt.** (adjective)

Dog shelters help pets **to be adopted.** (adverb)

Be careful not to confuse an infinitive with a prepositional phrase that begins with the preposition *to.* An infinitive ends with a verb form; a prepositional phrase ends with a noun or a pronoun.

Infinitive	I want **to help.**
Prepositional Phrase	Tell that **to Dad.**

CHAPTER 15

Infinitive Phrases

Like participles and gerunds, an infinitive can be combined with modifiers and complements to form an **infinitive phrase.**

15 C.7 An **infinitive phrase** is an infinitive with its modifiers and complements all working together as a noun, an adjective, or an adverb.

Notice the variations of an infinitive phrase. An infinitive, for example, can be followed by a complement, a modifier, or a prepositional phrase.

Noun	**To exercise a pet regularly** is very important. (subject)
	I hope **to find a pet soon.** (direct object)
Adjective	That is the agency **to contact for more information.**
Adverb	The veterinarians were happy **to help us.**

Sometimes the word *to* is omitted when an infinitive follows such verbs as *dare, feel, hear, help, let, make, need, see,* or *watch.* It is, nevertheless, understood to be there.

> Did you help **(to) rescue** the stray puppies?

Practice Your Skills

Identifying Infinitive Phrases

Write the infinitive phrases in the following sentences. Then underline each infinitive.

1. My brother wanted to convince my father of our need for a puppy.
2. One of our strategies was to find a friendly, trainable breed.
3. To convince Dad of our dedication would be the hardest part.
4. As we approached him, I tried not to appear anxious.
5. We presented our case to become owners of a puppy from the local shelter.
6. Our father left the room to consider our arguments.
7. We were soon to be granted permission for a furry friend.

Practice Your Skills

Determining the Uses of Infinitive Phrases

Write each infinitive phrase. Then label how each one is used: ***n.*** (noun), ***adj.*** (adjective), or ***adv.*** (adverb).

1. Jason was the first neighbor to meet our new puppy.
2. We have decided to name her Zoe.
3. Zoe was first to chase after us at the shelter.

Connect to Writing: Analyzing Poetry

Analyzing the Use of Infinitive Phrases

Read this poem by Emily Dickinson. Note particularly her use of the opening infinitive phrase. Then answer the questions on the next page.

> To make a prairie it takes a clover and one bee,
> One clover, and a bee,
> And revery.
> The revery alone will do,
> If bees are few.
>
> *—Emily Dickinson*

- What is the literal meaning of this poem?
- What is the figurative meaning of the poem?
- Why do you think Dickinson chose to begin the poem with an infinitive phrase?
- How does the infinitive phrase affect you as a reader?

Check Point: Mixed Practice

Write each verbal phrase. Then label the use of each one, using the following abbreviations: participle = *part.* gerund = *ger.* infinitive = *inf.* Note: Some sentences do not contain verbals.

(1) Born in New York City, Edith Newbold Jones came from a wealthy family. **(2)** Educated by private tutors and governesses at home, she started to write poetry at the age of 16. **(3)** Then she decided to marry Edward Wharton, a wealthy Boston banker. **(4)** It wasn't until after several years of a rather aimless marriage, however, that she began to write in earnest. **(5)** She began by contributing poems and stories to magazines. **(6)** Her first novel, *The Valley of Decision,* appeared in 1902. **(7)** After many years of success in the United States, Wharton chose to spend the latter part of her life in France.

(8) Many of Wharton's early books deal with the class structure existing in society and with people's resistance to social change. **(9)** Wharton disregarded this theme, however, in her famous novelette *Ethan Frome.* **(10)** This story is about simple New England people who are doomed to live within the narrow confines of convention. **(11)** After writing *The Age of Innocence* nine years later, she won a Pulitzer Prize. **(12)** In all, Wharton published more than 50 books.

CHAPTER 15

Misplaced and Dangling Modifiers

Lesson 4

15 D **Misplaced modifiers and dangling modifiers are common modifier problems. They can confuse the meaning of a sentence.**

All phrases except gerund and appositive phrases can be used as modifiers. Phrases used as modifiers should be placed near the word they modify. When a modifier is misplaced, the meaning of the sentence gets confused because the modifier appears to describe some other word.

15 D.1 A modifier that is placed too far away from the word it modifies is called a **misplaced modifier.**

Misplaced	We ate the apples **chatting on the porch.**
Correct	**Chatting on the porch,** we ate the apples.
Misplaced	We saw orchards **looking out the window.**
Correct	**Looking out the window,** we saw orchards.

CHAPTER 15

15 D.2 A **dangling modifier** is a phrase that is used as a modifier but does not describe any word in the sentence.

Be sure that the noun or pronoun that the modifying phrase is describing is in the sentence.

Dangling	**Strolling through the garden,** the vegetables looked luscious. (Who was strolling?)
Correct	**Strolling through the garden,** I admired the luscious vegetables.
Dangling	**Citing medical research,** broccoli is healthful. (Who did the citing?)
Correct	**Citing medical research,** my doctor says broccoli is healthful.

Practice Your Skills

Recognizing Misplaced and Dangling Modifiers

Write ***I*** if the sentence contains misplaced or dangling modifiers. If the sentence is correct, write ***C***.

1. I looked for the vitamins, unpacking the grocery bag.
2. Having eaten all but three sunflower seeds, the package was nearly empty.
3. Freshly picked, Roger carried a basket of grapes.
4. Having followed a healthful diet for years, the doctor congratulated Yoko.
5. Jane drinks milk four times a day with a high calcium content.
6. Asparagus, a good source of vitamin E, is part of a nutritional meal.
7. Tossed with Italian dressing, Freddie served the salad.
8. Experts recommend eating at least five servings of fruits and vegetables a day to prevent diseases.

Practice Your Skills

Correcting Misplaced or Dangling Modifiers

Rewrite the incorrect sentences in the preceding exercise. For each incorrect sentence, place the phrase closer to the word it modifies, or add words and change the sentence so that the phrase has a noun or a pronoun to modify. Add punctuation as needed.

Phrase Fragments Lesson 5

Even though a phrase may be as long as a sentence, it can never be a sentence because a phrase has no subject or verb.

15 E **When phrases are written as if they were sentences, they become phrase fragments.**

The following examples of phrase fragments are in **bold** type. Notice that they are incorrectly capitalized and punctuated as if they were sentences.

Prepositional Phrase	Henry Ford was born in Michigan. **On a prosperous family farm in today's Dearborn.**
Appositive Phrase	On July 30, 1863, Henry arrived. **The first of six Ford children.**
Participial Phrase	Ford left the family farm for Detroit. **Chosen for its industrial opportunities.**
Gerund Phrase	He earned a living for himself and his wife. **Running a sawmill.**
Infinitive Phrase	A promotion at work boosted his dream. **To devote time to his engineering inventions.**

When you edit your written work, you can correct phrase fragments in one of two ways: (1) add words to make them into separate sentences or (2) attach them to a related group of words that has a subject and a verb.

Sentence and Fragment	Student drivers are cautious. **Driving slowly, braking frequently, and parking away from other cars.**
Separate Sentences	Student drivers are cautious. **They drive slowly, brake frequently, and park away from other cars.**
Attached	**Driving slowly, braking frequently, and parking away from other cars,** student drivers are cautious.

You can find out more about other types of fragments on pages 663–664 and 726–727.

CHAPTER 15

Practice Your Skills

Recognizing Phrase Fragments

Label each group of words ***S*** for sentence or ***F*** for fragment.

1. On a winding road near the edge of town.
2. She learned to parallel park in the school parking lot.
3. To wear a seatbelt in the car.
4. Driving to the corner of Elm Street and Ash Road.
5. The officer from the Department of Public Transportation.
6. Passengers in the convertible were waving.
7. By turning onto the wrong street.
8. Affixed to the hood of his car.

Connect to Writing: Revising

Writing Complete Sentences

Rewrite each fragment in the exercise above as a complete sentence.

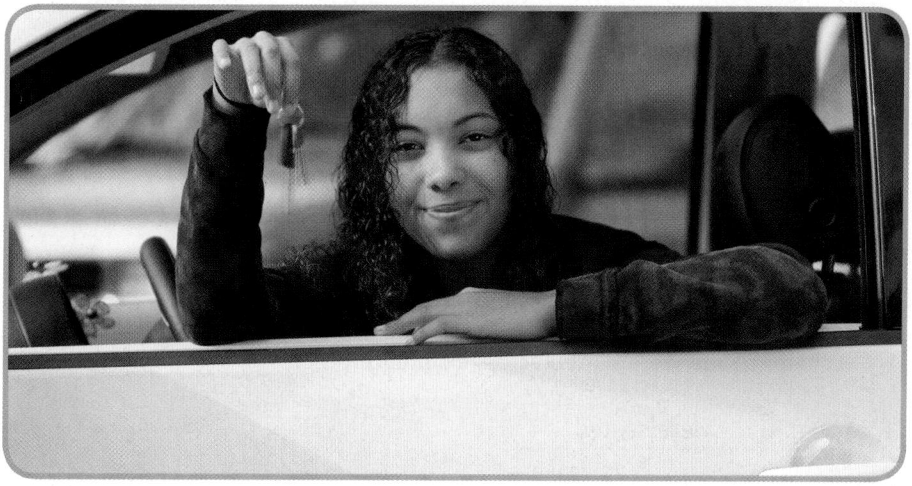

Connect to Writing: Editorial

Writing Complete Sentences

Your state wants to raise the driving age. You and your friends have discussed this issue many times. What does driving a car mean to you? Does it signify freedom or responsibility, for example? Is it a necessity for someone your age? Write an editorial for your local newspaper. Explain your thoughts. Use complete sentences and correct punctuation so that your ideas will be taken seriously.

Diagraming Phrases

Diagraming sentences can help you understand how the different kinds of phrases function in a sentence. Because prepositional phrases, appositive phrases, participial phrases, gerund phrases, and infinitive phrases all function in different ways, they are diagramed according to different rules.

Prepositional Phrases

An **adjectival** or **adverbial phrase** is always connected to the word it modifies. The preposition is placed on a connecting slanted line. The object of the preposition is placed on a horizontal line that is attached to the slanted line. The following example includes three adjectival phrases and one adverbial phrase. Notice that an adjectival phrase can modify the object of the preposition of another phrase.

The tickets to the theater on James Street were bought in a store at the mall.

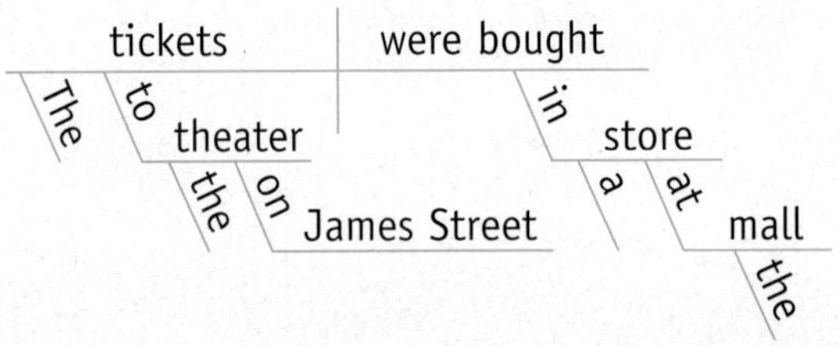

An **adverbial phrase** that modifies an adjective or an adverb needs an additional line.

In chemistry we were seated across from each other.

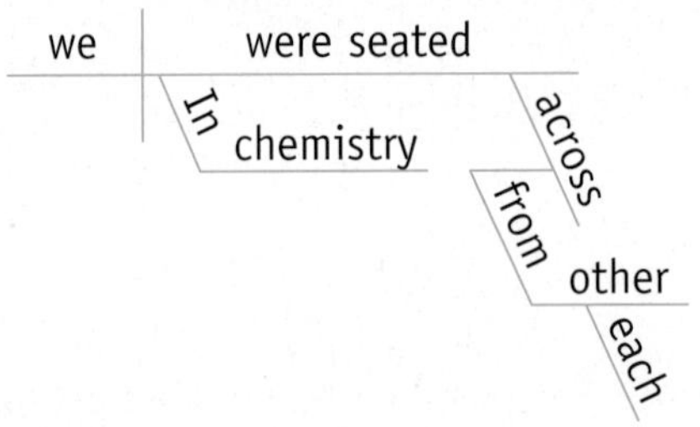

Appositives and Appositive Phrases

An **appositive** or **appositive phrase** is diagramed in parentheses next to the word it identifies or explains. Words in the appositive phrase are placed directly underneath it.

The hyacinth, a member of the lily family, is grown in many parts of the world.

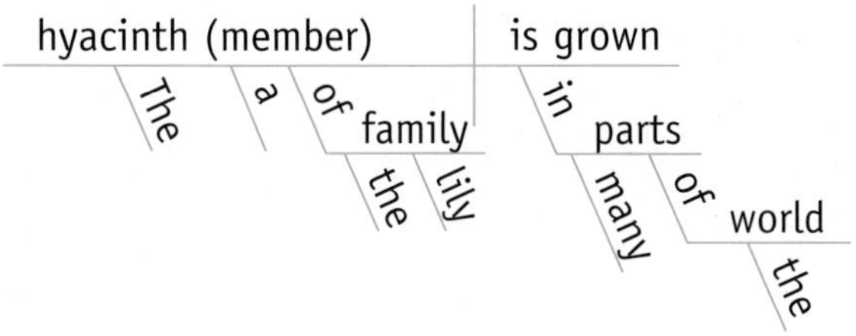

Participial Phrases

Because a **participial phrase** is always used as an adjective, it is diagramed under the word it modifies. The participle, however, is written on a curve. Notice in the following example that an adverb and a prepositional phrase make up part of the participial phrase.

Sprinting first across the line, Davis won the race.

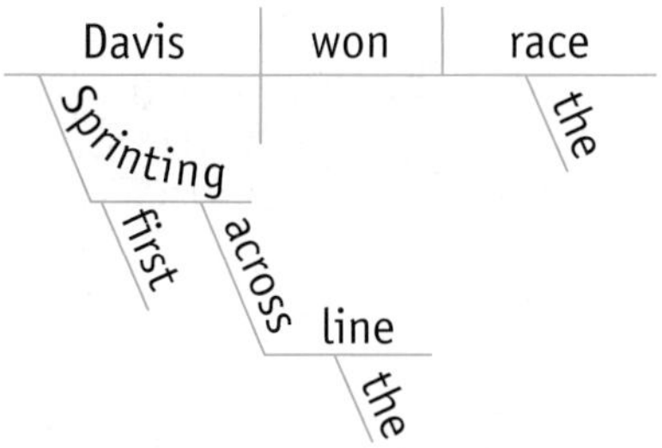

CHAPTER 15

Gerund Phrases

A **gerund phrase** is used as a noun. For this reason it is diagramed in any position a noun would be diagramed. In this diagram the gerund phrase is used as a direct object. You can see that it is diagramed on a pedestal, with the gerund curved on a step.

On Sunday afternoon I began studying my notes for the history test.

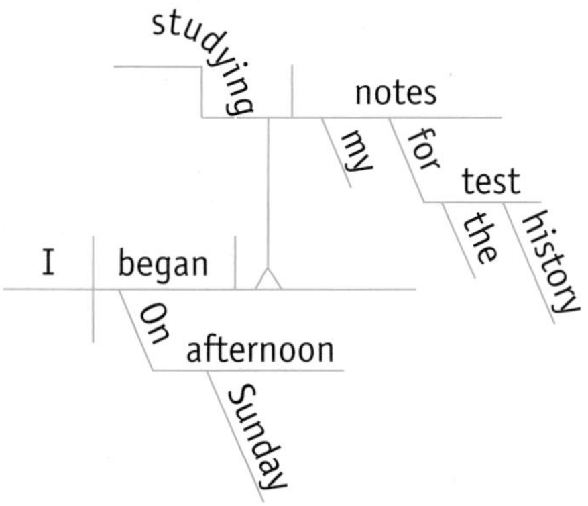

Infinitive Phrases

Because an **infinitive phrase** may be used as a noun, an adjective, or an adverb, it can be diagramed in one of several ways. The following example shows how an infinitive phrase used as a subject and an infinitive phrase used as a predicate nominative are diagramed. Notice that the word *action* functions as a direct object in the second infinitive phrase and is diagramed in that position.

To procrastinate is to delay action.

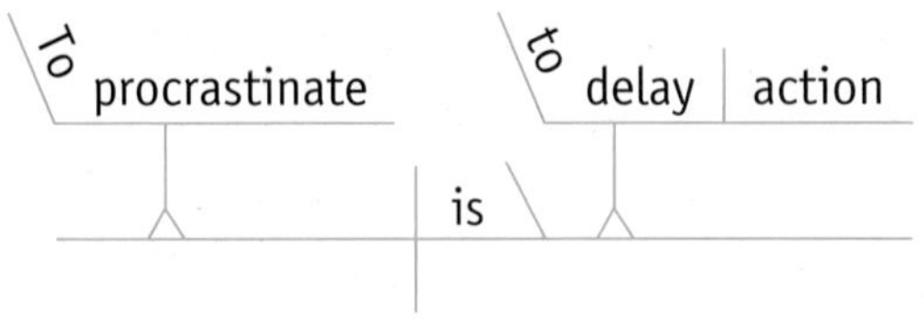

If the *to* of an infinitive is omitted from the sentence, it is placed in parentheses.

Practice Your Skills

Diagraming Phrases

Diagram the following sentences or copy them. If you copy them, draw one line under each subject and two lines under each verb. Then put parentheses around each phrase and label each one *prepositional, appositive, participial, gerund,* or *infinitive*.

1. During my vacation, I visited Texas.

2. My relatives live in Austin, the capital of Texas.

3. Riding to Dallas, I understood the huge size of Texas.

4. In the future, I want to fly from Austin to Dallas.

5. Learning about the history of Texas was interesting.

6. In 1836, Sam Houston led troops fighting for independence from Mexico.

7. The highlight of the trip was seeing a rodeo.

8. We did not try to ride the wild horses.

9. At home in Ohio, I still like to wear my ten-gallon hat.

10. I will always remember traveling through Texas.

Assess Your Learning

Identifying Phrases

Write the phrases in the following sentences. Then label each one *prepositional, appositive, participial, gerund,* or *infinitive.*

1. The forepaws of the raccoon look very much like small human hands.
2. Amy and Vanessa enjoyed watching the beautiful sunrise.
3. The bassoon is sometimes used in a musical work to create a humorous effect.
4. Jacques Cousteau, the great underwater explorer, helped invent the Aqua-Lung.

Identifying Phrases

Write the underlined phrases in the following paragraph. Then label each phrase *prepositional, appositive, participial, gerund,* or *infinitive.*

Igloos, **(1)** temporary or permanent dwellings, are really quite amazing structures. **(2)** Lighting a fire, for example, does not melt the igloo's ceilings or walls. A fire actually adds additional insulation **(3)** to an igloo. The largest problem **(4)** facing an igloo builder is **(5)** finding the right snow. The snow must be firm and compact but not too icy. Huge blocks of snow are cut and arranged **(6)** to form a dome. Any gaps **(7)** in the snow are then filled **(8)** with soft, fresh snow. The final tasks are **(9)** cutting an opening and **(10)** shaping the door.

Participial or Gerund?

Identify the underlined phrase as *participial* or *gerund.* Then choose the correct word in parentheses to complete the sentence.

1. I got a headache from (Brittany, Brittany's) singing in the next room.
2. I understand (him, his) wanting a job.
3. Yesterday I saw (you, your) walking along the beach.
4. Mother doesn't like (me, my) working so late.
5. We were proud of (them, their) winning the game.
6. Mr. Seidenberger didn't like (you, your) missing yesterday's band practice.
7. At the beach the children watched (him, his) throwing a disk to the dog.
8. Anastasia took a photograph of the (lion, lion's) roaring loudly in its cage.
9. (Roberto, Roberto's) pitching in the last inning helped us win the game.
10. The coach encourages (us, our) running five laps around the track every day.

Using Phrases

Write five sentences that follow the directions below. (The sentences may come in any order.) Write about one of the following topics or a topic of your choice: why you enjoy playing or watching sports or why you do not enjoy playing or watching sports.

Write a sentence that . . .

1. includes at least two prepositional phrases.
2. includes an appositive phrase.
3. includes an introductory participial phrase.
4. includes a gerund phrase.
5. includes an infinitive phrase.

Underline and label each phrase. Then check for correct punctuation in each sentence.

Phrases: Posttest

Directions

Write the letter of the term that correctly identifies the underlined phrase in each sentence.

(1) Preparing a résumé should not be a difficult chore. **(2)** The best résumés are specifically tailored to one specific job. **(3)** Doing a bit of homework beforehand can improve your chances of landing the job you want. **(4)** The complete package, résumé and cover letter, should be coherent and expressive of your best efforts. **(5)** The heading, displaying your name, address, phone number, and e-mail address, should be bold and readable. **(6)** You should include an objective, your immediate goal for the future. **(7)** An example of an objective might be to become a nurse's assistant in an urban hospital. **(8)** Include your work experiences from the most recent to the least recent. **(9)** In your descriptions avoid using lengthy sentences. **(10)** The language in an effective résumé is always clear and concise.

1. **A** prepositional
B participial
C gerund
D infinitive

2. **A** participial
B prepositional
C appositive
D gerund

3. **A** prepositional
B participial
C gerund
D infinitive

4. **A** infinitive
B gerund
C appositive
D participial

5. **A** prepositional
B participial
C gerund
D infinitive

6. **A** participial
B prepositional
C appositive
D gerund

7. **A** prepositional
B participial
C gerund
D infinitive

8. **A** infinitive
B prepositional
C appositive
D gerund

9. **A** prepositional
B participial
C gerund
D infinitive

10. **A** appositive
B prepositional
C appositive
D gerund

Writer's Corner

Snapshot

15 A A **phrase** is a group of related words that functions as a single part of speech and does not have a subject and verb. **Adjectival** and **adverbial phrases** are prepositional phrases that modify other parts of speech. (pages 682–685)

15 B An **appositive** is a noun or pronoun that identifies or explains another noun or pronoun next to it in a sentence. When an appositive has modifiers, it is called an **appositive phrase.** (pages 686–687)

15 C A **verbal** is a verb form that is used as a noun, adjective, or adverb instead of a verb. The three kinds of verbals are **participles, gerunds,** and **infinitives.** (pages 688–695)

15 D A **misplaced modifier** is a phrase that is placed too far away from the word it modifies. A **dangling modifier** is a modifier that does not describe any noun or pronoun in the sentence. (pages 696–697)

15 E A **phrase fragment** is a phrase that is written as if it were a sentence. (pages 698–699)

Power Rules

Fix **phrase fragments** by adding words to turn the phrase into a sentence or by attaching the phrase to an existing sentence. (pages 698–699)

Before Editing

Sergio scored a goal. *During the last minute.*

At last night's soccer game. I lost my voice. *Cheering for my team.*

After Editing

Sergio scored a goal. *He made the goal during the last minute.*

At last night's soccer game, I lost my voice *cheering for my team.*

Editing Checklist ✓

Use this checklist when editing your writing.

✓ Did I make sure that all my sentences are complete? (See pages 656–662.)
✓ Did I use adjectival and adverbial phrases to vary my sentences or to combine sentences? (See pages 682–685.)
✓ Did I use appositives to explain nouns and pronouns? (See pages 686–687.)
✓ Did I use commas to set off nonessential and certain introductory phrases? (See pages 689 and 926–927.)
✓ Did I use participial, gerund, and infinitive phrases to add action and liveliness to my writing? (See pages 688–695.)
✓ Did I place all of my modifiers close to the word or words they describe? (See pages 696–697.)

CHAPTER 15

Use the Power

Think of phrases as the colors on a painter's palette. Just as an artist uses colors to bring a painting to life, you can add phrases to sentences to make your writing vivid and colorful.

On Saturday, Chloe and Clara went to Allstate Arena to see Jackson Dylan, one of their favorite singers. Standing in the aisles, they were able to see the dancers on the stage. During the concert, they showed their appreciation by dancing and singing.

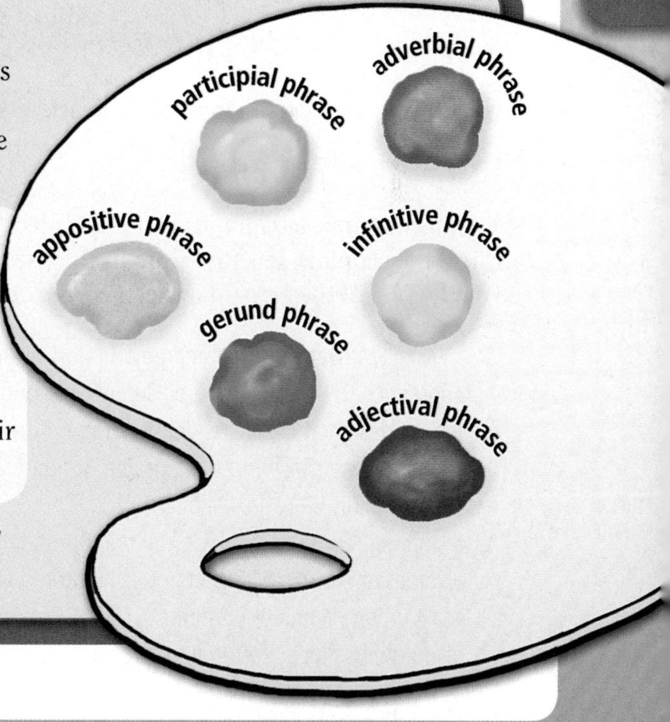

Add color to a recent composition by adding at least three phrases.

Clauses

World's Columbian Exposition, 1893

How can you use clauses to express subtle and precise meaning?

Clauses: Pretest 1

The following draft paragraphs about architect Daniel Burnham are hard to read because they contain several errors in the use of clauses. Revise the draft so that it reads correctly. One of the errors has been corrected as an example.

Architect Daniel Burnham, grew up in Chicago who was born in 1846. He was an apprentice to William Le Baron Jenney, although he did not go to school for architecture. Jenney designed the first steel skyscraper. Later partnered with John Wellborn Root. Their company was chosen to manage the design and installation. Of the 1893 World's Columbian Exposition. In Chicago, Illinois.

In addition to his work on the fair, Burnham designed the Flatiron Building in New York he also designed Union Station in Washington, D.C., and Orchestra Hall in Chicago. For large-scale urban planning, Burnham's 1909 "Plan of Chicago" became a model. An example of Burnham's ideas for urban planning is Chicago's vast Lake Michigan shoreline. The Field Museum of Natural History, the Shedd Aquarium, and the Museum of Science and Industry campuses are located. A stroll along Chicago's Navy Pier is just one more reminder. Of Burnham's architectural vision.

Clauses: Pretest 2

Directions

Write the letter of the term that correctly identifies each sentence or underlined part of a sentence.

(1) Lawyers may serve in private practice, government service, or labor unions. **(2)** About 75 percent of lawyers are in private practice. **(3)** Unlike English lawyers, who work either in offices or in courtrooms, American lawyers work in both. **(4)** Some private practitioners are trial lawyers; others are real estate lawyers or patent lawyers. **(5)** Lawyers continue learning even after passing the bar. **(6)** Lawyers must keep up with reading that applies to their specialties, and they often need extra coursework. **(7)** Before 1952, some law schools had required only two years of college study, but now they all require three. **(8)** After they were advised by the American Bar Association, law schools changed their requirements. **(9)** That most lawyers are well educated is clear. **(10)** Lawyers who pass the bar in one state are not necessarily qualified in other states.

1. **A** simple sentence
B compound sentence
C complex sentence
D compound-complex sentence

2. **A** simple sentence
B compound sentence
C complex sentence
D compound-complex sentence

3. **A** simple sentence
B compound sentence
C complex sentence
D compound-complex sentence

4. **A** simple sentence
B compound sentence
C complex sentence
D compound-complex sentence

5. **A** simple sentence
B compound sentence
C complex sentence
D compound-complex sentence

6. **A** simple sentence
B compound sentence
C complex sentence
D compound-complex sentence

7. **A** independent clause
B adverbial clause
C adjectival clause
D noun clause

8. **A** independent clause
B adverbial clause
C adjectival clause
D noun clause

9. **A** independent clause
B adverbial clause
C adjectival clause
D noun clause

10. **A** independent clause
B adverbial clause
C adjectival clause
D noun clause

Independent and Subordinate Clauses

Lesson 1

A paragraph consisting of only short, simple sentences would be dull to read and could even be confusing. When each idea is expressed in a separate sentence, the relationship between ideas may also be unclear. Combining sentences will add variety to your sentence structure. In this chapter you will learn how to combine ideas by using clauses to form compound and complex sentences.

16 A **A clause is a group of words that has a subject and a verb.**

Add color and interest to your writing by varying the structure of your sentences. Include various combinations of clauses, as in the paragraph below.

> In the early years of this nation, Americans were moving westward. As new lands were gained, new settlements sprang up. First there was Louisiana, which was bought from France. After people settled in the areas surrounding the Mississippi, they went west to explore the land.

CHAPTER 16

A clause can be independent or subordinate. An independent clause makes sense alone. A subordinate clause does not make sense alone.

16 A.1 An **independent (main) clause** can stand alone as a sentence because it expresses a complete thought.

An independent clause is called a sentence when it stands alone, but it is called a clause when it appears in a sentence with another clause. In the following examples, each subject is underlined once, and each verb is underlined twice. Notice that each independent clause could stand alone as a sentence.

independent clause — independent clause

Early Americans had few reliable maps, and the maps were changing constantly.

sentence — sentence

Early Americans had few reliable maps. The maps were changing constantly.

16 A.2 A **subordinate (dependent) clause** cannot stand alone because it does not express a complete thought.

Even though a subordinate clause has a subject and a verb, it does not express a complete thought. As a result, it cannot stand alone. A subordinate clause is dependent upon an independent clause to complete its meaning.

independent clause / subordinate clause
I will choose a route after I find my compass.

independent clause / subordinate clause
I found the compass, which was a gift from my grandfather.

When You Write

When writers want to persuade an audience of their viewpoint, they can acknowledge the opposing point of view by presenting it in a subordinate clause.

> **Although maps may be a valuable tool,** the Internet can help people find their way to places more conveniently and easily.

By beginning the statement with a subordinate clause, the writer lets the audience know that he or she has considered the value of maps but has found something more valuable.

Look at a recent persuasive composition and check to see if you can use a dependent clause to acknowledge and subordinate the opposing point of view.

Practice Your Skills

Distinguishing Between Independent and Subordinate Clauses

Label each underlined clause as ***I*** for independent or ***S*** for subordinate.

1. Because he was a younger son in a land-poor family, George Washington worked hard for acceptance as a Virginia gentleman.
2. When Washington was only eleven years old, his father died.
3. Washington wanted to run away to sea, but his mother stopped him.
4. George Washington did not attend college as the next five presidents did.
5. Washington, however, was a good student who excelled in mathematics.
6. A dominant figure in his early life was his older half-brother Lawrence, who married into the wealthy Fairfax family of Virginia.
7. After Washington turned seventeen, Lawrence got him a job as a surveyor.
8. For a few dollars a day, Washington mapped new lands on the frontier.

Uses of Subordinate Clauses Lesson 2

16 B **A subordinate clause can function as an adverb, an adjective, or a noun.**

Similar to a phrase, a subordinate clause can function as an adverb, an adjective, or a noun. The difference between a clause and a phrase is that a clause has a subject and a verb while a phrase does not.

Adverbial Clauses

16 B.1 An **adverbial clause** is a subordinate clause that is used as an adverb to modify a verb, an adjective, or an adverb.

CHAPTER 16

An adverbial clause can be used just like a single adverb or an adverbial phrase. The single adverb, the adverbial phrase, and the adverbial clause in the following examples all modify the verb *studied.*

Single Adverb	Jerry studied **carefully.**
Adverbial Phrase	Jerry studied **with great diligence.**
Adverbial Clause	Jerry studied **as though his life depended on it.**

An adverbial clause answers the same questions a single adverb answers: *How? When? Where? How much?* and *To what extent?* An adverbial clause also answers *Under what condition?* and *Why?* Although most adverbial clauses modify verbs, some modify adjectives or adverbs.

Modifying a Verb	I finished my lab report **before it was due.** (The clause answers *When?*)
	Because his microscope was broken, Peter borrowed one. (The clause answers *Why?*)
Modifying an Adjective	Mike is more nervous **than I am.** (The clause answers *To what extent?*)
Modifying an Adverb	Jan finished the experiment sooner **than I did.** (The clause answers *How much?*)

Subordinating Conjunctions

An adverbial clause begins with a word called a **subordinating conjunction.** Some words, such as *after, before, since,* and *until,* can also serve as prepositions in prepositional phrases.

COMMON SUBORDINATING CONJUNCTIONS				
after	as long as	even though	than	whenever
although	as much as	if	though	where
as	as though	in order that	unless	wherever
as far as	because	since	until	while
as if	before	so that	when	

An adverbial clause modifies the whole verb phrase.

Chris will quote chemistry facts ***as long as*** **anyone is listening.**

Whenever **you experiment,** you are testing theories.

The petri dish, ***when*** **it toppled,** was sitting on the ledge.

PUNCTUATION WITH ADVERBIAL CLAUSES

Place a comma after an introductory adverbial clause.

While you write the hypothesis, I will adjust the microscope.

If an adverbial clause interrupts an independent clause, surround it with commas.

The students, **after they had completed the experiments,** washed the equipment.

When the adverbial clause follows the independent clause, no comma is needed.

Ms. Carver will grade our lab reports **when she has the time.**

Practice Your Skills

Punctuating Adverbial Clauses

Write each adverbial clause. Then write ***I*** if the adverbial clause is punctuated incorrectly and **C** if it is punctuated correctly.

1. If you fill an ice cube tray with warm water your ice cubes will be clearer.

2. Nickel because it has exceptional ductility can be stretched into fine wire.

3. Before she becomes a Nobel Prize winner, Kylie must finish college.

CHAPTER 16

4. Magnesium after it is ignited burns with a brilliant white light.
5. Shelly began the experiment after she put on her safety goggles.

Connect to Writing: **Editing**

Punctuating Adverbial Clauses

Rewrite the sentences in the preceding exercise that are punctuated incorrectly, adding a comma or commas where needed.

Elliptical Clauses

16 B.2 An adverbial clause in which words are missing is called an **elliptical clause.**

Words in an adverbial clause are occasionally omitted to tighten the sentence or reduce repetition. Despite the omission, the words are understood to be there. Elliptical clauses often begin with *than* or *as,* as in the examples below.

Lee is a better artist **than I.**
(The completed elliptical clause reads "than I *[am]*.")
A tiny brush can change a portrait **as much as a large brush.**
(The completed elliptical clause reads "as a large brush *[can change a portrait]*.")

You can find out about pronouns in elliptical clauses on pages 797–798.

Practice Your Skills

Recognizing Elliptical Clauses

If the sentence contains an elliptical clause, write *yes.* If the sentence does not contain an elliptical clause, write *no.*

1. In New York there are many artists more talented than he.
2. Pat draws better than Lamar draws.
3. Lamar has better sculpting skills than Pat.
4. That tube of red paint contains nearly as much paint as the blue tube.
5. Rory is as talented as Kumar.
6. Dwayne is as eager to create as his younger brother.
7. Some paintbrushes are both delicate and expensive.
8. In the art show, Latoya won more awards than Emily.

Connect to Writing: Editing

Completing Elliptical Clauses

Write the completed version of each elliptical clause in the preceding exercise.

Adjectival Clauses

16 B.3 An **adjectival clause** is a subordinate clause that is used as an adjective to modify a noun or a pronoun.

You can use an adjectival clause as you would use a single adjective. The single adjective, the adjectival phrase, and the adjectival clause in the examples below all modify *officer.*

Single Adjective	The young military recruits shouted for the **chief** officer.
Adjectival Phrase	The young military recruits shouted for the officer **with the huge, blaring bullhorn.**
Adjectival Clause	The young military recruits shouted for the officer **who demanded their attention.**

An adjectival clause and a single adjective answer the same questions: *Which one(s)?* and *What kind?*

Which One(s)?	Sam is the new marine **who just shaved his head.**
What Kind?	The soldiers need haircuts **that all look alike.**

Relative Pronouns

An adjectival clause usually begins with a relative pronoun.

16 B.4 A **relative pronoun** relates an adjectival clause to its antecedent—the noun or pronoun the clause modifies.

RELATIVE PRONOUNS				
who	whom	whose	which	that

Quantico, ***which* is located in Virginia,** is a marine military base.

My cousin, ***who* is twenty-nine years old,** is a marine.

CHAPTER 16

Occasionally words such as *where* and *when* are also used to begin an adjectival clause.

This is the army base **where you will go first.**

Saturday is the day **when the recruits will arrive.**

The relative pronoun *that* is sometimes omitted from an adjectival clause. It is still understood to be there.

Is this the jacket **you will wear every day?**
(The complete adjectival clause is *[that] you will wear every day.*)

When You Write

To be concise, skilled writers avoid using adjectival clauses when one word will do. Notice the difference in these sentences.

The officers expected to see boots **that were polished.**

The officers expected to see **polished** boots.

Tighten the language of a recent composition by replacing wordy adjectival clauses with adjectives.

CHAPTER 16

Practice Your Skills

Recognizing Adjectival Clauses as Modifiers

Write the adjectival clause in each sentence. Then beside each clause, write the word it modifies.

1. The hero of *The Red Badge of Courage* is young Henry Fleming, who is afraid of battle.
2. His ideas of war were formed from books that he had read during his childhood.
3. Henry gets a less glamorous idea of war after arriving at the army camp, where he hears many gruesome stories.
4. Henry, who had imagined himself a hero, now begins to doubt his own courage.
5. Most of the book is a minute-by-minute description of Henry's first battle, where he finds out for himself about war and courage.

6. This first encounter, when Henry runs away in panic, prepares him for later battles.
7. Courage, which deserts Henry in the first battle, stays with him in the next; and he develops awareness and maturity.
8. Stephen Crane's classic war novel was one of the first books that told not only of many acts of heroism but also of the horrors of war.
9. At the time both Union and Confederate soldiers, whose feelings were accurately presented, praised the book.

Functions of a Relative Pronoun

Within the adjectival clause, the relative pronoun can function as a subject, a direct object, or an object of a preposition. It may also show possession.

Subject	Students **who are interested in international friends** can join a pen pal program. (*Who* is the subject of *are interested.*)
Direct Object	Having a pen pal is an exciting opportunity **students can enjoy for a lifetime.** (The understood relative pronoun *that* is the direct object of *can enjoy.*)
Object of a Preposition	The pen pal program **to which Alex belongs** was a fulfilling experience. (*Which* is the object of the preposition *to. To* is part of the clause.)
Possession	The Iranian student **whose letters arrived every month** became a good friend. (*Whose* shows possession.)

CHAPTER 16

PUNCTUATION WITH ADJECTIVAL CLAUSES

No punctuation is used with an adjectival clause that contains essential information needed to identify a person, place, or thing. A comma or commas, however, should set off an adjectival clause that is nonessential. A clause is nonessential if it can be removed without changing the basic meaning of the sentence. An adjectival clause that follows a proper noun is usually nonessential.

Essential My uncle **who lives in Sweden** wrote me a hilarious letter. (No commas are used because the clause is needed to identify which uncle.)

Nonessential Fredrik Rolfsson, **who lives in Sweden,** wrote me a hilarious letter. (Commas are used because the clause can be removed without changing the main meaning of the sentence.)

The relative pronoun *that* is frequently used in an essential clause, and *which* is often used in a nonessential clause.

CHAPTER 16

Practice Your Skills

Determining the Function of a Relative Pronoun

Write each adjectival clause. Then label the use of each relative pronoun, using the following abbreviations. If an adjectival clause begins with an understood *that,* write ***understood*** after the number and then write how *that* is used.

subject = *subj.* direct object = *d.o.*
object of a preposition = *o.p.* possession = *poss.*

1. The letter, which was written in Spanish and English, arrived for Alberto.
2. Beth told him a story that made him want to visit Ireland.
3. Lillian, whose e-mails were always brief, wrote her pen pal every week.
4. Ginger never found the address she lost last year.
5. The person to whom Leroy writes is moving to Kamnik, Slovenia.
6. Jason Morton, who was my father's pen pal 25 years ago, sends him a birthday card every year.
7. This is the same stationery I have used for the past two years.
8. Her stationery, which always has her name printed at the top, is yellow.
9. The Australian to whom you wrote last year will visit the United States soon.
10. He sends his letter via air mail, which takes a month to arrive at its destination.

Connect to Writing: Editing

Punctuating Adjectival Clauses

Rewrite the following paragraph, adding commas where necessary.

The World's Columbian Exposition which was built on 600 acres of Chicago swampland astonished the world in 1893. The scientific wonders that were being developed achieved notoriety. Electricity about which visitors, were curious was extensively used. The art that was on display introduced new American artists to the public. Now called the Museum of Science and Industry the Palace of Fine Arts where the art was displayed is the only surviving structure. Seventy-seven countries prepared exhibits that drew 25 million visitors.

CHAPTER 16

Connect to Writing: Explanation

Using Adjectival Clauses

Imagine creating a time capsule that would remain buried for 100 years and accurately reflect your life and culture. Write an explanation for the people who will eventually open the capsule, naming the ten items you included and giving reasons for your choices. Include at least two adjectival clauses.

Misplaced Modifiers

Because an adjectival clause works as a modifier, it should be placed as close to the word it describes as possible. A clause placed too far away from the word it modifies is called a **misplaced modifier.**

Misplaced	I saw Dr. Miller at the clinic, **who has always been my favorite.**
Correct	At the clinic I saw Dr. Miller, **who has always been my favorite.**

Practice Your Skills

Identifying Misplaced Modifiers

Write ***MM*** for misplaced modifier if the underlined modifier is placed incorrectly in the sentence. If the underlined modifier is placed correctly, write **C** for correct.

1. Reading the magazines, we sat in the waiting room that we brought.
2. We read a magazine in the lobby, which was full of local and national news.
3. Greg had a bandage on his arm that was waterproof.
4. The nurse called his name, and he stood up from the chair in which he was sitting.
5. The thermometer measured his temperature, which was under his tongue.
6. The nurse calculated his blood pressure, which was somewhat above normal.

Connect to Writing: Revising

Correcting Misplaced Modifiers

Rewrite the sentences from the preceding exercise that contain misplaced modifiers. Use a comma or commas where needed.

CHAPTER 16

Noun Clauses

A noun clause can be used in the same way that a single noun is used.

16 B.5 A **noun clause** is a subordinate clause that is used as a noun.

The following examples show some functions noun clauses can serve in a sentence.

Subject	**Whoever has the birthday** gets all the gifts.
Direct Object	Do you know **when the party starts?**
Indirect Object	Give **whoever answers the door** this invitation.
Object of a Preposition	They made cookies for **whoever doesn't like cake.**
Predicate Nominative	Good friends, not gifts, are **what truly counts at a birthday party.**

The words in the box below often introduce a noun clause. *Who, whom, whose, which,* and *that* can also be used as relative pronouns to introduce adjectival clauses. For this reason do not rely on the introductory words themselves to identify a clause. Instead, determine how a clause is used in a sentence.

COMMON INTRODUCTORY WORDS FOR NOUN CLAUSES				
how	what	where	who	whomever
if	whatever	whether	whoever	whose
that	when	which	whom	why

Practice Your Skills

Identifying Noun Clauses

Write the noun clause in each sentence. Then label each one using the following abbreviations.

subject = *subj.* object of a preposition = *o.p.*
direct object = *d.o.* predicate nominative = *p.n.*
indirect object = *i.o.*

1. The invitation stated that Taylor's surprise party would begin at 7:00 P.M.
2. A gag gift is what her friends wanted to buy her for her birthday.
3. That Taylor loves surprises is no surprise to her best friends.
4. Have you thought at all about where you will look for a gift?
5. Give whoever comes to the house a noisy horn and a party hat.

Connect to Writing: Encyclopedia Entry

Using Clauses

Though scientists can explain many phenomena, there are still unsolved mysteries in nature. In fact, reading about Bigfoot, the Abominable Snowman, and other legendary creatures is almost a national pastime. Contribute to the *Who's Who of Unsolved Mysteries* encyclopedia by describing your own legendary creature. For effective writing, use adverbial, adjectival, and noun clauses in your entry.

Check Point: Mixed Practice

Write the ten subordinate clauses in the following paragraphs. Then label the use of each one, using the following abbreviations:

adverb = *adv.* noun = *n.*
adjective = *adj.*

(1) The most unusual of all reptiles may be the tuatara, which lives on the offshore coastal islets of New Zealand. **(2)** The tuatara is the sole survivor of a group of reptiles that are known to scientists today by their fossil remains. **(3)** What is so unusual about the tuatara is that it has three eyes! **(4)** On top of the tuatara's head is a small third eye, which is protected by a hard, transparent scale. **(5)** Although the optic nerve is completely developed, the iris, which is the colored portion of the eye, is missing. **(6)** How the tuatara uses its third eye is a mystery, but scientists are looking for an explanation.

(7) Even though other lizards have three eyes, their third eye is covered and is no longer useful. **(8)** A long time ago, many creatures had three eyes. **(9)** The tuatara, however, is the only living creature that has kept its third eye virtually intact.

CHAPTER 16

Kinds of Sentence Structure

Lesson 3

16 C **All sentences are classified as simple, compound, complex, or compound-complex.**

The classification of a sentence is determined by the number and kind of clauses in it.

16 C.1 A **simple sentence** consists of one independent clause.

In the examples below, the subject is underlined once and the verb is underlined twice.

> Next year I will earn my pilot's license.

A simple sentence can have a compound subject, a compound verb, or both.

> My brother and I were taught but were not licensed to fly a plane.

16 C.2 A **compound sentence** consists of two or more independent clauses.

You can combine simple sentences into compound sentences to help reduce the monotony in a paragraph. Independent clauses should be combined in a compound sentence, however, only if they are closely related.

> [independent clause] [independent clause]
> The flight was due at noon, but it will be an hour late.
> [independent clause] [independent clause]
> The captain landed the plane, the steward announced the arrival, and
> [independent clause]
> the crew unloaded the passengers.

You can learn about punctuating a compound sentence on pages 924–926 and 955–957.

CHAPTER 16

16 C.3 A **complex sentence** consists of one independent clause and one or more subordinate clauses.

independent clause / subordinate clause
I need some new luggage that is good for air travel.

independent clause
Dallas/Fort Worth International Airport got its name
subordinate clause
because it lies between the two cities.

independent clause / subordinate clause
Many travelers share the belief that airports are the most stressful places on earth.

You can learn about punctuating a complex sentence on page 728.

16 C.4 A **compound-complex sentence** consists of two or more independent clauses and one or more subordinate clauses.

independent clause / independent clause
Children can ride on airplanes, but their attention spans are so short
subordinate clause
that they can become very restless.

When you punctuate compound-complex sentences, follow the rules for both compound and complex sentences.

CHAPTER 16

Practice Your Skills

Classifying Sentences

Label each sentence *simple, compound, complex,* or *compound-complex.* If the sentence is punctuated incorrectly, write ***I.***

1. The author Herman Melville was born in New York to a prosperous family.
2. Melville's father whose business eventually failed died when Melville was only twelve years old.
3. Because of the family's severe financial difficulties Melville needed a job.
4. Melville seemed ashamed of his family's loss of status and the remainder of his life was spent seeking security.
5. Melville halfheartedly tried being a clerk and a teacher, but he eventually signed onto a whaling boat that was headed for the South Seas.
6. When his ship reached the Marquesas Islands the young Herman Melville jumped ship and lived among the Marquesan people for a while.
7. Eventually he became homesick and headed back home to New York City.

8. Melville then wrote several novels that were based on his sea experiences.
9. *Moby Dick,* one of his novels, was based on his own experience aboard a whaling ship and on an old sailor's yarn about a huge albino whale that was named Mocha Dick.
10. Melville could not sustain his early writing pace but he did complete *Billy Budd* just before his death.

Connect to Writing: Editing

Punctuating Sentences

In the preceding exercise, five of the sentences were punctuated incorrectly. Rewrite the sentences, adding a comma or commas where needed.

Connect to Writing: Tribute Speech

Using Various Kinds of Sentence Structure

Write a tribute speech about a favorite author. Imagine you are introducing this author to an auditorium full of other fans. Use various kinds of sentence structure to add interest to your speech.

When You Write

A paragraph with nothing but simple sentences becomes dull and monotonous to read. On the other hand, a paragraph with only complex or compound-complex sentences can be confusing. A paragraph that includes a combination of different kinds of sentences is by far the most interesting.

Select a paragraph from a recent composition that could use more sentence variety. Revise the paragraph so that it reads with more fluency.

Clause Fragments Lesson 4

16 D **A subordinate clause becomes a clause fragment when it stands alone.**

Only an independent clause can function by itself as a complete sentence. When a subordinate clause is punctuated as a sentence, it becomes a **clause fragment.** In the following examples, clause fragments are in **bold** type.

Adverbial Clause Fragment	**Since there are no repair shops along the trails.** A mountain bike owner should know how to fix flat tires.
Corrected	Since there are no repair shops along the trails, a mountain bike owner should know how to fix flat tires.
Adjectival Clause Fragment	Summer bikers often ride on ski trails. **That you want to walk on.**
Corrected	Summer bikers often ride on ski trails that you want to walk on.

You can correct a clause fragment by adding or changing words to make a complete thought, or you can attach the fragment to a related sentence next to it.

Sentence and Fragment	Mountain bikers are adventurous athletes. **Who ride down steep hills, twist around trees, and hop over rocks.**
Separate Sentences	Mountain bikers are adventurous athletes. They ride down steep hills, twist around trees, and hop over rocks.
Attached	Mountain bikers are adventurous athletes who ride down steep hills, twist around trees, and hop over rocks.

You can learn more about fragments on pages 663–664 and 698–699.

Practice Your Skills

Recognizing Clause Fragments

Write ***S*** if the word group is a sentence or ***F*** if the word group is a fragment.

1. Even though our tires were flat.
2. Because he couldn't avoid the fallen logs.
3. Which route did they take?
4. The pedaling was slow going up the steep hill.
5. Where she tumbled over the handlebars.
6. When they jumped up unharmed.
7. After a long day of riding, we went home.
8. Since we forgot our helmets for the ride.

Connect to Writing: Revising

Correcting Clause Fragments

Use each fragment in the preceding exercise in a complete sentence. Add capital letters and punctuation where needed.

Connect to Writing: Persuasive Speech

Using Clauses

Imagine that you desperately want a new mountain bike, but your parents are unsure about spending the money. Prepare a brief, but persuasive, speech that will convince them the investment is worthwhile. To add variety to your writing, include clauses at the beginning of at least two sentences.

Check Point: Mixed Practice

Rewrite the following paragraphs, correcting clause fragments. Add capital letters and punctuation where needed.

Robert Frost was born in San Francisco. When Frost was ten years old. His father died. After he and his mother moved to New England. Where his family had lived for nine generations. He briefly attended Dartmouth and Harvard.

Since he was determined to make his writing successful. Frost and his family moved to England. There he published two volumes of poetry that were extremely popular. During the following years, he received four Pulitzer Prizes for his poetry. Frost became the Poet Laureate of the United States.

Run-on Sentences Lesson 5

A run-on sentence bombards readers with too much information in one sentence. Lack of proper punctuation is one of the leading causes of run-on sentences.

16 E **A run-on sentence is two or more sentences written as one sentence and separated by a comma or no mark of punctuation at all.**

A sentence that contains two complete thoughts separated by a comma is also known as a **comma splice.** The following examples show two types of run-on sentences:

Comma Splice	Diamonds discovered in their natural settings would be recognizable only to expert miners, also they do not look like the diamonds found in stores.
With No Punctuation	Diamonds can be found all over the world the United States is not well known for its diamond mining.

You can correct a run-on sentence in one of three ways: Separate the complete thoughts into separate sentences, combine the thoughts into a compound sentence, or create a complex sentence by converting one of the thoughts into a subordinate clause.

Run-on Sentence	A polished diamond has a brilliant luster, an unpolished diamond resembles frosted glass.
Separate Sentences	A polished diamond has a brilliant luster. An unpolished diamond resembles frosted glass.
Compound Sentence	A polished diamond has a brilliant luster, but an unpolished diamond resembles frosted glass. (comma and a conjunction)
Compound Sentence	A polished diamond has a brilliant luster; an unpolished diamond resembles frosted glass. (semicolon)
Complex Sentence	Although a polished diamond has a brilliant luster, an unpolished diamond resembles frosted glass.

Practice Your Skills

Recognizing Run-on Sentences

Label each of the following examples as RO for run-on or S for sentence.

1. Today there are some metals more costly than gold, I never knew that.

2. Rubies can be more valuable than diamonds of the same size and quality, my mother loves rubies and hopes to find ruby earrings to match her antique necklace.

3. Jeannie's grandmother wanted Jeannie to have the diamond earrings that she had received as a wedding gift from her husband, Jeannie's grandfather.

4. There are about 100 minerals valued as gems, many of the 100, however, are found in two or more colors.

5. Diamonds have been cherished since ancient times in addition to that they may be colorless, white, yellow, green, or even blue.

6. The Hope diamond is 25.60 millimeters long, 21.78 millimeters wide, and 12.00 millimeters deep.

7. In 1974, the Hope diamond was removed from its setting and was found to weigh 45.52 carats.

8. Tracy saw the Hope diamond on display at the Smithsonian Museum, which is in Washington, D.C.

9. The Hope diamond has left the Smithsonian only four times since it was donated, it has been exhibited in Paris, France; traveled to Johannesburg, South Africa; and twice has been to New York City, once on display and once for cleaning.

10. Veronica will never own a diamond as big as the Hope diamond, and she says that is just fine with her.

Connect to Writing: Editing

Correcting Run-on Sentences

Correct the run-on sentences in the preceding exercise. Write them as separate sentences or as compound or complex sentences. Add capital letters and punctuation where needed.

Check Point: Mixed Practice

Write the following sentences, correcting each clause fragment or run-on sentence. Add capital letters and punctuation where needed.

1. Article Three of the Constitution establishes the Supreme Court, it is the highest court in the land.
2. Although James Fenimore Cooper had intended to become a farmer. He turned to writing instead.
3. Andrew Jackson was the only president to pay off the final installment of the national debt he did this in 1835.
4. After Belva Lockwood argued a case before the Supreme Court. She was nominated in 1884 for president.
5. President Pierce graduated from Bowdoin College, schoolmates of his were Longfellow and Hawthorne.

Connect to Writing: Editing a Passage

Run-on Sentences

Read the following excerpt. Rewrite the passage using correct sentences. Then compare your version with the original, and think about the reasons why the author might have chosen to use run-on sentences as he did.

> Great uncle on my mother's side—mother's side, I said—got killed on a horse and it never singed a hair on that horse and it killed him graveyard dead they had to cut his belt off him where it welded the buckle shut and I got a cousin aint but four years oldern me was struck down in his own yard comin from the barn and it paralyzed him all down one side and melted his fillins in his teeth and soldered his jaw shut.
>
> —Cormac McCarthy, ***All the Pretty Horses***

Diagraming Sentences

Each clause in a sentence—whether it is independent or subordinate—is diagramed on a separate baseline.

Compound Sentences Each independent clause in a sentence is diagramed like a simple sentence. The clauses are joined at the verbs with a broken line on which the conjunction is placed.

That restaurant looks expensive, but prices are rather reasonable.

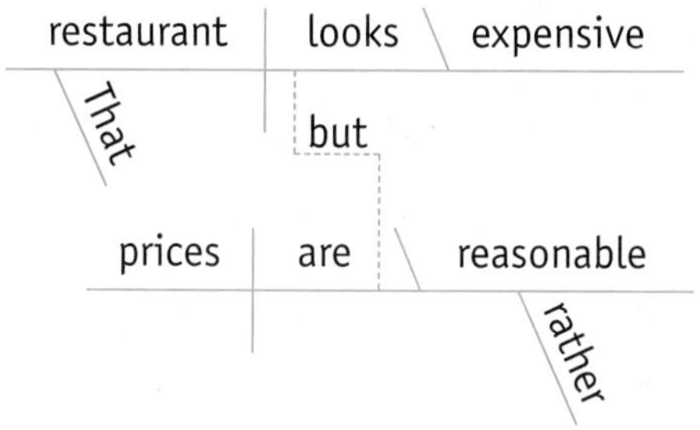

CHAPTER 16

Complex Sentences An adverbial or adjectival clause that appears in a complex sentence is diagramed beneath the independent clause it modifies. The subordinating conjunction in an adverbial clause goes on a broken line that connects the modified verb, adverb, or adjective in the independent clause to the verb in the adverbial clause.

After you type a report, you should proofread it.

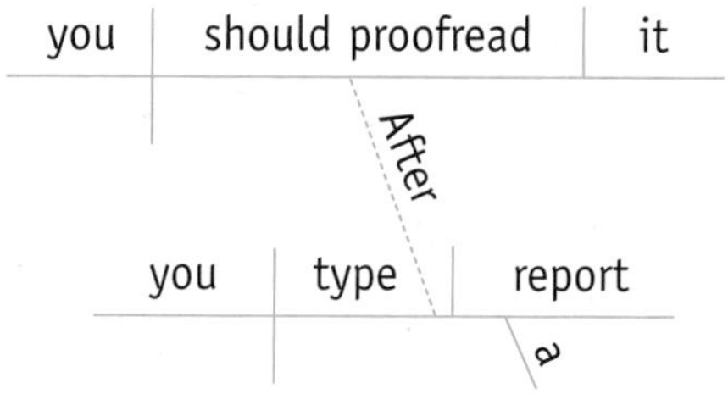

The **relative pronoun** in an adjectival clause is connected by a broken line to the noun or the pronoun the clause modifies.

Amy, whom I met in Texas, is visiting me.

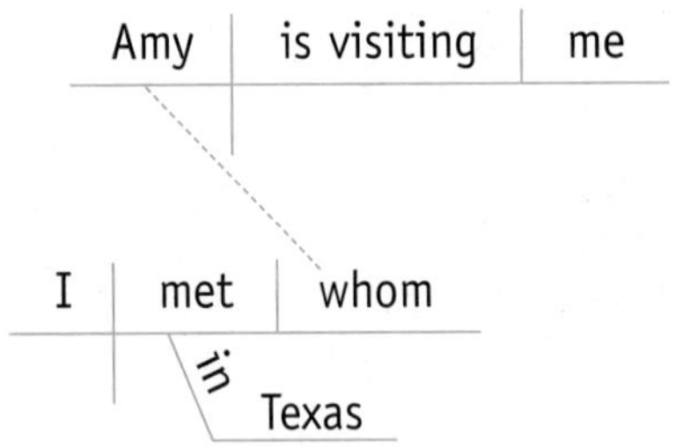

A **noun clause** is diagramed on a pedestal. Put the pedestal where a single noun with the same function would appear. In the following diagram, the noun clause is used as the subject.

What I do should not affect you.

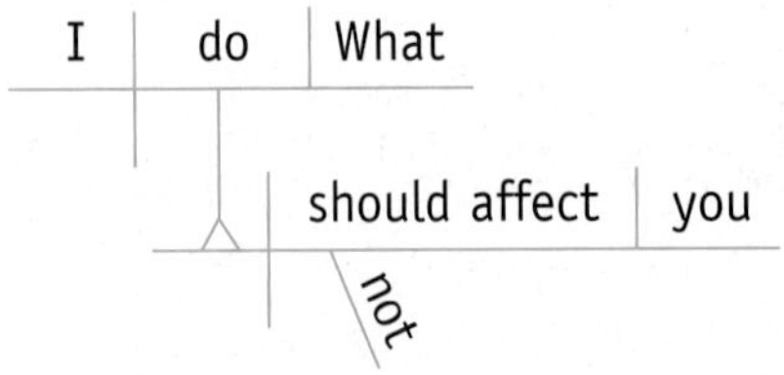

Compound-Complex Sentences To diagram this kind of sentence, apply what you just learned about diagraming compound and complex sentences.

Practice Your Skills

Diagraming Sentences

Diagram the following sentences or copy them. If you copy them, draw one line under each subject and two lines under each verb. Then put parentheses around each subordinate clause and label each one *adverbial, adjectival,* or *noun.*

1. Hurricanes are powerful tropical storms that usually occur in late summer.
2. Hurricanes can bring tons of rain, but powerful winds usually cause the most damage.
3. The eye of the hurricane, which forms at its center, is calm.
4. Hurricanes weaken when they hit land.
5. What you do during a hurricane is important.

Assess Your Learning

Identifying Clauses

Write each subordinate clause. Then label each one *adverbial, adjectival,* or *noun.*

1. Did you know that fish are used to make glue?
2. When Gertrude Ederle swam the English Channel, she was only nineteen years old.
3. Invertebrate animals that have six legs and segmented bodies are called insects.
4. He who hesitates is lost.
5. Some scientists believe that sunspots are storms in the lower atmosphere of the sun.
6. Stars are seen best when there is no moon.
7. "That the future may learn from the past" is the motto of Colonial Williamsburg.
8. As a dolphin swims, it emits a steady clicking sound.
9. More than half of all Americans live in the same state where they were born.
10. Food that you swallow reaches your stomach in only four to eight seconds.
11. Have you ever thought about how the Internet works?
12. A big question is whether or not life exists in other galaxies.

Classifying Sentences

Label each sentence *simple, compound, complex,* or *compound-complex.*

1. Dracula, who is one of the earliest film monsters, is a vampire.
2. When he bites his victims, they too become vampires.
3. Eventually Dracula is destroyed by sunlight and a wooden stake through his heart.
4. Do you remember what Frankenstein looks like?
5. He is made from parts of dead bodies, and a bolt of electricity brings him to life.

6. At the end of the classic film, he gets trapped in a windmill and is burned to death.
7. Godzilla is sometimes called "The King of the Monsters" because he is 200 feet tall and weighs several tons.
8. King Kong is a man-eating ape, but he has a tender side because he falls in love with Ann Darrow.
9. Mighty Joe Young is another monster ape, but he is a good monster.
10. He is one of the few monsters who does not get killed at the end of the movie.

Using Sentence Structure

Write five sentences that follow the directions below. (The sentences may come in any order.) Write about one of the following topics or a topic of your choice: your favorite monster, a new end to an old monster movie, a monster you have created.

1. Write a simple sentence.
2. Write a complex sentence with an introductory adverbial clause.
3. Write a complex sentence with an adjectival clause.
4. Write a compound sentence.
5. Write a complex sentence with a noun clause.

Label each sentence and check its punctuation.

Clauses: Posttest

Directions

Write the letter of the term that correctly identifies each sentence or underlined part of a sentence.

(1) In classical economic theory, the factors of production include land, labor, and capital. **(2)** Capital consists of property or wealth that produces income. **(3)** Money capital includes bank deposits, but property capital includes stocks or bonds. **(4)** Some economists think that education should be included within capital; it is, after all, a source of income. **(5)** Capital generally refers to assets. **(6)** A corporation is a legal entity because it may be treated more or less as a person. **(7)** A corporation may own property since it may also incur debts. **(8)** Corporations are often run by a board of directors that sets policy and determines the direction of the company. **(9)** A corporation is defined by how it distributes its stock. **(10)** When the government establishes a corporation, it is called a public corporation.

1. A simple sentence
B compound sentence
C complex sentence
D compound-complex sentence

2. A simple sentence
B compound sentence
C complex sentence
D compound-complex sentence

3. A simple sentence
B compound sentence
C complex sentence
D compound-complex sentence

4. A simple sentence
B compound sentence
C complex sentence
D compound-complex sentence

5. A simple sentence
B compound sentence
C complex sentence
D compound-complex sentence

6. A independent clause
B adverbial clause
C adjectival clause
D noun clause

7. A independent clause
B adverbial clause
C adjectival clause
D noun clause

8. A independent clause
B adverbial clause
C adjectival clause
D noun clause

9. A independent clause
B adverbial clause
C adjectival clause
D noun clause

10. A independent clause
B adverbial clause
C adjectival clause
D noun clause

Writer's Corner

Snapshot

16 A A **clause** is a group of words that has a subject and predicate. An **independent clause** expresses a complete thought. A **subordinate clause** does not express a complete thought and cannot stand alone as a sentence. (pages 710–711)

16 B A **subordinate clause** can function as an adverb, an adjective, or a noun. (pages 712–722)

16 C A sentence can be **simple, compound, complex,** or **compound-complex,** depending on the number and the kind of clauses in it. (pages 723–725)

16 D A **clause fragment** is a subordinate clause that is punctuated like a sentence. (pages 726–727)

16 E A **run-on sentence** is two or more sentences that are written as one sentence. (pages 728–730)

Power Rules

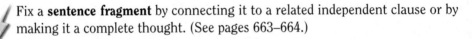

Fix a **sentence fragment** by connecting it to a related independent clause or by making it a complete thought. (See pages 663–664.)

Before Editing	After Editing
President Theodore Roosevelt is one of the faces of Mount Rushmore. *Which is in South Dakota.*	President Theodore Roosevelt is one of the faces of Mount Rushmore, *which is in South Dakota.*

Revise a **run-on sentence** by adding the correct punctuation or by writing it as separate sentences. (See pages 728–730.)

Before Editing	After Editing
The carnival has lots of rides, Marsha likes the Ferris wheel best.	The carnival has lots of rides. Marsha likes the Ferris wheel best.

Editing Checklist

Use this checklist when editing your writing.

- ✓ Did I use subordinating conjunctions to show relationships between ideas? (page 713)
- ✓ Did I use adverbial and adjectival clauses to add variety and detail to my sentences? (pages 712–720)
- ✓ Did I use noun clauses to make my sentences clear and specific? (page 721)
- ✓ Did I place adjectival clauses correctly to avoid misplaced modifiers? (page 720)
- ✓ Did I use commas correctly with adjectival and adverbial clauses? (pages 713 and 718)
- ✓ Did I use a combination of simple, compound, complex, and compound-complex sentences to add variety and interest to my writing? (pages 723–725)
- ✓ Did I correct any clause fragments and run-on sentences? (pages 726–730)

CHAPTER 16

Use the Power

Using a variety of sentence types will guarantee that your writing does not get monotonous. The following passage shows the power of using different sentence types and varying their length.

> This is Tiffany, walking back home. Start with the boots. They are big and heavy boots, much repaired by her father, and they belonged to various sisters before her; she wears several pairs of socks to keep them on. They are *big*. Tiffany sometimes feels she is nothing more than a way of moving boots around.
>
> —Terry Pratchett, *The Wee Free Men*

When you revise your writing, be sure to check the variety of your sentence types. Use a mix of simple, compound, complex, and compound-complex sentences to achieve fluency and enhance your meaning.

Unit 5

Usage

In the last unit you examined the structural backbone of the English language. Now you will add "flesh" to its bones and help the language "walk." You will learn to use verbs that agree with their subjects, pronouns that accurately represent the nouns they are replacing, and adjectives and adverbs that precisely convey your meaning. You will learn to write in an active rather than a passive voice, and to use problem words—such as *whom, lie,* and *which*—with confidence. Because it will give you the power to communicate effectively in classrooms, in workplaces, and with nearly all English-speakers around the globe, mastering this conventional English usage is sure to join, or "tether," you to the world.

Language tethers us to the world; without it we spin like atoms. —*Penelope Lively*

Using Verbs

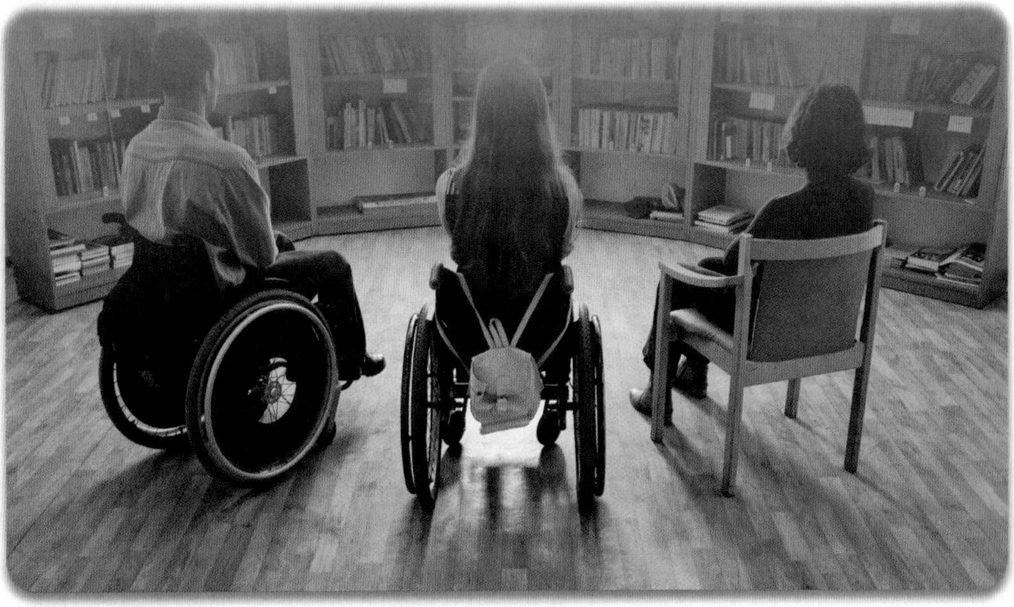

How can using verbs in just the right way spark your descriptions and make your writing shine?

Using Verbs: Pretest 1

The following draft paragraph about attending an art exhibit is hard to read because it contains several errors in the use of verbs. Revise the paragraph so that it reads correctly. One of the errors has been corrected as an example.

A growing trend in television programming ~~are~~ is reality television. Unlike traditional TV shows, reality programs will be about everyday people. Some reality shows has put people in extreme situations. Other programs will have showcased peoples' talents or alternative lifestyles. There has been a time when news broadcasts and game shows was the only reality programming on television. Today, viewers will be watching just about anything, including courtroom proceedings. From cooking shows to scavenger hunts reality television has been bringing people together around the world. Why do you think reality television programs is so popular? I wonder what people is watching in the future?

Using Verbs: Pretest 2

Directions

Read the passage and choose the word or group of words that belongs in each underlined space. Write the letter of the correct answer.

The Jamestown settlement __(1)__ many hardships during its early days. In 1609, its leader, Captain John Smith, __(2)__ and had to return to England. The following winter __(3)__ to be the severest test for the struggling colony. With insufficient provisions and few remaining crops, so many people __(4)__ from lack of food that historians later __(5)__ this period *the starving time.*

Fortunately supplies from visiting ships managed __(6)__ the colony. The leaders then immediately __(7)__ long-term plans for survival. In 1612, a colonist named John Rolfe __(8)__ the colony's first tobacco crop. Having developed a successful method of curing, or preserving, the crop, Rolfe __(9)__ it to England. If it __(10)__ not for this valuable export, Jamestown might never have become a permanent settlement.

1. A endure
B has endured
C endured
D will have endured

2. A is injured
B had injured
C will be injured
D was injured

3. A proving
B proved
C had been proved
D was proving

4. A have died
B will die
C did die
D died

5. A call
B will call
C called
D had called

6. A to have saved
B to be saved
C to save
D to be saving

7. A making
B made
C having made
D will be making

8. A rose
B had risen
C raised
D have raised

9. A exported
B had exported
C will export
D exports

10. A were
B was
C is
D has been

The Principal Parts of Verbs Lesson 1

Mistakes in the use of verbs account for approximately half of all errors in speech and writing. This chapter will review the many forms of a verb and the uses of those forms. Each verb in the English language has four basic forms called the verb's **principal parts.** You need to know the principal parts of a verb because all the tenses of a verb are formed from them.

17 A The **principal parts** of a verb are the **present, the present participle, the past,** and **the past participle.**

Notice in the following examples that helping verbs are needed with the present participle and the past participle when either is used as the main verb of a sentence.

Present	I **cook** dinner once a week.
Present Participle	I ***am*** **cooking** dinner tonight.
Past	I **cooked** dinner last week.
Past Participle	I ***have*** **cooked** dinner many times.

Regular Verbs

The majority of verbs form their past and past participle in the same way.

17 A.1 A **regular verb** forms its past and past participle by adding *-ed* or *-d* to the present.

Notice that the present participle is formed by adding *-ing* to the present form and the past participle is formed by adding *-ed* or *-d* to the present form. Following are the four principal parts of regular verbs.

Present	Present Participle	Past	Past Participle
wash	(is) washing	washed	(have) washed
hope	(is) hoping	hoped	(have) hoped
drop	(is) dropping	dropped	(have) dropped

When endings such as *-ing* and *-ed* are added to some verbs like *hope* and *drop,* the spelling changes. If you are unsure of the spelling of a verb form, look it up in a dictionary.

When You Write and Speak

Be careful not to drop the *-ed* or *-d* endings from the past or the past participle of a verb when you write or speak. This commonly happens with such verbs as *asked, helped, looked, seemed, supposed, talked, used,* and *walked.*

Incorrect	I **use** to cook lasagna every Sunday night.
Correct	I **used** to cook lasagna every Sunday night.

Practice Your Skills

Determining the Principal Parts of Regular Verbs

Make four columns on your paper. Label them *Present, Present Participle, Past,* and *Past Participle.* Then write the four principal parts of the following verbs.

1. ask
2. trim
3. use
4. play
5. stop
6. end
7. mend
8. boil
9. wait
10. suppose

Irregular Verbs

17 A.2 An **irregular verb** does not form its past and past participle by adding *-ed* or *-d* to the present.

The irregular verbs in the charts on the following pages have been divided into groups by the way they form their past and past participle. Helping verbs have been added to remind you that all present and past participles must have one of these helping verbs when they are used as a verb in a sentence.

CHAPTER 17

Group 1 These verbs have the same form for the present, past, and past participle.

IRREGULAR VERBS GROUP 1			
Present	**Present Participle**	**Past**	**Past Participle**
burst	(is) bursting	burst	(have) burst
cost	(is) costing	cost	(have) cost
hit	(is) hitting	hit	(have) hit
hurt	(is) hurting	hurt	(have) hurt
let	(is) letting	let	(have) let
put	(is) putting	put	(have) put

Group 2 These verbs have the same form for the past and past participle.

CHAPTER 17

IRREGULAR VERBS GROUP 2			
Present	**Present Participle**	**Past**	**Past Participle**
bring	(is) bringing	brought	(have) brought
buy	(is) buying	bought	(have) bought
catch	(is) catching	caught	(have) caught
feel	(is) feeling	felt	(have) felt
find	(is) finding	found	(have) found
get	(is) getting	got	(have) got or gotten
hold	(is) holding	held	(have) held
keep	(is) keeping	kept	(have) kept
lead	(is) leading	led	(have) led
leave	(is) leaving	left	(have) left
lose	(is) losing	lost	(have) lost
make	(is) making	made	(have) made
say	(is) saying	said	(have) said
sell	(is) selling	sold	(have) sold
send	(is) sending	sent	(have) sent
teach	(is) teaching	taught	(have) taught
tell	(is) telling	told	(have) told
win	(is) winning	won	(have) won

Practice Your Skills

Using Correct Verb Forms

Write the past or the past participle of each verb in parentheses.

1. My family (find) chairs on the porch and watched the rain.
2. Last week we all (buy) new raincoats.
3. Where have you (put) your raincoat, Stephanie?
4. Mom should have (make) raincoats mandatory attire for today.
5. Has Jennifer (leave) without her coat again?
6. She (catch) a cold last time it rained.
7. Bryce (get) wet even with his umbrella.
8. He has never (hold) the umbrella up straight.
9. Our instructor (teach) us about thunderstorms.
10. I have (keep) studying about rain.
11. I (feel) very knowledgeable about rain clouds after that class.
12. Tim (buy) an extra book about thunderstorms.
13. My grandmother often (say) rain brings laughter to life.
14. Kelly (win) a ribbon for her science project about lightning.
15. Jeff (tell) me about scientists who chase storms.

CHAPTER 17

Connect to Writing: Editing

Correcting Verb Forms

Rewrite each sentence, correcting the verb form. If the verb form is correct, write **C**.

1. Our teacher has teached us about Walt Whitman.
2. She brang in many books about this poet.
3. Like Benjamin Franklin and Mark Twain, Whitman holded an apprentice job in the printing business.
4. Whitman find a literary and intellectual culture in the printing office.
5. For a few years, Whitman making a living as a newspaper editor and journalist.

Group 3 These irregular verbs form the past participle by adding *-n* to the past.

IRREGULAR VERBS GROUP 3			
Present	**Present Participle**	**Past**	**Past Participle**
break	(is) breaking	broke	(have) broken
choose	(is) choosing	chose	(have) chosen
freeze	(is) freezing	froze	(have) frozen
speak	(is) speaking	spoke	(have) spoken
steal	(is) stealing	stole	(have) stolen

Group 4 These irregular verbs form the past participle by adding *-n* to the present.

CHAPTER 17

IRREGULAR VERBS GROUP 4			
Present	**Present Participle**	**Past**	**Past Participle**
blow	(is) blowing	blew	(have) blown
draw	(is) drawing	drew	(have) drawn
drive	(is) driving	drove	(have) driven
give	(is) giving	gave	(have) given
grow	(is) growing	grew	(have) grown
know	(is) knowing	knew	(have) known
see	(is) seeing	saw	(have) seen
take	(is) taking	took	(have) taken
throw	(is) throwing	threw	(have) thrown

Practice Your Skills

Using Correct Verb Forms

Write the past or the past participle of each verb in parentheses.

1. Have any of your friends (choose) a college yet?
2. Ben (steal) some time to research colleges.
3. Have you ever (drive) around a college campus?
4. I think I (see) students walking on the university lawn.
5. I wonder who (draw) the murals on the campus buildings.
6. The statue of the school mascot has (break) again.
7. Have you (take) the required entrance exams?

8. She (throw) out some sample exam questions.
9. I (freeze) when she asked me about my grades.
10. I (give) her a copy of my grade reports.
11. The guidance counselor's smile has (blow) away any doubts.
12. Enrollment in state colleges has (grow) this past year.
13. Jake (know) last year what colleges he would visit.
14. It (take) me longer to decide which ones I liked.
15. My parents have (give) me advice on completing applications.

Connect to Writing: Editing

Correcting Verb Forms

Rewrite each sentence, correcting the verb form. If the verb form is correct, write **C**.

1. The "Underground Railroad" growed from a loose network of antislavery Americans.
2. These heroes threw a lifeline to fugitive slaves.
3. The Underground Railroad was also know as the Liberty Line.
4. Reaching the North gived the slaves freedom but not always safety.
5. Professional slave catchers and Southern officials often took fugitives back to the owners for rewards.

Group 5 These irregular verbs form the past and the past participle by changing a vowel.

IRREGULAR VERBS GROUP 5

Present	Present Participle	Past	Past Participle
begin	(is) beginning	began	(have) begun
drink	(is) drinking	drank	(have) drunk
ring	(is) ringing	rang	(have) rung
shrink	(is) shrinking	shrank	(have) shrunk
sing	(is) singing	sang	(have) sung
sink	(is) sinking	sank	(have) sunk
swim	(is) swimming	swam	(have) swum

Group 6 These irregular verbs form the past and the past participle in other ways.

IRREGULAR VERBS GROUP 6

Present	Present Participle	Past	Past Participle
come	(is) coming	came	(have) come
do	(is) doing	did	(have) done
eat	(is) eating	ate	(have) eaten
fall	(is) falling	fell	(have) fallen
go	(is) going	went	(have) gone
ride	(is) riding	rode	(have) ridden
run	(is) running	ran	(have) run
tear	(is) tearing	tore	(have) torn
wear	(is) wearing	wore	(have) worn
write	(is) writing	wrote	(have) written

Practice Your Skills

Using Correct Verb Forms

Write the past or the past participle of each underlined verb. Then label each one *past* or *past participle.*

1. The rodeo rider had fall across the horse.
2. Have you ever ride one of the ponies at a rodeo?
3. The hog-tying contest begin ten minutes ago.
4. My cousin James do well in the bull-riding competition.
5. The horses were so thirsty they drink a gallon of water from the bucket.
6. Frank's spirits sink when he saw his low score on the scoreboard.
7. Skye's horse tear a muscle in its leg.
8. Your horse run into the barn after the contest.
9. The newspaper reporter write an article about the famous calf-roping contest.
10. The rodeo clown sing silly songs to distract the bulls.

Practice Your Skills

Supplying Correct Verb Forms

Complete each pair of sentences by supplying the correct forms of the verb in parentheses.

1. (come) We ___ to the prom in my Dad's car. You should have ___ with us.
2. (wear) Have you ever ___ a strapless dress? I ___ one to the prom last year.
3. (swim) The table decorations were small bowls of goldfish, which had ___ in circles all night. They ___ in circles while we danced in circles.
4. (begin) Have they ___ taking photographs yet? They ___ 20 minutes ago.
5. (do) Dave ___ his famous dance move on the dance floor. He has ___ that for two years straight.

Connect to Writing: Editing

Correcting Verb Forms

Rewrite the following sentences, using the correct form of the verbs. If the verb form is correct, write **C**.

1. Have you torn the car ads out of the newspaper?
2. Should we have went to the car dealership by now?
3. I have never rode in this kind of car.
4. Has the test vehicle ran out of gas?
5. Felicia wore her sunglasses for the drive.
6. We have sang along with the radio for ten minutes.
7. Her spirits sunk at the thought of the car's price tag.
8. The costs have shrunk with the added discount.
9. Darren has hurt his finger in the door.
10. Kevin had not losed his chance to test-drive the truck.

Connect to Writing: Business Letter

Using Verb Forms

Imagine you have recently purchased a new car. Consider what aspects of the vehicle you particularly enjoy and which features disappoint you. Write a letter to the manufacturer explaining your feelings about the car. When you have completed your letter, edit it for errors in verb forms.

Six Problem Verbs Lesson 2

17 B The verb pairs *lie* and *lay, rise* and *raise,* and *sit* and *set* are easily confused.

lie and *lay*

17 B.1 *Lie* means "to rest or recline." *Lie* is never followed by a direct object. *Lay* means "to put or set (something) down." *Lay* is usually followed by a direct object.

You can learn about direct objects on page 665.

Present	Present Participle	Past	Past Participle
lie	(is) lying	lay	(have) lain
lay	(is) laying	laid	(have) laid

Lie	Our cats always **lie** in the hammock.
	One **is lying** there now.
	They **lay** there yesterday afternoon.
	They **have lain** there all day.
Lay	**Lay** the cats' toys on the shelf. (You lay what? *Toys* is the direct object.)
	Jeff **is laying** the cats' toys on the shelf.
	His sister **laid** the toys on the shelf this morning.
	Usually I **have laid** the toys on the shelf.

When You Write

Be careful to express yourself clearly when using the verb *to lie,* meaning "to be dishonest." Often only a context clue will indicate meaning.

Incorrect	He is **lying** on the witness stand.
Correct	He is **lying** about his alibi on the witness stand.

rise and *raise*

17 B.2 *Rise* means "to move upward" or "to get up." *Rise* is never followed by a direct object. *Raise* means "to lift up," "to increase," or "to grow." *Raise* is usually followed by a direct object.

Present	Present Participle	Past	Past Participle
rise	(is) rising	rose	(have) risen
raise	(is) raising	raised	(have) raised

Rise

Rise up and start your morning chores.

The kids **are rising** just after dawn.

My father **rose** at 5:00 AM yesterday morning.

My parents **have risen** before sunrise for a week.

Raise

Raise the windows carefully.

(You raise what? *Windows* is the direct object.)

He **is raising** the front windows.

He **raised** the upstairs windows, also.

He **has raised** the windows each day.

CHAPTER 17

sit and *set*

17 B.3 *Sit* means "to rest in an upright position." *Sit* is never followed by a direct object. *Set* means "to put or place (something)." *Set* is usually followed by a direct object.

Present	Present Participle	Past	Past Participle
sit	(is) sitting	sat	(have) sat
set	(is) setting	set	(have) set

Sit

Sit and read a book.

She **is sitting** in a comfortable chair.

She **sat** there all day.

She **has** often **sat** there with her books.

Set	**Set** the book on the table. (You set what? *Book* is the direct object.) He **is setting** the book on the table. He **set** the book on the table last night. He **has set** the book by his bed.

Practice Your Skills

Recognizing Problem Verbs

Write the verb in each sentence, and then write **C** if the form is correct or ***I*** if the form is incorrect.

1. Our family sat down for dinner together.
2. We have sit down for family meals for many years now.
3. My father lays the dishes on the table.
4. I am sitting the table with silverware.
5. Mom sits near the oven timer.
6. She has risen the lids off the steaming pots.
7. Our dog Zoe is laying on the floor near the table.
8. She always lays there during our dinner.
9. Zoe raised to her feet to see the food.
10. She sat down by the baby's high chair.

Connect to Writing: Editing

Correcting Problem Verbs

Rewrite the preceding incorrect sentences, using the correct verb forms.

Connect to Writing: Description

Using Problem Verbs

Write a short description of a familiar spot, such as your room. Use at least two of the six problem verbs reviewed in this chapter.

Verb Tense Lesson 3

17 C The time expressed by a verb is called the tense of a verb.

When you know the four principal parts of a verb, you can easily form the six tenses: the **present, past, future, present perfect, past perfect,** and **future perfect.**

In the following examples, the six tenses of *fly* are used to express action at different times.

Present	She often **flies** on business.
Past	She **flew** to Wisconsin yesterday.
Future	She **will fly** to Ohio next week.
Present Perfect	She **has flown** over 100,000 miles.
Past Perfect	She **had** not **flown** much before last year.
Future Perfect	By the end of the year, she **will have flown** over 200,000 miles.

CHAPTER 17

Uses of the Tenses

You will use the six basic tenses—three simple tenses and three perfect tenses—to show whether something is happening now, has happened in the past, or will happen in the future. All of these tenses can be formed from the four principal parts of a verb and the helping verbs *have, has, had, will,* and *shall.*

17 C.1 **Present tense** is used mainly to express an action that is going on now, an action that happens regularly, or an action that is usually constant or the same.

To form the present tense, use the present form (the first principal part of the verb) or add *-s* or *-es* to the present form.

Present Tense	**Listen** to this music. (current action)
	I **enjoy** rock and roll music. (regular action)
	The guitarist **plays** loudly. (constant action)

17 C.2 Use the **historical present tense** when you want to relate a past action as if it were happening in the present. Use the **literary present tense** when you are writing about literature.

Historical Present Tense	Henry David Thoreau **urges** his followers to lead a simple life.
Literary Present Tense	In *Walden,* Thoreau **tells** of his experiences living in an isolated cabin.

17 C.3 **Past tense** is used to express an action that already took place or was completed in the past.

To form the past tense of a regular verb, add *-ed* or *-d* to the present form. Check a dictionary for the past form of an irregular verb or look for it on pages 744 and 746–748.

Past Tense	We **traveled** to the beach last summer.
	Hillary **swam** in the ocean for the first time.

CHAPTER 17

17 C.4 **Future tense** is used to express an action that will take place in the future.

To form the future tense, use the helping verb *shall* or *will* with the present form. In formal English *shall* is used with *I* and *we,* and *will* is used with nouns and *you, he, she, it,* and *they.* In informal speech, *shall* and *will* are used interchangeably with *I* and *we*—except *shall* is still often used with *I* and *we* for questions.

Future Tense	I **shall travel** back to the beach again.
	Hillary **will swim** in the ocean waves too.

Another way to express a future action is to use a present-tense verb with an adverb or a group of words that indicate, or specify, a future time.

Future Tense	She **swims** tomorrow in the competition.

17 C.5 **Present perfect tense** has two uses: to express an action that was completed at some indefinite time in the past and to express an action that started in the past and is still going on.

To form the present perfect tense, add *has* or *have* to the past participle.

Present Perfect Tense	We **have traveled** here twice before. (action completed at a definite time) Hillary **has swum** in pools for years. (action that is still going on)

17 C.6 **Past perfect tense** expresses an action that took place before some other action.

To form the past perfect tense, add *had* to the past participle.

Past Perfect Tense	We **had traveled** to the mountains before we traveled to the beach. Hillary **had swum** in lakes before she saw the ocean. (one action completed before another)

17 C.7 **Future perfect tense** expresses an action that will take place before another future action or time.

To form the future perfect tense, add *shall have* or *will have* to the past participle.

Future Perfect Tense	I **shall have traveled** over 2,000 miles by August. By next month Hillary **will have swum** in two oceans. (action completed before a specific time)

CHAPTER 17

Verb Conjugation

17 C.8 A **conjugation** is a list of all the singular and plural forms of a verb in its various tenses.

Following is a conjugation of the irregular verb *see.* Its forms are *see, seeing, saw, seen.*

CONJUGATION OF *SEE* SIMPLE TENSES	
Present	
Singular	**Plural**
I see	we see
you see	you see
he, she, it sees	they see
Past	
Singular	**Plural**
I saw	we saw
you saw	you saw
he, she, it saw	they saw
Future	
Singular	**Plural**
I shall/will see	we shall/will see
you will see	you will see
he, she, it will see	they will see
PERFECT TENSES	
Present Perfect	
Singular	**Plural**
I have seen	we have seen
you have seen	you have seen
he, she, it has seen	they have seen
Past Perfect	
Singular	**Plural**
I had seen	we had seen
you had seen	you had seen
he, she, it had seen	they had seen

CHAPTER 17

Future Perfect	
Singular	**Plural**
I shall/will have seen	we shall/will have seen
you will have seen	you will have seen
he, she, it will have seen	they will have seen

The present participle is used only to conjugate the progressive forms of a verb. You can learn about these forms on pages 764–765.

The verb *be* is highly irregular; consequently, its conjugation is very different from other irregular verbs. Its forms include *am, is,* and *are* in the present; the present particple *being; was* and *were* in the past; and the past particple *been.*

CONJUGATION OF *BE* SIMPLE TENSES	
Present	
Singular	**Plural**
I am	we are
you are	you are
he, she, it is	they are
Past	
Singular	**Plural**
I was	we were
you were	you were
he, she, it was	they were
Future	
Singular	**Plural**
I shall/will be	we shall/will be
you will be	you will be
he, she, it will be	they will be

Conjugation of *Be* continued

PERFECT TENSES	
Present Perfect	
Singular	**Plural**
I have been	we have been
you have been	you have been
he, she, it has been	they have been
Past Perfect	
Singular	**Plural**
I had been	we had been
you had been	you had been
he, she, it had been	they had been
Future Perfect	
Singular	**Plural**
I shall/will have been	we shall/will have been
you will have been	you will have been
he, she, it will have been	they will have been

CHAPTER 17

Practice Your Skills

Identifying Verb Tenses

Write the tense of each underlined verb.

1. *My Antonia* by Willa Cather is on the reading list.
2. Cather wrote many of her books about life in Nebraska and the American Southwest.
3. She has been called one of America's foremost novelists.
4. Her books show the tough, dignified life of immigrant farm families.
5. Our class will study Cather's *O Pioneers!* next month.
6. Cather had worked as a newspaperwoman and teacher in Pittsburgh, Pennsylvania.
7. *Death Comes for the Archbishop* has been one of her most highly acclaimed books.
8. Cather had written poetry before writing novels.
9. She was proud of her pioneer ancestors.
10. Willa Cather became a Pulitzer Prize winner in 1923.

Practice Your Skills

Choosing Correct Verb Tenses

Write the correct form of the verb in parentheses. Be prepared to name the tense you chose and to tell why that tense is correct.

1. Tammy told us that she (is working, had worked) on her research paper the night before.
2. Last month in history class, we (receive, received) the research paper assignment.
3. For the past three months, I have (make, made) A's on all my research papers.
4. After researching our topics yesterday, we (become, became) more knowledgeable.
5. Last Thursday I (begin, began) to research my project.

CHAPTER 17

Connect to Writing: Editing

Friendly Letter: Verb Tenses

Imagine that you are training to swim the English Channel. Write a letter to your parents telling them about your typical day. Describe what you do each morning—when you get up, what you eat, how you train, and with whom you work. Then describe your afternoon and evening activities. Finally, discuss what accomplishing this athletic feat will mean to you. Use your imagination to make this letter sound realistic and enthusiastic. After you have written the letter, underline all the verbs you have used. Above each verb, label its tense.

Connect to Writing: Historical Narrative

Using Verb Tenses

You are a tour guide in historic Lexington, Massachusetts, and must prepare for tomorrow's group of junior-high history students. Based on what you know, write a brief narrative of the first battle of the American Revolution, which took place in Lexington. Be sure to use correct verb tenses in your account.

CHAPTER 17

Check Point: Mixed Practice

Write the correct form of the verb in parentheses. Be prepared to identify the tense you chose and to tell why that tense is correct.

1. Sue suddenly realized she (promised, had promised) to meet Phil at the shoe store.
2. She arrived just as he (is, was) about to leave.
3. She (was, had been) glad he was still there.
4. After laughing about the close call, they (walks, walked) into the store together.
5. Every shelf (displayed, has displayed) athletic shoes.
6. Just then a saleswoman came along, and Sue (ask, asked) her for advice.
7. What shoes shall I (buy, have bought) for a marathon?
8. For the past two months, Phil (suggested, had suggested) that they train together.
9. Ever since they ran a 5K race, they (were, have been) dedicated runners.
10. They (started, have started) their marathon training right after the shopping trip.

Common Problems Using Tenses — Lesson 4

All actions do not take place at the same time. More often than not, you will want to say or write that one event happened before another event happened or that one event will follow another. The following examples will help you choose the tenses and verb forms that will best express your meaning.

17 D **The tense of the verbs you use depends on the meaning you want to express.**

Past Tenses

If you want to express two past events that happened at the same time, use the past tense for both. If you want to tell about an action that happened before another past action, use the past perfect to express the action that happened first.

Past/Past	I **bought** (past) tickets when I **was** (past) in Ohio. (Both events happened at the same time.)
Past/Past Perfect	Li **said** (past) he **had bought** (past perfect) tickets by mail. (The buying of the tickets took place before Li said anything.)

CHAPTER 17

When You Speak

When speaking, do not use the words *would have* in a clause starting with *if* when that clause expresses the earlier of two past actions. Instead, use the past perfect tense to express the earlier action.

Incorrect	**If** Tim **would have finished** his paper on time, he could have gone to the concert.
Correct	**If** Tim **had finished** his paper on time, he could have gone to the concert.

Present and Past Tenses

Occasionally you will also need to use a combination of present and past tense verbs.

Present/Past	I **believe** (present) that she **attended** (past) the concert last night. (*Believe* is in the present because it describes action that is happening now, but *attended* is in the past because it happened at a definite time in the past.)
Past/Present Perfect	Ever since she **heard** (past) that song, she **has sung** (present perfect) it continually. (*Heard* is in the past tense because it occurred at a definite time in the past, but *has sung* is in the present perfect because it started in the past and is still going on.)

CHAPTER 17

Past Participles

Participles, like verbs, have present and past tenses to express specific time.

Present Participle	seeing
Past Participle	seen

17 D.1 Use *having* with a past participle in a participial phrase to show that one action was completed before another one.

Incorrect	**Finishing** the tour, the band **decided** to go on vacation.
Correct	**Having finished** the tour, the band **decided** to go on vacation. (The use of *having* with the past participle *finished* shows that the band completed the tour before deciding to go on vacation.)

You can learn more about participial phrases on pages 351 and 688–690.

Present and Perfect Infinitives

Like participles, infinitives also have different forms.

INFINITIVES OF *SEE*	
Present Infinitive	to see
Perfect Infinitive	to have seen

17 D.2 To express an action that takes place *after* another action, use the **present infinitive.** To express an action that takes place *before* another action, use the **perfect infinitive.**

Present Infinitive	For months we had hoped **to attend** the concert. (The attending came *after* the hoping.)
Perfect Infinitive	I feel very fortunate **to have found** good seats at the concert. (The finding of good seats came *before* the feeling fortunate.)

You can learn more about infinitives on pages 693–694.

Practice Your Skills

Identifying Shifts in Tense

If the underlined verb in a sentence incorrectly shifts in tense, write ***I.*** If the verb is correct, write **C.**

1. Everyone woke up early when Dad starts the lawn mower.
2. By the time we finished breakfast, he has mowed the entire yard.
3. I think that he enjoyed it.
4. Emily scratched her arm when she plants a rosebush.
5. Dad sharpened the clippers before he trims the hedge.
6. Beth had bought seeds before she plants a flower garden.
7. For months we planned to dig up the old tree stump in the backyard.
8. Last week when my other siblings labored in the yard, my brother avoided work.

Connect to Writing: Editing

Correcting Verb Tenses

Rewrite the sentences you marked ***I*** in the previous exercise, correcting the verb tenses.

Progressive and Emphatic Verb Forms

In addition to the six basic tenses, every verb has six **progressive forms** and an **emphatic form** for the present and past tenses.

Progressive Forms

17 D.3 The **progressive forms** are used to express continuing or ongoing action. To write the progressive forms, add a present, past, future, or perfect tense of the verb *be* to the present participle.

Notice in the following examples that all of the progressive forms end in *-ing*.

Present Progressive	I am seeing.
Past Progressive	I was seeing.
Future Progressive	I will (shall) be seeing.
Present Perfect Progressive	I have been seeing.
Past Perfect Progressive	I had been seeing.
Future Perfect Progressive	I will (shall) have been seeing.

CHAPTER 17

The **present progressive** form shows an ongoing action that is taking place now.

I **am seeing** this movie for the first time.

Occasionally the present progressive can also show action in the future when the sentence contains an adverb or a phrase that indicates the future—such as *tomorrow* or *next month.*

Tomorrow I **am seeing** a movie at the new theater near my house.

The **past progressive** form shows an ongoing action that took place in the past.

I **was seeing** a movie when I remembered my dentist appointment.

The **future progressive** form shows an ongoing action that will take place in the future.

I **will be seeing** a movie for two hours tomorrow.

The **present perfect progressive** form shows an ongoing action that is continuing in the present.

I **have been seeing** movies every Saturday night for several years now.

The **past perfect progressive** form shows an ongoing action in the past that was interrupted by another past action.

I **had been seeing** a movie until the film broke.

The **future perfect progressive** form shows a future ongoing action that will have taken place by a stated future time.

This Saturday I **will have been seeing** movies for ten years.

Emphatic Forms

17 D.4 The **emphatic forms** of the present and past tense of verbs are mainly used to show emphasis or force. To write the present emphatic, add *do* or *does* to the present tense of a verb. To write the past emphatic, add *did* to the present tense.

Present	I **see** a movie every week.
Present Emphatic	I **do see** a movie every week.
Past	I **saw** a movie yesterday.
Past Emphatic	I **did see** a movie yesterday.

The emphatic forms are also used in some negative statements and questions.

Negative Statement	The sisters **did**n't **see** the same movie.
Question	**Do** they ever **see** the same movie?

Practice Your Skills

Recognizing Progressive and Emphatic Forms

Write whether each underlined verb is a progressive or emphatic form. Then name the tense.

1. I <u>am studying</u> about the scientist Robert Boyle.

2. I <u>have been reading</u> about his contributions to the field of chemistry.

3. Boyle <u>did become</u> famous for his dedication to the scientific method.

4. I <u>do believe</u> Boyle was the first chemist to isolate and collect a gas.

5. Boyle <u>had been researching</u> gases when he formulated the law of physics that bears his name.

6. Our class <u>will be learning</u> about Boyle's Law, which states that under conditions of constant temperature, the pressure and volume of a gas are inversely proportional.

7. Boyle never <u>did support</u> some of Aristotle's theories about elements.

8. <u>Did</u> Boyle ever <u>prove</u> him wrong?

9. I <u>have been hearing</u> that Boyle was one of the founding members of the scientific organization known as the Royal Society of London.

10. I <u>will have been reading</u> one of his books, *The Skeptical Chemist,* for three months now.

Check Point: Mixed Practice

Rewrite the following paragraph, changing each incorrect verb form. (You will need to change ten.)

Mark Twain was born Samuel Langhorne Clemens in Florida, Missouri. He growed up in the Mississippi River town of Hannibal, the main setting for his famous novels *The Adventures of Huckleberry Finn* and *The Adventures of Tom Sawyer.* He leaved school to become a printer, but his first job is as a reporter. Later he choose a career as a steamboat pilot, but he is leaving the river when the Civil War started. Then he begin to write. Clemens maked two great contributions to American literature: clever use of local language and humor. Rather than used the stiff, formal language of English writers, he wrote as people speaked. He use that very language to create his celebrated brand of humor.

Active and Passive Voice

Lesson 5

The **voice** of a verb indicates whether the subject is doing the action or the subject is receiving the action. Some verbs can be used in the active voice or in the passive voice.

17 E **The active voice indicates that the subject is performing the action. The passive voice indicates that the action of the verb is being performed upon the subject.**

Notice in the following examples that the verb in the active voice has a direct object, making it a **transitive verb.** The verb in the passive voice, however, does not have a direct object.

Active Voice	The tornado **leveled** two buildings. (d.o.: buildings) (The subject *tornado* is performing the action. *Buildings* is the direct object.)
Passive Voice	Two buildings **were leveled** by the tornado. (The action of the verb is being performed upon the subject *buildings. Were leveled* has no direct object.)

Most verbs in the active voice can also be used in the passive voice.

Active Voice	Keith **made** an announcement about the tornado. (d.o.: announcement)
Passive Voice	The announcement about the tornado **was made** by Keith. (no direct object)

When the active voice is changed to the passive voice, the direct object becomes the subject. In the preceding examples, *announcement* is the direct object when the verb is active; it becomes the subject when the verb is passive.

CHAPTER 17

Verbs in the passive voice consist of some form of the verb *be* plus a past participle—such as *were leveled* and *was made.*

Some transitive verbs can have an indirect object in addition to a direct object. When such a verb and its objects are changed to the passive voice, either of the two objects can become the subject of the sentence. The other object remains an object and is called a **retained object** (r.o.).

Active Voice	The meteorologist gave every radio **station** (i.o.) the **message.** (d.o.)
Passive Voice	Every radio station was given the **message** (r.o.) by the meteorologist.
Passive Voice	The message was given every radio **station** (r.o.) by the meteorologist.

Practice Your Skills

Recognizing Active and Passive Voice

Write the verb in each sentence. Then label each one ***A*** for *active* or ***P*** for *passive.*

1. George Washington's beloved dogs were treated as members of the family.
2. Abraham Lincoln's family called their dog Fido.
3. Teddy Roosevelt's children played with a one-legged rooster.
4. The Roosevelts' pony was given rides in the White House elevator.
5. A hole was chewed in the French Ambassador's pants by their dog Pete.
6. Woodrow Wilson's sheep grazed on the White House lawn.
7. William Howard Taft owned a cow named Pauline.
8. Warren Harding's dogs were trained to do tricks.
9. A cabinet chair was reserved for his dog Laddie Boy.
10. The dogs often performed at cabinet meetings.

Use of Voice in Writing

17 E.1 As a general rule, avoid using the passive voice. Sentences are clearer, more forceful, and less wordy when they are written in **active voice.**

Active Voice	Our school **sponsored** the car wash.
Passive Voice	The car wash **was sponsored** by our school.

17 E.2 Use the **passive voice** when the doer of the action is unknown or unimportant, or to emphasize the receiver of the action or the results.

Passive Voice	Old rags **were brought** to the car wash. (doer unknown or unimportant)
	Jerry **was elected** as car wash treasurer. (emphasis on receiver)
	Tips **were donated** by car owners. (emphasis on results)

Practice Your Skills

Using Active and Passive Voice

Write the verb or verbs in each sentence and label each verb *active* or *passive.*

1. Jazz music was developed by African Americans around 1900.
2. Jazz was influenced by folk music, and popular music was influenced by jazz.
3. Musicians Charlie Parker and Dizzy Gillespie rose to fame during the Jazz Era.
4. The artists improvised many jazz songs.
5. In jazz music the written scores often are used merely as guides.
6. Benny Goodman greatly influenced swing music.
7. Solo improvisations were executed by Count Basie's bands.
8. The bebop style of jazz was developed largely by Parker and Gillespie.
9. Pop and jazz standards were transformed by Gillespie's talents.
10. Inspiration was found by many jazz musicians.

Connect to Writing: Revising

Using Active and Passive Voice

Rewrite the passive-voice sentences in the previous exercise, changing the passive voice to the active voice if appropriate. If a sentence is better in the passive voice, write **C**.

Connect to Speaking and Writing: Vocabulary Review

Using the Vocabulary of Grammar

With a partner, talk about the difference between active voice and passive voice. Then write short definitions of the two terms. Finally, write a sentence in active voice. Exchange it with your partner. Try to change your partner's sentence from active to passive voice.

Mood Lesson 6

17 F The mood of a verb is the way in which a verb expresses an idea.

In English, there are three moods: indicative, imperative, and subjunctive.

17 F.1 The **indicative mood** is used to state a fact or to ask a question.

17 F.2 The **imperative mood** is used to give a command or to make a request.

Since the indicative mood is used to state facts or ask questions, it is the mood used most often in both writing and speaking.

Indicative	Improved nutrition **has contributed** to the increased height of Americans.
	Junk food **has caused** some people to be unhealthy.
Imperative	**Eat** more fruits and vegetables.
	Drink fewer soft drinks and more water.

CHAPTER 17

17 F.3 The **subjunctive mood** is used to express a condition contrary to fact or a possibility that begins with words such as *if, as if,* or *as though.* It is also used to express a wish, command, or request after the word *that.*

Contrary to Fact or Possibility	If spinach **were** like candy, he would eat more of it. (Spinach is not like candy.)
	You are acting as if he **were** ill. (He is not ill, or he may possibly be ill.)
A Wish	I wish she **were** healthy again. (*That* is omitted as understood: *I wish (that) she were healthy again.*)
Command/Request	I demand *that* I **be** fed healthier food. (If not in the subjunctive mood, the subject and verb would be *I am.*)
	We suggest *that* she **hire** a nutrition expert. (If not in the subjunctive mood, the subject and verb would be *she hires.*)

In English, the subjunctive verb forms differ from the indicative forms in only two situations.

The **present subjunctive** uses the base form of the verb for all persons and numbers, including the third-person singular, while indicative verbs use the *-s* form.

Indicative	Mrs. Smith **is** the school's nutritionist.
Subjunctive	We suggested that Mrs. Smith **be** the school's nutritionist.

In the present subjunctive, the verb *to be* is always *be.*

She recommended that all high school students **be** aware of good nutrition.

The **past subjunctive** form of the verb *to be* is *were* for all persons and numbers.

If I **were** you, I would listen to her.

Although the subjunctive mood is not used much today, it still shows up in a number of idiomatic expressions such as the following.

Subjunctive Expressions	**Be** that as it may,
	Far **be** it from me to. . . .

CHAPTER 17

Practice Your Skills

Using Subjunctive Mood

Write the correct form of the verb in parentheses.

1. If I (was, were) you, I would apply for the job.
2. I wish I (was, were) qualified for the position.
3. I would feel as if I (was, were) extremely successful.
4. We suggest that he (is, be) hired for the job.
5. Kathy wishes she (was, were) employed too.
6. If he (was, were) more ambitious, he would succeed in his job.
7. My older brother recommends that Sandy (takes, take) the written test.
8. If he (was, were) more experienced, I would hire him.
9. I wish I (was, were) the boss.
10. The boss suggested that I (am, be) given a raise.

Check Point: Mixed Practice

Write the correct form of the verb in parentheses. Be prepared to identify the tense you chose and to tell why that tense is correct.

1. Jeff suddenly remembered that he (promised, had promised) to take his nephew to the zoo.
2. They reached the zoo just as the gates (open, opened).
3. I wish that he (was, were) not afraid of the monkeys.
4. The polar bear dived into the water and in a few minutes (appears, appeared) on the other side of the ice.
5. Yesterday the koala bears (broke, had broken) several branches of the eucalyptus tree.
6. Just then a tour guide walked by, and we (ask, asked) him for directions to the lion cages.
7. If I (was, were) five years old, I would be afraid of lions.
8. For the past month, Joel (talked, has talked) about seeing the lions.
9. At the elephant cages, one creature filled its trunk with water and (give, gave) itself a cool shower.
10. I wish I (was, were) a zoo employee.

Connect to Writing: Revising

Changing Verbs to Active Voice

Rewrite the following sentences, changing passive-voice verbs to active voice, if appropriate.

> Last week, our small school was in the path of a tornado. Our safety was at risk. We were scared and confused. For a while all seemed lost. Then an idea came to us. We decided to sing. Our spirits were lifted by that song. We sang another and another until all danger was gone.

Connect to Writing: Descriptive Paragraph

Using Subjunctive Mood

Imagine you are at an employment office and must describe to the counselor what kind of job you have always wanted. Write a paragraph describing your dream job. Use subjunctive mood where appropriate.

Chapter Review

Assess Your Learning

Using the Correct Verb Form

Write the past or past participle form of each verb in parentheses.

1. Mr. Miller (bring) several watermelons to the town's picnic.
2. Lake Matoba has (freeze) over after several weeks of winter.
3. The sun (rise) at 5:15 A.M. behind heavy clouds.
4. Hurry! The orchestra has (begin) to play the overture.
5. I should have (send) the documents by overnight express mail.
6. After weeks of our hacking, the enemy's code was finally (break).
7. Last year all of the visitors (wear) name tags at the company's luncheon.
8. If I (be) kinder to Michele, I would feel a lot better about myself.
9. Although warned that the old chair was fragile, Otto (sit) in it anyway.
10. Andy's cat has (lie) on the sunny windowsill all morning.
11. He (send) the package to the wrong address in New York City.
12. I have (do) my best.
13. Has he ever (drive) a car with a standard shift before?
14. Uncle Herb hadn't (see) his nephew Ryan for almost three years.
15. My cousin Kate and I (run) in the Boston Marathon last year.

Choosing the Correct Tense

Write the correct form of the verb in parentheses.

1. For our parents' anniversary, we made dinner, cleaned up, and (took, have taken) them to a Paul Simon concert.
2. When Mr. Butler inspected his orchard, he found that the hurricane (destroyed, had destroyed) several trees.
3. Study for the test as if it (was, were) the final exam of the semester.
4. The firefighters left the station immediately and (arrive, arrived) at the scene of the fire six minutes later.

5. If you keep the gelatin in the refrigerator, it (set, will set) in an hour.
6. LaShawna treated me as if I (was, were) sick.
7. Mrs. Angeletti (is, has been) on the school board for the past three years.
8. After the boat left Provincetown, no one (saw, has seen) it again.
9. Many covered bridges in New England (stood, have stood) for more than 100 years.
10. To (rise, raise) the head of the bed, press this button on the remote control.

Writing Sentences

Write five sentences that follow the directions below. Write about ways in which you can help save the environment.

1. Write a sentence using *having* with a past participle.
2. Write a sentence that includes a perfect infinitive.
3. Write a sentence in the subjunctive mood beginning with *As if.*
4. Write a sentence with one verb in the active voice and another in the passive voice.
5. Write a sentence in the imperative mood.

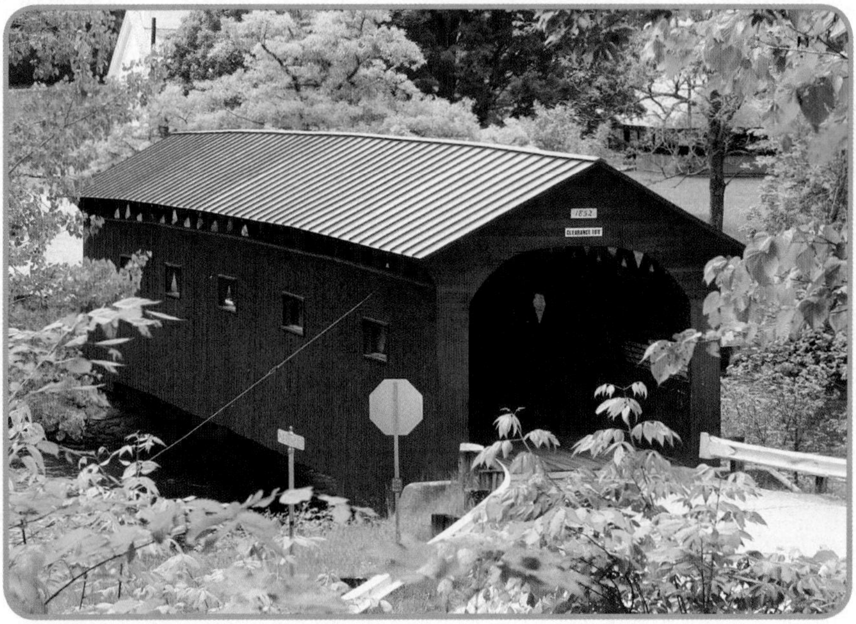

Using Verbs: Posttest

Directions

Read the passage and choose the word or group of words that belongs in each underlined space. Write the letter of the correct answer.

By 3000 B.C., both Middle Eastern and Egyptian sculptors __(1)__ reliefs, or slightly raised figures, in walls and columns. About the same time, Aegean islanders __(2)__ to carve figures from white marble. Early Chinese sculptors __(3)__ famous for figures of bronze, jade, and clay. Many people today __(4)__ the Greeks and Romans the best ancient sculptors of the West. The smooth, flowing lines and expressive faces of their works later __(5)__ European sculptors. Strangely, this classical style __(6)__ to have been lost during the Middle Ages. Between A.D. 500 and 1400, the feudal states of Europe __(7)__, and their sculpture consisted mostly of intricate Anglo-Saxon icons and statues of saints. Donatello, Michelangelo, Cellini, and Bernini __(8)__ among the greatest sculptors of the Renaissance. Together they __(9)__ the Greco-Roman style but added greater expressiveness and deeper emotion to the faces and bodies of their works. Even today, some of these sculptures __(10)__ so realistic that they seem to breathe and move.

1. A carve
B will carve
C were carving
D have carved

2. A begin
B have begun
C began
D are beginning

3. A have been
B will have been
C will be
D were

4. A are considering
B had considered
C consider
D are considered

5. A are inspiring
B were inspiring
C inspire
D inspired

6. A seems
B is seeming
C are seeming
D were seeming

7. A arise
B arose
C are risen
D arisen

8. A were
B will have been
C are being
D will be

9. A will have revived
B do revive
C were reviving
D revived

10. A have been appearing
B appear
C were appearing
D had been appearing

Writer's Corner

Snapshot

17 A The **principal parts of a verb** are the **present,** the **present participle,** the **past,** and the **past participle.** (pages 742–749)

17 B The verb pairs *lie* and *lay, rise* and *raise,* and *sit* and *set* can be easily confused. (pages 750–752)

17 C The time expressed by a verb is called the **tense** of a verb. (pages 753–760)

17 D The **tense** of the verbs you use depends on the meaning you want to express. (pages 761–766)

17 E The **active voice** indicates that the subject is performing the action. The **passive voice** indicates that the action of the verb is being performed upon the subject. (pages 767–769)

17 F The **mood** of a verb—**indicative, imperative,** or **subjunctive**—is the way in which a verb expresses an idea. (pages 770–772)

Power Rules

Use correct past tense forms of regular and irregular verbs. (pages 742–766)

Before Editing	After Editing
Logan *rehearse* his speech several times.	Logan *rehearsed* his speech several times.
She *find* her missing watch under the bed.	She *found* her missing watch under the bed.
He *selled* his old bike.	He *sold* his old bike.

Use a consistent verb tense except when a change is clearly necessary. (pages 753–766)

Before Editing	After Editing
He researched guitars before he *buy* an acoustic one.	He researched guitars before he *bought* an acoustic one.

Editing Checklist ✓

Use this checklist when editing your writing.

✓ Did I use the correct verb forms of both regular and irregular verbs? (See pages 742–749.)
✓ Did I use the six basic verb tenses correctly? (See pages 753–760.)
✓ Did I correct unnecessary shifts in tense? (See pages 761–766.)
✓ Did I use the progressive verb forms correctly? (See pages 764–765.)
✓ Did I use the emphatic past and present verb forms correctly? (See page 765.)
✓ Did I use active voice to make my sentences more powerful? (See pages 767–769.)
✓ Did I use the indicative mood to state a fact or ask a question? (See page 770.)
✓ Did I use the imperative and subjunctive moods correctly? (See pages 770–771.)

CHAPTER 17

Use the Power

Use this chart to help you form verb tenses correctly.

	Past	Present	Future
Simple	past tense form *She drove.*	base form *She drives.*	*will* + base form *She will drive.*
Perfect	*had* + past participle *She had driven.*	*have* or *has* + past participle *She has driven.*	*will have* + past participle *She will have driven.*
Progressive	*was* or *were* + present participle *She was driving.*	*am, is,* or *are* + present participle *She is driving.*	*will be* + present participle *She will be driving.*
Perfect Progressive	*had been* + present participle *She had been driving.*	*has* or *have been* + present participle *She has been driving.*	*will have been* + present participle *She will have been driving.*
Emphatic	*did* + present tense *She did drive.*	*do + present tense* *She does drive.*	no future emphatic form

Review your recent writing for proper use of past, present, and future tenses.

Using Pronouns

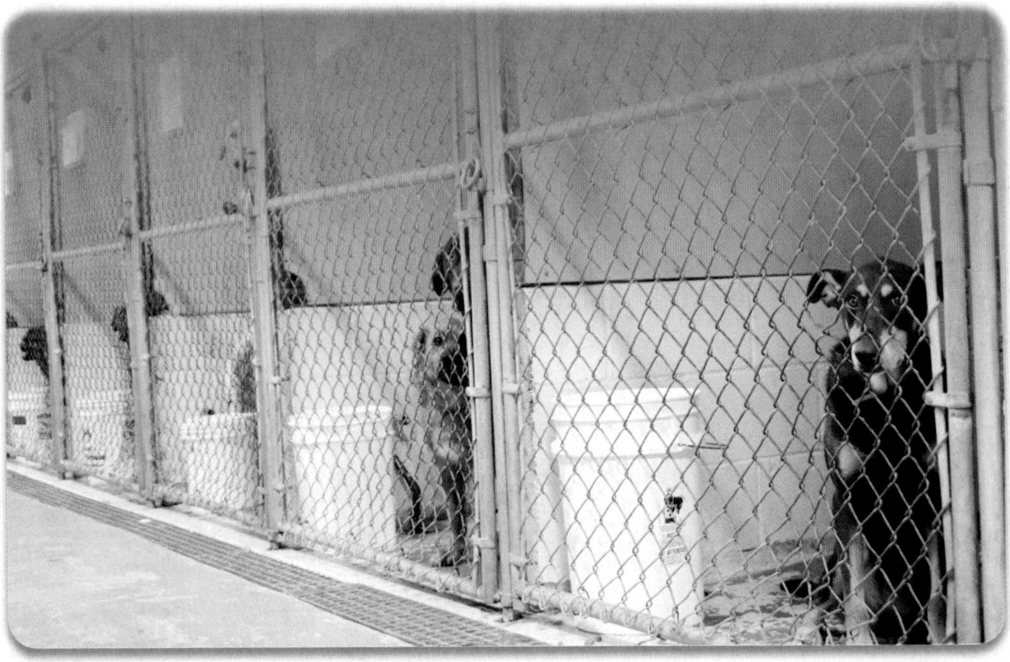

How can you use pronouns to make your writing fluid and accurate?

Using Pronouns: Pretest 1

The following draft paragraph about volunteering is hard to read because it contains several pronoun errors. Revise the paragraph so that it reads correctly. The first error has been corrected as an example.

The local animal shelter is looking for volunteers. My brother Eric and ~~me~~ I love animals. Me and him hope to be veterinarians one day. Yesterday, us two rode our bikes to the shelter. We walked up to the counter to learn how him and I could help. The two women their gave us there personal assistance. They gave he and I the grand tour. They told us that every day this shelter and others like them take in dozens of animals in need of homes. Eric and me couldn't believe them dogs and cats sitting bravely, waiting to be adopted. I decided to write an article for your school newspaper about they. Throughout the summer, me and Eric returned to the shelter every weekend.

Using Pronouns: Pretest 2

Directions

Read the passage and choose the pronoun that belongs in each underlined space. Write the letter of the correct answer.

At the rehearsal for the awards ceremony, Mrs. Graham, the class advisor, assigned __(1)__ juniors our seats on the stage. Although the teachers helped, we students did all of the work __(2)__. Throughout the rehearsal no one knew the winners' names. Everyone guessed __(3)__ would win. José, the class president, had several chances to look at the list of winners, but __(4)__ knew that __(5)__ looking at it would be wrong. Before the awards are given out, Susan or Tanya will give __(6)__ speech. __(7)__ do you think the faculty speaker will be? At one point José called for Mrs. Mason, the principal. However, because of the loud noise and confusion in the auditorium, getting __(8)__ attention seemed hopeless. José had wanted to know from __(9)__ he should get the awards that night. Not even Mrs. Graham __(10)__ understood José's question. As a result no one showed up with the awards that night.

1. **A** us
B ourselves
C we
D themselves

2. **A** himself
B herself
C ourselves
D themselves

3. **A** who
B whose
C whom
D whomever

4. **A** his
B him
C he
D himself

5. **A** him
B his
C he
D himself

6. **A** she
B her
C their
D theirs

7. **A** Whom
B Whose
C Whomever
D Who

8. **A** she
B her
C hers
D herself

9. **A** who
B whom
C whoever
D whose

10. **A** herself
B hers
C she
D her

CHAPTER 18

The Cases of Personal Pronouns

Lesson 1

Most pronouns have different forms to show how they are used in a sentence. The pronoun *I,* for example, is used as a subject or as a predicate nominative. The pronoun *me* is used as an object, and *my* or *mine* shows possession. The changes in form for pronouns, and nouns as well, occur because nouns and pronouns have **case.**

18 A **Case is the form of a noun or a pronoun that indicates its use in a sentence.**

English has three cases: the **nominative (or subjective) case, the objective case,** and **the possessive case.** Many pronouns change form for each case.

NOMINATIVE CASE	
(Used for subjects and predicate nominatives)	
Singular	I, you, he, she, it
Plural	we, you, they
OBJECTIVE CASE	
(Used for direct objects, indirect objects, and objects of prepositions)	
Singular	me, you, him, her, it
Plural	us, you, them
POSSESSIVE CASE	
(Used to show ownership or possession)	
Singular	my, mine, your, yours, his, her, hers, its
Plural	our, ours, your, yours, their, theirs

You and *it* are the same in both nominative and objective cases.

Practice Your Skills

Determining Case

Write the personal pronouns in each sentence. Then using the following abbreviations, write the case of each one.

nominative = *nom.* objective = *obj.* possessive = *pos.*

1. They haven't finalized the plans for their trip yet.
2. I hope he finds his lost luggage.
3. Does she know that we are meeting her at the airport?

4. This suitcase belongs to either him or her.
5. My car is parked closer than hers.
6. Remind me to give my sister her boarding pass.
7. Please meet us on the plane near our seats.

The Nominative Case

18 A.1 The **nominative case** is used for subjects and predicate nominatives.

The personal pronouns in the nominative case are *I, you, he, she, it, we,* and *they.*

Pronouns as Subjects

A pronoun can be the subject of an independent clause or a dependent clause.

They are traveling to New Mexico.

She was packing her bags when **I** called.

To determine the pronouns for a compound subject, check to make sure they are in the nominative case. There is a test you can use to check them. Say each pronoun separately.

Randy Jackson and (he, him) planned the trip.

He planned the trip.

Him planned the trip.

The nominative case *he* is the correct form to use.

Randy Jackson and **he** planned the trip.

This test also works if both subjects are pronouns.

CHAPTER 18

Pronouns as Predicate Nominatives

18 A.2 A **predicate nominative** follows a linking verb and identifies, renames, or explains the subject.

That is **she** near the airport gate.

It is common to use an objective case pronoun as a predicate nominative in casual conversation, as in *That's her* or *It's me,* but avoid this construction in written work.

That is **he.** It is **I.**

Sometimes the wording becomes awkward when pronouns are used as predicate nominatives. The awkwardness can usually be avoided by turning the sentence around.

Awkward	The copilots are **he** and **she.**
Turned Around	**He** and **she** are the copilots.

You can see lists of common linking verbs on pages 632–633. See pages 668–669 for more information about predicate nominatives.

CHAPTER 18

Nominative Case Pronouns Followed by Appositives

18 A.3 A pronoun in the nominative case that has a nominative appositive will not be affected by the appositive.

To check whether you have used the correct pronoun, mentally drop the appositive from the sentence.

We *copilots* will be flying soon. (We will be flying soon.)

Nominative Case Pronouns as Appositives

When a pronoun is part of an appositive to a noun that is a subject or a predicate nominative, the pronoun should be in the nominative case.

The copilots, Jack Ryan and **she,** will stand near the door as we exit.
(*Jack Ryan* and *she* are appositives to the subject *copilots.* Since a subject is in the nominative case, an appositive to the subject is also in the nominative case.)

Power Your Writing: Who or What?

Using appositive phrases in your writing gives the reader necessary information—the who and the what—to stay involved and interested in your writing. In the sentence below, the appositive phrase in bold type adds important information about the word *proportion.* The appositive phrase is set off by two commas.

Appositive Phrase	Proportion, **the relation of one part to another,** is determined by the observing eye.

An appositive phrase also helps streamline your writing.

Two Sentences	I was taken out of the Davis School. It was the elementary school across the street.
Appositive Phrase	I was taken out of the Davis School, **the elementary school across the street.**

Revise a recent composition by adding at least three appositive phrases.

CHAPTER 18

Practice Your Skills

Determining Pronouns

Turn each sentence around, making the predicate nominative the subject. Decide which pronoun is correct and say the sentence again.

1. The passengers in this row are she and (I, me).
2. The flight attendants were Sally and (them, they).
3. The girl sitting by the window is (her, she).
4. Sitting in the first-class cabin were (he, him) and (she, her).
5. The first passengers off the plane were (us, we).

Practice Your Skills

Using Pronouns in the Nominative Case

Write the correct form of the pronoun in parentheses.

1. Susan and (he, him) are planning a trip to Santa Fe.
2. (We, Us) neighbors will meet them there for the holiday weekend.
3. The other friends asked to go along were Brenda and (her, she).
4. The most experienced travelers, Mark and (I, me), will choose the hotel.
5. Neither (he, him) nor (me, I) had ever visited Santa Fe.

Practice Your Skills

Supplying Pronouns in the Nominative Case

Complete each sentence by writing an appropriate pronoun in the nominative case. (Do not use *you* or *it.*) Then write how the pronoun is used.

subject = *subj.*　　predicate nominative = *p.n.*　　appositive = *app.*

1. Nathan and ___ made homemade pizza.
2. ___ chefs were happy to cook for our friends.
3. The first guests were Jeff, Susan, and ___.
4. Are ___ the friends you met at the grocery store?
5. Because ___ was late, ___ missed the first pizza.

Connect to Writing: Editing

Using Pronouns Correctly

Rewrite the following sentences, correcting any errors in the use of pronouns. If a sentence is correct, write **C.**

1. Connie and her are planning to take the SAT.
2. Are you and he taking it as well?
3. Signing up for the Saturday exam were him and me.
4. The Greenes and they are going to help us study.

CHAPTER 18

Connect to Writing: Editing

Using Nominative Case Pronouns

You and your best friend won a trip to Florence, Italy. Using the photograph at the right as inspiration, write a postcard to your family, describing what you and your friend have seen and done on vacation. At least three sentences should include a compound subject, a compound predicate nominative, or a compound appositive.

The Objective Case

The personal pronouns in the objective case are *me, you, him, her, it, us,* and *them.*

18 A.4 The **objective case** is used for direct objects, indirect objects, objects of prepositions, and objects of verbals.

Pronouns as Direct and Indirect Objects

18 A.5 A pronoun used as a direct object will answer the question *Whom?* after an action verb. A pronoun used as an indirect object will answer the question *To whom?* or *For whom?* after a verb.

Direct Objects	The editor asked **me** about the deadline. Interview **her** for the story.
Indirect Objects	Frank gave **us** a lead on the story. (*Lead* is the direct object.) Send **him** an e-mail about your idea. (*e-mail* is the direct object.)

You can learn more about direct and indirect objects on pages 665–667.

Pronouns as Objects of Prepositions

18 A.6 A prepositional phrase begins with a preposition and ends with a noun or a pronoun called the **object of a preposition.**

A pronoun used as the object of a preposition is in the objective case.

Will you talk with **us?** (*With us* is the prepositional phrase.)

The student told his story to **me.** (*To me* is the prepositional phrase.)

Check to see that any pronoun used in a compound object of a preposition is in the objective case. You can do this by saying each pronoun separately.

Our editor was very proud of Matt and (she, her).

Our editor was very proud of **she.** (incorrect)

Our editor was very proud of **her.**

Our editor was very proud of Matt and **her.** (*her* is correct)

When You Speak

People often will use nominative case pronouns after the preposition *between* in an effort to sound formal or correct. However, all pronouns used as objects of a preposition should be in the objective case.

Incorrect	The comment was *between he and I.*
Correct	The comment was *between him and me.*

You can find a list of common prepositions on pages 643–644. You can learn more about objects of prepositions on page 644.

Practice Your Skills

Using Pronouns as Objects

Write the correct form of the pronoun in parentheses. Then label the use of each pronoun as follows.

direct object = *d.o.* indirect object = *i.o.*
object of preposition = *o.p.*

1. We interviewed the students and (they, them) for the staff reporter job.
2. Did you give Peg and (she, her) the writing test?
3. The editor interviewed Max and (he, him).
4. I waited with Jessica and (they, them) in the hallway until it was my turn.
5. The editor chose Daniel and (he, him) as staff photographers.

Pronouns as Objects of Verbals

18 A.7 Participles, gerunds, and infinitives are all verbals. Because verbals are verb forms, they can take objects. The object of a verbal is in the objective case.

To find the object, say the verbal and then ask *whom?*

Participial Phrase	Seeing **her** at the press conference, Steve introduces himself to his new employer. (The phrase is *seeing her at the press conference.* Seeing whom? *Her* is the object of the participle.)
Gerund Phrase	Asking **him** for an interview made Jordan anxious. (The phrase is *asking him for an interview.* Asking whom? *Him* is the object of the gerund.)

Infinitive Phrase	Tell Lisa to call **me** at the office before noon. (The phrase is *to call me at the office before noon.* To call whom? *Me* is the object of the infinitive.)

When the object of a verbal is compound, say each pronoun separately.

Interviewing Jason and (they, them) wasn't easy for the reporter.

Interviewing **they** wasn't easy for the reporter.

Interviewing **them** wasn't easy for the reporter.

The objective case *them* is the correct form to use.

Interviewing Jason and **them** wasn't easy for the reporter.

You can learn more about verbals on pages 688–695.

Objective Case Pronouns Followed by Appositives

Sometimes a pronoun in the objective case will have an appositive. The appositive will never affect the case of the pronoun it identifies or explains. To check whether you have used the correct pronoun, mentally drop the appositive from the sentence.

Give **us** *reporters* our new assignments so we can leave.
(*Us* is used as an indirect object. *Give us our new assignments so we can leave.*)

Objective Case Pronouns as Appositives

Occasionally a pronoun itself will be part of an appositive to a noun that is a direct object, an indirect object, or an object of a preposition. When it is, the pronoun should be in the objective case.

Mr. Talbot sent two reporters, Marcia and **me,** to the press conference.
(*Marcia* and *me* are appositives to the direct object *reporters.* Since a direct object is in the objective case, an appositive to a direct object is also in the objective case.)

When You Speak and Write

People use appositives in the objective case to clarify information. The compound appositives provide details that might be unknown to the listener or reader.

Vague	The editor gave **us** summer jobs cleaning the office.
Clear	The editor gave **us, Max and me,** summer jobs cleaning the office.

Practice Your Skills

Choosing the Correct Pronoun

Read each sentence aloud, saying each pronoun separately. Then repeat the sentence, using the correct pronoun.

1. A veteran reporter offered him and (me, I) advice.
2. She gave Jeff and (us, we) tape recorders for interviews.
3. Katie interviewed the store owners and (they, them) for the story.
4. She sent Millie and (her, she) a copy of the final story.
5. Several readers called the editor and (he, him) with constructive feedback.

Practice Your Skills

Using Pronouns in the Objective Case

Write the correct form of the pronoun in parentheses.

1. I asked some Minnesota historians and (they, them).
2. They gave (we, us) students information on Minnesota's early leaders.
3. Interviewing the governor and (he, him) was impossible.
4. Informing (they, them) of the history project, we asked graciously for help.
5. Send your questions to any legislator—Mr. Smith, Ms. Jones, or (she, her).
6. The politicians gave (we, us) interesting information.
7. Ms. Jones told (I, me) about Minnesota's first governor, Henry H. Sibley.
8. Henry A. Swift followed the first two governors, (he, him) and Alexander Ramsey.
9. The timeline of Minnesota history was completed by (we, us) students of Mr. Kemp's class.
10. Mr. Kemp plans to ask Stacy and (she, her) what they learned about Minnesota.

Practice Your Skills

Supplying Pronouns in the Objective Case

Complete each sentence by writing an appropriate pronoun in the objective case. (Do not use *you* or *it.*) Then use the following abbreviations to write how each pronoun is used.

direct object = *d.o.*
indirect object = *i.o.*
object of a preposition = *o.p.*
object of a verbal = *o.v.*
appositive = *app.*

1. Tell ___ the story of Sir Edmund Hillary's expedition.
2. The world praised ___ for his accomplishments.
3. Between you and ___, I am still amazed at his feat.
4. Historians call the first people to climb Mount Everest, ___ and Tenzing Norgay, true adventurers.
5. Some Nepalese guides offered to lead the group and ___.

Connect to Writing: Editing

Using Objective Case Pronouns

Rewrite the following sentences, correcting any errors in the use of pronouns. If a sentence is correct, write **C**.

1. Try to stall Oliver and she until six o'clock.
2. Horns were purchased by the party hosts, Alvin and he.
3. To Barry and I, the surprise plan was flawless.
4. Call Kevin and he before the party guests arrive.
5. My sister and Alvin include Diana and I in their schemes.

Connect to Speaking and Writing: Vocabulary Review

Using the Vocabulary of Grammar

With a partner, talk about the meanings of the terms *nominative case* and *objective case.* Then write short definitions of each term.

The Possessive Case

The personal pronouns in the possessive case are *my, mine, your, yours, his, her, hers, its, our, ours, their,* and *theirs.*

18 A.8 The **possessive case** is used to show ownership or possession.

Possessive case pronouns are most often used before a noun or by themselves.

Before A Noun	**Her** cat is beautiful.
By Themselves	Those kittens are **mine,** but which are **yours?**

Be careful not to confuse certain personal pronouns in the possessive case with contractions. A personal pronoun in the possessive case never includes an apostrophe. *Its, your, their,* and *theirs* are possessive pronouns. *It's, you're, they're,* and *there's* are contractions and include apostrophes.

CHAPTER 18

Possessive Pronoun	**Its** fur is orange and white.
Contraction	**It's** a tabby cat, not a Siamese.
Possessive Pronoun	**Their** kittens are still nursing.
Contraction	**They're** the parents of those kittens.
Possessive Pronoun	It is **your** choice.
Contraction	**You're** picking one from the litter next week, aren't you?
Possessive Pronoun	That shy kitten is **theirs.**
Contraction	**There's** only one solid white kitten.

Possessive Pronouns with Gerunds

18 A.9 When a pronoun comes directly in front of a gerund, it should be in the possessive case—in just the same way a possessive pronoun would come in front of a noun.

There is a good chance of **his** adopting a kitten.
(The gerund phrase is *adopting a kitten.* It is used as an object of the preposition *of.* Since *adopting* is a gerund, it should be preceded by a possessive pronoun: *his adopting.*)

Sue appreciated **your** *caring for the kittens yesterday.*
(The gerund phrase is *caring for the kittens yesterday.* It is used as the direct object. Sue appreciated what? Your caring for the kittens. Since *caring* is a gerund, it should be preceded by a possessive pronoun: *your caring.*)

A common error is to put a nominative or an objective case pronoun before a gerund phrase—instead of a possessive case pronoun.

Incorrect	There is a good chance of **him** adopting a kitten.
Incorrect	Sue appreciated **you** caring for the kittens yesterday.

Since a gerund and a participle are both verb forms that end in *-ing,* they are easy to confuse. A participle is used as an adjective; it would never be preceded by a possessive pronoun.

Gerund	**Our** *adopting kittens* appeared on television. (The gerund phrase is the subject. Since *adopting* is a gerund, it is preceded by a possessive pronoun.)
Participle	The neighbors watched **us** *adopting kittens.* (*Us* is a direct object in this sentence. The neighbors watched what? Us. Since *us* is a direct object, it is in the objective case. The participial phrase is used as an adjective to describe *us.*)

You can learn more about gerunds on pages 691–692 and more about participles on pages 688–690.

Practice Your Skills

Using Pronouns in the Possessive Case

Write the correct form of the word in parentheses.

1. (Theirs, There's) is the kitten with the white feet.
2. Everyone was amazed at (my, me) choosing so quickly.
3. Who objected to (your, you're) adopting two kittens?
4. Dad advised against (them, their) bringing home more than one.
5. That sweet cat couldn't be (ours, our's), could it?
6. After choosing a cat, we will need to pick (its, it's) veterinarian.

Practice Your Skills

Supplying Pronouns in Possessive Cases

Complete each sentence by writing appropriate pronouns. (Do not use *you* or *it.*)

1. They met us at ___ local movie theater.
2. Rebecca showed him where ___ friends were sitting.
3. Tessa ate ___ popcorn before the movie began.
4. Peter told us about ___ working at the theater.
5. ___ buying her ticket early saved time.

Connect to Writing: Editing

Using Possessive Pronouns

Rewrite each sentence using the correct possessive pronoun.

1. Who disliked you're choice of seating for today's movie?
2. I think you choosing the back row this time was terrific.
3. After watching it's previews, I don't want to see that action movie.
4. We friends are cheering ours favorite stars as they triumph over adversity.
5. There is no chance of him seeing the movie twice in one day.
6. He's trading seats will improve my view of my favorite hero.
7. This popcorn is mine, but where is there's?
8. I suppose you balancing snacks was for attention.

CHAPTER 18

Check Point: Mixed Practice

Write each pronoun that is in the wrong case. Beside it, write the correct form of the pronoun. If a sentence is correct, write **C** after the number.

1. With some help from Fred and I, the Baxters made their own movie.
2. Shall I give the videotapes to Stephen or he?
3. Linda, Lou, and me act as students.
4. Haven't you heard about us making the movie?
5. The only witnesses to the filming were she and I.
6. Convincing Robert and they to join us wasn't as hard as it first seemed.
7. The producer of the film will be Jan or him.
8. Manuel invited you and I to preview the movie.
9. Kimberly told me about you entering the film festival.
10. He will go to the festival with Mike and me.

Pronoun Problems Lesson 2

We all have unique speech patterns, most of which are fine to use in informal conversation. At other times, however, it is probably best to use the correct forms. This includes the correct use of pronouns.

18 B **Common problems with pronouns include the misuse of *who* and *whom*, incomplete comparisons, and misuse of reflexive and intensive pronouns.**

Who or *Whom?*

Who and *whoever* are pronouns that have different forms for each case—just as personal pronouns do.

WHO/WHOEVER	
Nominative Case	who, whoever
Objective Case	whom, whomever
Possessive Case	whose

Who and *whoever* and their related pronouns are used in questions and in subordinate clauses.

18 B.1 The correct case of *who* is determined by how the pronoun is used in a question or a clause.

Nominative Case — **Who** invented the electric telegraph? (subject)

Objective Case — **Whom** did you contact? (direct object)

From **whom** did you learn Morse code? (object of the preposition *from*)

CHAPTER 18

When You Write

In casual conversation you may hear people say, "Who did you see?" This use of *who* is generally accepted in informal situations; however, it should be avoided in written work or in formal situations, such as a job interview or a speech.

In clauses, forms of *who* are often used as the first word of an adjectival clause or a noun clause. The form you use depends on how the pronoun is used within the clause—not on any word outside the clause.

The following examples show how forms of *who* and *whom* are used in adjectival clauses.

Nominative Case	Samuel F. B. Morse is the man **who invented the electric telegraph.** (*Who* is the subject of *invented.*)
Objective Case	Morse is the American inventor **whom we studied.** (*Whom* is the direct object of *studied.* We studied *whom.*)
	Morse is the person **about whom I was just reading.** (*Whom* is the object of the preposition *about.*)

The following examples show how forms of *who* and *whoever* are used in noun clauses.

Nominative Case	Give **whoever asks** this Morse code message. (*Whoever* is the subject of *asks.*)
	Do you know **who the sender is?** (*Who* is a predicate nominative. The sender is *who.*)
Objective Case	Test **whomever you want** on Morse code. (*Whomever* is the direct object of *want.* You want *whomever.*)
	Brad likes **whomever he works with.** (*Whomever* is the object of the preposition *with.* He works with *whomever.*)

CHAPTER 18

Sometimes questions and clauses contain an interrupting expression, such as *I believe, we know, do you suppose,* or *she hopes.* Before you decide the case of a pronoun, mentally drop the expression so that the choice will be easier to make.

Who do you think helped with the creation of the National Academy of Design?
(Who helped with the creation? *Who* is the subject of *helped.*)

I'm learning about Samuel Morse, **who** I know helped with the creation of the National Academy of Design.
(I'm learning about Samuel Morse, **who** helped. *Who* is the subject of *helped.*)

You can learn more about adjective and noun clauses on pages 715–722.

Practice Your Skills

Using Who *and Its Related Pronouns*

Write the correct form of the pronoun in parentheses. Then using the following abbreviations, write how each pronoun is used.

subject = *subj.*	direct object = *d.o.*
predicate nominative = *p.n.*	object of a preposition = *o.p.*

1. Samuel Morse, (who, whom) first aspired to be an artist, was known for his portrait paintings.
2. Of (who, whom) did he paint portraits?
3. Many were wondering (who, whom) would paint a portrait of Marquis de Lafayette.
4. Then the artist, (who, whom) had earned worldwide recognition, wanted to paint more than portraits.
5. Morse, (who, whom) invented the electric telegraph, also invented a code for the instrument.
6. From (who, whom) did he get his idea?
7. (Whoever, Whomever) received his first telegraph message was part of history.
8. I don't know to (who, whom) he sent his first message, which said, "What hath God wrought?"
9. Morse is a man (who, whom) several nations honored.
10. Morse is a man (who, whom) experimented with submarine cable telegraphy.

Connect to Writing: Editing

Using Who *and* Whom *Correctly*

Rewrite each sentence, correcting any pronoun errors. If the sentence is correct, write **C**.

1. Whom has ever sent a telegram?
2. To who did you send the telegram?
3. Sharon, whom has grandparents in France, receives a telegram on her birthday every year.
4. Rob, who has studied science, knows the difference between a telegram and a telegraph message.
5. Ken and he were joking about whom could whistle better Morse code messages.

CHAPTER 18

Connect to Writing: Narrative

Using Forms of Who

Your music teacher has asked you to write a 150-word essay titled "The Greatest Musician Who Ever Lived." Choose a musician—living or dead, famous or obscure—whom you feel deserves this designation. Write a short essay for your teacher, explaining why you feel this person is important. Use the following forms of *who* correctly at least once: *who, whom, whoever,* and *whomever.*

Pronouns in Comparisons

Problems sometimes arise when pronouns are used in comparisons—especially when a comparison is an elliptical clause.

18 B.2 An **elliptical clause** is a subordinate clause that begins with *than* or *as* and that has words omitted. The words omitted are understood to be there.

Rick admires Ellen more **than I.**

Rick admires Ellen more **than me.**

Both of the preceding examples are correct—depending upon what words are missing.

Rick admires Ellen more **than I admire Ellen.**
(*I* is correct because *I* is the subject of *admire.*)

Rick admires Ellen more **than he admires me.**
(Now *me* is correct because *me* is the direct object of the verb *admires.*)

18 B.3 In an elliptical clause, use the form of the pronoun you would use if the clause were completed.

You can decide the case of a pronoun in an elliptical clause by mentally completing the clause. Then choose the form of the pronoun that expresses the meaning you want. Some elliptical clauses can express only one meaning.

Are you as tired as (I, me)?

Are you as tired **as I am?**

You can learn more about elliptical clauses on page 714.

Practice Your Skills

Using Pronouns in Elliptical Clauses

Write each sentence, completing the elliptical clause. Be sure to choose the pronoun that is correct for each clause. Then underline the pronoun you chose.

1. Brian missed the volunteer project meeting because he didn't awake as early as (I, me).

2. The volunteers on the house-building team think Tina's sister is stronger than (she, her).

3. You did a better job painting the doors than (we, us).

4. Lynn spent more time measuring the wood than (I, me).

5. Does Julie hammer as quickly as (she, her)?

6. Because he has built other houses before, I'm sure Burt is more confident than (I, me).

7. Art likes volunteering as much as (we, us).

8. Carl knows more about installing kitchen plumbing than (he, him).

9. Do you think Betsy is a better volunteer than (I, me)?

10. Joseph seems much closer to the volunteers than (I, me).

11. During the building project, our leader thanked Kim more than (I, me).

12. After the wiring was complete, Roy had to admit that Louis was as good an electrician as (he, him).

13. I think Patrick likes the volunteers more than (I, me).

14. No one can install windows as well as (he, him).

15. Claire could see that the new home owners were as excited as (she, her).

Connect to Writing: Revising

Using Elliptical Clauses

Rewrite the following sentences, correcting any elliptical clauses. If the sentence is correct, write **C.** Be prepared to explain your answers.

1. For working in perfect harmony, no volunteer team is as good as them.

2. Within the past year, my younger brother has built as many houses as me.

3. When the volunteers are inspired, nobody works as hard as them.

4. After the fifth project, none of the volunteers were as tired as her.

5. For motivation, there is no one as inspiring as him.

Reflexive and Intensive Pronouns

Reflexive and intensive pronouns are easy to recognize because they end in *-self* or *-selves.* These pronouns are often used for emphasis.

REFLEXIVE AND INTENSIVE PRONOUNS	
Singular	myself, yourself, himself, herself, itself
Plural	ourselves, yourselves, themselves

18 B.4 **Reflexive pronouns** always refer back to a previous noun or pronoun in the sentence.

Reflexive Pronouns Tom was counting to **himself.**

The boys had never found **themselves** among such junk before.

18 B.5 **Intensive pronouns** are used to emphasize a noun or another pronoun in the sentence.

Intensive Pronouns Benjamin **himself** was responsible for the garage-sale money.

The organizers **themselves** seemed to be buying the items.

Reflexive or intensive pronouns should never be used by themselves. They must have an antecedent in the same sentence.

Incorrect Lexi and **myself** are the only browsers.

Correct Lexi and **I** are the only browsers.

You can learn more about pronouns on pages 209 and 623–627.

CHAPTER 18

Practice Your Skills

Using Reflexive and Intensive Pronouns

Write the reflexive and intensive pronouns in the following sentences. Then write ***I*** if the pronoun is *incorrect* and **C** if the pronoun is *correct.*

1. Jane and himself bought the last of the folding chairs.
2. They themselves purchased one item, an old blender.
3. Jesse seemed to be wondering to herself about the mahogany table.
4. My sister and myself negotiated on the price of a chair.
5. I had never seen himself become so attached to junk.
6. She herself had admired the monkey statue for years.
7. Bob and I were both looking for neon signs for ourselves.
8. They themself were responsible for carrying the table.

CHAPTER 18

Connect to Writing: Editing

Replacing Reflexive and Intensive Pronouns

Write the pronoun that correctly replaces the incorrect pronoun in each sentence in the preceding exercise.

Check Point: Mixed Practice

Find and write each pronoun that is used incorrectly. Then write the pronoun correctly. If a sentence is correct, write ***C.***

1. For whom are you buying that lamp?
2. Paul has never been at a garage sale earlier than me.
3. The men in the blue truck rushed to the owner, whom they feared had sold the lawn mower.
4. Zelda and herself are efficient garage sale hostesses.
5. I get frustrated because Alli shops much faster than I.
6. I always give advice to whomever is interested.
7. The owner negotiated a price with Mrs. Randle, who was holding a vase.
8. Can Ned find as many bargains as him?
9. I could see that Lucy was now buying as much as me.
10. Raymond, who I believe is having a garage sale next weekend, just bought our old sofa.

Pronouns and Their Antecedents

Lesson 3

18 C **A pronoun and its antecedent, the word that a pronoun refers to or replaces, must agree.**

18 C.1 A single pronoun must agree in **number** and **gender** with its antecedent.

Number is the term used to indicate whether a noun or a pronoun is singular or plural. **Gender** is the term used to indicate whether a noun or a pronoun is masculine, feminine, or neuter.

GENDER			
Masculine	he	him	his
Feminine	she	her	hers
Neuter	it	its	

CHAPTER 18

Agreement between a single antecedent and a pronoun usually presents no problem.

Maria carefully laced up **her** soccer shoes.
(*Maria* is singular and feminine; therefore, *her* is correct because it is also singular and feminine.)

Members of the team warmed up before **they** began to practice.
(*Members* is plural; therefore, *they* is plural.)

If the antecedent of a pronoun is two or more words, remember the following two rules.

18 C.2 When two or more singular antecedents are joined by *or, nor, either/or,* or *neither/nor,* use a singular pronoun to refer to them.

In the following example, Lana *or* Emma will bring a ball—not both of them. As a result, the pronoun must be singular because it is referring to only one person.

Either Lana or Emma will bring **her** ball to soccer practice.

When one antecedent is singular and the other is plural, the pronoun agrees with the closer antecedent.

Either Gerry or the Davis twins will bring **their** cameras.

Neither my parents nor my uncle has **his** camera.

18 C.3 When two or more singular antecedents are joined by *and* or *both/and,* use a plural pronoun to refer to them.

The conjunctions in this rule indicate more than one. In the following example, both *Ted and Paulo*—two people—cleaned the uniforms. Therefore, the pronoun referring to Ted and Paulo is plural.

Ted and Paulo cleaned **their** uniforms for Saturday's game.

18 C.4 When the gender of an antecedent is not obvious, use the phrase *his or her* to refer to the antecedent.

Each player must bring **his or her** uniform to the game.

Overusing *his or her* in a short passage can become tiresome. You can often avoid this problem by rewriting such sentences, using plural forms.

All players must bring **their** uniforms to the game.

Practice Your Skills

Making Pronouns Agree with Their Antecedents

Write the pronoun that correctly completes each sentence.

1. If any boy wants to try out for the boys' soccer team, ▒ should report to the soccer field this afternoon.
2. All members of the team have been measured for ▒ new uniforms.
3. Both Liz and Chris won ▒ varsity soccer letters.
4. Will you ask Sarah or Lisa to stop by after practice with ▒ cleats?
5. Either David or his brothers will take you to practice in ▒ old station wagon.
6. Neither Sheila nor Sasha can get ▒ varsity letter until next year.

7. Examine this game plan and observe how each player has ▒ own strategic role.
8. Mom and Dad prefer to stand near the goal because ▒ can see more.
9. Both Nancy and Pauline like ▒ new soccer coach.
10. Neither Ray nor his teammates have been able to find ▒ ball.

Connect to Writing: Editing

Using Pronouns and Antecedents

Rewrite the following sentences, correcting any errors in pronoun-antecedent agreement.

1. Our team has so many trophies that we don't know what to do with it.
2. Either Pepe or Jon will drive their car to soccer practice.
3. Both Mary and Ellen have finished practicing her drills.
4. Neither Alma nor her sisters want to meet her coach.
5. I kicked the ball to Sal, but he hasn't kicked them back.

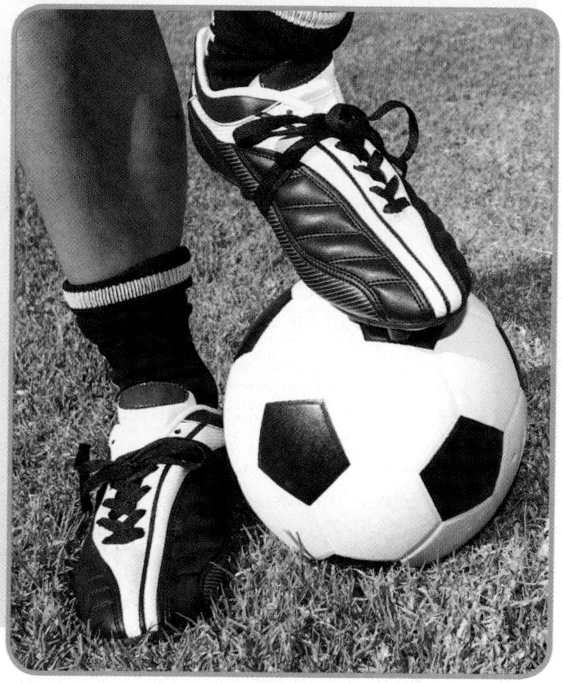

CHAPTER 18

Connect to Writing: Journal Entry

Using Pronouns and Antecedents Correctly

When was the first time you realized that you were no longer a carefree child? Write a journal entry to your future self, capturing as many details and specifics as you can about an event or incident that first made you realize you were growing up. Be sure to check that you used pronouns and antecedents correctly.

Indefinite Pronouns as Antecedents

The common indefinite pronouns can be divided in three groups based on their number.

COMMON INDEFINITE PRONOUNS	
Singular	anybody, anyone, each, either, everybody, everyone, neither, nobody, no one, one, somebody, someone
Plural	both, few, many, several
Singular/Plural	all, any, most, none, some

18 C.5 A personal pronoun must be singular if its antecedent is a singular indefinite pronoun (in the singular group listed above).

One of the girls works for **her** father during the summer.

18 C.6 A personal pronoun must be plural if its antecedent is a plural indefinite pronoun (in the plural group listed above).

Both of the students submitted **their** résumés.

18 C.7 When the antecedent of a personal pronoun is one of the singular/plural indefinite pronouns, the personal pronoun must agree in number and gender with the noun to which the indefinite pronoun refers (the noun is underlined in the examples below).

Some of the application had mistakes on **it.** (singular)

Most of the students have found **their** summer jobs. (plural)

Occasionally, the gender of a singular indefinite pronoun is not known. Standard English solves this problem by using *his or her* or by rewriting the sentence using the plural form.

Everyone must submit **his or her** job application by the end of this week.

All of the students must submit **their** job applications by the end of this week.

CHAPTER 18

Practice Your Skills

Making Pronouns Agree

Write the pronoun that correctly completes each sentence.

1. Each of the boys straightened ___ tie before the interview.
2. None of the parents want ___ children to work during the school year.
3. Neither of the students finished typing ___ résumé.
4. Both of the employees hired ___ staff already.
5. Someone left ___ notebook in the interviewer's office.

Connect to Writing: Editing

Using Pronouns and Antecedents

Rewrite the following sentences, correcting any errors in pronoun-antecedent agreement. If the sentence is correct, write C.

1. Jenny and Ruth work in her mother's office.
2. None of the bosses want his employees to be late.
3. The summer job had its tough responsibilities.
4. Two of my friends started her jobs in June.
5. Neither of the boys brought his résumé.

CHAPTER 18

Check Point: Mixed Practice

Write the pronoun in parentheses that correctly completes each sentence.

1. The Romans called (his, their) god of the sky Jupiter.
2. In Greek mythology the people called (her, their) gods' ruler Zeus.
3. Zeus's breastplate could be identified by (its, their) symbols.
4. Zeus had several shrines in (his, their) name.
5. One of the shrines was famous for (its, their) oracle.
6. Zeus's father, Cronus, was not a good father to (his, their) children.
7. Rhea, Zeus's mother, hid (their, her) son on a secluded island.
8. Zeus rescued (his, their) siblings eventually.
9. Neither Poseidon nor Hades had (their, his) brother's power of the sky.
10. Both Ares and Hebe called Zeus (his, their) father.
11. Some of Zeus's children used (his, their) powers wisely.
12. Everyone looked to Zeus's son, Hermes, for (his, their) good luck and wealth.
13. Zeus threw thunderbolts at (his, their) enemies.

Unclear, Missing, or Confusing Antecedents

Lesson 4

When you edit your written work, always make sure each pronoun is in the correct case and has a clear antecedent. When antecedents are missing or vague, your writing will become confusing or even misleading.

18 D **Personal pronouns should clearly refer to a specific antecedent.**

Unclear Antecedents

Someone reading your written work should never have to stop to figure out your meaning because some pronouns—such as *it, they, this,* and *that*—only vaguely refer to their antecedents. As you edit your work, replace any such pronouns with specific antecedents to avoid any possible confusion or misunderstanding.

CHAPTER 18

Unclear Ray stood in the outfield and threw **it** 30 yards.
(The antecedent of *it* is not clear. However, the context of the sentence suggests that the pronoun *it* refers to a ball.)

Clear Ray stood in the outfield and threw **the ball** 30 yards.

Unclear When you are tired of listening to the game, hand **them** to me.
(The antecedent of *them* is not clear. The sentence suggests that the pronoun *them* refers to headphones.)

Clear When you are tired of listening to the game, hand **the headphones** to me.

Unclear The umpire stopped to check the ball for defects. **This** caused the game to end late.
(*This* has no clear antecedent, but the context of the sentence suggests that time was lost.)

Clear The umpire stopped to check the ball for defects. **This delay** caused the game to end late.

Unclear I was nervous about speaking because **you** are afraid of making a mistake.
(*You* is used incorrectly because the speaker is referring to himself.

Clear I was nervous about speaking because **I** was afraid of making a mistake.

Missing Antecedents

Occasionally pronouns are written without any antecedent. To correct this kind of mistake, you often have to rewrite the sentence.

Missing	In the play **it** shows how love conquers all. (The antecedent of *it* is missing.)
Clear	The **play** shows how love conquers all.
Missing	In Los Angeles **they** have many young actors. (The antecedent of *they* is missing.)
Clear	**Los Angeles** has many young actors.

Confusing Antecedents

Readers can easily confuse the meaning of a sentence when a pronoun has more than one possible antecedent.

Confusing	Remove the plant from the container and place **it** in the ground. (What should be placed in the ground, the plant or the container?)
Clear	Remove the plant from the container and place **the plant** in the ground.
Confusing	If the rabbits eat the plants, place chicken wire over **them.** (Should the rabbits or the plants be put under wire?)
Clear	Place chicken wire over the **plants** if the rabbits eat them.

CHAPTER 18

Practice Your Skills

Identifying Pronoun-Antecedent Errors

Write ***I*** if the sentence contains a pronoun-antecedent error and **C** if the sentence is correct.

1. If gardeners do not wear sunscreen in the yard, it can cause blisters.
2. In my neighborhood they grow pansies in the winter.
3. Ida told Maya, "You have won the 'Yard of the Month' award."
4. I was nervous about starting the lawn mower for the first time because you're afraid of breaking it.
5. After gardening, he had ant bites on both arms, but they soon healed.
6. My neighbors water their plants every few days, because you can't expect the flowers to live unless you water frequently.

7. In its first chapter, the book describes how to fertilize properly.
8. Rachel got the mower and pushed it across the grass.
9. Ann told Mai that her dog digs up rose bushes.
10. If the gardeners don't kill the weeds, spray them with poison.

Connect to Writing: Revising

Using Pronouns and Antecedents Correctly

Rewrite the incorrect sentences from the previous exercise, correcting unclear, missing, or confusing antecedents.

Check Point: Mixed Practice

Write the correct form of the pronoun in parentheses.

1. Come run with Melba and (I, me).
2. Some of the boys couldn't find (his, their) best running shoes.
3. My uncle was surprised to hear of (me, my) training for a marathon.
4. Lu can sprint to the finish line much faster than (I, me).
5. Joshua and (I, me) are going to the track meet.
6. (Who, Whom) did you say wanted to run with us?
7. Are you sure it was Lee and (she, her) at the front of the pack?
8. Will you take (I, me) with you to the marathon?
9. (We, Us) runners feel good and fit after each day's run.
10. The person to (whom, who) you should direct your questions is Coach Henry.
11. To (who, whom) should I speak about running?
12. Ken gave up soccer for (he's, his) track practice.
13. The runners (ourselves, themselves) seemed alert.
14. Kay didn't run as fast as (she, her) can.
15. Ron drank more orange juice than (I, me).

Assess Your Learning

Using Pronouns in the Correct Case

Write the correct form of the pronoun in parentheses.

1. Where did Juan and (he, him) go last night after they left the party?
2. (Who, Whom) do you think is the best candidate for the job?
3. Everyone thinks that Mr. Robb and (he, him) should run for office.
4. Ms. Kelly was amazed at (us, our) selling so many ads for the program.
5. Are you and (she, her) going to the final football game?
6. Mom promised a special treat to (whoever, whomever) raked the leaves.
7. Ask Gail, her sisters, and (they, them) to dinner.
8. Senator Ruiz spoke with (we, us) honor society members at the awards ceremony.
9. We selected two students, Allison and (he, him), to plan the paper drive.
10. Did you notice whether it was Dmitri or (he, him) in the science lab?
11. Come here and sit between McKenna and (I, me).
12. Some of the boys couldn't find (his, their) bicycle helmets.
13. My uncle was surprised to hear of (me, my) building my own stereo.
14. Kathleen can memorize each week's spelling words much faster than (I, me).
15. (Who, Whom) did you say wanted to talk to me?

Eliminating Errors

From the choices in parentheses, write the word that correctly completes each sentence.

1. From (who, whom) did you borrow that calculator?
2. The class will be impressed at (us, our) tasteful decorating of the room.
3. Do you think Lucia is a better dancer than (she, her)?
4. Mr. Portland chose two of our classmates, Jenna and (she, her), to greet the mayor when she arrives.
5. Amanda has chosen this kitten for (its, it's) gentleness.

Making Pronouns Agree with Antecedents

Write the pronoun that correctly completes each sentence.

1. Neither of the boys on the corner had an identification card with ___.
2. Did all of the teachers send ___ students to the library at the same time?
3. Each of my aunts likes flowers on ___ kitchen table.
4. Both Carol and Tanya entered pictures of ___ pets in the photo contest.
5. Have you ever seen a bird training ___ young?

Writing Sentences

Write five sentences that follow the directions below.

1. Write a sentence using an appropriate word before a gerund.
2. Write a sentence that includes a pronoun in the correct case in an elliptical clause.
3. Write a sentence that includes an indefinite pronoun at the beginning of a subordinate clause.
4. Write a sentence that includes a pronoun in the correct case in an appositive.
5. Write a sentence that includes an intensive pronoun.

Using Pronouns: Posttest

Directions

Read the passage and choose the pronoun that belongs in each underlined space. Write the letter of the correct answer.

Chief Joseph

At the age of 31, Joseph became the chief of the Nez Perce tribe in 1871. __(1)__ and his tribe made __(2)__ home in the Wallowa Valley in northeastern Oregon. Although some tribes fought against the invading white settlers, the Nez Perce were a peaceful nation. Since the Lewis and Clark expedition, the tribe had maintained good relations with white settlers. Joseph had also spent much of his early childhood among Christian missionaries. No one wanted peace more than __(3)__. Speaking of the settlers, Joseph once said, "__(4)__ stole a great many horses from __(5)__, and __(6)__ could not get __(7)__ back because we were Indians." He added, "Indians had no friends to plead __(8)__ cause before the law councils."

Eventually a great battle began when one of the white soldiers raised __(9)__ gun and shot two Nez Perce Indians. __(10)__ do you think finally won?

1. **A** He
B Him
C His
D Himself

2. **A** their
B them
C themselves
D they

3. **A** he
B his
C him
D them

4. **A** Them
B Themselves
C They
D Their

5. **A** we
B us
C ourselves
D our

6. **A** we
B us
C our
D ourselves

7. **A** they
B themselves
C them
D their

8. **A** we
B us
C our
D ourselves

9. **A** their
B theirs
C his
D him

10. **A** Who
B Whose
C Whom
D Whomever

Writer's Corner

Snapshot

18 A **Case** indicates a noun or pronoun's use in a sentence. Nouns and pronouns have three cases: **nominative, objective,** and **possessive.** (pages 780–792)

18 B Common problems with pronouns include the misuse of *who* and *whom,* incomplete comparisons, and misuse of reflexive and intensive pronouns. (pages 793–800)

18 C The pronoun and its **antecedent** must agree in number and gender. (pages 801–805)

18 D Every personal pronoun should clearly refer to a specific antecedent to avoid unclear, missing, or confusing references. (pages 806–808)

CHAPTER 18

Power Rules

Use **subject** forms of pronouns in subject position. Use **object** forms of pronouns in object position. (pages 781–789)

Before Editing	After Editing
Darnel and *him* made the team.	Darnel and *he* made the team.
They will meet *we* at the campsite.	They will meet *us* at the campsite.

When using **sound-alikes,** choose the word with your intended meaning. (page 790)

Before Editing	After Editing
When can I see *you're* puppy? (*you're* is a contraction of *you are*)	When can I see *your* puppy? (*your* is the possessive form of *you*)
Their ready for the race to begin. (*their* is the possessive form of *they*)	*They're* ready for the race to begin. (*they're* is the contraction of *they are*)
Their is a spider on the counter. (*their* is the possessive form of *they*)	*There* is a spider on the counter. (*there* means *in that place*)
I think *its* almost time to leave. (*its* is the possessive form of *it*)	I think *it's* almost time to leave. (*it's* is a contraction of *it is*)

Editing Checklist

Use this checklist when editing your writing.

- ✓ Did I use nominative pronouns as subjects or predicate nominatives? (See pages 780–784.)
- ✓ Did I use objective pronouns as direct objects, indirect objects, or objects of prepositions? (See pages 785–786.)
- ✓ Did I use possessive pronouns to show ownership? (See pages 790–792.)
- ✓ Did I use *who* and *whom* correctly in questions? (See pages 793–796.)
- ✓ Did I use pronouns correctly when making comparisons? (See pages 797–798.)
- ✓ Did I use reflexive pronouns to show emphasis and intensive pronouns to emphasize nouns or pronouns in a sentence? (See pages 799–800.)
- ✓ Did I make each pronoun agree with its antecedent in number and gender? (See pages 801–805.)
- ✓ Did I make sure all pronouns have clear antecedents? (See pages 806–808.)

CHAPTER 18

Use the Power

Use pronouns to avoid repetition. When you use a pronoun to replace a noun, it must agree in gender and number. Use the following example to see how each pronoun agrees with its antecedent.

Matthew was in an auto accident. He has to use a wheelchair for a month. His friend Marta has been helping him get between classes, since they both have the same schedule. Yesterday Marta had an appointment, so she called Matthew to let him know she would not be able to help.

"Thanks for the warning," he said, "I'll probably ask Taquisha to help me out. Or maybe I will be able to get around on my own."

Revise a recent composition by adding pronouns.

CHAPTER 19

Subject and Verb Agreement

Gertrude Stein

How can you use subject-verb agreement to make the meaning of your writing clear?

Subject and Verb Agreement: Pretest 1

The first draft below contains several errors in subject and verb agreement. The first error, in which the singular verb *was* is replaced by the plural *were,* is corrected. How would you revise the draft to be sure all subjects and verbs agree?

Ernest Hemingway, F. Scott Fitzgerald, and Gertrude Stein ~~was~~ were part of a group of writers who chose to live and work in Europe following World War I. Disillusioned by the realities of war, these writers sets out for Paris and eventually become representatives of what we now call the "lost generation." Other Americans also seeked answers abroad, including Ezra Pound and T. S. Eliot. Some literary critics credits this group for ushering in the modern writing that replaced the elaborate style of Victorian writing.

During this time, writers abroad was freely developing their own voice. Hemingway does not shy away from writing about his generation's search for meaning in this new era. His stories also often addresses his time as a journalist in Spain and as an ambulance volunteer in Italy. Two of his most popular works, *The Sun Also Rises* and *A Farewell to Arms,* is about life during WWI and the years that followed.

Subject and Verb Agreement: Pretest 2

Directions

Write the letter of the best way to write the underlined word or words in each sentence. If an underlined part contains no error, write ***D.***

1. Most of the world's diamond supply originate in Africa.
2. A basket of oranges were sent to us from Florida.
3. Every stick and twig was gathered for the campfire.
4. Neither radar nor unmarked police cars has been eliminating speeding.
5. Has they left for Connecticut yet?

1. A were originated
B originates
C are originating
D No error

2. A was sent
B have been sent
C are sent
D No error

3. A were gathered
B are gathered
C being gathered
D No error

4. A eliminating
B are eliminating
C was eliminating
D No error

5. A Will they leave
B Did they left
C Have they left
D No error

Agreement of Subjects and Verbs Lesson 1

The subject and the verb of a sentence should fit as snugly as a hand in a glove. Subjects and verbs that fit together are said to be in **agreement.** This chapter will help you understand which ones fit together and which ones do not.

19 A **A verb must agree with its subject in number.**

19 A.1 **Number** is used to indicate whether a noun or a pronoun is singular or plural.

You know that nouns can be *singular* (one) or *plural* (more than one). The plurals of most nouns are formed by adding *-s* or *-es* to the singular form. A few nouns form their plurals irregularly; for example, *men* is the plural of *man.* Certain pronouns also form their plurals by changing form.

NOUNS		PRONOUNS	
Singular	**Plural**	**Singular**	**Plural**
diamond	diamonds	I	we
bus	buses	you	you
lady	ladies	he, she, it	they
child	children		
mouse	mice		
foot	feet		
goose	geese		
cactus	cacti		

Verbs in the present tense also have singular and plural forms. Verbs in the third person singular end in *-s* or *-es.* Most plural forms of verbs do *not* end in *-s* or *-es.*

Third Person Singular	(He, She, It) **runs.**
Other Forms	(I, You, We, They) **run.** (*I* and *you* are used with the plural form of *run.*)

In the following box are the singular and plural forms of the irregular verbs *be, have,* and *do* in the present tense and *be* in the past tense. Notice that *be* has irregular forms for both the singular and plural in the past tense as well.

PRESENT TENSE	
Singular	**Plural**
I **am, have, do**	we **are, have, do**
you **are, have, do**	you **are, have, do**
he, she, it **is, has, does**	they **are, have, do**

PAST TENSE	
Singular	**Plural**
I **was**	we **were**
you **were**	you **were**
he, she, it **was**	they **were**

Since a subject and a verb both have number, they must agree in a sentence.

19 A.2 A singular subject takes a singular verb. A plural subject takes a plural verb.

The diamond sparkles.
The city bus is late.
The child was here.
He has my jewelry.

The diamonds sparkle.
All the city buses are late.
The children were here.
They have my jewelry.

Be, have, and *do* are also often used as helping verbs. When they are, they must agree in number with the subject.

19 A.3 The first helping verb must agree in number with the subject.

Rob **is** buying a gift.
The men **have been** making a spaghetti dinner.
Mary Ellen **did** finish law school.

CHAPTER 19

Practice Your Skills

Making Subjects and Verbs Agree

Write the form of the verb in parentheses that agrees with each subject.

1. He (sings, sing).
2. Kids (smiles, smile).
3. Wayne (is, are) speaking.
4. The cats (was, were) fed.
5. The apples (is, are) bad.
6. Mom (has, have) cooked.
7. She (has, have) mine.
8. He (stirs, stir).
9. The bell (rings, ring).
10. Jan (whistles, whistle).
11. Bread (bakes, bake).
12. Liz (was, were) laughing.
13. They (has, have) helped.
14. Food (was, were) cleared.
15. They (has, have) eaten.
16. Pies (was, were) served.

Connect to Writing: Revising

Correcting Subject and Verb Agreement

Rewrite each sentence, making sure the subject and verb agree.

1. I has a chore during dinnertime.
2. Mom expect me to set the table each evening.
3. This responsibility are enjoyable for me.
4. The two forks belongs on the left side of the plate.
5. The glasses sits to the upper right of the plate.

Connect to Writing: Writing Sentences

Using Subject and Verb Agreement

Create your own sentences using the directions. Write a sentence that:

1. Tells about a household chore that is your responsibility.
2. Describes how you feel about doing this chore and how often you do it.
3. Includes the word *they* and the past tense of the verb *is*.
4. Includes the word *my* and the present tense of the verb *have*.

Interrupting Words

Agreement between a subject and a verb is usually easy to recognize when the subject and the verb are side by side. When a phrase or a clause interrupts them, you may mistakenly make the verb agree with a word close to it rather than with the subject.

19 A.4 The agreement of a verb and subject is not changed by any interrupting words.

Notice that the subjects and verbs in the following examples agree in number—regardless of the words that come between them.

Prepositional Phrase	The drums on the top shelf are mine. (The plural verb *are* agrees with the plural subject *drums,* even though *shelf* is closer to the verb.)
Participial Phrase	The instruments sitting by the door are waiting to be tuned. (*Are* agrees with *instruments,* not *door.*)
Negative Statement	The final performance, not the practices, is what Kim enjoys. (*Is* agrees with *performance,* not *practices.*)
Adjectival Clause	The drummers who attend the competition are excused from third period. (*Are* agrees with the word *drummers,* not with *competition.*)

Occasionally a prepositional phrase beginning with a compound preposition—such as *in addition to, as well as, along with,* or *together with*—will interrupt a subject and a verb. In this case, the verb still agrees with the subject, not the object of the preposition.

A snare drum, as well as some other instruments, was kept in the band closet.
(*Was* agrees with *drum,* not with *instruments.*)

Practice Your Skills

Making Interrupted Subjects and Verbs Agree

Write the subject in each sentence. Then write the form of the verb in parentheses that agrees with the subject.

1. The top membranes of a drum (is, are) called heads.
2. The constant motion of drumming (causes, cause) soreness in the hands.
3. The drum, as well as other instruments, (has, have) many ceremonial uses worldwide.
4. A drum made entirely of resonant solid materials (is, are) classified as an idiophone.
5. The drummers who are playing with Robert (is, are) sophomores.
6. The drums used in an orchestra (is, are) usually timpani.

7. The snare drum, as well as the bass drum, (is, are) played in marching bands.
8. The drumsticks wrapped with maroon tape (is, are) on the chair.
9. Many types of conga drums (come, comes) from Afro-Cuban origin.
10. Lessons from Randy (was, were) helpful in developing techniques.

Connect to Writing: Editing

Making Interrupted Subjects and Verbs Agree

Write the verb in each sentence. If the verb does not agree with the subject, write the correct form. If the verb does agree with the subject, write **C.**

1. The drums that were in the band closet looks old.
2. Training, as well as discipline, are needed to make a talented musician.
3. The shells of drums tends to be made of wood, metal, or pottery.
4. The instruments played by the marching band belong to the high school.
5. The tambourines of medieval Europe was traditionally played by a woman.

Check Point: Mixed Practice

Write the subject in each sentence. Then write the form of the verb in parentheses that agrees with the subject.

1. Some drums of Africa (was, were) believed to protect tribal royalty.
2. Experts in European history (says, say) that timpani were often associated with royalty.
3. Kevin, not his brothers, (hopes, hope) to buy some bongos this summer.
4. Only two percussionists in the school's marching band (was, were) chosen to attend the competition.
5. The drumsticks sold at that store (is, are) cheaper.
6. The Japanese tsuzumi drum (is, are) shaped like an hourglass.
7. Mr. Thurman, one of our band directors, (gives, give) motivating advice.
8. The darabuka, a goblet-shaped drum, (come, comes) from the Middle East.

Connect to Writing: Description

Making Subjects and Verbs Agree

Do you have a favorite instrument? Describe to a friend who is hearing impaired how the instrument sounds and which specific characteristics of the instrument appeal to you. Check your description for subject and verb agreement.

Common Agreement Problems

Lesson 2

Be aware of problems that may arise to cause confusion as you strive to maintain subject-verb agreement in your writing.

19 B **Compound subjects, indefinite pronouns as subjects, and subjects in inverted order are behind three common agreement problems.**

Compound Subjects

Remember the following two rules when making a verb agree with two or more subjects.

19 B.1 When subjects are joined by *or, nor, either/or,* or *neither/nor,* the verb agrees with the closer subject.

Either Donna or Rico was the presenter for book report day.
(*Was* agrees with the closer subject *Rico.*)

Poems or novels **are** described on book report day.
(*Are* agrees with the closer subject *novels.*)

This rule applies even when one subject is singular and the other is plural.

Neither the title nor the co-authors **were** mentioned before the presentation.
(*Were* agrees with the closer subject *co-authors*—even though *title* is singular.)

The second rule involving compound subjects is based on other conjunctions.

19 B.2 When subjects are joined by *and* or *both/and,* the verb is plural.

The conjunctions *and* and *both/and* always suggest more than one. Since more than one is plural, the verb must be plural also—whether the individual subjects are singular, plural, or a combination of singular and plural.

The written report and the oral presentation are graded together.
(Two things—the *report* and the *presentation*—are graded. The verb, therefore, must be plural to agree with both.)

Three tapes and a filmstrip were used as additional research for the report.
(Even though *filmstrip* is singular, the verb is still plural because the *filmstrip* and the *tapes*—together—were used as research.)

CHAPTER 19

There are exceptions to the second rule. Two subjects joined by *and* occasionally refer to only one person or one thing. In such a case, the verb must be singular.

The student and author was given a special award at the banquet.
(*Student* and *author* refer to the same person.)

Cheese and crackers was one of the appetizers.
(*Cheese* and *crackers* is considered one item.)

The words *every* and *each* are the basis of another exception. If one of these words comes before a compound subject that is joined by *and*, each subject is considered separately and the verb must be singular to agree.

Every student and teacher was invited to the banquet.

Each chair and bench was occupied.

CHAPTER 19

When You Write

When thinking about which verb agrees in number with a subject, remember this mnemonic phrase: Each and every *each* and *every* with a compound subject is followed by a singular verb.

Look back at a recent composition to be sure your subjects and verbs agree.

Practice Your Skills

Making Verbs Agree with Compound Subjects

Write the correct form of the verb in parentheses.

1. Neither the luggage nor the boys (is, are) ready to go.
2. Curvy roads, bumpy terrain, and warm weather often (make, makes) her carsick.
3. A map or good directions (is, are) needed for the trip.
4. Every brook and creek along the way (has, have) dried up during the drought.
5. Either a gas station or a convenience store (is, are) a good place to stop.
6. Ham and cheese (is, are) my favorite traveling snack.
7. The size of the car and its roomy seats (is, are) perfect for traveling.
8. Neither Kim nor the twins (is, are) traveling with us.

9. Yesterday the trees and the telephone wires along the highway (was, were) covered in ice.
10. Each child and parent (was, were) wearing a seatbelt.

Connect to Writing: **Editing**

Correcting Subject and Verb Agreement with Compound Subjects

Write the verb in each sentence. If the verb does not agree with the subject, write the correct form. If the verb does agree with the subject, write **C.**

1. Most adults and children enjoys traveling.
2. Neither the backseat nor the trunk have enough space to hold Lucy's suitcase.
3. Our travel agent, who also happens to be one of our aunts, are also our neighbor.
4. Your steering and braking were cautious.

CHAPTER 19

Indefinite Pronouns as Subjects

Indefinite pronouns have number. Some are singular, some are plural, and some can be either singular or plural.

19 B.3 A verb must agree in number with an indefinite pronoun used as a subject.

COMMON INDEFINITE PRONOUNS	
Singular	another, anybody, anyone, anything, each, either, everybody, everyone, everything, much, neither, nobody, no one, one, somebody, someone, something
Plural	both, few, many, others, several
Singular/Plural	all, any, most, none, some

A singular verb agrees with a singular indefinite pronoun, and a plural verb agrees with a plural indefinite pronoun.

Singular Either of the picnic tables is fine for our gathering.

Plural Both of my coolers have delicious food and drinks in them.

The number of an indefinite pronoun in the last group below is determined by the object of the preposition that follows the pronoun in the sentence.

Singular or Plural

Most of my picnic basket is empty.

Most of the deviled eggs **were** eaten by Sam.

None of my family **has** eaten.

None of my friends **have** eaten.

Practice Your Skills

Making Verbs Agree with Indefinite Pronoun Subjects

Write the subject in each sentence. Next to each, write the form of the verb in parentheses that agrees with the subject.

1. None of the salad (has, have) been eaten.
2. Anyone in the junior class (is, are) invited.
3. Some of the afternoon (was, were) windy.
4. Many of my friends (has, have) kites.
5. A few of our dishes (was, were) broken at the picnic.
6. All of the girls at the picnic (was, were) hungry.
7. Some of the drinks (was, were) warmed by the sun.
8. Each of those drinks (was, were) once cold.
9. No one in the group (likes, like) deviled eggs.
10. Not one of the dogs there (was, were) misbehaving.

Connect to Writing: Revising

Making Indefinite Pronoun Subjects and Verbs Agree

Rewrite the following sentences, correcting errors in subject-verb agreement. If a sentence is correct, write **C**.

1. Everyone in my neighborhood are at the picnic today.
2. Neither of the Smiths were planning to stay home.
3. Any of the cooks are capable of grilling great burgers.
4. Most of my friends has brought a Frisbee or soccer ball.
5. Everybody in the neighborhood are planning to attend next year's picnic.

Subjects in Inverted Order

A subject usually comes before the verb in a sentence. Sometimes, a sentence is written in **inverted order,** with the subject following the verb or part of the verb phrase. Regardless of where a subject is located in a sentence, the verb must agree with it.

19 B.4 The subject and the verb of an **inverted sentence** must agree in number.

When you are looking for the subject in an inverted sentence, turn the sentence around to its natural order. To have the sentence make sense, you must occasionally drop *here* or *there* when you put the sentence into its natural order.

Inverted Order	In Oak Park, Illinois, is the birthplace of Ernest Hemingway. (The *birthplace* of Ernest Hemingway ***is*** in Oak Park, Illinois.)
Question	Has Hemingway's biography been read by your literary group? (Hemingway's *biography* **has** *been read* by your literary group.)
	Do Hemingway's works still have relevance? (Hemingway's *works* still **do** have relevance.)
Sentences Beginning with *Here* and *There*	Here is *The Old Man and the Sea.* (*The Old Man and the Sea* **is** here.)
	There are many Hemingway novels in our library. (Many Hemingway *novels* **are** in our library.)

You can learn more about inverted sentences on pages 659–660.

Practice Your Skills

Making Verbs Agree with Subjects in Inverted Order

Write the correct form of the verb in parentheses.

1. Serving as an ambulance driver in Italy during World War I (was, were) Ernest Hemingway.
2. There (is, are) the place where he was injured.
3. Where (was, were) his first newspaper job?
4. There (is, are) some years when Hemingway was a correspondent during two later wars.

CHAPTER 19

5. (Was, Were) other famous authors journalists too?
6. After World War I, Hemingway and his wife (was, were) living in Paris.
7. Here (comes, come) the other expatriate writers to live in Paris.
8. (Do, Does) many other writers move to Paris?
9. There (is, are) where Hemingway met Ezra Pound.
10. In many of his novels (was, were) examples of his adventurous spirit.

Connect to Writing: Editing

Correcting Subject and Verb Agreement in Inverted Sentences

Write the verb in each sentence. If the verb does not agree with the subject, write the correct form. If the verb does agree with the subject, write **C**.

1. Does his first novel or his last novel describe the bullfighting life?
2. There is many simple, economical sentences in Hemingway's stories.
3. In his stories was many deprived, cynical characters.
4. How does Ali and Paul like the book they are reading?
5. There is several short stories in the *Hemingway Reader.*

CHAPTER 19

Check Point: Mixed Practice

Find and write the verbs that do not agree with their subjects. Then write them correctly. If a sentence is correct, write **C**.

1. One of the largest tomatoes from their garden this year weighs two pounds.
2. The rows of vegetables was full of zucchini and beets.
3. A fruit I wish we could grow in the garden are bananas.
4. There are two pairs of garden gloves, but people are always losing them.
5. Both Sharon and Doug pulls weeds in the garden.
6. Our guidebook about gardens have been read so often, the cover is worn.
7. Last year a huge bell pepper were grown in our garden.
8. Are there documented proof that the peppers were the city's largest?
9. The success of summer gardens in Texas are dependent upon watering techniques.
10. Much of my garden holds tomatoes.
11. A few of my friends cans the tomatoes.
12. The squash plants in that row have orange blossoms.
13. Their vines has wandered through the corn.
14. Doug or his brothers does plan to plant radishes before spring is finished.

Other Agreement Problems — Lesson 3

19 C **Other situations that cause agreement problems include contractions, collective nouns, words expressing time, and titles.**

Collective Nouns

You may recall that a **collective noun** names a group of people or things. A collective noun may be either singular or plural—depending on how it is used in a sentence.

COMMON COLLECTIVE NOUNS			
band	congregation	flock	orchestra
class	crew	gang	swarm
colony	crowd	herd	team
committee	family	league	tribe

19 C.1 Use a singular verb with a collective noun subject that is thought of as a unit. Use a plural verb with a collective noun subject that is thought of as individual parts.

The orchestra is playing a new symphony.
(The orchestra is working together as a whole unit in the sentence. As a result, the verb is singular.)

The orchestra are taking their places in the pit.
(The members of the orchestra are acting independently in this sentence—each one taking his or her own seat. As a result, the verb is plural.)

Words Expressing Amounts or Times

Subjects that express amounts, measurements, weights, or times usually are considered single units. However, they often have plural forms.

19 C.2 A subject that expresses an amount, a measurement, a weight, or a time is usually considered singular and takes a singular verb.

CHAPTER 19

Quantity	**Five** miles **is** the distance to the performance hall. (one unit of distance)
	One hundred dollars **was** donated to the symphony. (one sum of money)
	Two thirds of the choir **has** arrived. (one part of a group)
Time	Six **months is** needed to learn the music. (one period of time)

If an amount, a measurement, a weight, or a time is being thought about in its individual parts, the verb must be plural. Notice how the following subjects tell *how many*.

Eight dollars were scattered on the donation table.

Two hours have passed quickly.

The Number of, A Number of

Although the expressions in the title above are very similar, the adjective *the* takes a singular verb and the article *a* takes a plural verb.

19 C.3 Use a singular verb with ***the number of*** and a plural verb with ***a number of.***

The number **of** men in the orchestra **has** increased greatly over the past two years. (singular)

A number **of** musicians **were** noticed after the performance. (plural)

Singular Nouns That Have a Plural Form

Some words *look* plural because they end in *-s.* They are singular, however, because they name single things, such as one type of disease or one area of knowledge. Some examples follow.

SINGULAR NOUNS WITH PLURAL FORMS			
mathematics	economics	gallows	mumps
news	physics	molasses	social studies

CHAPTER 19

19 C.4 Use a singular verb with certain subjects that are plural in form but singular in meaning.

Gymnastics is my favorite form of exercise.

Mumps is a very uncomfortable illness.

There are similar words, however, that are usually plural, and some others that can be either singular or plural—depending on how they are used in a sentence. If you are confused by a particular noun, it sometimes helps to check the dictionary.

SIMILAR NOUNS	
Usually Plural	barracks, data, eyeglasses, media, pliers, scissors, shears, slacks, trousers
Singular/Plural	acoustics, athletics, headquarters, politics

The pliers are rusty. (plural)

Politics is usually a controversial subject.
(singular—the science of government)

Politics are on his mind day and night.
(plural—political practices or policies)

When a word that is usually plural is preceded by *pair of,* the verb is singular because it agrees with the singular noun *pair.*

Singular	Your pair of slacks **is** pressed.
Plural	Your slacks **are** pressed.

CHAPTER 19

Practice Your Skills

Making Subjects and Verbs Agree

Write the correct form of the verb in parentheses.

1. Three fourths of the orchestra (was, were) present for the rehearsal.
2. The news of the musician's illness (was, were) not good.
3. The mumps (is, are) serious enough to keep him from performing this weekend.
4. The number of musicians getting sick lately (is, are) increasing.
5. The performance committee (is, are) discussing where to take the next tour.
6. My extra pair of violin bows (is, are) broken too.
7. Miguel's percussion group (practice, practices) every Wednesday evening.
8. Thirty-five years (is, are) the average age of the musicians in our orchestra.

Connect to Writing: Revising

Correcting Subject and Verb Agreement

Rewrite the following sentences, correcting errors in subject and verb agreement. If a sentence is correct, write **C.**

1. Are twenty-five dollars too much to pay to see the symphony?
2. Ten percent of the orchestra are the percussion section.
3. The orchestra are still debating the contract terms.

Doesn't or *Don't*?

Doesn't and *don't* are contractions. To avoid a mistake, always say the two words of a contraction separately when checking for agreement with a subject. Also keep in mind which contractions are singular and which are plural.

CONTRACTIONS	
Singular	does**n't**, has**n't**, is**n't**, was**n't**
Plural	do**n't**, have**n't**, are**n't**, were**n't**

19 C.5 The verb part of a contraction must agree in number with the subject.

> Mr. Barry **does**n't usually assign homework on Friday.
>
> We **do**n't know when the report is due.

In addition to *doesn't* and *don't,* the verb part of all contractions must agree with the subject.

> The junior class **has**n't had their prom yet.
>
> The juniors **have**n't eaten lunch today.

Subjects with Linking Verbs

A predicate nominative follows a linking verb and renames or identifies the subject. Sometimes a subject and its predicate nominative will not have the same number. Still, the verb always agrees with the subject.

19 C.6 A verb agrees with the subject of a sentence, not with the predicate nominative.

Poems are Sarah's favorite literary form.
(The plural verb *are* agrees with the plural subject *poems*—even though the predicate nominative *form* is singular.)

Sarah's favorite literary form is poems.
(In this sentence *is* agrees with the subject *form*—not with the plural predicate nominative *poems*.)

CHAPTER 19

When You Write

When you read a sentence aloud and the predicate nominative and the subject sound awkward, try to rewrite it to make the predicate nominative and subject agree.

Awkward	Sarah's favorite literary **form is poems.**
Better	Sarah's favorite literary **form is poetry.**

Look back at a recent composition to be sure predicate nominatives and their subjects do not sound awkward.

You can learn more about linking verbs on pages 632–634.

Titles

Many titles are composed of several words, some of which may be plural in form. A title, nevertheless, is singular and takes a singular verb because it is the name of one book or one work of art. Names of businesses and organizations that include more than one word are also considered singular.

19 C.7 A title is singular and takes a singular verb.

Works of Robert Frost contains many of my favorite poems.

The Library of Congress has a poetry consultant called the Poet Laureate.

Practice Your Skills

Making Subjects and Verbs Agree

Write the correct form of the verb in parentheses.

1. "Mushrooms" (is, are) the title of a poem by Sylvia Plath.

2. Trees (is, are) his favorite poetry topic.

3. Adam (doesn't, don't) want to read his poem aloud.

4. The last stanza (hasn't, haven't) been finished yet.

5. One characteristic of the haiku (is, are) unrhymed lines.

6. The League of Poets (is, are) holding its annual meeting at the library.

7. Maria's chief concern then (was, were) her lost poetry books and files.

Connect to Writing: Editing

Making the Subject and Verb Agree

Write the verb in each sentence. If the verb does not agree with the subject, write the correct form. If the verb does agree with the subject, write **C**.

1. The lines in a haiku is specific lengths.

2. My brother don't like to read his poetry aloud.

3. "The Road Not Taken" are the name of a famous poem by Robert Frost.

4. Hasn't anyone read his work?

5. Poems is created in many styles.

Connect to Speaking and Writing: Basic Vocabulary

Using Subjects and Verbs that Agree

Go over the meanings of the terms *compound subject, indefinite pronoun, inverted order, contraction,* and *linking verbs.* Then think about the impact these kinds of constructions can have on the verbs you use when writing. Next, write three sentences, each of which contains one of the following:

- a compound subject
- an indefinite pronoun as a subject
- a subject that begins "A number of."

Read your sentences to a partner, but leave out the verb and ask your partner to supply the missing word.

Check Point: Mixed Practice

Write the verbs that do not agree with the subjects. Then write those verbs correctly.

(1) There is nearly 3,500 pieces of space debris orbiting the earth. **(2)** These include spent rockets, fragments of wrecked satellites, and miscellaneous nuts, bolts, and ceramic tiles. **(3)** Satellites that are functional, as well as junk, is catalogued and tracked by the North American Aerospace Defense Command, NORAD.

(4) There is good reasons for monitoring this space trash. **(5)** For one thing, even a chunk of metal as small as a grapefruit become a deadly weapon if it falls to the earth. **(6)** More frightening still, a piece of space litter on a radar screen could easily be mistaken for an enemy missile.

(7) The chances of real danger, however, is slim. **(8)** Some of the many recorded objects now in orbit is in "deep space." **(9)** At approximately 3,000 miles up, atmospheric drag and gravitational pull is minimal. **(10)** The pieces closer to the earth fall out of orbit at a rate of more than one a day. **(11)** Most of the pieces burns up on reentry. **(12)** One of the most memorable exceptions were *Skylab,* whose pieces landed in Western Australia and in the Indian Ocean in July 1979. **(13)** It were described as fiery rainfall.

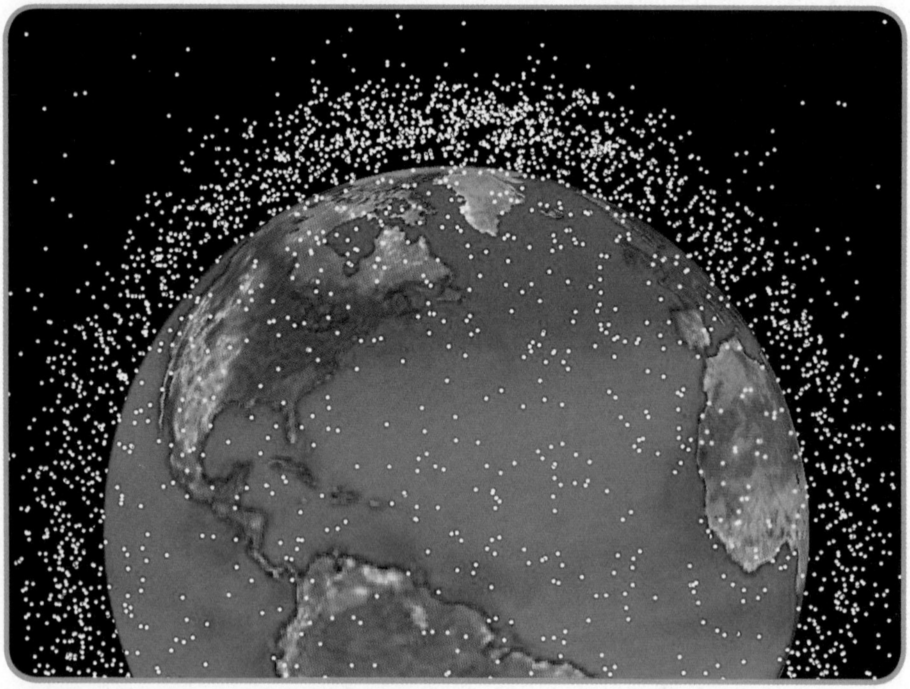

Assess Your Learning

Making Subjects and Verbs Agree

Write the correct form of each verb in parentheses.

1. The quarterback and the halfback (has, have) worked together for weeks on that new play.
2. Each magazine and newspaper (was, were) returned to its place after study hall.
3. Neither the Harris brothers nor José (is, are) playing in today's game.
4. Approximately 26 miles (is, are) the distance run by Olympic marathon runners.
5. The committee (was, were) finally able to agree on the subject.
6. The outcome of the class elections (is, are) being announced at the assembly today.
7. There (has, have) been three sites mentioned for the Junior Prom.
8. Mathematics (has, have) always interested me.
9. In the back of the drawer (was, were) the missing argyle socks.
10. Tanya (doesn't, don't) look as though she has just jogged five miles.
11. Encyclopedias (is, are) filled with useful information.
12. Neither of the morning flights (is, are) on schedule.
13. We and she (has, have) always wanted to visit Nantucket.
14. (Has, Have) the train arrived yet?
15. An elegant science (is, are) physics.

Editing for Agreement

Rewrite the paragraph, correcting any mistakes in subject-verb agreement.

(1) Hawaii are actually a chain of 132 islands, although most people considers only the eight easternmost islands as making up the state. **(2)** Most of Hawaii's inhabitants lives on Oahu, where Honolulu, the capital, be located. **(3)** Polynesians once comprised the bulk of the native population; however, people of Samoan, Filipino, Korean, Japanese, and Chinese ancestry has contributed as well to its ethnic makeup. **(4)** This tropical paradise were unknown to the rest of the world until Captain James Cook discovered it in 1778. **(5)** Captain Cook called the islands the Sandwich Islands after the Earl of Sandwich in England. **(6)** Today anyone visiting the Hawaiian Islands actually visit one of the United States—a state rich in resources, history, and heritage. **(7)** Traditional customs like the hula dance, the luau, and the lei, for example, is recognized throughout the world.

Writing Sentences

Write five sentences that follow the directions below. Then underline each subject once and each verb twice.

1. Write a sentence that includes a sum of money as the subject.
2. Write a sentence that includes the title of a book as the subject.
3. Write a question.
4. Write a sentence that includes *doesn't* or *don't.*
5. Write a sentence that includes a collective noun as the subject.

Subject and Verb Agreement: Posttest

Directions

Write the letter of the best way to write the underlined word or words in each sentence. If an underlined part contains no error, write ***D.***

1. One of the oak trees in our backyard <u>were struck</u> by lightning last night.
2. The iridescent colors reflected in the mirror <u>were</u> breathtaking.
3. A number of hockey sticks <u>was left</u> on the locker room floor after the game.
4. <u>Don't</u> he drive a red pickup truck?
5. Either Amanda or her sisters <u>goes</u> to the meeting every weekend.

1. A was struck
B are being struck
C are struck
D No error

2. A is
B be
C was
D No error

3. A are left
B is left
C were left
D No error

4. A Hasn't
B Isn't
C Doesn't
D No error

5. A is going
B go
C has gone
D No error

Writer's Corner

Snapshot

19 A A **verb** must agree with its **subject** in number. (pages 816–820)

19 B **Compound subjects, indefinite pronouns as subjects,** and **subjects in inverted order** can pose agreement problems. (pages 821–826)

19 C Other situations that cause agreement problems include **contractions, collective nouns, words expressing time,** and **titles.** (pages 827–834)

Power Rules

Be sure that every sentence has a subject and predicate. **The subject and verb must agree.** (pages 814–839)

Before Editing	After Editing
Each player *hope* to impress the scouts.	Each player *hopes* to impress the scouts.
The crowd at the parade *grow* bigger each year.	The crowd at the parade *grows* bigger each year.
Tran and Wayan *rebuilds* computers.	Tran and Wayan *rebuild* computers.
The class *need* to agree on an outing.	The class *needs* to agree on an outing.

CHAPTER 19

Editing Checklist

Use this checklist when editing your writing.

- ✓ Did I make singular subjects take singular verbs and plural subjects take plural verbs? (See pages 816–820.)
- ✓ Did I make verbs agree with compound subjects? (See pages 821–823.)
- ✓ Did I use singular verbs with singular indefinite pronouns and plural verbs with plural indefinite pronouns? (See pages 823–824.)
- ✓ Did I make subjects and verbs in inverted order agree? (See pages 825–826.)
- ✓ Did I use verbs that agreed with collective nouns? (See page 827.)
- ✓ Did I make verbs agree with singular nouns that have plural forms? (See pages 829–830.)

Use the Power

Use your knowledge of academic language as you check for subject-verb agreement problems. Most of the problems arise because the subject is not accurately identified, either because of compounds, inverted order, contractions, or other interfering elements. Using your knowledge of academic language, mentally clear away all the parts of a sentence except the subject and verb. Then you'll be able to match a singular subject with a singular verb, and a plural subject with a plural verb.

The aroma of freshly baked pies and oatmeal cookies drift^s through the cozy house.

Write about a dessert you could eat anytime, anywhere. Describe what it looks like, smells like, tastes like, and how it feels in your mouth. Be sure your subjects and verbs agree.

Using Adjectives and Adverbs

How can you use adjectives and adverbs to show precise relationships among your ideas?

Using Adjectives and Adverbs: Pretest 1

The following first draft contains several errors in the use of adjectives and adverbs. The first error is corrected. How would you revise the draft to correct the remaining errors?

For more than 100 years, the Nobel Foundation has been recognizing the ~~most~~ best individual achievements in the fields of physics, chemistry, physiology or medicine, literature, and peace. The Nobel Prize is the more widely known award in the world. Alfred Nobel bequeathed his substantial wealth to the establishment of the Nobel Prize. He wanted people recognized for their greatest contributions to humanity. His family couldn't scarcely believe his last will and testament. They had few interest in the goodly works of others. Eventually, Nobel's wishes were heeded, and the Nobel Foundation was established.

The first Nobel Prizes were awarded in 1901. Since then, the intelligentest people in the world have won the award. Nelson Mandela may be the amazingest person to win the Nobel Peace Prize. My favoritest author, William Faulkner, won the Nobel Prize in Literature in 1949. Would you rather win the Nobel Peace Prize or the Nobel Prize for Literature?

CHAPTER 20

Using Adjectives and Adverbs: Pretest 2

Directions

Read the passage and choose the word or group of words that belongs in each underlined space. Write the letter of the correct answer.

Lizards and salamanders are both cold-blooded, which means that they cannot keep their bodies much __(1)__ than their surroundings. Because they are __(2)__ to control their body temperatures, lizards live __(3)__ in the __(4)__ areas of the country where the ground never freezes. Those that make their homes in __(5)__ areas dig burrows and hibernate in winter. Lizards, however, thrive in the tropics and in __(6)__ desert areas. Should the sun become __(7)__ than they can stand, they lie in the shade or go underground. Lizards vary __(8)__ in size, although most range between __(9)__ inches and a foot or so. Monitor lizards tend to be __(10)__ large.

1. A warmest
B warmer
C more warm
D warm

2. A able
B less able
C unable
D more able

3. A mostly
B not hardly
C seldom
D never

4. A less temperate
B seldom temperate
C least temperate
D temperate

5. A coldest
B most cold
C colder
D more colder

6. A dry
B drier
C most dry
D driest

7. A most hottest
B hotter
C hottest
D hot

8. A less greatly
B more greatly
C greatly
D great

9. A more fewer
B fewest
C fewer
D a few

10. A quite
B never
C seldom
D ever

Comparison of Adjectives and Adverbs Lesson 1

Both adjectives and adverbs have more than one form. The additional forms are used when two or more people or things are being compared. Most adjectives and adverbs show three degrees of comparison: the **positive,** the **comparative,** and the **superlative**.

20 A Adjectives and adverbs are modifiers. Most modifiers show degrees of comparison by changing their form.

When no comparison is being made, the **positive degree** is used. It is the basic form of an adjective or an adverb.

Adjective	This maple tree is **tall.**
Adverb	Jerome climbs **efficiently.**
	Roy **efficiently** climbs trees.

When two people, things, or actions are being compared, the **comparative degree** is used. The comparative form varies, depending on the adjective or adverb being used. Notice that *–er* is added to *tall* and that *more* is used with *efficiently.*

Adjective	This maple tree is **taller** than the oak tree in the front yard.
Adverb	Jerome climbs rocks and trees **more efficiently** than Roy.
	Jerome **more efficiently** climbs the maple tree than Roy.

When more than two people, things, or actions are being compared, the **superlative degree** is used. Notice that *–est* is added to *tall* and that *most* is used with *efficiently.*

Adjective	This tree is the **tallest** tree in the neighborhood.
Adverb	Of all the kids in the park, Jerome climbs the **most efficiently.**

Below are examples of the three degrees of comparison.

Positive	I study **hard** to get **good** grades. (*Hard* is an adverb and *good* is an adjective).
Comparative	He studies **harder** to get **better** grades.
Superlative	She studies **hardest** to get the **best** grades.

Regular Comparisons

Most adjectives and adverbs form their comparative and superlative degrees the same way. The comparative and superlative forms of most modifiers are determined by the number of syllables an adjective or adverb has.

One-Syllable Modifiers

20 A.1 Add *–er* to form the comparative degree and *–est* to form the superlative degree of one-syllable modifiers.

ONE-SYLLABLE MODIFIERS		
Positive	**Comparative**	**Superlative**
thick	thicker	thickest
strong	stronger	strongest
fast	faster	fastest

CHAPTER 20

Two-Syllable Modifiers

Some two-syllable modifiers use *more* and *most* to form the comparative and superlative degrees because they would sound awkward or would be impossible to pronounce if *–er* or *–est* was added. The *more* and *most* forms are also used for all adverbs that end in *–ly*. If you are not sure how to form the comparative and superlative degrees of a two-syllable modifier, you should check a dictionary.

20 A.2 Use *–er* or ***more*** to form the comparative and *–est* or ***most*** to form the superlative degree of two-syllable modifiers.

TWO-SYLLABLE MODIFIERS		
Positive	**Comparative**	**Superlative**
busy	busier	busiest
playful	more playful	most playful
often	more often	most often
brightly	more brightly	most brightly

Three-Syllable Modifiers

Modifiers with three or more syllables always form their comparative and superlative degrees by using *more* and *most*.

20 A.3 Use ***more*** to form the comparative and ***most*** to form the superlative degree of modifiers with three or more syllables.

MODIFIERS WITH THREE OR MORE SYLLABLES		
Positive	**Comparative**	**Superlative**
talented	more talented	most talented
convenient	more convenient	most convenient
nervously	more nervously	most nervously

CHAPTER 20

Less and *least* are used to form negative comparisons.

NEGATIVE COMPARISONS		
Positive	**Comparative**	**Superlative**
talented	less talented	least talented
convenient	less convenient	least convenient
nervously	less nervously	least nervously

Irregular Comparisons

20 A.4 Never add ***–er*** and ***–est*** to the comparative and superlative degrees of these irregular modifiers.

IRREGULAR MODIFIERS		
Positive	**Comparative**	**Superlative**
bad/badly/ill	worse	worst
good/well	better	best
little	less	least
many/much	more	most

Practice Your Skills

Comparing with Modifiers

Write each modifier and its comparative and superlative forms.

1. warm
2. steadily
3. heavy
4. spectacular
5. bad
6. fast
7. great
8. easily
9. good
10. quietly

Practice Your Skills

Using the Correct Form of Comparison

Write the correct form of the modifier in parentheses.

1. Which of the two paths to the beach is (closer, closest)?
2. Jacob is the (slower, slowest) of all the windsurfers.
3. That is the (quieter, quietest) surf I have ever heard.
4. Which of the two lifeguard towers is (nearer, nearest)?
5. The seagulls are (noisier, noisiest) of all.
6. *The Sun* is the (more, most) seaworthy of the two boats.
7. The crab is the (more, most) interesting creature here.
8. Of the three beaches, which one do you like (more, most)?
9. Is your beach bag (heavier, heaviest) than my bag?
10. I use my beach towel (less, least) than my beach chair.

Power Your Language: Adjectives Come Lately

Most adjectives come before the noun or the pronoun they modify. Sometimes, however, they follow the noun or the pronoun. Notice in the following sentence how Kurt Vonnegut uses adjectives in his story "Harrison Bergeron."

> "Even as I stand here—" he bellowed, "crippled, hobbled, sickened—I am a greater ruler than any man who ever lived!"

The highlighted adjectives might be called "adjectives come lately" because they come after the noun they describe. Since they are "extra" details, there is punctuation before them, usually a comma or a dash.

Check Point: Mixed Practice

Write the correct form of the modifier in parentheses.

1. Elaine can tread water (longer, longest) than Erika.
2. Which of those two crabs did you like (better, best)?
3. I think the temperature is (higher, highest) now than it was an hour ago.
4. Of all the state's beautiful beaches, this one is the (more, most) popular.
5. Sun damage is (worse, worst) during the midday hours than during any other time of day.
6. Sunscreen is used (more, most) widely by vacationers on the beach this year than last year.
7. Charlene is the (friendlier, friendliest) of all the beach volleyball players.
8. Of the three waves you surfed, which seemed (more, most) challenging?
9. That lifeguard can run (faster, fastest) than Jerry.
10. I found the (more, most) beautiful shells of all on Captiva Island.
11. Of all the shells we collected, I like the white scallop (less, least).
12. Sanibel is (farther, farthest) south than Captiva.
13. The biking is (best, better) than the canoeing.
14. The gulf waters are the (bluer, bluest) in the world.

Connect to Writing:

Paragraph of Comparison and Contrast

Write a short paragraph in which you compare and contrast two summer vacation activities you have engaged in. You might compare and contrast swimming at the beach with riding bikes or playing baseball with playing soccer. Decide which activity you like the best, giving reasons for your choice. Use the correct form of modifiers as you make your comparison.

Connect to Writing: Content-Based Vocabulary

Using Adjectives and Adverbs in Comparisons

Write an explanatory paragraph describing what you have learned about the three degrees of comparison in adjectives and adverbs: positive, comparative, and superlative. Write a short definition of each degree of comparison in your own words. Then write four sentences, one using an adjective in the positive degree, one using an adverb in the comparative degree, and one each using an adjective and an adverb in the superlative degree,.

Problems with Comparisons — Lesson 2

20 B **When using adjectives and adverbs for comparison, avoid making double comparisons, illogical comparisons, and comparisons of members of a group to themselves.**

Double Comparisons

Use only *one* method of forming the comparative and superlative degrees of a modifier. Using both methods simultaneously results in a **double comparison.**

20 B.1 Do not use both *–er* and ***more*** to form the comparative degree, or both *–est* and ***most*** to form the superlative degree of modifiers.

Double Comparison	This exam is **more harder** than the last one.
Correct	This exam is **harder** than the last one.
Double Comparison	The last day of class is the **most happiest** day of my life!
Correct	The last day of class is the **happiest** day of my life!

CHAPTER 20

Illogical Comparisons

When you write a comparison, be sure you compare two or more similar things. When you compare different things, the comparison is illogical.

20 B.2 Compare only items of a similar kind.

Illogical Comparison	Seniors' **exams** are more difficult than **sophomores.** (Exams are being compared with sophomores.)
Logical Comparison	Seniors' **exams** are more difficult than sophomores' **exams.** (Seniors' exams are being compared to similar exams.)
Illogical Comparison	The **material** in the final exam for astronomy is harder than the weekly **quiz.** (Material is being compared to quiz.)
Logical Comparison	The **material** in the final exam for astronomy is harder than the **material** in the weekly quiz. (Exam material is being compared to similar material.)

Other and Else in Comparisons

Sometimes in your writing you will compare one or more people or things with other people or things. When you make such comparisons, be sure you do not appear to compare people or things with themselves.

20 B.3 Add ***other*** or ***else*** when comparing a member of a group with the rest of the group.

Incorrect	That test is longer than any exam in our biology book. (Since the test is an exam, it is being compared with itself.)
Correct	That test is longer than any **other** exam in our biology book. (By adding *other,* the test is now being compared only with the other exams.)
Incorrect	Kim has made more *A*'s this semester than anyone in the class. (Since Kim is a student in the class, she is being compared with herself.)
Correct	Kim has made more *A*'s this semester than anyone **else** in the class. (By adding the word *else,* Kim is now being compared only with the other students in the class.)

CHAPTER 20

Practice Your Skills

Recognizing Mistakes with Comparisons

Write **C** if the comparison in the sentence is correct or ***I*** if the comparison is incorrect. Rewrite the incorrect sentences.

1. Grand Canyon National Park's size is larger than my hometown.
2. The canyon's history goes back farther than America's history.
3. The geysers are more old than any of the park's natural wonders.
4. This year's group is more determined to hike the canyon than last year's group was.
5. Our family's trip to the Grand Canyon was more enjoyabler than the Bryans'.
6. Our tour guide's donkeys are tougher than any pack animals in the area.
7. I believe the Grand Canyon's geological features are more interesting than Yellowstone National Park's geological features.
8. One year the Grand Canyon National Park attracted more visitors than any national park.

Connect to Writing: Descriptive Paragraph

Using Adjectives and Adverbs

Imagine you have just returned from two rafting trips. One trip took you down the Colorado River through the Grand Canyon. The other journey led you down a peaceful river or lake in your own state. Describe what you experienced and how the two trips were different. Use vivid adjectives and adverbs, as well as proper comparisons.

Check Point: Mixed Practice

Rewrite the following sentences, correcting each mistake in the use of comparisons.

1. Wilbur Wright's birthday was earlier than his brother.
2. Is their aviation story more famous than any American inventor?
3. When they were boys, Wilbur and Orville were better at kite-flying than the neighborhood boys.
4. They made a second toy helicopter that was more larger than their first toy helicopter.
5. I read that the Wright brothers invented the first practical airplane before any inventor.
6. Their idea for designing airplane wings in a wind tunnel was more better than other specialists.
7. In 1902, their glider flew successfuller than professionally engineered gliders.
8. Their most earliest engine-powered flight flew in 1903.
9. The most successfullest flight lasted 12 seconds in the air.
10. At Kitty Hawk the Wrights proved that planes could be balanced most best by pilots, rather than by built-in engineering devices.

Problems with Modifiers Lesson 3

20 C **Be aware of special problems when using adjectives and adverbs. Know whether to use an adjective or adverb, *good* or *well,* or *bad* or *badly.* Be alert for double negatives.**

Adjective or Adverb?

Adjectives are usually easy to recognize because they answer the following questions.

Which One? She moved the **sturdy** hurdle off the track.

What Kind? The stadium crowd was **large** and **friendly.**

How Many? The runners ran **four** laps.

How Much? The runners' **extensive** practice led to success.

Some verbs—including *grew* and *felt*—can be either linking verbs or action verbs. When they are used as linking verbs, they are often followed by an adjective.

Linking Verb The relay baton felt very **heavy.**
(*Felt* is used as a linking verb.)

Action Verb Tim felt blindly for the baton.
(*Felt* is used as an action verb.)

You can learn more about linking verbs on pages 632–633. See pages 632–633 for a complete list of additional linking verbs.

You may recall that adverbs describe verbs, adjectives, and other adverbs. Because adverbs can be placed almost anywhere in a sentence, you can ask the questions on the next page to find them.

Where?	The sprinter ran **back** to her place.
When?	Our team won the relay **today.**
How?	He jumped out of the blocks **quickly.**
To What Extent?	The winner was **extremely** fast in the 200-meter race.
	The crowd cheered **very** loudly when our team won.

Because so many adverbs end in *–ly,* they are usually easy to recognize. Remember that a few adjectives—such as *daily* and *early*—also end in *–ly.*

Adverb	The tired players act **lively.** (*Lively* tells how the players act.)
Adjective	The **lively** team cheered all the way home. (*Lively* tells what kind of team it was.)

A few words—such as *first, hard, high, late,* and *long*—are the same whether they are used as an adverb or an adjective.

Adverb	The team practices **late** on Wednesday nights. (*Late* tells when the team practices.)
Adjective	The **late** practice helped the runners improve their speed. (*Late* tells what kind of practice it was.)

Connect to Speaking and Listening: Classroom Materials

Using Adjectives and Adverbs in Comparisons

Discuss with a partner the difference between adjectives and adverbs. What questions does an adjective answer? What questions does an adverb answer? In turn, create sentences that use the words *high, low, late, long, wide,* and *early,* asking your partner to identify whether each is used as an adverb or an adjective. Decide together if each answer was correct, and why or why not.

Good or *Well*?

Good is always an adjective. *Well* is usually used as an adverb. *Well* is used as an adjective when it means "in good health" or "satisfactory."

20 C.1 Use *good* as an adjective; use *well* as an adverb unless it means "in good health" or "satisfactory."

Adjective	Earl is a **good** runner.
Adverb	Earl runs **well.**
Adjective	Earl finally feels **well.** (in good health)

Bad or *Badly*?

Bad is an adjective and often follows a linking verb. *Badly* is used as an adverb.

20 C.2 Use *bad* as an adjective; use *badly* as an adverb.

Adjective	The sweaty running shoes smelled **bad.**
Adverb	He took the loss **badly.**

When You Speak and Write

In casual conversations, it is acceptable to use *bad* or *badly* after the verb *feel.* In formal writing, however, always use *bad* as an adjective and *badly* as an adverb.

In Writing	I feel bad about the misunderstanding.
In Conversation	I feel badly about the misunderstanding.

Check over any compositions in which you used the word *bad* or the word *badly* to be sure you used them correctly.

Double Negatives

A **double negative** is an expression that uses two negative words to express one negative meaning.

20 C.3 Avoid double negatives.

Double negatives cause confusion because the two negatives cancel each other out. For example, if you say, "There isn't no more time," it is hard to tell if you mean, "There is no time," or "There is more time."

COMMON NEGATIVES			
but ("only")	neither	none	nothing
barely	never	not (*n't*)	only
hardly	no	no one	scarcely

Double Negative	I do**n't** have **no** time to run tonight.
Correct	I do**n't** have time to run tonight.
Double Negative	There is**n't hardly** any time left.
Correct	There is **hardly** any time left.

CHAPTER 20

Practice Your Skills

Recognizing Mistakes with Modifiers

Write **C** if the modifiers are used correctly in a sentence. Write ***I*** if they are used incorrectly.

1. When training for a race, you should measure your heart rate accurate.
2. Finishing a race feels more wonderfully than not completing a race.
3. For a freshman, Karen runs well.
4. The trainer careful counted all the equipment.
5. Michael shouldn't never have tried to run while he was ill.
6. Jennifer and her relay partners work good together.
7. On the day after the race, Gene's muscles were so stiff he couldn't hardly move.
8. Timothy looked nervously as he stretched his legs.
9. The injured foot hurt bad.

Connect to Writing: Revising

Correcting Mistakes with Modifiers

Rewrite the preceding incorrect sentences, correcting the use of modifiers.

Check Point: Mixed Practice

Write the following paragraphs, correcting each mistake in the use of modifiers.

(1) Mercury is the planet most nearest the sun. **(2)** It is more smaller than any planet in the solar system. **(3)** Its diameter is about one-third that of Earth. **(4)** Because of its smaller size, Mercury's gravity is weaker than Earth's. **(5)** One hundred kilograms on Earth would weigh only 37 kilograms on Mercury.

(6) Scientists knew hardly nothing about the surface of Mercury until *Mariner 10,* an unpiloted spacecraft, made fly-by observations in 1974 and 1975. **(7)** The photographs taken of about one third of Mercury turned out good. **(8)** They showed that Mercury's surface was similar to the moon. **(9)** The rocky landscape on Mercury is marked by broad plains, a few large ringed basins, and highlands studded with more smaller craters. **(10)** The plains were formed by lava. **(11)** Basins were formed when rock masses from space collided forceful with Mercury. **(12)** The most largest basin has a diameter of 1,300 kilometers and is ringed by mountains. **(13)** Most of the craters were formed when rocky masses smashed into the planet's surface.

(14) Because of Mercury's hottest surface, scientists thought that hardly no water couldn't ever exist there. **(15)** However, in 1991, scientists bounced radio waves off Mercury, and a more bright reflection returned from its north pole. **(16)** One explanation is the presence of ice on or near the surface in areas that no sunlight scarcely touches.

Connect to Writing: Speech

Using Modifiers

Imagine you will be speaking at the welcome assembly for younger students entering high school for the first time. Write a speech describing the most challenging part of being in high school. Use vivid adjectives and adverbs. Ask yourself the following questions:

- Which situations have been difficult?
- Where have I gone for help?
- What did I learn from my first year of high school?

Check your work for correct use of modifiers.

Chapter Review

Assess Your Learning

Correcting Errors with Modifiers

Write the following sentences, correcting each error.

1. With so many low-flying planes overhead, we couldn't scarcely hear the guide.
2. Today the donations to our scholarship fund reached their most highest level.
3. Does the movie end happy?
4. Our yard is much smaller than the Jacksons.
5. The library in our town is larger than any library in the country.
6. This suit fits good, even though it's a hand-me-down from my brother.
7. The most largest snowflake on record was eight inches wide.
8. Wasn't there no one at the camp who could build a fire?
9. The Grand Coulee Dam produces more hydroelectric power than any dam in the United States.
10. Which city is the largest, Buenos Aires or Rio de Janeiro?
11. The banana has been called the most ancientest fruit in existence.
12. Dan can swim 300 yards easy.
13. At 282 feet below sea level, California's Death Valley has a lower elevation than any place in the United States.

Editing for the Correct Use of Modifiers

Read the following paragraphs. Then find and write the seven errors in the use of adjectives or adverbs. Beside each error write the correct form.

(1) Animals are amazing creatures. **(2)** For example, which animal do you think jumps highest, the tiger or the thoroughbred racehorse? **(3)** The answer is the tiger; it can jump 13 feet. **(4)** That is 5 feet more higher than the horse can jump. **(5)** Still, the tiger is not the most greatest jumper in the animal kingdom. **(6)** A puma can jump real high—23 feet. **(7)** In the small animal category, a cat can jump about 6 feet. **(8)** Don't never be afraid to match your cat against a dog in a jumping contest.

(9) Did you know that dolphins and sharks are good jumpers too? **(10)** The killer whale can jump farther than any sea mammal, with an average of 20 feet. **(11)** In a contest between a killer whale and a Mako shark, which one do you think would win the award for the best jumper? **(12)** The shark would win because it can cover 25 feet in one leap.

Writing Sentences

Write five sentences that follow the directions below. If a subject is not given for a sentence, you might write about a memorable nature scene.

1. Write a sentence using a negative expression and an adverb.
2. Write a sentence with a superlative adjective or a superlative adverb.
3. Write a sentence that correctly contrasts the sizes of a very small and a very large structure.
4. Write a sentence about an object in nature. Use a positive adjective and a comparative adverb.
5. Write a sentence about two people you know who are very different in some way.

Using Adjectives and Adverbs: Posttest

Directions

Read the passage below about oceanographer Robert Ballard and choose the word or words that belong in each underlined space. Write the letter of the correct answer.

Ballard's research off Italy's coast took ocean archaeology __(1)__ than ever before. Ballard, whose __(2)__ finds included the *Titanic* and the *Bismarck,* announced the discovery of five Roman ships. Until now, marine archaeology had been __(3)__ confined to coastal waters __(4)__ than 200 feet deep.

Using a remote-controlled vehicle, the *Jason,* the explorers retrieved artifacts from the __(5)__ ships. The ships seemed to be from Roman times, __(6)__ lost in storms on the Rome-to-North Africa trade route. One vessel dated from about 100 B.C., __(7)__ than any other ship they had found. Its hold was full of ancient jars used for bulk goods. Another ship carried blocks of marble, __(8)__ ready to assemble into some kind of building.

The upper hulls of the ships had been destroyed by wood borers, but the timbers buried in the mud were __(9)__ preserved. The *Jason* was able to pick up even the __(10)__ glassware.

1. **A** deep
B deeply
C deepest
D deeper

2. **A** most early
B earliest
C most earliest
D more earliest

3. **A** largely
B most largely
C least largely
D more largely

4. **A** little
B lesser
C least
D less

5. **A** most old
B most older
C old
D less old

6. **A** more likely
B likelier
C likely
D less likelier

7. **A** earlier
B most early
C more early
D more earlier

8. **A** apparent
B apparently
C most apparently
D least apparently

9. **A** more best
B good
C less better
D well

10. **A** delicater
B less delicate
C most delicate
D more delicater

CHAPTER 20

Writer's Corner

Snapshot

20 A Adjectives and adverbs are **modifiers.** Most modifiers show the degree of comparison by changing form. (pages 842–846)

20 B When using adjectives and adverbs for comparison, avoid problems with **double comparisons, illogical comparisons,** and comparisons of members of a group to themselves. (pages 847–849)

20 C Be aware of special problems when using adjectives and adverbs. Know whether to use an adjective or adverb, *good* or *well,* or *bad* or *badly.* Be alert for double negatives. (pages 850–854)

CHAPTER 20

Power Rules

Avoid using double negatives. Use only one negative form for a single negative idea. (page 853)

Before Editing	After Editing
Gilli *doesn't* want *nothing*.	Gilli *doesn't* want *anything*.
I *didn't* do *nothing* last weekend.	I *didn't* do *anything* last weekend.

Some adverbs have a negative meaning. **Avoid forming double negatives by using negative words with these adverbs.** (page 853)

Before Editing	After Editing
She won't hardly miss the noise.	*She won't* miss the noise.
I *couldn't scarcely* believe what happened.	I *could scarcely* believe what happened.
They *won't barely* notice the small dent.	They *will barely* notice the small dent.

Editing Checklist

Use this checklist when editing your writing.

Did I use the correct forms of adjectives and adverbs to show degrees of comparison? (See pages 842–846.)

Did I avoid double comparisons and double negatives? (See pages 847 and 853.)

Did I compare similar things in my writing? (See page 847.)

Did I use *other* or *else* when comparing a member of a group with the rest of the group? (See page 848.)

Did I use adverbs and adjectives correctly in my writing? (See pages 850–851.)

Did I generally use *good* as an adjective and *well* as an adverb and *bad* as an adjective and *badly* as an adverb? (See page 852.)

Use the Power

Use these graphics to help you understand the regular and irregular comparative and superlative forms.

Regular Comparative: That blue is dark, but this blue is *darker.*

dark

darker

Regular Superlative: Jake is a big dog. Ralph is the *biggest*.

big

biggest

Irregular Comparative: Andrew has *many* shoes, but Calvin has *more* shoes.

many

more

Irregular Superlative: Emelda has the *most* shoes.

most

A Writer's Glossary of Usage

January has 31 days. That is a fact. It would be incorrect to say January has 25 days. Unlike factual information, written or spoken English is often not a matter of correctness but one of appropriateness. Understanding what is appropriate in a given situation is important in English usage.

The region in which you grew up has influenced your speech from early childhood. Ethnic background and education have influenced it as well. These factors have contributed to the richness and the diversity of the English language today. They have also created the use of two different levels of the English language: standard and nonstandard.

Standard English refers to the conventions of usage accepted most widely by English-speaking people throughout the world. Writers, television and radio personalities, government officials, and most public figures usually use Standard English in both written and spoken presentations. Standard English differs for formal and informal situations.

Nonstandard English is generally is defined as one that draws negative attention to itself in situations where Standard English is the norm and the expectation. Although lacking the generally accepted and preferred conventions of usage, Nonstandard English is correct in some circumstances. It should be avoided when circumstances dictate the use of Standard English as discussed in the preceding section. Nonstandard English is influenced by regional dialects, as well as by other factors, such as slang. Most writers use Standard English when they write but some use Nonstandard English to recreate the conversation of people from particular locales. This was John Steinbeck's purpose in the following passage.

> Casy said, "I been walkin' aroun' in the country. Ever'body's askin' that. What we comin' to? Seems to me we don't never come to nothin'. Always on the way. Always goin' and goin'. . . .
>
> —John Steinbeck, *The Grapes of Wrath*

Usage is a matter of convention, and it changes over time. Not everyone always agrees on what usage is correct. In the case of complex or contested usage, consult references, such as *Merriam-Webster's Dictionary of English Usage* and *Garner's Modern American Usage,* for a resolution.

Formal English has a wide range of applications, including legal documents, business letters, and well-written compositions. Writers who use formal English strictly follow conventional rules of grammar, usage, and mechanics. Contractions, colloquialisms, and some common expressions are avoided. The following example of formal English is an excerpt from the speech Ralph Ellison delivered in 1953 when he received the National Book Award for his novel *Invisible Man.*

> . . . On its profoundest level American experience is of a whole. Its truth lies in its diversity and swiftness of change. Through forging forms of the novel worthy of it, we achieve not only the promise of our lives, but we anticipate the resolution of those world problems of humanity which for a moment seem to those who are in awe of statistics completely insoluble.
>
> —Ralph Ellison, "Brave Words for a Startling Occasion"

Informal English follows the rules and the conventions of Standard English; it is merely used on other occasions. It is most often used in magazines, newspapers, advertising, and much of the fiction that is being written today. Informal English includes words and expressions that would sound out of place in formal writing. Shortcuts, such as contractions, are often included. Informal English is also used by most educated people in their everyday conversations. The following example of informal English was written by newspaper columnist Andy Rooney.

> There are two kinds of savers. The first is the practical saver who keeps string, bags, and old aluminum foil as a practical matter. And then there's the sentimental saver. The sentimental saver can't stand the idea of throwing out any memory of his life.
>
> —Andy Rooney, *A Few Minutes with Andy Rooney*

The following glossary of usage covers common usage problems. As you go through the items, notice that some of them refer to Standard and Nonstandard English. The glossary has been arranged alphabetically so that you can use it as a reference tool.

a, an Use *a* before words beginning with a consonant sound and *an* before words beginning with a vowel sound. Always keep in mind that this rule applies to sounds, not letters. For example, *an hour ago* is correct because the *h* is silent.

I would like to live in **a** house in the country.

Why don't we plan **an** early departure to search for one?

accept, except *Accept* is a verb meaning "to receive with consent." *Except* is usually a preposition meaning "but" or "other than."

I **accept** all your suggestions **except** this one.

adapt, adopt Both of these words are verbs. *Adapt* means "to adjust." *Adopt* means "to take as your own."

If we **adopt** your plans, we can **adapt** them to our needs.

USAGE GLOSSARY

advice, advise *Advice* is a noun that means "a recommendation." *Advise* is a verb that means "to recommend."

I **advise** you to follow your parents' **advice.**

affect, effect *Affect* is usually a verb that means "to influence" or "to act upon." *Effect* is usually a noun that means "a result" or "an influence." As a verb, *effect* means "to accomplish" or "to produce."

Was your decision **affected** by his comments?

Don't let his comments have a negative **effect** on you. (noun)

Your suggestions **effected** an increase in sales. (verb)

all ready, already *All ready* means "completely ready." *Already* means "previously."

The cast was **all ready** for opening night.

They had **already** practiced for weeks.

all together, altogether *All together* means "in a group." *Altogether* means "wholly" or "thoroughly."

We tenants should complain to the landlord **all together.**

Are you **altogether** sure that's the right thing to do?

allusion, illusion Both of these words are nouns. An *allusion* is "an implied or indirect reference; a hint." An *illusion* is "something that deceives or misleads."

> The magician created the **illusion** that he had turned silver into gold.
>
> He pretended to "have the Midas touch," an **allusion** to the legendary king whose touch turned everything into gold.

a lot These two words are often written as one. There is no such word as "alot." *A lot,* even when it is written as two words, should be avoided in formal writing. (Do not confuse *a lot* with *allot,* which is a verb that means "to distribute by shares.")

Informal	He gave us **a lot** of help.
Formal	He gave us **much** help.
	Was the scholarship money **allotted** evenly?

among, between Both of these words are prepositions. *Among* is used when referring to three or more people or things. *Between* is usually used when referring to two people or things.

> We shared a large pizza **among** the three of us.
>
> Since I don't like black olives, we divided them **between** Jerry and Mark.

amount, number *Amount* refers to a quantity. *Number* refers to things that can be counted.

> How can you feed such a large **number** of people with such a small **amount** of food?

When You Use Technology

The spell check feature on your word processing or e-mail software can be very helpful. It can help you check your spelling as you compose or edit your writing. Be careful, however, because a spelling check will not edit your work. For example, spell check will not flag your writing when you incorrectly use *altar* when *alter* is the right choice. You can usually find the spelling feature in the Edit or the Tools menu of your software. You can also set most current programs to mark misspelled words as you type. Look in the Preferences menu to activate this feature.

Practice Your Skills

Finding the Correct Word

Write the word in parentheses that correctly completes each sentence.

1. (A lot of, Many) students procrastinate about going through the college application process.
2. They often don't (accept, except) the (advice, advise) of a guidance counselor.
3. Some students are under the (allusion, illusion) that having a high ACT or SAT score guarantees college acceptance.
4. GPA, community service, and extracurricular activities are (among, between) the factors that colleges consider.
5. In other words, colleges usually look at a large (amount, number) of factors (all together, altogether) rather than just one or two factors.
6. A college application essay (ain't, isn't) always a mandatory requirement.
7. Many colleges, however, have (adapted, adopted) the policy of requiring (a, an) essay.
8. It is essential to (adapt, adopt) the essay to the designated topic and particular college.
9. The (affect, effect) of a well-expressed essay can favorably (affect, effect) a college's decision.
10. You should have (all ready, already) begun the process; don't wait until everyone has applied to college (accept, except) you.

USAGE GLOSSARY

Connect to Writing: Revising

Recognizing Correct Usage

Rewrite the following list of *Do's* and *Don'ts* for college applications, changing the words that are used incorrectly.

1. **Do** allow parents, teachers, and guidance counselors to advise you. **Don't** exclude the advise or instincts your own mind offers.
2. **Do** list achievements and honors you have all ready received. **Don't** adopt a superior attitude about your accomplishments.
3. **Do** provide many factual supporting details if you have to write an essay. **Don't** create an allusion about yourself.
4. **Do** include allusions to add interest. **Don't** forget that inflated language and wordiness effect your reader unfavorably.
5. **Do** except the fact that it requires your time and effort. **Don't** forget that the amount of time and effort spent is worthwhile.

any more, anymore Do not use *any more* for *anymore. Any more* refers to quantity. The adverb *anymore* means "from now on" or "at present" and is usually used in a negative statement.

Do you have **any more** clothes for sale?

No, I don't sell clothes **anymore.**

anywhere, everywhere, nowhere, somewhere Do not add *–s* to any of these words.

Nonstandard	That key must be here **somewheres.**
Standard	That key must be here **somewhere.**

as far as This expression is sometimes confused with "all the farther," which is nonstandard English.

Nonstandard	This is **all the farther** the bus will take us.
Standard	This is **as far as** the bus will take us.

at Do not use *at* after *where.*

Nonstandard	Can you tell us **where** we're **at?**
Standard	Can you tell us **where** we are?

a while, awhile *A while* is an expression made up of an article and a noun. This expression is used mainly after a preposition. *Awhile* is an adverb.

After exercising for **a while,** no one said anything.

The coach suggested that we rest **awhile** before continuing.

bad, badly *Bad* is an adjective and often follows a linking verb. *Badly* is used as an adverb.

Nonstandard	I have felt **badly** all week. (linking verb)
Standard	I have felt **bad** all week. (linking verb)
Standard	I **badly** wanted to feel better. (action verb)

You can learn more about using adjectives and adverbs on pages 840–859.

USAGE GLOSSARY

because Do not use *because* after *the reason*. Use one or the other.

Nonstandard	**The reason** I fell is **because** I wasn't looking where I was going.
Standard	I fell **because** I wasn't looking where I was going.
Standard	**The reason** I fell is **that** I wasn't looking where I was going.

being as, being that These expressions should be replaced with *because* or *since*.

Nonstandard	**Being that** the motor on the boat wouldn't start, I began to row.
Standard	**Since** the motor on the boat wouldn't start, I began to row.

beside, besides *Beside* is always a preposition that means "by the side of." As a preposition, *besides* means "in addition to." As an adverb, *besides* means "also" or "moreover."

At the airport, I placed our coats **beside** the luggage. (by the side of)

Besides my parents, my sister was there to see us off. (in addition to)

When our flight was cancelled, we were given a night's stay in a hotel and breakfast **besides.** (also)

USAGE GLOSSARY

both Never use *the* before *both.*

Nonstandard	**The both** of them were absent today.
Standard	**Both** of them were absent today.

both, each *Both* refers to two persons or objects together, but *each* refers to an individual person or object.

Although **both** artists have equal talent, **each** has her own style.

bring, take *Bring* indicates motion toward the speaker. *Take* indicates motion away from the speaker.

Please **take** these books to the English office and then **bring** the cart back to me.

Practice Your Skills

Finding the Correct Word

Write the word in parentheses that correctly completes each sentence.

1. No one enjoyed writing (any more, anymore) than F. Scott Fitzgerald.
2. Not earning his degree, he failed to go (all the farther, as far as) he would have liked at Princeton.
3. The writings of Fitzgerald (bring, take) us back to the Roaring '20s.
4. (Beside, Besides) the Roaring '20s, this era was also known as the Jazz Age.
5. *The Great Gatsby,* a novel about the Jazz Age, was received (bad, badly) and took quite (a while, awhile) before it became successful.
6. Fitzgerald and his wife Zelda traveled widely searching for happiness but found it (nowhere, nowheres).
7. (Being as, Since) they lived in Paris for (a while, awhile), Fitzgerald and Ernest Hemingway became good friends.
8. Although (both, each) admired the other's works, they (both, each) had a distinctive writing style.

USAGE GLOSSARY

Connect to Writing: Revising

Recognizing Correct Usage

Rewrite the following paragraphs, changing the words that are used incorrectly.

Besides enjoying international success, Ernest Hemingway had an impact on other authors being that many imitated his style. He received the Nobel Prize for Literature and the Pulitzer Prize, the both of them prestigious awards. The reason for the Pulitzer Prize was because of the artistic merit of *The Old Man and the Sea,* a short novel of a heroic old fisherman who badly wants to land a "great fish." Hemingway often created characters whom life had treated bad but who behaved with courage and stoicism, each characteristics of his "code hero."

Both Hemingway's short stories and novels mirrored his interests in life. Besides writing about fishing and hunting, he also wrote about boxing and bullfighting. Like Fitzgerald, Hemingway resided in Paris quite a while. In the 1930s, he left France and settled in Key West, Florida, where he resided at for many years.

Although he died in 1961, every year brings many people to Ernest Hemingway Festivals that celebrate his life and works. If you attend one somewheres, plan to stay awhile. Take a camera, since you will find many interesting exhibits as well as Hemingway "look-alikes."

Practice Your Skills

Writer's Craft: Analyzing the Use of Style

Writers have distinctive ways of expressing themselves. Every aspect of the use that writers make of language—including words, phrases, and sentences—is known as **style.** This excerpt from *The Great Gatsby,* which speaks of the main character and his dream, demonstrates F. Scott Fitzgerald's style. Read it and then follow the instructions.

And as I sat there brooding on the old, unknown world, I thought of Gatsby's wonder when he first picked out the green light at the end of Daisy's dock. He had come a long way to this blue lawn, and his dream must have seemed so close that he could hardly fail to grasp it. He did not know that it was already behind him, somewhere back in that vast obscurity beyond the city, where the dark fields of the republic rolled on under the night.

—F. Scott Fitzgerald, *The Great Gatsby*

Write a personal response to the excerpt above by analyzing Fitzgerald's style and how it affects you. Support your response by making specific references to the text. Include at least five of the words listed below. Be sure to use each choice correctly.

- *accept/except*
- *affect/effect*
- *allusion/illusion*
- *among/between*
- *amount/number*
- *bad/badly*
- *both/each*

USAGE GLOSSARY

can, may *Can* expresses ability. *May* expresses possibility or permission.

Rita **can** type eighty words per minute.

May I take a typing course, too?

can't help but Use a gerund instead of *but.*

Nonstandard	I **can't help but remember** our good times at school.
Standard	**I can't help remembering** our good times at school.

capital, capitol A *capital* is the chief city of a state. Also, names are written with *capital* letters, people invest *capital*, and a person can receive *capital* punishment. A *capitol* is the building in which the legislature meets.

> We toured the **capitol** in Hartford, the **capital** of Connecticut.

coarse, course *Coarse* is an adjective that means "loose or rough in texture" or "crude and unrefined." *Course* is a noun that means "a way of acting or proceeding" or "a path, road, or route." Also, people play the game of golf on a *course*, students take *courses* in school, and an appetizer is one *course* of a meal. *Course* is also the word used in the parenthetical expression *of course.*

> Bermuda grass has a very **coarse** texture.
>
> **Of course,** I learned how to identify different types of grasses from the **course** I took.

continual, continuous Both of these words are adjectives. *Continual* means "frequently repeated." *Continuous* means "uninterrupted."

> The **continual** advertisements on radio and television are very distracting.
>
> During the regular programming, there is a **continuous** hum on my television.

USAGE GLOSSARY

different from Use this phrase instead of *different than. Different than,* however, can be used informally when it is followed by a clause.

Informal	Ana found life on her uncle's ranch **different than** she had expected.
Formal	Ana found life on her uncle's ranch **different from** what she had expected.
Standard	Her opinion about life on the ranch is **different from** mine.

discover, invent Both of these words are verbs. *Discover* means "to find or get knowledge of for the first time." *Invent* means "to create or produce for the first time." Something that is discovered has always existed but has been unknown. Something that is invented has never existed before.

> While some scientists were still **discovering** facts about the moon, other scientists were **inventing** a spaceship to take astronauts there.

doesn't, don't *Doesn't* is singular and should be used only with singular nouns and the personal pronouns *he, she,* and *it. Don't* is plural and should be used with plural nouns and the personal pronouns *I, you, we,* and *they.*

Nonstandard	She **don't** live here anymore.
Standard	She **doesn't** live here anymore.
Nonstandard	Skiing **don't** appeal to me.
Standard	Skiing **doesn't** appeal to me.

done *Done* is the past participle of the verb *do.* When *done* is used as a verb, it must be preceded by one or more helping verbs.

Nonstandard	I **done** my homework already.
Standard	I **have done** my homework already.

USAGE GLOSSARY

double negative Words such as *hardly, never, no, not,* and *nobody* are considered negatives. Do not use two negatives in a sentence.

Nonstandard	I do**n't never** eat lunch in the cafeteria.
Standard	I do**n't** ever eat lunch in the cafeteria.
Standard	I **never** eat lunch in the cafeteria.

You can learn more about the use of negatives on page 853.

emigrate, immigrate Both of these words are verbs. *Emigrate* means "to leave a country to settle elsewhere." *Immigrate* means "to enter a foreign country to live there." A person emigrates *from* a country and immigrates *to* another country.

In 1954, Grandfather **emigrated** from Russia.
He **immigrated** to Israel.

etc. *Etc.* is an abbreviation for a Latin phrase, *et cetera,* which means "and other things." Never use the word *and* with *etc.* If you do, what you are really saying is "and and other things." It is best not to use this abbreviation at all in formal writing.

Informal	To make the posters for the advertising campaign, we will need poster board, markers, paint, **etc.**
Formal	To make the posters for the advertising campaign, we will need poster board, markers, paint, and **other art supplies.**

farther, further *Farther* refers to distance. *Further* means "additional" or "to a greater degree or extent."

Is the cabin much **farther?**

If we don't find it soon, we'll need **further** directions.

fewer, less *Fewer* is plural and refers to things that can be counted. *Less* is singular and refers to quantities and qualities that cannot be counted.

Fewer apples will make **less** applesauce.

former, latter *Former* is the first of two people or things. *Latter* is the second. (Use *first* and *last* for three or more.)

For our book report, we had a choice of a novel or a biography. I chose the **former;** Beth chose the **latter.**

Practice Your Skills

Finding the Correct Word

Write the word in parentheses that correctly or best completes each sentence.

1. It (can, may) be said that Christopher Reeve was (discovered, invented) by a vast audience when he starred in the movie *Superman* in 1978.
2. This role was much (different from, different than) his part in the television soap opera *Love of Life.*
3. The (coarse, course) of Reeve's life changed dramatically when he was paralyzed from the neck down in 1995.
4. With the courage and example he showed the world, you (can't help but realize, can't help realizing) that he became a real "superman."
5. Of (coarse, course), he had already been active in many worthwhile projects before his accident.
6. He didn't allow his injury to curtail his support of those projects; instead, he supported more causes after his accident rather than (fewer, less).
7. Reeve used his condition and influence to (farther, further) humanitarian causes, such as research, funding, education, and (other activities, etc.) for spinal-cord injuries.

Connect to Writing: Revising

Recognizing Correct Usage

Rewrite the following paragraphs, changing the words that are used incorrectly.

The duties of a physical therapist include assessing a patient's needs and prescribing a coarse of treatment. The former must take place before the latter. Conditions requiring therapy can range in severity from a strained muscle to a catastrophic injury such as the one Christopher Reeve endured. Although one is much different than the other in terms of severity, a therapist's job is to invent a treatment program that results in less pain and one that don't cause farther damage. Rehabilitating a patient often requires continual conferencing with other professionals to ensure they done everything possible to meet the patient's needs.

Therapists don't never just deal with a patient's injury or illness. To achieve a continual recovery, therapists often instruct patients and their families on how to provide care at home. This approach usually results in less repeat cases. Ultimately, the expert care by therapists and the progress made by patients are like capitol gains on an investment.

good, well *Good* is an adjective and often follows a linking verb. *Well* is an adverb and often follows an action verb. However, when *well* means "in good health" or "satisfactory," it is an adjective.

The plot of that book sounds **good.** (adjective)

I wish I could write **well.** (adverb)

Since you don't feel **well,** why don't you finish exercising later? (adjective, "in good health")

You can learn more about using good *and* well *on page 852.*

had of Do not use *of* after *had*.

Nonstandard	If I **had of** taken typing, I could get that job.
Standard	If I **had** taken typing, I could get that job.

have, of Never substitute *of* for the verb *have*. When speaking, many people make a contraction of *have*. For example, someone might say, "We should've left sooner." Because *'ve* sounds like *of*, *of* is often mistakenly substituted for *have* in writing.

Nonstandard	I **could of** worked this weekend.
Standard	I **could have** worked this weekend.

hear, here *Hear* is a verb that means "to perceive by listening." *Here* is an adverb that means "in this place."

From **here** I could **hear** everything they said.

hole, whole *Hole* is an opening. *Whole* means "complete or entire unit."

The **hole** is so big that a **whole** orange can fit into it.

imply, infer Both of these words are verbs. *Imply* means "to suggest" or "to hint." *Infer* means "to draw a conclusion by reasoning or from evidence." A speaker implies; a listener infers. *Implication* and *inference* are the noun forms.

Julie's comment **implied** that what I had **inferred** from John's remarks was wrong.

Connect to Speaking and Writing

Although the words *imply* and *infer* are often used interchangeably, there is a clear difference between the two. When you read literature, what the writer *implies* is the basis on which you *infer* or draw a conclusion in order to analyze a piece of literature. When you write an analysis, be sure to use these words correctly.

in, into Use *into* when you want to express motion from one place to another.

The boxes **in** the car should be brought **into** the house.

irregardless Do not substitute this word for *regardless*. The prefix *ir-* and the suffix *-less* both mean "without." It is a double negative.

Nonstandard	I am going through with my plans **irregardless** of the consequences.
Standard	I am going through with my plans **regardless** of the consequences.

its, it's *Its* is a possessive pronoun and means "belonging to it." *It's* is a contraction for *it is.*

The jury defended **its** guilty verdict.

It's not surprising to me that they found him guilty.

kind, sort, type These words are singular and should be preceded by *this* or *that. Kinds, sorts,* and *types* are plural and should be preceded by *these* or *those.*

Do you like this **kind** of flower?

Do you like these **kinds** of flowers?

kind of, sort of Never substitute these expressions for *rather* or *somewhat*.

Nonstandard	That test was **kind of** hard.
Standard	That test was **rather** hard.

USAGE GLOSSARY

knew, new *Knew,* the past tense of the verb *know,* means "was acquainted with." *New* is an adjective that means "recently made" or "just found."

I **knew** you would wear your **new** wool sports coat for the class picture.

learn, teach Both of these words are verbs. *Learn* means "to gain knowledge." *Teach* means "to instruct."

Nonstandard	Wanda **learned** me how to use the microwave oven.
Standard	Wanda **taught** me how to use the microwave oven.
Standard	I **learned** how to use the microwave oven by reading the instructions.

leave, let Both of these words are verbs. *Leave* means "to depart." *Let* means "to allow" or "to permit."

Nonstandard	**Leave** me handle this matter for you.
Standard	**Let** me handle this matter for you.
Standard	I can work on it before I **leave** the office.

Practice Your Skills

Finding the Correct Word

Write the word in parentheses that correctly completes each sentence.

1. To gain admission (in, into) most four-year colleges, (its, it's) required that you take at least two years of a foreign language.

2. (This type, These types) of courses should prepare you (good, well) for advanced work in a language.

3. You can (hear, here) the language assignments spoken on tapes in a language lab.

4. (Hear, Here) you can develop (good, well) listening and practice skills.

5. In time, you (should have, should of) also developed a (rather, sort of) authentic pronunciation.

6. Your instructor will (learn, teach) you historical facts about the (knew, new) country.

7. (Its, It's) culture and people will be explored as well.

8. The (kind, kinds) of language courses offered vary.

9. The most common ones offered (in, into) high school are French, German, and Spanish.

10. However, in some high schools, Chinese, Japanese, and Russian are a part of the (hole, whole) curriculum.

Connect to Writing: Revising

Recognizing Correct Usage

Rewrite the following paragraphs, changing the words that are used incorrectly.

Irregardless of the language you choose to learn, you will have a whole in your education if you don't at least experience the delight of communicating in a different language. Learning a second language can open a whole knew world to you. Its possible that it could lead you in a profession such as interpreter. Today many companies require their employees to speak a second language well. Don't make the mistake of realizing later in life that you could of landed a certain job if you had studied a foreign language.

Another rewarding benefit is that it promotes well feelings among people of different countries. If you travel abroad and already know how to speak the language, it will infer that you value the other culture. It's value is priceless in broadening your global horizons.

Practice Your Skills

Writer's Craft: Analyzing an Autobiography

Writers often use autobiographical writing to express their feelings. In this excerpt from *Barrio Boy,* Ernesto Galarza poignantly relates his feelings of isolation from the perspective of a young immigrant in America who does not speak English. Examine his work carefully and then answer the question below.

> America was all around us, in and out of the *barrio.* Abruptly we had to forget the ways of shopping in a *mercado* and learn those of shopping in a corner grocery or in a department store. The Americans paid no attention to the Sixteenth of September, but they made a great commotion about the Fourth of July. In Mazatlán, Don Salvador had told us, saluting and marching as he talked to our class, that the *Cinco de Mayo* was the most glorious date in human history. The Americans had not even heard about it.
>
> —Ernesto Galarza, *Barrio Boy*

Explain in your own words why the narrator feels isolated.

USAGE GLOSSARY

lie, lay *Lie* means "to rest or recline." *Lie* is never followed by a direct object. Its principal parts are *lie, lying, lay,* and *lain. Lay* means "to put or set (something) down." *Lay* is usually followed by a direct object. Its principal parts are *lay, laying, laid,* and *laid.*

I will **lie** down and rest if you will **lay** the blanket over me.

You can learn more about using the verbs lie *and* lay *on page 750.*

like, as *Like* is a preposition that introduces a prepositional phrase. *As* is usually a subordinating conjunction that introduces an adverbial clause. Although *like* is sometimes used informally as a subordinating conjunction, it should be avoided in formal speaking and writing situations.

Informal	Jenny retold the story **like** it had happened.
Formal	Jenny retold the story just **as** it had happened. (clause)
Formal	**Like** me, she left out no details. (prepositional phrase)

loose, lose *Loose* is usually an adjective that means "not tight." *Lose* is a verb that means "to misplace" or "not to have in your possession any longer."

I was afraid I might **lose** those **loose** papers in my English notebook.

may be, maybe *May be* is a form of the verb *be*. *Maybe* is an adverb that means "perhaps."

This **may be** your last chance to apply.

Maybe you should talk to the manager today.

most, almost *Most* is a noun, a pronoun, or an adjective that modifies a noun or a pronoun. *Almost*, which means "nearly," is an adverb. Do not substitute *most* for *almost*.

Nonstandard	Brad finished **most** all of the repair work on his car last night.
Standard	Brad finished **almost** all of the repair work on his car last night.
Standard	**Most** students agree he is an outstanding automobile mechanic.

nor, or Use *neither* with *nor* and *either* with *or.*

Neither carnations **nor** roses look appropriate in that vase.

Either tulips **or** daffodils would be a better choice.

of Prepositions such as *inside, outside,* and *off* should not be followed by *of.*

Nonstandard	Please take the towels **off of** the clothesline.
Standard	Please take the towels **off** the clothesline.

ought Never use *have* or *had* with *ought*.

Nonstandard	I **hadn't ought** to eat this late.
Standard	I **ought not** to eat this late.

passed, past *Passed* is the past tense of the verb *pass*. As a noun *past* means "a time gone by." As an adjective *past* means "just gone" or "elapsed." As a preposition *past* means "beyond."

In the **past,** when I wondered if she had come home, time **passed** slowly for me. (*past* as a noun, *passed* as a verb)

For the **past** few days, I have been driving **past** her house to be sure. (*past* as an adjective and then as a preposition)

USAGE GLOSSARY

precede, proceed Both words are verbs. *Precede* means "to be, go, or come ahead of something else." *Proceed* means "to move along a course," "to advance," or "to continue after a pause."

In the procession the faculty **preceded** the graduating class.

Then they **proceeded** to their reserved seats.

principal, principle The adjective *principal* means "main" or "chief." As a noun *principal* means "head of a school" or "leader." *Principle* is a noun synonymous with *law, truth, doctrine,* or *code of conduct.*

Our **principal,** Mrs. Dobbin, was the **principal** speaker.

She urged the graduates to live by moral **principles.**

USAGE GLOSSARY

respectfully, respectively *Respectfully* is the adverbial form of the noun *respect,* which means "high regard or esteem." *Respectively* means "in the order given."

He **respectfully** asked each student to answer the question.

The winner said that Phoenix, Columbus, and Albany are the capitals of Arizona, Ohio, and New York, **respectively.**

rise, raise *Rise* means "to move upward" or "to get up." *Rise* is never followed by a direct object. Its principal parts are *rise, rising, rose,* and *risen. Raise* means "to lift (something) up," "to increase," or "to grow something." *Raise* is usually followed by a direct object. Its principal parts are *raise, raising, raised,* and *raised.*

Please **rise** to sing the national anthem as they **raise** the American flag.

You can learn more about using the verbs rise *and* raise *on page 751.*

Practice Your Skills

Finding the Correct Word

Write the word in parentheses that correctly completes each sentence.

1. Most students are interested in (almost, most) all the journalism courses offered.

2. Creating products (like, as) newspapers, yearbooks, and literary magazines (may be, maybe) part of the course.

3. As students (precede, proceed) in courses designed to teach about newspapers, they (had ought, ought) to gain a variety of skills.

4. For example, (may be, maybe) a student will be assigned the task of interviewing the school (principal, principle).
5. One approach might be to (raise, rise) an important issue, such as the effectiveness of school policy.
6. (Preceding, Proceeding) the interview, questions need to be prepared to keep the conversation from (loosing, losing) its focus; for example, the questions should neither be arranged in too (loose, lose) an order (nor, or) should they stray (off, off of) the topic.
7. As a matter of (principal, principle), an interview should be conducted (respectfully, respectively).
8. (Respectfully, Respectively), the order of arrangements should involve setting up a designated time, preparing advance questions, and conducting the interview.
9. Once students have (passed, past) the test by conducting a successful interview, they can rely on (passed, past) experience for future ones.
10. (As, Like) local newspapers, the (principal, principle) parts of a typical school newspaper might include editorials, feature stories, and sports coverage.

USAGE GLOSSARY

Connect to Writing: Revising

Recognizing Correct Usage

Rewrite the following paragraphs, changing the words that are used incorrectly.

Journalism teachers lie down specific criteria for the course. Sales, layout, and photography raise other possibilities for the development of skills. Advertisement sales outside the school community are sometimes needed. Learning how to approach a business owner respectfully and how to establish good public relations is essential to avoid loosing an account.

Preceding the actual layout of the newspaper, students develop skills like planning and designing. Visual appeal of a newspaper ought to be one of its principle components. The final layout must be past across the teacher's desk for approval. Of course, the principals of good photography must also be utilized. The final grade for journalism class depends on several factors, such as the quality of writing, an original and objective reporting style, and past performance of duties.

To raise to another course level, students must master the basic requirements. If pursued properly, journalism classes may be considered an excellent training ground and may lay the foundation for aspiring journalists.

Practice Your Skills

Advertisement: Correct Usage

Choose a product that you think is great, like a bicycle or roller blades. Think about how you might change the item or create a new product. Then brainstorm ideas to include in an advertisement for your product.

- Name the product.
- List the audience you want to attract.
- Create a catchy phrase or slogan.
- Highlight strengths of the product.
- Choose a statement that will challenge the audience to try the product.

Write an advertisement using your ideas and correctly using at least five of the following words: *loose/lose, may be/maybe, most/almost, like/as, precede/proceed, rise/raise.*

says, said Do not use the present tense *says*, when you should use the past tense, *said*.

Nonstandard	After Jim struck out, Paul **says,** "My turn!"
Standard	After Jim struck out, Paul **said,** "My turn!"

-self, -selves A reflexive or an intensive pronoun that ends in *-self* or *-selves* should not be used as a subject. (Never use "hisself" or "theirselves.")

Nonstandard	Dad and **myself** are the only ones at home.
Standard	Dad and **I** are the only ones at home.

shall, will Formal English uses *shall* with first person pronouns and *will* with second and third person pronouns. Today, however, *shall* and *will* are used interchangeably with *I* and *we*, except that *shall* is still used with first person pronouns for questions.

Shall we take a vote on the proposed amendment to the club's bylaws?

They **will** announce the results tomorrow.

sit, set *Sit* means "to rest in an upright position." *Sit* is rarely followed by a direct object. Its principal parts are *sit, sitting, sat,* and *sat. Set* means "to put or place (something)." *Set* is usually followed by a direct object. Its principal parts are *set, setting, set,* and *set.*

Sit in that chair while I **set** your purse on the coffee table.

You can learn more about using the verbs sit *and* set *on pages 751–752.*

USAGE GLOSSARY

some, somewhat *Some* is either a pronoun or an adjective that modifies a noun or a pronoun. *Somewhat* is an adverb that modifies an adjective or another adverb.

Nonstandard	Mom is feeling **some** better today than she was yesterday.
Standard	Mom is feeling **somewhat** better today than she was yesterday.

suppose to, supposed to Be sure to add the *d* to *suppose* when it is followed by *to.*

Nonstandard	I was **suppose to** visit my grandparents this weekend.
Standard	I was **supposed to** visit my grandparents this weekend.

than, then *Than* is usually a subordinating conjunction and is used for comparisons. *Then* is an adverb that means "at that time" or "next."

My report is shorter **than** yours.

Let me present mine first, and **then** you can present yours.

that, which, who *That* refers to animals, things, and sometimes people. It always begins an essential clause. *Which* refers to animals and things. *Who* refers to people.

The novel **that** the teacher assigned was *Moby Dick.*

Moby Dick, **which** is required reading for juniors, is about a giant white whale.

Herman Melville, **who** is the author of this classic, used his extensive travels and experiences in his writing.

their, there, they're *Their* is a possessive pronoun. *There* is usually an adverb, but sometimes it can also begin an inverted sentence. *They're* is a contraction for *they are.*

They're here for **their** annual checkup.

Please have a seat over **there** until the nurse calls you.

theirs, there's *Theirs* is a possessive pronoun. *There's* is a contraction for *there is.*

There's our car, but where is **theirs?**

them, those Use *those* as a subject or a modifier, never *them.*

Nonstandard	**Them** are the ones I'm selling. (subject)
Standard	**Those** are the ones I'm selling.
Nonstandard	Do you really plan to sell **them** antiques? (adjective)
Standard	Do you really plan to sell **those** antiques?

this here, that there Avoid using *here* and *there* in addition to *this* and *that.*

Nonstandard	**That there** horse likes **this here** saddle.
Standard	**That** horse likes **this** saddle.

this, that, these, those *This* and *that* modify singular nouns. *These* and *those* modify plural nouns.

Nonstandard	I plan to buy **these** brand of jeans.
Standard	I plan to buy **this** brand of jeans.

threw, through *Threw* is the past tense of the verb *throw. Through* is a preposition that means "in one side and out the other."

When Matt **threw** the baseball, it exploded **through** the window.

USAGE GLOSSARY

Practice Your Skills

Finding the Correct Word

Write the word in parentheses that correctly completes each sentence.

1. The role of guidance counselors has changed (some, somewhat) from (their, there, they're) previous role.

2. In today's complex society, (theirs, there's) a wider range of concerns that students face (than, then) years ago.

3. Close attention is paid to parents and students (which, who) are new to the community.

4. (Their, There, They're) encouraged to meet in individual sessions to plan their schedules.

5. (Them, Those) planning sessions held (there, they're) at school help acclimate both parents and students to a new experience.

6. Most counselors (shall, will) offer orientation sessions in the classrooms.

7. (Threw, Through) these sessions, counselors explain the services available.

8. They also clearly (sit, set) the standard procedure to follow.

Connect to Writing: Revising

Recognizing Correct Usage

Rewrite the following paragraphs, changing the words that are used incorrectly.

This here is only the beginning of a year that offers many challenges. Guidance counselors theirselves are greatly involved in ensuring that students don't just set back and neglect to sign up for important tests. They monitor these types of problems by sending out notices and by calling students individually into there offices. Of special importance are seniors, particularly those in danger of failing. After the effort the counselors exert, it is disheartening for them to learn that one of their students through away chances for graduation through negligence.

Yet theirs more than one problem with which counselors must deal. Sometimes they experience an overwhelming feeling of responsibility as they deal with issues concerning drugs, family, and peers. One innovative program in recent years has been the peer counseling program, who features students acting as counselors for other students. Guidance counselors often help set the standards; and than, after training, the peer counselors act as mediators between students who are having problems with one another.

to, too, two *To* is a preposition. *To* also begins an infinitive. *Too* is an adverb, which modifies a verb, an adjective, or another adverb. *Two* is a number.

We had **to** drive **two** miles before reaching a rest stop.

We hurried **to** the picnic area before it got **too** crowded.

try to Use *try to* instead of *try and,* which is nonstandard.

Nonstandard	I will **try and** save you a seat.
Standard	I will **try to** save you a seat.

use to, used to Be sure to add the *d* to *use* when it is followed by *to.*

Nonstandard	I **use to** like chocolate, but now I don't.
Standard	I **used to** like chocolate, but now I don't.

way, ways Do not substitute *ways* for *way* to refer to distance.

Nonstandard	We were still a long **ways** from shore.
Standard	We were still a long **way** from shore.

weak, week *Weak* is an adjective that means "not strong." *Week* is a noun that means "a period of seven days."

I have felt too **weak** to leave the house for a whole **week.**

what Do not substitute *what* for *that.*

Nonstandard	The apartment **what** we rented is too small.
Standard	The apartment **that** we rented is too small.

USAGE GLOSSARY

when, where Do not use *when* or *where* directly after a linking verb in a definition.

Nonstandard	Early in the morning is **when** it is best to work in the garden.
Standard	Early in the morning is the best time to work in the garden.
Nonstandard	Horticulture is **where** you cultivate plants.
Standard	Horticulture is the study of cultivating plants.

where Do not substitute *where* for *that.*

Nonstandard	I learned **where** he was telling the truth.
Standard	I learned **that** he was telling the truth.

who, whom *Who,* a pronoun in the nominative case, is used either as a subject or a predicate nominative. *Whom,* a pronoun in the objective case, is used mainly as a direct object, an indirect object, or an object of a preposition.

Who delivered your new boat? (subject)

From **whom** did you buy it? (object of a preposition)

You can learn more about using who *and* whom *on pages 793–795.*

whose, who's *Whose* is a possessive pronoun. *Who's* is a contraction for *who is.*

Whose car are you parking?

Who's waiting for you in the driveway?

your, you're *Your* is a possessive pronoun. *You're* is a contraction.

I suppose that what **you're** looking for is **your** new jacket.

Practice Your Skills

Finding the Correct Word

Write the word in parentheses that correctly completes each sentence.

1. If you're interested in famous historical landmarks, (you're, your) travels might take you through New York Harbor (to, too, two) Ellis Island and the Statue of Liberty.

2. Battery Park and Liberty State Park are the (to, too, two) places where you can board a ferry to visit them.

3. Between 1892 and 1954, some twelve million immigrants for (who, whom) America was a haven came to Ellis Island.

4. It (use to, used to) be a clearing station for immigrants (who, whom) sought freedom from social injustice.

5. Those (who's, whose) relatives remained behind often had dreams of their immigrating (to, too, two).

6. Letters (that, what) told stories of the many opportunities in America made them willing to travel a long (way, ways).

7. They read (that, where) living and working conditions were superior to those in their own lands.

8. Immigrants also told of the problems they encountered from some of the people at Ellis Island who would (try and, try to) take advantage of them.

9. Others were separated from their families a (weak, week) or more because of the possibility of contagious disease.

10. Even to those (weak, week) from their trip, the trouble they endured was worth the promise of a better life.

Connect to Writing: Revising

Recognizing Correct Usage

Rewrite the following paragraphs, changing the words that are used incorrectly.

If you had been one of those immigrants, try to imagine the joy your sure to have experienced when you're eyes beheld the Statue of Liberty. In her hands were placed to important symbols of liberty, a torch and a law book. Even the light from the torch what was visible to the incoming passengers brought hope. When they were a long way from shore, they could see its glow.

France, from whom America received the statue, presented it as a symbol of international friendship. Frédéric Bartholdi, whom designed the statue, made trips to America to promote the idea too. The statue, whose size was enormous, had to be transported in sections. The Statue of Liberty, who's name was also Liberty Enlightening the World, weighed over two hundred tons. On its pedestal, that was paid for by the American people, are the inspiring words of a sonnet by Emma Lazarus that speaks to those who give our country its diversity.

USAGE GLOSSARY

Practice Your Skills

Explanatory Paragraph: Correct Usage

Read the sonnet below carefully. Then follow the instructions.

Not like the brazen giant of Greek fame,
With conquering limbs astride from land to land;
Here at our sea-washed, sunset gates shall stand
A mighty woman with a torch, whose flame
Is the imprisoned lightning, and her name
Mother of Exiles. From her beacon-hand
Glows world-wide welcome; her mild eyes command
The air-bridged harbor that twin cities frame,
"Keep, ancient lands, your storied pomp!" cries she
With silent lips. "Give me your tired, your poor,
Your huddled masses yearning to breathe free,
The wretched refuse of your teeming shore.
Send these, the homeless, tempest-tost to me,
I lift my lamp beside the golden door!"

—*Emma Lazarus,* "The New Colossus"

Imagine you are doing peer tutoring for a student who has difficulty with usage of the words *like, to, shall, whose, that, your,* and *these*. Write a paragraph that explains why these seven words, some of which appear more than once, are used correctly in "The New Colossus."

Check Point: Mixed Practice

Write the word in parentheses that correctly completes each sentence.

1. From the time the first (emigrants, immigrants) to America (emigrated, immigrated) from (their, there, they're) native lands, they struggled to have others (accept, except) them.
2. (Their, There, They're) also arose a need to (adapt, adopt) to a style of life (different from, different than) that which they had known before.
3. Many (bad, badly) wanted to preserve (their, there) culture even while (adapting, adopting) new customs.
4. Much has been accomplished (all ready, already), but we need to go (farther, further) in our acceptance.
5. (Raising, Rising) cultural awareness (precedes, proceeds) cultural acceptance.
6. (It's, Its) necessary to (learn, teach) the former and to (learn, teach) the latter.
7. (Discovering, Inventing) a (whole, hole) (knew, new) concept isn't needed; (discovering, inventing) what (all ready, already) exists is needed.
8. (Fewer, Less) emphasis on a narrow view of our world (shall, will) result in (fewer, less) misunderstandings and incidences of prejudice.
9. Although we (shall, will) never eradicate all prejudice, we must make a (continual, continuous) effort to (farther, further) the cause of cultural acceptance for all.
10. The diversity in our country (had ought, ought) to be celebrated (among, between) all nationalities.

Unit 6

Mechanics

As the headline on the opposite page shows, careless punctuation can seriously muddle a sentence's meaning. Did the writer mean to say that a man was mistakenly sold as a pet fish? Avoiding confusion is the primary reason humans invented mechanics, or conventions, for their languages. In this unit you will learn the importance of inserting a hyphen between the words *man* and *eating* when you want them to work together to describe a carnivorous fish. You will also learn to spell correctly by recognizing common spelling patterns, and to show respect for people, places, and things by properly capitalizing and italicizing their names. And proper language mechanics will also help amuse and surprise your readers—but only when that is your intention.

MAN EATING PIRANHA MISTAKENLY SOLD AS PET FISH

—newspaper headline

Capital Letters

How can you use capitalization to clarify your writing?

Capital Letters: Pretest 1

The following first draft contains several errors in capitalization. The first error has been corrected by adding marks to show that the *l* should be capitalized in the name *Lewis*. How would you revise the paragraph to be sure capital letters are used correctly?

Authors such as C. S. lewis and J. R. R. Tolkien created unforgettable fantasy lands in their books. Tolkien's *the Hobbit* is filled with places such as The lonely mountain, the Iron hills, and Wilderland. In *the Lion, the Witch, and The Wardrobe,* Peter, Susan, Edmond, and lucy discover a fascinating world called narnia. Try looking at your surroundings through the eyes of a Fantasy writer. Perhaps you would label the track at your school as the road to Discipline, and the public swimming pool as the Sea of relaxation. You might call your world skoolia or something more imaginative. What title would you give a book about your fantasy land? That might depend on the characters in your fantasy, and what happens to them. Could the title be *Rami, Jermaine, and the witch in the Locker?*

Capital Letters: Pretest 2

Directions

Read the passage and decide which word or words should be capitalized in each underlined part. Write the letter of the correct answer. If the underlined part contains no error, write ***D.***

Wyoming is the only **(1)** State that had its origins in the four principal U.S. **(2)** annexations: the louisiana purchase in 1803, the annexation of Texas in 1845, the **(3)** cession of oregon by the british in 1846, and the land taken at the **(4)** end of the mexican war in 1848. One popular Wyoming attraction is **(5)** Old Faithful in Yellowstone National Park.

1. A State that had its Origins
B state that had its Origins
C state that had its origins
D No error

2. A Annexations: The Louisiana Purchase
B annexations: the Louisiana Purchase
C annexations: The Louisiana Purchase
D No error

3. A cession of Oregon by the British
B Cession of Oregon by the British
C cession of Oregon by the british
D No error

4. A End of the Mexican War
B end of the Mexican war
C end of the Mexican War
D No error

5. A old faithful in Yellowstone National Park
B old faithful in yellowstone national park
C Old Faithful in Yellowstone National park
D No error

First Words and the Pronoun *I* Lesson 1

Before the printing press was invented, every letter in every word was a capital letter. Today, capital letters have special uses that provide clues to guide readers. Applied correctly, capitalization can make your writing flow smoothly.

Capital letters are attention getters. They are taller and larger than lowercase letters.

21 A Capitalize the beginning of a sentence or a line of poetry, parts of a letter or an outline, and the pronoun *I*.

Sentences and Poetry

A capital letter at the beginning of every sentence is a signal to the reader that a new idea is beginning. In a poem the capital letters represent new lines and also suggest emphasis on that first word. These clues are essential to the reader's understanding.

CHAPTER 21

21 A.1 Capitalize the first word of a sentence or of a line of poetry.

Sentence **M**y favorite poet is Emily Dickinson.

Lines of Poetry
A bird came down the walk:
He did not know I saw.
—Emily Dickinson

When You Write

Some modern poets don't follow the capitalization rule. Here is an example from the poem "All in green my love went riding":

All in green went my love riding
on a great horse of gold
into the silver dawn.
—E. E. Cummings

Since your attention is not drawn to the beginning of each line, you might notice other things about the poem instead. When you quote a poem, copy it exactly as the poet has written it.

Parts of a Letter

21 A.2 Capitalize the first word in the greeting and in the closing of a letter.

PARTS OF A LETTER		
Greetings	**D**ear Grandmother,	**T**o whom it may concern:
Closings	**W**ith love,	**S**incerely yours,

Outlines

Use a capital letter to begin each part of an outline.

21 A.3 Capitalize the first word of each item in an outline and the letters that begin major subsections of the outline.

I. **T**he poetry of E. E. Cummings
   A. **U**nusual capitalization
   B. **U**nique arrangement of lines on page
II. **T**he poetry of Emily Dickinson
   A. **S**hort lines
   B. **U**se of dashes

The Pronoun *I*

21 A.4 Capitalize the pronoun *I*, both alone and in contractions.

I sleep better if **I**'ve read a good book before bedtime.

I don't know when **I**'ll finish writing this story.

The first word of a direct quotation is also capitalized. Learn about capitalizing quotations on page 968.

Connect to Speaking and Writing: Peer Consultation

Using Capitals in an Outline

With a partner, write an outline for a short skit you would like to perform. Talk about what you will include in the skit, and then work on the outline together. Use capital letters correctly when creating your outline.

CHAPTER 21

Practice Your Skills

Using Capitalization

Write the letter of the item in each pair that is capitalized correctly.

1. a. I can't believe I'm going to meet Toni Morrison!
b. I can't believe i'm going to meet Toni Morrison!

2. a. did you read Morrison's novel *Beloved?*
b. Did you read Morrison's novel *Beloved?*

3. a. Does the film *Beloved* include the book's supernatural elements?
b. does the film *Beloved* include the book's supernatural elements?

4. a. I wrote a letter that began, "to my favorite author."
b. I wrote a letter that began, "To my favorite author."

5. a. Then I signed it, "your loyal fan."
b. Then I signed it, "Your loyal fan."

6. a. Also, I decided i'd enclose the poem I wrote.
b. Also, I decided I'd enclose the poem I wrote.

7. a. It begins, "Chained by fear, / I know only that Beloved is near."
b. It begins, "chained by fear, / I know only that Beloved is near."

Connect to Writing: Editing

Using Capital Letters

Correctly write each word that should be capitalized.

dear Margaret,

i'm returning your copy of *The Sound and the Fury* by William Faulkner. thanks for lending it to me; i liked it even though the story is a little surreal. i especially liked the way Faulkner tells parts of the story from various characters' points of view. i started wondering what kind of life Faulkner led and if his life influenced his stories. would you look at this outline that i started? it's all i have so far, but i'll add more.

I. the life of William Faulkner
  A. lived 1897–1962
  B. native of Mississippi
  C. later lived in Hollywood
  D. southern life influenced his work

i'm not sure what to write as my next main point—i'm doing more research.

Your friend,
Andie

Proper Nouns Lesson 2

Beginning a noun with a capital letter can tell a reader that it is a **proper noun**—that it names a particular person, place, or thing.

21 B **Capitalize proper nouns and their abbreviations.**

There are many types of proper nouns, including names of particular persons, geographical names, and names of time periods. The rule for each type of proper noun follows.

Names of Particular Persons and Animals

21 B.1 Names of particular persons and animals should be capitalized. Also capitalize the initials that stand for people's names.

NAMES	
Persons	Amy, **E**rnest **W**arner, **N**orman **A.** **G**oldstein
Animals	**M**uffin, **T**rigger, **L**addie, **L**ightning, **B**aron

Some surnames have two capital letters. In those names the letter following *De, Mc, Mac, O,* and *St.* should be capitalized. Names do vary. It is always best to ask individuals exactly how their names are spelled and capitalized.

NAMES WITH TWO CAPITALS				
De**N**ise	**M**c**N**air	**M**ac**D**uffee	**O'N**eil	St. **C**lair

An abbreviation that follows a person's name also should be capitalized.

ABBREVIATIONS	
Margaret M. Perry, **M.D.**	Edward J. Lee, **S**r.

Capitalize common nouns that are clearly personified.

Admire **N**ature in her green finery.

CHAPTER 21

Geographical Names

21 B.2 Geographical names, which include places, bodies of water, celestial bodies and their abbreviations, initials, and acronyms, should be capitalized.

GEOGRAPHICAL NAMES	
Streets, Highways	Brook Road (Rd.), Route (Rt.) 6, Mason Turnpike (Tpk.), Forty-second Street (The second part of a hyphenated numbered street is not capitalized.)
Cities, States	Salt Lake City, Utah (UT); Santa Fe, New Mexico (NM); Memphis, Tennessee (TN)
Counties, Parishes, Townships	Chickasaw County, Jefferson Parish, Plymouth Township
Countries	Poland, Nigeria, United States
Sections of a Country	the Northeast, the Midwest, the Pacific Northwest, the Sun Belt (Compass directions do not begin with a capital letter: *Go east to Kent Road.*)
Continents	North America, Africa, Australia
World Regions	the Northern Hemisphere, South Pole
Islands	Santa Rosa, Corsica, Hawaiian Islands
Mountains	Rocky Mountains (Mts.), Mount (Mt.) Rainier, El Capitan
Parks	Olympic National Park, Kenny State Park, Big Bend National Park
Bodies of Water	Arctic Ocean, Lake Erie, Chesapeake Bay, Wappapello Reservoir, Gulf of Mexico, Niagara Falls
Stars	North Star, Sirius, Vega, Antares
Constellations	Andromeda, Orion, Ursa Minor (the Little Dipper)
Planets	Mercury, Saturn, Uranus, Earth (Do not capitalize *sun* or *moon*. Also, do not capitalize *earth* if it is preceded by the word *the*.)

You can learn more about proper nouns on pages 620–621.

CHAPTER 21

Practice Your Skills

Using Capitalization

Write the following items, using capitalization where needed.

1. south of clay city
2. matthew r. royan, jr.
3. the philippine islands
4. a port on the black sea
5. a river in kentucky
6. the big dipper
7. the mississippi river
8. my dog jiggers
9. the southeast
10. an island off the coast of maine
11. lake louise
12. the u.s.
13. mt. everest
14. the macgregors' house
15. fifty-fifth st.
16. a country in europe

Practice Your Skills

Using Capitalization

Write the letter of the item that uses capitalization correctly.

1. a. T. J. Owenson
b. t. j. Owenson
2. a. the Earth
b. the earth
3. a. Sunshine hwy.
b. Sunshine Hwy.
4. a. the Little dipper
b. the Little Dipper
5. a. Rock Creek
b. Rock creek
6. a. Lima, peru
b. Lima, Peru
7. a. the appalachian Mts.
b. the Appalachian Mts.
8. a. the U.S. Virgin Islands
b. the U.S. Virgin islands
9. a. the Moon
b. the moon
10. a. Santa Fe historic national trail
b. Santa Fe Historic National Trail

Connect to Writing: Vocabulary

Using Capitals in Geographical Names

With a partner, look over all the types of geographical names listed in the chart on the left page. Go down the list together and, using a separate piece of paper, write two additional names for each entry on the chart. For example, at "Countries" you might add United Arab Emirates or China and at "Islands" you might add Puerto Rico or Cuba. Once you have completed your chart, write a short account of which entry was the hardest to find additional examples for, and why.

Connect to Writing: Editing

Using Capital Letters

Write each sentence, capitalizing each word that should begin with a capital letter.

1. tokyo is on honshu, japan's largest island.
2. Did you know that france is bordered on the north by the english channel and on the south by spain and the mediterranean sea?
3. Charon, pluto's only moon, was discovered from the earth with the aid of a powerful telescope.
4. No fish can live in either the great salt lake in utah or the dead sea in the middle east.
5. Jacksonville, florida, is on the st. john's river, twelve miles from the atlantic ocean.

CHAPTER 21

Names of Groups

21 B.3 Names of groups, including the names of organizations, businesses, institutions, government bodies, political parties, and teams, should be capitalized.

NAMES OF GROUPS	
Organizations	the **N**ational **F**ootball **L**eague (**NFL**), the **H**umane **S**ociety, **B**righton **H**igh **S**tudents' **A**ssociation (**A**ssoc.), the **A**merican **M**edical **A**ssociation (**AMA**)
Businesses	**M**atrix **O**il **C**orporation (**C**orp.); **S**eagraves, **W**hitney and **C**ompany (**C**o.); **D**ouber and **A**ssociates (**A**ssoc.)
Institutions	**P**erkins **S**chool for the **B**lind, **M**iddlebury **H**igh **S**chool, **G**reenwood **H**ospital (Words such as *school, college,* and *hospital* are not capitalized unless they are part of a proper noun.)
Government Bodies and Agencies	**D**epartment of the **I**nterior, the **S**upreme **C**ourt, **C**ongress, **U**nited **S**tates **T**reasury, the **H**ouse of **C**ommons
Political Parties	the **R**epublican party, a **D**emocrat
Teams	**F**armington **C**oyotes, **F**orest **H**igh **F**ighting **F**alcons

Specific Time Periods, Events, and Documents

21 B.4 Specific time periods, including the days and months of the year, holidays, special events, and historical events, periods, and documents, are capitalized.

TIMES, EVENTS, AND DOCUMENTS	
Days, Months	Sunday (Sun.), Saturday (Sat.), January (Jan.), December (Dec.) (Do not capitalize seasons—such as spring and winter—unless they are part of a proper noun: Spring Fling.)
Holidays	the Fourth of July, Veterans Day
Special Events	the Mardi Gras, the Super Bowl, the New York Marathon
Historical Events	the Boxer Rebellion, the Battle of Shiloh, the Boston Tea Party, the Vietnam War, the Atlantic Charter, the New Deal
Periods	the Victorian Period, the Industrial Revolution, the Middle Ages, the Renaissance, Byzantine Empire
Time Abbreviations	B.C. B.C.E./A.D., AM/PM, CST (Central Standard Time)
Documents	the First Amendment to the United States Constitution, the Bill of Rights, the Declaration of Independence, the Dred Scott Decision, the Paris Peace Treaty of 1783

A preposition that is part of a proper noun is not usually capitalized.

Names of Nationalities, Races, Languages, and Religions

21 B.5 Names of nationalities, races, ethnic groups, languages, and religions, including religious holidays and references, are capitalized.

NATIONALITIES, RACES, LANGUAGES, AND RELIGIONS	
Nationalities	Italians, an American, the French, Koreans, Russians, the Swiss
Races and Ethnic Groups	Caucasian, Asian, Hispanic, African American
Languages	English, Swahili, Polish, Hebrew
Computer Languages	Cobol, Java, Visual Basic
Religions	Baptist, Roman Catholic, Hindu
Religious References	Jehovah, the New Testament, the Holy Spirit, the Koran, God
Religious Holidays	Easter, Purim, Kwanzaa, Hanukkah

Other Proper Nouns

21 B.6 Other proper nouns should also begin with capital letters.

OTHER PROPER NOUNS	
Awards	**N**obel **P**eace **P**rize, the **G**rammy **A**wards, a **G**olden **G**lobe
Brand Names	**N**ew **F**oam soap, **T**riangles frozen pizza, **M**int **L**eaf mouthwash (The product itself is not capitalized.)
Bridges, Buildings	**B**rooklyn **B**ridge, **K**ennedy **C**enter, **E**iffel **T**ower, the **G**ateway **A**rch, the **E**mpire **S**tate **B**uilding
Memorials, Monuments	**L**incoln **M**emorial, the **T**omb of the **U**nknown **S**oldier, the **W**ashington **M**onument
Technological Terms	**I**nternet, **W**eb, **W**orld **W**ide **W**eb, **W**eb site, **W**eb page
Vehicles	***D**iscovery* (space shuttle), ***O**rient **E**xpress* (train), the ***S**anta **M**aria* (ship) (Names of vehicles are also italicized.)
Names of Courses	**W**oodworking II, **E**nglish, **H**istory III, **L**atin, **B**iology 101 (Unnumbered courses such as history and science are not capitalized.)

CHAPTER 21

Connect to Writing: **Summary**

Using Capital Letters

You have chosen a United States president to write about, and you are planning a summary of his major accomplishments. Using biographies, reference works, and magazine articles (and perhaps even video- and audiotapes), take notes on this president's achievements. Arrange your notes from most important to least important. Write a first draft of your summary. As you revise and edit, check for the correct use of capital letters. Finally, write a neat final copy.

When You Write

Titles of some Web sites and digital products don't follow conventional capitalization rules. Some start with lowercase letters; others include two capital letters in a single word. Check the company's Web site for accurate spelling.

Microsoft PowerPoint® Apple iPhone® YouTube MySpace

Practice Your Skills

Capitalizing Proper Nouns

Write the following items, using capitalization where needed.

1. biology and french
2. a college in the south
3. the steel company of america
4. capagna's products soup
5. the social security act
6. access to the internet
7. the battle of bunker hill
8. a chevrolet convertible
9. department of defense
10. the University of iowa
11. the magna carta
12. the house of representatives
13. thunder lake lodge
14. the guggenheim museum in new york
15. the war of 1812
16. mother's day

Practice Your Skills

Using Capital Letters

Correctly write each word that should be capitalized.

1. One of the first photocopiers was marketed by the rectigraph company of rochester, new york, in the early days of the twentieth century.

2. Testing of the early space shuttle *enterprise* ended on october 26, 1977, at edwards air force base.

3. the crash of the new york stock exchange in 1929 started the great depression in the united states.

4. Volleyball was invented in 1895 by william g. morgan in holyoke, massachusetts.

5. The sixteenth amendment to the constitution, passed by congress in 1913, made income tax a legal fact of U.S. life.

6. The highest uninhabited point in the United States is mount mckinley in alaska; the lowest point is death valley in california.

7. Among the most widely spoken languages in the world today are chinese, english, and russian.

8. Booker t. washington founded the tuskegee institute.

9. The cathedral of cologne near the rhine river in germany took 300 years to build.

10. President lincoln issued the emancipation proclamation on september 22, 1862.

Check Point: Mixed Practice

Write correctly each word that should begin with a capital letter.

(1) after getting married in 1764, abigail and john adams moved to a little farm in massachusetts. **(2)** a year later the english parliament passed the stamp act, which taxed the colonies. **(3)** from then on, john became involved in matters of government, leaving abigail to manage the household.

(4) from 1774 to 1776, john was in philadelphia with the continental congress, and letter writing became john and abigail's main means of communication. **(5)** In june of 1775, she wrote about hearing a battle near bunker hill in charlestown. **(6)** a year later she heard washington's cannon fire during the capture of dorchester heights. **(7)** she and her children also watched the fleet from england sail out of the harbor after the boston tea party. **(8)** in 1800, abigail moved into the white house with john, who was the second president of the united states.

CHAPTER 21

Connect to Writing: Chronology

Using Capital Letters

Create a timeline or other document showing a technological development from the 1940s or 1950s through the present. You might choose the development of the Internet, fast foods, modes of transportation, and so on. Be sure all proper nouns are capitalized.

Connect to Writing: Fantasy Map

Capitalizing Proper Nouns

Continue to investigate the works of J. R. R. Tolkien, C. S. Lewis, and other favorite fantasy writers. Think of a fantasy land that you would like to write about. Draw a small map of the places you create in your imagination, labeling them with descriptive proper nouns. Create a map like the one shown here. Begin all proper nouns with capital letters and double-check for accuracy.

Proper Adjectives Lesson 3

A **proper adjective** is formed from a proper noun. Since proper nouns begin with a capital letter, most proper adjectives also begin with capital letters.

21 C Capitalize most proper adjectives.

PROPER NOUNS AND ADJECTIVES	
Proper Nouns	**A**laska, **C**ongress
Proper Adjectives	**A**laskan oil, **C**ongressional session

Some proper adjectives keep the same form as the proper noun.

UNCHANGED PROPER ADJECTIVES	
Proper Noun	**F**lorida, **F**riday
Proper Adjectives	**F**lorida oranges, **F**riday traffic

A few proper adjectives have become so commonplace in the English language that they are no longer capitalized.

COMMONPLACE PROPER ADJECTIVES		
china cup	plaster of **p**aris	**p**asteurized milk

Sometimes a proper adjective is part of a hyphenated adjective. Capitalize only the part that is a proper adjective. Occasionally, both parts of a hyphenated adjective will be proper adjectives.

HYPHENATED PROPER ADJECTIVES	
European-made cars	un-**A**merican attitudes
Indo-**E**uropean language	**F**rench-**C**anadian art
Pulitzer-**P**rize-winning novel	

CHAPTER 21

Practice Your Skills

Capitalizing Proper Adjectives

Write the letter of the item that is capitalized correctly.

1. a. the Dallas-fort worth Airport
b. the Dallas-Fort Worth Airport

2. a. the February Forecast
b. the February forecast

3. a. a New Jersey farmer
b. a New jersey farmer

4. a. the republican leaders
b. the Republican leaders

5. a. Canadian architecture
b. canadian Architecture

6. a. French-style homes
b. French-Style homes

7. a. an English-Speaking city
b. an English-speaking city

8. a. the Canadian-american border
b. the Canadian-American border

9. a. a British citizen
b. a British Citizen

10. a. a Roman numeral
b. a Roman Numeral

Connect to Writing: Editing

Capitalizing Proper Adjectives

Correctly write each word that should be capitalized in this menu.

SUNDAY SPECIALS

Entrées

southern fried steak
alaskan king crab
steamed maine lobster
flounder with italian seasonings

Side Dishes

creamed idaho potatoes
spanish rice
waldorf salad
japanese vegetables

Desserts

baked washington apples
new york cheesecake

Beverages

sumatran roast coffee
chinese green tea

Titles Lesson 4

Capital letters emphasize the importance of titles of persons and works of art.

21 D Capitalize the titles of persons and works of art.

Titles with Names of Persons

21 D.1 Capitalize a title showing office, rank, or profession when the title comes before a person's name.

Before a Name	Have you met **D**r. Jordan of Highview Regional Hospital?
Used Alone	Our regular **d**octor was out of town.
Before a Name	The speaker will be **C**ongresswoman Gill.
Used Alone	Have you met the **c**ongresswoman from our district?

Do not capitalize the prefix *ex-* or the suffix *-elect* when either is connected to a title.

The speakers tonight will be **e**x-Senator Burton and Mayor-**e**lect Rodini.

Titles Used Alone

21 D.2 Capitalize a title that is used alone when it is being substituted for a person's name in direct address.

Used as a Name	I'd like to make a collect call to my parents, **O**perator.
Not Used as a Name	The **o**perator helped me place my call.
High Government Official	The **P**resident held a dinner for the visiting dignitaries.

The titles for the United States President, Vice President, and Chief Justice, and for the Queen of England, are often capitalized when they stand alone. However, *president* and *vice president* are capitalized when they stand alone only if they refer to the *current* president and vice president.

Was George Bush the president who preceded William J. Clinton, or was it Ronald Reagan?

Titles Showing Family Relationships

21 D.3 Capitalize titles showing family relationships when they come before a person's name or when they are substituted for a person's name in direct address.

Before a Name	Will **A**unt Kate like this movie?
Used as a Name in Direct Address	I wrote a poem for you, **M**om. Do you think **D**ad will like it?

Titles showing family relationships should not be capitalized when they are preceded by a possessive noun or pronoun—unless they are considered a part of a person's name.

Not Part of a Name	My **g**randfather taught photography.
Part of a Name	Did your **U**ncle Harley teach art?

Titles of Written Works and Other Works of Art

21 D.4 Capitalize the first and last words and all important words in the titles of the following: books, stories, poems, newspapers and newspaper articles, magazines and magazine articles, movies, plays, television series, musical songs and compositions, and works of art.

Do not capitalize a short preposition, a coordinating conjunction, or an article—unless it is the first or last word in a title.

TITLES OF WORKS	
Books and Chapter Titles	Jack London's book ***The Call of the Wild*** the chapter "**T**he **S**ounding of the **C**all"
Short Stories	"**T**he **B**lack **C**at" by Edgar Allan Poe
Poems	"**T**he **H**ighwayman" by Alfred Noyes
Newspapers and Newspaper articles	the ***Washington Post*** (The word *the* before the title of a newspaper or a periodical is usually not capitalized. One exception is *The New York Times*.) "**M**aya **A**ngelou **S**peaks to **L**ocal **E**leventh-**G**rade **C**lass"
Magazines and Magazine Articles	***Seventeen, Road and Track, Muscle*** "**T**eenagers and **W**eekend **J**obs"
Movies	***Ever After, The Sixth Sense***
Plays	***The Member of the Wedding*** by Carson McCullers
Television Series	***Law and Order, The Simpsons***
Musical Compositions	Mendelssohn's "**V**iolin **C**oncerto in **E** **M**inor"
Works of Art	Rembrandt's painting ***The Polish Rider***

You can learn about using italics and quotation marks with titles on pages 961–965.

Practice Your Skills

Capitalizing Titles

Correctly write each word that should be capitalized. If a sentence is correct, write **C**.

1. Would you rather watch *survivor* or a *friends* rerun tonight?
2. Have you ever read Poe's poem "the raven," dad?
3. My grandmother and Jack's aunt read *home and garden* magazine.
4. One of my favorite paintings is *the accolade* by Edmund Blair Leighton.
5. As the president entered the room, the band began to play "hail to the chief."
6. Which singer performed "My Heart Will Go On" for the film *Titanic?*

Check Point: Mixed Practice

Write each word in each question that should begin with a capital letter. Then write the answer to the question, if you can!

1. is neptune or uranus closer to earth?
2. did robert frost write the poem "stopping by woods on a snowy evening"?
3. does buffalo or rochester lie at the east end of lake erie on the niagara river?
4. was shea stadium in new york city or in cincinnati?
5. did franklin roosevelt or martin luther king, jr., say, "i have been to the mountain"?
6. is *the grapes of wrath* by john steinbeck about people from oklahoma or people from rhode island?
7. did the treaty of versailles end the spanish-american war or world war I?
8. does the most valuable player in the national football league win the jim thorpe trophy or the heisman trophy every year?
9. in which state is grand canyon national park, arizona or nevada?
10. during president carter's term in office, who was his vice president?
11. is the north star in the bowl of the big dipper or the tail of the little dipper?
12. what famous author lived at walden pond?
13. three well-known railroads are the reading, the pennsylvania, and the short line. which well-known railroad is missing?
14. what was the name of king arthur's wife?
15. is the acropolis located in the greek city of athens or sparta?
16. was christopher columbus's nationality italian or spanish?
17. were the incas or the aztecs of Mexico conquered by cortés in 1521?
18. who was the first roman catholic president of the united states?
19. the united states and what other country were involved in the louisiana purchase?
20. does the play *our town* take place in grover's corners, vermont?

Connect to Writing: PowerPoint™ Presentation

Titles

The librarian at your school has asked you to create a set of PowerPoint™ slides to present to sophomores. Each slide is to feature a written work or work of art that these students will be learning about next year when they become juniors. For each title give a short (one or two sentences) description that will interest the students in the work. Edit your presentation for correct capitalization. For long books you might also list sample chapters.

Assess Your Learning

Using Capital Letters Correctly

Write the following items, using capital letters wherever they are needed.

1. henry ford's original *model t*
2. summer on cape cod
3. exodus 2:3 in the bible
4. the *wall street journal*
5. west on bently highway
6. the american revolution
7. the monroe doctrine
8. an egyptian tomb
9. the justice department
10. st. mary's catholic church
11. the panama canal
12. fifty-sixth street
13. american history
14. congressman ted angelino
15. the fourth of july
16. my sister jeanne

Editing for Correct Capitalization

Rewrite the following sentences, substituting capital letters for lowercase letters wherever needed.

1. the hawaiian islands are actually the tops of a 1,600-mile-long range of underwater mountains.
2. "tell me, mom, will grandfather willis spend christmas with us this year?"
3. the movie *lust for life* was based on the life of the artist vincent van gogh.
4. before she wrote her first novel, *so big*, edna ferber worked for her hometown newspaper, the *appleton daily crescent*.
5. the first of the breed of morgan horses was a stallion named justin morgan.

6. I read about an Englishwoman who made a record crossing, sailing from the canary islands to the west indies.
7. my brother carlos was just promoted to captain in the fulton police department.
8. a speech by senator payne highlighted the graduation ceremony at western institute of technology.
9. after spending our two-week vacation in the midwest, we headed east to pennsylvania.
10. although the constitution states that a senator must be at least thirty years old, henry clay became a member of the senate at twenty-nine.
11. during my senior year, I'm going to take english history, spanish II, english, trigonometry, chemistry, and art II.
12. the most famous geysers are in yellowstone national park, on north island in new zealand, and in iceland.
13. the planet smaller than mars is mercury.
14. who wrote the lovely poem, "when lilacs last in the dooryard bloomed"?
15. when are aunt hilda and uncle harold leaving woonsocket, rhode island, to visit their relatives in connecticut?

Writing Sentences

Write five sentences that follow the directions below. Check for correct capitalization.

1. Write a sentence about a foreign or out-of-state university you might like to attend. Include the city, state or province, and country in which the university is located.
2. Write a sentence about a favorite play, poem, novel, short story, or other written work. Include the author of the work.
3. Write a sentence about a foreign city you would like to visit someday. Mention a particular site or sites you would visit.
4. Write a sentence about one of your favorite relatives. Mention the city, state or province, and country in which he or she lives.
5. Write a sentence about your favorite artwork and favorite musical composition, naming the artist and the composer.

Capital Letters: Posttest

Directions

Read the passage and decide which word or words should be capitalized in each underlined part. Write the letter of the correct answer. If the underlined part contains no error, write ***D.***

Virginia is a historically rich state. In 1606, Captain John Smith established the **(1)** first Permanent English Settlement in America. Today in the **(2)** harbor of Jamestown island, you can tour **(3)** *Godspeed,* a trans-atlantic ship that brought the first colonists to America. Stories say that Pocahontas, a **(4)** powhatan indian princess, saved the life of Captain John Smith by interceding with her father, the chief. Later, in 1619, Virginians formed the first democratically elected **(5)** legislature, the house of burgesses.

CHAPTER 21

1. A first permanent English settlement
B first permanent English Settlement
C First Permanent English Settlement
D No error

2. A Harbor of Jamestown Island
B Harbor of Jamestown island
C harbor of Jamestown Island
D No error

3. A *Godspeed,* a Trans-Atlantic ship
B *Godspeed,* a trans-Atlantic ship
C *godspeed,* a trans-Atlantic Ship
D No error

4. A Powhatan indian Princess
B Powhatan Indian princess
C Powhatan Indian Princess
D No error

5. A Legislature, the House of Burgesses
B Legislature, the house of Burgesses
C legislature, the House of Burgesses
D No error

Writer's Corner

Snapshot

21 A Use capital letters at the beginning of a sentence or a line of poetry, in parts of a letter or an outline, and in the pronoun *I.* (pages 892–894)

21 B Capitalize proper nouns and their abbreviations. (pages 895–902)

21 C Capitalize most proper adjectives. (pages 903–904)

21 D Capitalize the titles of persons and works of art. (pages 905–908)

Power Rules

Be sure that every statement in your writing that **begins with a capital letter** is a complete sentence, not a sentence fragment. (pages 663–664)

Before Editing	After Editing
When I visit my grandparents. I usually bring them a treat.	*When I visit my grandparents,* I usually bring them a treat.
Jon's father. A great artist. Has an exhibit at a downtown art gallery.	*Jon's father, a great artist,* has an exhibit at a downtown art gallery.
I prefer writing my essays in the library. *Because it's always so quiet.*	I prefer writing my essays in the library *because it's always so quiet.*

Check for **run-on sentences** and separate them by **capitalizing the first word of the second sentence** or making other appropriate changes, such as adding a conjunction and/or punctuation. (pages 728–730)

Before Editing	After Editing
LeBron walked the dog Abe took out the trash.	LeBron walked the dog. Abe took out the trash.
The pizza arrived we took our places in front of the big game on the TV.	*When the pizza arrived,* we took our places in front of the big game on the TV.

Editing Checklist

Use this checklist when editing your writing.

- ✓ Did I capitalize first words in each sentence? (See page 892.)
- ✓ Did I capitalize the pronoun *I*? (See page 893.)
- ✓ Did I capitalize the right parts of letters and outlines? (See page 893.)
- ✓ Did I capitalize proper nouns and their abbreviations? (See pages 895–902.)
- ✓ Did I capitalize proper adjectives? (See pages 903–904.)
- ✓ Did I identify the titles of persons and works of art and know when to capitalize them? (See pages 905–908.)
- ✓ Did I edit my work for mistakes in capitalization? (See pages 890–913.)

Use the Power

Capital letters draw attention to certain words and the beginnings of sentences. Use the rules below to help you understand how to use correct capitalization in your writing.

Rule: Capitalize the **first word** in every sentence.
City-living will always be my preference.

Rule: Always capitalize the pronoun *I*.
What **I** love most about cities is the hustle and bustle.

Rule: Capitalize **proper nouns.**
Ideally, **I**'ll have a chance to live in some foreign cities, like **London** and **Madrid**.

Rule: Capitalize **proper adjectives.**
I wouldn't mind attending a **British** or **Spanish** school.

Rule: Capitalize **titles** of persons and works of art.
I envy my **Uncle** Francisco, who has seen the **Mona Lisa**.

CHAPTER 21

CHAPTER 22

CHAPTER 22

End Marks and Commas

How can you create meaning through the careful use of end marks and commas?

End Marks and Commas: Pretest 1

The following first draft contains several errors in the use of end marks and commas. The first two errors have been corrected. How would you revise the rest of the draft so that all end marks and commas are used correctly?

In 1976, Alex Haley published *Roots*, which became an extremely popular book. Like Haley, most people are interested in their roots—where they came from who their ancestors were and what they were like. People want to have continuity in their lives they want to be linked to the past. Thus most families have traditions from the past that they carry on today. Perhaps they do something special on certain holidays eat special foods that their grandparents or great-grandparents ate, or practice other rituals. Can you think of a tradition from your past that is carried on in your family today. Haley's book also inspired many people to become genealogists tracing their family's roots way back in time.

End Marks and Commas: Pretest 2

Directions

Read the passage and write the letter of the answer that correctly punctuates each underlined part. If the underlined part contains no error, write ***D***.

When the major leagues finally became integrated in 1948, Leroy Paige should have been too **(1)** old too slow and too beat up to strike anyone out. **(2)** Leroy, known as Satchel, was ready, nevertheless, to show off **(3)** his own, unparalleled talent. **(4)** On July 9, 1948 Satchel walked to the mound at Cleveland's Municipal Stadium. As the Cleveland manager handed him the **(5)** ball the crowd roared. At the age of 42, Satchel shut down the St. Louis Browns for two straight innings.

1. **A** old, too slow, and too
B old, too slow, and, too
C old too slow, and too
D No error

2. **A** Leroy, known as Satchel
B Leroy known as Satchel,
C Leroy known as Satchel
D No error

3. **A** his own, unparalleled,
B his own unparalleled
C his own unparalleled,
D No error

4. **A** On July 9, 1948,
B On July 9 1948,
C On July 9 1948
D No error

5. **A** ball the crowd roared!
B ball, the crowd, roared.
C ball, the crowd roared!
D No error

Kinds of Sentences and End Marks Lesson 1

The purpose of all sentences is to communicate. Within this broad category, however, there are four kinds of sentences—each with a particular function.

22 A **Depending on its function, a sentence can be declarative, imperative, interrogative, or exclamatory.**

The end mark you use in a sentence is determined by the intent of the sentence. Most sentences make a statement or express an opinion.

22 A.1 A **declarative sentence** makes a statement or expresses an opinion and ends with a period (**.**).

The following examples are both declarative sentences, even though the second example contains an indirect question.

CHAPTER 22

Bicycles are a common means of transportation to school**.**

I don't know where the auditorium is**.**

(The direct question would be *Where is the auditorium?*)

Another function of a sentence is to give directions, make requests, or give commands. Generally *you* is the understood subject of these sentences.

22 A.2 An **imperative sentence** gives a direction, makes a request, or gives a command. It ends with either a period or an exclamation point (**.** or **!**).

If a command is given in a normal tone of voice, it is followed by a period when written. If it expresses strong feeling, it is followed by an exclamation point.

Meet me in the library**.**

(normal tone of voice)

Don't touch my experiment**!**

(emotional tone of voice)

Occasionally an imperative sentence is stated as a question, but no reply is expected. Since the purpose of the sentence remains the same—to make a request—the sentence is followed by a period or by an exclamation point.

Will you please pass your test papers forward**.**
(normal tone of voice)

Would you stop that**!**
(emotional tone of voice)

A third function of a sentence is to ask a question—whether it is completely or incompletely expressed.

22 A.3 An **interrogative sentence** asks a question and ends with a question mark (**?**).

Does anyone in the cafeteria want to trade lunches with me**?**

What**?** I couldn't hear you.

The fourth function of a sentence is to express strong feeling, such as excitement or anger. Avoid overusing this type of sentence, for it can very quickly lose its impact.

22 A.4 An **exclamatory sentence** expresses strong feeling or emotion and ends with an exclamation point (**!**).

You passed your test with flying colors**!**

That was my homework you threw away**!**

We're thrilled we won the competition**!**

When an interjection expresses strong feeling or emotion, it is followed by an exclamation point.

No**!** You may not leave early for lunch.

Yes**!** I would love to go on the field trip.

Oh**!** I forgot my permission slip.

You can find out more about interjections on page 646.

When You Read

The next time you are traveling in a car, notice the imperative commands and declarative statements on signs all around you. Because these signs are meant for people in moving vehicles, they use only a few words. Some signs use punctuation to increase their impact.

STOP YIELD SLOW

Hurry! Sale ends Friday**.**

Right lane **MUST** turn right**.**

CHAPTER 22

Practice Your Skills

Classifying Sentences

Write an appropriate end mark for each sentence. Then label each sentence using the following abbreviations.

declarative = ***d.***	imperative = ***imp.***
interrogative = ***int.***	exclamatory = ***ex.***

1. Read the next two chapters in your biology textbook by Friday

2. Mr. Kent asked Kate whether she had taken her SAT last semester

3. Take out a sheet of paper for a pop quiz

4. Did Toby drive you to school today

5. Run or we'll miss the bus

6. Do you think the test will be postponed because of the fire alarm

7. May I please have your attention

8. There's smoke coming from the cafeteria

9. I don't know what the homework assignment is for American history

Connect to Writing: Business Letter

Using End Marks

You have decided to apply for an after-school job at the department store where your mother works. Write a cover letter for your application, addressing it to Ms. Nguyen, Director of Human Resources. Describe your interest in a specific position and your relevant background. Explain why you would be an excellent employee. Use at least one sentence of each type, and use end marks appropriately. Edit your letter carefully, and then write a neat final copy.

Connect to Writing: **Editing**

Using End Marks

Write the following speech, adding appropriate end marks.

Good morning, students This is your principal speaking How many of you have part-time jobs after school How many of you would like a part-time job but do not have transportation to the business district of town Well, I have exciting news for you The school board has approved an experimental work program here on campus Yes You heard me correctly Starting next week, students can work after-school jobs here on campus These jobs will include yard care, janitorial services, kitchen work, tutoring, office work, and other similar jobs All jobs will pay at least minimum wage Also, you are automatically eligible for time off to study for any major test Are you interested Help me show the school board that our campus can make this idea work You can stop by the main office for an application Hurry There are only a limited number of positions for this trial phase Thank you, and have a good day

Other Uses of Periods

Besides ending sentences, periods have other uses.

Periods with Abbreviations

Abbreviations are useful when you are writing quickly. They save time when you are taking notes from books or during lectures. They also are useful when writing e-mail messages. Most abbreviations, however, should be avoided in formal writing.

22 A.5 Use a period after most abbreviations.

The following list contains some abbreviations that are acceptable in formal writing. Use the dictionary to find the spelling and the punctuation of other abbreviations.

ABBREVIATIONS

Titles with Names	Mr.	Ms.	Mrs.	Jr.	Sr.
	Lt.	Capt.	Gen.	Sen.	Gov.
	Rev.	Dr.	Hon.	Prof.	Sgt.
Initials for Names	E. E. Cummings			T. S. Eliot	
	F. Scott Fitzgerald			J. D. Salinger	
Times with Numbers	a.m.	p.m.	B.C.	A.D.	B.C.E.

ABBREVIATIONS					
Addresses	Ave.	St.	Blvd.	Rt.	Dept.
	Rd.	Dr.	Ct.	Apt.	P.O. Box
Organizations and Companies	Co.	Inc.	Corp.	Assoc.	

When You Speak and Write

Some organizations and companies are known by abbreviations that stand for their full names. When we speak, we say the abbreviation rather than the whole name, for example, "What is the finding of the FAA about the cause of the crash?" (not the *Federal Aviation Administration*). When written, most of these abbreviations do not use periods. A few other common abbreviations also do not include periods.

IRS = Internal Revenue Service	kg = kilogram
ROM = read-only memory	CD = compact disc

A declarative sentence that ends with an abbreviation needs only one period. An interrogative or an exclamatory sentence that ends with an abbreviation needs both marks of punctuation.

The lecture starts at 6:45 p.m.

Does your bus leave at 6:45 p.m.?

Today almost everyone uses the post office's two-letter state abbreviations, which do not include periods. You can find a list of these state abbreviations at the front of most telephone books. The following chart lists a few examples.

STATE ABBREVIATIONS		
AR = Arkansas	KY = Kentucky	OR = Oregon
GA = Georgia	ME = Maine	TX = Texas
HI = Hawaii	MI = Michigan	UT = Utah
IL = Illinois	NM = New Mexico	VA = Virginia

Periods with Outlines

22 A.6 Use a period after each number or letter that shows a division in an outline.

I. Narration
 A. First-person narrators
  1. Use *I*
  2. Don't always give their names
 B. Omniscient narrators
II. Setting

You can learn about capitalization with outlines on page 893.

Practice Your Skills

Using End Marks

Write the abbreviation for each item. Use periods where needed. If you are unsure of a particular abbreviation, look it up in a dictionary.

1. foot
2. Street
3. ounce
4. February
5. volume
6. New Mexico
7. Major
8. meter
9. Fahrenheit
10. United Nations

Connect to Writing: Revising

Using Abbreviations

Write each sentence, using the abbreviation for the item specified in parentheses.

1. The poem "Trees" was written by Sergeant Joyce Kilmer. (title of author)
2. Which author's books do you like better, Clive Staples Lewis or David Herbert Lawrence? (initials for first and middle names)
3. Nathaniel Hawthorne lived from Anno Domini 1804 to 1864. (time)
4. Did Aristotle live from 384 to 322 before Christ? (time)
5. Please read Arthur Miller's *Death of a Salesman* by tomorrow at 10:00 ante meridiem. (time)
6. The Internal Revenue Service publishes lengthy guidelines. (organization)
7. *The Life of Charlotte Brontë* was published in 1857 by Missus Gaskell. (title of woman)
8. Where can I find copies of all speeches by Doctor Martin Luther King, Junior? (titles)

22 B **The comma (,) is used to separate items and to enclose items.**

Commas That Separate

Commas are needed to separate similar items that come next to each other in a sentence. Without commas, a reader would not know where one item stopped and another item began. By clarifying your meaning with commas, you will ensure your reader's understanding.

Items in a Series

A **series** is three or more similar items listed in consecutive order. Words, phrases, or clauses can be written as a series.

22 B.1 Use commas to separate items in a series.

Words	Kittens, puppies, hamsters, and fish are popular pets. (nouns)
	Fido barked, jumped, and whined all day. (verbs)
Phrases	I searched for my hermit crab in its terrarium, on my desk, and throughout my house.
Clauses	I don't know where he came from, whose dog he is, or how we can find his owner.

When a conjunction connects the last two items in a series, a comma is optional. In some situations, the comma before the conjunction can help avoid confusion.

Confusing	We feed Tabby tuna, beef and liver cat food. (Is it a beef and liver mix, or two separate cat foods?)
Clear	We feed Tabby tuna, beef, and liver cat food.

If conjunctions connect all the items in a series, no commas are needed. The meaning is clear.

Each of the dog groomers worked quickly **and** efficiently **and** quietly during the afternoon rush.

When You Write

Some expressions, such as *franks and beans,* are thought of as single items. When you write one of these expressions in a series, it should be considered one item.

We were offered three kinds of sandwiches: *ham and cheese, peanut butter and jelly,* and *tuna.*

CHAPTER 22

Adjectives Before a Noun

22 B.2 In certain situations, use a comma to separate two adjectives that directly precede a noun and that are not joined by a conjunction.

Our parrot made loud, strange sounds.

The nimble, stealthy cat was stalking the parrot.

To decide whether a comma should be placed between two adjectives, use the following test. Read the sentence with *and* between the adjectives. If the sentence sounds natural, a comma is needed.

Comma Needed	The loud, frequent thunder frightened Rex. (*Loud and frequent thunder* sounds natural. You can also reverse the adjectives: *frequent and loud thunder.*)
Comma Not Needed	I brushed Rex's fluffy golden fur. (*Fluffy and golden fur* does not sound natural, nor could you reverse the adjectives.)

Usually no comma is needed after a number or after an adjective that refers to size, shape, or age. For example, no commas are needed in the following expressions.

Adjective Expressions	five small turtles	an old gray cat
	round yellow eyes	oval floppy ears

Practice Your Skills

Using Commas to Separate

Write ***I*** if a sentence needs a comma or commas. Write **C** if a sentence does not need any commas. Rewrite the incorrect sentences adding commas where needed.

1. Bears and woodchucks and prairie dogs sleep for months at a time when the weather is cold.
2. Housecats enjoy sleeping on warm TVs in sunny windows and in baskets of laundry.
3. Young elephants antelopes rhinos dolphins and hippos are called calves.
4. The young of dogs and seals and foxes are called pups.
5. Leopards are sly agile and alert animals.
6. The small black ant can lift fifty times its own weight and pull thirty times its own weight.

Connect to Writing: Informative Speech

Using Commas to Separate

You volunteered to speak to children at a day care center about the wildlife in your area. What can you tell them about the birds, mammals, and insects they might find in their own backyards? How can you help them understand that all creatures deserve respect and compassion? Write an informative speech, using commas to separate items in lists and to separate adjectives when necessary. Edit your writing for correct usage of commas and end punctuation, and then write the final copy.

Compound Sentences

Placing a comma before a coordinating conjunction is one way to separate the independent clauses of a compound sentence. *And, but, or, nor, for,* and *yet* are all coordinating conjunctions.

22 B.3 Use a comma to separate the independent clauses of a compound sentence if the clauses are joined by a coordinating conjunction.

The appetizers are ready, **and** dinner will be here shortly.

Your dinner was delicious, **but** I can't eat another bite.

No comma is needed in a very short compound sentence—unless the conjunction *yet* or *for* separates the independent clauses.

No Comma	I made quiche **but** no one ate it.
Comma	I could not eat, **for** I wasn't hungry.

Be careful not to confuse a sentence that has one subject and a compound verb with a compound sentence that has two sets of subjects and verbs. A comma is not placed between the parts of a compound verb.

Compound Sentence	I cook breakfast each morning, and John cooks dinner each evening. (A comma is needed.)
Compound Verb	I worked late last night and didn't cook today. (No comma is needed.)

A semicolon can also be used between independent clauses that are not separated by a conjunction.

You can learn more about punctuation with clauses on pages 713 and 718.

CHAPTER 22

Practice Your Skills

Using Commas with Compound Sentences

Write each word that should be followed by a comma, adding the comma. If a sentence does not need a comma, write **C**.

(1) Until the late 1800s, toothpicks were not disposable for they were made from feather quills. **(2)** Today most toothpicks are made from birch wood but others are made from plastic. **(3)** In 1869, Charles Forster noticed Brazilians carving toothpicks from wood and he marketed the idea. **(4)** Birch logs are cut into blocks and steamed. **(5)** A special cutting instrument then cuts the wood into thin sheets for the wood must now be dried. **(6)** Next the sheets of dried wood are cut into small cards and fed into a shaping machine. **(7)** This machine cuts and shapes 12,000 toothpicks per minute yet the process is not over. **(8)** The toothpicks are then polished and pointed. **(9)** Finally, another machine packs the toothpicks into boxes and it packs one box per second. **(10)** Either a wooden toothpick or a plastic one will serve you well.

Connect to Writing: Editing

Using Commas in Compound Sentences

Write the following sentences, adding commas where needed and removing those that are incorrectly placed. If a sentence is correct, write **C**.

1. The term *hors d'oeuvre* is French and, it means "outside the work."
2. Toothpicks, cheese, and olives are the ingredients for simple hors d'oeuvres.
3. Hors d'oeuvres are served before a meal or they may be served alone at receptions and parties.
4. Bite-sized food on toothpicks is a popular type of hors d'oeuvre yet many people prefer something more elegant or unusual.
5. Place a single small shrimp on a butter cracker and drizzle it with lemon juice.

CHAPTER 22

Introductory Structures

Certain introductory words, phrases, and clauses are separated from the rest of the sentence by a comma.

22 B.4 Use a comma after certain introductory structures.

Following are examples of introductory words that should be followed by commas.

Words	**Yes,** that is my constellation map. (*No, now, oh, well,* and *why* are other introductory words that are set off by commas—unless they contribute to the meaning of a sentence: **Yes** *was his answer*.)
Prepositional Phrases	**In the night sky,** Jessie saw the brilliant northern lights. (A comma comes after a prepositional phrase of four or more words.)
Participial Phrases	**Studying the sky,** I recognized the wispy cirrus clouds.
Adverbial Clauses	**After we took off,** the pilot flew to an altitude of 10,000 feet.

You will notice that the punctuation of shorter phrases can vary. Also, do not place a comma after a phrase or phrases that are followed by a verb.

Others	**In July 2000,** 255 students purchased passes and visited the planetarium. (A comma follows a phrase that ends in a number.)
	Besides Mary, Lou is the newest pilot in the training program. (A comma is used to prevent confusion.)
	Behind that low building is a dirt runway. (No comma is used because the introductory phrase is followed by the verb.)

Practice Your Skills

Using Commas with Introductory Structures

Write the introductory words, adding a comma after each one. If a sentence does not need a comma, write **C**.

1. If you disregard the sun the nearest star to Earth is more than four light-years away.
2. Shining brightly above the horizon at sunrise or sunset Venus is sometimes mistaken for a beacon.
3. Well cumulus clouds are somewhat horizontal on the bottom and domed on top.
4. In the layer of the atmosphere called the troposphere clouds and other weather conditions occur.
5. Extending from ten to thirty-one miles above the earth's surface the stratosphere has a temperature of between 45°C and 75°C.
6. On May 4, 1961 a manned balloon flew to a height of 21.5 miles.
7. In the night sky of the Northern Hemisphere is the aurora borealis, beautiful bands of light.
8. Also known as the northern lights the aurora borealis is caused by ionized particles from the sun crashing into Earth's air molecules.
9. In 1969 235,857 miles were traversed by the high-tech spacecraft *Apollo*.
10. When *Apollo 11* landed on the moon it made history.

Connect to Writing: Editing

Using Commas

Write the following sentences, adding commas where needed and removing those that are incorrectly placed. If a sentence is correct, write **C.**

1. Oh don't forget the upcoming trip to the planetarium.
2. On Friday afternoon we will take a short field trip.
3. Teaching, the lesson on constellations I realized many of you were unfamiliar with the night sky.
4. Because of so many city lights it is hard to see complete constellations anymore.
5. Now please remember to bring in your consent forms for our trip to the planetarium.

CHAPTER 22

Commonly Used Commas

There are a few other rules for commas that you use almost daily.

Commas with Dates and Addresses

22 B.5 Use commas to separate the elements in dates and addresses.

Notice in the following examples that a comma is used to separate the last item in a date or the last item in an address from the rest of the sentence.

Saturday**,** June 20**,** 2009**,** my older brother finished writing his autobiography.

We arrived in Austin**,** Texas**,** in the middle of a hot spell.

Write to Hanson Studios**,** 400 Wellwyn Highway**,** Portland**,** Connecticut 06480**,** for free samples.

(No comma is placed between the state and the ZIP code.)

No commas are used with just a month and a year.

My autobiography should be finished by June 2015.

Commas in Letters

22 B.6 Use a comma after the salutation of a friendly letter and after the closing of all letters.

SALUTATIONS AND CLOSINGS		
Salutations	Dear Aunt Ruth**,**	Dear Cathy**,**
Closings	Sincerely yours**,**	Love**,**
	Yours truly**,**	Sincerely**,**

Using too many commas can be as confusing as not using enough commas. Use commas only where a rule indicates they are needed—only where they make the meaning of your writing clear.

You can learn about using commas with direct quotations on pages 969–970.

CHAPTER 22

Practice Your Skills

Using Commas

Write each word or number that should be followed by a comma, adding the comma. (The abbreviations without periods in items 5 and 6 are correct.)

1. On February 10, 1992 Alex Haley passed away.
2. Haley published *Roots: Saga of an American Family* in 1976 and it won the National Book Award.
3. Born in New York in August 1921 Haley grew up in Henning, Tennessee.
4. On December 14, 1978 Haley's childhood home was listed in the National Register of Historic Places.
5. You can visit the offices of the National Register at 800 N. Capitol Street, NW, Washington, DC between 9:00 a.m. and 4:00 p.m.
6. Write to the National Register Reference Desk, National Park Service, 1849 C Street, NW, (2280) Washington, DC 20240 for site nomination forms.
7. In 1965 Haley published *The Autobiography of Malcolm X: As Told to Alex Haley.*
8. On February 21, 1965 Malcolm X was assassinated.
9. The home of Malcolm X at 3448 Pinkney Street in Omaha, Nebraska was torn down less than five years after his death.
10. On March 29 1993 Denzel Washington did not win the Academy Award for his portrayal in the title role in *Malcolm X* despite a powerful performance.

Connect to Writing: Editing

Using Commas in Letters, Dates, and Addresses

Write the following letter, adding commas where needed.

February 3 2010

Dear Grandmother

I have just finished reading *Roots* by Alex Haley, and the story made me wonder about my own roots. I want to start learning about your side of the family first. I know you were born on November 24, 1942 and got married after college. Is it correct that your wedding was in June 1960? Unfortunately, I don't know much else, other than the fact that I was born on January 2, 1997 to your son! I would like to come visit you the weekend of March 15 and talk about our roots. Would that be okay? If you want to write me a letter before then, please send it to 138 Nelson Ave., Austin, TX 78759 and I will start my research early!

Love
Corey

CHAPTER 22

Check Point: Mixed Practice

Write the following paragraph, adding commas where needed. (There are 20 missing commas.)

(1) Benjamin Franklin was born on January 17 1706 in Boston Massachusetts. **(2)** He was the fifteenth child and youngest son of a soapmaker and candlemaker. **(3)** His formal schooling ended after two years and the young Franklin was apprenticed to an older brother in his printing shop. **(4)** Working long hard hours young Franklin still managed to educate himself. **(5)** He taught himself grammar algebra geometry and philosophy. **(6)** When Franklin had a disagreement with his brother he moved to Philadelphia. **(7)** After several years he became an author and publisher and in the following years he became much more. **(8)** He established a reputation as a scientist a statesman an inventor a businessman a philosopher and a humanitarian. **(9)** During the Revolutionary War Franklin even helped to draft the Declaration of Independence.

Connect to Writing: Personal Essay

Using Commas to Separate

Most people want to be linked to their past. What tradition from your family's past is carried on today? Perhaps it is a traditional celebration with special food and tales of your family's history. Write a short essay about this tradition. Add descriptive details, and check for correct use of commas and end marks.

Commas That Enclose

Some sentences contain expressions that interrupt the flow and are not necessary to understanding the sentence. If one of these interrupting expressions comes in the middle of a sentence, two commas are needed to set it off from the rest of the sentence. An interrupting expression at the beginning or end of a sentence requires only one comma.

Commas in Direct Address

Any name, title, or other word that is used to address someone directly is set off by commas. These interrupting expressions are called nouns of **direct address.**

22 B.7 Use commas to enclose nouns of direct address.

Juan, please feed the fish.

I understand**, Elena,** how much you want a parrot.

Where are your ferrets**, Meredith?**

When You Read and Write

When writing dialogue, a writer often uses direct address to help the reader keep track of speakers. Read the passage below and decide which character speaks last.

> When she finally straightened up, her face was tense with excitement in a way that I had never seen before.
> "**John,**" she said, looking into my eyes.
> "Yes, **Miss Merrill**?"
> "This butterfly has hooks on its wings."
>
> —David Klass, *California Blue*

Connect to Reading, Speaking, and Listening: Vocabulary

Using Inflection to Understand Sentences

You use the inflection of your voice to make meaning clear when speaking. In writing, you use commas and end marks. Play this game: Read a few statements from a written text without inflection or pauses, such as "This is what I want and I will have it this way" or "Indeed I understand exactly where you are coming from." Have a partner say each as a simple statement, a question, and an exclamation. You must suggest where commas should be placed and the end mark that would be appropriate at the end of each sentence.

Parenthetical Expressions

A **parenthetical expression** acts as a transition or as a comment on the main idea of the sentence. When speaking, you naturally pause slightly—both before and after a parenthetical expression.

22 B.8 Use commas to enclose parenthetical expressions.

The following is a list of common parenthetical expressions.

COMMON PARENTHETICAL EXPRESSIONS			
after all	for instance	I know (think)	of course
at any rate	however	in fact	on the contrary
by the way	I believe	in my opinion	on the other hand
consequently	I guess	moreover	therefore
for example	I hope	nevertheless	to tell the truth

CHAPTER 22

On the other hand, I like the larger dog house better.

The horse**, by the way,** is hungry.

We were able to afford the cockatiel**, for instance.**

The expressions listed in the box above are set off by commas only if they interrupt a sentence. Notice the difference between the following examples.

Commas	Your dog**, to tell the truth,** is undernourished.
No Commas	She needs **to tell the truth** to him.

22 B.9 Use commas to enclose **contrasting expressions,** which usually begin with *not.* A contrasting expression is considered a type of parenthetical expression.

It is the chow chow of Chinese origin**, not the poodle,** that has a black tongue.

Parentheses and dashes are also used to set off parenthetical expressions.

You can learn about parentheses and dashes on pages 984–986.

Appositives

An **appositive,** including its modifiers, identifies or explains a noun or a pronoun in a sentence.

22 B.10 Use commas to enclose most appositives and their modifiers.

Their car, **that old red convertible,** is as slow as a desert tortoise.

I want a cat, **an orange-striped one.**

An appositive is not set off by commas if it identifies a person or a thing by telling which one or ones. Usually these appositives are names and have no modifiers.

The puppies were born in the year **2009.** (Which year?)

The book *Moby Dick* was made into a movie with Gregory Peck as Captain Ahab. (Which book?)

Adjectives are not appositives. By definition appositives are nouns or pronouns. Titles and degrees in the appositive position are also set off by commas.

Titles	Stephen R. Malory, **Sr.,** sold me these hamsters and gerbils.
Degrees	Gretchen Winters, **D.D.S.,** earned her degree at Yale.

You can learn more about appositives on pages 175 and 686–687.

Practice Your Skills

Using Commas with Interrupters

Write each word that should be followed by a comma. If a sentence does not need any commas, write **C.**

1. Alaskan brown bears the tallest of all bears may grow to a height of nine feet.
2. The dodo a clumsy and short-legged bird had become extinct by the end of the seventeenth century.
3. Tell me Donald did you know a chameleon's tongue is as long as its body?
4. During the 1840s, whaling ships small but sturdy vessels would leave New England and stay away for years.
5. Certain plants in Africa by the way can survive several years without rain.

6. Melissa did you know that beavers can grow nearly four feet long from the tip of the nose to the tip of the tail?
7. Beavers animals that are comfortable on land and in water have webbed feet for swimming and sharp teeth for gnawing wood.
8. Of course you must remember that pets should be fed nutritiously.
9. The gorilla not the chimpanzee looks large and fierce.
10. Please consult Dr. K. J. Jones Jr. about the veterinary needs of your horses.
11. I found out Christy that a hummingbird can fly up to 60 mph.
12. Moreover, the ruby-throated hummingbird migrates 500 miles from North America to Mexico in the winter.

Connect to Writing: Editing

Editing for Commas

Write each sentence, adding commas where needed and removing them where they are incorrectly placed. If a sentence is correct, write **C**.

1. I enjoyed reading the book, *All Creatures Great and Small,* by James Herriot.
2. I have not however, read the other books by Herriot.
3. My favorite book for a long time by the way was, *Black Beauty* by Anna Sewell.
4. The horse, a young black one, told the story himself.
5. I know of course that horses can't talk.

CHAPTER 22

Connect to Writing: Descriptive Paragraph

Using Commas that Enclose

What is your favorite type of food? Is it Mexican or Italian? Have you ever tried Indian cuisine or Japanese sushi? Write a description of one dish that you are familiar with. Describe the ingredients and other facts about the dish. Use appositives and parenthetical expressions. Edit your work for correct usage of commas and end marks, and then write the final copy to make available to your classmates. *Bon appétit!*

Nonessential Elements

Like the other interrupters you have just reviewed, some participial phrases and some clauses are not needed to make the meaning of a sentence clear or complete. Such phrases and clauses are **nonessential,** or **nonrestrictive.**

22 B.11 Use commas to set off a **nonessential,** or **nonrestrictive,** participial phrase or clause.

To decide whether a phrase or a clause is or is not essential, read the sentence without it. If the phrase or the clause could be removed without changing the basic meaning of the sentence, it is nonessential. A phrase or a clause that modifies a proper noun is almost always nonessential.

Nonessential Participial Phrase	Fajitas**, made with beef and tortillas,** are a Mexican dish. *(Fajitas are a Mexican dish.)*
Nonessential Adjectival Clause	Manicotti**, which is my favorite Italian dish,** is a cheese-filled pasta. *(Manicotti is a cheese-filled pasta.)*

A clause or phrase is **essential,** or **restrictive,** if it identifies a person or thing by answering the question *Which one?* If the phrase or the clause were removed, the meaning of the sentence would be unclear or incomplete. An adjectival clause that begins with *that* is usually essential.

22 B.12 No commas are used if a participial phrase or clause is **restrictive,** or **essential** to the meaning of a sentence.

Essential Participial Phrase	The chef **named Terrence** cooks today. (*The chef cooks today.* The phrase is needed to identify which chef.)
Essential Adjectival Clause	The dessert **that you ordered** was taken to the wrong table. (*The dessert was taken to the wrong table.* The clause is needed to identify which dessert was taken to the wrong table.)

CHAPTER 22

Practice Your Skills

Using Commas with Nonessential Elements

Write each sentence, adding a comma or commas where needed. If a sentence does not need any commas, write **C**.

(1) Carrots contain vitamin A which is essential to good vision. **(2)** Magnesium found in green vegetables such as spinach and asparagus is good for your muscles. **(3)** Allium which helps strengthen the immune system occurs in white vegetables. **(4)** Vegetables in which you'll find allium are onions, garlic, leeks, and others. **(5)** Beta-carotene widely regarded as a powerful antioxidant is in orange and red vegetables. **(6)** The blueberries that we love in our pancakes and muffins are very healthy for us. **(7)** Blueberries along with beets and red grapes have anthocyanins in them. **(8)** Anthocyanins which are antioxidants help fight the damages of pollution. **(9)** Curcumin is an antioxidant that also has an anti-inflammatory effect. **(10)** Corn, yellow peppers, and summer squash which are all yellow contain curcumin.

CHAPTER 22

Check Point: Mixed Practice

Write the following paragraphs, adding commas where needed. (There are 16 missing commas.)

(1) On May 14 1804 about forty men and a dog set out from St. Louis Missouri to explore the northwestern part of what is now the United States. **(2)** The leaders of the expedition Meriwether Lewis and William Clark had been commissioned by President Thomas Jefferson. **(3)** Over two years later they brought back a great deal of information about the Louisiana Territory which Jefferson had just purchased from France. **(4)** On their long dangerous trip they received enormous help from a young Indian woman named Sacagawea.

(5) As the expedition journeyed west it was Sacagawea the principal guide who acted as interpreter and who found food in the wilderness. **(6)** Because Sacagawea spoke Shoshone she was instrumental in trading horses with these people. **(7)** Many of the plants she harvested were also used for medicinal purposes. **(8)** Moreover her presence with the expedition was a sign of peace to various Indian groups. **(9)** The success of Lewis and Clark opened the way for new exploration but no one knows how successful they would have been if Sacagawea had not been along. **(10)** Today some historians number Sacagawea among America's most important women.

Chapter Review

Assess Your Learning

Understanding Kinds of Sentences and End Marks

Write each sentence and its appropriate end mark. Then label each one ***D*** for declarative, ***IN*** for interrogative, ***IM*** for imperative, or ***E*** for exclamatory.

1. Corn is one of the largest farm crops in the United States
2. Did you say the opossum is related to the kangaroo
3. Follow these directions carefully
4. I asked whether he had swum in the Great Salt Lake
5. I don't care for the sharp taste of kumquats
6. We just won the championship game
7. Why didn't you take that job
8. Don't skate on that thin ice
9. That's the best news I've heard all week
10. Please turn off the lights when you're finished

Using Commas Correctly

Write each sentence, adding a comma or commas where needed. If a sentence needs no commas, write ***C***.

1. From the bark of the birch tree the Native Americans built watertight portable boats.
2. Ernest Hemingway grew up in Oak Park Illinois but he spent his summers in Michigan.
3. The train arriving at 6:42 p.m. is from Chicago.
4. By midnight the heavy dense fog had descended on the highway and traffic ground to a halt.
5. Well have you decided what you're going to do?
6. During Admiral Byrd's first expedition to the South Pole he had to become accustomed to the long freezing Antarctic nights.
7. A *palindrome* is a word or a sentence that reads the same backward as it does forward.
8. Three weeks before Lola had applied for a summer job in the Catskills.
9. Paderewski one of the greatest concert pianists of all time was also a premier of Poland.

10. On September 21 1784 the first daily newspaper in the United States was published in Philadelphia Pennsylvania.

11. When Alexander Calder's huge mobiles are pushed by air currents the delicately balanced sculptures move.

12. Playing the part of Harry in the musical Marvin Dawson is hilarious.

13. *A Tale of Two Cities* which is set in Paris France is a historical novel.

14. The Milky Way which appears in the sky as a hazy band really contains millions of huge stars.

15. Florida's state bird is the mockingbird and Maine's is the chickadee.

Writing Sentences

Write five sentences that follow the directions below.

1. Write a sentence with two or more introductory prepositional phrases.

2. Write a sentence with an introductory participial phrase.

3. Write a sentence that includes two sets of appositives.

4. Write a sentence that begins with an adverbial clause and ends with an independent clause.

5. Write a sentence made up of two independent clauses joined by *and.*

End Marks and Commas: Posttest

Directions

Read the passage and write the letter of the answer that correctly punctuates each underlined part. If the underlined part contains no error, write ***D***.

(1) Diana Golden a world champion skier and a superb athlete also takes five-day treks through the desert—alone. Although she would never mention **(2)** it she has only one leg. Looking back at her **(3)** childhood Diana remembers being the last one chosen for school teams. That is when she took up skiing, which was not a school sport. She became a good skier, but everything changed one day when she was twelve. Doctors found cancer in her **(4)** leg, and immediately removed it. Over the years this strong, courageous girl took up skiing again. Before she graduated from high school, reporters were calling her a **(5)** champion a hero and a role model.

1. **A** Diana Golden, a world champion skier and a superb athlete,
B Diana Golden a world champion skier, and a superb athlete
C Diana Golden a world champion skier and a superb athlete,
D No error

2. **A** it, she has only, one leg.
B it she has only one leg.
C it, she has only one leg.
D No error

3. **A** childhood, Diana remembers,
B childhood, Diana remembers
C childhood Diana remembers,
D No error

4. **A** leg and immediately removed it.
B leg and, immediately, removed it.
C leg, and immediately, removed it.
D No error

5. **A** champion a hero, and a role
B champion, a hero, and a role
C champion, a hero, and a role,
D No error

CHAPTER 22

Writer's Corner

Snapshot

22 A Depending on its function, a sentence may be **declarative, imperative, interrogative,** or **exclamatory.** (pages 916–918)

22 B The **comma (,)** is used to separate items and to enclose items. (pages 922–936)

Power Rules

Be sure that every statement in your writing is a **complete sentence, not a fragment.** (pages 663–664)

Before Editing	After Editing
If I decide to have a party. I think I'll e-mail the invitations.	*If I decide to have a party,* I think I'll e-mail the invitations.
Planning a menu I can afford. Could be challenging and fun.	*Planning a menu I can afford* could be challenging and fun.
I'll talk to Roxie about whom to invite. *Because I trust her opinions.*	I'll talk to Roxie about whom to invite *because I trust her opinions.*

Check for **run-on sentences** and fix them by adding a conjunction and/or a comma or by separating the sentences into two complete sentences with the proper end marks. (pages 728–730)

Before Editing	After Editing
We decided to adopt a dog, we found a shelter with many to choose from.	We decided to adopt a dog, *and* we found a shelter with many to choose from.
My brother and I argued about which to adopt, we finally agreed on a lively little terrier.	My brother and I argued about which to adopt. *We finally agreed on a lively little terrier.*
We took the dog home, we started to train it.	*After* we took the dog home, we started to train it.

Editing Checklist

Use this checklist when editing your writing.

- ✓ Did I use a period to end sentences that made a statement or expressed an opinion? (See page 916.)
- ✓ Did I use a period or exclamation point to end sentences that gave a command or made a request? (See pages 916–917.)
- ✓ Did I use a question mark to end sentences that asked a question? (See page 917.)
- ✓ Did I use an exclamation point to end sentences that expressed strong feelings? (See page 917.)
- ✓ Did I correctly use commas to separate items in my writing? (See pages 922–928.)
- ✓ Did I use commas where they were needed to make my writing clear? (See pages 922–936.)
- ✓ Did I use commas to enclose expressions that would otherwise interrupt the flow of the sentence? (See pages 931–936.)

CHAPTER 22

Use the Power

The purpose of a sentence tells you which end punctuation to use. Use the sentences below to see how end marks can sometimes completely change the meaning or clarity of a sentence.

Grandma is sending a text message.
Grandma is sending a text message?

Think of a text message you would like to send to one of your grandparents. Use correct end marks and commas as you express your thoughts.

Other Punctuation

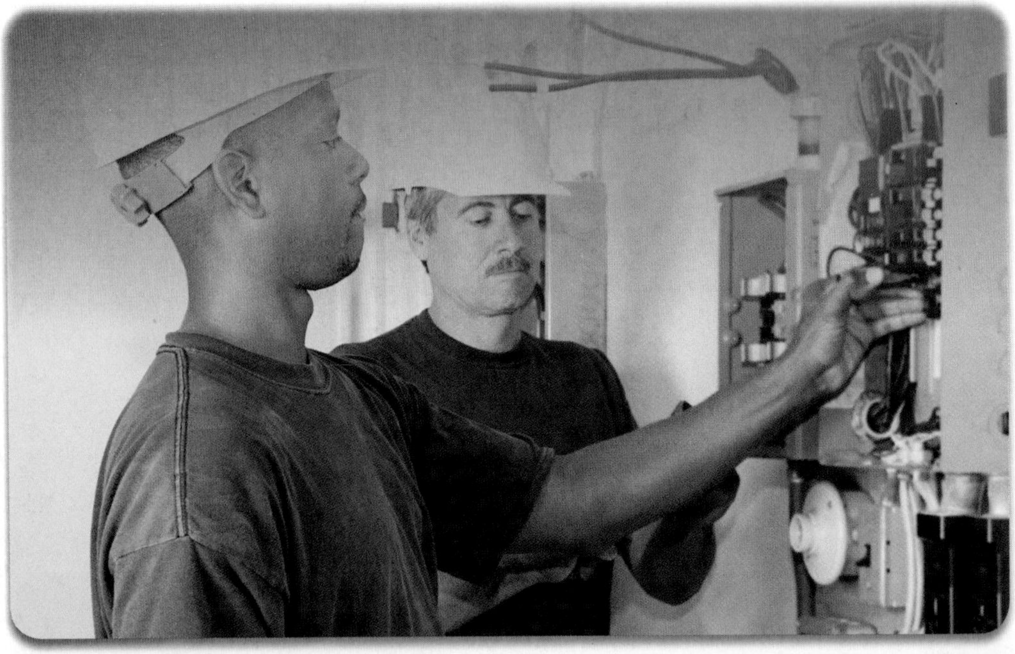

How can you use the right punctuation to communicate your ideas clearly and enhance your writing style?

Other Punctuation: Pretest 1

The following first draft of a speech contains several punctuation errors. The first two errors have been corrected. How would you revise the draft to correct the remaining errors?

Welcome everybody. Id like you to look at the booklet you were given at the door. The chart of occupations (see pages 3–4) lists both high tech and low-tech jobs. George Crandel he's our speaker for today is in the construction business. Crandel once wrote, I believe that it the construction business is as essential to our future as the high-tech industry is." Crandel's Construction Company established 1985 builds the office buildings that make high tech jobs possible. Moreover, many people don't realize that trade workers for example electricians, sheet metal workers, and plumbers make more than many office workers make. At the end of the twentieth century, a sheet metal worker's hourly wage about $18.00 was similar to the wage of entry level computer programmers.

Other Punctuation: Pretest 2

Directions

Read the passage and write the letter of the answer that correctly punctuates each underlined part. If the underlined part contains no error, write D.

(1) <u>Ive been interested</u> in animals since before I can **(2)** <u>remember," said Jane</u> Goodall. Even her favorite childhood **(3)** <u>books for instance, Tarzan</u> were about animals. At the age of seven, Jane read **(4)** <u>The Story of Dr. Dolittle</u>, a book about an Englishman who talks to animals and lives in Africa. **(5)** "<u>Afterward" Jane said "I</u> made up my mind to go to Africa."

1. **A** I've been interested
B "I've been interested
C "Ive been interested
D No error

2. **A** remember" said Jane
B remember." said Jane
C remember, said Jane
D No error

3. **A** books (for instance, Tarzan)
B books [for instance, *Tarzan*]
C books—for instance, *Tarzan*—
D No error

4. **A** (The Story of Dr. Dolittle)
B "The Story of Dr. Dolittle"
C *The Story of Dr. Dolittle*
D No error

5. **A** "Afterward," Jane said, "I
B "Afterward," Jane said. "I
C "Afterward" Jane said, "I
D No error

Apostrophes Lesson 1

Although end marks and commas are the most frequently used punctuation marks, other marks of punctuation are important also. A contraction without an apostrophe or a direct quotation without quotation marks, for example, can be as confusing to read as several sentences that run together without any end marks.

23 A The apostrophe (') is used to show possession and to create contractions.

Apostrophes to Show Possession

An apostrophe is used to signal a reader that nouns and certain pronouns show possession.

CHAPTER 23

Possessive Forms of Nouns

The possessive of a singular noun is formed differently from the possessive of a plural noun.

23 A.1 Add **'s** to form the possessive of a singular noun.

Do not add or omit any letters when writing the possessive of a singular noun—just add *'s* at the end.

fruit + 's = fruit's	The fruit**'s** flavor is sweet.
Ben + 's = Ben's	Ben**'s** fruit pies are delicious.

Singular compound nouns and the names of most businesses and organizations form their possessives in the same way that other singular nouns do.

A jack-in-the-box**'s** image is the logo for Village Toy Shop**'s** sign.

23 A.2 Add only an apostrophe to form the possessive of a plural noun that ends in **s**.

To form the possessive of a plural noun, look at the ending of the noun. That ending will determine how you form the possessive. If the noun ends in *s,* add an apostrophe.

students + ' = students'	The students' lunch hour is over.
Adamses + ' = Adamses'	The Adamses' parents brought lunch for them.

23 A.3 If a plural noun does not end in *s,* add *'s* to form the possessive, just as you would to a singular noun that does not end in *s.*

men + 's = men's	The men**'s** contributions to the
women + 's = women's	bake sale equal the women**'s.**
mice + 's = mice's	The mice**'s** teeth marks on the cheese were obvious.

FORMING THE POSSESSIVE OF PLURAL NOUNS

Plural	Ending	Add		Possessive
cats	*s*	'	=	cats**'** toys
boxes	*s*	'	=	boxes**'** tags
women	no *s*	*'s*	=	women**'s** clothes
geese	no *s*	*'s*	=	geese**'s** habit

Do not confuse a possessive with the simple plural form of a noun.

Possessive	The **cake's** frosting was chocolate.
Plural	The frosting on the **cakes** was chocolate.

Practice Your Skills

Forming Possessive Nouns

Write the possessive form of each noun.

1. brother
2. editor
3. Peter
4. Joneses
5. sister-in-law
6. Denver
7. men
8. ox
9. life
10. chairs
11. president
12. teacher
13. plumber
14. children
15. geese

Practice Your Skills

Using Possessive Nouns

Write *a* or **b** to indicate the choice that is written correctly.

1. **a.** an orchards' trees
   b. an orchard's trees
2. **a.** several trees' leaves
   b. several tree's leaves
3. **a.** the oxens' cart
   b. the oxen's cart
4. **a.** one carts' crates
   b. one cart's crates
5. **a.** 24 crates' of apples
   b. 24 crates of apples
6. **a.** my father-in-law's crop
   b. my father's-in-law crop
7. **a.** the Peñas' farm
   b. the Peñases farm
8. **a.** one farm's buildings
   b. one farms' buildings
9. **a.** two building's rooms
   b. two buildings' rooms
10. **a.** ten rooms of storage
    b. ten rooms' of storage

Connect to Writing: Editing

Using Apostrophes

Correctly write each word that needs an apostrophe or an apostrophe and *s*.

1. I am preparing for the juniors bake sale.
2. The holiday fund-raising committee plans are to raise 500 dollars.
3. What is the recipe for Kris Clark apple pie?
4. Look in Kris notebook.
5. The president-elect lemon cookies will be a best seller.
6. Caroline bought fresh lemons and limes at Owen Organic Food Store.
7. Please hand me Rob boxes of banana muffins.
8. All of the boxes lids are missing.
9. Where are all the other bakers items?
10. Rick left his apple crisp and John cake in his school locker.

Possessive Forms of Pronouns

Unlike nouns, personal pronouns do not use an apostrophe to show possession. Instead, they change form. The possessive pronouns listed in the chart below do not require apostrophes.

POSSESSIVE PRONOUNS			
my, mine	his	its	their, theirs
your, yours	her, hers	our, ours	

23 A.4 The possessive forms of personal pronouns and the pronoun *who* do not use apostrophes.

His drawing is on the shelf. **Her** drawing is hanging on the wall.
Whose drawing do you like better, **hers, his,** or **mine?**

Do not confuse a contraction with a possessive pronoun. A possessive pronoun, such as the word *your,* does not require an apostrophe. A contraction, such as the word *you're,* does require an apostrophe.

Possessive Pronouns	its	your	their	theirs
Contractions	it's (it is)	you're (you are)	they're (they are)	there's (there is)

You can learn more about contractions on pages 790 and 831.

Add *'s* to form the possessive of some indefinite pronouns.

SOME INDEFINITE PRONOUNS
anybody, anyone, everybody, everyone, nobody, one, no one, somebody, someone

23 A.5 Add ***'s*** to form the possessive of some indefinite pronouns.

Everyone**'s** ballot had been counted by midnight.

We should hold the meeting at someone**'s** home.

Practice Your Skills

Using Possessive Pronouns

Write the correct form of the words in parentheses.

1. Almost (everybody's, everybodies') idea of a good date is a movie.
2. These movie tickets are (there's, theirs).
3. The movie they plan to see is (everyones', everyone's) favorite.
4. This popcorn is (ours, our's), but you can have some.
5. This soda has lost (it's, its) carbonation.
6. Is this box of chocolate-coated raisins (her's, hers)?
7. (Nobody's, Nobodys') ticket was checked at the door.
8. The seats over there are (theirs, theirs').
9. Which seat is (your's, yours)?
10. Mine is the one next to (his, his').

CHAPTER 23

Connect to Writing: Editing

Using Possessive Pronouns

Rewrite each incorrect possessive form of a pronoun. If a sentence is correct, write **C**.

1. Are these somebodies' tickets?
2. The dinner reservations and theater tickets are ours.
3. It's our six-month anniversary.
4. Will you two be going in you're date's car?
5. Yes, her's is more reliable than mine.
6. Everyones attention is on your beautiful dress.
7. You're new blue shirt looks very nice too.
8. I borrowed someone's digital camera to take pictures.
9. Put your arm through his' arm.
10. This picture will be everybodys favorite.

Apostrophes to Show Joint or Separate Ownership

Correctly used, apostrophes can identify joint or separate ownership. One apostrophe can be used to show joint ownership in the same way one apostrophe is used to show single ownership.

23 A.6 Add **'s** to only the last word to show joint ownership.

In the following example, the boat belongs to both Nancy and Dan. Therefore, an apostrophe is added to only Dan's name.

The *Water Bug* is Nancy and Dan**'s** boat.

If one of the words showing joint ownership is a possessive pronoun, the noun must also show possession.

The *Water Bug* is Nancy**'s** and **his** boat.

23 A.7 Add **'s** to each word to show separate ownership.

In the following example, both Nancy and Dan have hats; therefore, an apostrophe is added to each name.

Nancy**'s** and Dan**'s** hats are in the cabin.

Apostrophes with Nouns Expressing Time or Amount

When you use a noun that expresses time or amount as an adjective, write it in the possessive form.

23 A.8 Use an apostrophe with the possessive form of a noun that expresses time or amount.

I get one week**'s** vacation this summer.

I'll buy fifty dollars**'** worth of hiking equipment and go to the mountains.

Other words that express time include such words as *minute, day, hour, month,* and *year*.

Practice Your Skills

Using Apostrophes

Write correctly each word that needs an apostrophe or an apostrophe and an ***s***.

1. Both Amy and Jo research papers were informative.
2. It takes at least five weeks time to lose ten pounds.
3. Several months worth of regular exercise will pay off.
4. Weightlifting is Coach Bellows and Coach Warren favorite exercise.
5. They have nearly a thousand pounds worth of weights in the weight room.
6. Dr. Reem and Dr. McMill advice is to alternate bodybuilding with cardiovascular workouts.
7. An hour worth of aerobics is plenty.
8. In four to six weeks time, you'll start seeing results.
9. Amy or Jo paper will surely win the fitness essay contest.
10. They inspired my sister-in-law and my workout plans.

Connect to Writing: Editing

Using Apostrophes

Rewrite correctly the incorrect possessive forms in the following advertisement.

MARK'S AND MARIA FITNESS CENTER

Welcome to Mark and Maria Fitness Center. Your membership entitles you to twenty hours worth of gym time per week. Each week unused hours may not be accrued for following weeks.

Make every day workout count!

Megan and LaTasha step aerobics classes:

9:00 AM (Megan)	This class is designed with the beginner and the intermediate fitness levels in mind.
10:00 AM (LaTasha)	This class is designed for the advanced or the very fit person abilities.

Clint and Jared kickboxing class:

7:00 PM	Clint's and Jared class is for all fitness levels. This hour of your time is well spent!

Please note that the employee's-of-the-month parking slot is not to be used by club members.

Check Point: Mixed Practice

Correctly write each underlined word as a possessive form.

1. What is the assignment in Mr. Clark class?
2. We had only a few minutes review time before the test.
3. When is Anne oral report scheduled?
4. After a month delay, we have received our art supplies.
5. Where are the Peterson twins desks?
6. The Petersons desks are those two over there.
7. This book is mine, but who's is that one?
8. Chris and Tara work shows great improvement.
9. They're academic improvement reflects a semester worth of diligent study.
10. The editor-in-chief praise was a pleasant surprise.

Other Uses of Apostrophes

Apostrophes with Contractions

An apostrophe takes the place of missing letters in a contraction.

23 A.9 Use an apostrophe in a contraction to show where one or more letters have been omitted.

CONTRACTIONS		
I ~~ha~~ve = I've	there ~~i~~s = there's	let ~~u~~s = let's
is n~~o~~t = isn't	he ~~wi~~ll = he'll	~~of the~~ clock = o'clock

No letters are added or moved around in a contraction except in the contraction for *will not,* which is *won't.*

Practice Your Skills

Writing Contractions

Write the contraction for each pair of words.

1. have not
2. we have
3. that is
4. I have
5. there is
6. is not
7. I am
8. will not
9. they are
10. were not
11. I would
12. has not
13. you are
14. does not
15. who is

Connect to Writing: Editing

Writing Contractions

Write contractions for words that can be combined. If a contraction is written incorrectly, rewrite it.

1. We are'nt watering our lawn every day this summer.
2. We do not want to waste water.
3. Its' evident that the lawn can survive with less water.
4. Also, we are going to plant various kinds of cacti.
5. They are hardy dry-weather plants.
6. Moreover, theyl'l bloom with colorful blossoms.

CHAPTER 23

Apostrophes with Certain Plurals

To prevent confusion, certain items form their plurals by adding *'s.*

23 A.10 Add ***'s*** to form the plural of lowercase letters, some capital letters, and some words used as words.

Did you mean to write *b***'s** or *d***'s?**

Small children have difficulty forming *O***'s.**

The plurals of most other letters, symbols, numerals, and words used as words can be formed by adding *s*. Be aware that some writers prefer to add *'s* to form these plurals also.

There are too many *if***s** in that sentence.

Important information is often marked with ***s.**

Apostrophes with Certain Dates

An apostrophe is also used when numbers are dropped from a date.

23 A.11 Use an apostrophe to show that numbers are omitted in a date.

I took a course in handwriting analysis in '11. (2011)

I enjoyed reading these old letters from '65. (1965)

Practice Your Skills

Using Apostrophes

Rewrite each underlined letter, number, symbol, or word that is incorrectly written. Write C if a sentence is correct.

1. Class, you are to learn the following facts about Spanish, and there will be no *ifs* or *buts* about it!
2. I placed *s on your handouts next to important items.
3. When you learn Spanish, you must learn to roll your *rs*.
4. If Spanish is your first language, it is difficult to pronounce *ss* and *ts* together in English, as in *stop*.
5. A local Mexican phone number has six digits, written in pairs separated by –s.
6. Spanish does not use apostrophes with *ss* to form possessive nouns.
7. While in English $s refer to dollars, in Spanish $s often refer to pesos.
8. In Spanish, +s and –s are used as symbols for addition and subtraction.
9. In Spanish, September 10, 09, would be written 10 Septiembre 09.
10. Many Spanish speakers pronounce the *xs* like *hs* in the words *Mexico* and *Oaxaca*.

CHAPTER 23

Connect to Writing: Editing

Editing for Apostrophes with Plurals and Dates

Rewrite the following paragraphs, adding apostrophes with plurals and dates where needed.

In 09 I started learning Spanish. First I learned that in Spanish, *j*s are pronounced like *h*s in English. I also learned that *a*s are always pronounced "ah" as in *spa,* not with a long *a,* as in *cake. E*s are pronounced like the *e* in *bed* and *shred.* Like the *a*s, the *e*s are not pronounced with the long vowel sound; however, the *i*s do have the long *e* sound, as in *me*. The *o*s are long, as in *no*, while the *u*s have the vowel sound you hear in *moon*.

The following year, in 10, I learned more: double *l*s (*ll*) are pronounced like English *y*s, and *ñ*s are pronounced like *n* and *y* combined. When writing exclamatory sentences, you write *!*s at the beginning and the end of the sentence (with the first exclamation point written upside down). Likewise, *?*s are written at the beginning and end of a question (with the first one written upside down).

CHAPTER 23

Connect to Writing: Personal Experience

Apostrophes

Learning another language can be both fun and challenging. Write an informal speech about an experience you had learning words and pronunciations in another language. Use apostrophes as needed with possessive forms, joint or separate ownership, times, amounts, contractions, and the plurals of letters, symbols, and words. Edit your use of apostrophes and then write the final copy.

Semicolons and Colons

Lesson 2

23 B **The most common use for a semicolon (;) is to separate the independent clauses of a compound sentence. A colon (:) is primarily used to introduce a list of items.**

Semicolons

Two independent clauses not properly joined result in a **run-on sentence.** There are, however, several ways to join the independent clauses of a compound sentence. Using a comma and a conjunction is one way.

Run-On	I bought a world map my family uses it.
Corrected	I bought a world map**,** **and** my family uses it.

Clauses in a compound sentence can also be joined by a semicolon when there is no conjunction.

23 B.1 Use a semicolon between closely related clauses of a compound sentence when they are not joined by a conjunction.

I bought a world map**;** my family uses it.

CHAPTER 23

When You Speak and Write

When we speak, we sometimes pause only slightly between sentences or clauses—as if they were joined by a semicolon. In your writing, remember that only closely related clauses should be joined by a semicolon. Ideas not closely related belong in separate sentences.

Joined	I bought another map**;** this one was topographical.
Separated	I bought a topographical map**.** I had previously studied land features in an encyclopedia.

You can learn more about run-on sentences on pages 728–730.

Semicolons with Conjunctive Adverbs and Transitional Words

Independent clauses in compound sentences can also be joined by semicolons and certain conjunctive adverbs or transitional words.

The following are lists of common conjunctive adverbs and transitional words.

COMMON CONJUNCTIVE ADVERBS		
accordingly	furthermore	otherwise
also	hence	similarly
besides	however	still
consequently	instead	therefore
finally	nevertheless	thus

COMMON TRANSITIONAL WORDS		
as a result	in addition	in other words
for example	in fact	on the other hand

CHAPTER 23

23 B.2 Use a semicolon between clauses in a compound sentence that are joined by certain conjunctive adverbs or transitional words.

> The mountain was tall**;** nevertheless, I climbed it.
>
> The river wasn't very wide**;** in fact, it was narrow.

Notice in the preceding examples that the conjunctive adverb *nevertheless* and the transitional words *in fact* are preceded by a semicolon and followed by a comma.

Some transitional words and conjunctive adverbs can also be used as parenthetical expressions within a single clause. In this case, commas are used.

> The hike up the mountain, **however,** left me dehydrated.
> (A comma is placed before and after a parenthetical expression.)

You can learn more about parenthetical expressions on page 932.

Semicolons to Avoid Confusion

23 B.3 Use a semicolon instead of a comma in certain situations to avoid confusion.

In most of your writing, a comma will be used before a conjunction separating the clauses in a compound sentence. However, a semicolon is used instead of a comma between the clauses of a compound sentence if there are commas within a clause.

> Do not put away these maps**,** surveys**,** and charts**;** for the test is starting now.

Normally, commas are used to separate the items in a series. Sometimes, however, a semicolon is necessary for clarity.

23 B.4 Use a semicolon instead of a comma between items in a series if the items themselves contain commas.

> We will study various islands of the world on Friday**,** May 29**;** Tuesday**,** June 2**;** and Friday**,** June 5.

You can learn more about using commas on pages 922–936.

CHAPTER 23

Practice Your Skills

Using Semicolons

Write ***I*** if the sentence does not use semicolons and commas correctly. Write **C** if the sentence is correct.

(1) Cambodia's flag is mostly red and blue a white silhouette of a temple is centered on it. **(2)** Cambodia has a rich religious heritage for example, the temples at Angkor and Angkor Wat are the largest group of religious buildings in the world. **(3)** Buddhism is the dominant religion in Cambodia; the country is 88 percent Buddhist. **(4)** Temperatures and humidity in Cambodia are high, in fact the country has a tropical monsoon climate. **(5)** The rainy season is from May to October the dry season is from November to April. **(6)** Until the 1970s, Cambodia relied completely on its own agriculture however war ruined the country's economy. **(7)** Cambodia produces rice, rubber, and corn, but the country remains poverty-stricken. **(8)** France ruled Cambodia for nearly a hundred years however, the country became an independent monarchy in 1954.

Connect to Writing: Editing

Using Semicolons and Commas

Rewrite the incorrect sentences from the preceding exercise, using semicolons and commas where needed.

Colons

Although colons are used most often to introduce a list of items, they also have other uses.

Colons with Lists

The most common use of a colon is to signal a list of items that is about to follow in a sentence.

23 B.5 Use a colon before most lists of items, especially when a list comes after an expression such as *the following.*

The parrot family includes the following birds**:** the kea, the parakeet, the cockatoo, and the macaw.

CHAPTER 23

A colon, however, never follows a verb or a preposition.

No Colon	Last week we learned about hummingbirds, bowerbirds, and cranes.
Colon	Last week we learned about these birds**:** hummingbirds, bowerbirds, and cranes.
No Colon	The plumage of the crane includes brownish feathers, grayish feathers, or white feathers.
Colon	The colors of the crane's plumage are these**:** brown, gray, and white.

Remember that commas separate items in a series. You can learn more on pages 922–923.

Colons with Certain Independent Clauses

23 B.6 Use a colon between independent clauses when the second clause explains or restates the first.

We learned how crickets chirp**:** male crickets rub their wings together.

The crocodile's snout is different from the alligator's snout**:** the crocodile's is longer.

The kakapo is an unusual parrot that lives in New Zealand**:** it does not fly.

Colons with Long Formal Quotations

23 B.7 Use a colon to introduce a long formal quotation.

> Henry David Thoreau once said: "A truly good book is something as natural, and as unexpectedly fair and perfect, as a wild flower discovered on the prairies of the West or in the jungles of the East."

You can learn more about writing long quotations on pages 353 and 975.

Colons with Conventional Situations

23 B.8 Use a colon in certain conventional situations.

COLONS IN CONVENTIONAL SITUATIONS	
Between Hours and Minutes	4:15 a.m. OR 4:15 AM
Between Biblical Chapters and Verses	Romans 6:23
Between Periodical Volumes and Pages	*America* 157:12–15
After Salutations in Business Letters	Dear Sir or Madam:
Between Titles and Subtitles	*Babe: Pig in the City*

Practice Your Skills

Using Colons

Write *I* if the sentence needs a colon or does not use colons correctly. Write *C* if the sentence is correct.

1. Among the most intelligent animals are the chimpanzee, the gorilla, the dolphin, and the elephant.

2. Many reptiles are protected by law turtles, alligators, and some snakes.

3. *Debugging* can mean two things removing insects from your house or removing glitches from your computer.

4. These animals are considered endangered species: the Bengal tiger, the California condor, and the blue whale.

5. Now I know how the "house wren" got its name it will build nests in old shoes, hats, and mailboxes.

6. The following Bible verses mention doves Psalms 55 6, Isaiah 60 8, and Matthew 10 16.

Connect to Writing: Editing

Using Colons

Rewrite the incorrect sentences from the preceding exercise, using colons correctly.

Check Point: Mixed Practice

Rewrite the following sentences, adding semicolons, colons, and commas where needed.

1. Most of the potatoes grown in the United States come from three states Idaho Washington and Maine.
2. William Faulkner won two Pulitzer Prizes moreover he was awarded the Nobel Prize for literature in 1949.
3. Lancaster Pennsylvania Princeton New Jersey and Annapolis Maryland have all been capitals of the United States.
4. By 1983, the Statue of Liberty was in need of extensive repairs consequently a citizens' group raised millions of dollars for its restoration.
5. The Liberty Bell in Independence Hall was first cast in London in 1752 it was recast in Philadelphia a year later.
6. North Carolina is a major producer of textiles electronic equipment and furniture and it is also a rich agricultural state.
7. The first telephone directory, which was issued in 1878, was quite small in fact it included only about fifty names.
8. The first woman to become governor of Connecticut was Ella T. Grasso she held office from 1975 to 1980.
9. Candidates for the United States presidency must have three major qualifications be at least thirty-five years old be a native-born citizen and have lived in this country for at least fourteen years.
10. One of the longest continuous borders in the world lies between the United States and Canada it extends 3,987 miles.
11. In 1779, Eli Whitney applied for a patent on the cotton gin but it was delayed by an epidemic of yellow fever.

Italics (Underlining) Lesson 3

23 C **Italics are used to indicate certain titles and names, foreign words, and the use of a word used as a word. If you are writing by hand, underline whatever should be italicized.**

Italics	*The Book of Sand* is a collection of eerie short stories.
Underlining	Jorge Luis Borges wrote The Book of Sand.

23 C.1 Italicize (underline) letters, numbers, and words used as words. Also italicize (underline) foreign words that are not generally used in English.

Letters, Numbers	I can't tell the difference between your *z*'s and your *2*'s.
Words, Phrases	The word *garb* means "attire; clothing."
Foreign Words	*Garb* is derived from the Italian word *garbo,* which means "elegance."

Only the *z* and the *2* in the first example are italicized—not the *'s*.

23 C.2 Italicize (underline) the titles of long written or musical works that are published as a single unit. Also italicize (underline) the titles of paintings and sculptures and the names of vehicles.

Long works include books, periodicals, newspapers, full-length plays, and very long poems. Long musical compositions include operas, symphonies, ballets, and albums. Vehicles include airplanes, ships, trains, and spacecraft. Titles of movies and radio and TV series should also be italicized (underlined).

Books	Robert Louis Stevenson wrote the novel *Treasure Island.*
	Where is my copy of 101 Famous Poems?
Magazines	I subscribe to *Writer's Digest.*
	I have subscribed to Studies in Short Fiction in the past.
Newspapers	I enjoy the entertainment and the editorial section of the *New Orleans Times-Picayune*.
	(*The* is generally not considered part of the title of a newspaper or a magazine.)
	I read the Chicago Tribune in the E-edition.

CHAPTER 23

Plays and Movies	I enjoyed Shakespeare's play *A Midsummer Night's Dream.* The 1999 film A Midsummer Night's Dream was directed by Michael Hoffman.
Television Series	There is a surprise in just about every episode of *Heroes.* American Idol is one of the most popular reality TV shows.
Long Musical Compositions	Luciano Pavarotti made his debut in the opera *La Bohème.* Schubert composed Winterreise in 1827.
Works of Art	*La Civilisation Tarasque: Dying Material* is a painting by Diego Rivera. David is a sculpture by Michelangelo.
Names of Vehicles	*Apollo 11* carried the first human astronauts to the moon. Air Force One is the name given to the president's airplane.

You can learn more about the capitalization of titles on pages 905–908.

CHAPTER 23

Practice Your Skills

Using Italics (Underlining)

Write and underline each letter, number, word, or group of words that should be italicized. (The names of awards are not italicized.)

1. Ernest Hemingway's book The Old Man and the Sea won the Pulitzer Prize for literature in 1953.

2. A famous Winslow Homer painting is Boys in a Pasture.

3. The long-running TV series Frasier contains frequent references to literature, art, and opera.

4. Lorraine Hansberry wrote the play A Raisin in the Sun.

5. Have you ever heard Verdi's opera Otello?

6. The 1927 film The Jazz Singer ended the era of silent films.

7. On display at the Museum of Modern Art in New York City is Henry Moore's sculpture titled Family Group.

8. The French word franc is an abbreviation for the Latin term Francorum Rex, which means "King of the Franks."

9. The film 1492 chronicles the voyage of the Niña, the Pinta, and the Santa Maria under Columbus's direction.

10. The letters lou in Maya Angelou's name are pronounced with a long o sound, not a long u sound.

Connect to Writing: Editing

Using Italics (Underlining)

Rewrite each sentence, correcting mistakes in italics. If a sentence does not need any italics, or has used them correctly, write C. (The names of awards are not italicized.)

1. In 1996, Richard Ford won a Pulitzer Prize for his novel Independence Day.
2. The play *Billy Elliot: The Musical* won a Tony Award in 2009.
3. *The Hunt for Red October,* starring Sean Connery, is a movie about a submarine named Red October.
4. In May 1999, the Dixie Chicks' album Wide Open Spaces won Album of the Year at the Country Music Awards.
5. After playing Erica Kane on All My Children since 1970, Susan Lucci won an Emmy award in 1999.
6. Don McLean's album American Pie contains the song "Vincent," which is about Vincent van Gogh.
7. The song mentions van Gogh's painting Starry Night and the artist's tragic death.
8. Slumdog Millionaire, directed by Danny Boyle, won an Oscar for Best Film in 2009.
9. I learned that the Spanish words la isla bonita mean "the pretty island."
10. There is a song entitled "La Isla Bonita" on Madonna's album The Immaculate Collection.

CHAPTER 23

Connect to Writing: Reading List

Italics (Underlining)

You and two friends are spending the weekend at the beach, and you are in charge of "beach entertainment." What will the three of you read while lying in the shade of your beach umbrellas? Write a list of written works that the three of you would enjoy. Remember to italicize or underline appropriate titles.

Quotation Marks and Ellipses

Fiction writers use conversation to provide realism and to reveal important information, such as the characters' feelings, beliefs, and attitudes. Knowing how to use quotation marks is imperative when writing creatively. Quotation marks are equally important when writing term papers. Supporting your thesis with facts often involves using the words of others—words that require using quotation marks.

Ellipses are used when words in a quotation are condensed or expunged. Use ellipses to let the reader know when words have been left out of a quotation.

23 D **Quotation marks are placed at the beginning and at the end of certain titles and uninterrupted quotations. Ellipses indicate that words have been removed.**

Quotation Marks with Titles

In the last section, you learned that titles of long works of art and publications are italicized (underlined). Usually these long works are composed of smaller parts, such as chapters. The titles of such smaller parts should be enclosed in quotation marks.

23 D.1 Use quotation marks to enclose the titles of chapters, articles, essays, stories, one-act plays, short poems, songs, episodes from a TV series, and movements from a musical composition.

Chapters in a Book	"Hester at Her Needle" is the fifth chapter in *The Scarlet Letter* by Nathaniel Hawthorne.
Poems	Yesterday we read Mary Austin's poem "The Grass on the Mountain" in our anthology *America Speaks.*
Articles in Magazines or Newspapers	"Jim Dandy," an article about novelist Jim Magnuson, was in *Texas Monthly.*
	Have you read "Local Literary Legends" in today's newspaper?
Television Episodes	"On Deadly Ground" is an episode of *Walker, Texas Ranger,* starring Chuck Norris.
Songs	"I'll Be There for You" is a song on the CD entitled *Friends.*

Practice Your Skills

Using Quotation Marks with Titles

Write each title, adding quotation marks or italics (underlining) where needed.

1. In 1899, Scott Joplin became famous when he wrote the ragtime song Maple Leaf Rag.
2. Tomorrow we will discuss the article Teenage Musical Prodigies in the latest edition of USA Today.
3. One movement from Gustav Holst's orchestral suite The Planets is called Uranus, the Magician.
4. The short story By the Waters of Babylon by Stephen Vincent Benét takes place in a futuristic world.
5. Judy Garland sings Somewhere over the Rainbow in the movie The Wizard of Oz.
6. Evelyn Tooley Hunt's poem Taught Me Purple is included in the anthology Modern American Poetry.
7. I read the chapter Musical Suffering: The Life of Billie Holiday in the book Great Blues Artists.

CHAPTER 23

Connect to Writing: Editing

Using Quotation Marks and Italics

Rewrite the following assignment sheet, adding and changing quotation marks and italics (underlining) where needed.

THIS WEEK'S SCHEDULE FOR JUNIOR ENGLISH	
Monday	Discuss Lord of the Flies. By today, read through chapter 5, Beasts from Water.
Tuesday	Discuss these poems: Hiawatha's Childhood, by Longfellow; The Daffodils, by Wordsworth; and The Raven, by Poe.
Wednesday	Watch a pre-recorded episode of the TV series Great Books; this episode is titled Aldous Huxley's Brave New World.
Thursday	Discuss the article A Conversation with Amy Tan.
Friday	Listen to and discuss the song Afternoons and Coffeespoons, performed by Crash Test Dummies. Then read and discuss The Love Song of J. Alfred Prufrock by T. S. Eliot, which contains the line "I have measured out my life with coffee spoons."

Check Point: Mixed Practice

Write each title, adding quotation marks or italics (underlining) where needed.

1. From an Internet bookstore, you can order an issue of the literary magazine Zoetrope: All-Story.
2. I have read through the third chapter of the book A Tree Grows in Brooklyn.
3. This history chapter is entitled February: Valentine's Day Massacre.
4. I just found an amusing book of poetry: Spam-Ku: Tranquil Reflections on Luncheon Loaf, edited by John Cho.
5. Have you listened to Diana Krall's album All for You: A Dedication to The Nat King Cole Trio?
6. Her song Hit That Jive Jack was written by Johnny Alston and Skeets Tolbert.
7. I bought a poster of The Scream, an expressionist painting by Edvard Munch.
8. I always peruse the Los Angeles Times, a newspaper to which I subscribe.

Quotation Marks with Direct Quotations

A **direct quotation**—a person's exact words—is enclosed in quotation marks. Quotation marks do not enclose an **indirect quotation**—a paraphrase of someone's words.

A direct quotation uses a **speaker tag,** a phrase such as *Josh replied* or *asked Mary,* that indicates who is speaking. Direct quotations can be placed before or after a speaker tag. A quotation can also be interrupted by a speaker tag.

23 D.2 Use quotation marks to enclose a person's exact words.

Direct Quotation	Eddie said, **"**Wayne is a good friend.**"**
Indirect Quotation	Eddie said that Wayne is a good friend. (*That* often signals an indirect quotation.)

No matter where the speaker tag occurs, quotation marks enclose only the person's exact words. Notice in the third example below that two sets of quotation marks are needed because quotation marks do not enclose the speaker tag.

Before	**"**This poem is about friendship,**"** Kay said.
After	Kay said, **"**This poem is about friendship.**"**
Interrupted	**"**This poem,**"** Kay said, **"**is about friendship.**"**

Only one set of quotation marks is needed to enclose any number of quoted sentences—unless the quotation is interrupted by a speaker tag.

> Kay said, **"**This poem is about friendship. The author wrote it for a friend who had recently moved away. It expresses how much she misses their daily talks.**"**

Practice Your Skills

Using Quotation Marks with Direct Quotations

Write ***I*** if quotation marks are used incorrectly. Write **C** if quotation marks are used correctly.

1. Katherine Mansfield stated, I always felt that the great comfort of friendship was that one had to explain nothing."

2. "Friendship will not stand the strain of very much good advice for very long," Robert Lynd said.

3. "When people are friendly, a Chinese proverb says, even water is sweet."

4. None is so rich as to throw away a friend, "states a Turkish proverb."

5. Another Turkish proverb states, "He who seeks a faultless friend remains friendless."

6. Eleanor Roosevelt said, "Friendship with oneself is all-important." "Without it one cannot be friends with anyone else in the world."

7. "Good friendships are fragile things," Ralph Bourne once said, "and require as much care as any other precious thing."

8. "Give and take makes good friends, states a Scottish proverb."

Connect to Writing: Editing

Using Quotation Marks with Direct Quotations

Rewrite the incorrect sentences from the preceding exercise, using quotation marks correctly. In this exercise place a comma or an end mark that follows a quotation *inside* the closing quotation marks.

Connect to Speaking and Listening: Classroom Interaction

Using Quotation Marks

Find a novel with plenty of dialogue that uses quotation marks. With a partner, take turns reading a page of conversation between the characters. As you read, indicate where the quotation marks are placed by saying, "Begin quote" and "End quote." Tell your partner beforehand that you will be indicating a few quotation marks where they do not belong and that it is his or her job to correct you when this happens.

Capital Letters with Direct Quotations

23 D.3 Begin each sentence of a direct quotation with a capital letter.

"Poetry provides the one permissible way of saying one thing and meaning another,**"** Robert Frost wrote.

Robert Frost wrote, **"P**oetry provides the one permissible way of saying one thing and meaning another.**"** (*Two* capital letters are needed—one for the first word of the sentence and one for the first word of the quotation.)

"Poetry,**"** Robert Frost wrote, **"**provides the one permissible way of saying one thing and meaning another.**"** (*Provides* does not begin with a capital letter because it is in the middle of the quotation.)

CHAPTER 23

Practice Your Skills

Using Capital Letters with Direct Quotations

Write ***I*** if the sentence does not use quotation marks and capital letters correctly. Write **C** if the sentence is correct.

1. John Maynard Keynes once said, "Ideas shape the course of history."
2. "To grow older is a new venture in itself, Johann von Goethe once wrote.
3. "A German proverb reads, even the smallest eel hopes to become a whale."
4. "Attention is a hard thing to get from people," Francis A. Baker commented.
5. "Every calling is great," Oliver Wendell Holmes observed, "when greatly pursued."
6. "To change and to improve," a German proverb states, "Are two different things."
7. When you have to make a choice and don't make it, "William James stated," that is in itself a choice.
8. Gertrude Stein said, "the things I like most are the names of the states of the United States. they make music and they are poetry."
9. "People of many kinds ask questions, but few and rare people listen to the answers. why?" asked Janet Erskine Stuart.

Connect to Writing: Editing

Using Capital Letters with Direct Quotations

Write each incorrect sentence from the preceding exercise, adding capital letters and quotation marks where needed.

Commas with Direct Quotations

A comma creates a pause in speech and a visual separation between a quotation and a speaker tag.

23 D.4 Use a comma to separate a direct quotation from a speaker tag. Place the comma inside the closing quotation marks.

Notice in the following examples that when the speaker tag follows the quotation, the comma goes inside the closing quotation marks.

"A pithy saying is a short yet meaningful saying," Lynda explained to us.
(The comma goes *inside* the closing quotation marks.)

Lynda explained to us, "A pithy saying is a short yet meaningful saying."
(The comma follows the speaker tag.)

"A pithy saying," Lynda explained to us, "is a short yet meaningful saying."
(*Two* commas are needed to separate the speaker tag from the parts of an interrupted quotation. The first comma goes *inside* the closing quotation marks.)

CHAPTER 23

When You Write

When writing dialogue, vary the location of the speaker tags to provide variety. Also note that the location of the speaker tag can place emphasis on the speaker or on the speech.

Emphasis on Speaker	Carla suggested, "Definitely use quotations to reinforce your ideas."
Emphasis on Speech	"Definitely use quotations to reinforce your ideas," Carla suggested.

Practice Your Skills

Using Commas with Direct Quotations

Write *I* if the sentence uses commas, capital letters, or quotation marks incorrectly. Write *C* if the sentence is correct.

1. "the hand will not reach for what the heart does not long for," states a Welsh proverb.

2. A German proverb says "When a person is happy, he does not hear the clock strike."

3. "Happiness is not a horse" a Russian proverb states. "You cannot harness it."

4. An Arabic proverb says, "He who has health has hope, and he who has hope has everything."

5. "Help your brother's boat across states a Hindu proverb and your own will reach the shore."

6. A person with little learning," a Burmese proverb concludes "is like the frog who thinks its puddle a great sea."

7. A Russian proverb states, "A kind word is like a spring day."

CHAPTER 23

Connect to Writing: Editing

Punctuating Direct Quotations

Rewrite the incorrect sentences from the preceding exercise, adding commas, capital letters, and quotation marks where needed.

End Marks with Direct Quotations

A period follows a quotation that is a statement or an opinion—just as it does a regular sentence.

23 D.5 Place a period inside the closing quotation marks when the end of the quotation comes at the end of a sentence.

He said, **"**I enjoy reading about history**.""**

(The period goes inside the closing quotation marks.)

"I enjoy reading about history,**"** he said**.**

(The period follows the speaker tag, and a comma separates the quotation from the speaker tag.)

"I enjoy,**"** he said, **"**reading about history**."**

(The period goes *inside* the closing quotation marks.)

A quotation can also end with a question mark or an exclamation point. When it does, place the question mark or the exclamation point inside the closing quotation marks.

She asked, **"**When was the Civil War**?"**

"When was the Civil War**?"** she asked.
(A period follows the speaker tag.)

"When,**"** she asked, **"**was the Civil War**?"**

The exclamation point also goes *inside* the closing quotation marks in the following three examples.

He exclaimed, **"**This is a great book about Lincoln**!"**

"This is a great book about Lincoln**!"** he exclaimed.
(A period follows the speaker tag.)

"This is,**"** he exclaimed, **"**a great book about Lincoln**!"**

A quotation of two or more sentences, of course, can include various end marks.

"Did you see the historical book exhibit**?"** Laine asked. **"**I bought ten new books**!"**

The question marks and the exclamation points in the examples above are placed inside the closing quotation marks because they are part of the quotation. Occasionally a question or an exclamatory statement will include a direct quotation.

23 D.6 Place the question mark or the exclamation point *outside* the closing quotation marks when the sentence itself is a question or exclamation.

Did Nancy say, **"**The history test is multiple choice**"?**
(The whole sentence is the question, not the quotation.)

I was so relieved when the teacher said, **"**I had to cancel the history test**"!**
(The whole sentence is exclamatory, not the quotation.)

Notice that in the two preceding examples, the end marks for the sentences themselves are omitted. *Two* end marks would be distracting to a reader.

When You Speak and Write

When you speak a sentence that expresses intense emotion, you usually shout, scream, exclaim, or cry out. You'll notice, therefore, that in an exclamatory sentence writers use these words—*shouted, screamed, exclaimed,* for example—instead of *said* or *stated.* These specific, colorful words and the exclamation point work together to communicate urgency, danger, or strong emotion.

Practice Your Skills

Using End Marks with Direct Quotations

Write ***I*** if end marks or commas are used incorrectly. Write **C** if the sentence is correct. Rewrite the incorrect sentences.

1. "Alexander the Great became the king of Macedonia at age twenty", my friend Alex informed me.

2. "Isn't Pancho Villa a famous historical outlaw in Mexico" asked Phil?

3. "Exactly," exclaimed the historian! "His real name was Francisco Villa."

4. "At age 57," said my music teacher, "Marian Anderson became the first African American to sing with New York's Metropolitan Opera."

5. "In 1976" said Coach Carol "the Romanian gymnast Nadia Comaneci earned the first score of 10 in Olympic gymnastic history"

6. I exclaimed "Impressive."

7. Daw Aung San Suu Kyi, a human rights activist, won the 1991 Nobel Peace Prize for her nonviolent resistance to the military government in Burma." said my history teacher.

Connect to Writing: Short Story

Using Direct Quotations

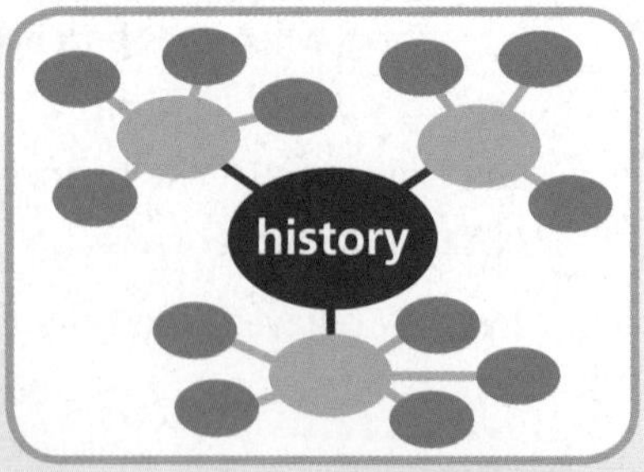

Make a cluster diagram with the word *history* in the center and write down historical events, eras, and figures of the past that are interesting to you. Choose one area of the cluster to be the basis for a short story. List and organize all of your events in a logical order. Then write the first draft of a science fiction story that involves traveling back in time. Include dialogue to make your story more interesting. As you revise and edit your story, pay particular attention to the correct punctuation of the dialogue.

Check Point: Mixed Practice

Rewrite each sentence, adding capital letters, quotation marks, and other punctuation marks where needed.

1. William Feather said finishing a good book is like leaving a good friend
2. a book is like a garden carried in the pocket declares a Chinese proverb
3. there is more treasure in books the famous cartoonist Walt Disney once stated than in all the pirates' loot on Treasure Island
4. a book is good, bad, or medium for me remarked Lillian Hellman, the author and playwright but I usually don't know the reasons why
5. Theodore Haecker mused there are people who talk like books. Happily there are also books that talk like people

Other Uses of Quotation Marks

Long quotations in reports and conversations between two or more people in a story require some special applications of quotation marks.

CHAPTER 23

Unusual Uses of Words

Quotation marks can draw attention to a word that is used in an unusual way.

23 D.7 Use quotation marks to enclose slang words, technical terms, invented words, and words used to show sarcasm or irony.

Slang	"Flick" is a slang term for a movie.
Technical Terms	The "sprockets" on a reel of film are the holes along the edges.
Invented Words	Informative commercials that run as long as a TV program are known as "infomercials." (invented word)
Sarcasm or Irony	This so-called "special program" was really an infomercial.

Connect to Writing: Opinion

Unusual Uses of Words

Write a short opinion piece using quotation marks to set off two or three words used ironically or sarcastically.

When You Speak

When a speaker wants to convey irony or sarcasm, he or she uses the saying "quote, unquote" along with the word being used ironically.

Written	That "art" looks like a paint spill.
Spoken	That quote, unquote art looks like a paint spill.

Dictionary Definitions

When you write a dictionary definition within a piece of writing, you will have to include both italics and quotation marks.

23 D.8 When writing a word and its definition in a sentence, italicize (underline) the word, but use quotation marks to enclose the definition.

Definitions of Words	The word *antenna* can mean either "a sense organ on an insect's head" or "a signal-receiving device on a TV."

Dialogue

A **dialogue** is a conversation that takes place between two or more people.

23 D.9 When writing dialogue, begin a new paragraph each time the speaker changes.

The following dialogue from "Shiloh" takes place between Mabel and her son-in-law Leroy. Each time the speaker changes, a new paragraph begins. Notice that actions and descriptions are included within the same paragraph in which each character speaks.

> "What's that thing?" Mabel says to Leroy in a loud voice, pointing to a tangle of yarn on a piece of canvas.
>
> Leroy holds it up for Mabel to see. "It's my needlepoint," he explains. "This is a *Star Trek* pillow cover."
>
> "That's what a woman would do," says Mabel. "Great day in the morning!"
>
> "All the big football players on TV do it," he says.
>
> —Bobbie Ann Mason, "Shiloh"

CHAPTER 23

If the speaker's sentences form more than one paragraph, begin each paragraph with a quotation mark, but place a closing quotation mark at the end of the last paragraph only.

> Mr. Davis said with a smile, "Television, as you know, is that magical box in your living room that receives your favorite programs by radio wave or cable.
>
> "In the beginning, only a few channels were available, and people turned the channel knob by hand to change channels. You, however, probably never experienced that because you are the remote-control generation.
>
> "And that brings us to today's lesson: How to Repair a Remote Control."

Long Passages

Whenever you are quoting a passage of five or more lines, use a **block quote.** In a block quote, the quoted material is set off from the body of the text by indenting either the left margin or both the left and right margins. Notice in the example below that no quotation marks are used around a block quote.

> . . . While some kinds of noise are clearly distracting, others may be merely white noise. Some examples can be found in this passage from "On Noise," by Seneca:
>
>> Among the things which create a racket all around me without distracting me at all I include the carriages hurrying by in the street, the carpenter who works in the same block, a man in the neighbourhood who saws, and this fellow tuning horns and flutes at the Trickling Fountain and emitting blasts instead of music.
>
> One can assume that Seneca would not willingly submit himself . . .

When you write a term paper, be sure to consult your teacher's guidelines or the style handbook that your class uses. Follow that format consistently.

You can learn more about citing sources on pages 452–459.

Quotations Within Quotations

Occasionally a direct quotation will include a title or another quotation. A distinction is made between the two sets of quotation marks.

23 D.10 Use single quotation marks to enclose a quotation or certain titles within a quotation.

Ms. Rainier said, "Please read the article 'Teens on TV.'"

Nell asked, "Is the article 'Teens on TV' interesting?"

A quotation within a quotation follows all the rules covered in this section. Notice, however, in the first example above that the closing single quotation mark and the closing double quotation marks come together after the period.

Practice Your Skills

Using Quotation Marks

Write ***I*** if quotation marks are used incorrectly. Write **C** if the sentence is correct. Rewrite the incorrect sentences.

1. "Did you know that the song 'I Don't Want to Miss a Thing" is from the movie *Armageddon?*" asked Derrick.

2. Heather added, "I also recognized the song 'La Grange.'"

3. "I suppose, though, that one of the most well-known movie songs is "My Heart Will Go On" from *Titanic,*" remarked Ted.

4. Rosa said, "My mom told me that one of the most popular movie songs for her generation was 'Maria' from *West Side Story.*

5. The word *sitcom* means situation comedy.

6. Rachel asked, "Is tonight's episode of *House* called Remorse?"

7. Ian rented all the *Star Wars* movies for a "Star-Wars-athon."

8. This comedy is a waste of air time.

9. My mother says that my homework is watching the TV and texting my friends.

10. In my opinion, there is nothing real about reality TV.

Connect to Writing: Interview

Using Quotation Marks

Imagine you are able to interview someone you have read about in history books. Would it be Cleopatra? John F. Kennedy? Select a setting and a topic for your conversation. Then write an imaginary conversation between that person and you. Write either a formal interview or a casual conversation. When you have finished, carefully edit the dialogue for the correct use of punctuation, capitalization, and indentation. Use variety when placing your speaker tags.

Ellipses

23 D.11 Use ellipses to indicate omissions in quoted passages or pauses in written passages.

Original Passage "You can play no part but Pyramus; for Pyramus is a sweet-faced man, a proper man, as one shall see in a summer's day, a most lovely gentlemanlike man: therefore you must needs play Pyramus."
(Quince's exact words in *A Midsummer Night's Dream*)

Quoted Passage "You can play no part but Pyramus; for Pyramus is . . . a most lovely gentlemanlike man . . . ."
(The first ellipsis indicates where some of Quince's words have been left out. The second ellipsis indicates that more of Quince's dialogue follows in the original sentence. This ellipsis is followed by the period.)

Written Passage "Well . . . Let me think about it," I said.
(This ellipsis indicates that the speaker paused.)

Practice Your Skills

Using Ellipses

Rewrite the following paragraph from *Saint George and the Dragon,* omitting the underlined portions and inserting ellipses as needed.

Once more the Red Cross Knight mounted and attacked the dragon. Once more in vain. Yet the beast had never before felt such a mighty stroke from the hand of any man, and he was furious for revenge. With his waving wings spread wide, he lifted himself high from the ground, then, stooping low, snatched up both horse and man to carry them away. High above the plain he bore them as far as a bow can shoot an arrow, but even then the knight still struggled until the monster was forced to lower his paws so that both horse and rider fought free. With the strength of three men, again the knight struck. The spear glanced off the scaly neck, but it pierced the dragon's left wing, spread broad above him, and the beast roared like a raging sea in a winter storm.

—Retold by Margaret Hodges

Connect to Writing: Revising

Using Ellipses

Write a shortened version of this passage, using ellipses to indicate where you omit words.

Now from the furnace inside himself, the dragon threw huge flames that covered all the heavens with smoke and brimstone so that the knight was forced to retreat to save his body from the scorching fire. Again, weary and wounded with his long fight, he fell. When gentle Una saw him lying motionless, she trembled with fear and prayed for his safety.

But he had fallen beneath a fair apple tree, its spreading branches covered with red fruit, and from that tree dropped a healing dew that the deadly dragon did not dare to come near. Once more the daylight faded and night spread over the earth. Under the apple tree the knight slept.

—from *Saint George and the Dragon*
Retold by Margaret Hodges

CHAPTER 23

Connect to Writing: Sequel

Writing with Ellipses

For your classmates' entertainment, continue the story above of the battle between the dragon and the knight. After you have written two or three paragraphs, underline words and phrases that you could remove without changing the basic meaning of the paragraphs. Then write a final version, adding ellipses where you removed text.

Other Marks of Punctuation Lesson 5

23 E **The hyphen has several uses, such as dividing a word at the end of a line and separating parts of compound words. Dashes, parentheses, and brackets are used to separate words from the rest of the sentence.**

Hyphens

A **hyphen** is used to divide words at the end of a line.

Hyphens with Divided Words

23 E.1 Use a **hyphen** (-) to divide a word at the end of a line.

If a word must be divided, use the following guidelines.

GUIDELINES FOR DIVIDING WORDS

1. Divide words only between syllables.

sig·na·ture:	sig-nature or signa-ture		

2. Never divide a one-syllable word.

verse	silk	lung	soup

3. Never separate a one-letter syllable from the rest of the word.

Do Not Break	e·vent	a·mong	i·tem

4. Hyphenate after two letters at the end of a line, but do not force a two-letter word ending to the next line.

Break	de-cay	ex-pand	re-lief
Do Not Break	time·ly	liv·er	strick·en

5. Usually divide words containing double consonants between the double consonants.

sum-mit	lat-tice	ham-mer	fol-low

6. Divide hyphenated words only after the hyphens.

hand-to-mouth	daughter-in-law	sixty-one

7. Do not divide a proper noun or a proper adjective.

Bernstein	Montana	African	Victorian

Look in a dictionary to find where a word can be divided between syllables.

CHAPTER 23

Practice Your Skills

Using Hyphens to Divide Words

Write each word, using a hyphen or hyphens to show each place where the word can be divided at the end of a line. If a word should not be divided at the end of a line, write *no.*

1. rate
2. handful
3. indent
4. happened
5. again
6. bitter
7. lava
8. charity
9. fault
10. runner
11. hamster
12. ten-foot
13. driven
14. molasses
15. fast-food

Connect to Writing: Editing

Dividing Words with Hyphens

Some of the following words have been divided incorrectly. Rewrite each word, using a hyphen or hyphens to show where the word can be divided. If a word is correct, write *C.*

1. ca-nvas
2. dis-pense
3. tel-evision
4. two-tone
5. shorts
6. doll
7. carr-iage
8. fixed-rate
9. Linda
10. en-velope
11. Wil-liam
12. friend-ly
13. comp-uter
14. carp-et
15. ant-hology

CHAPTER 23

Hyphens with Certain Numbers

Hyphens are needed when you write out certain numbers.

23 E.2 Use a hyphen when writing out the compound numbers from ***twenty-one*** through ***ninety-nine.***

Thirty-two chairs were built by students in the shop class.

We are waiting for materials to make forty-five hardwood jewelry boxes.

Hyphens with Some Compound Nouns and Adjectives

Some compound nouns and adjectives need one or more hyphens.

23 E.3 Use one or more hyphens to separate the parts of some compound nouns and adjectives. Also use one or more hyphens between words that make up a compound adjective in front of a noun.

HYPHENATED COMPOUND WORDS	
Compound Nouns	half-dollar, make-believe, right-of-way, stand-in, attorney-at-law, send-off
Compound Adjectives	high-energy, off-line, fiber-optic, long-term, face-to-face, third-class

A hyphen is used only when a compound adjective comes before a noun—not when it follows a linking verb and comes after the noun it describes.

Adjective Before a Noun This is a **well-built** rocking chair.

Adjective After a Noun This rocking chair is **well built.**

A hyphen is used only when a fraction is used as an adjective—not when it is used as a noun.

Fraction Used as an Adjective A **one-fourth** minority of the students take shop class now.

Fraction Used as a Noun **One third** of the students will take shop class next semester.

Never use a hyphen between an adverb ending in *-ly* and an adjective.

That math test was a **fairly easy** one. (no hyphen)

My answers were **amazingly accurate.** (no hyphen)

CHAPTER 23

Hyphens with Certain Prefixes

Several prefixes and one suffix are always separated from their root words by a hyphen.

23 E.4 Use a hyphen after the prefixes *ex-*, *self-*, and *all-* and before the suffix *-elect*. Also use a hyphen with all prefixes before a proper noun or a proper adjective.

HYPHENATED PREFIXES AND SUFFIXES			
ex-chairman	self-taught	all-time	senator-elect
ex-governor	self-assured	all-around	mayor-elect
pre-World War I tension		pro-American film	
post-Renaissance figurine		mid-July sale	

CHAPTER 23

Practice Your Skills

Using Hyphens

Correctly write each word that should be hyphenated. If no word in the sentence needs a hyphen, write *C*.

1. Each student has a can of paint that is one third full.
2. We will paint furniture that was made in the mid nineteenth century.
3. Is this American made furniture?
4. I have completed two thirds of my project.
5. Every student made an all out effort to finish the furniture attractively.
6. An ex teacher of Monroe High School's shop class sells refurbished furniture.
7. Three fourths of his income is from furniture sales.
8. Have you decided which piece to paint for your prospective in laws?

Connect to Writing: Editing

Using Hyphens

Some of the hyphens in these sentences are used incorrectly; others are missing. Write each sentence correctly. If a sentence is correct, write **C**.

1. One half of the wood is cedar.
2. Please hand me a two foot length of board.
3. This simple gold frame will look good with my pre Raphaelite painting.
4. I need more two penny nails to finish this project.
5. Wait. I still have one fourth of a bag left.
6. This project is entirely self financed.

Hyphens to Avoid Confusion

Without a hyphen, some words would be difficult to read.

23 E.5 Use a hyphen to prevent confusion.

re-press the clothes
(prevents confusion with the word *repress*)

re-sign the contract
(prevents confusion with the word *resign*)

Practice Your Skills

Using Hyphens

Write the correct word in parentheses.

1. You must (re-dress, redress) the wrong you've done to your sister.
2. Please (re-dress, redress) your little brother, for he spilled juice on his clothes.
3. Mom and Dad would like the upholsterer to (re-cover, recover) this old chair.
4. Did you (re-cover, recover) your stolen camera?
5. My family lives in a (coop, co-op).
6. Chickens live in a (coop, co-op).
7. Give me your shirt again, Bill, and I'll (repress, re-press) it with the warm iron.
8. I've tried to (repress, re-press) the horrible memory of twisting my ankle in front of my parents' guests.
9. Dad will (re-sign, resign) his job today and take a better job across town.
10. If we want to continue living here, we must (re-sign, resign) our lease.

Connect to Writing: Editing

Using Hyphens

Rewrite the following sentences, adding or removing hyphens as needed. If a sentence is correct, write C.

1. Dad, do you want to help me recollect the papers that fell from the shelf?

2. I am in charge of the children's re-creation at the family reunion.

3. It took my younger sister six weeks to re-cover from her foot surgery.

4. Your gerbils will not re-produce if you keep them in separate cages.

5. My parents performed a formal recreation of their marriage ceremony.

Dashes, Parentheses, and Brackets

Dashes, parentheses, and brackets are used to separate words and phrases. Do not overuse these punctuation marks and do not substitute them for other marks of punctuation, such as commas or colons.

Dashes

Dashes are similar to commas, but they indicate a greater separation between words than commas do. Dashes should be used in the following situations.

23 E.6 Use **dashes** (—) to set off an abrupt change in thought.

Several computers—six in all—crashed this morning.

I need the software that—oh, here it is.

Use dashes to set off an appositive that is introduced by words such as *that is, for example,* or *for instance.*

If you damage your computer—for example, with water, hard impacts, or unauthorized repairs—your warranty will be void.

Spamming—that is, sending unsolicited, annoying e-mails—will cause your account to be canceled.

23 E.7 Use dashes to set off a parenthetical expression or an appositive that includes commas. Also use dashes to call special attention to a phrase.

Special symbols—trademark, copyright, and dashes—do not appear on the keyboard.

You can buy that software at any computer store—or on the Internet, for that matter—for under 50 dollars.

23 E.8 Use dashes to set off a phrase or a clause that summarizes or emphasizes what has preceded it.

Java, C++, and Visual Basic—these are the programming languages I know.

The manual and the CD—I need these to install the software.

When you write a dash, remember that it is twice as long as a hyphen. If you are using a typewriter, use two hyphens to make a dash. If you are using a computer, you can look under "Insert" for the dash or em-dash symbol (—), or you can type two hyphens to make a dash (--). (Some word processing programs will automatically convert two hyphens into one dash.)

CHAPTER 23

Parentheses

Parentheses separate additional information or an explanation that is added, but not needed, from the rest of the sentence. Definitions and dates are sometimes put in parentheses. When using parentheses, remember that they come in pairs.

23 E.9 Use **parentheses** (**( )**) to enclose information that is not related closely to the meaning of the sentence.

To decide whether you should use parentheses, read the sentence without the parenthetical material. If the meaning and structure of the sentence are not changed, then add parentheses.

Please affix inventory tags to each PC **(**personal computer**)** in the office.

Alexander Graham Bell **(**1847–1922**)** invented the telephone and many other machines.

Keep in mind that parenthetical additions to sentences slow readers down and interrupt their train of thought. As a result, you should always limit the amount of parenthetical material that you add to any one piece of writing.

When the closing parenthesis comes at the end of a sentence, the end mark usually goes outside of the parenthesis.

> Born in Scotland, Bell immigrated to Canada when he was twenty-three years old **(**1870**).**

Occasionally the end mark goes inside the parenthesis if the end mark actually belongs with the parenthetical material.

> In 1872, Bell opened a school in Boston for teachers of the deaf. **(**His father had been asked to take the position but was unable to do so.**)**

CHAPTER 23

Brackets

You may need to use brackets when writing a report or research paper that includes quoted passages.

23 E.10 Use **brackets** ([ ]) to enclose an explanation within quoted material that is not part of the quotation.

> Laura Mitchell wrote, "Benjamin Franklin was a printer there **[**Philadelphia**]** and published Poor Richard's Almanac."

Brackets also enclose parenthetical material added to material that is already within parentheses.

> Benjamin Franklin **(**printer, politician, and inventor **[**1706–1790**])** identified electricity in lightning with his famous kite experiment.

Following is a summary of when to use certain kinds of punctuation.

PUNCTUATING PARENTHETICAL INFORMATION

Parenthetical (nonessential) information is always set off from the rest of the sentence by special punctuation. Depending on how important the parenthetical material is, use one of the following marks of punctuation.

- Use commas (**,**) to enclose information that is loosely related to the rest of the sentence yet is nonessential. This method is the most common.
- Use parentheses (**( )**) to enclose information that is not essential to the meaning of the sentence but that adds an interesting point.
- Use dashes (**—**) to signal a break in the train of thought or to emphasize parenthetical information.
- Use brackets (**[ ]**) to enclose your own words inserted into a quotation.

CHAPTER 23

Practice Your Skills

Using Dashes, Parentheses, and Brackets

Write *I* if the sentence is punctuated incorrectly. Write *C* if it is punctuated correctly.

1. A television receiver—a cathode-ray tube receives signals and projects images onto the television screen.

2. A catalytic converter, which is placed in a car's exhaust system reduces pollution.

3. Is it possible a modern computer 100 years ago?

4. The funding request (which had to receive governmental approval was denied.

5. Here's what the textbook says: "The people who work on AI artificial intelligence projects include programmers."

6. Bar codes—a series of thick and thin black lines—represent product information.

Connect to Writing: Editing

Using Dashes, Parentheses, and Brackets

Rewrite the incorrect sentences you identified in the preceding exercise using dashes, commas, parentheses, and brackets correctly.

Check Point: Mixed Practice

Rewrite the following sentences, inserting hyphens, parentheses, dashes, and brackets as needed.

1. Mercy Otis Warren poet, dramatist, and historian was the sister of James Otis, an activist during the American Revolution.
2. Harry Houdini birth name Eric Weiss was born in Hungary in 1874 and became a famous magician in the United States.
3. Houdini was an escape artist that is, he "magically" escaped from handcuffs, straitjackets, and other restraints.
4. The self confident Houdini exposed fraudulent psychics and swindlers.
5. Sara Teasdale 1884–1933 won the Columbia University prize for poetry for her collection titled *Love Songs.*

Check Point: Mixed Practice

Rewrite the following paragraphs, adding any punctuation marks that are needed.

American Indians Mohawks, to be precise have built virtually all of New York Citys skyline. Mohawks were quickly recognized for their grace agility and balance and many seem to have little fear of walking on narrow girders and beams at high altitudes. These qualities have earned Mohawks high-paying positions as riveters in many cities New York Boston and Chicago for example.

In 1886, Mohawks first received recognition for their great skill they participated in the construction of a long bridge spanning Canadas St. Lawrence River. Their reputation quickly spread consequently thousands of Mohawks were hired during Manhattans building boom 1920s–1930s. They played a major role at various construction sites the Empire State Building Rockefeller Center and other famous landmarks.

Connect to Writing: Comparison-Contrast Speech

Using All Punctuation

Are you planning for a high-tech or a low-tech career? You and your classmates can help each other determine some of the pros and cons in both types of professions. Write a paragraph in which you compare and contrast the two types of occupations. Use end marks, commas, quotation marks, colons, semicolons, dashes, parentheses, and brackets as needed. Edit your work for all punctuation. Then write the final copy to present to the class.

Chapter Review

Assess Your Learning

Using Correct Punctuation

Write each sentence, adding and correcting punctuation where needed.

1. A string quartet has four instruments the first violin the second violin the viola and the cello.
2. Faults are thick where love is thin states a Danish proverb.
3. Sean bought running shoes a sweatshirt and a headband and any day now he plans to start jogging.
4. Dont touch the casserole dish John bellowed Its very hot!
5. The mule cannot reproduce it is the sterile offspring of a donkey and a horse.
6. During the summer our attic became unbearably hot as a result our landlord installed an exhaust fan.
7. Davy Crockett famous hunter pioneer and frontier hero was born in Limestone, Tennessee.
8. Where is this months issue of Sports Illustrated Jennifer inquired.
9. Everyones help contributed to the governor elects victory.
10. Sue received the most votes in the election 142 in all.
11. Shells have been used for all sorts of curious things money ornaments buttons and horns.
12. Andrea told him My brother in laws orange groves werent affected by the frost.

Editing for Correct Punctuation

Write each sentence correctly, adding any needed punctuation. (Underline any items that should be italicized.) If a sentence contains no error, write C.

1. I will subtract points from your compositions if your os look like cs, Mrs. Henderson warned.
2. When was The Star-Spangled Banner adopted as the national anthem of the United States Amanda asked
3. Gary and Bills editorial appeared in Sundays paper?
4. In 1883 William Cody he was famous as Buffalo Bill helped form a traveling Wild West circus!
5. Back home the days were cool moist and cloudy but here they were hot and sunny.
6. "Dave's umbrella," Mr. Harrington said, "was lost."
7. A warm spring day a quiet stream and the trout jumping above the water what more could anyone ask for?
8. The bus left St. Louis an hour late nevertheless we made our connection in Chicago.
9. Its almost five miles from the Carters cabin to the lake.
10. The taste buds can detect the following tastes sweet sour bitter and salty.

CHAPTER 23

Writing Sentences

Write five sentences that follow the directions below.

1. Write a sentence using a set of dashes.
2. Write a sentence using single and double quotation marks and a semicolon.
3. Write a sentence using a set of double quotation marks and a set of hyphens.
4. Write a sentence using parentheses and a colon.
5. Write a sentence that includes a well-known saying.

Other Punctuation: Posttest

Directions

Read the passage and write the letter of the answer that correctly punctuates each underlined part. If the underlined part contains no error, write D.

In the seventh grade, Ann became a fan of the **(1)** TV series "Star Trek." **(2)** "Thats when I realized Ann **(3)** said, "That I would need technical skills if I wanted to be a space explorer." Years later at the University of California, she took the **(4)** following subjects calculus, physics, and chemistry. Reflecting on her past, Ann has said, **(5)** "I wouldn't be working now with marine mammals **(6)** I am enchanted by them if I had not wanted to be a space explorer as a seventh-grade student." At the Hubbs-Sea World Research Institute, she studied the effects of human-made noise on marine animals.

1. A TV series, "Star Trek."
B TV series *Star Trek.*
C TV series—Star Trek.
D No error

2. A "Thats when I realized,"
B "That's when I realized,"
C "That's when I realized"
D No error

3. A said. "That I would
B said, "that I would
C said "that I would
D No error

4. A following subjects (calculus,
B following: subjects, calculus,
C following subjects: calculus,
D No error

5. A I wouldnt be working
B "I wouldnt be working,
C "I wouldnt be working
D No error

6. A —I am enchanted by them—
B [I am enchanted by them]
C 'I am enchanted by them'
D No error

CHAPTER 23

Writer's Corner

Snapshot

23 A **Apostrophes (')** are used with nouns and some pronouns to show possession. They are also used in contractions. (pages 944–954)

23 B The most common use for a **semicolon (;)** is to separate the independent clauses of a compound sentence. A **colon (:)** is primarily used to introduce a list of items. (pages 955–960)

23 C **Italics** are used to indicate certain titles and names, foreign words, and the use of a word used as a word. If you are writing by hand, **underline** whatever should be italicized. (pages 961–963)

23 D **Quotation marks (" ")** are placed at the beginning and end of certain titles and uninterrupted quotations. **Ellipses (. . .)** indicate that words have been removed. (pages 964–978)

23 E A **hyphen (-)** is used to divide a word at the end of a line. **Dashes (—)**, **parentheses (( ))**, and **brackets ([ ])** are used to separate certain words or groups of words from the rest of the sentence. (pages 979–988)

Power Rules

Check for **run-on sentences** and fix them by adding a conjunction and/or punctuation. (pages 728–730)

Before Editing	After Editing
Our band has really improved *we're hoping to make a CD this summer.*	Our band has really improved; *we're hoping to make a CD this summer.*
I didn't begin music lessons until I was thirteen *most kids start earlier.*	I didn't begin music lessons until I was thirteen. *Most kids start earlier.*

Use standard ways to **make nouns possessive.** (pages 944–946)

Before Editing	After Editing
My *sister* books are piled on her bed.	My *sister's* books are piled on her bed.
She should put them in my *parents* study.	She should put them in my *parents'* study.

Editing Checklist

Use this checklist when editing your writing.

- ✓ Did I use apostrophes correctly with possessive forms of nouns and possessive pronouns? (See pages 944–948.)
- ✓ Did I use semicolons and colons correctly? (See pages 955–960.)
- ✓ Did I italicize the titles of books, movies, works of art, magazines, newspapers, long works, and certain words? (See pages 961–963.)
- ✓ Did I use quotation marks with titles of certain short works and direct quotations? (See pages 964–973.)
- ✓ Did I use hyphens to divide words or when writing compound nouns and numbers? (See pages 979–982.)
- ✓ Did I use dashes, parentheses, and brackets to set off information and clarify my writing? (See pages 984–987.)

CHAPTER 23

Use the Power

Use these graphics to help you understand the importance of punctuation in everyday life.

"Quotation Marks"	"Dancing Queen" is my mom's favorite song.
Apostrophe '	Has anyone found Julie's contact lens?
Dash —	Have fun at the beach—and don't forget your hat.
Semicolon ;	We heard about Pete's accident; we're going to the hospital to visit him.
Colon :	Dear Mom and Dad:
Italics *abc*	*Born on the Fourth of July* is a powerful book.
Hyphen -	Reggie's act was a first-class performance.
Ellipses ...	"You haven't been very friendly lately ... and I hope you'll tell me why, " said Noah.
[Brackets]	"The museum's collection [of medieval music] is truly outstanding."
(Parentheses)	Some people consider Abraham Lincoln (1809–1865) our greatest president.

Write a paragraph that uses as many of the punctuation marks listed above as possible.

Spelling Correctly

How can you communicate your message effectively by using accurate spelling?

Spelling Correctly: Pretest 1

The following first draft contains several spelling errors. The first error, in which *whole* has been misspelled *hole*, has been corrected. How would you revise the draft to correct the remaining spelling errors?

In the ~~hole~~ whole world, there are only six human-made machines. This statment seems totaly unbelieveable when you consider the endiless variety of machines that humanes use to help them do their work. In fact, every machine is simpley a combinetion of these six machines. Consider a machine you may have some familiarity with—the bicicle. What simple machines are combined in the createon of the bicicle? First, their's the wheel and axle. That's unmistakeable. The wheels, the driving wheel, and the geares are all examples of a wheel and axle. When you push the petals, you are actually useing levers, and the chain is basicaly a pulley arrangment in which two gears with a chain around them are powered by the leveres.

Spelling Correctly: Pretest

Directions

Read the passage. Write the letter of the answer that correctly respells each underlined word. If the word is correct, write *D.*

Anton hopes to find a job in the **(1)** foriegn service when he graduates. He may join the Peace **(2)** Core as a way of learning more about his chosen field. Even in that **(3)** unpayed position, the experience he can gain will be **(4)** invaluble. Many **(5)** alumnuses of that institution have later obtained overseas jobs. Anton is **(6)** optamistic about the future. He **(7)** believes that **(8)** coperation is possible, and he thinks that peace is an **(9)** achieveable goal, even in a world filled with **(10)** nucular weapons.

1. **A** forein
B foreign
C forreign
D No error

2. **A** Corpse
B Corp
C Corps
D No error

3. **A** unpaid
B unpayd
C unpaied
D No error

4. **A** invalueble
B invaluable
C invalubal
D No error

5. **A** alumnus
B alumnas
C alumni
D No error

6. **A** optimistic
B optomistic
C optermistic
D No error

7. **A** beleaves
B beleives
C beleifs
D No error

8. **A** cooperation
B coroporation
C cowoperation
D No error

9. **A** acheiveable
B acheivable
C achievable
D No error

10. **A** nuclear
B nukelear
C newclear
D No error

Strategies for Learning to Spell

Learning to spell involves a variety of senses. You use your senses of hearing, sight, and touch to spell a word correctly. Here is a five-step strategy that many people have used successfully as they learned to spell unfamiliar words.

1 Auditory

Say the word aloud. Answer these questions.

- Where have I heard or read this word before?
- What was the context in which I heard or read the word?

2 Visual

Look at the word. Answer these questions.

- Does this word divide into parts? Is it a compound word? Does it have a prefix or a suffix?
- Does this word look like any other word I know? Could it be part of a word family I would recognize?

3 Auditory

Spell the word to yourself. Say the word the way it is spelled. Answer these questions.

- How is each sound spelled?
- Are there any surprises? Does the word follow spelling rules I know, or does it break the rules?

4 Visual/Kinesthetic

Write the word as you look at it. Answer these questions.

- Have I written the word clearly?
- Are my letters formed correctly?

5 Visual/Kinesthetic

Cover up the word. Visualize it. Write it. Answer this question.

- Did I write the word correctly?

If the answer is no, return to step 1.

Spelling Strategies

When you write, you want your readers to think about your message. You don't want them to get bogged down trying to figure out what words you meant to write. Understanding strategies for spelling will help you communicate clearly.

Use a dictionary. If you're not sure how to spell a word, or if a word you've written doesn't "look right," check the word in a dictionary. Sometimes when you are writing, you may not want to stop to look up a word. Instead, circle the word to remind you to look it up later.

Proofread your writing carefully. Watch for misspellings and for words you're not sure you spelled correctly. If you use a computer, do not rely on the spell-check to find all spelling errors. When you type the word *there,* the computer can't know that you really meant to type *their* or *they're*.

Be sure you are pronouncing words correctly. "Swallowing" syllables or adding extra syllables can cause you to misspell a word.

Make up mnemonic devices. A sentence like "**Critic**s **critic**ize" can help you remember that the *s* sound in *criticize* is spelled with *c*. "The **chap**eron is a fine **chap**" can help you remember that *chaperon* begins with the letters *ch* even though the sound is *sh*.

Keep a spelling journal. Use it to record the words that you've had trouble spelling. Here are some suggestions for organizing your spelling journal.

- Write the word correctly.
- Write the word again, underlining or circling the part of the word that gave you trouble.
- Write a tip that will help you remember how to spell the word in the future.

optimistic	**optimistic**	**I am optimistic every vowel is i except the first one.**

Practice Your Skills

Recognizing Misspelled Words

Identify the misspelled word in each set. Then write the word correctly. Use a dictionary to check your work.

1.	(a) unforgetable	(b) veteran	(c) sizable
2.	(a) referee	(b) resign	(c) extrorindary
3.	(a) organick	(b) luxury	(c) eventually
4.	(a) prestige	(b) similiar	(c) thesaurus
5.	(a) dissatisfied	(b) rebel	(c) brillant
6.	(a) mathmatics	(b) athletics	(c) together
7.	(a) fasinating	(b) incident	(c) bureau
8.	(a) illegal	(b) permanant	(c) forty
9.	(a) illustrate	(b) coupon	(c) advertisment
10.	(a) punctual	(b) resteraunt	(c) disguise

Practice Your Skills

Pronouncing Words

Practice saying each syllable in the following words to help you spell the words correctly. Check a dictionary if you are not sure of the correct pronunciation.

1. nu•cle•ar

2. per•se•ver•ance

3. pop•u•lace

4. syr•up

5. cit•i•zen

6. con•sci•en•tious

7. des•per•ate

8. mo•not•o•nous

9. bib•li•og•ra•phy

10. po•et•ry

Spelling Patterns Lesson 1

Understanding spelling patterns can help you spell many words correctly. The following information should clarify these patterns and explain how to form plurals and add prefixes and suffixes to words.

24 A **Spelling patterns—such as *i* before *e* except after *c*—apply to many words and can help you spell many different words correctly.**

Words with *ie* and *ei*

24 A.1 When you spell words with *ie* or *ei*, *i* comes before *e* except when the letters follow *c* or when they stand for the sound long *a*.

IE AND *EI*			
Examples	***ie***	gr**ie**vance	bel**ie**ve
	ei* after *c	c**ei**ling	dec**ei**ve
	sounds like ***a***	r**ei**gn	**ei**ght
Exceptions	profic**ie**nt	forf**ei**t	n**ei**ther
	consc**ie**nce	h**ei**fer	**ei**ther
	anc**ie**nt	l**ei**sure	prot**ei**n
	effic**ie**nt	h**ei**r	h**ei**ght
	spec**ie**s	w**ei**rd	s**ei**ze

The rule about the *ie*/*ei* spelling patterns only applies when the two letters occur in the same syllable and spell just one vowel sound. It does not apply when *i* and *e* appear in different syllables.

IE AND *EI* IN DIFFERENT SYLLABLES			
d**e•i**sm	r**e•i**nvent	fanc**i•e**r	sc**i•e**ntist

Words with *-sede, -cede,* and *-ceed*

24 A.2 Words that end with a syllable that sounds like "seed" are usually spelled with *-cede.* Only one word in English is spelled with *-sede,* and only three words are spelled with *-ceed.*

-SEDE, -CEDE, AND *-CEED*				
Examples	con**cede**	re**cede**	pre**cede**	se**cede**
Exceptions	super**sede**	pro**ceed**	suc**ceed**	ex**ceed**

CHAPTER 24

WORD ALERT

Word parts that sound like "seed" are never spelled *seed* except in words that have to do with seeds or sowing seeds. A misspelling could produce a homophone with a very different meaning.

recede—[verb] to go or move back
The flood waters finally **receded.**

reseed—[verb] to sow again
We **reseeded** the meadow with wildflower seeds.

Practice Your Skills

Using Spelling Patterns

Write each word, adding *ie* or *ei.* If you are not sure about a spelling, check the dictionary.

1. w ▢ ght	**6.** p ▢ rce	**11.** dec ▢ ve	**16.** med ▢ val
2. s ▢ ge	**7.** for ▢ gn	**12.** hyg ▢ ne	**17.** retr ▢ ve
3. br ▢ f	**8.** gr ▢ ve	**13.** l ▢ sure	**18.** prot ▢ n
4. f ▢ rce	**9.** y ▢ ld	**14.** rec ▢ ve	**19.** perc ▢ ve
5. v ▢ l	**10.** rel ▢ ve	**15.** w ▢ rd	**20.** n ▢ ther

Practice Your Skills

Using Spelling Patterns

Write each word, adding *-sede, -ceed,* or *-cede.* Use a dictionary to check your work.

1. ex ▢	**4.** suc ▢	**7.** pro ▢	**10.** pre ▢
2. con ▢	**5.** super ▢	**8.** ac ▢	
3. se ▢	**6.** inter ▢	**9.** re ▢	

Connect to Writing: Editing

Using Spelling Patterns

Read this narrative and rewrite the underlined words that have been spelled incorrectly. Use a dictionary to check your work.

Student 1: You know that new person in our science class? My nieghbor says he's the hier to a huge fortune!

Student 2: The hier to a huge fortune going to public school? That's hard to beleive. In fact, it's pretty inconcievable.

Student 1: Not everyone who's rich is concieted. Maybe he's not even rich yet. Maybe he won't recieve his fortune until he's ancient.

Student 2: I didn't say rich people were conceited. But it would be wierd for someone who's really rich to go to a regular public school instead of a fancy private school.

Student 1: Maybe his parents want him to succede as a regular kid. However, as the recipeint of a fortune, he would be able to take college courses at his liesure. His life will no doubt be influenced by the reciept of money.

Student 2: I think your fascination with this kid exseeds normal interest. Why don't you introduce yourself and procede to get to know him? That would be the best way to relieve your curiosity.

CHAPTER 24

WORD ALERT

Conceited and *conceded* sound alike, but they have very different meanings.

conceited—[adjective] having an exaggerated opinion of oneself; vain. The winner was accomplished in debate, but he was also very **conceited.**

conceded—[verb] admitted as true or certain; acknowledged. She **conceded** one point during the debate but refused to give up the argument. The candidate **conceded** defeat before all the votes in the district were in.

Plurals Lesson 2

These examples will explain how to form the plurals of nouns. When in doubt about a spelling, check a dictionary.

24 B **Many nouns form their plurals by adding *s* or *es*. There are exceptions.**

Regular Nouns

24 B.1 To form the plural of most nouns, simply add *s.*

MOST NOUNS				
Singular	plumber	almanac	course	maze
Plural	plumber**s**	almanac**s**	course**s**	maze**s**

24 B.2 If a noun ends with *s, ch, sh, x,* or *z,* add *es* to form the plural.

S, CH, SH, X, AND *Z*					
Singular	atla**s**	pea**ch**	a**sh**	ta**x**	blint**z**
Plural	atlas**es**	peach**es**	ash**es**	tax**es**	blintz**es**

Nouns Ending with *y*

24 B.3 Add *s* to a noun ending with a vowel and *y.*

VOWELS AND *Y*				
Singular	birthd**ay**	vall**ey**	bu**oy**	all**oy**
Plural	birthday**s**	valley**s**	buoy**s**	alloy**s**

24 B.4 Change the *y* to *i* and add *es* to a noun ending with a consonant and *y.*

CONSONANTS AND *Y*				
Singular	bo**dy**	sala**ry**	fanta**sy**	chari**ty**
Plural	bod**ies**	salar**ies**	fantas**ies**	charit**ies**

CHAPTER 24

Practice Your Skills

Forming Plurals

Write the plural form of each noun. Use a dictionary to check your work.

1. lawyer	**6.** delivery	**11.** specialty	**16.** church
2. journey	**7.** referee	**12.** radish	**17.** comedy
3. tax	**8.** display	**13.** inequity	**18.** vase
4. inquiry	**9.** actress	**14.** nephew	**19.** flurry
5. satire	**10.** alley	**15.** convoy	**20.** triangle

Connect to Writing: Editing

Spelling Plural Nouns

Change the underlined nouns from singular to plural. Use a dictionary to check your work.

The Strauss family is one of the most famous <u>family</u> in music history. What's interesting about the <u>Strauss</u> is that both father and son became <u>musician</u> against the <u>wish</u> of their <u>parent</u>. The elder Johann Strauss played violin and joined a dance orchestra. Later he formed his own orchestra that toured many <u>country</u> in Europe. His son Johann also followed a musical career against his father's <u>wish</u>. He formed his own successful orchestra.

In those <u>day</u>, the waltz was the most popular of all <u>dance</u> in European <u>city</u>. Both <u>Strauss</u> were famous for <u>waltz</u>. The younger Johann composed more than 400 <u>waltz</u>. The most famous of his <u>composition</u> is the "Blue Danube Waltz."

Nouns Ending with *o*

24 B.5 Add *s* to a noun ending with a vowel and *o*.

VOWELS AND *O*				
Singular	studi**o**	curi**o**	stere**o**	kangar**oo**
Plural	studio**s**	curio**s**	stereo**s**	kangaroo**s**

24 B.6 Add *s* to form the plural of musical terms ending in *o*.

MUSICAL TERMS WITH *O*				
Singular	sopran**o**	cell**o**	tri**o**	concertin**o**
Plural	soprano**s**	cello**s**	trio**s**	concertino**s**

24 B.7 The plurals of nouns ending in a consonant and *o* do not follow a regular pattern.

CONSONANTS AND *O*				
Singular	auto	ego	hero	embar**go**
Plural	autos	egos	her**oes**	embar**goes**

When you are not sure how to form the plural of a word that ends with *o,* consult a dictionary. If the dictionary shows more than one plural form, use the first form listed. If the dictionary does not give a plural form, the plural is usually formed by adding *s.*

Nouns Ending in *f* or *fe*

24 B.8 To form the plural of some nouns ending in *f* or *fe,* just add *s.*

F AND *FE*				
Singular	gulf	sheriff	fi**fe**	wai**f**
Plural	gulfs	sheriffs	fi**fes**	wai**fs**

CHAPTER 24

24 B.9 For some nouns ending in *f* or *fe,* change the *f* or *fe* to *v* and add *es.*

F AND *FE* TO *V*				
Singular	wife	half	loaf	self
Plural	wives	halves	loaves	selves

Because there is no sure way to tell which rule applies, consult a dictionary to check the plural form of a word that ends with *f* or *fe.*

Practice Your Skills

Forming Plurals

Write the plural form of each of these nouns. Check a dictionary to be sure you've formed the plural correctly.

1. alto
2. echo
3. photo
4. solo
5. shampoo
6. ratio
7. concerto
8. silo
9. cuckoo
10. potato
11. chief
12. wolf
13. chef
14. tariff
15. life
16. hoof
17. roof
18. shelf
19. proof
20. scarf

Connect to Writing: Editing

Spelling Plural Nouns

Correct the spelling errors below. Use a dictionary to check your work.

All over the world, there are disagreements and confusing storys about animals. In Australia, the kangaroo is the national animal, and most people love the kangaroo. But kangarooes can destroy people's yards and ruin crops. So for some people, kangaroos are nuisances instead of national treasures. Wolfs have a similar problem in the United States. Many people were delighted when wolves were reintroduced into places like Yellowstone National Park. But nearby ranchers and farmers say that the wolves feed themselfs by taking the lifes of domestic animals. For them, the people who helped bring back the wolfs are anything but heros.

Other Plural Forms

24 B.10 Irregular plurals are not formed by adding *s* or *es*.

IRREGULAR PLURALS				
Singular	man	woman	ox	mouse
Plural	men	women	ox**en**	m**ice**
Singular	child	foot	goose	tooth
Plural	child**ren**	f**ee**t	g**ee**se	t**ee**th

24 B.11 Some nouns have the same form for singular and plural.

SAME SINGULAR AND PLURAL					
Swiss	cattle	species	moose	Sioux	series
corps	deer	scissors	pliers	sheep	trousers

WORD ALERT

Do not confuse *corps* with *corpse*. The *p* and *s* are silent in the word *corps*.

corps—[pronounced kôr, plural *corps*] a group of people associated with some work or organization. They rely on a small **corps** of dedicated workers.

corpse—[pronounced kôrps, plural *corpses*] a dead body, especially of a person. The main character in the mystery novel discovered an unknown **corpse** in the library.

CHAPTER 24

Foreign Plurals

24 B.12 The plurals of some foreign words are formed as they are in their original language. With some foreign words, there are two ways to form the plural.

FOREIGN WORDS				
Examples	alumn**us**	gen**us**	cris**is**	dat**um**
	alumn**i**	gen**era**	cris**es**	dat**a**
Exceptions	formul**a** formul**as** or formul**ae**		ind**ex** ind**exes** or ind**ices**	
	cact**us** cact**uses** or cact**i**		phenomen**on** phenomen**a** or phenomen**ons**	

Check a dictionary when you form the plural of foreign words. When two forms are given, the first one is preferred.

Practice Your Skills

Forming Plurals

Write the plural form of each of these nouns. Check a dictionary, if necessary, to be sure you've written the preferred plural form.

1. focus
2. goose
3. trout
4. opus
5. rice
6. louse
7. moose
8. Chinese
9. minimum
10. gateau
11. synopsis
12. salmon
13. corps
14. tooth
15. die
16. appendix
17. neurosis
18. stimulus
19. optimum
20. criterion

Connect to Writing: Editing

Spelling Plural Nouns

Check each underlined plural noun in this passage. If the plural is formed incorrectly, write the correct form. Use a dictionary to check your work.

(1) The king's dinner table was laden with elaborate dishes, all enticing stimuluses for the king's enormous appetite. **(2)** The dishes were prepared by endless corpses of chefs who worked around the clock. The king loved to eat—anything and everything. **(3)** For him there were two criterions for a good meal. There had to be lots of food and it had to taste good. **(4)** The king might start with a dozen smoked trout. **(5)** Next he might consume six or seven whole poached salmons. Just finding enough food for the king was a challenge. **(6, 7)** When there were no more geese or deers to be found, the desperate chefs were often forced to cook **(8, 9)** opossums and mooses to satisfy the king's boundless appetite. **(10)** While the king ate all the meat and fish, his subjects ate only rices and beans.

CHAPTER 24

Compound Nouns

24 B.13 Most **compound nouns** are made plural in the same way as other nouns. The letter *s* or *es* is added to the end of the word. However, when the main word in a compound noun appears first, that word becomes plural.

COMPOUND NOUNS			
Examples	chair**man**	hour**glass**	step**child**
	chair**men**	hour**glasses**	step**children**
Exceptions	**sister**-in-law	**hanger**-on	**poet** laureate
	sisters-in-law	**hangers**-on	**poets** laureate

Numerals, Letters, Symbols, and Words as Words

24 B.14 To form the plurals of most letters, symbols, numerals, and words used as words, add an *s.* To prevent confusion, it is best to use an apostrophe and *s* with lowercase letters, some capital letters, and some words used as words.

Examples The *$***s** over his head signify that he is greedy.

All the sentences in her letter ended with *!***s.**

*But***s** and *and***s** are conjunctions.

Were you born in the 1990**s**?

Exceptions This letter is full of *I***'s** and *me***'s.**

All the *like***'s** in this paragraph should be replaced with *as***'s.**

How do you form your capital *S***'s?**

CHAPTER 24

Practice Your Skills

Forming Plurals

Write the plural form for each item. Use a dictionary to check your work.

1. musk-ox
2. *and*
3. 30
4. by-product
5. groomsman
6. editor-in-chief
7. bride-to-be
8. &
9. mayor-elect
10. attorney-at-law
11. jackknife
12. *good*
13. doorman
14. 2010
15. snapdragon

Connect to Writing: Editing

Forming Plurals

Decide if the underlined plurals in this newspaper article are formed correctly. If any are incorrect, write the correct form. Use a dictionary to check your work.

> Twin sisters Elizabeth and Emily Hatfield will wed twin brothers Andrew and Alan Madsen in a double wedding on June 10. Both bride-to-bes will wear family heirloom gowns. Emily will wear her great-grandmother's wedding gown from the 1920s. Elizabeth will wear her grandmother's gown from the 1940's. The maid of honors will wear the gowns that were worn by the maids of honor at the original weddings. The bridesmaids' gowns will also reflect the fashions of the 1920's or the 1940s.
>
> The sisters are similar, and they are very close. When they speak, their sentences contain more *wes* than *Is*. "We've been twins all our lives," says Elizabeth, "now we'll be sister-in-laws too!"

CHAPTER 24

Check Point: Mixed Practice

Write the plural form of each of these words. Use a dictionary whenever necessary.

1. 6	**6.** pinto	**11.** series	**16.** scissors
2. libretto	**7.** *to*	**12.** blowfish	**17.** schema
3. focus	**8.** oasis	**13.** '90	**18.** ostrich
4. concerto	**9.** hero	**14.** premium	**19.** *why*
5. serum	**10.** hoof	**15.** spin-off	**20.** *hello*

Connect to Writing: Opinion Paragraph

Using Plurals

What would it be like to be a twin? How would you feel if there were another person who looked just like you? Write an opinion paragraph telling what you think being a twin would be like. If you really are a twin, tell about your own experience. Use at least ten plural nouns in your paragraph.

Connect to Reading and Writing: Classroom Vocabulary

English Vocabulary and Spelling

This chapter has introduced you to new terms you will use often in your study of English grammar. To keep track of these new words and phrases, such as *regular nouns, compound nouns, words used as words, prefixes,* and *suffixes,* make a booklet that lists and tells about them.

Spelling Numbers Lesson 3

24 C Some numbers are written as numerals while other numbers are written as words.

The following generalizations can help you decide how to write numbers in your writing.

Numerals or Number Words

24 C.1 Spell out numbers that can be written in one or two words. Use numerals for other numbers. Always spell out a number that begins a sentence.

Our committee worked for **four** hours.

We sent out **890** invitations to our band concert.

Five hundred eighty-three people bought tickets.

When you have a series of numbers, and some are just one or two words, but others are not, use numerals for them all.

There are **800** seats in our high school auditorium. All but **25** seats were filled on Thursday night. Friday night's performance was sold out. On Saturday night, **781** people attended. All together, **2,356** people saw our play.

Ordinal Numbers

24 C.2 Always spell out numbers used to tell the order.

The **first** time we did the play, everyone was nervous.

By our **third** performance, we had calmed down a little.

WORD ALERT

Words such as *once* or *twice* have no numeral substitutes. Remember to spell them out.

once—[adverb] completed one time. Emily forgot her lines only **once.**

twice—[adverb] repeated two times. The play was great; I watched it **twice.**

Numbers in Dates

24 C.3 Use a numeral for a date when you include the name of the month. Always use numerals for the year.

Examples The play *Our Town* opened on **April 14.**

Thornton Wilder won the Pulitzer Prize for *The Skin of Our Teeth* in **1943.**

Exception Our show closed on the **sixteenth** of April.
(Always spell out ordinal numbers.)

Practice Your Skills

Spelling Numbers

Complete each sentence with the correct form of the number in parentheses. Some of the answers are correct already.

1. (1897) Thornton Wilder was born in ____.
2. (41) He was ____ years old when he wrote *Our Town.*
3. (3) *Our Town* is a play in ____ acts.
4. (1938) Wilder won the Pulitzer Prize for *Our Town* in ____.
5. (2) It was the ____ time he'd won a Pulitzer Prize.
6. (1) His ____ was for the novel *The Bridge of San Luis Rey.*
7. (3) He won a ____ Pulitzer Prize for the play *The Skin of Our Teeth.*
8. (22,462) There are ____ secondary schools in the United States.
9. (80) *Our Town* has probably been performed in ____ percent of them.
10. (17,696) ____ schools would have presented *Our Town.*

Connect to Writing: Editing

Writing Numbers

Correct any mistakes in the numbers below. Use a dictionary to check your work.

There are 194 nations in the world. The second smallest nation is one you may never have heard of. It is called Tuvalu, and it is made up of 9 ring-shaped coral islands, called atolls, in the Pacific Ocean. Though it is three hundred fifty miles from the north of Tuvalu to the south, the total land area of Tuvalu is only about ten square miles. The population of Tuvalu is estimated at nine thousand eight hundred thirty-one. If you compare Tuvalu with Washington, D.C., you discover that the geographic area of Washington, D.C., is ten times greater than the entire nation of Tuvalu, and 62 times as many people live there.

Prefixes and Suffixes

24 D **A prefix is one or more syllables placed in front of a base word to form a new word. A suffix is one or more syllables placed after a base word to change its part of speech and possibly also its meaning.**

24 D.1 When you add a **prefix,** the spelling of the base word does not change.

PREFIXES	
in + visible = **in**visible	**mis** + step = **mis**step
co + operate = **co**operate	**re** + entry = **re**entry
dis + jointed = **dis**jointed	**il** + legal = **il**legal

24 D.2 Most of the time when adding a **suffix,** simply affix it to the end of the word.

SUFFIXES	
bear + **able** = bear**able**	slow + **ly** = slow**ly**
hope + **ful** = hope**ful**	hope + **less** = hope**less**

Suffixes *-ness* and *-ly*

24 D.3 The suffixes *-ness* and *-ly* are added to most base words without any spelling changes.

-NESS AND *-LY*	
keen + **ness** = keen**ness**	total + **ly** = total**ly**
like + **ness** = like**ness**	fond + **ly** = fond**ly**

Words Ending in *e*

24 D.4 Drop the final e in the base word when adding a suffix that begins with a vowel.

SUFFIXES WITH VOWELS	
drive + **er** = driv**er**	believe + **able** = believ**able**
nature + **al** = natur**al**	scarce + **ity** = scarc**ity**

24 D.5 Keep the final *e* when the suffix begins with a consonant or when the base word ends with *ce* or *ge.*

SUFFIXES WITH CONSONANTS, ETC.		
Examples	amaze + **ment** = amaze**ment**	trace + **able** = trace**able**
	hope + **ful** = hope**ful**	courage + **ous** = courage**ous**
	notice + **able** = notice**able**	manage + **able** = manage**able**
Exceptions	argue + **ment** = argu**ment**	awe + **ful** = aw**ful**
	judge + **ment** = judg**ment**	true + **ly** = tru**ly**

WORD ALERT

Dying and *dyeing* are homophones. Be careful not to confuse them in your writing.

dying—[die + ing] ceasing to be alive; becoming dead. Crops are **dying** because of the drought.

dyeing—[dye + ing] giving color to a substance by adding dye. My friends are **dyeing** their hair bright red.

Practice Your Skills

Adding Prefixes and Suffixes

Combine these words with the prefixes and suffixes. Remember to make any necessary spelling changes. Use a dictionary to check your work.

1. re + elect
2. equal + ity
3. note + able
4. im + move + able
5. mile + age
6. over + rule
7. manage + able
8. argue + ment
9. pre + existing
10. care + ful
11. joy + ous
12. brave + ly
13. approve + al
14. imagine + ary
15. actual + ly
16. attract + ion

Words Ending with *y*

24 D.6 Keep the *y* when adding a suffix to words that end in a vowel and *y*. Change *y* to *i* when adding a suffix to words that end in a consonant and *y*.

SUFFIXES WITH *Y*		
Examples	buoy + **ant** = buoy**ant**	icy + **ly** = ic**ily**
	employ + **ment** = employ**ment**	stud**y** + **ous** = stud**ious**
Exceptions	thirty + **ish** = thirty**ish**	da**y** + **ly** = dai**ly**
	lobby + **ist** = lobby**ist**	sly + **ness** = sly**ness**

Doubling the Final Consonant

24 D.7 Sometimes you must double the final consonant when you add a suffix that begins with a vowel. Do this when the base word satisfies both these conditions: (1) It has only one syllable or is stressed on the final syllable and (2) It ends in one consonant preceded by one vowel.

CHAPTER 24

DOUBLE CONSONANTS		
One-Syllable Words	bag + y = ba**gg**y	spot + er = spo**tt**er
	hot + est = ho**tt**est	top + er = to**pp**er
Final Syllable Stressed	forget + able = forge**tt**able	remit + ance = remi**tt**ance
	omit + ed = omi**tt**ed	deter + ence = dete**rr**ence
	refer + al =refe**rr**al	concur + ent = concu**rr**ent

WORD ALERT

Be sure to divide words with double consonants correctly. If you are not sure, check the dictionary to determine where a word should be divided.

compress•ible **refer•ral**

Words Ending with *c*

24 D.8 When you add a suffix that begins with *e, i,* or *y* to a word that ends with *c* preceded by a single vowel, do not double the final *c.* Add the letter *k* after the *c* to retain the hard *c* sound.

FINAL C	
mimic + er = mimi**ck**er	shellac + ed = shella**ck**ed
panic + y = pani**ck**y	picnic + er = picni**ck**er

Practice Your Skills

Adding Suffixes

Combine these base words and suffixes. Remember to make any necessary spelling changes. Use a dictionary to check your work.

1. hobby + ist
2. plain + est
3. sad + en
4. picnic + er
5. steady + ly
6. regret + able
7. propel + er
8. lug + age
9. bother + some
10. swim + er
11. real + ist
12. six + ish
13. stop + age
14. red + ish
15. win + er
16. comfort + able
17. frolic + ing
18. slim + est
19. colic + y
20. remit + ance

Connect to Writing: Editing

Adding Suffixes and Other Endings

Rewrite this story beginning, correcting the words that are spelled incorrectly. Check your work by using a dictionary.

Once a year, the Science Club had a Beach Day. On that day, they visitted the beach and combinned picniking with studying marine life. This year, some students were feeling prankish. They planed a joke that they thought would be the height of sillyness. They would bring an exotic fish with them and pretend they had discovered it in a tidepool. Talking about it, they mimiced the shrieks of excitement that they imagined would follow the discovery.

They chose the uglyest, angriest-looking fish they could find. They took it with them in a plastic bag full of water. However, along the way, there was an unplaned-for occurence. The bag sprung a leak!

Connect to Writing: Narrative

Adding Suffixes and Other Endings

Continue the story about the students' prank started in the previous activity. Will the students carry out their prank as planned? What will their teacher do when the prank is discovered? Use five of the following words in your writing, adding the suffix or ending shown. Use a dictionary to check your work.

- panic + y
- commit + ed
- obey + ing
- angry + ly
- rely + able
- mad + er
- ecology + ist
- deny + ing
- betray + al
- biology + ist

Check Point: Mixed Practice

Add the prefix or suffix to each of these base words and write the new word. Use a dictionary to check your work.

1. believe + able
2. dizzy + ly
3. total + ly
4. argue + ment
5. notice + able
6. compel + able
7. lobby + ist
8. judge + ment
9. il + logical
10. dis + satisfied
11. outrage + ous
12. concur + ence
13. happy + ness
14. politic + ing
15. picnic + er
16. transfer + al
17. usual + ly
18. refer + al
19. stubborn + ness
20. study + ous
21. acknowledge + ment

Words to Master

Make it your goal to learn to spell these fifty words this year. Use them in your writing and practice writing them until spelling them correctly comes automatically.

a**cc**ident**ally**
advi**sa**ble
a**rr**ang**e**ment
believ**ab**le
ben**e**fit
bus**i**ness
camp**aign**
colu**mn**
conv**enie**nce
cor**ps**
c**ou**rt**e**ous
depend**ent**
descend**ant**
desi**ra**ble
di**ss**atisfied
emba**rr**a**ss**ment
ex**traor**dinary
for**eign**
fur**io**us
gover**n**ment
gramm**ar**
honor**a**ble
ho**rri**ble
i**rr**elev**ant**
i**rr**esist**ible**
justi**fi**able
lic**ense**
lin**ea**r
lu**xuri**ous
med**ie**val
mi**ss**pelled
mo**va**ble
nin**e**ty
noti**ce**able
nu**clear**
o**cc**u**rr**ence
op**tim**istic
particul**ar**
pa**st**ime
pecu**liar**
pro**nun**ciation
r**hy**me
r**hythm**
s**ei**ze
si**e**ge
surpr**ise**
temper**a**ment
temper**a**ture
unforge**tt**able
val**ua**ble

Chapter Review

Assess Your Learning

Spelling Words Correctly

Write the letter preceding the misspelled word in each group. Then write the word, spelling it correctly.

1. (a) illegible	(b) cellos	(c) echoes
(d) accessory	(e) believeable	
2. (a) acknowledge	(b) procede	(c) famous
(d) sandwiches	(e) either	
3. (a) picnicker	(b) selves	(c) ilogical
(d) buoys	(e) keenness	
4. (a) eighth	(b) decieve	(c) studios
(d) dizzily	(e) tariff	
5. (a) supersede	(b) matinee	(c) courageous
(d) transfered	(e) totally	
6. (a) loseing	(b) dissatisfied	(c) their
(d) foreign	(e) occurred	
7. (a) breathe	(b) sameness	(c) leisure
(d) halfs	(e) arguments	
8. (a) mosses	(b) management	(c) happier
(d) conceit	(e) outragous	
9. (a) sheriff	(b) soloes	(c) analysis
(d) sufficient	(e) representative	
10. (a) referred	(b) icily	(c) consciencious
(d) efficient	(e) counselors-at-law	

Spelling Correctly: Posttest

Directions

Read the passage. Write the letter of the answer that correctly respells each underlined word. If the word is correct, write D.

By studying advertising **(1)** campains of the past, advertising executives can determine which kinds of ads are **(2)** iresistable to consumers. Many **(3)** agencys have their own **(4)** specialties. One might focus on automobile commercials, for example, whereas another might churn out **(5)** extrordinary ads for cosmetics.

Most **(6)** CEOs would **(7)** conceed that advertising is **(8)** responsable for a huge volume of their **(9)** busness. For your product to be **(10)** noticeable in today's glutted market, your ads must be superior to everyone else's.

1. **A** campagnes
B campaigns
C campeigns
D No error

2. **A** irresistable
B iresistible
C irresistible
D No error

3. **A** agencies
B agentcies
C agences
D No error

4. **A** specialtys
B specialites
C speciallties
D No error

5. **A** extrardinary
B extrordinarry
C extraordinary
D No error

6. **A** CEO
B CEO'S
C CEOses
D No error

7. **A** concede
B consede
C conseed
D No error

8. **A** responseable
B responsible
C responsibal
D No error

9. **A** busyness
B business
C bussiness
D No error

10. **A** noticable
B noticeible
C noticible
D No error

CHAPTER 24

Writer's Corner

Snapshot

24 A **Spelling patterns**—such as *i* before *e* except after *c*—apply to many words and can help you spell many different words correctly. (pages 999–1001)

24 B To form the plural of most nouns, add *s* or *es*. Some nouns form their plurals in other ways. (pages 1002–1009)

24 C Some numbers are written as numerals while other numbers are written as words. (pages 1010–1011)

24 D A **prefix** is one or more syllables placed in front of a base word to form a new word. A **suffix** is one or more syllables placed after a base word to change its part of speech and possibly also its meaning. (pages 1012–1016)

CHAPTER 24

Power Rules

Homophones are **words that sound alike** but have different meanings. When you write, be sure you use the word with your intended meaning. It often helps to say contractions as two words. (pages 860–887)

Before Editing	After Editing
Can I compare *you're* notes to mine? (*You're* is a contraction of *you are.*)	Can I compare *your* notes to mine? (*Your* is the possessive form of *you.*)
Their doesn't seem to be room for us. (*Their* is the possessive form of *they.*)	*There* doesn't seem to be room for us. (*There* means *in that place.*)

When you write, avoid misusing or misspelling these **commonly confused words.** (pages 860–887)

Before Editing	After Editing
Marissa tried to raise the *moral* of her teammates. (*Moral* means *based on right or wrong.*)	Marissa tried to raise the *morale* of her teammates. (*Morale* means *confidence and enthusiasm.*)
It was hard to *breath* in that heat. (*Breath* refers to *air taken into the lungs.*)	It was hard to *breathe* in that heat. (*Breathe* refers to *the act of taking air into the lungs.*)

Editing Checklist

Use this checklist when editing your writing.

- ✓ Did I pay attention to spelling patterns in my writing? (See pages 999–1001.)
- ✓ Did I correctly form plurals of regular and irregular nouns? (See pages 1002–1005.)
- ✓ Did I use spelling strategies to form plurals of compound words, foreign words, and other plurals? (See pages 1006–1009.)
- ✓ Did I use a dictionary to check words I wasn't sure how to spell? (See pages 512 and 997.)
- ✓ Did I change the spelling of base words if needed when adding prefixes and/or suffixes? (See pages 1012–1016.)
- ✓ Did I carefully edit my writing for misspelled words? (See pages 996–997 and 1017.)

Use the Power

Some words or word parts sound the same but are spelled differently. Use a mnemonic device to help you remember how to spell difficult words.

WORD	MNEMONIC DEVICE
believe, deceive, eight, ancient, heir	*i* before *e* except after *c* (except when it's wEIrd)
their, there	**Their** feet take them here and **there.** (*Here* and *there* are places.)
succeed, proceed, exceed (*-ceed* vs. *-cede*)	Full sp**EED** ahead.
whether, weather	**Whether** to wear a jacket depends on the **weather.**
for, four	**Four** (the number) has four letters.
stationary, stationery	Station**A**ry is p**A**rked c**A**rs. Station**E**ry is **E**nvelopes and p**E**ns.

Write a joke or a poem that plays on two words that sound alike but have different spellings and meanings.

Language QuickGuide

The Power Rules

Researchers have found that certain patterns of language use offend educated people more than others and therefore affect how people perceive you. Since these patterns of language use have such an impact on future success, you should learn how to edit for the more widely accepted forms. The list below identifies ten of the most important conventions to master the Power Rules. Always check for them when you edit.

1. Use only one negative form for a single negative idea. (See page 853.)

Before Editing	After Editing
After I dropped it, my mp3 player *wasn't* worth *nothing.*	After I dropped it, my mp3 player *wasn't* worth *anything.*
There wasn't *nowhere* to keep my old comic book collection.	There wasn't *anywhere* to keep my old comic book collection.

2. Use mainstream past tense forms of regular and irregular verbs. (See pages 742–766.) You might try to recite and memorize the parts of the most common irregular verbs.

Before Editing	After Editing
I *swum* at the YMCA last night.	I *swam* at the YMCA last night.
Otto *fix* my car engine.	Otto *fixed* my car engine.
You should not have *did* that.	You should not have *done* that.
You *brung* me the wrong hammer.	You *brought* me the wrong hammer.

3. Use verbs that agree with the subject. (See pages 814–839.)

Before Editing	After Editing
She *don't* have any.	She *doesn't* have any.
The brussels sprouts and the shitake mushroom *tastes* good together.	The brussels sprouts and the shitake mushroom *taste* good together.
Either the shrubs or the tree *are* diseased.	Either the shrubs or the tree *is* diseased.
Neither the cat nor the dogs *is eating* the bird food.	Neither the cat nor the dogs *are eating* the bird food.

4. Use subject forms of pronouns in subject position. Use object forms of pronouns in object position. (See pages 781–789.)

Before Editing	After Editing
Her and Carla are wearing boots.	*She* and Carla are wearing boots.
Him and his hiking partner are going in the wrong direction.	*He* and his hiking partner are going in the wrong direction.
Her and *me* have much in common.	*She* and *I* have much in common.

5. Use standard ways to make nouns possessive. (See pages 944–946.)

Before Editing	After Editing
The *frogs* legs are powerful.	The *frog's* legs are powerful.
Carly was scratched by *cats* claws.	Carly was scratched by *cat's* claws.
Sybil marched across the *citys* border.	Sybil marched across the *city's* border.
The *trucks* brakes squealed loudly.	The *truck's* brakes squealed loudly.
All three *bikes* wheels deflated over the winter.	All three *bikes'* wheels deflated over the winter.

6. Use a consistent verb tense except when a change is clearly necessary. (See pages 753–766.)

Before Editing	After Editing
The power *goes* off during yesterday's storm.	The power *went* off during yesterday's storm.
I *play* video games for two hours yesterday.	I *played* video games for two hours yesterday.

7. Use sentence fragments only the way professional writers do, after the sentence they refer to and usually to emphasize a point. Fix all sentence fragments that occur before the sentence they refer to and ones that occur in the middle of a sentence. (See pages 663–664.)

Before Editing	After Editing
Today. Tanya is wearing sunglasses.	*Today,* Tanya is wearing sunglasses.
Writing a paper. *While the school band is playing next door is hard.* So I'm moving to the library.	Writing a paper *while the school band is playing next door is hard, so* I'm moving to the library.
We contributed 50% of our money to the charity. *The reason being that we wanted to help their worthy cause.*	We contributed 50% of our money to the charity *because we wanted to help their worthy cause.*

QUICKGUIDE

8. Use the best conjunction and/or punctuation for the meaning when connecting two sentences. Revise run-on sentences. (See pages 728–730.)

Before Editing	After Editing
Celia got an A in English, she celebrated.	*When* Celia got an A in English, she celebrated.
It snowed, I got out my sled.	*After* it snowed, I got out my sled.
I took a guess, my answer was wrong.	I took a guess, *but* my answer was wrong.

9. Use the contraction *'ve* (not *of*) when the correct word is *have,* or use the full word *have.* (See pages 872, 881, and 883.) **Use *supposed* instead of *suppose* and *used* instead of *use* when appropriate.**

Before Editing	After Editing
They should *of* sung the national anthem in the right key.	They should *have* sung the national anthem in the right key.
We might *of* gone a bit overboard with the sugar.	We might *have* gone a bit overboard with the sugar.
The songs would *of* sounded better if they'd been sung instead of played on a kazoo.	The songs would *have* sounded better if they'd been sung instead of played on a kazoo.
I was *suppose* to be home by dinnertime.	I was *supposed* to be home by dinnertime.
I *use* to take piano lessons, but then I switched to cello.	I *used* to take piano lessons, but then I switched to cello.

10. For sound-alikes and certain words that sound almost alike, choose the word with your intended meaning. (See pages 860–887.)

Before Editing	After Editing
Atticus wanted *too* clean the kitchen. (*too* means "also" or "in addition")	Atticus wanted *to* clean the kitchen. (*to* is part of the infinitive *to clean*)
I have *to* jobs, but I probably need three. (*to* means "in the direction of")	I have *two* jobs, but I probably need three. (*two* is a number)
You're tendrils could use a trim. (*you're* is a contraction of *you are*)	*Your* tendrils could use a trim. (*your* is the possessive form of *you*)
They're problem is obvious. (*they're* is a contraction of *they are*)	*Their* problem is obvious. (*their* is the possessive form of *they*)
Their you go again. (*their* is the possessive form of *they*)	*There* you go again. (*there* means "in that place")
Its unfortunate that Marcus lost in the first round of the chess tournament. (*its* is the possessive form of *it*)	*It's* unfortunate that Marcus lost in the first round of the chess tournament. (*it's* is a contraction of *it is*)

Nine Tools for Powerful Writing

In addition to using Power Rules to help you avoid errors, try using these nine powerful tools to help you turn good writing into excellent writing.

1. Elaborate by **explaining who or what with appositives.** (See page 175.)

An appositive is a noun or pronoun phrase that identifies or adds identifying information to the preceding noun.

We climbed into the taxi, **a tiny red Asian car.**

2. Create emphasis by **dashing it all.** (See page 93.)

When you are writing informally, dashes can create abrupt breaks that emphasize a word or group of words. Use one dash to set off words at the end of a sentence. Use a pair of dashes to set off words in the middle of a sentence.

Bicycles, motorbikes, and three-wheeled cyclos—**human-powered versions of our vehicle**—streamed around us on the street leading to the center of this Vietnamese town.

3. **Tip the scale** with adverbial clauses. (See page 307.)

Use subordinate clauses to tip the scale toward the idea in the main clause. Start the subordinate clause with words such as *although, if, because, until, while,* or *since*.

Although the absence of traffic signals would seem to invite chaos, vehicles snaked through town with an uncanny grace.

4. Let your adjectives **come lately or early.** (See page 202.)

Adjectives can add rich details to your sentences. Many adjectives work well when placed before the nouns they modify. For variety, try adding them after the noun.

Our driver, **serene and focused,** pressed the car's horn.

5. **Catch and release** related sentences with a semicolon. (See page 65.)

The semicolon combines a comma and a period. The period "catches" the idea in the words before the semicolon, signaling its end. The comma "releases" it and relates it to another idea. Semicolons invite the reader to supply the words or idea that connects what could be two separate sentences.

Travelers ahead of us responded with no visible **annoyance; they** simply made adjustments in speed or direction.

6. Answer the questions **Which one? What kind?** or **How many?** with adjectival clauses. Begin your clause with one of the relative pronouns: *that, which, who, whom*, or *whose*.

On our right, a man struggled to pedal a cyclo **that held a full-size mattress.**

7. Use the **power of 3s** to add style and emphasis with **parallelism.** (See page 250.)

One way to add power is to use a writing device called parallelism. Parallelism is the use of the same kind of word or group of words in a series of three or more.

On the sidewalk, a woman's brilliant blue tunic flashed in the sunlight. **On our left**, a motorbike buzzed past us, laden with its driver and a dozen live ducks hanging by their feet. **On our right**, a man struggled to pedal a cyclo that held a full-size mattress.

8. **Get into the action** with participial phrases. (See page 351.)

You can pack a lot of action into your sentences if you include an *–ing* verb, or "*–ing* modifier." Formally called a *present participial phrase,* these *–ing* modifiers describe a person, thing, or action in a sentence.

Pressing the horn again and again, our driver navigated his way through this stream of life.

9. Write with variety and coherence and **let it flow.** (See pages 145 and 440.)

Vary the length, structure, and beginnings of your sentences and use connecting words to help your writing flow smoothly.

We climbed into the taxi, a tiny red Asian car. Bicycles, motorbikes, and three-wheeled cyclos—human-powered versions of our vehicle—streamed around us on the street leading to the center of this Vietnamese town. Although the absence of traffic signals would seem to invite chaos, the mass of vehicles snaked through town with an uncanny grace. Our driver, serene and focused, pressed the car's horn. Travelers ahead of us responded with no visible annoyance; they simply made adjustments in speed or direction. I looked out the windows. On the sidewalk, a woman's brilliant blue tunic flashed in the sunlight. On our left, a motorbike buzzed past us, laden with its driver and a dozen live ducks hanging by their feet. On our right, a man struggled to pedal a cyclo that held a full-size mattress. Pressing the horn again and again, our driver navigated his way through this stream of life.

QUICKGUIDE

Grammar QuickGuide

This section presents an easy-to-use reference for the definitions of grammatical terms. The number on the colored tab tells you the chapter covering that topic. The page number to the right of each definition refers to the place in the chapter where you can find additional instruction, examples, and applications to writing.

13 The Parts of Speech

How can you combine the parts of speech to create vivid and exact sentences?

Nouns

13 A A **noun** is the name of a person, place, thing, or idea. **620**

- **13 A.1** **Concrete nouns** name people, places, or things. **Abstract nouns** name ideas and qualities. 620
- **13 A.2** **Common nouns** name any person, place, or thing. **Proper nouns** name a particular person, place, or thing. 621
- **13 A.3** **Compound nouns** are nouns that include more than one word. 621
- **13 A.4** **Collective nouns** name a group of people or things. 621

Pronouns

13 B A **pronoun** is a word that takes the place of one or more nouns. **623**

- **13 B.1** **Personal pronouns** are the most common kind of pronoun and can be divided into three groups: first person, second person, and third person. 623
- **13 B.2** A **reflexive pronoun** refers to the noun or the pronoun that is the subject of the sentence. It is needed to make the meaning of the sentence clear. 624
- **13 B.3** An **intensive pronoun** is not a necessary part of a sentence. It is included to add emphasis—or intensity—to a noun or another pronoun in the sentence. 624
- **13 B.4** **Indefinite pronouns** often refer to unnamed people or things. 625
- **13 B.5** A **demonstrative pronoun** is used to point out a specific person, place, or object. 626

QUICKGUIDE

13 B.6 An **interrogative pronoun** is used to ask a question. 626

Verbs

13 C A verb is a word that expresses action or a state of being. 628

13 C.1 An **action verb** tells what action a subject is performing. 628

13 C.2 An action verb that has an object is **transitive.** An action verb that has no object is **intransitive.** 628

13 C.3 A **verb phrase** is a main verb plus one or more helping verbs. 630

13 C.4 A **linking verb** links the subject with another word in the sentence. The other word either renames or describes the subject. 632

Adjectives and Adverbs

13 D Adjectives and adverbs are words that modify, or describe, other parts of speech. 635

13 D.1 An **adjective** is a word that modifies a noun or pronoun. 635

13 D.2 A **proper adjective** is a special kind of adjective. It is formed from a proper noun and begins with a capital letter. 636

13 D.3 **Compound adjectives** are adjectives that are made up of more than one word. 636

13 D.4 The words *a, an,* and *the* form a special group of adjectives called **articles.** 636

13 D.5 An **adverb** is a word that modifies a verb, an adjective, or another adverb. 639

Other Parts of Speech

13 E The three remaining parts of speech are prepositions, conjunctions, and interjections. 643

13 E.1 A **preposition** shows the relationship between a noun or a pronoun and another word in the sentence. 643

13 E.2 A **prepositional phrase** begins with a preposition and ends with a noun or a pronoun called the **object of a preposition.** 644

13 E.3 A **conjunction** connects words or groups of words. **Coordinating conjunctions** are single connecting words; **correlative conjunctions** are pairs of connecting words. 645

13 E.4 **Subordinating conjunctions** are used to introduce adverbial clauses. 645

13 E.5	An **interjection** is a word that expresses strong feeling or emotion.	646

14 The Sentence Base

How can you use sentences to paint powerful images and tell interesting stories?

Subjects and Predicates

14 A	**A sentence is a group of words that expresses a complete thought.**	**656**
14 A.1	A **subject** names the person, place, thing, or idea the sentence is about. A **predicate** tells something about the subject.	656
14 A.2	A **simple subject** is the main word in the complete subject. A simple **predicate,** or **verb,** is the main word or phrase in the complete predicate.	656
14 A.3	**Inverted order** means that the verb or part of a verb phrase comes before the subject.	659
14 A.4	**Understood *you*** occurs when the subject does not appear in the sentence.	659
14 A.5	A **compound subject** is two or more subjects in one sentence that have the same verb and are joined by a conjunction.	661
14 A.6	A **compound verb** is two or more verbs that have the same subject and are joined by a conjunction.	661

QUICKGUIDE

Sentence Fragments

14 B	**A sentence fragment is a group of words that does not express a complete thought.**	**663**

Complements

14 C	**A complement finishes the meaning of a sentence.**	**665**
14 C.1	A **direct object** is a noun or a pronoun that receives the action of the verb.	665
14 C.2	An **indirect object** answers the questions *To or for whom?* or *To or for what?* after an action verb.	666
14 C.3	An **objective complement** is a noun or an adjective that renames or describes the direct object.	667
14 C.4	**Subject complements** complete the meaning of linking verbs.	668

15 Phrases

How can you use phrases to add variety and clarity to your writing?

Prepositional Phrases

15 A **A phrase is a group of related words that function as a single part of speech. A phrase does not have a subject or a verb.** 682

15 A.1 An **adjectival phrase** is a prepositional phrase that is used to modify a noun or a pronoun. 682

15 A.2 An **adverbial phrase** is a prepositional phrase that is used to modify a verb, an adjective, or an adverb. 683

Appositives and Appositive Phrases

15 B **An appositive is a noun or a pronoun that identifies or explains another noun or pronoun next to it in the sentence.** 686

15 B.1 An appositive and its modifiers are called an **appositive phrase.** 686

Verbals and Verbal Phrases

15 C **A verbal is a verb form used as another part of speech.** 688

15 C.1 A **participle** is a verb form that is used as an adjective. 688

15 C.2 A **present participle** ends in *–ing;* a **past participle** has a regular ending of *–ed* or an irregular ending of *–n, –t,* or *–en.* 688

15 C.3 A **participial phrase** is a participle with its modifiers and complements—all working together as an adjective. 688

15 C.4 A **gerund** is a verb form that is used as a noun. 691

15 C.5 A **gerund phrase** is a gerund with its modifiers and complements all working together as a noun. 691

15 C.6 An **infinitive** is a verb form that usually begins with *to.* It is used as a noun, an adjective, or an adverb. 693

15 C.7 An **infinitive phrase** is an infinitive with its modifiers and complements all working together as a noun, an adjective, or an adverb. 693

Misplaced and Dangling Modifiers

15 D **Misplaced modifiers and dangling modifiers are common modifier problems. They can confuse the meaning of a sentence.** 696

15 D.1 A modifier that is placed too far away from the word it modifies is called a **misplaced modifier.** 696

15 D.2 A **dangling modifier** is a phrase that is used as a modifier but does not describe any word in the sentence. 696

Phrase Fragments

15 E When phrases are written as if they were sentences, they become phrase fragments. **698**

16 Clauses

How can you use clauses to express subtle and precise meaning?

Independent and Subordinate Clauses

16 A A clause is a group of words that has a subject and a verb. **710**

16 A.1 An **independent (main) clause** can stand alone as a sentence because it expresses a complete thought. 710

16 A.2 A **subordinate (dependent) clause** cannot stand alone because it does not express a complete thought. 711

QUICKGUIDE

Uses of Subordinate Clauses

16 B A subordinate clause can function as an adverb, an adjective, or a noun. **712**

16 B.1 An **adverbial clause** is a subordinate clause that is used as an adverb to modify a verb, an adjective, or an adverb. 712

16 B.2 An adverbial clause in which words are missing is called an **elliptical clause.** 714

16 B.3 An **adjectival clause** is a subordinate clause that is used as an adjective to modify a noun or a pronoun. 715

16 B.4 A **relative pronoun** relates an adjectival clause to its antecedent—the noun or pronoun the clause modifies. 715

16 B.5 A **noun clause** is a subordinate clause that is used as a noun. 721

Kinds of Sentence Structure

16 C All sentences are classified as simple, compound, complex, or compound-complex. **723**

16 C.1 A **simple sentence** consists of one independent clause. 723

16 C.2 A **compound sentence** consists of two or more independent clauses. 723

16 C.3 A **complex sentence** consists of one independent clause and one or more subordinate clauses. 724

16 C.4 A **compound-complex sentence** consists of two or more independent clauses and one or more subordinate clauses. 724

Clause Fragments

16 D A subordinate clause becomes a clause fragment when it stands alone. 726

Run-on Sentences

16 E A run-on sentence is two or more sentences written as one sentence and separated by a comma or no mark of punctuation at all. 728

QUICKGUIDE

Usage QuickGuide

This section presents an easy-to-use reference for the explanations of how various grammatical elements are and should be used. The number on the colored tab tells you the chapter covering that topic. The page number to the right of each definition refers to the place in the chapter where you can find additional instruction, examples, and applications to writing. You can also refer to the Writer's Glossary of Usage (pages 860–887) for help with commonly confused usage items.

17 Using Verbs

How can using verbs in just the right way spark your descriptions and make your writing shine?

QUICKGUIDE

The Principal Parts of Verbs

17 A **The principal parts of a verb are the present, the present participle, the past, and the past participle.** 742

17 A.1 A **regular verb** forms its past and past participle by adding *–ed* or *–d* to the present. 742

17 A.2 An **irregular verb** does not form its past and past participle by adding *–ed* or *–d* to the present. 743

Six Problem Verbs

17 B **The verb pairs *lie* and *lay, rise* and *raise,* and *sit* and *set* are easily confused.** 750

17 B.1 *Lie* means "to rest or recline." *Lie* is never followed by a direct object. *Lay* means "to put or set (something) down." *Lay* is usually followed by a direct object. 750

17 B.2 *Rise* means "to move upward" or "to get up." *Rise* is never followed by a direct object. *Raise* means "to lift up," "to increase," or "to grow." *Raise* is usually followed by a direct object. 751

17 B.3 *Sit* means "to rest in an upright position." *Sit* is never followed by a direct object. *Set* means "to put or place (something)." *Set* is usually followed by a direct object. 751

Verb Tense

17 C **The time expressed by a verb is called the tense of a verb.** **753**

17 C.1 **Present tense** is used mainly to express an action that is going on now, an action that happens regularly, or an action that is usually constant or the same. 753

17 C.2 Use the **historical present tense** when you want to relate a past action as if it were happening in the present. Use the **literary present tense** when you are writing about literature. 754

17 C.3 **Past tense** is used to express an action that already took place or was completed in the past. 754

17 C.4 **Future tense** is used to express an action that will take place in the future. 754

17 C.5 **Present perfect tense** has two uses: to express an action that was completed at some indefinite time in the past and to express an action that started in the past and is still going on. 754

17 C.6 **Past perfect tense** expresses an action that took place before some other action. 755

17 C.7 **Future perfect tense** expresses an action that will take place before another future action or time. 755

17 C.8 A **conjugation** is a list of all the singular and plural forms of a verb in its various tenses. 756

QUICKGUIDE

Common Problems Using Tenses

17 D **The tense of the verbs you use depends on the meaning you want to express.** **761**

17 D.1 Use *having* with a past participle in a participial phrase to show that one action was completed before another one. 762

17 D.2 To express an action that takes place *after* another action, use the **present infinitive.** To express an action that takes place *before* another action, use the **perfect infinitive.** 763

17 D.3 The **progressive forms** are used to express continuing or ongoing action. To write the progressive forms, add a present, past, future, or perfect tense of the verb *be* to the present participle. 764

17 D.4 The **emphatic forms** of the present and past tense of verbs are mainly used to show emphasis or force. To write the present emphatic, add *do* or *does* to the present tense of a verb. To write the past emphatic, add *did* to the present tense. 765

Active and Passive Voice

Mood

QUICKGUIDE

18 Using Pronouns

How can you use pronouns to make your writing fluid and accurate?

The Cases of Personal Pronouns

18 A.6	A prepositional phrase begins with a preposition and ends with a noun or a pronoun called the **object of a preposition.**	785
18 A.7	Participles, gerunds, and infinitives are all verbals. Because verbals are verb forms, they can take objects. The object of a verbal is in the objective case.	786
18 A.8	The **possessive case** is used to show ownership or possession.	790
18 A.9	When a pronoun comes directly in front of a gerund, it should be in the possessive case—in just the same way a possessive pronoun would come in front of a noun.	790

Pronoun Problems

18 B	**Common problems with pronouns include the misuse of *who* and *whom,* incomplete comparisons, and misuse of reflexive and intensive pronouns.**	**793**
18 B.1	The correct case of *who* is determined by how the pronoun is used in a question or a clause.	793
18 B.2	An **elliptical clause** is a subordinate clause that begins with *than* or *as* and that has words omitted. The omitted words are understood to be there.	797
18 B.3	In an elliptical clause, use the form of the pronoun you would use if the clause were completed.	797
18 B.4	**Reflexive pronouns** always refer back to a previous noun or pronoun in the sentence.	799
18 B.5	**Intensive pronouns** are used to emphasize a noun or another pronoun in the sentence.	799

Pronouns and Their Antecedents

18 C	**A pronoun and its antecedent, the word that a pronoun refers to or replaces, must agree.**	**801**
18 C.1	A single pronoun must agree in **number** and **gender** with its antecedent.	801
18 C.2	When two or more singular antecedents are joined by *or, nor, either/or,* or *neither/nor,* use a singular pronoun to refer to them.	801
18 C.3	When two or more singular antecedents are joined by *and* or *both/and,* use a plural pronoun to refer to them.	802
18 C.4	When the gender of an antecedent is not obvious, use the phrase *his or her* to refer to the antecedent.	802

QUICKGUIDE

18 C.5	A personal pronoun must be singular if its antecedent is a singular indefinite pronoun.	804
18 C.6	A personal pronoun must be plural if its antecedent is a plural indefinite pronoun.	804
18 C.7	When the antecedent of a personal pronoun is one of the singular/plural indefinite pronouns, the personal pronoun must agree in number and gender with the noun to which the indefinite pronoun refers.	804

Unclear, Missing, or Confusing Antecedents

18 D	**Personal pronouns should clearly refer to a specific antecedent.**	**806**

19 Subject and Verb Agreement

QUICKGUIDE

How can you use subject-verb agreement to make the meaning of your writing clear?

Agreement of Subjects and Verbs

19 A	**A verb must agree with its subject in number.**	**816**
19 A.1	**Number** is used to indicate whether a noun or a pronoun is singular or plural.	816
19 A.2	A singular subject takes a singular verb. A plural subject takes a plural verb.	817
19 A.3	The first helping verb must agree in number with the subject.	817
19 A.4	The agreement of a verb and subject is not changed by any interrupting words.	819

Common Agreement Problems

19 B	**Compound subjects, indefinite pronouns as subjects, and subjects in inverted order are behind three common agreement problems.**	**821**
19 B.1	When subjects are joined by *or, nor, either/or,* or *neither/nor,* the verb agrees with the closer subject.	821
19 B.2	When subjects are joined by *and* or *both/and,* the verb is plural.	821
19 B.3	A verb must agree in number with an indefinite pronoun used as a subject.	823
19 B.4	The subject and the verb of an **inverted sentence** must agree in number.	825

Other Agreement Problems

19 C	**Other situations that cause agreement problems include contractions, collective nouns, words expressing time, and titles.**	**827**
19 C.1	Use a singular verb with a collective noun subject that is thought of as a unit. Use a plural verb with a collective noun subject that is thought of as individual parts.	827
19 C.2	A subject that expresses an amount, a measurement, a weight, or a time is usually considered singular and takes a singular verb.	827
19 C.3	Use a singular verb with ***the number of*** and a plural verb with ***a number of.***	829
19 C.4	Use a singular verb with certain subjects that are plural in form but singular in meaning.	829
19 C.5	The verb part of a contraction must agree in number with the subject.	831
19 C.6	A verb agrees with the subject of a sentence, not with the predicate nominative.	832
19 C.7	A title is singular and takes a singular verb.	832

QUICKGUIDE

20 Using Adjectives and Adverbs

How can you use adjectives and adverbs to show precise relationships among your ideas?

Comparison of Adjectives and Adverbs

20 A	**Adjectives and adverbs are modifiers. Most modifiers show degrees of comparison by changing their form.**	**842**
20 A.1	Add *–er* to form the comparative degree and *–est* to form the superlative degree of one-syllable modifiers.	843
20 A.2	Use ***–er*** or ***more*** to form the comparative and ***–est*** or ***most*** to form the superlative degree of two-syllable modifiers.	843
20 A.3	Use ***more*** to form the comparative and ***most*** to form the superlative degree of modifiers with three or more syllables.	844
20 A.4	Never add ***–er*** and ***–est*** to the comparative and superlative degrees of irregular modifiers.	844

QUICKGUIDE

Problems with Comparisons

20 B **When using adjectives and adverbs for comparison, avoid problems with double comparisons, illogical comparisons, and comparisons of members of a group to themselves.** **847**

- **20 B.1** Do not use both *–er* and ***more*** to form the comparative degree, or both ***–est*** and ***most*** to form the superlative degree of modifiers. 847
- **20 B.2** Compare only items of a similar kind. 847
- **20 B.3** Add ***other*** or ***else*** when comparing a member of a group with the rest of the group. 848

Problems with Modifiers

20 C **Be aware of special problems when using adjectives and adverbs. It's important to know whether to use an adjective or adverb, *good* or *well*, or *bad* or *badly*. Be alert for double negatives.** **850**

- **20 C.1** Use *good* as an adjective; use *well* as an adverb unless it means "in good health" or "satisfactory." 852
- **20 C.2** Use *bad* as an adjective; use *badly* as an adverb. 852
- **20 C.3** Avoid double negatives. 853

Mechanics QuickGuide

This section presents an easy-to-use reference for the mechanics of writing: capitalization, punctuation, and spelling. The number on the colored tab tells you the chapter covering that topic. The page number to the right of each definition refers to the place in the chapter where you can find additional instruction, examples, and applications to writing.

21 Capital Letters

How can you use capitalization to clarify your writing?

First Words and the Pronoun *I*

21 A	**Capitalize the beginning of a sentence or a line of poetry, parts of a letter or an outline, and the pronoun *I*.**	**892**
21 A.1	Capitalize the first word of a sentence or of a line of poetry.	892
21 A.2	Capitalize the first word in the greeting and in the closing of a letter.	893
21 A.3	Capitalize the first word of each item in an outline and the letters that begin major subsections of the outline.	893
21 A.4	Capitalize the pronoun *I*, both alone and in contractions.	893

Proper Nouns

21 B	**Capitalize proper nouns and their abbreviations.**	**895**
21 B.1	Names of particular persons and animals should be capitalized. Also capitalize the initials that stand for people's names.	895
21 B.2	Geographical names, which include places, bodies of water, celestial bodies and their abbreviations, initials, and acronyms, should be capitalized.	896
21 B.3	Names of groups, including the names of organizations, businesses, institutions, government bodies, political parties, and teams, should be capitalized.	898
21 B.4	Specific time periods, including the days and months of the year, holidays, special events, and historical events, periods, and documents, are capitalized.	899

QUICKGUIDE

21 B.5 Names of nationalities, races, languages, and religions, including religious holidays and references, are capitalized. 899

21 B.6 Other proper nouns should also begin with capital letters. 900

Proper Adjectives

21 C Capitalize most proper adjectives. 903

Titles

21 D Capitalize the titles of persons and works of art. 905

21 D.1 Capitalize a title showing office, rank, or profession when the title comes before a person's name. 905

21 D.2 Capitalize a title that is used alone when it is being substituted for a person's name in direct address. 905

21 D.3 Capitalize titles showing family relationships when they come before a person's name or when they are substituted for a person's name in direct address. 906

21 D.4 Capitalize the first and last words and all important words in the titles of the following: books, stories, poems, newspapers and newspaper articles, magazines and magazine articles, movies, plays, television series, musical songs and compositions, and works of art. 906

QUICKGUIDE

22 End Marks and Commas

How can you create meaning through the careful use of end marks and commas?

Kinds of Sentences and End Marks

22 A Depending on its function, a sentence can be declarative, imperative, interrogative, or exclamatory. 916

22 A.1 A **declarative sentence** makes a statement or expresses an opinion and ends with a period (.). 916

22 A.2 An **imperative sentence** gives a direction, makes a request, or gives a command. It ends with either a period or an exclamation point (. or !). 916

22 A.3 An **interrogative sentence** asks a question and ends with a question mark (?). 917

22 A.4 An **exclamatory sentence** expresses strong feeling or emotion and ends with an exclamation point (!). 917

22 A.5	Use a period after most abbreviations.	919
22 A.6	Use a period after each number or letter that shows a division in an outline.	921

Commas

22 B **The comma (,) is used to separate items and to enclose items.** **922**

22 B.1	Use commas to separate items in a series.	922
22 B.2	In certain situations, use a comma to separate two adjectives that directly precede a noun and that are not joined by a conjunction.	923
22 B.3	Use a comma to separate the independent clauses of a compound sentence if the clauses are joined by a coordinating conjunction.	924
22 B.4	Use a comma after certain introductory structures.	926
22 B.5	Use commas to separate the elements in dates and addresses.	928
22 B.6	Use a comma after the salutation of a friendly letter and after the closing of all letters.	929
22 B.7	Use commas to enclose nouns of direct address.	931
22 B.8	Use commas to enclose parenthetical expressions.	932
22 B.9	Use commas to enclose **contrasting expressions,** which usually begin with *not.* A contrasting expression is considered a type of parenthetical expression.	932
22 B.10	Use commas to enclose most appositives and their modifiers.	933
22 B.11	Use commas to set off a **nonessential** or **nonrestrictive** participial phrase or clause.	935
22 B.12	No commas are used if a participial phrase or clause is **restrictive** or **essential** to the meaning of a sentence.	935

QUICKGUIDE

23 Other Punctuation

How can you use the right punctuation to communicate your ideas clearly and enhance your writing style?

Apostrophes

23 A **The apostrophe (') is used to show possession and to create contractions.** **944**

23 A.1	Add *'s* to form the possessive of a singular noun.	944

23 A.2	Add only an apostrophe to form the possessive of a plural noun that ends in ***s.***	944
23 A.3	If a plural noun does not end in *s*, add ***'s*** to form the possessive, just as you would to a singular noun that does not end in *s.*	945
23 A.4	The possessive forms of personal pronouns and the pronoun *who* do not use apostrophes.	947
23 A.5	Add ***'s*** to form the possessive of some indefinite pronouns.	947
23 A.6	Add ***'s*** to only the last word to show joint ownership.	949
23 A.7	Add ***'s*** to each word to show separate ownership.	949
23 A.8	Use an apostrophe with the possessive form of a noun that expresses time or amount.	949
23 A.9	Use an apostrophe in a contraction to show where one or more letters have been omitted.	951
23 A.10	Add ***'s*** to form the plural of lowercase letters, some capital letters, and some words used as words.	952
23 A.11	Use an apostrophe to show that numbers are omitted in a date.	953

QUICKGUIDE

Semicolons and Colons

23 B	**The most common use for a semicolon (;) is to separate the independent clauses of a compound sentence. A colon (:) is primarily used to introduce a list of items.**	**955**
23 B.1	Use a semicolon between closely related clauses of a compound sentence when they are not joined by a conjunction.	955
23 B.2	Use a semicolon between clauses in a compound sentence that are joined by certain conjunctive adverbs or transitional words.	956
23 B.3	Use a semicolon instead of a comma in certain situations to avoid confusion.	957
23 B.4	Use a semicolon instead of a comma between items in a series if the items themselves contain commas.	957
23 B.5	Use a colon before most lists of items, especially when a list comes after an expression such as *the following.*	958
23 B.6	Use a colon between independent clauses when the second clause explains or restates the first.	958
23 B.7	Use a colon to introduce a long formal quotation.	959
23 B.8	Use a colon in certain conventional situations.	959

Italics (Underlining)

23 C	**Italics are used to indicate certain titles and names, foreign words, and the use of a word used as a word. If you are writing by hand, underline whatever should be italicized.**	**961**
23 C.1	Italicize (underline) letters, numbers, and words used as words. Also underline foreign words that are not generally used in English.	961
23 C.2	Italicize (underline) the titles of long written or musical works that are published as a single unit. Also italicize (underline) the titles of paintings and sculptures and the names of vehicles.	961

Quotation Marks and Ellipses

23 D	**Quotation marks are placed at the beginning and at the end of certain titles and uninterrupted quotations. Ellipses indicate that words have been removed.**	**964**
23 D.1	Use quotation marks to enclose the titles of chapters, articles, essays, stories, one-act plays, short poems, songs, episodes from a TV series, and movements from a musical composition.	964
23 D.2	Use quotation marks to enclose a person's exact words.	966
23 D.3	Begin each sentence of a direct quotation with a capital letter.	968
23 D.4	Use a comma to separate a direct quotation from a speaker tag. Place the comma inside the closing quotation marks.	969
23 D.5	Place a period inside the closing quotation marks when the end of the quotation comes at the end of a sentence.	970
23 D.6	Place the question mark or the exclamation point *outside* the closing quotation marks when the sentence itself is a question or exclamation.	971
23 D.7	Use quotation marks to enclose slang words, technical terms, invented words, and words used to show sarcasm or irony.	973
23 D.8	When writing a word and its definition in a sentence, italicize (underline) the word, but use quotation marks to enclose the definition.	974
23 D.9	When writing dialogue, begin a new paragraph each time the speaker changes.	974
23 D.10	Use single quotation marks to enclose a quotation or certain titles within a quotation.	976
23 D.11	Use ellipses to indicate omissions in quoted passages or pauses in written passages.	977

Other Marks of Punctuation

23 E **The hyphen has several uses, such as dividing a word at the end of a line and separating parts of a compound word. Dashes, parentheses, and brackets are used to separate words from the rest of the sentence.** **979**

23 E.1 Use a **hyphen** (-) to divide a word at the end of a line. 979

23 E.2 Use a hyphen when writing out the compound numbers ***twenty-one*** through ***ninety-nine.*** 980

23 E.3 Use one or more hyphens to separate the parts of some compound nouns and adjectives. Also use one or more hyphens between words that make up a compound adjective in front of a noun. 981

23 E.4 Use a hyphen after the prefixes *ex-*, *self-*, and *all-* and before the suffix *-elect.* Also use a hyphen with all prefixes before a proper noun or a proper adjective. 982

23 E.5 Use a hyphen to prevent confusion. 983

23 E.6 Use **dashes** (—) to set off an abrupt change in thought. 984

23 E.7 Use dashes to set off a parenthetical expression or an appositive that includes commas. Also use dashes to call special attention to a phrase. 985

23 E.8 Use dashes to set off a phrase or a clause that summarizes or emphasizes what has preceded it. 985

23 E.9 Use **parentheses** (**( )**) to enclose information that is not related closely to the meaning of the sentence. 985

23 E.10 Use **brackets** (**[ ]**) to enclose an explanation within quoted material that is not part of the quotation. 986

QUICKGUIDE

24 Spelling Correctly

How can you communicate your message effectively by using accurate spelling?

Spelling Patterns

24 A **Spelling patterns—such as *i* before *e* except after *c*—apply to many words and can help you spell many different words correctly.** **999**

24 A.1 When you spell words with *ie* or *ei, i* comes before *e* except when the letters follow *c* or when they stand for the sound long *a.* 999

24 A.2 Words that end with a syllable that sounds like "seed" are usually spelled with *–cede.* Only one word in English is spelled with *–sede,* and only three words are spelled with *–ceed.* 999

Plurals

Spelling Numbers

QUICKGUIDE

24 C.2 Always spell out numbers used to tell the order. 1010

24 C.3 Use a numeral for a date when you include the name of the month. Always use numerals for the year. 1011

Prefixes and Suffixes

24 D A prefix is one or more syllables placed in front of a base word to form a new word. A suffix is one or more syllables placed after a base word to change its part of speech and possibly also its meaning. 1012

24 D.1 When you add a **prefix,** the spelling of the base word does not change. 1012

24 D.2 Most of the time when adding a **suffix,** simply affix it to the end of the word. 1012

24 D.3 The suffixes –*ness* and –*ly* are added to most base words without any spelling changes. 1012

24 D.4 Drop the final *e* in the base word when adding a suffix that begins with a vowel. 1012

24 D.5 Keep the final *e* when the suffix begins with a consonant or when the base word ends with *ce* or *ge.* 1013

24 D.6 Keep the *y* when adding a suffix to words that end in a vowel and *y.* Change *y* to *i* when adding a suffix to words that end in a consonant and *y.* 1014

24 D.7 Sometimes you must double the final consonant when you add a suffix that begins with a vowel. Do this when the base word satisfies both these conditions: (1) It has only one syllable or is stressed on the final syllable and (2) It ends in one consonant preceded by one vowel. 1014

24 D.8 When you add a suffix that begins with *e, i,* or *y* to a word that ends with *c* preceded by a single vowel, do not double the final *c.* Add the letter *k* after the *c* to retain the hard *c* sound. 1015

QUICKGUIDE

Glossary

English	Español
A	
abbreviation shortened form of a word that generally begins with a capital letter and ends with a period	**abreviatura** forma reducida de una palabra que generalmente comienza con mayúscula y termina en punto
abstract summary of points of writing, presented in skeletal form	**síntesis** resumen de los puntos principales de un texto, presentados en forma de esquema
abstract noun noun that cannot be seen or touched, such as an idea, quality, or characteristic	**austantivo abstracto** sustantivo que no puede verse ni tocarse, como una idea, una cualidad o una característica
acronym an abbreviation formed by using the initial letters of a phrase or name (CIA—Central Intelligence Agency)	**acrónimo** abreviatura que se forma al usar las letras iniciales de una frase o de un nombre (CIA—Central Intelligence Agency [Agencia Central de Inteligencia])
action verb verb that tells what action a subject is performing	**verbo de acción** verbo que indica qué acción realiza el sujeto
active voice voice the verb is in when it expresses that the subject is performing the action	**voz activa** voz en que está el verbo cuando expresa que el sujeto está realizando la acción
adequate development quality of good writing in which sufficient supporting details develop the main idea	**desarrollo adecuado** cualidad de un texto bien escrito, en cual suficientes detalles de apoyo desarrollan la idea principal
adjectival clause subordinate clause used to modify a noun or pronoun	**cláusula adjetiva** cláusula subordinada utilizada para modificar a un sustantivo o a un pronombre
adjectival phrase prepositional phrase that modifies a noun or a pronoun	**frase adjetiva** frase preposicional que modifica a un sustantivo o a un pronombre
adjective word that modifies a noun or a pronoun	**adjetivo** palabra que modifica a un sustantivo o a un pronombre

English	Español
adverb word that modifies a verb, an adjective, or another adverb	**adverbio** palabra que modifica a un verbo, a un adjetivo o a otro adverbio
adverbial clause subordinate clause that is used mainly to modify a verb	**cláusula adverbial** cláusula subordinada que se utiliza principalmente para modificar a un verbo
adverbial phrase prepositional phrase that is used mainly to modify a verb	**frase adverbial** frase preposicional que se utiliza principalmente para modificar a un verbo
aesthetics study of beauty and artistic quality	**estética** estudio de la belleza y de las características del arte
alliteration repetition of a consonant sound at the beginning of a series of words	**aliteración** repetición de un sonido consonántico al comienzo de una serie de palabras
allusion reference to persons or events in the past or in literature	**alusión** referencia a personas o sucesos del pasado o de la literatura
analogy logical relationship between a pair of words	**analogía** relación lógica entre una pareja de palabras
analysis the process of breaking a whole into parts to see how the parts fit and work together	**análisis** proceso de separación de las partes de un todo para examinar cómo encajan y cómo funcionan juntas
antecedent word or group of words to which a pronoun refers	**antecedente** palabra o grupo de palabras a que hace referencia un pronombre
antithesis in literature, using contrasting words, phrases, sentences, or ideas for emphasis: *She was tough as nails and soft as spun sugar.*	**antítesis** en literatura, el uso de palabras, frases, oraciones o ideas contrastantes para producir énfasis: *Era dura como una piedra y con un corazón de oro.*
antonym word that means the opposite of another word	**antónimo** palabra que significa lo opuesto de otra palabra
appositive noun or pronoun that identifies or explains another noun or pronoun in a sentence	**aposición** sustantivo o pronombre que especifica o explica a otro sustantivo o pronombre en una oración

English	Español
article the special adjectives *a, an, the*	**artículo** adjetivos especiales *a (un/una), an (un/una)* y *the (el/la/los/las)*
assonance repetition of a vowel sound within words	**asonancia** repetición de un sonido vocálico en las palabras
audience person or persons who will read your work or hear your speech	**público** persona o personas que leerán tu trabajo o escucharán tu discurso
autobiography account of a person's life, written by that person	**autobiografía** relato de la vida de una persona, escrito por esa misma persona

B

English	Español
ballad a narrative song or poem. A *folk ballad* may be passed down by word of mouth for generations before being written down. A *literary ballad* is written in a style to imitate a folk ballad but has a known author.	**balada** canción o poema narrativo. Una *balada folclórica* puede transmitirse oralmente de generación en generación antes de que se ponga por escrito. Una *balada literaria* está escrita en un estilo que imita a la balada folclórica, pero se sabe quién es su autor.
bandwagon statement appeal that leads the reader to believe that everyone is using a certain product	**enunciado de arrastre** enunciado apelativo que lleva al lector a creer que todos usan cierto producto
bibliographic information information about a source, such as author, title, publisher, date of publication, and Internet address	**información bibliográfica** datos sobre una fuente: autor, título, editorial, fecha de publicación, dirección de Internet, etc
body one or more paragraphs composed of details, facts, and examples that support the main idea	**cuerpo** uno o más párrafos compuestos de detalles, hechos y ejemplos que apoyan la idea principal
brackets punctuation marks [ ] used to enclose information added to text or to indicate new text replacing the original quoted text; always used in pairs	**corchetes** signos de puntuación [ ] utilizados para encerrar la información añadida al texto o para indicar el texto nuevo que reemplaza al texto original citado; siempre se usan en parejas

English	Español
brainstorming prewriting technique of writing down ideas that come to mind about a given subject	**intercambio de ideas** técnica de preparación para la escritura que consiste en anotar las ideas que surgen sobre un tema
business letter formal letter that asks for action on the part of the receiver and includes an inside address, heading, salutation, body, closing, and signature	**carta de negocios** carta formal que solicita al destinatario que realice una acción e incluye dirección del destinatario, membrete, saludo, cuerpo, despedida y firma

C

case form of a noun or a pronoun that indicates its use in a sentence. In English there are three cases: the nominative case, the objective case, and the possessive case.	**caso** forma de un sustantivo o de un pronombre que indica su uso en una oración. En inglés hay tres casos: nominativo, objetivo y posesivo.
cause and effect method of development in which details are grouped according to what happens and why it happens	**causa y efecto** método de desarrollo en cual los detalles están agrupados según lo que sucede y por qué sucede
central idea the main or controlling idea of an essay	**idea central** idea principal o fundamental de un ensayo
characterization variety of techniques used by writers to show the personality of a character	**caracterización** varias técnicas utilizadas por los escritores para mostrar la personalidad de un personaje
chronological order the order in which events occur	**orden cronológico** orden en el que ocurren los sucesos
citation note that gives credit to the source of another person's paraphrased or quoted ideas	**cita** nota que menciona la fuente de donde se extrajeron las ideas, parafraseadas o textuales, de otra persona
claim in a persuasive speech or essay, a main position or statement supported with one or more examples and warrants	**afirmación** en un discurso o ensayo persuasivo, punto de vista o enunciado principal fundamentado con uno o más ejemplos y justificaciones

GLOSSARY

English	Español
clarity the quality of being clear	**claridad** cualidad de un texto de ser claro
classics literary works that withstand the test of time and appeal to readers from generation to generation and from century to century	**clásicos** obras literarias que superan la prueba del tiempo y atraen a los lectores de generación en generación y de un siglo a otro
classification method of development in which details are grouped into categories	**clasificación** método de desarrollo en el que los detalles están agrupados en categorías
clause fragment subordinate clause standing alone	**fragmento de cláusula** cláusula subordinada que aparece de forma independiente
clause group of words that has a subject and verb and is used as part of a sentence	**cláusula** grupo de palabras que tiene sujeto y verbo y se utiliza como parte de una oración
cliché overused expression that is no longer fresh or interesting to the reader	**cliché** expresión demasiado usada que ya no resulta original ni interesante para el lector
close reading reading carefully to locate specific information, follow an argument's logic, or comprehend the meaning of information	**lectura atenta** lectura minuciosa para identificar información específica, seguir un argumento lógico o comprender el significado de la información
clustering visual strategy a writer uses to organize ideas and details connected to the subject	**agrupación** estrategia visual que emplea un escritor para organizar las ideas y los detalles relacionados con el tema
coherence logical and smooth flow of ideas connected with clear transitions	**coherencia** flujo lógico de ideas que discurren conectadas con transiciones claras

English	Español
collaboration in writing, the working together of several individuals on one piece of writing, usually done during prewriting, including brainstorming and revising	**colaboración** en el ámbito de la escritura, el trabajo en común de varios individuos en un texto, usualmente durante la etapa de preparación para la escritura, incluida la técnica de intercambio de ideas y la tarea de revisión
collective noun noun that names a group of people or things	**sustantivo colectivo** sustantivo que designa un grupo de personas o cosas
colloquialism informal phrase or colorful expression not meant to be taken literally but understood to have particular non-literal meaning	**coloquialismo** frase informal o expresión pintoresca que no debe tomarse literalmente, pues tiene un significado figurado específico
common noun names any person, place, or thing	**sustantivo común** designa cualquier persona, lugar o cosa
comparative degree modification of an adjective or adverb used when two people, things, or actions are compared	**grado comparativo** forma de un adjetivo o adverbio que se usa cuando se comparan dos personas, cosas o acciones
compare and contrast method of development in which the writer examines similarities and differences between two subjects	**compara y contraste** método de desarrollo en cual el escritor examina las semejanzas y las diferencias entre dos temas
complement word or group of words used to complete a predicate	**complemento** palabra o grupo de palabras utilizadas para completar un predicado
complete predicate all the words that tell what the subject is doing or that tell something about the subject	**predicado completo** todas las palabras que expresan qué hace el sujeto o dicen algo acerca del sujeto
complete subject all the words used to identify the person, place, thing, or idea that the sentence is about	**sujeto completo** todas las palabras utilizadas para identificar la persona, el lugar, la cosa o la idea de la que trata la oración

English	Español
complex sentence sentence that consists of a dependent and an independent clause	**oración compleja** oración que consiste de una cláusula dependiente y una independiente
composition writing form that presents and develops one main idea	**composición** tipo de texto que presenta y desarrolla una idea principal
compound adjective adjective made up of more than one word	**adjetivo compuesto** adjetivo formado por más de una palabra
compound noun a single noun comprised of several words	**sustantivo compuesto** sustantivo individual formado por varias palabras
compound sentence consists of two simple sentences, usually joined by a comma and the coordinating conjunction *and, but, or,* or *yet*	**oración compuesta** consiste de dos oraciones simples, unidas generalmente por una coma y la conjunción coordinante *and (y), but (pero), or (o)* o *yet (sin embargo)*
compound subject two or more subjects in a sentence that have the same verb and are joined by a conjunction	**sujeto compuesto** dos o más sujetos en una oración que tienen el mismo verbo y están unidos por una conjunción
compound verb two or more verbs in one sentence that have the same subject and are joined by a conjunction	**verbo compuesto** dos o más verbos en una oración que tienen el mismo sujeto y están unidos por una conjunción
compound-complex sentence two or more independent clauses and one or more subordinate clauses	**oración compuesta-compleja** dos o más cláusulas independientes y una o más cláusulas subordinadas
concluding sentence a strong ending added to a paragraph that summarizes the major points, refers to the main idea, or adds an insight	**oración conclusiva** un final que se añade a un párrafo y que resume los puntos principales, se refiere a la idea principal o añade una reflexión.
conclusion a strong ending added to a paragraph or composition that summarizes the major points, refers to the main idea, and adds an insight	**conclusión** un final fuerte que se añade a un párrafo o a una composición y que resume los puntos principales, se refiere a la idea principal y añade una reflexión

English	Español
concrete noun person, place, or thing that can be seen or touched	**sustantivo concreto** una persona, un lugar o una cosa que puede verse o tocarse
conflict struggle between opposing forces around which the action of a work of literature revolves	**conflicto** lucha entre fuerzas opuestas alrededor de cual gira la acción de una obra literaria
conjunction word that joins together sentences, clauses, phrases, or other words	**conjunción** palabra que une dos oraciones, cláusulas, frases u otras palabras
conjunctive adverb an adverb used to connect two clauses	**adverbio conjuntivo** adverbio utilizado para conectar dos cláusulas
connotation meaning that comes from attitudes attached to a word	**connotación** significado que proviene de los valores vinculados a una palabra
consonance repetition of a consonant sound, usually in the middle or at the end of words	**consonancia** repetición de un sonido consonántico, usualmente en el medio o al final de las palabras
context clue clues to a word's meaning provided by the sentence, the surrounding words, or the situation in which the word occurs	**clave del contexto** pistas sobre el significado de una palabra proporcionadas por la oración, las palabras que la rodean o la situación en la que aparece la palabra
contraction word that combines two words into one and uses an apostrophe to replace one or more missing letters	**contracción** palabra que combina dos palabras en una y utiliza un apóstrofo en lugar de la(s) letra(s) faltante(s)
contradiction in a persuasive speech or essay, a logical incompatibility between two propositions made by the author	**contradicción** en un discurso o ensayo persuasivo, incompatibilidad lógica entre dos proposiciones hechas por el autor
controlling idea the main idea or thesis of an essay	**idea dominante** idea principal o tesis de un ensayo
cooperative learning strategy in which a group works together to achieve a common goal or accomplish a single task	**aprendizaje cooperativo** estrategia mediante cual los miembros de un grupo trabajan juntos para alcanzar una meta en común o llevar a cabo una tarea

GLOSSARY

English	Español
coordinating conjunction single connecting word used to join words or groups of words	**conjunción coordinante** palabra de conexión usada para unir palabras o grupos de palabras
correlative conjunction pairs of conjunctions used to connect compound subjects, compound verbs, and compound sentences	**conjunción correlativa** pares de conjunciones usadas para conectar los sujetos compuestos, los verbos compuestos y las oraciones compuestas
count noun a noun that names an object that can be counted (*grains of rice, storms, songs*)	**sustantivo contable** sustantivo que designa un objeto que se puede contar *(granos de arroz, tormentas, canciones)*
counter-argument argument offered to address opposing views in a persuasive composition	**contra-argumento** argumento que se ofrece para tratar las opiniones contrarias en una composición persuasiva
creative writing writing style in which the writer creates characters, events, and images within stories, plays, or poems to express feelings, perceptions, and points of view	**escritura creativa** estilo de escritura en cual el escritor crea los personajes, los sucesos y las imágenes de cuentos, obras de teatro o poemas para expresar sentimientos, percepciones y puntos de vista
critique a detailed analysis and assessment of a work such as a piece of writing	**crítica** análisis detallado y evaluación de una obra, como un texto escrito

D

dangling modifier phrase that has nothing to describe in a sentence	**modificador mal ubicado** frase que no describe nada en una oración
dash punctuation mark that indicates a greater separation of words than a comma	**raya** signo de puntuación que indica una separación mayor entre las palabras que una coma
declarative sentence a statement or expression of an opinion. It ends with a period.	**oración enunciativa** enunciado o expresión de una opinión. Termina en punto.

GLOSSARY

English

definition method of development in which the nature and characteristics of a word, object, concept, or phenomenon are explained

demonstrative pronoun word that substitutes for a noun and points out a person or thing

denotation literal meaning of a word

descriptive writing writing that creates a vivid picture of a person, an object, or a scene by stimulating the reader's senses

developmental order information that is organized so that one idea grows out of the preceding idea

Dewey decimal system system by which nonfiction books are arranged on shelves in numerical order according to ten general subject categories

dialect regional variation of a language distinguished by distinctive pronunciation and some differences in word meanings

dialogue conversation between two or more people in a story or play

direct object noun or a pronoun that answers the question *What?* or *Whom?* after an action verb

direct quotation passage, sentence, or words stated exactly as the person wrote or said them

Español

definición método de desarrollo en cual se explican la naturaleza y las características de una palabra, objeto, concepto o fenómeno

pronombre demostrativo palabra que está en lugar de un sustantivo y señala una persona o cosa

denotación significado literal de una palabra

texto descriptivo texto que crea una imagen vívida de una persona, un objeto o una escena por estimulando los sentidos del lector

orden de desarrollo información que está organizada de tal manera que una idea surge de la precedente

Sistema decimal de Dewey sistema por cual los libros de no ficción se ubican en los estantes en orden numérico según diez categorías temáticas generales

dialecto variación regional de un idioma caracterizada por una pronunciación distintiva y algunas diferencias en el significado de las palabras

diálogo conversación entre dos o más personas en un cuento o en una obra de teatro

objeto directo sustantivo o pronombre que responde la pregunta ¿Qué? *(What?)* o ¿Quién? *(Whom?)* después de un verbo de acción

cita directa pasaje, oración o palabras enunciadas exactamente como la persona las escribió o las dijo

English	Español
documentary a work composed of pieces of primary source materials or first-hand accounts such as interviews, diaries, photographs, film clips, etc.	**documental** obra compuesta por fragmentos de fuentes primarias o relatos de primera mano, como entrevistas, diarios, fotografías, fragmentos de películas, etc.
documentary images, interviews, and narration put together to create a powerful report	**documental** imágenes, entrevistas y narración que se combinan para crear un informe poderoso
double negative use of two negative words to express an idea when only one is needed	**negación doble** uso de dos palabras negativas para expresar una idea cuando sólo una es necesaria
drafting stage of the writing process in which the writer expresses ideas in sentences, forming a beginning, a middle, and an ending of a composition	**borrador** etapa del proceso de escritura en la cual el escritor expresa sus ideas en oraciones que forman el principio, el medio y el final de una composición

E

e-mail electronic mail that can be sent all over the world from one computer to another	**correo electrónico** mensaje electrónico que puede enviarse a cualquier lugar del mundo desde una computadora a otra
editing stage of the writing process in which the writer polishes his or her work by correcting errors in grammar, usage, mechanics, and spelling	**edición** etapa del proceso de escritura en la cual el escritor mejora su trabajo y corrige los errores de gramática, uso del lenguaje, aspectos prácticos y ortografía
elaboration addition of explanatory or descriptive information to a piece of writing, such as supporting details, examples, facts, and descriptions	**explicación** agregar información explicativa o descriptiva a un texto, como detalles de apoyo, ejemplos, hechos y descripciones

English	Español
electronic publishing various ways to present information through the use of technology. It includes desktop publishing (creating printed documents on a computer), audio and video recordings, and online publishing (creating a Web site).	**publicación electrónica o Ciberedición** varias maneras de presentar la información por el uso de la tecnología. Incluye la autoedición (crear documentos impresos en una computadora), las grabaciones de audio y video y la publicación en línea (crear un sitio web).
ellipses punctuation marks (. . .) used to indicate where text has been removed from quoted material or to indicate a pause or interruption in speech	**puntos suspensivos** signos de puntuación (. . .) utilizados para indicar dónde se ha quitado parte del texto de una cita o para indicar una pausa o una interrupción en el discurso
elliptical clause subordinate clause in which words are omitted but understood to be there	**cláusula elíptica** cláusula subordinada en cual se omiten palabras, pero se comprende que están implícitas
emoticons symbols used by e-mail users to convey emotions	**emoticonos** símbolos utilizados por los usuarios del correo electrónico para transmitir emociones
encyclopedia print or online reference that contains general information about a variety of subjects	**enciclopedia** obra de referencia, impresa o en línea, que contiene información general sobre varios temas
endnote complete citation of the source of borrowed material at the end of a research report	**nota final** cita completa de la fuente de la que se tomó información, colocada al final de un informe de investigación
essay composition of three or more paragraphs that presents and develops one main idea	**ensayo** composición de tres o más párrafos que presenta y desarrolla una idea principal
essential phrase or clause group of words essential to the meaning of a sentence; therefore, not set off with commas	**frase o cláusula esencial** grupo de palabras esencial para el significado de una oración; por lo tanto, no está encerrado entre comas
etymology history of a word, from its earliest recorded use to its present use	**etimología** historia de una palabra, desde su uso registrado más antiguo hasta su uso actual

GLOSSARY

English	Español
evidence facts and examples used to support a statement or proposition	**evidencia** hechos y ejemplos utilizados para fundamentar un enunciado o proposición
exclamatory sentence expression of strong feeling that ends with an exclamation point	**oración exclamativa** expresión de sentimiento intenso que termina con signo de exclamación
expository writing prose that explains or informs with facts and examples or gives directions	**texto expositivo** texto en prosa que explica o informa con hechos y ejemplos o da instrucciones
external coherence organization of the major components of a written piece (introduction, body, conclusion) in a logical sequence and flow, progressing from one idea to another while holding true to the central idea of the composition	**coherencia externa** organización de las partes principales de un trabajo escrito (introducción, cuerpo, conclusión) en una secuencia lógica que presenta fluidez y avanza de una idea a otra, pero sustentando la idea central de la composición

F

English	Español
fable story in which animal characters act like people to teach a lesson or moral	**fábula** relato en cual los personajes son animales que actúan como personas para enseñar una lección o una moraleja
fact statement that can be proven	**hecho** enunciado que puede probarse
feedback written or verbal reaction to an idea, a work, a performance, and so on, often used as a basis for improvement	**realimentación** reacción escrita u oral respecto de una idea, obra, representación, etc., que suele utilizarse como base para mejorarla
fiction prose works of literature, such as short stories and novels, which are partly or totally imaginary	**ficción** obras literarias en prosa, como cuentos y novelas, que son parcial o totalmente imaginarias
figurative language language that uses such devices as imagery, metaphor, simile, hyperbole, personification, or analogy to convey a sense beyond the literal meaning of the words	**lenguaje figurado** lenguaje que emplea recursos tales como imágenes, metáforas, símiles, hipérboles, personificación o analogía para transmitir un sentido que va más allá del sentido literal de las palabras

English	Español
flashback an interruption of the normal chronological order of the plot to narrate events that occurred earlier	**flash-back** interrupción del orden cronológico normal del argumento para narrar sucesos que ocurrieron anteriormente
folktale story that was told aloud long before it was written	**cuento folclórico** relato que se contaba en voz alta mucho antes de que fuera puesto por escrito
footnote complete citation of the source of borrowed material at the bottom of a page in a research report	**nota al pie** cita completa de la fuente de la que se tomó información, colocada en la parte inferior de una página de un informe de investigación
foreshadowing the use of hints or clues about what will happen later in the plot	**presagio** uso de pistas o claves sobre lo que sucederá posteriormente en el argumento
formal English conventional rules of grammar, usage, and mechanics	**inglés formal** reglas convencionales de gramática, uso del lenguaje y aspectos prácticos de la escritura
format (page) the way in which page elements, such as margins, heads, subheads, and sidebars, are arranged	**formato (página)** forma en que están organizados los elementos de la página, como los márgenes, encabezados, subtítulos y recuadros
fragment group of words that does not express a complete thought	**fragmento** grupo de palabras que no expresa un pensamiento completo
free verse poetry without meter or a regular, patterned beat	**verso libre** poesía sin metro fijo o patrón rítmico regular
freewriting prewriting technique of writing freely without concern for mistakes made	**escritura libre** técnica de preparación para la escritura que consiste en escribir libremente sin preocuparse por los errores cometidos
friendly letter writing form that may use informal language and includes a heading, greeting (salutation), body, closing, and signature	**carta amistosa** tipo de texto que puede usar un lenguaje informal e incluye membrete, saludo, cuerpo, despedida y firma

English	Español
G	
generalization a conclusion based on facts, examples, or instances	**generalización** conclusión basada en hechos, ejemplos o casos
generalizing forming an overall idea that explains something specific	**generalizando** formar una idea general que explica algo específico
genre a distinctive type or category of literature such as the epic, mystery, or science fiction	**género** tipo distintivo o categoría literaria, como la épica, las novelas de misterio, o la ciencia ficción
genre a distinctive type or category of text, such as personal narrative, expository essay, or short story	**género** tipo distintivo o categoría de texto, como la narración personal, el ensayo expositivo o el cuento
gerund phrase a gerund with its modifiers and complements working together as a noun	**frase de gerundio** un gerundio con sus modificadores y complementos, que funcionan juntos como un sustantivo
gerund verb form ending in *–ing* that is used as a noun	**gerundio** forma verbal que termina en *–ing* y puede usarse como sustantivo
glittering generality word or phrase that most people associate with virtue and goodness that is used to trick people into feeling positively about a subject	**generalidad entusiasta** palabra o frase que la mayoría de la gente asocia con la virtud y la bondad, y que se utiliza con el fin de engañar a las personas para que tengan una reacción positiva respecto de cierto tema
graphic elements (in poetry) in poetry, use of word position, line length, and overall text layout to express or reflect meaning	**elementos gráficos (en la poesía)** en poesía, el uso de la ubicación de las palabras, la extensión de los versos y la disposición general del texto para expresar o mostrar el significado
H	
helping verb auxiliary verb that combines with the main verb to make up a verb phrase	**verbo auxiliar** verbo que se emplea junto con el verbo principal para formar una frase verbal

GLOSSARY

English	Español
homographs words that are spelled alike but have different meanings and pronunciations	**homógrafos** palabras que se escriben de igual manera, pero tienen significados y pronunciaciones diferentes
homophones words that sound alike but have different meanings and spellings	**homófonos** palabras que suenan de igual manera, pero tienen significados diferentes y se escriben de manera distinta
hyperbole use of exaggeration or overstatement	**hipérbole** uso de la exageración o amplificación
hyphen punctuation mark used to divide words at the end of a line	**guión** signo ortográfico usado para separar las palabras al final de un renglón

I

idiom phrase or expression that has a meaning different from what the words suggest in their usual meanings	**modismo** frase o expresión que tiene un significado diferente de lo que sugieren habitualmente las palabras que la forman
imagery use of concrete details to create a picture or appeal to senses other than sight	**imaginería** uso de detalles concretos para crear una imagen o apelar a los otros sentidos además de la vista
imperative mood verb form used to give a command or to make a request	**modo imperativo** forma verbal usada para dar una orden o hacer un pedido
imperative sentence a request or command that ends with either a period or an exclamation point	**oración imperativa** pedido u orden que termina en punto con signo de exclamación
indefinite pronoun word that substitutes for a noun and refers to unnamed persons or things	**pronombre indefinido** palabra que sustituye a un sustantivo y alude a personas o cosas que no han sido identificadas
independent clause group of words that can stand alone as a sentence because it expresses a complete thought	**cláusula independiente** grupo de palabras que pueden formar por sí solas una oración porque expresan un pensamiento completo

GLOSSARY

English	Español
indicative mood verb form used to state a fact or to ask a question	**modo indicativo** forma verbal usada para enunciar un hecho o hacer una pregunta
indirect object noun or a pronoun that answers the question *To or from whom?* or *To or for what?* after an action word	**objeto indirecto** nombre o pronombre que responde la pregunta ¿A quién o para quién? (*To or from whom?*) o ¿A qué o para qué? (*To or for what?*) después de una palabra de acción
inference a reasonable conclusion drawn by the reader based on clues in a literary work	**inferencia** conclusión razonable que saca el lector basándose en las pistas de una obra literaria
infinitive verb form that usually begins with *to* and can be used as a noun, adjective, or adverb	**infinitivo** forma verbal que generalmente empieza con *to* y se puede usar como sustantivo, adjetivo o adverbio
informative writing writing that explains with facts and examples, gives directions, or lists steps in a process	**texto informativo** texto que explica algo con hechos y ejemplos, da instrucciones o enumera los pasos de un proceso
inquiring a prewriting technique in which the writer asks questions such as *Who? What? Where? Why?* and *When?*	**indagar** técnica de preparación para la escritura en cual el escritor hace preguntas como ¿Quién? (*Who?*), ¿Qué? (*What?*), ¿Dónde? (*Where?*), ¿Por qué? (*Why?*) y ¿Cuándo? (*When?*)
intensive pronoun word that adds emphasis to a noun or another pronoun in the sentence	**pronombre enfático** en una oración, palabra que añade énfasis a un sustantivo o a otro pronombre
interjection word that expresses strong feeling	**interjección** palabra que expresa un sentimiento intenso
internal coherence in a written piece, organization of ideas and/or sentences in a logical sequence and with a fluid progression	**coherencia interna** en un texto escrito, la organización de las ideas y/o de las oraciones en una secuencia lógica y con un desarrollo fluido
Internet global network of computers that are connected to one another with high speed data lines and telephone lines	**internet** red mundial de computadoras que están conectadas entre sí con líneas de datos y líneas telefónicas de alta velocidad

English	Español
interrogative pronoun pronoun used to ask a question	**pronombre interrogativo** pronombre utilizado para hacer una pregunta
interrogative sentence a question. It ends with a question mark.	**oración interrogativa** pregunta. Empieza y termina con signos de interrogación en español y termina con signo de interrogación en inglés.
intransitive verb action verb that does not pass the action from a doer to a receiver	**verbo intransitivo** verbo de acción que no transfiere la acción del agente a un receptor
introduction one or more paragraphs in an essay that introduce a subject, state or imply a purpose, and present a main idea	**introducción** en un ensayo, uno o más párrafos que presentan un tema, enuncian o sugieren un propósito y presentan una idea principal
introduction first paragraph of a composition that catches the reader's attention and states the main idea	**introducción** primer párrafo de una composición que capta la atención del lector y enuncia la idea principal
inverted order condition when the subject follows the verb or part of the verb phrase	**orden invertido** circunstancia en la que el sujeto sigue al verbo o a una parte de la frase verbal
irony a recognition and heightening of the difference between appearance and reality. *Situational irony* occurs when events turn out differently from what is expected; *dramatic irony* occurs when the audience has important information that a main character lacks.	**ironía** reconocimiento e intensificación de la diferencia entre la apariencia y la realidad. La *ironía situacional* ocurre cuando los sucesos resultan de manera diferente de lo esperado; la *ironía dramática* ocurre cuando el público tiene información importante de la que carece el personaje principal.
irregular verb verb that does not form its past and past participle by adding *–ed* or *–d* to the present tense	**verbo irregular** verbo que no forma el pasado o el participio pasado al agregar *–ed* o *–d* al tiempo presente

GLOSSARY

English	Español
J	
jargon specialized vocabulary used by a particular group of people	**jerga** vocabulario especializado usado por un grupo específico de personas
journal daily notebook in which a writer records thoughts and feelings	**diario** cuaderno en el que un escritor anota cada día sus pensamientos y sentimientos
juxtaposition two or more things placed side by side, generally in an unexpected combination	**yuxtaposición** dos o más cosas ubicadas una junto a la otra, generalmente en una combinación inesperada
L	
linking verb verb that links the subject with another word that renames or describes the subject	**verbo copulativo** verbo que conecta al sujeto con otra palabra que vuelve a nombrar o describe al sujeto
listening the process of comprehending, evaluating, organizing, and remembering information presented orally	**escuchar** proceso de comprender, evaluar, organizar y recordar la información presentada oralmente
literary analysis interpretation of a work of literature supported with appropriate details and quotations from the work	**análisis literario** interpretación de una obra literaria fundamentada con detalles apropiados y citas de la obra
loaded words words carefully chosen to appeal to one's hopes or fears rather than to reason or logic	**palabras tendenciosas** palabras escogidas cuidadosamente para apelar a las esperanzas o los temores del destinatario, en lugar de la razón o la lógica
M	
memo short for *memorandum*, a concise form of communication used to disseminate decisions, plans, policies and the like; used frequently in business settings	**memo** abreviatura de *memorándum*, forma concisa de comunicación usada para difundir decisiones, planes, políticas y cuestiones similares; utilizada frecuentemente en el ambiente de los negocios

English	Español
metaphor figure of speech that compares by implying that one thing is another	**metáfora** figura retórica que hace una comparación implícita entre dos cosas
meter rhythm of a specific beat of stressed and unstressed syllables found in many poems	**metro** ritmo con una cadencia específica de sílabas tónicas (acentuadas) y átonas (inacentuadas) que se halla en muchos poemas
misplaced modifier phrase or a clause that is placed too far away from the word it modifies, thus creating an unclear sentence	**modificador mal colocado** frase o cláusula ubicada demasiado lejos de la palabra que modifica, por lo que crea una oración poco clara
modifier word that makes the meaning of another word more precise	**modificador** palabra que hace más preciso el significado de otra palabra
mood overall atmosphere or feeling created by a work of literature	**atmósfera** clima o sentimiento general creado por una obra literaria
multimedia the use of more than one medium of expression or communication such as a presentation composed of visual images and audio soundtrack	**multimedia** uso de más de un medio de expresión o comunicación, como una presentación compuesta por imágenes visuales y una banda sonora de audio

N

English	Español
narrative writing writing that tells a real or an imaginary story with a clear beginning, middle, and ending	**texto narrativo** texto que relata una historia real o imaginaria con un principio, un medio y un final
narrator the person whose voice is telling the story	**narrador** persona cuya voz cuenta la historia
network a system of interconnected computers	**red** sistema de computadoras interconectadas
noncount noun a noun that names something that cannot be counted (*health, weather, music*)	**sustantivo no contable** sustantivo que designa algo que no se puede contar (la salud, el clima, la música)

GLOSSARY

English	Español
nonessential phrase or clause group of words that is not essential to the meaning of a sentence and is therefore set off with commas (also called *nonrestrictive phrase or clause*)	**frase o cláusula incidental** grupo de palabras que no es esencial para el significado de una oración y, por lo tanto, está encerrada entre comas (también llamada *frase o cláusula no restrictiva*)
nonfiction prose writing that contains facts about real people and real events	**no ficción** texto en prosa que contiene hechos sobre gente real y sucesos reales
nonstandard English less formal language used by people of varying regions and dialects; not appropriate for use in writing	**inglés no estándar** lenguaje menos formal utilizado por personas de diversas regiones y dialectos; inapropiado para usarlo en la escritura
noun a word that names a person, place, thing, or idea. A common noun gives a general name. A proper noun names a specific person, place, or thing and always begins with a capital letter. Concrete nouns can be seen or touched; abstract nouns can not.	**sustantivo** palabra que designa una persona, un lugar, una cosa o una idea. Un sustantivo común expresa un nombre general. Un sustantivo propio nombra una persona, un lugar o una cosa específica y siempre comienza con mayúscula. Los sustantivos concretos designan cosas que pueden verse o tocarse, mientras que los sustantivos abstractos no lo hacen.
noun clause a subordinate clause used like a noun	**cláusula nominal** cláusula subordinada usada como sustantivo
novel a long work of narrative fiction	**novela** obra extensa de ficción narrativa
nuance a small or subtle distinction in meaning	**matiz** diferencia de significado pequeña o sutil

O

object pronoun type of pronoun used for direct objects, indirect objects, and objects of prepositions	**pronombre objeto** tipo de pronombre utilizado para los objetos directos, objetos indirectos y objetos de preposiciones

GLOSSARY

English	Español
object word that answers the question *What?* or *Whom?*	**objeto** palabra que responde la pregunta ¿Qué? *(What?)* o ¿Quién? *(Whom?)*
objective not based on an individual's opinions or judgments	**objetivo** no basado en las opiniones o juicios de un individuo
objective complement a noun or an adjective that renames or describes the direct object	**complemento objetivo** sustantivo o adjetivo que vuelve a nombrar o describe al objeto directo
observing prewriting technique that helps a writer use the powers of observation to gather details	**observación** técnica de preparación para la escritura que ayuda a un escritor a usar su capacidad de observación para reunir detalles
occasion motivation for composing; the factor that prompts communication	**ocasión** motivación para componer; factor que da lugar a la comunicación
online connected to the Internet via a line modem connection	**en línea** conectado a la Internet a través de una conexión de módem
onomatopoeia the use of words whose sounds suggest their meaning	**onomatopeya** uso de palabras cuyos sonidos sugieren su significado
opinion a judgment or belief that cannot be absolutely proven	**opinión** juicio o creencia que no se puede probar completamente
oral interpretation performance or expressive reading of a literary work	**interpretación oral** representación o lectura expresiva de una obra literaria
order of importance or size way of organizing information by arranging details in the order of least to most (or most to least) pertinent	**orden de importancia o tamaño** manera de organizar la información poniendo los detalles en orden de menor a mayor (o de mayor a menor) pertinencia
outline information about a subject organized into main topics and subtopics	**esquema** información sobre un tema organizada en temas principales y subtemas

P

paragraph group of related sentences that present and develop one main idea	**párrafo** grupo de oraciones relacionadas que presentan y desarrollan una idea principal

GLOSSARY

English	Español
parallelism repetition of two or more similar words, phrases, or clauses creating emphasis in a piece of writing and easing readability	**paralelismo** repetición de dos o más palabras, frases o cláusulas similares que crea énfasis en un texto escrito y facilita su lectura
paraphrase restatement of an original work in one's own words	**paráfrasis** reescritura de una obra original con las propias palabras
parentheses punctuation marks ( ) used to enclose supplementary information not essential to the meaning of the sentence; always used in pairs	**paréntesis** signos de puntuación ( ) utilizados para encerrar información adicional que no es esencial para el significado de la oración; se usan siempre en parejas
parenthetical citation source title and page number given in parentheses within a sentence to credit the source of the information	**cita parentética** título de la fuente y número de página escritos entre paréntesis dentro de una oración para dar a conocer la fuente de la información
parody humorous imitation of a serious work	**parodia** imitación humorística de una obra seria
participial phrase participle that works together with its modifier and complement as an adjective	**frase participial** participio que funciona junto con su modificador y su complemento como adjetivo
participle verb form that is used as an adjective	**participio** forma verbal que se utiliza como adjetivo
parts of speech eight categories into which all words can be placed: noun, pronoun, verb, adjective, adverb, preposition, conjunction, and interjection	**categorías gramaticales** ocho categorías en las que pueden clasificarse todas las palabras: sustantivo, pronombre, verbo, adjetivo, adverbio, preposición, conjunción e interjección
passive voice the voice a verb is in when it expresses that the action of the verb is being performed upon the subject	**voz pasiva** voz en que está el verbo cuando expresa que la acción del verbo se realiza sobre el sujeto
peer conference a meeting with one's peers, such as other students, to share ideas and offer suggestions for revision	**conferencia de pares** reunión con los propios pares, como otros estudiantes, para compartir ideas y ofrecer sugerencias de corrección

GLOSSARY

English	Español
personal narrative narrative that tells a real or imaginary story from the writer's point of view	**narración personal** narración que cuenta una historia real o imaginaria desde el punto de vista del escritor
personal pronoun type of pronoun that renames a particular person or group of people. Pronouns can be categorized into one of three groups, dependent on the speaker's position: first person (*I*), second person (*you*), and third person (*she/he/it*).	**pronombre personal** tipo de pronombre que vuelve a nombrar a una persona o grupo de personas en particular. Los pronombres se pueden clasificar en tres grupos, según la posición del hablante: primera persona (*I* [yo]), segunda persona (*you* [tú]) y tercera persona (*she/he/it* [ella/él]).
personal writing writing that tells a real or imaginary story from the writer's point of view	**narración personal** texto que cuenta una historia real o imaginaria desde el punto de vista del escritor
personification giving human qualities to non-human subjects	**personificación** atribuir cualidades humanas a sujetos no humanos
persuasive writing writing that expresses an opinion and uses facts, examples, and reasons in order to convince the reader of the writer's viewpoint	**texto persuasivo** texto que expresa una opinión y emplea hechos, ejemplos y razones con el fin de convencer al lector del punto de vista del escritor
phrase group of related words that functions as a single part of speech and does not have a subject and a verb	**frase** grupo de palabras relacionadas que funciona como una sola categoría gramatical y no tiene un sujeto y un verbo
phrase fragment phrase written as if it were a complete sentence	**fragmento de frase** frase escrita como si fuera una oración completa
plagiarism act of using another person's words, pictures, or ideas without giving proper credit	**plagio** acción de usar las palabras, fotografías o ideas de otra persona sin reconocer su procedencia apropiadamente
play a piece of writing to be performed on a stage by actors	**obra de teatro** texto escrito para que los actores lo representen en un escenario

GLOSSARY

English	Español
plot sequence of events leading to the outcome or point of the story; contains a climax or high point, a resolution, and an outcome or ending	**argumento** secuencia de sucesos que lleva a la resolución del relato o propósito del mismo; contiene un clímax o momento culminante y una resolución o final
plural form of a noun used to indicate two or more	**plural** forma del sustantivo utilizada para indicar dos o más personas o cosas
poem highly structured composition that expresses powerful feeling with condensed, vivid language, figures of speech, and often the use of meter and rhyme	**poema** composición muy estructurada que expresa un sentimiento intenso mediante un lenguaje condensado y vívido, figuras retóricas y, frecuentemente, el uso de metro y rima
poetry form of writing that uses rhythm, rhyme, and vivid imagery to express feelings and ideas	**poesía** tipo de texto que utiliza ritmo, rima e imágenes vívidas para expresar sentimientos e ideas
point of view vantage point from which a writer tells a story or describes a subject	**punto de vista** posición de ventaja desde cual un escritor narra una historia o describe un tema
portfolio collection of work representing various types of writing and the progress made on them	**carpeta de trabajos** colección de obras que representan varios tipos de textos y el progreso realizado en ellos
positive degree adjective or adverb used when no comparison is being made	**grado positivo** adjetivo o adverbio usado cuando no se realiza una comparación
possessive pronoun a pronoun used to show ownership or possession	**pronombre posesivo** pronombre utilizado para indicar propiedad o posesión
predicate adjective adjective that follows a linking verb and modifies, or describes, the subject	**adjetivo predicativo** adjetivo que sigue a un verbo copulativo y modifica, o describe, al sujeto
predicate nominative noun or a pronoun that follows a linking verb and identifies, renames, or explains the subject	**predicado nominal** sustantivo o pronombre que sigue a un verbo copulativo e identifica, vuelve a nombrar o explica al sujeto

English	Español
predicate part of a sentence that tells what a subject is or does	**predicado** parte de la oración que indica qué es o qué hace el sujeto
prefix one or more syllables placed in front of a base word to form a new word	**prefijo** una o más sílabas colocadas adelante de la raíz de una palabra para formar una palabra nueva
preposition word that shows the relationship between a noun or a pronoun and another word in the sentence	**preposición** palabra que muestra la relación entre un sustantivo o un pronombre y otra palabra de la oración
prepositional phrase a group of words made up of a preposition, its object, and any words that describe the object (modifiers)	**frase preposicional** grupo de palabras formado por una preposición, su objeto y todas las palabras que describan al objeto (modificadores)
prewriting invention stage of the writing process in which the writer plans for drafting based on the subject, occasion, audience, and purpose for writing	**preescritura** etapa de invención del proceso de escritura en la cual el escritor planea un borrador basándose en el tema, la ocasión, el público y el propósito para escribir
principal parts of a verb the present, the past, and the past participle. The principal parts help form the tenses of verbs.	**partes principales de un verbo** presente, pasado y participio pasado. Las partes principales ayudan a formar los tiempos verbales.
progressive verb form verbs used to express continuing or ongoing action. Each of the six verb tenses has a progressive form.	**forma verbal progresiva** verbos usados para expresar una acción que continúa o está en curso. Cada uno de los seis tiempos verbales tiene una forma progresiva.
pronoun word that takes the place of one or more nouns. Three types of pronouns are *personal, reflexive,* and *intensive.*	**pronombre** palabra que está en lugar de uno o más sustantivos. Entre los tipos de pronombres están los pronombres personales, reflexivos y enfáticos.
proofreading carefully rereading and making corrections in grammar, usage, spelling, and mechanics in a piece of writing	**corregir** relectura atenta de un texto y corrección de la gramática, del uso del lenguaje, de la ortografía y de los aspectos prácticos de la escritura

English	Español
proofreading symbols a kind of shorthand that writers use to correct their mistakes while editing	**símbolos de corrección de textos** tipo de taquigrafía que usan los escritores para corregir sus errores cuando revisan un texto
propaganda effort to persuade by distorting and misrepresenting information or by disguising opinions as facts	**propaganda** intento de persuadir distorsionando y tergiversando la información o disfrazando de hechos las opiniones
proper adjective adjective formed from a proper noun	**adjetivo propio** adjetivo formado a partir de un sustantivo propio
protagonist the principal character in a story	**protagonista** personaje principal de un relato
publishing stage of the writing process in which the writer may choose to share the work with an audience	**publicar** etapa del proceso de escritura en la cual el escritor puede escoger dar a conocer su trabajo a un público
purpose reason for writing or speaking on a given subject	**propósito** razón para escribir o hablar sobre un tema dado

Q

quatrain four-line stanza in a poem	**cuarteta** en un poema, estrofa de cuatro versos

R

reader-friendly formatting page elements such as fonts, bullet points, line length, and heads adding to the ease of reading	**formato de fácil lectura** elementos que se agregan a la página escrita, como tipo de letra, viñetas, extensión de los renglones y encabezados para facilitar la lectura
Readers' Guide to Periodical Literature a print or online index of magazine and journal articles	**Guía para el lector de publicaciones periódicas** índice impreso o en línea de artículos de diarios y revistas
reflecting act of thinking quietly and calmly about an experience	**reflexionar** acción de pensar en silencio y con calma sobre una experiencia

GLOSSARY

English	Español
reflexive pronoun pronoun formed by adding *–self* or *–selves* to a personal pronoun; it is used to refer to or emphasize a noun or pronoun	**pronombre reflexivo** pronombre que se forma al agregar *–self* o *–selves* al pronombre personal; se usa para aludir a un sustantivo o a un pronombre o enfatizarlos
regular verb verb that forms its past and past participle by adding *–ed* or *–d* to the present	**verbo regular** verbo que forma el pasado o participio pasado al agregar *–ed* o *–d* al tiempo presente
relative pronoun pronoun that begins most adjectival clauses and relates the adjectival clause to the noun or pronoun it describes	**pronombre relativo** pronombre con el que comienza la mayoría de las cláusulas adjetivas y que relaciona la cláusula adjetiva con el sustantivo o pronombre que describe
repetition repeat of a word or phrase for poetic effect	**repetición** repetir una palabra o frase para lograr un efecto poético
report a composition of three or more paragraphs that uses specific information from books, magazines, and other sources	**informe** composición de tres o más párrafos que emplea información específica extraída de libros, revistas y otras fuentes
research paper a composition of three or more paragraphs that uses information drawn from books, periodicals, media sources, and interviews with experts	**artículo de investigación** composición de tres o más párrafos que utiliza información obtenida en libros, publicaciones periódicas, medios de comunicación y entrevistas con expertos en el tema
resolution the point at which the chief conflict or complication of a story is worked out	**resolución** momento en el que se resuelve el conflicto principal o complicación de un cuento
restrictive phrase or clause group of words essential to the meaning of a sentence; therefore, not set off with commas (also called *essential phrase or clause*)	**frase o cláusula restrictiva** grupo de palabras esencial para el significado de una oración; por lo tanto, no está encerrado entre comas (también llamada *frase o cláusula esencial*)
résumé summary of a person's work experience, education, and interests	**currículum vítae** resumen de la experiencia laboral, educación e intereses de una persona

GLOSSARY

English	Español
revising stage of the writing process in which the writer rethinks what is written and reworks it to increase its clarity, smoothness, and power	**revisar** etapa del proceso de escritura en la cual el escritor vuelve a pensar en lo que ha escrito y lo adapta para mejorar su claridad, fluidez y contundencia
rhetorical device a technique used to influence or persuade an audience	**recurso retórico** técnica usada para influir o persuadir al público
rhetorical device a writing technique, often employing metaphor and analogy, designed to enhance the writer's message	**recurso retórico** técnica de escritura, que suele emplear metáforas y analogías, destinada a realzar el mensaje del escritor
rhyme scheme regular pattern of rhyming in a poem	**esquema de rima** en un poema, patrón regular de rima
rhythm sense of flow produced by the rise and fall of accented and unaccented syllables	**ritmo** sensación de fluidez producida por el ascenso y descenso de sílabas tónicas (acentuadas) y átonas (inacentuadas)
root the part of a word that carries its basic meaning	**raíz** parte de una palabra que lleva en sí lo esencial del significado de la palabra
run-on sentence two or more sentences that are written as one sentence and are separated by a comma or have no mark of punctuation at all	**oración sin final** dos o más oraciones escritas como una sola oración y separadas por una coma o escritas sin ningún signo de puntación

S

English	Español
sarcasm an expression of contempt, often including irony	**sarcasmo** expresión de desprecio que suele incluir ironía
scheme a figure of speech, such as parallelism, that changes the normal arrangement of words	**esquema** figura retórica, como el paralelismo, que modifica la disposición normal de las palabras
script the written form of a dramatic performance, written by a playwright	**guión** forma escrita de un espectáculo dramático, realizada por un dramaturgo

English	Español
sensory details descriptive details that appeal to one of the five senses: seeing, hearing, touching, tasting, and smelling	**detalles sensoriales** detalles descriptivos que apelan a uno de los cinco sentidos: vista, oído, tacto, gusto y olfato
sentence group of words that expresses a complete thought	**oración** grupo de palabras que expresa un pensamiento completo
sentence base a subject, a verb, and a complement	**base de la oración** un sujeto, un verbo y un complemento
sentence combining method of combining short sentences into longer, more fluent sentences by using phrases and clauses	**combinación de oraciones** método de combinar oraciones breves para formar oraciones más largas y fluidas mediante el uso de frases y cláusulas
sentence fragment group of words that does not express a complete thought	**fragmento de oración** grupo de palabras que no expresa un pensamiento completo
sentence group of words that expresses a complete thought	**oración** grupo de palabras que expresa un pensamiento completo
sequential order the order in which details are arranged according to when they take place or when they are done	**orden secuencial** orden en que están organizados los detalles de acuerdo con el momento en que tienen lugar o cuándo se realizan
setting the place and time of a story	**ambiente** lugar y tiempo de un relato
short story well-developed story about characters facing a conflict or problem	**relato corto** relato bien desarrollado sobre personajes que se enfrentan a un conflicto o problema
simile figure of speech comparing two objects using the words *like* or *as*	**símil** figura retórica que compara dos objetos usando la palabra *como* (*like* or *as)*
simple predicate the main word or phrase in the complete predicate	**predicado simple** la palabra o la frase principal en el predicado completo
simple sentence a sentence that has one subject and one verb	**oración simple** oración que tiene un sujeto y un verbo
simple subject the main word in a complete subject	**sujeto simple** la palabra principal en un sujeto completo

English	Español
slang nonstandard English expressions that are developed and used by particular groups	**argot** expresiones propias del inglés no estándar desarrolladas y usadas por grupos específicos
sonnet a lyric poem of fourteen lines, usually in iambic pentameter, with rhymes arranged according to certain definite patterns	**soneto** poema lírico de catorce versos, usualmente en pentámetro yámbico, con rimas dispuestas según ciertos patrones definidos
sound devices ways to use sounds in poetry to achieve certain effects	**recursos sonoros** en poesía, formas de usar los sonidos para lograr ciertos efectos
spatial order the order in which details are arranged according to their physical location	**orden espacial** orden en el cual los detalles se organizan de acuerdo con su ubicación física
speaker tag in dialogue, text that indicates who is speaking; frequently includes a brief description of the manner of speaking	**identificador del interlocutor** en un diálogo, el texto que indica quién habla; suele incluir una breve descripción de la manera de hablar
speech an oral composition presented by a speaker to an audience	**discurso** composición oral presentada por un orador ante un público
Standard English proper form of the language that follows a set pattern of rules and conventions	**Inglés estándar** forma correcta del lenguaje que sigue un patrón establecido de reglas y convenciones
stanza group of lines in a poem that the poet decides to set together	**estrofa** en un poema, grupo de versos que el poeta decide colocar juntos
stereotype simplified concept of the members of a group based on limited experience with the group	**estereotipo** concepto simplificado de los miembros de un grupo que se basa en una experiencia limitada con el grupo
story within a story a story that is told during the telling of another story	**relato dentro de un relato** relato que se cuenta durante la narración de otro relato
style visual or verbal expression that is distinctive to an artist or writer	**estilo** expresión visual o verbal que es propia de un artista o escritor
subject (composition) topic of a composition or essay	**tema** idea principal de una composición o ensayo

GLOSSARY

GLOSSARY

English	Español
subject (grammar) word or group of words that names the person, place, thing, or idea that the sentence is about	**sujeto** palabra o grupo de palabras que nombran la persona, el lugar, la cosa o la idea de la que trata la oración
subject complement renames or describes the subject and follows a linking verb. The two kinds are predicate nominatives and predicate adjectives.	**complemento predicativo subjetivo** vuelve a nombrar o describe al sujeto y está a continuación de un verbo copulativo. Los dos tipos son los predicados nominales y los adjetivos predicativos.
subjunctive mood words such as *if, as if,* or *as though* that are used to express a condition contrary to fact or to express a wish	**modo subjuntivo** palabras como *if* (*si*), *as if* (*como si*) o *as though (como si)* que se usan para expresar la subjetividad o un deseo
subordinate clause group of words that cannot stand alone as a sentence because it does not express a complete thought	**cláusula subordinada** grupo de palabras que no puede funcionar por sí solo como una oración porque no expresa un pensamiento completo
subordinating conjunction single connecting word used in a sentence to introduce a dependent clause which is an idea of less importance than the main idea	**conjunción subordinante** palabra de conexión usada en una oración para introducir una cláusula dependiente que expresa una idea de menor importancia que la idea principal
subplot a secondary plot line that reinforces the main plot line	**subargumento** argumento secundario que refuerza la línea argumental principal
subtle meaning refined, intricate, or deep meaning, sometimes not noticed during the first encounter with a work of art	**significado sutil** significado delicado, intrincado o profundo que a veces no se nota durante el primer encuentro con una obra de arte
suffix one or more syllables placed after a base word to change its part of speech and possibly its meaning.	**sufijo** una o más sílabas colocadas después de la raíz de una palabra para modificar su categoría gramatical y, posiblemente, su significado
summary information written in a condensed, concise form, touching only on the main ideas	**resumen** información escrita en forma condensada y concisa, que incluye sólo las ideas principales

English	Español
superlative degree modification of an adjective or adverb used when more than two people, things, or actions are compared	**grado superlativo** forma de un adjetivo o adverbio que se usa cuando se comparan más de dos personas, cosas o acciones
supporting sentence sentence that explains or proves the topic sentence with specific details, facts, examples, or reasons	**oración de apoyo** oración que explica o prueba la oración principal con detalles específicos, hechos, ejemplos o razones
suspense in drama, fiction, and nonfiction, a build-up of uncertainty, anxiety, and tension about the outcome of the story or scene	**suspenso** en las obras de teatro, de ficción y de no ficción, acumulación de incertidumbre, ansiedad y tensión acerca de la resolución de la historia o escena
symbol an object, an event, or a character that stands for a universal idea or quality	**símbolo** objeto, suceso o personaje que representa una idea o cualidad universal
synonym word that has nearly the same meaning as another word	**sinónimo** palabra que significa casi lo mismo que otra palabra
synthesizing process by which information from various sources is merged into one whole	**sintetizar** proceso por cual se integra en un todo la información proveniente de varias fuentes

T

English	Español
tense the form a verb takes to show time. The six tenses are the *present, past, future, present perfect, past perfect,* and *future perfect*	**tiempo verbal** forma que toma un verbo para expresar el tiempo en que ocurre la acción. Los seis tiempos verbales son: presente, pasado, futuro, presente perfecto, pretérito perfecto y futuro perfecto
testimonial persuasive strategy in which a famous person encourages the purchase of a certain product	**testimonial** estrategia persuasiva en cual una persona famosa alienta a comprar un cierto producto
theme underlying idea, message, or meaning of a work of literature	**tema** idea, mensaje o significado subyacente de una obra literaria
thesaurus online or print reference that gives synonyms for words	**tesauro** (Diccionario de sinónimos) material de referencia en línea o impreso que ofrece alternativas para las palabras

English	Español
thesis statement statement of the main idea that makes the writing purpose clear	**enunciado de tesis** enunciado de la idea principal que pone en claro el propósito para escribir
tired word a word that has been so overused that it has been drained of meaning	**palabra gastada** palabra que se ha usado tanto que se ha vaciado de significado
tone writer's attitude toward the subject and audience of a composition (may also be referred to as the writer's *voice*)	**tono** actitud del escritor hacia el tema y destinatario de una composición (también puede denominarse voz del escritor)
topic sentence a sentence that states the main idea of the paragraph	**oración principal** oración que enuncia la idea principal del párrafo
transitions words and phrases that show how ideas are related	**elementos de transición** palabras y frases que muestran las ideas cómo están relacionadas
transitive verb an action verb that passes the action from a doer to a receiver	**verbo transitivo** verbo de acción que transfiere la acción de un agente a un destinatario
trope in literature, a figure of speech	**tropo** en literatura, un figura retórica

U

understatement an expression that contains less emotion than would be expected	**minimización** expresión que contiene menos emoción que la esperada
understood subject a subject of a sentence that is not stated	**sujeto tácito** sujeto de una oración que no está explícito
unity combination or ordering of parts in a composition so that all the sentences or paragraphs work together as a whole to support one main idea	**unidad** combinación u ordenamiento de las partes de una composición de tal manera que todas las oraciones o párrafos funcionen juntos como un todo para fundamentar una idea principal

V

verb phrase main verb plus one or more helping verbs	**frase verbal** verbo principal más uno o más verbos auxiliares
verb word used to express an action or state of being	**verbo** palabra usada para expresar una acción o un estado del ser

English	Español
verbal verb form that acts like another part of speech, such as an adjective or noun	**verbal** forma del verbo que funciona como otra categoría gramatical, tal como un adjetivo o un sustantivo
voice the particular sound and rhythm of the language the writer uses (closely related to *tone*)	**voz** sonido y ritmo particular del lenguaje que usa un escritor (estrechamente vinculado al tono)

W

English	Español
warrant in a persuasive speech or essay, connection made between a claim and the examples used to support the claim	**justificación** en un discurso o ensayo persuasivo, conexión que se hace entre una afirmación y los ejemplos usados para fundamentarla
wordiness use of words and expressions that add nothing to the meaning of a sentence	**palabrería** uso de palabras y expresiones que no añaden nada al significado de una oración
working thesis statement that expresses the possible main idea of a composition or research report	**hipótesis de trabajo** enunciado que expresa la posible idea principal de una composición o de un informe de investigación
works-cited page alphabetical listing of sources cited in a research paper	**página de obras citadas** lista alfabética de las fuentes citadas en un artículo de investigación
World Wide Web network of computers within the Internet capable of delivering multimedia content and text over communication lines into personal computers all over the globe	**red mundial de comunicación** red de computadoras dentro de la Internet capaz de transmitir contenido multimedia y textos, a través de líneas de comunicación, a las computadoras personales de todas partes del mundo
writing process recursive stages that a writer proceeds through in his or her own way when developing ideas and discovering the best way to express them	**proceso de escritura** etapas recurrentes que un escritor sigue a su manera cuando desarrolla ideas y descubre la mejor manera de expresarlas

GLOSSARY

Index

INDEX

Note: Italic locators (page numbers) indicate skill sets

INDEX

Note: Italic locators (page numbers) indicate skill sets

Note: Italic locators (page numbers) indicate skill sets

INDEX

B

INDEX

Note: Italic locators (page numbers) indicate skill sets

INDEX

Note: Italic locators (page numbers) indicate skill sets

INDEX

Note: Italic locators (page numbers) indicate skill sets

Note: Italic locators (page numbers) indicate skill sets

INDEX

Note: Italic locators (page numbers) indicate skill sets

Note: Italic locators (page numbers) indicate skill sets

INDEX

Note: Italic locators (page numbers) indicate skill sets

Note: Italic locators (page numbers) indicate skill sets

Note: Italic locators (page numbers) indicate skill sets

Note: Italic locators (page numbers) indicate skill sets

INDEX

INDEX

Note: Italic locators (page numbers) indicate skill sets

J

K

L

Note: Italic locators (page numbers) indicate skill sets

INDEX

Note: Italic locators (page numbers) indicate skill sets

Note: Italic locators (page numbers) indicate skill sets

INDEX

Note: Italic locators (page numbers) indicate skill sets

Note: Italic locators (page numbers) indicate skill sets

Note: Italic locators (page numbers) indicate skill sets

INDEX

Note: Italic locators (page numbers) indicate skill sets

INDEX

Note: Italic locators (page numbers) indicate skill sets

Note: Italic locators (page numbers) indicate skill sets

Note: Italic locators (page numbers) indicate skill sets

INDEX

R

Note: Italic locators (page numbers) indicate skill sets

INDEX

Note: Italic locators (page numbers) indicate skill sets

Note: Italic locators (page numbers) indicate skill sets

INDEX

Note: Italic locators (page numbers) indicate skill sets

Note: Italic locators (page numbers) indicate skill sets

T

Note: Italic locators (page numbers) indicate skill sets

Note: Italic locators (page numbers) indicate skill sets

Note: Italic locators (page numbers) indicate skill sets

W

Note: Italic locators (page numbers) indicate skill sets

INDEX

INDEX

Note: Italic locators (page numbers) indicate skill sets

Y

Z

Note: Italic locators (page numbers) indicate skill sets

INDEX

Image Credits

Every reasonable effort has been made to contact all copyright holders. If we have omitted anyone, please let us know and we will include a suitable acknowledgement in subsequent editions.

Art Resources: p. 230 © The Metropolitan Museum of Art / Art Resource, NY

Corbis: pp. 89 © Pool Photos / Retna Ltd. / Corbis, 695 Bettmann

CORBIS, 840 © Ted Spiegel / Corbis

Dreamstime: pp. 11, 17, 35, 36, 48, 52, 53, 55, 70, 71, 78, 92, 108, 116, 122, 123, 128, 139, 142, 150, 154, 164, 168, 181, 232, 240, 243, 249, 250, 262, 272, 274, 276, 278, 280, 285, 287, 288, 289, 298, 320, 341, 364, 375, 382, 383, 393, 396, 410, 412, 429, 431, 446, 451, 459, 464, 467, 472, 474, 481, 491, 505, 530, 586, 587, 617, 630, 634, 640, 650, 680, 707, 717, 722, 739, 740, 767, 774, 784, 813, 828, 831, 836, 838, 839, 859, 889, 890, 914, 927, 941, 953, 963

Getty Images: pp. 81 Archive Photos / Stringer / Hulton Archive / Getty Images, 394 Time & Life Pictures / Getty Images

iStockphoto: pp. 3, 99, 110, 131, 155, 156, 173, 176, 182, 195, 211, 227, 261, 264, 270, 298, 306, 367, 391, 433, 463, 470, 527, 618, 654, 662, 685, 697, 699, 737, 755, 760, 778, 796, 803, 913, 934, 942, 946, 948, 951, 954, 1007, 1008

Jupiter Images: pp. 4, 7, 8, 45, 57, 60, 63, 156, 163, 266, 271, 293, 306, 388, 445, 449, 493, 503, 504, 548, 706, 723, 734, 810, 849, 856, 978, 994, 1027

Library of Congress: pp. 255, 708, 814

© Mike Kelly: p. 221

NASA: p. 834

Northwind Picture Archives: p. 442

Randy Messer: p. 938

© Tony Kelly: p. 221

Wikimedia Commons: p. 719

Text Credits

From DEATH OF A SALESMAN by Arthur Miller, copyright 1949, renewed © 1977 by Arthur Miller. Used by permission of Viking Penguin, a division of Penguin Group (USA) Inc.

From GREAT ANIMALS OF THE MOVIES by Edward Edelson, copyright © 1980 by Edward Edelson. Used by permission of Doubleday, a division of Random House, Inc.

"A Mother in Mannville" from WHEN THE WHIPPOORWILL by Marjorie Kinnan Rawlings. Reprinted with the permission of Scribner, a Division of Simon & Schuster, Inc. Copyright © 1936, 1940 by Marjorie Kinnan Rawlings; copyright renewed 1964, 1968 by Norton Baskin. All rights reserved.

"The Point of No Comment" from MOVING VIOLATIONS by John Hockenberry. Copyright © 1995 John Hockenberry. Reprinted by permission of Hyperion. All rights reserved.